C000119063

The Journal to Stella

THE JOURNAL TO STELLA

THE
JOURNAL TO STELLA

BY

JONATHAN SWIFT

EDITED, WITH INTRODUCTION AND NOTES, BY

GEORGE A. AITKEN

METHUEN & CO.
36 ESSEX STREET W.C.
LONDON
1901

English
7-24-42
45755

PREFACE

THE history of the publication of the *Journal to Stella* is somewhat curious. On Swift's death twenty-five of the letters, forming the closing portion of the series, fell into the hands of Dr. Lyon, a clergyman who had been in charge of Swift for some years. The letters passed to a man named Wilkes, who sold them for publication. They accordingly appeared in 1766 in the tenth volume of Dr. Hawkesworth's quarto edition of Swift's works; but the editor made many changes in the text, including a suppression of most of the "little language." The publishers, however, fortunately for us, were public-spirited enough to give the manuscripts (with one exception) to the British Museum, where, after many years, they were examined by John Forster, who printed in his unfinished *Life of Swift* numerous passages from the originals, showing the manner in which the text had been tampered with by Hawkesworth. Swift himself, too, in his later years, obliterated many words and sentences in the letters, and Forster was able to restore not a few of these omissions. His zeal, however, sometimes led him to make guesses at words which are quite undecipherable. Besides Forster's work, I have had the benefit of the careful collation made by Mr. Ryland for his edition of 1897. Where these authorities differ I have usually found myself in agreement with Mr. Ryland, but I have felt justified in accepting some of Forster's readings which were rejected by him as uncertain; and the examination of the manuscripts has enabled me to make some additions and corrections of my own. Swift's writing is extremely small, and abounds in abbreviations. The difficulty of arriving at the true reading is therefore considerable, apart from the erasures.

The remainder of the *Journal*, consisting of the first forty letters, was published in 1768 by Deane Swift, Dr. Swift's second cousin. These letters had been given to Mrs. Whiteway in 1738, and by her to her son-in-law, Deane Swift. The originals have been lost, with the exception of the first, which, by some accident, is in the British Museum; but it is evident that Deane Swift took even greater liberties with the text than Hawkesworth. He substituted for "Ppt" the word "Stella," a name which Swift seems not to have used until some years later; he adopted the name "Presto" for Swift, and in other ways tried to give a greater literary finish to the letters. The whole of the correspondence was first brought together, under the title of the *Journal to Stella*, in Sheridan's edition of 1784.

Previous editions of the *Journal* have been but slightly annotated. Swift's letters abound with allusions to people of all classes with whom he came in contact in London, and to others known to Esther Johnson in Ireland; and a large proportion of these persons have been passed over in discreet silence by Sir Walter Scott and others. The task of the annotator has, of course, been made easier of late years by the publication of contemporary journals and letters, and of useful works of reference dealing with Parliament, the Army, the Church, the Civil Service, and the like, besides the invaluable *Dictionary of National Biography*. I have also been assisted by a collection of MS. notes kindly placed at my disposal by Mr. Thomas

Seccombe. I have aimed at brevity and relevance, but it is hoped that the reader will find all the information that is necessary. Here and there a name has baffled research, but I have been able to give definite particulars of a very large number of people—noblemen and ladies in society in London or Dublin, Members of Parliament, doctors, clergymen, Government officials, and others who have hitherto been but names to the reader of the *Journal*. Where there is no reference at the foot of the page, the note upon any person alluded to can readily be found by consulting the Index. I have corrected a good many errors in the older notes, but in dealing with so large a number of persons, some of whom it is difficult to identify, I cannot hope that I myself have escaped pitfalls.

G. A. A.

INTRODUCTION

WHEN Swift began to write the letters known as the *Journal to Stella*, he was forty-two years of age, and Esther Johnson twenty-nine. Perhaps the most useful introduction to the correspondence will be a brief setting forth of what is known of their friendship from Stella's childhood, the more specially as the question has been obscured by many assertions and theories resting on a very slender basis of fact.

Jonathan Swift, born in 1667 after his father's death, was educated by his uncle Godwin, and after a not very successful career at Trinity College, Dublin, went to stay with his mother, Abigail Erick, at Leicester. Mrs. Swift feared that her son would fall in love with a girl named Betty Jones, but, as Swift told a friend, he had had experience enough "not to think of marriage till I settle my fortune in the world, which I am sure will not be in some years; and even then, I am so hard to please that I suppose I shall put it off to the other world." Soon afterwards an opening for Swift presented itself. Sir William Temple, now living in retirement at Moor Park, near Farnham, had been, like his father, Master of the Irish Rolls, and had thus become acquainted with Swift's uncle Godwin. Moreover, Lady Temple was related to Mrs. Swift, as Lord Orrery tells us. Thanks to these facts, the application to Sir William Temple was successful, and Swift went to live at Moor Park before the end of 1689. There he read to Temple, wrote for him, and kept his accounts, and growing into confidence with his employer, "was often trusted with matters of great importance." The story— afterwards improved upon by Lord Macaulay—that Swift received only £20 and his board, and was not allowed to sit at table with his master, is wholly untrustworthy. Within three years of their first intercourse, Temple had introduced his secretary to William the Third, and sent him to London to urge the King to consent to a bill for triennial Parliaments.

When Swift took up his residence at Moor Park he found there a little girl of eight, daughter of a merchant named Edward Johnson, who had died young. Swift says that Esther Johnson was born on March 13, 1681; in the parish register of Richmond,[1] which shows that she was baptized on March 20, 1680–81, her name is given as Hester; but she signed her will "Esther," the name by which she was always known. Swift says, "Her father was a younger brother of a good family in Nottingham-shire, her mother of a lower degree; and indeed she had little to boast in her birth." Mrs. Johnson had two children, Esther and Ann, and lived at Moor Park as companion to Lady Giffard, Temple's widowed sister. Another member of the household, afterwards to be Esther's constant companion, was Rebecca Dingley, a relative of the Temple family.[2] She was a year or two older than Swift.

The lonely young man of twenty-two was both play-fellow and teacher of the delicate child of eight. How he taught her to write has been charmingly brought before us in the painting exhibited by Miss Dicksee at the Royal

---

[1] *Notes and Queries*, Sixth Series, x. 287.
[2] See letter from Swift to John Temple, February 1737. She was then "quite sunk with years and unwieldliness."

Academy a few years ago; he advised her what books to read, and instructed her, as he says, "in the principles of honour and virtue, from which she never swerved in any one action or moment of her life."

By 1694 Swift had grown tired of his position, and finding that Temple, who valued his services, was slow in finding him preferment, he left Moor Park in order to carry out his resolve to go into the Church. He was ordained, and obtained the prebend of Kilroot, near Belfast, where he carried on a flirtation with a Miss Waring, whom he called Varina. But in May 1696 Temple made proposals which induced Swift to return to Moor Park, where he was employed in preparing Temple's memoirs and correspondence for publication, and in supporting the side taken by Temple in the Letters of Phalaris controversy by writing *The Battle of the Books*, which was, however, not published until 1704. On his return to Temple's house, Swift found his old playmate grown from a sickly child into a girl of fifteen, in perfect health. She came, he says, to be "looked upon as one of the most beautiful, graceful, and agreeable young women in London, only a little too fat. Her hair was blacker than a raven, and every feature of her face in perfection."

On his death in January 1699, Temple left a will,[1] dated 1694, directing the payment of £20 each, with half a year's wages, to Bridget Johnson "and all my other servants"; and leaving a lease of some land in Monistown, County Wicklow, to Esther Johnson, "servant to my sister Giffard." By a codicil of February 1698, Temple left £100 to "Mr. Jonathan Swift, now living with me." It may be added that by her will of 1722, proved in the following year, Lady Giffard gave £20 to Mrs. Moss— Mrs. Bridget Johnson, who had married Richard Mose or

---

[1] *Athenæum*, Aug. 8, 1891.

Moss, Lady Giffard's steward. The will proceeds: "To Mrs. Hester (*sic*) Johnson I give £10, with the £100 I put into the Exchequer for her life and my own, and declare the £100 to be hers which I am told is there in my name upon the survivorship, and for which she has constantly sent over her certificate and received the interest. I give her besides my two little silver candlesticks."

Temple left in Swift's hands the task of publishing his posthumous works, a duty which afterwards led to a quarrel with Lady Giffard and other members of the family. Many years later Swift told Lord Palmerston that he stopped at Moor Park solely for the benefit of Temple's conversation and advice, and the opportunity of pursuing his studies. At Temple's death he was "as far to seek as ever." In the summer of 1699, however, he was offered and accepted the post of secretary and chaplain to the Earl of Berkeley, one of the Lords Justices, but when he reached Ireland he found that the secretaryship had been given to another. He soon, however, obtained the living of Laracor, Agher, and Rathbeggan, and the prebend of Dunlavin in St. Patrick's Cathedral, Dublin. The total value of these preferments' was about £230 a year, an income which Miss Waring seems to have thought enough to justify him in marrying. Swift's reply to the lady whom he had "singled out at first from the rest of women" could only have been written with the intention of breaking off the connection, and accordingly we hear no more of poor Varina.

At Laracor, a mile or two from Trim, and twenty miles from Dublin, Swift ministered to a congregation of about fifteen persons, and had abundant leisure for cultivating his garden, making a canal (after the Dutch fashion of Moor Park), planting willows, and rebuilding the vicarage.

As chaplain to Lord Berkeley, he spent much of his time in Dublin. He was on intimate terms with Lady Berkeley and her daughters, one of whom is best known by her married name of Lady Betty Germaine; and through them he had access to the fashionable society of Dublin. When Lord Berkeley returned to England in April 1701, Swift, after taking his Doctor's degree at Dublin, went with him, and soon afterwards published, anonymously, a political pamphlet, *A Discourse on the Contests and Dissentions in Athens and Rome.* When he returned to Ireland in September he was accompanied by Stella—to give Esther Johnson the name by which she is best known—and her friend Mrs. Dingley. Stella's fortune was about £1500, and the property Temple had left her was in County Wicklow. Swift, very much for his "own satisfaction, who had few friends or acquaintance in Ireland," persuaded Stella—now twenty years old—that living was cheaper there than in England, and that a better return was obtainable on money. The ladies took his advice, and made Ireland their home. At first they felt themselves strangers in Dublin; "the adventure looked so like a frolic," Swift says, "the censure held for some time as if there were a secret history in such a removal: which however soon blew off by her excellent conduct." Swift took every step that was possible to avoid scandal. When he was away, the ladies occupied his rooms; when he returned, they went into their own lodgings. When he was absent, they often stopped at the vicarage at Laracor, but if he were there, they moved to Trim, where they visited the vicar, Dr. Raymond, or lived in lodgings in the town or neighbourhood. Swift was never with Stella except in the presence of a third person, and in 1726 he said that he had not seen her in a morning "these dozen years, except once or twice in a journey."

During a visit to England in the winter of 1703–4 we find Swift in correspondence with the Rev. William Tisdall, a Dublin incumbent whom he had formerly known at Belfast. Tisdall was on friendly terms with Stella and Mrs. Dingley, and Swift sent messages to them through him. "Pray put them upon reading," he wrote, "and be always teaching something to Mrs. Johnson, because she is good at comprehending, remembering and retaining." But the correspondence soon took a different turn. Tisdall paid his addresses to Stella, and charged Swift with opposing his suit. Tisdall's letters are missing, but Swift's reply of April 20, 1704, puts things sufficiently clearly. "My conjecture is," he says, "that you think I obstructed your inclinations to please my own, and that my intentions were the same with yours. In answer to all which I will, upon my conscience and honour, tell you the naked truth. First, I think I have said to you before that, if my fortunes and humour served me to think of that state, I should certainly, among all persons upon earth, make your choice; because I never saw that person whose conversation I entirely valued but hers; this was the utmost I ever gave way to. And secondly, I must assure you sincerely that this regard of mine never once entered into my head to be an impediment to you." He had thought Tisdall not rich enough to marry; "but the objection of your fortune being removed, I declare I have no other; nor shall any consideration of my own misfortune, in losing so good a friend and companion as her, prevail on me, against her interest and settlement in the world, since it is held so necessary and convenient a thing for ladies to marry, and that time takes off from the lustre of virgins in all other eyes but mine. I appeal to my letters to herself whether I was your friend or not in the whole concern, though the part I designed to act in it was

purely passive." He had even thought "it could not be
decently broken," without disadvantage to the lady's credit,
since he supposed it was known to the town; and he had
always spoken of her in a manner far from discouraging.
Though he knew many ladies of rank, he had "nowhere
met with an humour, a wit, or conversation so agreeable,
a better portion of good sense, or a truer judgment of
men or things." He envied Tisdall his prudence and
temper, and love of peace and settlement, "the reverse of
which has been the great uneasiness of my life, and is
likely to continue so."

This letter has been quoted at some length because of
its great importance. It is obviously capable of various
interpretations, and some, like Dr. Johnson, have concluded that Swift was resolved to keep Stella in his power,
and therefore prevented an advantageous match by
making unreasonable demands. I cannot see any ground
for this interpretation, though it is probable that Tisdall's
appearance as a suitor was sufficiently annoying. There
is no evidence that Stella viewed Tisdall's proposal with
any favour, unless it can be held to be furnished by Swift's
belief that the town thought—rightly or wrongly—that
there was an engagement. In any case, there could be no
mistake in future with regard to Swift's attitude towards
Stella. She was dearer to him than anyone else, and his
feeling for her would not change, but for marriage he had
neither fortune nor humour. Tisdall consoled himself by
marrying another lady two years afterwards; and though
for a long time Swift entertained for him feelings of
dislike, in later life their relations improved, and Tisdall
was one of the witnesses to Swift's will.

The *Tale of a Tub* was published in 1704, and Swift
was soon in constant intercourse with Addison and the
other wits. While he was in England in 1705, Stella and

Mrs. Dingley made a short visit to London. This and a similar visit in 1708 are the only occasions on which Stella is known to have left Ireland after taking up her residence in that country. Swift's influence over women was always very striking. Most of the toasts of the day were his friends, and he insisted that any lady of wit and quality who desired his acquaintance should make the first advances. This, he says — writing in 1730 — had been an established rule for over twenty years. In 1708 a dispute on this question with one toast, Mrs. Long, was referred for settlement to Ginckel Vanhomrigh, the son of the house where it was proposed that the meeting should take place; and by the decision — which was in Swift's favour—" Mrs. Vanhomrigh and her fair daughter Hessy " were forbidden to aid Mrs. Long in her disobedience for the future. This is the first that we hear of Hester or Esther Vanhomrigh, who was afterwards to play so marked a part in the story of Swift's life. Born on February 14, 1690, she was now eighteen. Her father, Bartholomew Vanhomrigh, a Dublin merchant of Dutch origin, had died in 1703, leaving his wife a fortune of some sixteen thousand pounds. On the income from this money Mrs. Vanhomrigh, with her two daughters, Hester and Mary, were able to mix in fashionable society in London. Swift was introduced to them by Sir Andrew Fountaine early in 1708, but evidently Stella did not make their acquaintance, nor indeed hear much, if anything, of them until the time of the *Journal*.

Swift's visit to London in 1707–9 had for its object the obtaining for the Irish Church of the surrender by the Crown of the First-Fruits and Twentieths, which brought in about £2500 a year. Nothing came of Swift's interviews with the Whig statesmen, and after many disappointments he returned to Laracor (June 1709), and conversed with none but Stella and her card-playing friends, and Addison, now secretary to Lord Wharton.[1] Next year came the fall of the Whigs, and a request to Swift from the Irish bishops that he would renew the application for the First-Fruits, in the hope that there would be greater success with the Tories. Swift reached London in September 1710, and began the series of letters, giving details of the events of each day, which now form the *Journal to Stella.* " I will write something every day to MD," he says, " and make it a sort of journal; and when it is full I will send it, whether MD writes or no; and so that will be pretty; and I shall always be in conversation with MD, and MD with Presto." It is interesting to note that by way of caution these letters were usually addressed to Mrs. Dingley, and not to Stella.

The story of Swift's growing intimacy with the Tory leaders, of the success of his mission, of the increasing coolness towards older acquaintances, and of his services to the Government, can best be read in the *Journal* itself. In the meantime the intimacy with the Vanhomrighs grew rapidly. They were near neighbours of Swift's, and in a few weeks after his arrival in town we find frequent allusions to the dinners at their house (where he kept his best gown and periwig), sometimes with the explanation that he went there " out of mere listlessness," or because it was wet, or because another engagement had broken down. Only thrice does he mention the " eldest daughter ": once on her birthday; once on the occasion of a trick played him, when he received a message that she was suddenly very ill (" I rattled off the daughter "); and once to state that she was come of age, and was going to Ireland to look after her fortune. There is evidence

---

[1] *Journal*, May 4, 1711.

that " Miss Essy," or Vanessa, to give her the name by
which she will always be known, was in correspondence
with Swift in July 1710—while he was still in Ireland—
and in the spring of 1711;[1] and early in 1711 Stella
seems to have expressed surprise at Swift's intimacy with
the family, for in February he replied, " You say they are
of no consequence; why, they keep as good female
company as I do male; I see all the drabs of quality at
this end of the town with them." In the autumn Swift
seems to have thought that Vanessa was keeping company
with a certain Hatton, but Mrs. Long—possibly meaning
to give him a warning hint—remarked that if this were
so "she is not the girl I took her for; but to me she
seems melancholy."

In 1712 occasional letters took the place of the daily
journal to " MD," but there is no change in the affectionate
style in which Swift wrote. In the spring he had a long
illness, which affected him, indeed, throughout the year.
Other reasons which he gives for the falling off in his
correspondence are his numerous business engagements,
and the hope of being able to send some good news of an
appointment for himself. There is only one letter to
Stella between July 19 and September 15, and Dr. Birkbeck Hill argues that the poem " Cadenus and Vanessa "
was composed at that time.[2] If this be so, it must have
been altered next year, because it was not until 1713 that
Swift was made a Dean. Writing on April 19, 1726,
Swift said that the poem " was written at Windsor near
fourteen years ago, and dated: it was a task performed
on a frolic among some ladies, and she it was addressed to
died some time ago in Dublin, and on her death the copy
shewn by her executor." Several copies were in circulation,

---

[1] Craik's *Life of Swift*, 269.
[2] *Unpublished Letters of Dean Swift*, pp. 189–96.

and he was indifferent what was done with it; it was "only a cavalier business," and if those who would not give allowances were malicious, it was only what he had long expected.

From this letter it would appear that this remarkable poem was written in the summer of 1712; whereas the title-page of the pamphlet says it was "written at Windsor, 1713." Swift visited Windsor in both years, but he had more leisure in 1712, and we know that Vanessa was also at Windsor in that year. In that year, too, he was forty-four, the age mentioned in the poem. Neither Swift nor Vanessa forgot this intercourse: years afterwards Swift wrote to her, "Go over the scenes of Windsor. . . . Cad thinks often of these"; and again, "Remember the indisposition at Windsor." We know that this poem was revised in 1719, when in all probability Swift added the lines to which most exception can be taken. Cadenus was to be Vanessa's instructor:—

> "His conduct might have made him styled
> A father, and the nymph his child."

He had "grown old in politics and wit," and "in every scene had kept his heart," so that he now "understood not what was love." But he had written much, and Vanessa admired his wit. Cadenus found that her thoughts wandered—

> "Though she seemed to listen more
> To all he spoke than e'er before."

When she confessed her love, he was filled with "shame, disappointment, guilt, surprise." He had aimed only at cultivating the mind, and had hardly known whether she was young or old. But he was flattered, and though he could not give her love, he offered her friendship, "with gratitude, respect, esteem." Vanessa took him at his word, and said she would now be tutor, though he was not apt to learn :—

> "But what success Vanessa met
> Is to the world a secret yet.
> Whether the nymph to please her swain
> Talks in a high romantic strain;
> Or whether he at last descends
> To act with less seraphic ends;
> Or, to compound the business, whether
> They temper love and books together,
> Must never to mankind be told,
> Nor shall the conscious Muse unfold."

Such is the poem as we now have it, written, it must be remembered, for Vanessa's private perusal. It is to be regretted, for her own sake, that she did not destroy it.

Swift received the reward of his services to the Government—the Deanery of St. Patrick's, Dublin—in April 1713. Disappointed at what he regarded as exile, he left London in June. Vanessa immediately began to send him letters which brought home to him the extent of her passion; and she hinted at jealousy in the words, "If you are very happy, it is ill-natured of you not to tell me so, except 'tis what is inconsistent with my own." In his reply Swift dwelt upon the dreariness of his surroundings at Laracor, and reminded her that he had said he would endeavour to forget everything in England, and would write as seldom as he could.

Swift was back again in the political strife in London in September, taking Oxford's part in the quarrel between that statesman and Bolingbroke. On the fall of the Tories at the death of Queen Anne, he saw that all was over, and retired to Ireland, not to return again for twelve years. In the meantime the intimacy with Vanessa had been renewed. Her mother had died, leaving debts, and she

pressed Swift for advice in the management of her affairs.
When she suggested coming to Ireland, where she had
property, he told her that if she took this step he would
"see her very seldom." However, she took up her abode
at Celbridge, only a few miles from Dublin. Swift gave
her many cautions, out of " the perfect esteem and friendship" he felt for her, but he often visited her. She was
dissatisfied, however, begging him to speak kindly, and
at least to counterfeit his former indulgent friendship.
" What can be wrong," she wrote, " in seeing and advising
an unhappy young woman? You cannot but know that
your frowns make my life unsupportable." Sometimes he
treated the matter lightly; sometimes he showed annoyance; sometimes he assured her of his esteem and love,
but urged her not to make herself or him "unhappy
by imaginations." He was uniformly unsuccessful in
stopping Vanessa's importunity. He endeavoured, she
said, by severities to force her from him; she knew she was
the cause of uneasy reflections to him; but nothing would
lessen her "inexpressible passion."

Unfortunately he failed—partly no doubt from mistaken
considerations of kindness, partly because he shrank from
losing her affection—to take effective steps to put an end
to Vanessa's hopes. It would have been better if he had
unhesitatingly made it clear to her that he could not return
her passion, and that if she could not be satisfied with
friendship the intimacy must cease. To quote Sir Henry
Craik, " The friendship had begun in literary guidance: it
was strengthened by flattery: it lived on a cold and almost
stern repression, fed by confidences as to literary schemes,
and by occasional literary compliments: but it never came
to have a real hold over Swift's heart."

With 1716 we come to the alleged marriage with Stella.
In 1752, seven years after Swift's death, Lord Orrery, in

his *Remarks* on Swift, said that Stella was "the concealed, but undoubted, wife of Dr. Swift. . . . If my informations are right, she was married to Dr. Swift in the year 1716, by Dr. Ashe, then Bishop of Clogher." Ten years earlier, in 1742, in a letter to Deane Swift which I have not seen quoted before, Orrery spoke of the advantage of a wife to a man in his declining years; "nor had the Dean felt a blow, or wanted a companion, had he been married, or, in other words, had Stella lived." What this means is not at all clear. In 1754, Dr. Delany, an old friend of Swift's, wrote, in comment upon Orrery's *Remarks*, "Your account of his marriage is, I am satisfied, true." In 1789, George Monck Berkeley, in his *Literary Relics*, said that Swift and Stella were married by Dr. Ashe, "who himself related the circumstances to Bishop Berkeley, by whose relict the story was communicated to me." Dr. Ashe cannot have told Bishop Berkeley by word of mouth, because Ashe died in 1717, the year after the supposed marriage, and Berkeley was then still abroad. But Berkeley was at the time tutor to Ashe's son, and may therefore have been informed by letter, though it is difficult to believe that Ashe would write about such a secret so soon after the event. Thomas Sheridan, on information received from his father, Dr. Sheridan, Swift's friend, accepted the story of the marriage in his book (1784), adding particulars which are of very doubtful authenticity; and Johnson, in his *Lives of the Poets*, says that Dr. Madden told him that Stella had related her "melancholy story" to Dr. Sheridan before her death. On the other hand, Dr. Lyon, Swift's attendant in his later years, disbelieved the story of the marriage, which was, he said, "founded only on hearsay"; and Mrs. Dingley "laughed at it as an idle tale," founded on suspicion.

Sir Henry Craik is satisfied with the evidence for the marriage. Mr. Leslie Stephen is of opinion that it is inconclusive, and Forster could find no evidence that is at all reasonably sufficient; while Mr. Stanley Lane-Poole, Mr. Churton Collins, and others are strongly of opinion that no such marriage ever took place. A full discussion of the evidence would involve the consideration of the reliability of the witnesses, and the probability of their having authentic information, and would be out of place here. My own opinion is that the evidence for the marriage is very far from convincing, and this view seems to be confirmed by all that we know from his own letters of Swift's relations with Stella. It has been suggested that she was pained by reports of Swift's intercourse with Vanessa, and felt that his feelings towards herself were growing colder; but this is surmise, and no satisfactory explanation has been given to account for a form of marriage being gone through after so many years of the closest friendship. There is no reason to suppose that there was at the time any gossip in circulation about Stella, and if her reputation was in question, a marriage of which the secret was carefully kept would obviously be of no benefit to her. Moreover, we are told that there was no change in their mode of life; if they were married, what reason could there be for keeping it a secret, or for denying themselves the closer relationship of marriage? The only possible benefit to Stella was that Swift would be prevented marrying anyone else. It is impossible, of course, to disprove a marriage which we are told was secretly performed, without banns or licence or witnesses; but we may reasonably require strong evidence for so startling a step. If we reject the tale, the story of Swift's connection with Stella is at least intelligible; while the acceptance of this marriage introduces many puzzling circumstances, and makes it necessary to believe that during the remainder of Stella's life Swift repeatedly spoke of his wife as a friend, and of himself as one who had never

c

married.[1] What right have we to put aside Swift's plain
and repeated statements? Moreover, his attitude towards
Vanessa for the remaining years of her life becomes much
more culpable if we are to believe that he had given Stella
the claim of a wife upon him.[2]

From 1719 onwards we have a series of poems to Stella,
written chiefly in celebration of her birthday. She was
now thirty-eight (Swift says, "Thirty-four—we shan't
dispute a year or more."), and the verses abound in laughing but kindly allusions to her advancing years and wasting
form. Hers was "an angel's face a little cracked," but all
men would crowd to her door when she was fourscore.
His verses to her had always been

> " Without one word of Cupid's darts,
>   Of killing eyes, or bleeding hearts ;
>   With friendship and esteem possessed,
>   I ne'er admitted Love a guest."

Her only fault was that she could not bear the lightest
touch of blame. Her wit and sense, her loving care in
illness—to which he owed the fact that he was alive to
say it—made her the "best pattern of true friends." She
replied, in lines written on Swift's birthday in 1721, that
she was his pupil and humble friend. He had trained her
judgment and refined her fancy and taste :—

> " You taught how I might youth prolong
>   By knowing what was right and wrong;
>   How from my heart to bring supplies
>   Of lustre to my fading eyes ;

---

[1] In 1730 he wrote, " Those who have been married may form juster
ideas of that estate than I can pretend to do" (Dr. Birkbeck Hill's *Unpublished Letters of Dean Swift*, p. 237).

[2] Scott added a new incident which has become incorporated in the
popular conception of Swift's story. Delany is said to have met Swift
rushing out of Archbishop King's study, with a countenance of distraction,
immediately after the wedding. King, who was in tears, said, " You have

How soon a beauteous mind repairs
The loss of changed or falling hairs ;
How wit and virtue from within
Send out a smoothness o'er the skin
Your lectures could my fancy fix,
And I can please at thirty-six."

In 1723 Vanessa is said to have written to Stella or to Swift—there are discrepancies in the versions given by Sheridan and Lord Orrery, both of whom are unreliable—asking whether the report that they were married was true. Swift, we are told, rode to Celbridge, threw down Vanessa's letter in a great rage, and left without speaking a word.[1] Vanessa, whose health had been failing for some time, died shortly afterwards, having cancelled a will in Swift's favour. She left " Cadenus and Vanessa " for publication, and when someone said that she must have been a remarkable woman to inspire such a poem, Stella replied that it was well known that the Dean could write finely upon a broom-stick.

Soon after this tragedy Swift became engrossed in the Irish agitation which led to the publication of the *Drapier's Letters,* and in 1726 he paid a long-deferred visit to London, taking with him the manuscript of *Gulliver's Travels.* While in England he was harassed by bad news of Stella, who had been in continued ill-health for some years. His letters to friends in Dublin show how greatly he suffered. To the Rev. John Worrall he wrote, in a letter which he begged him to burn, " What you tell

just met the most unhappy man on earth; but on the subject of his wretchedness you must never ask a question." Will it be believed that Scott—who rejects Delany's inference from this alleged incident—had no better authority for it than "a friend of his (Delany's) relict "?

[1] This incident, for which there is probably some foundation of fact—we cannot say how much—has been greatly expanded by Mrs. Woods in her novel *Esther Vanhomrigh.* Unfortunately most of her readers cannot, of course, judge exactly how far her story is a work of imagination.

me of Mrs. Johnson I have long expected with great oppression and heaviness of heart. We have been perfect friends these thirty-five years. Upon my advice they both came to Ireland, and have been ever since my constant companions; and the remainder of my life will be a very melancholy scene, when one of them is gone, whom I most esteemed, upon the score of every good quality that can possibly recommend a human creature." He would not for the world be present at her death: "I should be a trouble to her, and a torment to myself." If Stella came to Dublin, he begged that she might be lodged in some airy, healthy part, and not in the Deanery, where too it would be improper for her to die. "There is not a greater folly," he thinks, "than to contract too great and intimate a friendship, which must always leave the survivor miserable." To Dr. Stopford he wrote in similar terms of the "younger of the two" "oldest and dearest friends I have in the world." "This was a person of my own rearing and instructing from childhood, who excelled in every good quality that can possibly accomplish a human creature. . . . I know not what I am saying; but believe me that violent friendship is much more lasting and as much engaging as violent love." To Dr. Sheridan he said, "I look upon this to be the greatest event that can ever happen to me; but all my preparation will not suffice to make me bear it like a philosopher nor altogether like a Christian. There hath been the most intimate friendship between us from our childhood, and the greatest merit on her side that ever was in one human creature towards another."[1] Pope alludes in a letter to Sheridan to the illness of Swift's "particular friend," but with the

---

[1] In October Swift explained that he had been in the country "partly to see a lady of my old acquaintance, who was extremely ill" (*Unpublished Letters of Dean Swift*, p. 198).

exception of another reference by Pope, and of a curiously flippant remark by Bolingbroke, the subject is nowhere mentioned in Swift's correspondence with his literary and fashionable friends in London.

Swift crossed to Ireland in August, fearing the worst; but Stella rallied, and in the spring of 1727 he returned to London. In August, however, there came alarming news, when Swift was himself suffering from giddiness and deafness. To Dr. Sheridan he wrote that the last act of life was always a tragedy at best: " it is a bitter aggravation to have one's best friend go before one." Life was indifferent to him; if he recovered from his disorder it would only be to feel the loss of " that person for whose sake only life was worth preserving. I brought both those friends over that we might be happy together as long as God should please; the knot is broken, and the remaining person you know has ill answered the end; and the other, who is now to be lost, is all that was valuable." To Worrall he again wrote (in Latin) that Stella ought not to be lodged at the Deanery; he had enemies who would place a bad interpretation upon it if she died there.

Swift left London for Dublin in September; he was detained some days at Holyhead by stress of weather, and in the private journal which he kept during that time he speaks of the suspense he was in about his " dearest friend."[1] In December Stella made a will—signed "Esther Johnson, spinster "—disposing of her property in the manner Swift had suggested. Her allusions to Swift are incompatible with any such feeling of resentment as is suggested by Sheridan. She died on January 28, 1728. Swift could

---

[1] There is a story that shortly before her death Swift begged Stella to allow herself to be publicly announced as his wife, but that she replied that it was then too late. The versions given by Delany and Theophilus Swift differ considerably, while Sheridan alters the whole thing by representing Swift as brutally refusing to comply with Stella's last wishes.

not bear to be present, but on the night of her death he
began to write his very interesting *Character of Mrs.
Johnson*, from which passages have already been quoted.
He there calls her "the truest, most virtuous and valuable
friend that I, or perhaps any other person, was ever
blessed with." Combined with excellent gifts of the mind,
"she had a gracefulness, somewhat more than human, in
every motion, word, and action. Never was so happy a
conjunction of civility, freedom, easiness, and sincerity."
Everyone treated her with marked respect, yet everyone
was at ease in her society. She preserved her wit, judgment, and vivacity to the last, but often complained of
her memory. She chose men rather than women for her
companions, "the usual topic of ladies' discourse being
such as she had little knowledge of and less relish."
"Honour, truth, liberality, good nature, and modesty
were the virtues she chiefly possessed, and most valued
in her acquaintance." In some Prayers used by Swift
during her last sickness, he begged for pity for "the
mournful friends of Thy distressed servant, who sink under
the weight of her present condition, and the fear of losing
the most valuable of our friends." He was too ill to be
present at the funeral at St. Patrick's. Afterwards, we are
told, a lock of her hair was found in his desk, wrapped
in a paper bearing the words, "Only a woman's hair."

Swift continued to produce pamphlets manifesting growing misanthropy, though he showed many kindnesses to
people who stood in need of help. He seems to have given
Mrs. Dingley fifty guineas a year, pretending that it came
from a fund for which he was trustee. The mental decay
which he had always feared—"I shall be like that tree,"
he once said, "I shall die at the top"—became marked
about 1738. Paralysis was followed by aphasia, and after
acute pain, followed by a long period of apathy, death

relieved him in October 1745. He was buried by Stella's side, in accordance with his wishes. The bulk of his fortune was left to found a hospital for idiots and lunatics.

There has been much rather fruitless discussion respecting the reason or reasons why Swift did not marry Stella; for if there was any marriage, it was nothing more than a form. Some have supposed that Swift resolved to remain unmarried because the insanity of an uncle and the fits and giddiness to which he was always subject led him to fear insanity in his own case. Others, looking rather to physical causes, have dwelt upon his coldness of temperament and indisposition to love; upon the repugnance he often showed towards marriage, and the tone of some of the verses on the subject written in his later years. Others, again, have found a cause in his parsimonious habits, in his dread of poverty, the effects of which he had himself felt, and in the smallness of his income, at least until he was middle-aged.[1] It may well be that one or all of these things influenced Swift's action. We cannot say more. He himself, as we have seen, said, as early as 1704, that if his humour and means had permitted him to think of marriage, his choice would have been Stella. Perhaps, however, there is not much mystery in the matter. Swift seems to have been wanting in passion; probably he was satisfied with the affection which Stella gave him, and did not wish for more. Such an attachment as his usually results in marriage, but not necessarily. It is not sufficiently remembered that the affection began in Stella's childhood. They were "perfect friends" for nearly forty years, and her advancing years in no way lessened his love, which was independent of beauty.

---

[1] There has also been the absurd suggestion that the impediment was Swift's knowledge that both he and Stella were the illegitimate children of Sir William Temple—a theory which is absolutely disproved by known facts.

Whether Stella was satisfied, who shall say? Mrs.
Oliphant thought that few women would be disposed
to pity Stella, or think her life one of blight or injury.
Mr. Leslie Stephen says, "She might and probably did
regard his friendship as a full equivalent for the sacrifice. . . . Is it better to be the most intimate friend
of a man of genius or the wife of a commonplace
Tisdall?" Whatever we may surmise, there is nothing to
prove that she was disappointed. She was the one star
which brightened Swift's storm-tossed course; it is well
that she was spared seeing the wreck at the end.

The *Journal to Stella* is interesting from many points of
view: for its bearing upon Swift's relations with Stella and
upon his own character; for the light which it throws upon
the history of the time and upon prominent men of the
day; and for the illustrations it contains of the social life
of people of various classes in London and elsewhere. The
fact that it was written without any thought of publication
is one of its greatest attractions. Swift jotted down his
opinions, his hopes, his disappointments, without thought
of their being seen by anybody but his correspondents.
The letters are transparently natural. It has been said
more than once that the *Journal*, by the nature of the case,
contains no full-length portraits, and hardly any sketches.
Swift mentions the people he met, but rarely stops to draw
a picture of them. But though this is true, the casual
remarks which he makes often give a vivid impression of
what he thought of the person of whom he is speaking, and
in many cases those few words form a chief part of our
general estimate of the man. There are but few people of
note at the time who are not mentioned in these pages.
We see Queen Anne holding a Drawing-room in her bed-
room: "she looked at us round with her fan in her mouth,

and once a minute said about three words to some that were nearest her." We see Harley, afterwards the Earl of Oxford, "a pure trifler," who was always putting off important business; Bolingbroke, "a thorough rake"; the prudent Lord Dartmouth, the other Secretary of State, from whom Swift could never "work out a dinner." There is Marlborough, "covetous as Hell, and ambitious as the prince of it," yet a great general and unduly pressed by the Tories; and the volatile Earl of Peterborough, "above fifty, and as active as one of five-and-twenty"—"the ramblingest lying rogue on earth." We meet poor Congreve, nearly blind, and in fear of losing his commissionership; the kindly Arbuthnot, the Queen's physician; Addison, whom Swift met more and more rarely, busy with the preparation and production of *Cato*; Steele, careless as ever, neglecting important appointments, and "governed by his wife most abominably"; Prior, poet and diplomatist, with a "lean carcass"; and young Berkeley of Trinity College, Dublin, "a very ingenious man and great philosopher," whom Swift determined to favour as much as he could. Mrs. Masham, the Duchess of Somerset, the Duchess of Shrewsbury, the Duchess of Hamilton, Lady Betty Germaine, and many other ladies appear with more or less distinctness; besides a host of people of less note, of whom we often know little but what Swift tells us.

Swift throws much light, too, on the daily life of his time. The bellman on his nightly rounds, calling "Paaast twelvvve o'clock"; the dinner at three, or at the latest, four; the meetings at coffee-houses; the book-sales; the visit to the London sights—the lions at the Tower, Bedlam, the tombs in Westminster Abbey, and the puppet-show; the terrible Mohocks, of whom Swift stood in so much fear; the polite "howdees" sent to friends by footmen; these and more are all described in the *Journal*. We read of curious habits and practices of fashionable ladies; of the snuff used by Mrs. Dingley and others; of the jokes— "bites," puns, and the like—indulged in by polite persons. When Swift lodged at Chelsea, he reached London either by boat, or by coach,—which was sometimes full when he wanted it,—or by walking across the "Five Fields," not without fear of robbers at night. The going to or from Ireland was a serious matter; after the long journey by road came the voyage (weather permitting) of some fifteen hours, with the risk of being seized or pursued by French privateers; and when Ireland was reached the roads were of the worst. We have glimpses of fashionable society in Dublin, of the quiet life at Laracor and Trim, and of the drinking of the waters at Wexford, where visitors had to put up with primitive arrangements: "Mrs. Dingley never saw such a place in her life."

Swift's own characteristics come out in the clearest manner in the *Journal*, which gives all his hopes and fears during three busy years. He was pleased to find on his arrival in London how great a value was set on his friendship by both political parties: "The Whigs were ravished to see me, and would lay hold on me as a twig while they are drowning;" but Godolphin's coldness enraged him, so that he was "almost vowing vengeance." Next day he talked treason heartily against the Whigs, their baseness and ingratitude, and went home full of schemes of revenge. "The Tories drily tell me I may make my fortune, if I please; but I do not understand them, or rather, I *do* understand them." He realised that the Tories might not be more grateful than others, but he thought they were pursuing the true interests of the public, and was glad to contribute what was in his power. His vanity was gratified by Harley inviting him to the private dinners with St.

John and Harcourt which were given on Saturdays, and by
their calling him Jonathan; but he did not hope too much
from their friendship: "I said I believed they would leave
me Jonathan, as they found me . . . but I care not."

Of Swift's frugal habits there is abundant evidence in
the *Journal*. When he came to town he took rooms on a
first floor, "a dining-room and bed-chamber, at eight
shillings a week; plaguy dear, but I spend nothing for
eating, never go to a tavern, and very seldom in a coach;
yet after all it will be expensive." In November he
mentions that he had a fire: "I am spending my second
half-bushel of coals." In another place he says, "People
have so left the town, that I am at a loss for a dinner. . . .
It cost me eighteenpence in coach-hire before I could find
a place to dine in." Elsewhere we find: "This paper does
not cost me a farthing: I have it from the Secretary's
office." He often complains of having to take a coach
owing to the dirty condition of the streets: "This rain
ruins me in coach-hire; I walked away sixpennyworth, and
came within a shilling length, and then took a coach, and
got a lift back for nothing."[1]

Swift's arrogance—the arrogance, sometimes, of a man
who is morbidly suspicious that he may be patronised—is
shown in the manner in which he speaks of the grand ladies
with whom he came in contact. He calls the Duke of

[1] It is curious to note the intimate knowledge of some of Swift's
peculiarities which was possessed by the hostile writer of a pamphlet
called *A Hue and Cry after Dr. S——t*, published in 1714. That piece
consists, for the most part, of extracts from a supposed Diary by Swift,
and contains such passages as these: "*Friday.* Go to the Club. . . . Am
treated. Expenses one shilling." "*Saturday.* Bid my servant get all
things ready for a journey to the country: mend my breeches; hire a
riding coat; borrow boots; sell my coals and candles; reckon with my
washerwoman, making her allow for old shirts, socks, dabbs and markees,
which she bought of me. . . . Six coaches of quality, and nine hacks,
this day called at my lodgings." "*Thursday.* The Earl looked queerly:
left him in a huff. Bid him send for me when he was fit for company.
. . . Spent ten shillings."

Ormond's daughters "insolent drabs," and talks of his "mistress, Ophy Butler's wife, who is grown a little charmless." When the Duchess of Shrewsbury reproached him for not dining with her, Swift said that was not so soon done; he expected more advances from ladies, especially duchesses. On another occasion he was to have supped at Lady Ashburnham's, "but the drab did not call for us in her coach, as she promised, but sent for us, and so I sent my excuses." The arrogance was, however, often only on the surface. It is evident that Swift was very kind in many cases. He felt deeply for Mrs. Long in her misfortunes, living and dying in an obscure country town. On the last illness of the poet Harrison he says, "I am very much afflicted for him, as he is my own creature. . . . I was afraid to knock at the door; my mind misgave me." He was "heartily sorry for poor Mrs. Parnell's death; she seemed to be an excellent good-natured young woman, and I believe the poor lad is much afflicted; they appeared to live perfectly well together." Afterwards he helped Parnell by introducing him to Bolingbroke and Oxford. He found kind words for Mrs. Manley in her illness, and Lady Ashburnham's death was "extremely moving. . . . She was my greatest favourite, and I am in excessive concern for her loss." Lastly, he was extraordinarily patient towards his servant Patrick, who drank, stopped out at night, and in many ways tried Swift's temper. There were good points about Patrick, but no doubt the great consideration which Swift showed him was due in part to the fact that he was a favourite of the ladies in Dublin, and had Mrs. Vanhomrigh to intercede for him.

But for the best example of the kindly side of Swift's nature, we must turn to what he tells us in the *Journal* about Stella herself. The "little language" which Swift used when writing to her was the language he employed when playing with Stella as a little child at Moor Park. Thackeray, who was not much in sympathy with Swift, said that he knew of "nothing more manly, more tender, more exquisitely touching, than some of these notes." Swift says that when he wrote plainly, he felt as if they were no longer alone, but " a bad scrawl is so snug it looks like a PMD." In writing his fond and playful prattle, he made up his mouth " just as if he were speaking it."[1]

Though Mrs. Dingley is constantly associated with Stella in the affectionate greetings in the *Journal*, she seems to have been included merely as a cloak to enable him to express the more freely his affection for her companion. Such phrases as " saucy girls," " sirrahs," " sauceboxes," and the like, are often applied to both; and sometimes Swift certainly writes as if the one were as dear to him as the other; thus we find, " Farewell, my dearest lives and delights, I love you better than ever, if possible, as hope saved, I do, and ever will. . . . I can count upon nothing, nor will, but upon MD's love and kindness. . . . And so farewell, dearest MD, Stella, Dingley, Presto, all together, now and for ever, all together." But as a rule, notwithstanding Swift's caution, the greetings intended for Stella alone are easily distinguishable in tone. He often refers to her weak eyes and delicate health. Thus he writes, " The chocolate is a present, madam, for Stella. Don't read this, you little rogue, with your little eyes; but give it to Dingley, pray now; and I will write as plain as the

[1] The "little language" is marked chiefly by such changes of letters (*e.g.*, l for r, or r for l) as a child makes when learning to speak. The combinations of letters in which Swift indulges are not so easy of interpretation. For himself he uses Pdfr, and sometimes Podefar or FR (perhaps Poor dear foolish rogue). Stella is Ppt (Poor pretty thing). MD (my dears) usually stands for both Stella and Mrs. Dingley, but sometimes for Stella alone. Mrs. Dingley is indicated by ME (Madam Elderly), D, or DD (Dear Dingley). The letters FW may mean Farewell, or Foolish Wenches. Lele seems sometimes to be There, there, and sometimes Truly.

skies." And again, "God Almighty bless poor Stella, and her eyes and head: what shall we do to cure them, poor dear life?" Or, "Now to Stella's little postscript; and I am almost crazed that you vex yourself for not writing. Can't you dictate to Dingley, and not strain your dear little eyes? I am sure 'tis the grief of my soul to think you are out of order." They had been keeping his birthday; Swift wished he had been with them, rather than in London, where he had no manner of pleasure: "I say Amen with all my heart and vitals, that we may never be asunder again ten days together while poor Presto lives." A few days later he says, "I wish I were at Laracor, with dear charming MD," and again, "Farewell, dearest beloved MD, and love poor poor Presto, who has not had one happy day since he left you." "I will say no more, but beg you to be easy till Fortune takes his course, and to believe MD's felicity is the great goal I aim at in all my pursuits." "How does Stella look, Madam Dingley?" he asks; "pretty well, a handsome young woman still? Will she pass in a crowd? Will she make a figure in a country church?" Elsewhere he writes, on receipt of a letter, "God Almighty bless poor dear Stella, and send her a great many birthdays, all happy and healthy and wealthy, and with me ever together, and never asunder again, unless by chance. . . . I can hardly imagine you absent when I am reading your letter or writing to you. No, faith, you are just here upon this little paper, and therefore I see and talk with you every evening constantly, and sometimes in the morning." The letters lay under Swift's pillow, and he fondled them as if he were caressing Stella's hand.

Of Stella herself we naturally have no direct account in the *Journal*, but we hear a good deal of her life in Ireland, and can picture what she was. Among her friends in and about Trim and Laracor were Dr. Raymond, the vicar of

Trim, and his wife, the Garret Wesleys, the Percevals, and
Mr. Warburton, Swift's curate. At Dublin there were Archdeacon Walls and his family; Alderman Stoyte, his wife
and sister-in-law; Dean Sterne and the Irish Postmaster-
General, Isaac Manley. For years these friends formed a
club which met in Dublin at each other's houses, to sup
and play cards (" ombre and claret, and toasted oranges "),
and we have frequent allusions to Stella's indifferent play,
and the money which she lost, much to Mrs. Dingley's
chagrin: " Poor Dingley fretted to see Stella lose that four
and elevenpence t'other night." Mrs. Dingley herself could
hardly play well enough to hold the cards while Stella went
into the next room. If at dinner the mutton was under-
done, and " poor Stella cannot eat, poor dear rogue," then
" Dingley is so vexed." Swift was for ever urging Stella to
walk and ride; she was " naturally a stout walker," and
" Dingley would do well enough if her petticoats were
pinned up." And we see Stella setting out on and returning from her ride, with her riband and mask: " Ah,
that riding to Laracor gives me short sighs as well as you,"
he says; " all the days I have passed here have been dirt
to those."

If the *Journal* shows us some of Swift's less attractive
qualities, it shows still more how great a store of humour,
tenderness, and affection there was in him. In these letters
we see his very soul; in his literary work we are seldom
moved to anything but admiration of his wit and genius.
Such daily outpourings could never have been written for
publication, they were meant only for one who understood
him perfectly; and everything that we know of Stella—
her kindliness, her wit, her vivacity, her loyalty—shows
that she was worthy of the confidence.

JOURNAL TO STELLA

LETTER I[1]

CHESTER, *Sept.* 2, 1710.

JOE[2] will give you an account of me till I got into the boat; after which the rogues made a new bargain, and forced me to give them two crowns, and talked as if we should not be able to overtake any ship: but in half an hour we got to the yacht; for the ships lay by [to] wait for my Lord Lieutenant's steward. We made our voyage in fifteen hours just. Last night I came to this town, and shall leave it, I believe, on Monday. The first man I met in Chester was Dr. Raymond.[3] He and Mrs. Raymond were here about levying a fine, in order to have power to sell their estate.

---

[1] Addressed "To Mrs. Dingley, at Mr. Curry's house over against the Ram in Capel Street, Dublin, Ireland," and endorsed by Esther Johnson, "Sept. 9. Received." Afterwards Swift added, "MD received this Sept. 9," and "Letters to Ireland from Sept. 1710, begun soon after the change of Ministry. Nothing in this."

[2] Beaumont is the "grey old fellow, poet Joe," of Swift's verses "On the little house by the Churchyard at Castlenock." Joseph Beaumont, a linen-merchant, is described as "a venerable, handsome, grey-headed man, of quick and various natural abilities, but not improved by learning." His inventions and mathematical speculations, relating to the longitude and other things, brought on mental troubles, which were intensified by bankruptcy, about 1718. He was afterwards removed from Dublin to his home at Trim, where he rallied; but in a few years his madness returned, and he committed suicide.

[3] Vicar of Trim, and formerly a Fellow of Trinity College, Dublin. In various places in his correspondence Swift criticises the failings of Dr. Anthony Raymond, who was, says Scott, "a particular friend." His unreliability in money matters, the improvidence of his large family, his peculiarities in grammar, his pride in his good manners, all these points are noticed in the *Journal* and elsewhere. But when Dr. Raymond returned to Ireland after a visit to London, Swift felt a little melancholy, and regretted that he had not seen more of him. In July 1713 Raymond was presented to the Crown living of Moyenet,

1

They have found everything answer very well. They both
desire to present their humble services to you: they do
not think of Ireland till next year. I got a fall off my horse,
riding here from Parkgate,[1] but no hurt; the horse understanding falls very well, and lying quietly till I get up. My
duty to the Bishop of Clogher.[2] I saw him returning from
Dunleary; but he saw not me. I take it ill he was not at
Convocation, and that I have not his name to my powers.[3]
I beg you will hold your resolution of going to Trim, and
riding there as much as you can. Let the Bishop of Clogher
remind the Bishop of Killala[4] to send me a letter, with one
enclosed to the Bishop of Lichfield.[5] Let all who write to
me, enclose to Richard Steele, Esq., at his office at the
Cockpit, near Whitehall.[6] But not MD; I will pay for their
letters at St. James's Coffee-house,[7] that I may have them
the sooner. My Lord Mountjoy[8] is now in the humour that
we should begin our journey this afternoon; so that I have
stole here again to finish this letter, which must be short or
long accordingly. I write this post to Mrs. Wesley,[9] and

[1] A small township on the estuary of the Dee, between twelve and thirteen
miles north-west of Chester. In the early part of the eighteenth century Parkgate was a rival of Holyhead as a station for the Dublin packets, which
started, on the Irish side, from off Kingsend.

[2] Dr. St. George Ashe, afterwards Bishop of Derry, who had been Swift's
tutor at Trinity College, Dublin. He died in 1718. It is this lifelong friend
who is said to have married Swift and Esther Johnson in 1716.

[3] The Commission to solicit for the remission of the First-Fruits and
twentieth parts, payable to the Crown by the Irish clergy, was signed by the
Archbishops of Armagh, Dublin, and Cashel, and the Bishops of Kildare,
Meath, and Killala.

[4] Dr. William Lloyd was appointed Bishop of Killala in 1690. He had
previously been Dean of Achonry.

[5] Dr. John Hough (1651-1743). In 1687 he had been elected President of
Magdalen College, Oxford, in place of the nominee of James II. Hough was
Bishop of Oxford, Lichfield, and Worcester successively, and declined the
primacy in 1715.

[6] Steele was at this time Gazetteer. The Cockpit, in Whitehall, looked
upon St. James's Palace, and was used for various Government purposes.

[7] This coffee-house, the resort of the Whig politicians, was kept by a man
named Elliot. It is often alluded to in the *Tatler* and *Spectator*.

[8] William Stewart, second Viscount Mountjoy, a friend and correspondent
of Swift's in Ireland. He was the son of one of William's generals, and was
himself a Lieutenant-General and Master-General of the Ordnance; he died
in 1728.

[9] Catherine, daughter of Maurice Keating, of Narraghmore, Kildare, and
wife of Garret Wesley, of Dangan, M.P. for Meath. She died in 1745. On

will tell her, that I have taken care she may have her bill of one hundred and fifteen pounds whenever she pleases to send for it; and in that case I desire you will send it her enclosed and sealed, and have it ready so, in case she should send for it: otherwise keep it. I will say no more till I hear whether I go to-day or no: if I do, the letter is almost at an end. My cozen Abigail is grown prodigiously old. God Almighty bless poo dee richar MD; and, for God's sake, be merry, and get oo health. I am perfectly resolved to return as soon as I have done my commission, whether it succeeds or no. I never went to England with so little desire in my life. If Mrs. Curry [1] makes any difficulty about the lodgings, I will quit them and pay her from July 9 last, and Mrs. Brent [2] must write to Parvisol [3] with orders accordingly. The post is come from London, and just going out; so I have only time to pray God to bless poor richr MD FW FW MD MD ME ME ME.

LETTER II

LONDON, *Sept.* 9, 1710.

I GOT here last Thursday,[4] after five days' travelling, weary the first, almost dead the second, tolerable the third, and well enough the rest; and am now glad of the fatigue, which has served for exercise; and I am at present well enough. The Whigs were ravished to see me, and would lay hold on

the death of Garret Wesley without issue in 1728, the property passed to a cousin, Richard Colley, who was afterwards created Baron Mornington, and was grandfather to the Duke of Wellington.

[1] The landlady of Esther Johnson and Mrs. Dingley.

[2] Swift's housekeeper at Laracor. Elsewhere Swift speaks of his "old Presbyterian housekeeper," "who has been my Walpole above thirty years, whenever I lived in this kingdom." "Joe Beaumont is my oracle for public affairs in the country, and an old Presbyterian woman in town."

[3] Isaiah Parvisol, Swift's tithe-agent and steward at Laracor, was an Irishman of French extraction, who died in 1718 (Birkbeck's *Unpublished Letters of Dean Swift*, 1899, p. 85).

[4] In some MS. Accounts of Swift's in the Forster Collection at South Kensington there is the following entry :—"Set out for England Aug. 31st on Thursday, 10 at night; landed at Parkgate Friday 1st at noon. Sept. 1, 1710, came to London. Thursday at noon, Sept. 7th, with Lord Mountjoy, etc. Mem. : Lord Mountjoy bore my expenses from Chester to London."

me as a twig while they are drowning,[1] and the great men making me their clumsy apologies, etc.   But my Lord Treasurer [2] received me with a great deal of coldness, which has enraged me so, I am almost vowing revenge.   I have not yet gone half my circle ; but I find all my acquaintance just as I left them.   I hear my Lady Giffard [3] is much at Court, and Lady Wharton [4] was ridiculing it t'other day ; so I have lost a friend there.   I have not yet seen her, nor intend it ; but I will contrive to see Stella's mother [5] some other way. I writ to the Bishop of Clogher from Chester ; and I now write to the Archbishop of Dublin.[6]   Everything is turning upside down ; every Whig in great office will, to a man, be infallibly put out ; and we shall have such a winter as hath not been seen in England.   Everybody asks me, how I came to be so long in Ireland, as naturally as if here were my being ; but no soul offers to make it so : and I protest I shall return to Dublin, and the Canal at Laracor,[7] with more

[1] In a letter to Archbishop King of the same date Swift says he was " equally caressed by both parties ; by one as a sort of bough for drowning men to lay hold of, and by the other as one discontented with the late men in power."

[2] The Earl of Godolphin, who was severely satirised by Swift in his *Sid Hamet's Rod*, 1710.   He had been ordered to break his staff as Treasurer on August 8.   Swift told Archbishop King that Godolphin was " altogether short, dry, and morose."

[3] Martha, widow of Sir Thomas Giffard, Bart., of County Kildare, the favourite sister of Sir William Temple, had been described by Swift in early pindaric verses as " wise and great."   Afterwards he was to call her " an old beast " (*Journal*,| Nov. 11, 1710).   Their quarrel arose, towards the close of 1709, out of a difference with regard to the publication of Sir William Temple's Works.   On the appearance of vol. v. Lady Giffard charged Swift with publishing portions of the writings from an unfaithful copy in lieu of the originals in his possession, and in particular with printing laudatory notices of Godolphin and Sunderland which Temple intended to omit, and with omitting an unfavourable remark on Sunderland which Temple intended to print.   Swift replied that the corrections were all made by Temple himself.

[4] Lord Wharton's second wife, Lucy, daughter of Lord Lisburn.   She died in 1716, a few months after her husband.   See Lady M. W. Montagu's *Letters*.

[5] Mrs. Bridget Johnson, who married, as her second husband, Ralph Mose or Moss, of Farnham, an agent for Sir William Temple's estate, was waiting-woman or companion to Lady Giffard.   In her will (1722) Lady Giffard left Mrs. Moss £20, " with my silver cup and cover."   Mrs. Moss died in 1745, when letters of administration were granted to a creditor of the deceased.

[6] Dr. William King (1650–1729), a Whig and High Churchman, had more than one difference with Swift during the twenty years following Swift's first visit to London in connection with the First-Fruits question.

[7] Swift's benefice, in the diocese of Meath, two miles from Trim.

satisfaction than ever I did in my life. The Tatler[1] expects
every day to be turned out of his employment; and the
Duke of Ormond,[2] they say, will be Lieutenant of Ireland.
I hope you are now peaceably in Presto's[3] lodgings; but I
resolve to turn you out by Christmas; in which time I shall
either do my business, or find it not to be done. Pray be at
Trim by the time this letter comes to you; and ride little
Johnson, who must needs be now in good case. I have
begun this letter unusually, on the post-night, and have
already written to the Archbishop; and cannot lengthen this.
Henceforth I will write something every day to MD, and
make it a sort of journal; and when it is full, I will send it,
whether MD writes or no; and so that will be pretty: and
I shall always be in conversation with MD, and MD with
Presto. Pray make Parvisol pay you the ten pounds immediately; so I ordered him. They tell me I am grown fatter,
and look better; and, on Monday, Jervas[4] is to retouch my
picture. I thought I saw Jack Temple[5] and his wife pass
by me to-day in their coach; but I took no notice of them.
I am glad I have wholly shaken off that family. Tell
the Provost,[6] I have obeyed his commands to the Duke of

<hr/>

[1] Steele, who had been issuing the *Tatler* thrice weekly since April 1709.
He lost the Gazetteership in October.

[2] James, second Duke of Ormond (1665-1745) was appointed Lord Lieutenant on the 26th of October. In the following year he became Captain-General
and Commander-in-Chief. He was impeached of high treason and attainted
in 1715; and he died in exile.

[3] "Presto," substituted by the original editor for "Pdfr," was suggested
by a passage in the *Journal* for Aug. 2, 1711, where Swift says that the
Duchess of Shrewsbury "could not say my name in English, but said Dr.
Presto, which is Italian for Swift."

[4] Charles Jervas, the popular portrait-painter, has left two portraits of Swift,
one of which is in the National Portrait Gallery, and the other in the Bodleian
Library.

[5] Sir William Temple's nephew, and son of Sir John Temple (died 1704),
Solicitor and Attorney-General, and Speaker of the Irish House of Commons.
"Jack" Temple acquired the estaté of Moor Park, Surrey, by his marriage
with Elizabeth, granddaughter of Sir William Temple, and elder daughter
of John Temple, who committed suicide in 1689. As late as 1706 Swift
received an invitation to visit Moor Park.

[6] Dr. Benjamin Pratt, Provost of Trinity College, Dublin, was appointed
Dean of Down in 1717. Swift calls him "a person of wit and learning," and
"a gentleman of good birth and fortune, . . . very much esteemed among
us" (*Short Character of Thomas, Earl of Wharton*). On his death in 1721

Ormond; or let it alone, if you please.   I saw Jemmy Leigh [1] just now at the Coffee-house, who asked after you with great kindness: he talks of going in a fortnight to Ireland. My service to the Dean,[2] and Mrs. Walls, and her Archdeacon.[3] Will Frankland's [4] wife is near bringing to-bed, and I have promised to christen the child.   I fancy you had my Chester letter the Tuesday after I writ.   I presented Dr. Raymond to Lord Wharton [5] at Chester.   Pray let me know when Joe gets his money.[6]   It is near ten, and I hate to send by the bellman.[7]   MD shall have a longer letter in a week, but I send this only to tell I am safe in London; and so farewell, etc.

Swift wrote, "He was one of the oldest acquaintance I had, and the last that I expected to die.   He has left a young widow, in very good circumstances.   He had schemes of long life. . . .   What a ridiculous thing is man!" (*Unpublished Letters of Dean Swift*, 1899, p. 106).

[1] A Westmeath landlord, whom Swift met from time to time in London. The Leighs were well acquainted with Esther Johnson.

[2] Dr. Enoch Sterne, appointed Dean of St. Patrick's, Dublin, in 1704. Swift was his successor in the deanery on Dr. Sterne's appointment as Bishop of Dromore in 1713.   In 1717 Sterne was translated to the bishopric of Clogher.   He spent much money on the cathedrals, etc., with which he was connected.

[3] Archdeacon Walls was rector of Castle Knock, near Trim.   Esther Johnson was a frequent visitor at his house in Queen Street, Dublin.

[4] William Frankland, Comptroller of the Inland Office at the Post Office, was the second son of the Postmaster-General, Sir Thomas Frankland, Bart. (see p. 7).   Luttrell (vi. 333) records that in 1708 he was made Treasurer of the Stamp Office, or, according to Chamberlayne's *Mag. Brit. Notitia* for 1710, Receiver-General.

[5] Thomas Wharton, Earl and afterwards Marquis of Wharton, had been one of Swift's fellow-travellers from Dublin.   Lord Lieutenant of Ireland under the Whig Government, from 1708 to 1710, Wharton was the most thoroughgoing party man that had yet appeared in English politics; and his political enemies did not fail to make the most of his well-known immorality.   In his Notes to Macky's *Characters* Swift described Wharton as "the most universal villain that ever I knew."   On his death in 1715 he was succeeded by his profligate son, Philip, who was created Duke of Wharton in 1718.

[6] This money was a premium the Government had promised Beaumont for his Mathematical Sleying Tables, calculated for the improvement of the linen manufacture.

[7] The bellman was both town-crier and night-watchman.

LETTER III

LONDON, *Sept.* 9, 1710.

AFTER seeing the Duke of Ormond, dining with Dr. Cockburn,[1] passing some part of the afternoon with Sir Matthew Dudley[2] and Will Frankland, the rest at St. James's Coffee-house, I came home, and writ to the Archbishop of Dublin and MD, and am going to bed. I forgot to tell you, that I begged Will Frankland to stand Manley's[3] friend with his father in this shaking season for places. He told me, his father was in danger to be out; that several were now soliciting for Manley's place; that he was accused of opening letters; that Sir Thomas Frankland[4] would sacrifice everything to save himself; and in that, I fear, Manley is undone, etc.

10. To-day I dined with Lord Mountjoy at Kensington; saw my mistress, Ophy Butler's[5] wife, who is grown a little charmless. I sat till ten in the evening with Addison and

[1] Dr. William Cockburn (1669–1739), Swift's physician, of a good Scottish family, was educated at Leyden. He invented an electuary for the cure of fluxes, and in 1730, in *The Danger of Improving Physick*, satirised the academical physicians who envied him the fortune he had made by his secret remedy. He was described in 1729 as "an old very rich quack."

[2] Sir Matthew Dudley, Bart., an old Whig friend, was M.P. for Huntingdonshire, and Commissioner of the Customs from 1706 to 1712, and again under George I., until his death in 1721.

[3] Isaac Manley, who was appointed Postmaster-General in Ireland in 1703 (Luttrell, v. 333). He had previously been Comptroller of the English Letter Office, a post in which he was succeeded by William Frankland, son of Sir Thomas Frankland. Dunton calls Manley "loyal and acute."

[4] Sir Thomas Frankland was Joint Postmaster-General from 1691 to 1715. He succeeded to the baronetcy on the death of his father, Sir William Frankland, in 1697, and he died in 1726. Macky describes Sir Thomas as "of a sweet and easy disposition, zealous for the Constitution, yet not forward, and indulgent to his dependants." On this Swift comments, "This is a fair character."

[5] Theophilus Butler, elected M.P. for Cavan, in the Irish Parliament, in 1703, and for Belturbet (as "the Right Hon. Theophilus Butler") in 1713. On May 3, 1710, Luttrell wrote (*Brief Relation of State Affairs*, vi. 577), "'Tis said the Earl of Montrath, Lord Viscount Mountjoy . . . and Mr. Butler will be made Privy Councillors of the Kingdom of Ireland." Butler—a contemporary of Swift's at Trinity College, Dublin—was created Baron of Newtown-Butler in 1715, and his brother, who succeeded him in 1723, was made Viscount Lanesborough. Butler's wife was Emilia, eldest daughter and co-heir of James Stopford, of Tara, County Meath.

Steele: Steele will certainly lose his Gazetteer's place, all the world detesting his engaging in parties.[1]   At ten I went to the Coffee-house, hoping to find Lord Radnor,[2] whom I had not seen.   He was there; and for an hour and a half we talked treason heartily against the Whigs, their baseness and ingratitude.   And I am come home, rolling resentments in my mind, and framing schemes of revenge: full of which (having written down some hints) I go to bed.   I am afraid MD dined at home, because it is Sunday; and there was the little half-pint of wine: for God's sake, be good girls, and all will be well.   Ben Tooke[3] was with me this morning.

11. Seven, morning.   I am rising to go to Jervas to finish my picture, and 'tis shaving - day, so good - morrow MD; but don't keep me now, for I can't stay; and pray dine with the Dean, but don't lose your money.   I long to hear from you, etc. — Ten at night.   I sat four hours this morning to Jervas, who has given my picture quite another turn, and now approves it entirely; but we must have the approbation of the town.   If I were rich enough, I would get a copy of it, and bring it over.   Mr. Addison and I dined together at his lodgings, and I sat with him part of this evening; and I am now come home to write an hour.   Patrick[4] observes, that the rabble here are much more inquisitive in politics than in Ireland.   Every day we expect changes, and the Parliament to be dissolved.   Lord Wharton expects every day to be out: he is working like a horse for elections; and, in short, I never saw so great a ferment among all sorts of people.   I had a miserable letter from Joe last

[1] No. 193 of the *Tatler*, for July 4, 1710, contained a letter from Downes the Prompter—not by Steele himself—in ridicule of Harley and his proposed Ministry.

[2] Charles Robartes, second Earl of Radnor, who died in 1723.   In the *Journal* for Dec. 30, 1711, Swift calls him "a scoundrel.

[3] Benjamin Tooke, Swift's bookseller or publisher, lived at the Middle Temple Gate.   Dunton wrote of him, "He is truly honest, a man of refined sense, and is unblemished in his reputation."   Tooke died in 1723.

[4] Swift's servant, of whose misdeeds he makes frequent complaints in the *Journal.*

Saturday, telling me Mr. Pratt [1] refuses payment of his money. I have told it Mr. Addison, and will to Lord Wharton; but I fear with no success.   However, I will do all I can.

12. To-day I presented Mr. Ford [2] to the Duke of Ormond; and paid my first visit to Lord President,[3] with whom I had much discourse; but put him always off when he began to talk of Lord Wharton in relation to me, till he urged it: then I said, he knew I never expected anything from Lord Wharton, and that Lord Wharton knew that I understood it so.   He said that he had written twice to Lord Wharton about me, who both times said nothing at all to that part of his letter.   I am advised not to meddle in the affair of the First-Fruits, till this hurry is a little over, which still depends, and we are all in the dark.   Lord President told me he expects every day to be out, and has done so these two months.   I protest, upon my life, I am heartily weary of this town, and wish I had never stirred.

13. I went this morning to the city, to see Mr. Stratford the Hamburg merchant, my old schoolfellow;[4] but calling at Bull's [5] on Ludgate Hill, he forced me to his house at Hampstead to dinner among a great deal of ill company; among the rest Mr. Hoadley,[6] the Whig clergyman, so famous for acting the contrary part to Sacheverell:[7] but to-

---

[1] Deputy Vice-Treasurer of Ireland.   In one place Swift calls him Captain Pratt; and in all probability he is the John Pratt who, as we learn from Dalton's *English Army Lists*, was appointed captain in General Erle's regiment of foot in 1699, and was out of the regiment by 1706.   In 1702 he obtained the Queen's leave to be absent from the regiment when it was sent to the West Indies.   Pratt seems to have been introduced to Swift by Addison.

[2] Charles Ford, of Wood Park, near Dublin, was a great lover of the opera and a friend of the Tory wits.   He was appointed Gazetteer in 1712.   Gay calls him "joyous Ford," and he was given to over-indulgence in conviviality. See Swift's poem on Stella at Wood Park.

[3] Lord Somers, to whom Swift had dedicated *The Tale of a Tub*, with high praise of his public and private virtues.   In later years Swift said that Somers "possessed all excellent qualifications except virtue."

[4] At the foundation school of the Ormonds at Kilkenny (see p. 10, note 6).

[5] A Whig haberdasher.

[6] Benjamin Hoadley, the Whig divine, had been engaged in controversy with Sacheverell, Blackall, and Atterbury.   After the accession of George I. he became Bishop of Bangor, Hereford, Salisbury, and Winchester in succession.

[7] Dr. Henry Sacheverell, whose impeachment and trial had led to the fall of the Whig Government.

morrow I design again to see Stratford. I was glad, how-
ever, to be at Hampstead, where I saw Lady Lucy [1] and
Moll Stanhope. I hear very unfortunate news of Mrs.
Long; [2] she and her comrade [3] have broke up house, and
she is broke for good and all, and is gone to the country:
I should be extremely sorry if this be true.

14. To-day, I saw Patty Rolt, [4] who heard I was in town;
and I dined with Stratford at a merchant's in the city, where
I drank the first Tokay wine I ever saw; and it is admirable, yet not to the degree I expected. Stratford is worth
a plum, [5] and is now lending the Government forty thousand
pounds; yet we were educated together at the same school
and university. [6] We hear the Chancellor [7] is to be suddenly

[1] Sir Berkeley Lucy, Bart., F.R.S., married Katherine, daughter of Charles
Cotton, of Beresford, Staffordshire, Isaac Walton's friend. Lady Lucy died
in 1740, leaving an only surviving daughter, Mary, who married the youngest
son of the Earl of Northampton, and had two sons, who became successively
seventh and eighth Earls of Northampton. Forster and others assumed that
"Lady Lucy" was a Lady Lucy Stanhope, though they were not able to identify
her. It was reserved for Mr. Ryland to clear up this difficulty. As he points
out, Lady Lucy's elder sister, Olive, married George Stanhope, Dean of Canterbury, and left a daughter Mary,—Swift's "Moll Stanhope,"—a beauty and a
madcap, who married, in 1712, William Burnet, son of Bishop Burnet, and
died in 1714. Mary, another sister of Lady Lucy's, married Augustine Armstrong, of Great Ormond Street, and is the Mrs. Armstrong mentioned by
Swift on Feb. 3, 1711, as a pretender to wit, without taste. Sir Berkeley
Lucy's mother was a daughter of the first Earl of Berkeley, and it was probably
through the Berkeleys that Swift came to know the Lucys.
[2] Ann Long was sister to Sir James Long, and niece to Colonel Strange-
ways. Once a beauty and a toast of the Kit-Cat Club, she fell into narrow
circumstances through imprudence and the unkindness of her friends, and
retired under the name of Mrs. Smythe to Lynn, in Norfolk, where she died
in 1711 (see *Journal*, December 25, 1711). Swift said, "She was the most
beautiful person of the age she lived in; of great honour and virtue, infinite
sweetness and generosity of temper, and true good sense" (Forster's *Swift*,
229). In a letter of December 1711, Swift wrote that she "had every valuable
quality of body and mind that could make a lady loved and esteemed."
[3] Said, I know not on what authority, to be Swift's friend, Mrs. Barton (see p.
20). But Mrs. Barton is often mentioned by Swift as living in London in 1710-11.
[4] One of Swift's cousins, who was separated from her husband, a man of
bad character, living abroad. Her second husband, Lancelot, a servant of
Lord Sussex, lived in New Bond Street, and there Swift lodged in 1727.
[5] £100,000.
[6] Francis Stratford's name appears in the Dublin University Register for
1686 immediately before Swift's. Budgell is believed to have referred to the
friendship of Swift and Stratford in the *Spectator*, No. 353, where he describes
two schoolfellows, and says that the man of genius was buried in a country
parsonage of £160 a year, while his friend, with the bare abilities of a common
scrivener, had gained an estate of above £100,000.
[7] William Cowper, afterwards Lord Cowper.

out, and Sir Simon Harcourt[1] to succeed him : I am come early home, not caring for the Coffee-house.

15. To-day Mr. Addison, Colonel Freind,[2] and I, went to see the million lottery[3] drawn at Guildhall. The jackanapes of bluecoat boys gave themselves such airs in pulling out the tickets, and showed white hands open to the company, to let us see there was no cheat. We dined at a country-house near Chelsea, where Mr. Addison often retires ; and to-night, at the Coffee-house, we hear Sir Simon Harcourt is made Lord Keeper ; so that now we expect every moment the Parliament will be dissolved ; but I forgot that this letter will not go in three or four days, and that my news will be stale, which I should therefore put in the last paragraph. Shall I send this letter before I hear from MD, or shall I keep it to lengthen ? I have not yet seen Stella's mother, because I will not see Lady Giffard ; but I will contrive to go there when Lady Giffard is abroad. I forgot to mark my two former letters ; but I remember this is Number 3, and I have not yet had Number 1 from MD ; but I shall by Monday, which I reckon will be just a fortnight after you had my first. I am resolved to bring over a great deal of china. I loved it mightily to-day.[4] What shall I bring?

16. Morning. Sir John Holland,[5] Comptroller of the Household, has sent to desire my acquaintance : I have a

---

[1] Sir Simon Harcourt, afterwards Viscount Harcourt, had been counsel for Sacheverell. On Sept. 19, 1710, he was appointed Attorney-General, and on October 19 Lord Keeper of the Great Seal. In April 1713 he became Lord Chancellor.

[2] This may be some relative of Dr. John Freind (see p. 65), or, more probably, as Sir Henry Craik suggests, a misprint for Colonel Frowde, Addison's friend (see *Journal*, Nov. 4, 1710). No officer named Freind or Friend is mentioned in Dalton's *English Army Lists*.

[3] See the *Tatler*, Nos. 124, 203. There are various allusions in the "Wentworth Papers" to this, the first State Lottery of 1710 ; and two bluecoat boys drawing out the tickets, and showing their hands to the crowd, as Swift describes them, are shown in a reproduction of a picture in a contemporary pamphlet given in Ashton's *Social Life in the Reign of Queen Anne*, i. 115.

[4] A few weeks later Swift wrote, "I took a fancy of resolving to grow mad for it, but now it is off."

[5] Sir John Holland, Bart., was a leading manager for the Commons in the impeachment of Sacheverell. He succeeded Sir Thomas Felton in the Comptrollership in March 1710.

mind to refuse him, because he is a Whig, and will, I suppose, be out among the rest; but he is a man of worth and learning. Tell me, do you like this journal way of writing? Is it not tedious and dull?

Night. I dined to-day with a cousin, a printer,[1] where Patty Rolt lodges, and then came home, after a visit or two; and it has been a very insipid day. Mrs. Long's misfortune is confirmed to me; bailiffs were in her house; she retired to private lodgings; thence to the country, nobody knows where: her friends leave letters at some inn, and they are carried to her; and she writes answers without dating them from any place. I swear, it grieves me to the soul.

17. To-day I dined six miles out of town, with Will Pate[2] the learned woollen-draper; Mr. Stratford went with me; six miles here is nothing: we left Pate after sunset, and were here before it was dark. This letter shall go on Tuesday, whether I hear from MD or no. My health continues pretty well; pray God Stella may give me a good account of hers! and I hope you are now at Trim, or soon designing it. I was disappointed to-night: the fellow gave me a letter, and I hoped to see little MD's hand; and it was only to invite me to a venison pasty to-day: so I lost my pasty into the bargain. Pox on these declining courtiers! Here is Mr. Brydges,[3] the Paymaster-General, desiring my acquaintance; but I hear the Queen sent Lord Shrewsbury[4] to assure him he may keep his place; and he promises me

[1] Dryden Leach (see p. 51).

[2] William Pate, "*bel esprit* and woollen-draper," as Swift called him, lived opposite the Royal Exchange. He was Sheriff of London in 1734, and died in 1746. Arbuthnot, previous to matriculating at Oxford, lodged with Pate, who gave him a letter of introduction to Dr. Charlett, Master of University College; and Pate is supposed to have been the woollen-draper, "remarkable for his learning and good-nature," who is mentioned by Steele in the *Guardian*, No. 141.

[3] James Brydges, son of Lord Chandos of Sudeley, was appointed Paymaster-General of Forces Abroad in 1707. He succeeded his father as Baron Chandos in 1714, and was created Duke of Chandos in 1729. The "princely Chandos", and his house at Canons suggested to Pope the Timon's villa of the "Epistle to Lord Burlington." The Duke died in 1744.

[4] Charles Talbot, created Duke of Shrewsbury in 1694, was held in great esteem by William III., and was Lord Chamberlain under Anne. In 1713 he became Lord Lieutenant of Ireland, and held various offices under George I.,

great assistance in the affair of the First-Fruits. Well, I must turn over this leaf to-night, though the side would hold another line; but pray consider this is a whole sheet; it holds a plaguy deal, and you must be content to be weary; but I'll do so no more. Sir Simon Harcourt is made Attorney-General, and not Lord Keeper.

18. To-day I dined with Mr. Stratford at Mr. Addison's retirement near Chelsea; then came to town; got home early, and began a letter to the *Tatler*,[1] about the corruptions of style and writing, etc., and, having not heard from you, am resolved this letter shall go to-night. Lord Wharton was sent for to town in mighty haste, by the Duke of Devonshire:[2] they have some project in hand; but it will not do, for every hour we expect a thorough revolution, and that the Parliament will be dissolved. When you see Joe, tell him Lord Wharton is too busy to mind any of his affairs; but I will get what good offices I can from Mr. Addison, and will write to-day to Mr. Pratt; and bid Joe not to be discouraged, for I am confident he will get the money under any Government; but he must have patience.

19. I have been scribbling this morning, and I believe shall hardly fill this side to-day, but send it as it is; and it is good enough for naughty girls that won't write to a body, and to a good boy like Presto. I thought to have sent this to-night, but was kept by company, and could not; and, to say the truth, I had a little mind to expect one post more for a letter from MD. Yesterday at noon died the Earl of Anglesea,[3] the great support of the Tories; so that employment of Vice-Treasurer of Ireland is again vacant. We were

until his death in 1718. "Before he was o. age," says Macaulay, "he was allowed to be one of the finest gentlemen and finest scholars of his time."

[1] See No. 230.

[2] William Cavendish, second Duke of Devonshire (1673–1729), who was Lord Steward from 1707 to 1710 and from 1714 to 1716. Afterwards he was Lord President of the Council. Swift's comment on Macky's character of this Whig nobleman was, "A very poor understanding."

[3] John Annesley, fourth Earl of Anglesea, a young nobleman of great promise, had only recently been appointed Joint Vice-Treasurer, Receiver-General, and Paymaster of the Forces in Ireland, and sworn of the Privy Council.

to have been great friends, and I could hardly have a loss that could grieve me more. The Bishop of Durham[1] died the same day. The Duke of Ormond's daughter[2] was to visit me to-day at a third place by way of advance,[3] and I am to return it to-morrow. I have had a letter from Lady Berkeley, begging me for charity to come to Berkeley Castle, for company to my lord,[4] who has been ill of a dropsy; but I cannot go, and must send my excuse to-morrow. I am told that in a few hours there will be more removals.

20. To-day I returned my visits to the Duke's daughters;[5] the insolent drabs came up to my very mouth to salute me. Then I heard the report confirmed of removals; my Lord President Somers; the Duke of Devonshire, Lord Steward; and Mr. Boyle,[6] Secretary of State, are all turned out to-day. I never remember such bold steps taken by a Court: I am almost shocked at it, though I did not care if they were all hanged. We are astonished why the Parliament is not yet dissolved, and why they keep a matter of that importance to the last. We shall have a strange winter here, between the struggles of a cunning provoked discarded party, and the triumphs of one in power; of both which I shall be an indifferent spectator, and return very peaceably to Ireland,

[1] Nichols, followed by subsequent editors, suggested that "Durham" was a mistake for "St. David's," because Dr. George Bull, Bishop of St. David's, died in 1710. But Dr. Bull died on Feb. 17, 1710, though his successor, Dr. Philip Bisse, was not appointed until November; and Swift was merely repeating a false report of the death of Lord Crewe, Bishop of Durham, which was current on the day on which he wrote. Luttrell says, on Sept. 19, "The Lord Crewe . . . died lately"; but on the 23rd he adds, "The Bishop of Durham is not dead as reported" (*Brief Relation*, vi. 630, 633).

[2] Lady Elizabeth ("Betty") Butler, who died unmarried in 1750.

[3] Swift wrote in 1734, "Once every year I issued out an edict, commanding that all ladies of wit, sense, merit, and quality, who had an ambition to be acquainted with me, should make the first advances at their peril: which edict, you may believe, was universally obeyed."

[4] Charles, second Earl of Berkeley (1649–1710), married Elizabeth, daughter of Baptist Noel, Viscount Campden. The Earl died on Sept. 24, 1710, and his widow in 1719. Swift, it will be remembered, had been chaplain to Lord Berkeley in Ireland in 1699.

[5] Lady Betty and Lady Mary Butler (see p. 44).

[6] Henry Boyle, Chancellor of the Exchequer from 1702 to 1708, was Secretary of State from 1708 to 1710, when he was succeeded by St. John. In 1714 he was created Baron Carleton, and he was Lord President from 1721 until his death in 1725.

when I have done my part in the affair I am entrusted with, whether it succeeds or no. To-morrow I change my lodgings in Pall Mall for one in Bury Street,[1] where I suppose I shall continue while I stay in London. If anything happens to-morrow, I will add it.—Robin's Coffee-house.[2] We have great news just now from Spain; Madrid taken, and Pampeluna. I am here ever interrupted.

21. I have just received your letter, which I will not answer now; God be thanked all things are so well. I find you have not yet had my second: I had a letter from Parvisol, who tells me he gave Mrs. Walls a bill of twenty pounds for me, to be given to you; but you have not sent it. This night the Parliament is dissolved: great news from Spain; King-Charles and Stanhope are at Madrid, and Count Staremberg has taken Pampeluna. Farewell. This is from St. James's Coffee-house. I will begin my answer to your letter to-night, but not send it this week. Pray tell me, whether you like this journal way of writing.—I don't like your reasons for not going to Trim. Parvisol tells me he can sell your horse. Sell it, with a pox? Pray let him know that he shall sell his soul as soon. What? sell anything that Stella loves, and may sometimes ride? It is hers, and let her do as she pleases: pray let him know this by the first that you know goes to Trim. Let him sell my grey, and be hanged.

LETTER IV

LONDON, *Sept.* 21, 1710.

HERE must I begin another letter, on a whole sheet, for fear saucy little MD should be angry, and think *much* that the paper is too *little*. I had your letter this night, as I

---

[1] On Sept. 29 Swift wrote that his rooms consisted of the first floor, a dining-room and bed-chamber, at eight shillings a week. On his last visit to England, in 1726, he lodged "next door to the Royal Chair" in Bury Street. Steele lived in the same street from 1707 to 1712; and Mrs. Vanhomrigh was Swift's next-door neighbour.

[2] In Exchange Alley. Cf. *Spectator*, No. 454: "I went afterwards to Robin's, and saw people who had dined with me at the fivepenny ordinary just before, give bills for the value of large estates."

told you just and no more in my last; for this must be taken
up in answering yours, saucebox.   I believe I told you where
I dined to-day ; and to-morrow I go out of town for two
days to dine with the same company on Sunday ; Molesworth[1]
the Florence Envoy, Stratford, and some others.   I heard
to-day that a gentlewoman from Lady Giffard's house had
been at the Coffee-house to inquire for me.   It was Stella's
mother, I suppose.   I shall send her a penny-post letter[2]
to - morrow, and contrive to see her without hazarding
seeing Lady Giffard, which I will not do until she begs my
pardon.

22. I dined to-day at Hampstead with Lady Lucy, etc., and
when I got home found a letter from Joe, with one enclosed
to Lord Wharton, which I will send to his Excellency, and
second it as well as I can ; but to talk of getting the Queen's
order is a jest.   Things are in such a combustion here, that
I am advised not to meddle yet in the affair I am upon,
which concerns the clergy of a whole kingdom ; and does he
think anybody will trouble the Queen about Joe ?   We shall,
I hope, get a recommendation from the Lord Lieutenant to
the trustees for the linen business, and I hope that will do ;
and so I will write to him in a few days, and he must have
patience.   This is an answer to part of your letter as well as
his.   I lied ; it is to-morrow I go to the country, and I won't
answer a bit more of your letter yet.

23. Here is such a stir and bustle with this little MD of
ours ; I must be writing every night ; I can't go to bed
without a word to them ; I can't put out my candle till I
have bid them good-night : O Lord, O Lord !   Well, I dined
the first time, to-day, with Will Frankland and his fortune :

---

[1] John Molesworth, Commissioner of the Stamp Office, was sent as Envoy to
Tuscany in 1710, and was afterwards Minister at Florence, Venice, Geneva,
and Turin.   He became second Viscount Molesworth in 1725, and died in
1731.

[2] Misson says, " Every two hours you may write to any part of the city or
suburbs : he that receives it pays a penny, and you give nothing when you put
it into the Post ; but when you write into the country both he that writes and
he that receives pay each a penny."   The Penny Post system had been taken
over by the Government, but was worked separately from the general Post.

she is not very handsome.   Did I not say I would go out of
town to-day ?   I hate lying abroad and clutter; I go to-
morrow in Frankland's chariot, and come back at night.
Lady Berkeley has invited me to Berkeley Castle, and Lady
Betty Germaine [1] to Drayton in Northamptonshire ; and I'll
go to neither.   Let me alone, I must finish my pamphlet.   I
have sent a long letter to Bickerstaff : [2] let the Bishop of
Clogher smoke [3] it if he can.   Well, I'll write to the Bishop
of Killala ; but you might have told him how sudden and
unexpected my journey was though.   Deuce take Lady
S——; and if I know D——y, he is a rawboned-faced fellow,
not handsome, nor visibly so young as you say : she sacrifices
two thousand pounds a year, and keeps only six hundred.
Well, you have had all my land journey in my second letter,
and so much for that.   So, you have got into Presto's
lodgings ; very fine, truly !   We have had a fortnight of the
most glorious weather on earth, and still continues : I hope
you have made the best of it.   Ballygall [4] will be a pure [5]
good place for air, if Mrs. Ashe makes good her promise.
Stella writes like an emperor : I am afraid it hurts your eyes ;
take care of that pray, pray, Mrs. Stella.   Can't you do what
you will with your own horse ?   Pray don't let that puppy
Parvisol sell him.   Patrick is drunk about three times a
week, and I bear it, and he has got the better of me ; but
one of these days I will positively turn him off to the wide

---

[1] The Countess of Berkeley's second daughter, who married, in 1706, Sir
John Germaine, Bart. (1650–1718), a soldier of fortune. Lady Betty Germaine
is said to have written a satire on Pope (Nichols' *Literary Anecdotes*, ii. 11),
and was a constant correspondent of Swift's. She was always a Whig, and
shortly before her death in 1769 she made a present of £100 to John Wilkes,
then in prison in the Tower. Writing of Lady Betty Butler (see p. 14) and
Lady Betty Germaine, Swift says elsewhere, " I saw two Lady Bettys this
afternoon ; the beauty of one, the good breeding and nature of the other,
and the wit of either, would have made a fine woman." Germaine obtained the
estate at Drayton through his first wife, Lady Mary Mordaunt — Lord
Peterborough's sister—who had been divorced by her first husband, the Duke
of Norfolk. Lady Betty was thirty years younger than her husband, and
after Sir John's death she remained a widow for over fifty years.

[2] The letter in No. 230 of the *Tatler*.

[3] Discover, find out. Cf. Shakespeare's *All's Well that Ends Well*, iii. 6 :
" He was first smoked by the old Lord Lafeu."

[4] A village near Dublin.   [5] Excellent.

2

world, when none of you are by to intercede for him.—Stuff
—how can I get her husband into the Charter-house? get
a —— into the Charter-house.—Write constantly! Why,
sirrah, don't I write every day, and sometimes twice a day to
MD? Now I have answered all your letter, and the rest
must be as it can be: send me my bill. Tell Mrs. Brent[1]
what I say of the Charter-house. I think this enough for
one night; and so farewell till this time to-morrow.

24. To-day I dined six miles out of town at Will Pate's,
with Stratford, Frankland, and the Molesworths,[2] and came
home at night, and was weary and lazy. I can say no more
now, but good-night.

25. I was so lazy to-day that I dined at next door,[3] and
have sat at home since six, writing to the Bishop of Clogher,
Dean Sterne, and Mr. Manley: the last, because I am in fear
for him about his place, and have sent him my opinion, what
I and his other friends here think he ought to do. I hope
he will take it well. My advice was, to keep as much in
favour as possible with Sir Thomas Frankland, his master here.

26. Smoke how I widen the margin by lying in bed when
I write. My bed lies on the wrong side for me, so that I am
forced often to write when I am up. Manley, you must
know, has had people putting in for his place already; and
has been complained of for opening letters. Remember that
last Sunday, September 24, 1710, was as hot as midsummer.
This was written in the morning; it is now night, and Presto
in bed. Here's a clutter, I have gotten MD's second letter,
and I must answer it here. I gave the bill to Tooke, and
so— Well, I dined to-day with Sir John Holland the
Comptroller, and sat with him till eight; then came home,
and sent my letters, and writ part of a lampoon,[4] which goes

---

[1] See p. 3.
[2] John Molesworth (see p. 16), and, probably, his brother Richard, afterwards
third Viscount Molesworth, who had saved the Duke of Marlborough's life at
the battle of Ramillies, and had been appointed, in 1710, colonel of a regiment
of foot.
[3] Presumably at Charles Ford's (see p. 9).
[4] *The Virtues of Sid Hamet the Magician's Rod*, published as a single
folio sheet, was a satire on Godolphin.

on very slow: and now I am writing to saucy MD; no wonder, indeed, good boys must write to naughty girls. I have not seen your mother yet; my penny-post letter, I suppose, miscarried: I will write another. Mr. S—— came to see me; and said M—— was going to the country next morning with her husband (who I find is a surly brute); so I could only desire my service to her.

27. To-day all our company dined at Will Frankland's, with Steele and Addison too. This is the first rainy day since I came to town; I cannot afford to answer your letter yet. Morgan,[1] the puppy, writ me a long letter, to desire I would recommend him for purse-bearer or secretary to the next Lord Chancellor that would come with the next Governor. I will not answer him; but beg you will say these words to his father Raymond,[2] or anybody that will tell him: That Dr. Swift has received his letter; and would be very ready to serve him, but cannot do it in what he desires, because he has no sort of interest in the persons to be applied to. These words you may write, and let Joe, or Mr. Warburton,[3] give them to him: a pox on him! However, it is by these sort of ways that fools get preferment. I must not end yet, because I cannot say good-night without losing a line, and then MD would scold; but now, good-night.

28. I have the finest piece of Brazil tobacco for Dingley that ever was born.[4] You talk of Leigh; why, he won't be in Dublin these two months: he goes to the country, then

[1] Apparently Marcus Antonius Morgan, steward to the Bishop of Kildare (Craik). Swift wrote to the Duke of Montagu on Aug. 12, 1713 (*Buccleuch MSS.*, 1899, i. 359), "Mr. Morgan of Kingstrope is a friend, and was, I am informed, put out of the Commission of Justice for being so."
[2] Dr. Raymond is called Morgan's "father" because he warmly supported Morgan's interests.
[3] The Rev. Thomas Warburton, Swift's curate at Laracor, whom Swift described to the Archbishop as "a gentleman of very good learning and sense, who has behaved himself altogether unblamably."
[4] The tobacco was to be used as snuff. About this time ladies much affected the use of snuff, and Steele, in No. 344 of the *Spectator*, speaks of Flavilla pulling out her box, "which is indeed full of good Brazil," in the middle of the sermon. People often made their own snuff out of roll tobacco, by means of rasps. 'On Nov. 3, 1711, Swift speaks of sending "a fine snuff rasp of ivory, given me by Mrs. St. John for Dingley, and a large roll of tobacco."

returns to London, to see how the world goes here in Parliament. Good-night, sirrahs; no, no, not night; I writ this in the morning, and looking carelessly I thought it had been of last night. I dined to-day with Mrs. Barton[1] alone at her lodgings; where she told me for certain, that Lady S——[2] was with child when she was last in England, and pretended a tympany, and saw everybody; then disappeared for three weeks, her tympany was gone, and she looked like a ghost, etc. No wonder she married when she was so ill at containing. Connolly[3] is out; and Mr. Roberts in his place, who loses a better here, but was formerly a Commissioner in Ireland. That employment cost Connolly three thousand pounds to Lord Wharton; so he has made one ill bargain in his life.

29. I wish MD a merry Michaelmas. I dined with Mr. Addison, and Jervas the painter, at Addison's country place; and then came home, and writ more to my lampoon. I made a *Tatler* since I came: guess which it is, and whether the Bishop of Clogher smokes it. I saw Mr. Sterne[4] to-day: he will do as you order, and I will give him chocolate for Stella's health. He goes not these three weeks. I wish I could send it some other way. So now to your letter, brave boys. I don't like your way of saving shillings: nothing vexes me but that it does not make Stella a coward in a coach.[5] I

---

[1] Katherine Barton, second daughter of Robert Barton, of Brigstock, Northamptonshire, and niece of Sir Isaac Newton. She was a favourite among the toasts of the Kit-Cat Club, and Lord Halifax, who left her a fortune, was an intimate friend. In 1717 she married John Conduitt, afterwards Master of the Mint.

[2] See p. 17.

[3] William Connolly, appointed a Commissioner of the Revenue in 1709, was afterwards Speaker of the Irish House of Commons. He died in 1729. Francis Robarts, appointed a Commissioner of the Revenue in 1692, was made a Teller of the Exchequer in England in 1704, and quitted that office, in September 1710, on his reappointment, in Connolly's place, as Revenue Commissioner in Ireland. In 1714 Robarts was removed, and Connolly again appointed Commissioner.

[4] Enoch Sterne, Collector of Wicklow and Clerk to the Irish House of Lords. Writing to Dr. Sterne on Sept. 26, Swift said, "I saw Collector Sterne, who desired me to present his service to you, and to tell you he would be glad to hear from you, but not about business."

[5] In his *Character of Mrs. Johnson* Swift says, "She was never known to cry out, or discover any fear, in a coach." The passage in the text is obscure. Apparently Esther Johnson had boasted of saving money by walking, instead of riding, like a coward.

don't think any lady's advice about my ear signifies two-pence: however I will, in compliance to you, ask Dr Cockburn. Radcliffe[1] I know not, and Barnard[2] I never see. Walls will certainly be stingier for seven years, upon pretence of his robbery. So Stella puns again; why, 'tis well enough; but I'll not second it, though I could make a dozen: I never thought of a pun since I left Ireland.—Bishop of Clogher's bill? Why, he paid it to me; do you think I was such a fool to go without it? As for the four shillings, I will give you a bill on Parvisol for it on t'other side of this paper; and pray tear off the two letters I shall write to him and Joe, or let Dingley transcribe and send them; though that to Parvisol, I believe, he must have my hand for. No, no, I'll eat no grapes; I ate about six the other day at Sir John Holland's; but would not give sixpence for a thousand, they are so bad this year. Yes, faith, I hope in God Presto and MD will be together this time twelvemonth. What then? Last year I suppose I was at Laracor; but next I hope to eat my Michaelmas goose at my two little gooses' lodgings. I drink no *aile* (I suppose you mean *ale*); but yet good wine every day, of five and six shillings a bottle. O Lord, how much Stella writes! pray don't carry that too far, young women, but be temperate, to hold out. To-morrow I go to Mr. Harley.[3] Why, small hopes from the Duke of Ormond: he loves me very well, I believe, and would, in my turn, give me something to make me easy; and I have good interest among his best friends. But I don't think of anything further than the business I am upon. You see I writ to Manley

---

[1] John Radcliffe (1650–1714), the well-known physician and wit, was often denounced as a clever empiric. Early in 1711 he treated Swift for his dizzi-ness. By his will, Radcliffe left most of his property to the University of Oxford.

[2] Charles Barnard, Sergeant-Surgeon to the Queen, and Master of the Barber Surgeons' Company. His large and valuable library, to which Swift afterwards refers, fetched great prices. Luttrell records Barnard's death in his diary for Oct. 12, 1710.

[3] Robert Harley, afterwards Earl of Oxford, had been appointed Chancellor of the Exchequer in August 1710. In May 1711 he was raised to the peerage and made Lord High Treasurer; and he is constantly referred to in the *Journal* as "Lord Treasurer." He was impeached in 1715, but was acquitted in 1717; he died in 1724.

before I had your letter, and I fear he will be out. Yes, Mrs. Owl, Bligh's corpse[1] came to Chester when I was there; and I told you so in my letter, or forgot it. I lodge in Bury Street, where I removed a week ago. I have the first floor, a dining-room, and bed-chamber, at eight shillings a week; plaguy deep, but I spend nothing for eating, never go to a tavern, and very seldom in a coach; yet after all it will be expensive. Why do you trouble yourself, Mistress Stella, about my instrument? I have the same the Archbishop gave me; and it is as good now the bishops are away. The Dean friendly! the Dean be poxed: a great piece of friendship indeed, what you heard him tell the Bishop of Clogher; I wonder he had the face to talk so: but he lent me money, and that's enough. Faith, I would not send this these four days, only for writing to Joe and Parvisol. Tell the Dean that when the bishops send me any packets, they must not write to me at Mr. Steele's; but direct for Mr. Steele, at his office at the Cockpit, and let the enclosed be directed for me: that mistake cost me eighteenpence the other day.

30. I dined with Stratford to-day, but am not to see Mr. Harley till Wednesday: it is late, and I send this before there is occasion for the bell; because I would have Joe have his letter, and Parvisol too; which you must so contrive as not to cost them double postage. I can say no more, but that I am, etc.

LETTER V

LONDON, *Sept.* 30, 1710.

HAN'T I brought myself into a fine *præmunire*,[2] to begin writing letters in whole sheets? and now I dare not leave it off. I cannot tell whether you like these journal letters: I believe they would be dull to me to read them

[1] The Right Hon. Thomas Bligh, M.P., of Rathmore, County Meath, died on Aug. 28, 1710. His son, mentioned later in the *Journal*, became Earl of Darnley.
[2] Penalty.

over; but, perhaps, little MD is pleased to know how Presto passes his time in her absence. I always begin my last the same day I ended my former. I told you where I dined to-day at a tavern with Stratford: Lewis,[1] who is a great favourite of Harley's, was to have been with us; but he was hurried to Hampton Court, and sent his excuse; and that next Wednesday he would introduce me to Harley. 'Tis good to see what a lamentable confession the Whigs all make me of my ill usage: but I mind them not. I am already represented to Harley as a discontented person, that was used ill for not being Whig enough; and I hope for good usage from him. The Tories drily tell me, I may make my fortune, if I please; but I do not understand them —or rather, I do understand them.

Oct. 1. To-day I dined at Molesworth's, the Florence Envoy; and sat this evening with my friend Darteneuf,[2] whom you have heard me talk of; the greatest punner of this town next myself. Have you smoked the *Tatler* that I writ?[3] It is much liked here, and I think it a pure[4] one. To-morrow I go with Delaval,[5] the Portugal Envoy, to dine with Lord Halifax near Hampton Court.[6] Your Manley's

[1] Erasmus Lewis, Under Secretary of State under Lord Dartmouth, was a great friend of Swift, Pope, and Arbuthnot. He had previously been one of Harley's secretaries, and in his *Horace Imitated, Book I. Ep. vii.*, Swift describes him as "a cunning shaver, and very much in Harley's favour." Arbuthnot says that under George I. Lewis kept company with the greatest, and was "principal governor" in many families. Lewis was a witness to Arbuthnot's will. Pope and Esther Vanhomrigh both left him money to buy rings. Lewis died in 1754, aged eighty-three.

[2] Charles Darteneuf, or Dartiquenave, was a celebrated epicure, who is said to have been a son of Charles II. Lord Lyttleton, in his *Dialogues of the Dead*, recalling Pope's allusions to him, selects him to represent modern *bon vivants* in the dialogue between Darteneuf and Apicius. See *Tatler* 252. Darteneuf was Paymaster of the Royal Works and a member of the Kit-Cat Club. He died in 1737.

[3] No. 230.   [4] Good, excellent.

[5] Captain George Delaval, appointed Envoy Extraordinary to the King of Portugal in Oct. 1710, was with Lord Peterborough in Spain in 1706. In May 1707 he went to Lisbon with despatches for the Courts of Spain and Portugal, from whence he was to proceed as Envoy to the Emperor of Morocco, with rich presents (Luttrell, vi. 52, 174, 192).

[6] Charles Montagu, Earl of Halifax, was Ranger of Bushey Park and Hampton Court, held many offices under William III., and was First Lord of the Treasury under George I., until his death in 1715. He was great as financier and as debater, and he was a liberal patron of literature.

brother, a Parliament-man here, has gotten an employment;[1]
and I am informed uses much interest to preserve his
brother: and, to-day, I spoke to the elder Frankland to
engage his father (Postmaster here); and I hope he will be
safe, although he is cruelly hated by all the Tories of Ireland.
I have almost finished my lampoon, and will print it for
revenge on a certain great person.[2]   It has cost me but three
shillings in meat and drink since I came here, as thin as the
town is.   I laugh to see myself so disengaged in these
revolutions.   Well, I must leave off, and go write to Sir
John Stanley,[3] to desire him to engage Lady Hyde as my
mistress to engage Lord Hyde[4] in favour of Mr. Pratt.[5]

2. Lord Halifax was at Hampton Court at his lodgings,
and I dined with him there with Methuen,[6] and Delaval,
and the late Attorney-General.[7]   I went to the Drawing-

[1] John Manley, M.P. for Bossiney, was made Surveyor-General on Sept.
30, 1710, and died in 1714.   In 1706 he fought a duel with another Cornish
member (Luttrell, vi. 11, 535, 635).   He seems to be the cousin whom Mrs. De
la Rivière Manley accuses of having drawn her into a false marriage.   For
Isaac Manley and Sir Thomas Frankland, see p. 7.
[2] The Earl of Godolphin (see p. 18).
[3] Sir John Stanley, Bart., of Northend, Commissioner of Customs, whom
Swift knew through his intimate friends the Pendarves.   His wife, Anne,
daughter of Bernard Granville, and niece of John, Earl of Bath, was aunt to
Mary Granville, afterwards Mrs. Delany, who lived with the Stanleys at their
house in Whitehall.
[4] Henry, Viscount Hyde, eldest son of Laurence Hyde, Earl of Rochester,
succeeded his father in the earldom in 1711, and afterwards became Earl of
Clarendon.   His wife, Jane, younger daughter of Sir William Leveson Gower,
—who married a daughter of John Granville, Earl of Bath,—was a beauty, and
the mother of two beauties—Jane, afterwards Countess of Essex (see Journal,
Jan. 29, 1712), and Catherine, afterwards Countess of Queensberry.   Lady
Hyde was complimented by Prior, Pope, and her kinsman, Lord Lansdowne,
and is said to have been more handsome than either of her daughters.   She
died in 1725 ; her husband in 1753.   Lord Hyde became Joint Vice-Treasurer
for Ireland in 1710 ; hence his interest with respect to Pratt's appointment.
[5] See p. 9.
[6] Sir Paul Methuen (1672–1757), son of John Methuen, diplomatist and
Lord Chancellor of Ireland.   Methuen was Envoy and Ambassador to Portugal
from 1697 to 1708, and was M.P. for Devizes from 1708 to 1710, and a Lord
of the Admiralty.   Under George I. he was Ambassador to Spain, and held
other offices.   Gay speaks of "Methuen of sincerest mind, as Arthur grave,
as soft as womankind," and Steele dedicated to him the seventh volume of
the Spectator.   In his Notes on Macky's Characters, Swift calls him "a
profligate rogue . . . without abilities of any kind."
[7] Sir James Montagu was Attorney-General from 1708 to Sept. 1710, when
he resigned, and was succeeded by Sir Simon Harcourt.   Under George I.
Montagu was raised to the Bench, and a few months before his death in 1723
became Chief Baron of the Exchequer.

room before dinner (for the Queen was at Hampton Court), and expected to see nobody; but I met acquaintance enough. I walked in the gardens, saw the cartoons of Raphael, and other things; and with great difficulty got from Lord Halifax, who would have kept me to-morrow to show me his house and park, and improvements. We left Hampton Court at sunset, and got here in a chariot and two horses time enough by starlight. That's something charms me mightily about London; that you go dine a dozen miles off in October, stay all day, and return so quickly: you cannot do anything like this in Dublin.[1] I writ a second penny-post letter to your mother, and hear nothing of her. Did I tell you that Earl Berkeley died last Sunday was se'nnight, at Berkeley Castle, of a dropsy? Lord Halifax began a health to me to-day; it was the Resurrection of the Whigs, which I refused unless he would add their Reformation too: and I told him he was the only Whig in England I loved, or had any good opinion of.

3. This morning Stella's sister[2] came to me with a letter from her mother, who is at Sheen; but will soon be in town, and will call to see me: she gave me a bottle of palsy-water,[3] a small one, and desired I would send it you by the first convenience, as I will; and she promises a quart bottle of the same: your sister looked very well, and seems a good modest sort of girl. I went then to Mr. Lewis, first secretary to Lord Dartmouth,[4] and favourite to Mr. Harley, who is to introduce me to-morrow morning. Lewis had with him one Mr. Dyot,[5] a Justice of Peace, worth twenty thousand pounds,

[1] The turnpike system had spread rapidly since the Restoration, and had already effected an important reform in the English roads. Turnpike roads were as yet unknown in Ireland.

[2] Ann Johnson, who afterwards married a baker named Filby.

[3] An infusion of which the main ingredient was cowslip or palsy-wort.

[4] William Legge, first Earl of Dartmouth (1672–1750), was St. John's fellow Secretary of State. Lord Dartmouth seems to have been a plain, unpretending man, whose ignorance of French helped to throw important matters into St. John's hands.

[5] Richard Dyot was tried at the Old Bailey, on Jan. 13, 1710–11, for counterfeiting stamps, and was acquitted, the crime being found not felony, but only breach of trust. Two days afterwards a bill of indictment was found against him for high misdemeanour.

a Commissioner of the Stamp Office, and married to a sister of
Sir Philip Meadows,[1] Envoy to the Emperor.   I tell you this,
because it is odds but this Mr. Dyot will be hanged ; for he
is discovered to have counterfeited stamped paper, in which
he was a Commissioner; and, with his accomplices, has
cheated the Queen of a hundred thousand pounds.   You
will hear of it before this come to you, but may be not so
particularly ; and it is a very odd accident in such a man.
Smoke Presto writing news to MD.   I dined to-day with
Lord Mountjoy at Kensington, and walked from thence this
evening to town like an emperor.   Remember that yesterday,
October 2, was a cruel hard frost, with ice ; and six days ago
I was dying with heat.   As thin as the town is, I have more
dinners than ever ; and am asked this month by some people,
without being able to come for pre-engagements.   Well, but
I should write plainer, when I consider Stella cannot read,[2]
and Dingley is not so skilful at my ugly hand.   I had to-
night a letter from Mr. Pratt, who tells me Joe will have
his money when there are trustees appointed by the Lord
Lieutenant for receiving and disposing the linen fund ; and
whenever those trustees are appointed, I will solicit whoever is Lord Lieutenant, and am in no fear of succeeding.   So
pray tell or write him word, and bid him not be cast down ;
for Ned Southwell [3] and Mr. Addison both think Pratt in
the right.   Don't lose your money at Manley's to-night,
sirrahs.

   4. After I had put out my candle last night, my landlady
came into my room, with a servant of Lord Halifax, to desire
I would go dine with him at his house near Hampton Court ;

[1] Sir Philip Meadows (1626-1718) was knighted in 1658, and was Ambassador
to Sweden under Cromwell.   His son Philip (died 1757) was knighted in 1700,
and was sent on a special mission to the Emperor in 1707.   A great-grandson
of the elder Sir Philip was created Earl Manvers in 1806.
   [2] Her eyes were weak.
   [3] The son of the Sir Robert Southwell to whom Temple had offered Swift as
a "servant" on his going as Secretary of State to Ireland in 1690.   Edward
Southwell (1671-1730) succeeded his father as Secretary of State for Ireland in
1702, and in 1708 was appointed Clerk to the Privy Council of Great Britain.
Southwell held various offices under George I. and George II., and amassed a
considerable fortune.

but I sent him word, I had business of great importance that hindered me, etc. And to-day I was brought privately to Mr. Harley, who received me with the greatest respect and kindness imaginable : he has appointed me an hour on Saturday at four, afternoon, when I will open my business to him ; which expression I would not use if I were a woman. I know you smoked it ; but I did not till I writ it. I dined to-day at Mr. Delaval's, the Envoy for Portugal, with Nic Rowe [1] the poet, and other friends ; and I gave my lampoon to be printed. I have more mischief in my heart; and I think it shall go round with them all, as this hits, and I can find hints. I am certain I answered your 2d letter, and yet I do not find it here. I suppose it was in my 4th : and why N. 2d, 3d ; is it not enough to say, as I do, 1, 2, 3 ? etc. I am going to work at another *Tatler* : [2] I'll be far enough but I say the same thing over two or three times, just as I do when I am talking to little MD ; but what care I ? they can read it as easily as I can write it : I think I have brought these lines pretty straight again. I fear it will be long before I finish two sides at this rate. Pray, dear MD, when I occasionally give you any little commission mixed with my letters, don't forget it, as that to Morgan and Joe, etc., for I write just as I can remember, otherwise I would put them all together. I was to visit Mr. Sterne to-day, and give him your commission about handkerchiefs : that of chocolate I will do myself, and send it him when he goes, and you'll pay me when *the giver's bread*,[3] etc. To-night I will read a pamphlet, to amuse myself. God preserve your dear healths !

5. This morning Delaval came to see me, and we went together to Kneller's,[4] who was not in town. In the way we

---

[1] Nicholas Rowe (1674–1718), dramatist and poet laureate, and one of the first editors of Shakespeare, was at this time under-secretary to the Duke of Queensberry, Secretary of State for Scotland.

[2] No. 238 contains Swift's "Description of a Shower in London."

[3] This seems to be a vague allusion to the text, "Cast thy bread upon the waters," etc.

[4] Sir Godfrey Kneller (1646–1723), the fashionable portrait-painter of the period.

met the electors for Parliament-men :[1] and the rabble came about our coach, crying, " A Colt, a Stanhope," etc.   We were afraid of a dead cat, or our glasses broken, and so were always of their side.   I dined again at Delaval's ; and in the evening, at the Coffee-house, heard Sir Andrew Fountaine [2] was come to town.   This has been but an insipid sort of day, and I have nothing to remark upon it worth threepence : I hope MD had a better, with the Dean, the Bishop, or Mrs. Walls.[3]   Why, the reason you lost four and eightpence last night but one at Manley's was, because you played bad games : I took notice of six that you had ten to one against you : Would any but a mad lady go out twice upon Manilio, Basto, and two small diamonds ?[4]   Then in that game of spades, you blundered when you had ten-ace ; I never saw the like of you : and now you are in a huff because I tell you this.   Well, here's two and eightpence halfpenny towards your loss.

6. Sir Andrew Fountaine came this morning, and caught me writing in bed.   I went into the city with him ; and we dined at the Chop-house with Will Pate,[5] the learned woollen-

[1] At the General Election of 1710 the contest at Westminster excited much interest.   The number of constituents was large, and the franchise low, all householders who paid scot and lot being voters.   There were, too, many houses of great Whig merchants, and a number of French Protestants.   But the High Church candidates, Cross and Medlicott, were returned by large majorities, though the Whigs had chosen popular candidates — General Stanhope, fresh from his successes in Spain, and Sir Henry Dutton Colt, a Herefordshire gentleman.

[2] Sir Andrew Fountaine (1676-1753), a distinguished antiquary, of an old Norfolk family, was knighted by William III. in 1699, and inherited his father's estate at Norfolk in 1706.   He succeeded Sir Isaac Newton as Warden of the Mint in 1727, and was Vice-Chamberlain to Queen Caroline. He became acquainted with Swift in Ireland in 1707, when he went over as Usher of the Black Rod in Lord Pembroke's Court.

[3] See p. 6.   The Bishop was probably Dr. Moreton, Bishop of Meath (see *Journal*, July 1, 1712).

[4] The game of ombre—of Spanish origin—is described in Pope's *Rape of the Lock.*   See also the *Compleat Gamester*, 1721, and *Notes and Queries*, April 8, 1871.   The ace of spades, or Spadille, was always the first trump ; the ace of clubs (Basto) always the third.   The second trump was the worst card of the trump suit in its natural order, *i.e.* the seven in red and the deuce in black suits, and was called Manille.   If either of the red suits was trumps, the ace of the suit was fourth trump (Punto).   Spadille, Manille, and Basto were " matadores," or murderers, as they never gave suit.

[5] See p. 12.

draper: then we sauntered at China-shops[1] and booksellers; went to the tavern, drank two pints of white wine, and never parted till ten: and now I am come home, and must copy out some papers I intend for Mr. Harley, whom I am to see, as I told you, to-morrow afternoon; so that this night I shall say little to MD, but that I heartily wish myself with them, and will come as soon as I either fail, or compass my business. We now hear daily of elections; and, in a list I saw yesterday of about twenty, there are seven or eight more Tories than in the last Parliament; so that I believe they need not fear a majority, with the help of those who will vote as the Court pleases. But I have been told that Mr. Harley himself would not let the Tories be too numerous, for fear they should be insolent, and kick against him; and for that reason they have kept several Whigs in employments, who expected to be turned out every day; as Sir John Holland the Comptroller, and many others. And so get you gone to your cards, and your claret and orange, at the Dean's; and I'll go write.

7. I wonder when this letter will be finished: it must go by Tuesday, that's certain; and if I have one from MD before, I will not answer it, that's as certain too. 'Tis now morning, and I did not finish my papers for Mr. Harley last night; for you must understand Presto was sleepy, and made blunders and blots. Very pretty that I must be writing to young women in a morning fresh and fasting, faith. Well, good-morrow to you; and so I go to business, and lay aside this paper till night, sirrahs.—At night. Jack How[2] told Harley that if there were a lower place in hell than another, it was reserved for his porter, who tells lies so gravely, and with so civil a manner. This porter I have had to deal with, going this evening at four to visit Mr. Harley, by his own

---

[1] In the *Spectator*, No. 337, there is a complaint from "one of the top China women about town," of the trouble given by ladies who turn over all the goods in a shop without buying anything. Sometimes they cheapened tea, at others examined screens or tea-dishes.

[2] The Right Hon. John Grubham Howe, M.P. for Gloucestershire, an extreme Tory, had recently been appointed Paymaster of the Forces. He is mentioned satirically as a patriot in sec. 9 of *The Tale of a Tub*.

appointment. But the fellow told me no lie, though I suspected every word he said. He told me his master was just gone to dinner, with much company, and desired I would come an hour hence : which I did, expecting to hear Mr. Harley was gone out; but they had just done dinner. Mr. Harley came out to me, brought me in, and presented to me his son-in-law Lord Doblane [1] (or some such name) and his own son,[2] and, among others, Will Penn [3] the Quaker : we sat two hours drinking as good wine as you do; and two hours more he and I alone; where he heard me tell my business; entered into it with all kindness; asked for my powers, and read them ; and read likewise a memorial [4] I had drawn up, and put it in his pocket to show the Queen ; told me the measures he would take; and, in short, said everything I could wish : told me, he must bring Mr. St. John [5] (Secretary of State) and me acquainted; and spoke so many things of personal kindness and esteem for me, that I am inclined half to believe what some friends have told me, that he would do everything to bring me over. He has desired to dine with me (what a comical mistake was that!). I mean he has desired me to dine with him on Tuesday ; and after four hours being with him, set me down at St. James's Coffee-house in a hackney-coach. All this is odd and comical, if you consider him and me. He knew my Christian name very well. I could not forbear saying thus much upon this matter, although you will think it tedious. But I'll tell you ;

[1] George Henry Hay, Viscount Dupplin, eldest son of the sixth Earl of Kinnoull, was made a Teller of the Exchequer in August, and a peer of Great Britain in December 1711, with the title of Baron Hay. He married, in 1709, Abigail, Harley's younger daughter, and he succeeded his father in the earldom of Kinnoull in 1719.

[2] Edward Harley, afterwards Lord Harley, who succeeded his father as Earl of Oxford in 1724. He married Lady Henrietta Cavendish Holles, daughter of the Duke of Newcastle, but died without male issue in 1741. His interest in literature caused him to form the collection known as the Harleian Miscellany.

[3] William Penn (1644–1718), the celebrated founder of Pennsylvania. Swift says that he "spoke very agreeably, and with much spirit."

[4] This "Memorial to Mr. Harley about the First-Fruits" is dated Oct. 7, 1710.

[5] Henry St. John, created Viscount Bolingbroke in July 1712. In the quarrel between Oxford and Bolingbroke in 1714, Swift's sympathies were with Oxford.

you must know, 'tis fatal[1] to me to be a scoundrel and a prince the same day : for, being to see him at four, I could not engage myself to dine at any friend's ; so I went to Tooke,[2] to give him a ballad, and dine with him ; but he was not at home : so I was forced to go to a blind[3] chop-house, and dine for tenpence upon gill-ale,[4] bad broth, and three chops of mutton ; and then go reeking from thence to the First Minister of State. And now I am going in charity to send Steele a *Tatler*, who is very low of late. I think I am civiller than I used to be ; and have not used the expression of " you in Ireland " and "we in England " as I did when I was here before, to your great indignation.—They may talk of the you know what ;[5] but, gad, if it had not been for that, I should never have been able to get the access I have had ; and if that helps me to succeed, then that same thing will be serviceable to the Church. But how far we must depend upon new friends, I have learnt by long practice, though I think among great Ministers, they are just as good as old ones. And so I think this important day has made a great hole in this side of the paper ; and the fiddle-faddles of to-morrow and Monday will make up the rest ; and, besides, I shall see Harley on Tuesday before this letter goes.

8. I must tell you a great piece of refinement[6] of Harley. He charged me to come to him often : I told him I was loth to trouble him in so much business as he had, and desired I might have leave to come at his levee ; which he immediately refused, and said, that was not a place for friends to come to. 'Tis now but morning ; and I have got a foolish trick, I must say something to MD when I wake, and wish them a good-morrow ; for this is not a shaving-day, Sunday, so I have time enough : but get you gone, you rogues, I must go write : yes, 'twill vex me to the blood if any of these long letters

---

[1] *I.e.*, it is decreed by fate. So Tillotson says, "These things are fatal and necessary."
[2] See p. 8.
[3] Obscure. Hooker speaks of a "blind or secret corner."
[4] Ale served in a gill measure.
[5] Scott suggests that the allusion is to *The Tale of a Tub*.
[6] An extravagant compliment.

should miscarry: if they do, I will shrink to half-sheets again; but then what will you do to make up the journal? there will be ten days of Presto's life lost; and that will be a sad thing, faith and troth.—At night. I was at a loss to-day for a dinner, unless I would have gone a great way, so I dined with some friends that board hereabout,[1] as a spunger;[2] and this evening Sir Andrew Fountaine would needs have me go to the tavern; where, for two bottles of wine, Portugal and Florence, among three of us, we had sixteen shillings to pay; but if ever he catches me so again, I'll spend as many pounds: and therefore I have it among my extraordinaries: but we had a neck of mutton dressed à la Maintenon, that the dog could not eat: and it is now twelve o'clock, and I must go sleep. I hope this letter will go before I have MD's third. Do you believe me? and yet, faith, I long for MD's third too: and yet I would have it to say, that I writ five for two. I am not fond at all of St. James's Coffee-house,[3] as I used to be. I hope it will mend in winter; but now they are all out of town at elections, or not come from their country houses. Yesterday I was going with Dr. Garth[4] to dine with Charles Main,[5] near the Tower, who has an employment there: he is of Ireland; the Bishop of Clogher knows him well: an honest, good-natured fellow, a thorough hearty laugher, mightily beloved by the men of wit: his mistress is never above a cook-maid. And so, good-night, etc.

9. I dined to-day at Sir John Stanley's; my Lady Stanley[6] is one of my favourites: I have as many here as the Bishop of Killala has in Ireland. I am thinking what scurvy company I shall be to MD when I come back: they know everything of me already: I will tell you no more, or I shall have nothing to say, no story to tell, nor any kind of thing. I was

---

[1] See p. 62.
[2] L'Estrange speaks of "trencher-flies and spungers."
[3] See p. 2.
[4] Samuel Garth, physician and member of the Kit-Cat Club, was knighted in 1714. He is best known by his satirical poem, *The Dispensary*, 1699.
[5] Gay speaks of "Wondering Main, so fat, with laughing eyes" (*Mr. Pope's Welcome from Greece*, st. xvii.).
[6] See p. 24, note 3.

very uneasy last night with ugly, nasty, filthy wine, that turned sour on my stomach. I must go to the tavern: oh, but I told you that before. To-morrow I dine at Harley's, and will finish this letter at my return; but I can write no more now, because of the Archbishop: faith, 'tis true; for I am going now to write to him an account of what I have done in the business with Harley:[1] and, faith, young women, I'll tell you what you must count upon, that I never will write one word on the third side in these long letters.

10. Poor MD's letter was lying so huddled up among papers, I could not find it: I mean poor Presto's letter. Well, I dined with Mr. Harley to-day, and hope some things will be done; but I must say no more: and this letter must be sent to the post-house, and not by the bellman.[2] I am to dine again there on Sunday next; I hope to some good issue. And so now, soon as ever I can in bed, I must begin my 6th to MD as gravely as if I had not written a word this month: fine doings, faith! Methinks I don't write as I should, because I am not in bed: see the ugly wide lines. God Almighty ever bless you, etc.

Faith, this is a whole treatise; I'll go reckon the lines on the other sides. I've reckoned them.[3]

LETTER VI

LONDON, *Oct.* 10, 1710.

SO, as I told you just now in the letter I sent half an hour ago, I dined with Mr. Harley to-day, who presented me to the Attorney-General, Sir Simon Harcourt, with much compliment on all sides, etc. Harley told me he had shown my memorial to the Queen, and seconded it very heartily; and he desires me to dine with him again on Sunday, when he promises to settle it with Her Majesty,

---

[1] See the letter of Oct. 10, 1710, to Archbishop King.   [2] See p. 6.
[3] " Seventy-three lines in folio upon one page, and in a very small hand," (Deane Swift).

3

before she names a Governor:[1] and I protest I am in hopes
it will be done, all but the forms, by that time; for he loves
the Church.   This is a popular thing, and he would not have
a Governor share in it; and, besides, I am told by all hands,
he has a mind to gain me over.   But in the letter I writ last
post (yesterday) to the Archbishop, I did not tell him a
syllable of what Mr. Harley said to me last night, because
he charged me to keep it secret; so I would not tell it. to
you, but that, before this goes, I hope the secret will be over.
I am now writing my poetical "Description of a Shower in
London," and will send it to the *Tatler*.[2]   This is the last
sheet of a whole quire I have written since I came to town.
Pray, now it comes into my head, will you, when you go to
Mrs. Walls, contrive to know whether Mrs. Wesley[3] be in
town, and still at her brother's, and how she is in health, and
whether she stays in town.   I writ to her from Chester, to
know what I should do with her note; and I believe the poor
woman is afraid to write to me: so I must go to my business,
etc.

11. To-day at last I dined with Lord Mountrath,[4] and
carried Lord Mountjoy, and Sir Andrew Fountaine with me;
and was looking over them at ombre till eleven this evening
like a fool: they played running ombre half-crowns; and Sir
Andrew Fountaine won eight guineas of Mr. Coote;[5] so I am
come home late, and will say but little to MD this night.   I
have gotten half a bushel of coals, and Patrick, the extravagant whelp, had a fire ready for me; but I picked off the
coals before I went to bed.   It is a sign London is now
an empty place, when it will not furnish me with matter for
above five or six lines in a day.   Did you smoke in my last
how I told you the very day and the place you were playing
at ombre?   But I interlined and altered a little, after I had

---

[1] *I.e.*, Lord Lieutenant.
[2] *Tatler*, No. 238.
[3] See p. 2.
[4] Charles Coote, fourth Earl of Mountrath, and M.P. for Knaresborough.
He died unmarried in 1715.
[5] Henry Coote, Lord Mountrath's brother.   He succeeded to the earldom in
1715, but died unmarried in 1720.

received a letter from Mr. Manley, that said you were at it in his house, while he was writing to me; but without his help I guessed within one day. Your town is certainly much more sociable than ours. I have not seen your mother yet, etc.

12. I dined to-day with Dr. Garth and Mr. Addison, at the Devil Tavern [1] by Temple Bar, and Garth treated; and 'tis well I dine every day, else I should be longer making out my letters: for we are yet in a very dull state, only inquiring every day after new elections, where the Tories carry it among the new members six to one. Mr. Addison's election [2] has passed easy and undisputed; and I believe if he had a mind to be chosen king, he would hardly be refused. An odd accident has happened at Colchester: one Captain Lavallin,[3] coming from Flanders or Spain, found his wife with child by a clerk of Doctors' Commons, whose trade, you know, it is to prevent fornications: and this clerk was the very same fellow that made the discovery of Dyot's [4] counterfeiting the stamp-paper. Lavallin has been this fortnight hunting after the clerk, to kill him; but the fellow was constantly employed at the Treasury, about the discovery he made: the wife had made a shift to patch up the business, alleging that the clerk had told her her husband was dead, and other excuses; but t'other day somebody told Lavallin his wife had intrigues before he married her: upon which he goes down in a rage, shoots his wife through the head, then falls on his sword; and, to make the matter sure, at the same time discharges a pistol through his own head, and died on the spot, his wife surviving him about two hours, but in what circumstances of mind and body is terrible to imagine. I have finished my poem on the "Shower," all but the beginning; and am going on with my *Tatler*. They have fixed about

---

[1] The Devil Tavern was the meeting-place of Ben Jonson's Apollo Club. The house was pulled down in 1787.

[2] Addison was re-elected M.P. for Malmesbury in Oct. 1710, and he kept that seat until his death in 1719.

[3] Captain Charles Lavallée, who served in the Cadiz Expedition of 1702, and was appointed a captain in Colonel Hans Hamilton's Regiment of Foot in 1706 (Luttrell, v. 175, vi. 640; Dalton's *English Army Lists*, iv. 126).

[4] See p. 25.

fifty things on me since I came: I have printed but three.[1] One advantage I get by writing to you daily, or rather you get, is, that I shall remember not to write the same things twice; and yet, I fear, I have done it often already: but I will mind and confine myself to the accidents of the day; and so get you gone to ombre, and be good girls, and save your money, and be rich against Presto comes, and write to me now and then: I am thinking it would be a pretty thing to hear sometimes from saucy MD; but do not hurt your eyes, Stella, I charge you.

13. O Lord, here is but a trifle of my letter written yet; what shall Presto do for prittle-prattle, to entertain MD? The talk now grows fresher of the Duke of Ormond for Ireland; though Mr. Addison says he hears it will be in commission, and Lord Galway [2] one. These letters of mine are a sort of journal, where matters open by degrees; and, as I tell true or false, you will find by the event whether my intelligence be good; but I do not care twopence whether it be or no. — At night. To-day I was all about St. Paul's, and up at the top like a fool, with Sir Andrew Fountaine and two more; and spent seven shillings for my dinner like a puppy: this is the second time he has served me so; but I will never do it again, though all mankind should persuade me, unconsidering puppies! There is a young fellow here in town we are all fond of, and about a year or two come from the University, one Harrison,[3] a little pretty fellow, with a

[1] The *Tatler*, No. 230, *Sid Hamet's Rod*, and the ballad (now lost) on the Westminster Election (see p. 28).
[2] The Earl of Galway (1648-1720), who lost the battle of Almanza to the Duke of Berwick in 1707. Originally the Marquis de Ruvigny, a French refugee, he had been made Viscount Galway and Earl of Galway successively by William III.
[3] William Harrison, the son of a doctor at St. Cross, Winchester, had been recommended to Swift by Addison, who obtained for him the post of governor to the Duke of Queensberry's son. In Jan. 1711 Harrison began the issue of a continuation of Steele's *Tatler* with Swift's assistance, but without success. In May 1711 St. John gave Harrison the appointment of secretary to Lord Raby, Ambassador Extraordinary at the Hague, and in Jan. 1713 Harrison brought the Barrier Treaty to England. He died in the following month, at the age of twenty-seven, and Lady Strafford says that "his brother poets buried him, as Mr. Addison, Mr. Philips, and Dr. Swift." Tickell calls him "that much loved youth," and Swift felt his death keenly. Harrison's best poem is *Woodstock Park*, 1706.

great deal of wit, good sense, and good nature; has written
some mighty pretty things; that in your 6th *Miscellanea*,[1]
about the Sprig of an Orange, is his: he has nothing to live
on but being governor to one of the Duke of Queensberry's [2]
sons for forty pounds a year. The fine fellows are always
inviting him to the tavern, and make him pay his club.
Henley [3] is a great crony of his: they are often at the tavern
at six or seven shillings reckoning, and he always makes the
poor lad pay his full share. A colonel and a lord were at
him and me the same way to-night: I absolutely refused,
and made Harrison lag behind, and persuaded him not to go
to them. I tell you this, because I find all rich fellows have
that humour of using all people without any consideration of
their fortunes; but I will see them rot before they shall
serve me so. Lord Halifax is always teasing me to go down
to his country house, which will cost me a guinea to his
servants, and twelve shillings coach-hire; and he shall be
hanged first. Is not this a plaguy silly story? But I am
vexed at the heart; for I love the young fellow, and am
resolved to stir up people to do something for him: he is a
Whig, and I will put him upon some of my cast Whigs; for
I have done with them; and they have, I hope, done with
this kingdom for our time. They were sure of the four
members for London above all places, and they have lost
three in the four.[4] Sir Richard Onslow,[5] we hear, has lost

---

[1] The last volume of Tonson's *Miscellany*, 1708.

[2] James Douglas, second Duke of Queensberry and Duke of Dover (1662–1711), was appointed Joint Keeper of the Privy Seal in 1708, and third Secretary of State in 1709. Harrison must have been "governor" either to the third son, Charles, Marquis of Beverley (born 1698), who succeeded to the dukedom in 1711, or to the fourth son, George, born in 1701.

[3] Anthony Henley, son of Sir Robert Henley, M.P. for Andover, was a favourite with the wits in London. He was a strong Whig, and occasionally contributed to the *Tatler* and Maynwaring's *Medley*. Garth dedicated *The Dispensary* to him. Swift records Henley's death from apoplexy in August 1711.

[4] Sir William Ashurst, Sir Gilbert Heathcote, and Mr. John Ward were replaced by Sir Richard Hoare, Sir George Newland, and Mr. John Cass at the election for the City in 1710. Scott was wrong in saying that the Whigs lost also the fourth seat, for Sir William Withers had been member for the City since 1707.

[5] Sir Richard Onslow, Bart., was chosen Speaker of the House of Commons in 1708. Under George I. he was Chancellor of the Exchequer, and was

for Surrey; and they are overthrown in most places. Lookee, gentlewomen, if I write long letters, I must write you news and stuff, unless I send you my verses; and some I dare not; and those on the "Shower in London" I have sent to the *Tatler*, and you may see them in Ireland. I fancy you will smoke me in the *Tatler* I am going to write; for I believe I have told you the hint. I had a letter sent me to-night from Sir Matthew Dudley, and found it on my table when I came in. Because it is extraordinary, I will transcribe it from beginning to end. It is as follows : " Is the Devil in you? Oct. 13, 1710." I would have answered every particular passage in it, only I wanted time. Here is enough for to-night, such as it is, etc.

14. Is that tobacco at the top of the paper,[1] or what? I do not remember I slobbered. Lord, I dreamt of Stella, etc., so confusedly last night, and that we saw Dean Bolton[2] and Sterne[3] go into a shop : and she bid me call them to her, and they proved to be two parsons I know not; and I walked without till she was shifting, and such stuff, mixed with much melancholy and uneasiness, and things not as they should be, and I know not how : and it is now an ugly gloomy morning. —At night. Mr. Addison and I dined with Ned Southwell, and walked in the Park ; and at the Coffee-house I found a letter from the Bishop of Clogher, and a packet from MD. I opened the Bishop's letter ; but put up MD's, and visited a lady just come to town ; and am now got into bed, and going to open your little letter : and God send I may find MD well, and happy, and merry, and that they love Presto as they do fires. Oh, I will not open it yet! yes I will! no

elevated to the peerage as Baron Onslow in 1716. He died in the following year.

[1] " The upper part of the letter was a little besmeared with some such stuff; the mark is still on it " (Deane Swift).

[2] John Bolton, D.D., appointed a prebendary of St. Patrick's in 1691, became Dean of Derry in 1699. He died in 1724. Like Swift, Bolton was chaplain to Lord Berkeley, the Lord Lieutenant, and, according to Swift, he obtained the deanery of Derry through Swift having declined to give a bribe of £1000 to Lord Berkeley's secretary. But Lord Orrery says that the Bishop of Derry objected to Swift, fearing that he would be constantly flying backwards and forwards between Ireland and England.

[3] See p. 6, note 2.

I will not! I am going; I cannot stay till I turn over.[1]
What shall I do? My fingers itch; and now I have it in my
left hand; and now I will open it this very moment.—I have
just got it, and am cracking the seal, and cannot imagine
what is in it; I fear only some letter from a bishop, and it
comes too late; I shall employ nobody's credit but my own.
Well, I see though— Pshaw, 'tis from Sir Andrew Fountaine.
What, another! I fancy that's from Mrs. Barton;[2] she told
me she would write to me; but she writes a better hand
than this: I wish you would inquire; it must be at Dawson's[3]
office at the Castle. I fear this is from Patty Rolt, by the
scrawl. Well, I will read MD's letter. Ah, no; it is from
poor Lady Berkeley, to invite me to Berkeley Castle this
winter; and now it grieves my heart: she says, she hopes
my lord is in a fair way of recovery;[4] poor lady! Well, now
I go to MD's letter: faith, it is all right; I hoped it was
wrong. Your letter, N. 3, that I have now received, is dated
Sept. 26; and Manley's letter, that I had five days ago, was
dated Oct. 3, that's a fortnight difference: I doubt it has
lain in Steele's office, and he forgot. Well, there's an end of
that: he is turned out of his place;[5] and you must desire
those who send me packets, to enclose them in a paper
directed to Mr. Addison, at St. James's Coffee - house: not
common letters, but packets: the Bishop of Clogher may
mention it to the Archbishop when he sees him. As for your
letter, it makes me mad: slidikins, I have been the best boy
in Christendom, and you come with your two eggs a penny.—
Well; but stay, I will look over my book: adad, I think
there was a chasm between my N. 2 and N. 3. Faith, I will
not promise to write to you every week; but I will write

---

[1] "That is, to the next page; for he is now within three lines of the bottom of
the first" (Deane Swift).
[2] See p. 20.
[3] Joshua Dawson, secretary to the Lords Justices. He built a fine house in
Dawson Street, Dublin, and provided largely for his relatives by the aid of the
official patronage in his hands.
[4] He had been dead three weeks (see pp. 14, 25).
[5] In *The Importance of the Guardian Considered*, Swift says that Steele, "to
avoid being discarded, thought fit to resign his place of Gazetteer."

every night, and when it is full I will send it; that will be
once in ten days, and that will be often enough: and if you
begin to take up the way of writing to Presto, only because
it is Tuesday, a Monday bedad it will grow a task; but write
when you have a mind.—No, no, no, no, no, no, no, no—
Agad, agad, agad, agad, agad, agad; no, poor Stellakins.[1]
Slids, I would the horse were in your—chamber! Have not
I ordered Parvisol to obey your directions about him? And
han't I said in my former letters that you may pickle him,
and boil him, if you will? What do you trouble me about your
horses for? Have I anything to do with them?—Revolutions
a hindrance to me in my business? Revolutions to me in my
business? If it were not for the revolutions, I could do
nothing at all; and now I have all hopes possible, though
one is certain of nothing; but to-morrow I am to have an
answer, and am promised an effectual one. I suppose I have
said enough in this and a former letter how I stand with
new people; ten times better than ever I did with the old;
forty times more caressed. I am to dine to-morrow at Mr.
Harley's; and if he continues as he has begun, no man has
been ever better treated by another. What you say about
Stella's mother, I have spoken enough to it already. I
believe she is not in town; for I have not yet seen her.
My lampoon is cried up to the skies; but nobody suspects me
for it, except Sir Andrew Fountaine: at least they say nothing
of it to me. Did not I tell you of a great man who received
me very coldly?[2] That's he; but say nothing; 'twas only a
little revenge. I will remember to bring it over. The
Bishop of Clogher has smoked my *Tatler*,[3] about shortening
of words, etc. But, God so![4] etc.

---

[1] As Swift never used the name "Stella" in the *Journal*, this fragment of
his "little language" must have been altered by Deane Swift, the first editor.
Forster makes the excellent suggestion that the correct reading is "sluttikins,"
a word used in the *Journal* on Nov. 28, 1710. Swift often calls his correspondents "sluts."

[2] Godolphin, who was satirised in *Sid Hamet's Rod* (see p. 4).

[3] No. 230.

[4] "This appears to be an interjection of surprise at the length of his journal"
(Deane Swift).

15. I will write plainer if I can remember it; for Stella must not spoil her eyes, and Dingley can't read my hand very well; and I am afraid my letters are too long: then you must suppose one to be two, and read them at twice. I dined to-day with Mr. Harley: Mr. Prior[1] dined with us. He has left my memorial with the Queen, who has consented to give the First - Fruits and Twentieth Parts,[2] and will, we hope, declare it to-morrow in the Cabinet. But I beg you to tell it to no person alive; for so I am ordered, till in public: and I hope to get something of greater value. After dinner came in Lord Peterborow:[3] we renewed our acquaintance, and he grew mightily fond of me. They began to talk of a paper of verses called "Sid Hamet." Mr. Harley repeated part, and then pulled them out, and gave them to a gentleman at the table to read, though they had all read them often. Lord Peterborow would let nobody read them but himself: so he did; and Mr. Harley bobbed[4] me at every line, to take notice of the beauties. Prior rallied Lord Peterborow for author of them; and Lord Peterborow said he knew them to be his; and Prior then turned it upon me, and I on him. I am not guessed at all in town to be the author; yet so it is: but that is a secret only to you.[5] Ten to one whether you see them in Ireland; yet here they run prodigiously. Harley presented me to Lord President of Scotland,[6] and Mr. Benson,[7] Lord of the Treasury. Prior

---

[1] Matthew Prior, poet and diplomatist, had been deprived of his Commissionership of Trade by the Whigs, but was rewarded for his Tory principles in 1711 by a Commissionership of Customs.

[2] "The twentieth parts are 12d. in the £1 paid annually out of all ecclesiastical benefices as they were valued at the Reformation. They amount to about £500 per annum; but are of little or no value to the Queen after the offices and other charges are paid, though of much trouble and vexation to the clergy" (Swift's "Memorial to Mr. Harley").

[3] Charles Mordaunt, the brilliant but erratic Earl of Peterborough, had been engaged for two years, after the unsatisfactory inquiry into his conduct in Spain by the House of Lords in 1708, in preparing an account of the money he had received and expended. The change of Government brought him relief from his troubles; in November he was made Captain-General of Marines, and in December he was nominated Ambassador Extraordinary to Vienna.

[4] Tapped, nudged.   [5] *I.e.*, told only to you.

[6] Sir Hew Dalrymple (1652–1737), Lord President of the Court of Session, and son of the first Viscount Stair.

[7] Robert Benson, a moderate Tory, was made a Lord of the Treasury in

and I came away at nine, and sat at the Smyrna[1] till eleven, receiving acquaintance.

16. This morning early I went in a chair, and Patrick before it, to Mr. Harley, to give him another copy of my memorial, as he desired; but he was full of business, going to the Queen, and I could not see him; but he desired I would send up the paper, and excused himself upon his hurry. I was a little baulked; but they tell me it is nothing. I shall judge by next visit. I tipped his porter with half a crown; and so I am well there for a time at least. I dined at Stratford's in the City, and had Burgundy and Tokay: came back afoot like a scoundrel: then went with Mr. Addison and supped with Lord Mountjoy, which made me sick all night. I forgot that I bought six pounds of chocolate for Stella, and a little wooden box; and I have a great piece of Brazil tobacco for Dingley,[2] and a bottle of palsy-water[3] for Stella: all which, with the two handkerchiefs that Mr. Sterne has bought, and you must pay him for, will be put in the box, directed to Mrs. Curry's, and sent by Dr. Hawkshaw,[4] whom I have not seen; but Sterne has undertaken it. The chocolate is a present, madam, for Stella. Don't read this, you little rogue, with your little eyes; but give it to Dingley, pray now; and I will write as plain as the skies: and let Dingley write Stella's part, and Stella dictate to her, when she apprehends her eyes, etc.

17. This letter should have gone this post, if I had not been taken up with business, and two nights being late out; so it must stay till Thursday. I dined to-day with your Mr.

August 1710, and Chancellor of the Exchequer in the following June, and was raised to the peerage as Baron Bingley in 1713. He died in 1731.

[1] The Smyrna Coffee-house was on the north side of Pall Mall, opposite Marlborough House. In the *Tatler* (Nos. 10, 78) Steele laughed at the "cluster of wise heads" to be found every evening at the Smyrna; and Goldsmith says that Beau Nash would wait a whole day at a window at the Smyrna, in order to receive a bow from the Prince or the Duchess of Marlborough, and would then look round upon the company for admiration and respect.

[2] See p. 19.

[3] See p. 25.

[4] An Irish doctor, with whom Swift invested money.

Sterne,[1] by invitation, and drank Irish wine;[2] but, before we parted, there came in the prince of puppies, Colonel Edgworth;[3] so I went away. This day came out the *Tatler*, made up wholly of my "Shower," and a preface to it. They say it is the best thing I ever writ, and I think so too. I suppose the Bishop of Clogher will show it you. Pray tell me how you like it. Tooke is going on with my *Miscellany*.[4] I'd give a penny the letter to the Bishop of Killaloe[5] was in it: 'twould do him honour. Could not you contrive to say, you hear they are printing my things together; and that you with the bookseller had that letter among the rest: but don't say anything of it as from me. I forget whether it was good or no; but only having heard it much commended, perhaps it may deserve it. Well, I have to-morrow to finish this letter in, and then I will send it next day. I am so vexed that you should write your third to me, when you had but my second, and I had written five, which now I hope you have all: and so I tell you, you are saucy, little, pretty, dear rogues, etc.

18. To-day I dined, by invitation, with Stratford and others, at a young merchant's in the City, with Hermitage and Tokay, and stayed till nine, and am now come home. And that dog Patrick is abroad, and drinking, and I cannot get my night-gown. I have a mind to turn that puppy away: he has been drunk ten times in three weeks. But I han't time to say more; so good-night, etc.

[1] Enoch Sterne, Collector of Wicklow and Clerk to the House of Lords in Ireland.

[2] Claret.

[3] Colonel Ambrose Edgworth, a famous dandy, who is supposed to have been referred to by Steele in No. 246 of the *Tatler*. Edgworth was the son of Sir John Edgworth, who was made Colonel of a Regiment of Foot in 1689 (Dalton, iii. 59). Ambrose Edgworth was a Captain in the same regiment, but father and son were shortly afterwards turned out of the regiment for dishonest conduct in connection with the soldiers' clothing. Ambrose was, however, reappointed a Captain in General Erle's Regiment of Foot in 1691. He served in Spain as Major in Brigadier Gorge's regiment; was taken prisoner in 1706; and was appointed Lieutenant-Colonel of Colonel Thomas Allen's Regiment of Foot in 1707.

[4] This volume of *Miscellanies in Prose and Verse* was published by Morphew in 1711.

[5] Dr. Thomas Lindsay, afterwards Bishop of Raphoe.

19. I am come home from dining in the city with Mr.
Addison, at a merchant's; and just now, at the Coffee-house,
we have notice that the Duke of Ormond was this day
declared Lord Lieutenant at Hampton Court, in Council. I
have not seen Mr. Harley since; but hope the affair is done
about First-Fruits. I will see him, if possible, to-morrow
morning; but this goes to-night. I have sent a box to Mr.
Sterne, to send to you by some friend: I have directed it
for Mr. Curry, at his house; so you have warning when it
comes, as I hope it will soon. The handkerchiefs will be
put in some friend's pocket, not to pay custom. And so here
ends my sixth, sent when I had but three of MD's: now I
am beforehand, and will keep so; and God Almighty bless
dearest MD, etc.

LETTER VII

LONDON, *Oct.* 19, 1710.

O FAITH, I am undone! this paper is larger than the
    other, and yet I am condemned to a sheet; but, since
it is MD, I did not value though I were condemned to a
pair. I told you in my letter to-day where I had been, and
how the day passed; and so, etc.

20. To-day I went to Mr. Lewis, at the Secretary's office,
to know when I might see Mr. Harley; and by and by comes
up Mr. Harley himself, and appoints me to dine with him
to-morrow. I dined with Mrs. Vanhomrigh,[1] and went to
wait on the two Lady Butlers;[2] but the porter answered
they were not at home: the meaning was, the youngest,
Lady Mary, is to be married to-morrow to Lord Ashburnham,[3]
the best match now in England, twelve thousand pounds a
year, and abundance of money. Tell me how my "Shower" is

[1] The first mention of the Vanhomrighs in the *Journal*. Swift had made
their acquaintance when he was in London in 1708.
[2] Lady Elizabeth and Lady Mary (see p. 14, and below).
[3] John, third Lord Ashburnham, and afterwards Earl of Ashburnham (1687-
1737), married, on Oct. 21, 1710, Lady Mary Butler, younger daughter of the
Duke of Ormond. She died on Jan. 2, 1712-3, in her twenty-third year. She
was Swift's "greatest favourite," and he was much moved at her death.

liked in Ireland: I never knew anything pass better here.
I spent the evening with Wortley Montagu[1] and Mr.
Addison, over a bottle of Irish wine. Do they know anything in Ireland of my greatness among the Tories? Everybody reproaches me of it here; but I value them not. Have
you heard of the verses about the "Rod of Sid Hamet"? Say
nothing of them for your life. Hardly anybody suspects me
for them; only they think nobody but Prior or I could write
them. But I doubt they have not reached you. There is
likewise a ballad full of puns on the Westminster Election,[2]
that cost me half an hour: it runs, though it be good for
nothing. But this is likewise a secret to all but MD. If
you have them not, I will bring them over.

21. I got MD's fourth to-day at the Coffee-house. God
Almighty bless poor, dear Stella, and her eyes and head!
What shall we do to cure them? poor, dear life! Your disorders are a pull-back for your good qualities. Would to
Heaven I were this minute shaving your poor, dear head,
either here or there! Pray do not write, nor read this letter,
nor anything else; and I will write plainer for Dingley to
read from henceforward, though my pen is apt to ramble
when I think whom I am writing to. I will not answer
your letter until I tell you that I dined this day with Mr.
Harley, who presented me to the Earl of Stirling,[3] a Scotch
lord; and in the evening came in Lord Peterborow. I stayed
till nine before Mr. Harley would let me go, or tell me anything of my affair. He says the Queen has now granted the
First-Fruits and Twentieth Parts; but he will not give me
leave to write to the Archbishop, because the Queen designs
to signify it to the Bishops in Ireland in form; and to take

---

[1] Edward Wortley Montagu, grandson of the first Earl of Sandwich, and
M.P. for Huntingdon. He was a great friend of Addison's, and the second
volume of the *Tatler* was dedicated to him. In 1712 he married the famous
Lady Mary Pierrepont, eldest daughter of the Duke of Kingston, and under
George I. he became Ambassador Extraordinary to the Porte. He died in
1761, aged eighty.
[2] See p. 28. No copy of these verses is known.
[3] Henry Alexander, fifth Earl of Stirling, who died without issue in 1739.
His sister, Lady Judith Alexander, married Sir William Trumbull, Pope's friend.

notice, that it was done upon a memorial from me; which, Mr. Harley tells me he does to make it look more respectful to me, etc.; and I am to see him on Tuesday. I know not whether I told you that, in my memorial which was given to the Queen, I begged for two thousand pounds a year more, though it was not in my commission; but that, Mr. Harley says, cannot yet be done, and that he and I must talk of it further: however, I have started it, and it may follow in time. Pray say nothing of the First-Fruits being granted, unless I give leave at the bottom of this. I believe never anything was compassed so soon, and purely done by my personal credit with Mr. Harley, who is so excessively obliging, that I know not what to make of it, unless to show the rascals of the other party that they used a man unworthily who had deserved better. The memorial given to the Queen from me speaks with great plainness of Lord Wharton. I believe this business is as important to you as the Convocation disputes from Tisdall.[1] I hope in a month or two all the forms of settling this matter will be over; and then I shall have nothing to do here. I will only add one foolish thing more, because it is just come into my head. When this thing is made known, tell me impartially whether they give any of the merit to me, or no; for I am sure I have so much, that I will never take it upon me.—Insolent sluts! because I say Dublin, Ireland, therefore you must say London, England: that is Stella's malice.—Well, for that I will not answer your letter till to-morrow-day, and so and so: I will go write something else, and it will not be much; for 'tis late.

---

[1] "These words, notwithstanding their great obscurity at present, were very clear and intelligible to Mrs. Johnson: they referred to conversations, which passed between her and Dr. Tisdall seven or eight years before; when the Doctor, who was not only a learned and faithful divine, but a zealous Church-Tory, frequently entertained her with Convocation disputes. This gentleman, in the year 1704, paid his addresses to Mrs. Johnson" (Deane Swift). The Rev. William Tisdall was made D.D. in 1707. Swift never forgave Tisdall's proposal to marry Esther Johnson in 1704, and often gave expression to his contempt for him. In 1706 Tisdall married, and was appointed Vicar of Kerry and Ruavon; in 1712 he became Vicar of Belfast. He published several controversial pieces, directed against Presbyterians and other Dissenters.

22. I was this morning with Mr. Lewis, the under-secretary to Lord Dartmouth, two hours, talking politics, and contriving to keep Steele in his office of stamped paper : he has lost his place of Gazetteer, three hundred pounds a year, for writing a *Tatler*,[1] some months ago, against Mr. Harley, who gave it him at first, and raised the salary from sixty to three hundred pounds. This was devilish ungrateful ; and Lewis was telling me the particulars : but I had a hint given me, that I might save him in the other employment : and leave was given me to clear matters with Steele. Well, I dined with Sir Matthew Dudley, and in the evening went to sit with Mr. Addison, and offer the matter at distance to him, as the discreeter person ; but found party had so possessed him, that he talked as if he suspected me, and would not fall in with anything I said. So I stopped short in my overture, and we parted very drily ; and I shall say nothing to Steele, and let them do as they will ; but, if things stand as they are, he will certainly lose it, unless I save him ; and therefore I will not speak to him, that I may not report to his disadvantage. Is not this vexatious ? and is there so much in the proverb of proffered service ? When shall I grow wise ? I endeavour to act in the most exact points of honour and conscience ; and my nearest friends will not understand it so. What must a man expect from his enemies ? This would vex me, but it shall not ; and so I bid you good-night, etc.

23. I know 'tis neither wit nor diversion to tell you every day where I dine ; neither do I write it to fill my letter ; but I fancy I shall, some time or other, have the curiosity of seeing some particulars how I passed my life when I was absent from MD this time ; and so I tell you now that I dined to-day at Molesworth's, the Florence Envoy, then went to the Coffee-house, where I behaved myself coldly enough to Mr. Addison, and so came home to scribble. We dine together to-morrow and next day by invitation ; but I shall

---

[1] No. 193 of the *Tatler*, for July 4, 1710, contained a letter from Downes the Prompter in ridicule of Harley's newly formed Ministry. This letter, the authorship of which Steele disavowed, was probably by Anthony Henley.

alter my behaviour to him, till he begs my pardon, or else we shall grow bare acquaintance. I am weary of friends; and friendships are all monsters, but MD's.

24. I forgot to tell you, that last night I went to Mr. Harley's, hoping—faith, I am blundering, for it was this very night at six; and I hoped he would have told me all things were done and granted: but he was abroad, and came home ill, and was gone to bed, much out of order, unless the porter lied. I dined to-day at Sir Matthew Dudley's, with Mr. Addison, etc.

25. I was to-day to see the Duke of Ormond; and, coming out, met Lord Berkeley of Stratton,[1] who told me that Mrs. Temple,[2] the widow, died last Saturday, which, I suppose, is much to the outward grief and inward joy of the family. I dined to-day with Addison and Steele, and a sister of Mr. Addison, who is married to one Mons. Sartre,[3] a Frenchman, prebendary of Westminster, who has a delicious house and garden; yet I thought it was a sort of monastic life in those cloisters, and I liked Laracor better. Addison's sister is a sort of a wit, very like him. I am not fond of her, etc.

26. I was to-day to see Mr. Congreve,[4] who is almost blind with cataracts growing on his eyes; and his case is, that he must wait two or three years, until the cataracts are riper, and till he is quite blind, and then he must have them couched; and, besides, he is never rid of the gout, yet he looks young and fresh, and is as cheerful as ever. He is younger by three years or more than I; and I am twenty

---

[1] William Berkeley, fourth Baron Berkeley of Stratton, was sworn of the Privy Council in September 1710, and was appointed Chancellor of the Duchy of Lancaster. He married Frances, youngest daughter of Sir John Temple, of East Sheen, Surrey, and died in 1740.

[2] Probably the widow of Sir William Temple's son, John Temple (see p. 5). She was Mary Duplessis, daughter of Duplessis Rambouillet, a Huguenot.

[3] The Rev. James Sartre, who married Addison's sister Dorothy, was Prebendary and Archdeacon of Westminster. He had formerly been French pastor at Montpelier. After his death in 1713 his widow married a Mr. Combe, and lived until 1750.

[4] William Congreve's last play was produced in 1700. In 1710, when he was forty, he published a collected edition of his works. Swift and Congreve had been schoolfellows at Kilkenny, and they had both been pupils of St. George Ashe—afterwards Bishop of Clogher—at Trinity College, Dublin. On Congreve's death, in 1729, Swift wrote, "I loved him from my youth."

years younger than he. He gave me a pain in the great toe, by mentioning the gout. I find such suspicions frequently, but they go off again. I had a second letter from Mr. Morgan,[1] for which I thank you: I wish you were whipped, for forgetting to send him that answer I desired you in one of my former, that I could do nothing for him of what he desired, having no credit at all, etc. Go, be far enough, you negligent baggages. I have had also a letter from Parvisol, with an account how my livings are set; and that they are fallen, since last year, sixty pounds. A comfortable piece of news! He tells me plainly that he finds you have no mind to part with the horse, because you sent for him at the same time you sent him my letter; so that I know not what must be done. It is a sad thing that Stella must have her own horse, whether Parvisol will or no. So now to answer your letter that I had three or four days ago. I am not now in bed, but am come home by eight; and, it being warm, I write up. I never writ to the Bishop of Killala, which, I suppose, was the reason he had not my letter. I have not time, there is the short of it.—As fond as the Dean[2] is of my letter, he has not written to me. I would only know whether Dean Bolton[3] paid him the twenty pounds; and for the rest, he may kiss—And that you may ask him, because I am in pain about it, that Dean Bolton is such a whipster. 'Tis the most obliging thing in the world in Dean Sterne to be so kind to you. I believe he knows it will please me, and makes up, that way, his other usage.[4] No, we have had none of your snow, but a little one morning; yet I think it was great snow for an hour or so, but no longer. I had heard of Will Crowe's[5] death before, but not the foolish circumstance that hastened his end. No, I have taken care that

---

[1] See p. 19.   [2] Dean Sterne.
[3] See p. 38.
[4] When he became Dean he withheld from Swift the living of St. Nicholas Without, promised in gratitude for the aid rendered by Swift in his election.
[5] Crowe was a Commissioner for Appeals from the Revenue Commissioners for a short time in 1706, and was Recorder of Blessington, Co. Wicklow. In his *Short Character of Thomas, Earl of Wharton*, 1710, Swift speaks of Wharton's "barbarous injustice to . . . poor Will Crowe."

Captain Pratt[1] shall not suffer by Lord Anglesea's death.[2]   I
will try some contrivance to get a copy of my picture from
Jervas.   I will make Sir Andrew Fountaine buy one as for
himself, and I will pay him again, and take it, that is, provided I have money to spare when I leave this.—Poor John!
is he gone? and Madam Parvisol[3] has been in town! Humm.
Why, Tighe[4] and I, when he comes, shall not take any
notice of each other; I would not do it much in this town,
though we had not fallen out.—I was to-day at Mr. Sterne's
lodging: he was not within; and Mr. Leigh is not come to
town; but I will do Dingley's errand when I see him.
What do I know whether china be dear or no?   I once took
a fancy of resolving to grow mad for it, but now it is off; I
suppose I told you in some former letter.   And so you only
want some salad-dishes, and plates, and etc.   Yes, yes, you
shall.   I suppose you have named as much as will cost five
pounds.—Now to Stella's little postscript; and I am almost
crazed that you vex yourself for not writing.   Cannot you
dictate to Dingley, and not strain your little, dear eyes?   I
am sure it is the grief of my soul to think you are out of
order.   Pray be quiet; and, if you will write, shut your eyes,
and write just a line, and no more, thus, "How do you do,
Mrs. Stella?"   That was written with my eyes shut.   Faith,
I think it is better than when they are open: and then
Dingley may stand by, and tell you when you go too high or
too low.—My letters of business, with packets, if there be
any more occasion for such, must be enclosed to Mr. Addison,
at St. James's Coffee-house: but I hope to hear, as soon as I
see Mr. Harley, that the main difficulties are over, and that
the rest will be but form.—Take two or three nutgalls, take
two or three —galls, stop your receipt in your—I have no
need on't.   Here is a clutter!   Well, so much for your letter,
which I will now put up in my letter-partition in my cabinet,
as I always do every letter as soon as I answer it.   Method

[1] See p. 9.   [2] See p. 13.   [3] See p. 3.
[4] Richard Tighe, M. P. for Belturbet, was a Whig, much disliked by Swift.
He became a Privy Councillor under George I.

is good in all things. Order governs the world. The Devil
is the author of confusion. A general of an army, a minister
of state; to descend lower, a gardener, a weaver, etc. That
may make a fine observation, if you think it worth finishing;
but I have not time. Is not this a terrible long piece for one
evening? I dined to-day with Patty Rolt at my cousin
Leach's,[1] with a pox, in the City: he is a printer, and prints
the *Postman*, oh hoo, and is my cousin, God knows how, and
he married Mrs. Baby Aires of Leicester; and my cousin
Thomson was with us: and my cousin Leach offers to bring
me acquainted with the author of the *Postman*;[2] and says
he does not doubt but the gentleman will be glad of my
acquaintance; and that he is a very ingenious man, and a
great scholar, and has been beyond sea. But I was modest
and said, may be the gentleman was shy, and not fond of
new acquaintance; and so put it off: and I wish you could
hear me repeating all I have said of this in its proper tone,
just as I am writing it. It is all with the same cadence with
" Oh hoo," or as when little girls say, " I have got an apple,
miss, and I won't give you some." It is plaguy twelvepenny
weather this last week, and has cost me ten shillings in
coach and chair hire. If the fellow that has your money
will pay it, let me beg you to buy Bank Stock with it, which
is fallen near thirty per cent. and pays eight pounds per cent.
and you have the principal when you please: it will certainly
soon rise. I would to God Lady Giffard would put in the
four hundred pounds she owes you,[3] and take the five per
cent. common interest, and give you the remainder. I will
speak to your mother about it when I see her. I am resolved

---

[1] Dryden Leach, of the Old Bailey, formerly an actor, was son of Francis
Leach. Swift recommended Harrison to employ Leach in printing the continuation of the *Tatler*; but Harrison discarded him. (See *Journal*, Jan. 16,
1710–11, and Timperley's *Literary Anecdotes*, 600, 631).

[2] The *Postman*, which appeared three days in the week, written by M.
Fonvive, a French Protestant, whom Dunton calls "the glory and mirror of
news writers, a very grave, learned, orthodox man." Fonvive had a universal
system of intelligence, at home and abroad, and "as his news is early and
good, so his style is excellent."

[3] Sir William Temple left Esther Johnson the lease of some property in
Ireland.

to buy three hundred pounds of it for myself, and take up what I have in Ireland; and I have a contrivance for it, that I hope will do, by making a friend of mine buy it as for himself, and I will pay him when I can get in my money. I hope Stratford will do me that kindness. I'll ask him to-morrow or next day.

27. Mr. Rowe[1] the poet desired me to dine with him to-day. I went to his office (he is under-secretary in Mr. Addison's place that he had in England), and there was Mr. Prior; and they both fell commending my " Shower " beyond anything that has been written of the kind: there never was such a " Shower " since Danae's, etc. You must tell me how it is liked among you. I dined with Rowe; Prior could not come: and after dinner we went to a blind tavern,[2] where Congreve, Sir Richard Temple,[3] Estcourt,[4] and Charles Main,[5] were over a bowl of bad punch. The knight sent for six flasks of his own wine for me, and we stayed till twelve. But now my head continues pretty well; I have left off my drinking, and only take a spoonful mixed with water, for fear of the gout, or some ugly distemper; and now, because it is late, I will, etc.

28. Garth and Addison and I dined to-day at a hedge[6] tavern; then I went to Mr. Harley, but he was denied, or not at home: so I fear I shall not hear my business is done before this goes. Then I visited Lord Pembroke,[7] who is just come

[1] See p. 27.

[2] An out-of-the-way or obscure house. So Pepys (*Diary*, Oct. 15, 1661): "To St. Paul's Churchyard to a blind place where Mr. Goldsborough was to meet me."

[3] Sir Richard Temple, Bart., of Stowe, a Lieutenant-General who saw much service in Flanders, was dismissed in 1713 owing to his Whig views, but on the accession of George I. was raised to the peerage, and was created Viscount Cobham in 1718. He died in 1749. Congreve wrote in praise of him, and he was the "brave Cobham" of Pope's first *Moral Essay*.

[4] Richard Estcourt, the actor, died in August 1712, when his abilities on the stage and as a talker were celebrated by Steele in No. 468 of the *Spectator*. See also *Tatler*, Aug. 6, 1709, and *Spectator*, May 5, 1712. Estcourt was " providore" of the Beef-Steak Club, and a few months before his death opened the Bumper Tavern in James Street, Covent Garden.

[5] See p. 32.

[6] Poor, mean. Elsewhere Swift speaks of " the corrector of a hedge press in Little Britain," and " a little hedge vicar."

[7] Thomas Herbert, eighth Earl of Pembroke, was Lord Lieutenant from

to town; and we were very merry talking of old things; and I hit him with one pun. Then I went to see the Ladies Butler, and the son of a whore of a porter denied them: so I sent them a threatening message by another lady, for not excepting me always to the porter. I was weary of the Coffee-house, and Ford[1] desired me to sit with him at next door; which I did, like a fool, chatting till twelve, and now am got into bed. I am afraid the new Ministry is at a terrible loss about money: the Whigs talk so, it would give one the spleen; and I am afraid of meeting Mr. Harley out of humour. They think he will never carry through this undertaking. God knows what will come of it. I should be terribly vexed to see things come round again: it will ruin the Church and clergy for ever; but I hope for better. I will send this on Tuesday, whether I hear any further news of my affair or not.

29. Mr. Addison and I dined to-day with Lord Mountjoy; which is all the adventures of this day.—I chatted a while to-night in the Coffee-house, this being a full night; and now am come home, to write some business.

30. I dined to-day at Mrs. Vanhomrigh's, and sent a letter to poor Mrs. Long,[2] who writes to us, but is God knows where, and will not tell anybody the place of her residence. I came home early, and must go write.

31. The month ends with a fine day; and I have been walking, and visiting Lewis, and concerting where to see Mr. Harley. I have no news to send you. Aire,[3] they say, is taken, though the Whitehall letters this morning say quite the contrary: 'tis good, if it be true. I dined with Mr. Addison and Dick Stewart, Lord Mountjoy's brother;[4] a treat of Addison's. They were half-fuddled, but not I; for I mixed water with my wine, and left them together

April 1707 to December 1708. A nobleman of taste and learning, he was, like Swift, very fond of punning, and they had been great friends in Ireland.
[1] See p. 9. [2] See p. 10.
[3] A small town and fortress in what is now the Pas de Calais.
[4] Richard Stewart, third son of the first Lord Mountjoy (see p. 2), was M.P. at various times for Castlebar, Strabane, and County Tyrone. He died in 1728.

between nine and ten; and I must send this by the bell-man, which vexes me, but I will put it off no longer. Pray God it does not miscarry. I seldom do so; but I can put off little MD no longer. Pray give the under note to Mrs. Brent.

I am a pretty gentleman; and you lose all your money at cards, sirrah Stella. I found you out; I did so.

I am staying before I can fold up this letter, till that ugly D is dry in the last line but one. Do not you see it? O Lord, I am loth to leave you, faith—but it must be so, till the next time. Pox take that D; I will blot it, to dry it.

LETTER VIII

LONDON, *Oct.* 31, 1710.

SO, now I have sent my seventh to your fourth, young women; and now I will tell you what I would not in my last, that this morning, sitting in my bed, I had a fit of giddiness: the room turned round for about a minute, and then it went off, leaving me sickish, but not very: and so I passed the day as I told you; but I would not end a letter with telling you this, because it might vex you: and I hope in God I shall have no more of it. I saw Dr. Cockburn[1] to-day, and he promises to send me the pills that did me good last year; and likewise has promised me an oil for my ear, that he has been making for that ailment for somebody else.

Nov. 1. I wish MD a merry new year. You know this is the first day of it with us.[2] I had no giddiness to-day; but I drank brandy, and have bought a pint for two shillings. I sat up the night before my giddiness pretty late, and writ very much; so I will impute it to that. But I never eat fruit, nor drink ale; but drink better wine than you do, as I

---

[1] See p. 7.
[2] Swift, Esther Johnson, and Mrs. Dingley seem to have begun their financial year on the 1st of November. Swift refers to "MD's allowance" in the *Journal* for April 23, 1713.

did to-day with Mr. Addison at Lord Mountjoy's: then went
at five to see Mr. Harley, who could not see me for much
company; but sent me his excuse, and desired I would dine
with him on Friday; and then I expect some answer to this
business, which must either be soon done, or begun again;
and then the Duke of Ormond and his people will interfere
for their honour, and do nothing. I came home at six, and
spent my time in my chamber, without going to the Coffee-
house, which I grow weary of; and I studied at leisure, writ
not above forty lines, some inventions of my own, and some
hints, and read not at all, and this because I would take care
of Presto, for fear little MD should be angry.

2. I took my four pills last night, and they lay an hour in
my throat, and so they will do to-night. I suppose I could
swallow four affronts as easily. I dined with Dr. Cockburn
to-day, and came home at seven; but Mr. Ford has been with
me till just now, and it is near eleven. I have had no
giddiness to-day. Mr. Dopping[1] I have seen; and he tells
me coldly, my "Shower" is liked well enough; there's your
Irish judgment! I writ this post to the Bishop of Clogher.
It is now just a fortnight since I heard from you. I must have
you write once a fortnight, and then I will allow for wind and
weather. How goes ombre? Does Mrs. Walls[2] win constantly, as she used to do? And Mrs. Stoyte;[3] I have not
thought of her this long time: how does she? I find we
have a cargo of Irish coming for London: I am sorry for it;
but I never go near them. And Tighe is landed; but Mrs.
Wesley,[4] they say, is going home to her husband, like a fool.
Well, little monkeys mine, I must go write; and so good-
night.

---

[1] Samuel Dopping, an Irish friend of Stella's, who was probably related to
Anthony Dopping, Bishop of Meath (died 1697), and to his son Anthony (died
1743), who became Bishop of Ossory.
[2] See p. 6.
[3] The wife of Alderman Stoyte, afterwards Lord Mayor of Dublin. Mrs.
Stoyte and her sister Catherine; the Walls; Isaac Manley and his wife;
Dean Sterne, Esther Johnson and Mrs. Dingley, and Swift, were the principal
members of a card club which met at each other's houses for a number
of years.
[4] See p. 2.

3. I ought to read these letters I write, after I have done ;
for, looking over thus much, I found two or three literal
mistakes, which should not be when the hand is so bad. But
I hope it does not puzzle little Dingley to read, for I think I
mend : but methinks, when I write plain, I do not know
how, but we are not alone, all the world can see us. A bad
scrawl is so snug, it looks like a PMD.[1] We have scurvy
Tatlers of late : so pray do not suspect me. I have one or
two hints I design to send him, and never any more : he does
not deserve it. He is governed by his wife most abominably,[2]
as bad as ———. I never saw her since I came ; nor has he ever
made me an invitation : either he dares not, or is such a
thoughtless Tisdall [3] fellow, that he never minds [4] it. So what
care I for his wit ? for he is the worst company in the world,
till he has a bottle of wine in his head. I cannot write
straighter in bed, so you must be content.—At night in
bed. Stay, let me see where's this letter to MD amoug these
papers ? Oh ! here. Well, I will go on now ; but I am very
busy (smoke the new pen). I dined with Mr. Harley to-day,
and am invited there again on Sunday. I have now leave to
write to the Primate and Archbishop of Dublin, that the
Queen has granted the First-Fruits ; but they are to take no
notice of it, till a letter is sent them by the Queen's orders
from Lord Dartmouth, Secretary of State, to signify it. The
bishops are to be made a corporation, to dispose of the
revenue, etc. ; and I shall write to the Archbishop of Dublin
to-morrow (I have had no giddiness to-day). I know not
whether they will have any occasion for me longer to be
here ; nor can I judge till I see what letter the Queen sends
to the bishops, and what they will do upon it. If despatch

[1] "This cypher stands for Presto, Stella, and Dingley ; as much as to say, it
looks like us three quite retired from all the rest of the world " (Deane Swift).
[2] Steele's "dear Prue," Mary Scurlock, whom he married as his second wife
in 1707, was a lady of property and a "cried-up beauty." She was somewhat of a prude, and did not hesitate to complain to her husband, in and out
of season, of his extravagance and other weaknesses. The other lady to whom
Swift alludes is probably the Duchess of Marlborough
[3] See p. 46.
[4] Remembers : an Irish expression.

be used, it may be done in six weeks; but I cannot judge. They sent me to-day a new Commission, signed by the Primate and Archbishop of Dublin,[1] and promise me letters to the two archbishops here; but mine a — for it all. The thing is done, and has been so these ten days; though I had only leave to tell it to-day. I had this day likewise a letter from the Bishop of Clogher, who complains of my not writing; and, what vexes me, says he knows you have long letters from me every week. Why do you tell him so? 'Tis not right, faith: but I won't be angry with MD at distance. I writ to him last post, before I had his; and will write again soon, since I see he expects it, and that Lord and Lady Mountjoy[2] put him off upon me, to give themselves ease. Lastly, I had this day a letter from a certain naughty rogue called MD, and it was N. 5; which I shall not answer to-night, I thank you. No, faith, I have other fish to fry; but to-morrow or next day will be time enough. I have put MD's commissions in a memorandum paper. I think I have done all before, and remember nothing but this to-day about glasses and spectacles and spectacle cases. I have no commission from Stella, but the chocolate and hand-kerchiefs; and those are bought, and I expect they will be soon sent. I have been with, and sent to, Mr. Sterne, two or three times to know; but he was not within. Odds my life, what am I doing? I must go write and do business.

4. I dined to-day at Kensington, with Addison, Steele, etc., came home, and writ a short letter to the Archbishop of Dublin, to let him know the Queen has granted the thing, etc. I writ in the Coffee-house, for I stayed at Kensington till

1 This new Commission, signed by Narcissus Marsh, Archbishop of Armagh, and William King, was dated Oct. 24, 1710.· In this document Swift was begged to take the full management of the business of the First-Fruits into his hands, the Bishops of Ossory and Killala—who,were to have joined with him in the negotiations—having left London before Swift arrived. But before this Commission was despatched the Queen had granted the First - Fruits and Twentieth Parts to the Irish clergy.

2 Lady Mountjoy, wife of the second Viscount Mountjoy (see p. 2), was Anne, youngest daughter of Murrough Boyle, first Viscount Blessington, by his second wife, Anne, daughter of Charles Coote, second Earl of Mountrath. After Lord Mountjoy's death she married John Farquharson, and she died in 1741.

nine, and am plaguy weary; for Colonel Proud [1] was very ill company, and I will never be of a party with him again; and I drank punch, and that and ill company has made me hot.

5. I was with Mr. Harley from dinner to seven this night, and went to the Coffee-house, where Dr. Davenant [2] would fain have had me gone and drink a bottle of wine at his house hard by, with Dr. Chamberlen, [3] but the puppy used so many words, that I was afraid of his company; and though we promised to come at eight, I sent a messenger to him, that Chamberlen was going to a patient, and therefore we would put it off till another time: so he, and the Comptroller, [4]

[1] Forster suggests that Swift wrote "Frowd" or "Frowde," and there is every reason to believe that this was the case. No Colonel Proud appears in Dalton's *Army Lists*. A Colonel William Frowde, apparently third son of Sir Philip Frowde, Knight, by his third wife, Margaret, daughter of Sir John Ashburnham, was appointed Lieutenant-Colonel in Colonel Farrington's (see p. 59) Regiment of Foot in 1694. He resigned his commission on his appointment to the First Life Guards in 1702, and he was in this latter regiment in 1704. In November and December 1711 Swift wrote of Philip Frowde the elder (Colonel William Frowde's brother) as "an old fool," in monetary difficulties. It is probable that Swift's Colonel Proud (? Frowde) was not Colonel William Frowde, but his nephew, Philip Frowde, junior, who was Addison's friend as Oxford, and the author of two tragedies and various poems. Nothing seemt known of Philip Frowde's connection with the army, but he is certainly called "Colonel" by Swift, Addison, and Pope (see Forster's *Swift*, 159; Addison's *Works*, v. 324; Pope's *Works*, v. 177, vi. 227). Swift wrote to Ambrose Philips in 1705, "Col. Froud is just as he was, very friendly and *grand rêveur et distrait*. He has brought his poems almost to perfection." It will be observed that when Swift met Colonel "Proud" he was in company with Addison, as was also the case when he was with Colonel "Freind" (see p. 11).

[2] Charles Davenant, LL.D., educated at Balliol College, Oxford, was the eldest son of Sir William Davenant, author of *Gondibert*. In Parliament he attacked Ministerial abuses with great bitterness until, in 1703, he was made secretary to the Commissioners appointed to treat for a union with Scotland. To this post was added, in 1705, an Inspector-Generalship of Exports and Imports, which he retained until his death in 1714. *Tom Double*, a satire on his change of front after obtaining his place, was published in 1704. In a Note on Macky's character of Davenant, Swift says, "He ruined his estate, which put him under a necessity to comply with the times." Davenant's *True Picture of a Modern Whig, in Two Parts*, appeared in 1701-2; in 1707 he published *The True Picture of a Modern Whig revived, set forth in a third dialogue between Whiglove and Double*, which seems to be the piece mentioned in the text, though Swift speaks of the pamphlet as "lately put out."

[3] Hugh Chamberlen, the younger (1664-1728), was a Fellow of the College of Physicians and Censor in 1707, 1717, and 1721. Atterbury and the Duchess of Buckingham and Normanby were among his fashionable patients. His father, Hugh Chamberlen, M.D., was the author of the Land Bank Scheme of 1693-94.

[4] Sir John Holland (see p. 11).

and I, were prevailed on by Sir Matthew Dudley to go to his house, where I stayed till twelve, and left them. Davenant has been teasing me to look over some of his writings that he is going to publish; but the rogue is so fond of his own productions, that I hear he will not part with a syllable; and he has lately put out a foolish pamphlet, called *The Third Part of Tom Double*; to make his court to the Tories, whom he had left.

6. I was to-day gambling [1] in the City to see Patty Rolt, who is going to Kingston, where she lodges; but, to say the truth, I had a mind for a walk to exercise myself, and happened to be disengaged: for dinners are ten times more plentiful with me here than ever, or than in Dublin. I won't answer your letter yet, because I am busy. I hope to send this before I have another from MD: it would be a sad thing to answer two letters together, as MD does from Presto. But when the two sides are full, away the letter shall go, that is certain, like it or not like it; and that will be about three days hence, for the answering-night will be a long one.

7. I dined to-day at Sir Richard Temple's, with Congreve, Vanbrugh, Lieutenant-General Farrington,[2] etc. Vanbrugh, I believe I told you, had a long quarrel with me about those verses on his house;[3] but we were very civil and cold. Lady Marlborough used to tease him with them, which had made him angry, though he be a good-natured fellow. It was a Thanksgiving-day,[4] and I was at Court, where the Queen passed us by with all Tories about her; not one Whig:

---

[1] Swift may mean either rambling or gambolling.

[2] Thomas Farrington was appointed Colonel of the newly raised 29th Regiment of Foot in 1702. He was a subscriber for a copy of the *Tatler* on royal paper (Aitken, *Life of Steele*, i. 329, 330).

[3] In *The History of Vanbrugh's House*, Swift described everyone as hunting for it up and down the river banks, and unable to find it, until at length they—

"—— in the rubbish spy
A thing resembling a goose pie."

Sir John Vanbrugh was more successful as a dramatist than as an architect, though his work at Blenheim and elsewhere has many merits.

[4] For the successes of the last campaign.

Buckingham,[1] Rochester,[2] Leeds,[3] Shrewsbury,[4] Berkeley of Stratton,[5] Lord Keeper Harcourt,[6] Mr. Harley, Lord Pembroke,[7] etc.; and I have seen her without one Tory. The Queen made me a curtsey, and said, in a sort of familiar way to Presto, "How does MD?" I considered she was a Queen, and so excused her.[8] I do not miss the Whigs at Court; but have as many acquaintance there as formerly.

8. Here's ado and a clutter! I must now answer MD's fifth; but first you must know I dined at the Portugal Envoy's [9] to-day, with Addison, Vanbrugh, Admiral Wager,[10] Sir Richard Temple,[11] Methuen,[12] etc. I was weary of their company, and stole away at five, and came home like a good boy, and studied till ten, and had a fire, O ho! and now am in bed. I have no fireplace in my bed-chamber; but 'tis very warm weather when one's in bed. Your fine cap,[13] Madam Dingley, is too little, and too hot: I will have

---

[1] John Sheffield, third Earl of Mulgrave, was created Duke of Buckingham and Normanby in 1703, and died in 1721. On Queen Anne's accession he became Lord Privy Seal, and on the return of the Tories to power in 1710 he was Lord Steward, and afterward (June 1710) Lord President of the Council. The Duke was a poet, as well as a soldier and statesman, his best known work being the *Essay on Poetry*. He was Dryden's patron, and Pope prepared a collected edition of his works.

[2] Laurence Hyde, created Earl of Rochester in 1682, died in 1711. He was the Hushai of Dryden's *Absalom and Achitophel*, "the friend of David in distress." In 1684 he was made Lord President of the Council, and on the accession of James II., Lord Treasurer; he was, however, dismissed in 1687. Under William III. Rochester was Lord Lieutenant of Ireland, an office he resigned in 1703; and in September 1710 he again became Lord President. His imperious temper always stood in the way of popularity or real success.

[3] Sir Thomas Osborne, Charles II.'s famous Minister, was elevated to the peerage in 1673, and afterwards was made successively Earl of Danby, Marquis of Caermarthen, and Duke of Leeds. On Nov. 29, 1710, a few days after this reference to him, the Duke was granted a pension of £3500 a year out of the Post Office revenues. He died in July 1712, aged eighty-one, and soon afterwards his grandson married Lord Oxford's daughter.

[4] See p. 12.   [5] See p. 48.   [6] See p. 11.   [7] See p. 52.
[8] This is, of course, a joke; Swift was never introduced at Court.
[9] Captain Delaval (see p. 23).
[10] Admiral Sir Charles Wager (1666–1743) served in the West Indies from 1707 to 1709, and gained great wealth from the prizes he took. Under George I. he was Comptroller of the Navy, and in 1733 he became First Lord of the Admiralty, a post which he held until 1742.
[11] See p. 52.   [12] See p. 24.
[13] Isaac Bickerstaff's "valentine" sent him a nightcap, finely wrought by a maid of honour to Queen Elizabeth (*Tatler*, No. 141). The "nightcap" was

that fur taken off; I wish it were far enough; and my old velvet cap is good for nothing. Is it velvet under the fur? I was feeling, but cannot find: if it be, 'twill do without it: else I will face it; but then I must buy new velvet: but may be I may beg a piece. What shall I do? Well, now to rogue MD's letter. God be thanked for Stella's eyes mending; and God send it holds; but faith you writ too much at a time: better write less, or write it at ten times. Yes, faith, a long letter in a morning from a dear friend is a dear thing. I smoke a compliment, little mischievous girls, I do so. But who are those *Wiggs* that think I am turned Tory? Do you mean Whigs? Which *Wiggs* and *wat* do you mean? I know nothing of Raymond, and only had one letter from him a little after I came here. [Pray remember Morgan.] Raymond is indeed like to have much influence over me in London, and to share much of my conversation. I shall, no doubt, introduce him to Harley, and Lord Keeper, and the Secretary of State. The *Tatler* upon Ithuriel's spear[1] is not mine, madam. What a puzzle there is betwixt you and your judgment! In general you may be sometimes sure of things, as that about *style*,[2] because it is what I have frequently spoken of; but guessing is mine a—, and I defy mankind, if I please. Why, I writ a pamphlet when I was last in London, that you and a thousand have seen, and never guessed it to be mine. Could you have guessed the " Shower in Town " to be mine? How chance you did not see that before your last letter went? but I suppose you in Ireland did not think it worth mentioning. Nor am I suspected for the lampoon; only Harley said he smoked me; (have I told you so before?) and some others knew it. 'Tis called " The Rod of Sid Hamet." And I have written several other things that I hear commended, and nobody suspects me for them; nor you shall not know till I see you again. What do you mean, " That

a periwig with a short tie and small round head, and embroidered nightcaps were worn chiefly by members of the graver professions.
[1] *Tatler*, No. 237.   [2] *Tatler*, No. 230.

boards near me, that I dine with now and then?"   I know no
such person: I do not dine with boarders.[1]   What the pox!
You know whom I have dined with every day since I left
you, better than I do.   What do you mean, sirrah?   Slids,
my ailment has been over these two months almost.   Impudence, if you vex me, I will give ten shillings a week
for my lodging; for I am almost st—k out of this with the
sink, and it helps me to verses in my "Shower."[2]   Well,
Madam Dingley, what say you to the world to come?
What ballad?   Why go look, it was not good for much:
have patience till I come back: patience is a gay thing as,
etc.   I hear nothing of Lord Mountjoy's coming for Ireland.
When is Stella's birthday? in March?   Lord bless me, my
turn at Christ Church;[3] it is so natural to hear you write
about that, I believe you have done it a hundred times; it
is as fresh in my mind, the verger coming to you; and why
to you?   Would he have you preach for me?   O, pox on
your spelling of Latin, *Johnsonibus atque*, that is the way.
How did the Dean get that name by the end?   'Twas
you betrayed me: not I, faith; I'll not break his head.
Your mother is still in the country, I suppose; for she
promised to see me when she came to town.   I writ to her
four days ago, to desire her to break it to Lady Giffard, to
put some money for you in the Bank, which was then fallen
thirty per cent.   Would to God mine had been here, I
should have gained one hundred pounds, and got as good
interest as in Ireland, and much securer.   I would fain
have borrowed three hundred pounds; but money is so
scarce here, there is no borrowing, by this fall of stocks.
'Tis rising now, and I knew it would: it fell from one
hundred and twenty-nine to ninety-six.   I have not heard
since from your mother.   Do you think I would be so un-
kind not to see her, that you desire me in a style so.

---

[1] See pp. 32, 68.
[2] " Returning home at night, you'll find the sink
      Strike your offended sense with double stink."
                          (" Description of a City Shower, ll. 5, 6.)
[3] Christ Church Cathedral, Dublin (see p. 93).

melancholy? Mrs. Raymond,[1] you say, is with child: I am sorry for it; and so is, I believe, her husband. Mr. Harley speaks all the kind things to me in the world; and, I believe, would serve me, if I were to stay here; but I reckon in time the Duke of Ormond may give me some addition to Laracor. Why should the Whigs think I came to England to leave them? Sure my journey was no secret. I protest sincerely, I did all I could to hinder it, as the Dean can tell you, although now I do not repent it. But who the Devil cares what they think? Am I under obligations in the least to any of them all? Rot 'em, for ungrateful dogs; I will make them repent their usage before I leave this place. They say here the same thing of my leaving the Whigs; but they own they cannot blame me, considering the treatment I have had. I will take care of your spectacles, as I told you before, and of the Bishop of Killala's; but 1 will not write to him, I have not time. What do you mean by my fourth, Madam Dinglibus? Does not Stella say you have had my fifth, Goody Blunder? You frighted me till I looked back. Well, this is enough for one night. Pray give my humble service to Mrs. Stoyte. and her sister, Kate is it, or Sarah?[2] I have forgot her name, faith. I think I will even (and to Mrs. Walls and the Arch-deacon) send this to-morrow: no, faith, that will be in ten days from the last. I will keep it till Saturday, though I write no more. But what if a letter from MD should come in the meantime? Why then I would only say, "Madam, I have received your sixth letter; your most humble servant to command, Presto"; and so conclude. Well, now I will write and think a little, and so to bed, and dream of MD.

9. I have my mouth full of water, and was going to spit it out, because I reasoned with myself, how could I write when my mouth was full? Han't you done things like that, reasoned wrong at first thinking? Well, I was to see Mr. Lewis this morning, and am to dine a few days hence, as he tells me, with Mr. Secretary St. John; and I must

[1] See p. 1.   [2] See p. 55.

contrive to see Harley soon again, to hasten this business
from the Queen. I dined to-day at Lord Mountrath's,[1] with
Lord Mountjoy,[2] etc.; but the wine was not good, so I
came away, stayed at the Coffee-house till seven, then came
home to my fire, the maidenhead of my second half-bushel,
and am now in bed at eleven, as usual. 'Tis mighty warm;
yet I fear I should catch cold this wet weather, if I sat an
evening in my room after coming from warm places: and I
must make much of myself, because MD is not here to take
care of Presto; and I am full of business, writing, etc., and
do not care for the Coffee-house; and so this serves for all
together, not to tell it you over and over, as silly people do;
but Presto is a wiser man, faith, than so, let me tell you,
gentlewomen. See, I am got to the third side; but, faith,
I will not do that often; but I must say something early
to-day, till the letter is done, and on Saturday it shall go;
so I must leave something till to-morrow, till to-morrow and
next day.

10. O Lord, I would this letter was with you with all my
heart! If it should miscarry, what a deal would be lost!
I forgot to leave a gap in the last line but one for the seal,
like a puppy; but I should have allowed for night, good-
night; but when I am taking leave, I cannot leave a bit,
faith; but I fancy the seal will not come there. I dined
to-day at Lady Lucy's, where they ran down my "Shower";
and said, "Sid Hamet" was the silliest poem they ever read;
and told Prior so, whom they thought to be author of it.
Don't you wonder I never dined there before? But I am
too busy, and they live too far off; and, besides, I do not
like women so much as I did. [MD, you must know, are
not women.] I supped to-night at Addison's, with Garth,
Steele, and Mr. Dopping; and am come home late. Lewis
has sent to me to desire I will dine with some company I
shall like. I suppose it is Mr. Secretary St. John's appointment. I had a letter just now from Raymond, who is
at Bristol, and says he will be at London in a fortnight,

[1] See p. 34.   [2] See p. 2.

and leave his wife behind him; and desires any lodging in the house where I am: but that must not be. I shall not know what to do with him in town: to be sure, I will not present him to any acquaintance of mine; and he will live a delicate life, a parson and a perfect stranger! Paaast twelvvve o'clock,[1] and so good-night, etc. Oh! but I forgot, Jemmy Leigh is come to town; says he has brought Dingley's things, and will send them with the first convenience. My parcel, I hear, is not sent yet. He thinks of going for Ireland in a month, etc. I cannot write tomorrow, because—what, because of the Archbishop; because I will seal my letter early; because I am engaged from noon till night; because of many kind of things; and yet I will write one or two words to-morrow morning, to keep up my journal constant, and at night I will begin my ninth.

11. Morning by candlelight. You must know that I am in my nightgown every morning between six and seven, and Patrick is forced to ply me fifty times before I can get on my nightgown; and so now I will take my leave of my own dear MD for this letter, and begin my next when I come home at night. God Almighty bless and protect dearest MD. Farewell, etc.

This letter's as long as a sermon, faith.

LETTER IX

LONDON, *Nov.* 11, 1710.

I DINED to-day, by invitation, with the Secretary of State, Mr. St. John. Mr. Harley came in to us before dinner, and made me his excuses for not dining with us, because he was to receive people who came to propose advancing money to the Government: there dined with us only Mr. Lewis,

---

[1] The bellman's accents. Cf. Pepys' *Diary*, Jan. 16, 1659–60: "I staid up till the bellman came by with his bell just under my window as I was writing of this very line, and cried, 'Past one of the clock, and a cold, frosty, windy morning.'"

and Dr. Freind[1] (that writ "Lord Peterborow's Actions in Spain"). I stayed with them till just now between ten and eleven, and was forced again to give my eighth to the bellman, which I did with my own hands, rather than keep it till next post. The Secretary used me with all the kindness in the world. Prior came in after dinner; and, upon an occasion, he (the Secretary) said, "The best thing I ever read is not yours, but Dr. Swift's on Vanbrugh"; which I do not reckon so very good neither.[2] But Prior was damped, until I stuffed him with two or three compliments. I am thinking what a veneration we used to have for Sir William Temple, because he might have been Secretary of State at fifty; and here is a young fellow, hardly thirty, in that employment.[3] His father is a man of pleasure,[4] that walks the Mall, and frequents St. James's Coffee - house, and the chocolate-houses; and the young son is principal Secretary of State. Is there not something very odd in that? He told me, among other things, that Mr. Harley complained he could keep nothing from me, I had the way so much of getting into him. I knew that was a refinement; and so I told him, and it was so: indeed, it is hard to see these great men use me like one who was their betters, and the puppies with you in Ireland hardly regarding me : but

[1] John Freind, M.D. (1675-1728), was a younger brother of the Robert Freind, of Westminster School, mentioned elsewhere in the *Journal*. Educated under Dr. Busby at Westminster, he was in 1694 elected a student of Christ Church, where he made the acquaintance of Atterbury, and supported Boyle against Bentley in the dispute as to the authorship of the letters of Phalaris. In 1705 he attended the Earl of Peterborough to Spain, and in the following year wrote a defence of that commander (*Account of the Earl of Peterborough's Conduct in Spain*). A steady Tory, he took a share in the defence of Dr. Sacheverell; and in 1723, when M.P. for Launceston, he fell under the suspicion of the Government, and was sent to the Tower. On the accession of George II., however, he came into favour with the Court, and died Physician to the Queen.

[2] See p. 59.

[3] St. John was thirty-two in October 1710. He had been Secretary at War six years before, resigning with Harley in 1707. Swift repeats this comparison elsewhere. Temple was forty-six when he refused a Secretaryship of State in 1674.

[4] Sir Henry St. John seems to have continued a gay man to the end of his life. In his youth he was tried and convicted for the murder of Sir William court in a duel (Scott). In 1716, after his son had been attainted, he was de Viscount St. John. He died in 1742, aged ninety.

there are some reasons for all this, which I will tell you when we meet. At coming home, I saw a letter from your mother, in answer to one I sent her two days ago. It seems she is in town; but cannot come out in a morning, just as you said; and God knows when I shall be at leisure in an afternoon: for if I should send her a penny-post letter, and afterwards not be able to meet her, it would vex me; and, besides, the days are short, and why she cannot come early in a morning, before she is wanted, I cannot imagine. I will desire her to let Lady Giffard know that she hears I am in town; and that she would go to see me, to inquire after you. I wonder she will confine herself so much to that old beast's humour. You know I cannot in honour see Lady Giffard,[1] and consequently not go into her house. This I think is enough for the first time.

12. And how could you write with such thin paper? (I forgot to say this in my former.) Cannot you get thicker? Why, that's a common caution that writing-masters give their scholars; you must have heard it a hundred times. 'Tis this:

> " If paper be thin,
> Ink will slip in;
> But, if it be thick,
> You may write with a stick."[2]

I had a letter to-day from poor Mrs. Long,[3] giving me an account of her present life, obscure in a remote country town, and how easy she is under it. Poor creature! 'tis just such an alteration in life, as if Presto should be banished from MD, and condemned to converse with Mrs. Raymond. I dined to-day with Ford, Sir Richard Levinge,[4] etc., at a

---

[1] See p. 4.

[2] "Swift delighted to let his pen run into such rhymes as these, which he generally passes off as old proverbs" (Scott). Many of the charming scraps of " Old Ballads " and " Old Plays " at the head of Scott's own chapters are in reality the result of his own imagination.

[3] See p. 10.

[4] Sir Richard Levinge, Bart., had been Solicitor-General for Ireland from 1704 to 1709, and was Attorney-General from 1711 to 1714. Afterwards he was Speaker of the Irish House of Commons and Chief-Justice of the Common Pleas in Ireland.

place where they board,[1] hard by. I was lazy, and not very well, sitting so long with company yesterday. I have been very busy writing this evening at home, and had a fire: I am spending my second half-bushel of coals; and now am in bed, and 'tis late.

13. I dined to-day in the City, and then went to christen Will Frankland's[2] child; and Lady Falconbridge[3] was one of the godmothers: this is a daughter of Oliver Cromwell, and extremely like him by his pictures that I have seen. I stayed till almost eleven, and am now come home and gone to bed. My business in the City was, to thank Stratford for a kindness he has done me, which now I will tell you. I found Bank Stock was fallen thirty-four in the hundred, and was mighty desirous to buy it; but I was a little too late for the cheapest time, being hindered by business here; for I was so wise to guess to a day when it would fall. My project was this: I had three hundred pounds in Ireland; and so I writ to Mr. Stratford in the City, to desire he would buy me three hundred pounds in Bank Stock, and that he should keep the papers, and that I would be bound to pay him for them; and, if it should rise or fall, I would take my chance, and pay him interest in the meantime. I showed my letter to one or two people who understand those things; and they said money was so hard to be got here, that no man would do it for me. However, Stratford, who is the most generous man alive, has done it: but it costs one hundred pounds and a half, that is, ten shillings; so that three hundred pounds cost me three hundred pounds and thirty shillings. This was done about a week ago, and I can have five pounds for my bargain already. Before it fell, it was one hundred and thirty pounds; and we are sure it will be the same again. I told you I writ to your mother, to desire that Lady Giffard

---

[1] See pp. 32, 62. [2] See p. 6.

[3] Thomas Belasyse, second Viscount Fauconberg, or Falconbridge (died 1700), a nobleman of hereditary loyalty, married, in 1657, the Protector's youngest daughter, Mary Cromwell, who is represented as a lady of high talent and spirit. She died on March 14, 1712. Burnet describes her as "a wise and worthy woman," who would have had a better prospect of maintaining her father's post than either of her brothers.

would do the same with what she owes you; but she tells your mother she has no money. I would to God all you had in the world was there. Whenever you lend money, take this rule, to have two people bound, who have both visible fortunes; for they will hardly die together; and, when one dies, you fall upon the other, and make him add another security: and if Rathburn (now I have his name) pays you in your money, let me know, and I will direct Parvisol accordingly: however, he shall wait on you and know. So, ladies, enough of business for one night. Paaaaast twelvvve o'clock. I must only add, that, after a long fit of rainy weather, it has been fair two or three days, and is this day grown cold and frosty; so that you must give poor little Presto leave to have a fire in his chamber morning and evening too; and he will do as much for you.

14. What, has your Chancellor[1] lost his senses, like Will Crowe?[2] I forgot to tell Dingley that I was yesterday at Ludgate, bespeaking the spectacles at the great shop there, and shall have them in a day or two. This has been an insipid day. I dined with Mrs. Vanhomrigh, and came gravely home, after just visiting the Coffee - house. Sir Richard Cox,[3] they say, is sure of going over Lord Chancellor, who is as arrant a puppy as ever ate bread: but the Duke of Ormond has a natural affection to puppies; which is a thousand pities, being none himself. I have been amusing myself at home till now, and in bed bid you good-night.

15. I have been visiting this morning, but nobody was at home, Secretary St. John, Sir Thomas Hanmer,[4] Sir

[1] Richard Freeman, Chief Baron, was Lord Chancellor of Ireland from 1707 until his death in November 1710.

[2] See p. 49.

[3] Sir Richard Cox, Bart. (1650–1733), was Lord Chancellor of Ireland from 1703 to 1707. In 1711 he was appointed Chief-Justice of the Queen's Bench, but he was removed from office on the death of Queen Anne. His zealous Protestantism sometimes caused his views to be warped, but he was honest and well-principled.

[4] Sir Thomas Hanmer, Bart. (1676–1746), succeeded Bromley as Speaker in 1714. In February 1713 Swift said, "He is the most considerable man in the House of Commons." His edition of Shakespeare was published by the University of Oxford in 1743–44. Pope called it "pompous," and sneered at Hanmer's "superior air" (*Dunciad*, iv. 105).

Chancellor Cox-comb, etc. I attended the Duke of Ormond with about fifty other Irish gentlemen at Skinners' Hall, where the Londonderry Society laid out three hundred pounds to treat us and his Grace with a dinner. Three great tables with the dessert laid in mighty figure. Sir Richard Levinge and I got discreetly to the head of the second table, to avoid the crowd at the first: but it was so cold, and so confounded a noise with the trumpets and hautboys, that I grew weary, and stole away before the second course came on; so I can give you no account of it, which is a thousand pities. I called at Ludgate for Dingley's glasses, and shall have them in a day or two; and I doubt it will cost me thirty shillings for a microscope, but not without Stella's permission; for I remember she is a virtuoso. Shall I buy it or no? 'Tis not the great bulky ones, nor the common little ones, to impale a louse (saving your presence) upon a needle's point; but of a more exact sort, and clearer to the sight, with all its equipage in a little trunk that you may carry in your pocket. Tell me, sirrah, shall I buy it or not for you? I came home straight, etc.

16. I dined to-day in the city with Mr. Manley,[1] who invited Mr. Addison and me, and some other friends, to his lodging, and entertained us very handsomely. I returned with Mr. Addison, and loitered till nine in the Coffee-house, where I am hardly known, by going so seldom. I am here soliciting for Trounce; you know him: he was gunner in the former yacht, and would fain be so in the present one: if you remember him, a good, lusty, fresh-coloured fellow. Shall I stay till I get another letter from MD before I close up this? Mr. Addison and I meet a little seldomer than formerly, although we are still at bottom as good friends as ever, but differ a little about party.

17. To-day I went to Lewis at the Secretary's office; where I saw and spoke to Mr. Harley, who promised, in a few days, to finish the rest of my business. I reproached him for putting me on the necessity of minding him of it,

[1] See p. 24.

and rallied him, etc., which he took very well. I dined
to-day with one Mr. Gore, elder brother to a young merchant
of my acquaintance; and Stratford and my other friend
merchants dined with us, where I stayed late, drinking claret
and burgundy; and am just got to bed, and will say no
more, but that it now begins to be time to have a letter from
my own little MD; for the last I had above a fortnight ago,
and the date was old too.

18. To-day I dined with Lewis and Prior at an eating-
house, but with Lewis's wine. Lewis went away, and Prior
and I sat on, where we complimented one another for an
hour or two upon our mutual wit and poetry. Coming home
at seven, a gentleman unknown stopped me in the Pall Mall,
and asked my advice; said he had been to see the Queen
(who was just come to town), and the people in waiting
would not let him see her; that he had two hundred
thousand men ready to serve her in the war; that he knew
the Queen perfectly well, and had an apartment at Court,
and if she heard he was there, she would send for him
immediately; that she owed him two hundred thousand
pounds, etc., and he desired my opinion, whether he should
go try again whether he could see her; or because, perhaps,
she was weary after her journey, whether he had not better
stay till to-morrow. I had a mind to get rid of my companion,
and begged him of all love to go and wait on her immediately;
for that, to my knowledge, the Queen would admit him;
that this was an affair of great importance, and required
despatch: and I instructed him to let me know the success
of his business, and come to the Smyrna Coffee-house, where
I would wait for him till midnight; and so ended this
adventure. I would have fain given the man half a crown;
but was afraid to offer it him, lest he should be offended;
for, beside his money, he said he had a thousand pounds a
year. I came home not early; and so, madams both, good-
night, etc.

19. I dined to-day with poor Lord Mountjoy, who is ill of
the gout; and this evening I christened our coffee-man

Elliot's[1] child, where the rogue had a most noble supper, and Steele and I sat among some scurvy company over a bowl of punch; so that I am come home late, young women, and can't stay to write to little rogues.

20. I loitered at home, and dined with Sir Andrew Fountaine at his lodging, and then came home: a silly day.

21. I was visiting all this morning, and then went to the Secretary's office, and found Mr. Harley, with whom I dined; and Secretary St. John, etc., and Harley promised in a very few days to finish what remains of my business. Prior was of the company, and we all dine at the Secretary's to-morrow. I saw Stella's mother this morning: she came early, and we talked an hour. I wish you would propose to Lady Giffard to take the three hundred pounds out of her hands, and give her common interest for life, and security that you will pay her: the Bishop of Clogher, or any friend, would be security for you, if you gave them counter-security; and it may be argued that it will pass better to be in your hands than hers, in case of mortality, etc. Your mother says, if you write, she will second it; and you may write to your mother, and then it will come from her. She tells me Lady Giffard has a mind to see me, by her discourse; but I told her what to say, with a vengeance. She told Lady Giffard she was going to see me: she looks extremely well. I am writing[2] in my bed like a tiger; and so good-night, etc.

22. I dined with Secretary St. John; and Lord Dartmouth, who is t'other Secretary, dined with us, and Lord Orrery[3] and Prior, etc. Harley called, but could not dine with us, and would have had me away while I was at dinner; but I did

---

[1] Elliot was keeper of the St. James's Coffee-house (see p. 2).

[2] Forster suggested that the true reading is "writhing." If so, it is not necessary to suppose that Lady Giffard was the cause of it. Perhaps it is the word "tiger" that is corrupt.

[3] The Hon. Charles Boyle (1676–1731), of the Boyle and Bentley controversy, succeeded to the peerage as Lord Orrery in 1703. When he settled in London he became the centre of a Christ Church set, a strong adherent of Harley's party, and a member of Swift's "club." His son John, fifth Earl of Orrery, published *Remarks on the Life and Writings of Jonathan Swift* in 1751.

not like the company he was to have. We stayed till eight, and I called at the Coffee-house, and looked where the letters lie; but no letter directed for Mr. Presto: at last I saw a letter to Mr. Addison, and it looked like a rogue's hand; so I made the fellow give it me, and opened it before him, and saw three letters all for myself: so, truly, I put them in my pocket, and came home to my lodging. Well, and so you shall hear: well, and so I found one of them in Dingley's hand, and t'other in Stella's, and the third in Domville's.[1] Well, so| you shall hear; so, said I to myself, What now, two letters from MD together? But I thought there was something in the wind; so I opened one, and I opened t'other; and so you shall hear, one was from Walls. Well, but t'other was from our own dear MD; yes it was. O faith, have you received my seventh, young women, already? Then I must send this to-morrow, else there will be old[2] doings at our house, faith.—Well, I won't answer your letter in this: no, faith, catch me at that, and I never saw the like. Well; but as to Walls, tell him (with service to him and wife, etc.) that I have no imagination of Mr. Pratt's[3] losing his place: and while Pratt continues, Clements is in no danger; and I have already engaged Lord Hyde[4] he speaks of, for Pratt and twenty others; but, if such a thing should happen, I will do what I can. I have above ten businesses of other people's now on my hands, and, I believe, shall miscarry in half. It is your sixth I now have received. I writ last post to the Bishop of Clogher again. Shall I send this to-morrow? Well, I will, to oblige MD. Which would you rather, a short letter every week, or a long one every fortnight? A long one; well, it shall be done, and so good-night. Well, but is

[1] William Domville, a landed proprietor in County Dublin, whom Swift called "perfectly as fine a gentleman as I know."
[2] On May 16, 1711, Swift wrote, "There will be an old to do." The word is found in Elizabethan writers in the sense of "more than enough." Cf. *Macbeth*, ii. 3: "If a man were porter of hell gate, he should have old turning the key."
[3] See p. 9. Clements was related to Pratt, the Deputy Vice-Treasurer, and was probably the Robert Clements who became Deputy Vice-Treasurer, and whose grandson Robert was created Earl of Leitrim in 1795.
[4] See p. 24.

this a long one?   No, I warrant you: too long for naughty
girls.

23. I only ask, have you got both the ten pounds, or only
the first; I hope you mean both.   Pray be good housewives;
and I beg you to walk when you can, for health.   Have you
the horse in town? and do you ever ride him? how often?
Confess.   Ahhh, sirrah, have I caught you?   Can you contrive to let Mrs. Fenton[1] know, that the request she has
made me in her letter I will use what credit I have to bring
about, although I hear it is very difficult, and I doubt I shall
not succeed?   Cox is not to be your Chancellor: all joined
against him.   I have been supping with Lord Peterborow at
his house, with Prior, Lewis, and Dr. Freind.   'Tis the
ramblingest lying rogue on earth.   Dr. Raymond is come to
town: 'tis late, and so I bid you good-night.

24. I tell you, pretty management!   Ned Southwell told
me the other day he had a letter from the bishops of Ireland,
with an address to the Duke of Ormond, to intercede with
the Queen to take off the First-Fruits.   I dined with him
to-day, and saw it, with another letter to him from the
Bishop of Kildare,[2] to call upon me for the papers, etc.;
and I had last post one from the Archbishop of Dublin, telling
me the reason of this proceeding; that, upon hearing the
Duke of Ormond was declared Lord Lieutenant, they met;
and the bishops were for this project, and talked coldly of
my being solicitor, as one that was favoured by t'other party,
etc., but desired that I would still solicit.[3]   Now the wisdom
of this is admirable; for I had given the Archbishop an

---

[1] Swift's sister Jane, who had married a currier in Bride Street, named
Joseph Fenton, a match to which Swift strongly objected.   Deane Swift says
that Swift never saw his sister again after the marriage; he had offered her
£500 if she would show a "proper disdain" of Fenton.   On her husband's
dying bankrupt, however, Swift paid her an annuity until 1738, when she died
in the same lodging with Esther Johnson's mother, Mrs. Bridget Mose, at
Farnham (Forster's *Swift*, pp. 118–19).

[2] Welbore Ellis, appointed Bishop of Kildare in 1705.   He was translated to
Meath in 1731, and died three years later.

[3] The expression of the Archbishop is, "I am not to conceal from you that
some expressed a little jealously, that you would not be acceptable to the
present courtiers; intimating that you were under the reputation of being a
favourite of the late party in power" (King to Swift, Nov. 2, 1710).

account of my reception from Mr. Harley, and how he had
spoken to the Queen, and promised it should be done; but
Mr. Harley ordered me to tell no person alive. Some time
after, he gave me leave to let the Primate and Archbishop
know that the Queen had remitted the First-Fruits; and that
in a short time they should have an account of it in form
from Lord Dartmouth, Secretary of State. So while their
letter was on the road to the Duke of Ormond and Southwell, mine was going to them with an account of the thing
being done. I writ a very warm answer[1] to the Archbishop
immediately; and showed my resentments, as I ought,
against the bishops; only, in good manners, excepting himself. I wonder what they will say when they hear the thing
is done. I was yesterday forced to tell Southwell so, that
the Queen had done it, etc.; for he said, my Lord Duke would
think of it some months hence, when he was going for
Ireland; and he had it three years in doing formerly, without any success. I give you free leave to say, on occasion,
that it is done; and that Mr. Harley prevailed on the Queen
to do it, etc., as you please. As I hope to live, I despise the
credit of it, out of an excess of pride; and desire you will
not give me the least merit when you talk of it; but I would
vex the bishops, and have it spread that Mr. Harley had
done it: pray do so. Your mother sent me last night a
parcel of wax candles, and a bandbox full of small plum-
cakes. I thought it had been something for you; and,
without opening them, sent answer by the maid that brought
them, that I would take care to send the things, etc.; but
I will write her thanks. Is this a long letter, sirrahs? Now,
are you satisfied? I have had no fit since the first: I drink
brandy every morning, and take pills every night. Never
fear, I an't vexed at this puppy business of the bishops,

---

[1] This indignant letter is dated Nov. 23, 1710. It produced an apolo-
getic reply from the Archbishop (Nov. 30, 1710), who represented that the
letter to Southwell was a snare laid in his way, since if he declined signing it,
it might have been interpreted into disrespect to the Duke of Ormond. Of
the bishops King said, "You cannot do yourself a greater service than to
bring this to a good issue, to their shame and conviction."

although I was a little at first. I will tell you my reward:
Mr. Harley will think he has done me a favour; the Duke
of Ormond, perhaps, that I have put a neglect on him; and
the bishops in Ireland, that I have done nothing at all. So
goes the world. But I have got above all this, and, perhaps,
I have better reason for it than they know: and so you shall
hear no more of First-Fruits, dukes, Harleys, archbishops, and
Southwells.

I have slipped off Raymond upon some of his countrymen, to
show him the town, etc., and I lend him Patrick. He desires
to sit with me in the evenings; upon which I have given
Patrick positive orders that I am not within at evenings.

LETTER X

LONDON, *Nov.* 25, 1710.

I WILL tell you something that's plaguy silly: I had forgot
to say on the 23d in my last, where I dined; and because
I had done it constantly, I thought it was a great omission,
and was going to interline it; but at last the silliness of it
made me cry, Pshah, and I let it alone. I was to-day to see
the Parliament meet; but only saw a great crowd; and Ford
and I went to see the tombs at Westminster, and sauntered
so long I was forced to go to an eating-house for my dinner.
Bromley[1] is chosen Speaker, *nemine contradicente*: Do you
understand those two words? And Pompey, Colonel Hill's[2]
black, designs to stand Speaker for the footmen.[3] I am

---

[1] William Bromley (died 1732) was M.P. for the University of Oxford. A
good debater and a strong High Churchman, he was Secretary of State from
August 1713 until the Queen's death in the following year.

[2] Colonel, afterwards Major-General, John Hill (died 1735) was younger
brother of Mrs. Masham, the Queen's favourite, and a poor relation of the
Duchess of Marlborough. He was wounded at Mons in 1709, and in 1711
was sent on an unsuccessful expedition to attack the French settlements
in North America. In 1713 he was appointed to command the troops at
Dunkirk.

[3] "The footmen in attendance at the Houses of Parliament used at this time to
form themselves into a deliberative body, and usually debated the same points
with their masters. It was jocularly said that several questions were lost by
the Court party in the menial House of Lords which were carried triumphantly

engaged to use my interest for him, and have spoken to
Patrick to get him some votes. We are now all impatient
for the Queen's speech, what she will say about removing the
Ministry, etc. I have got a cold, and I don't know how;
but got it I have, and am hoarse: I don't know whether
it will grow better or worse. What's that to you? I
won't answer your letter to-night. I'll keep you a little
longer in suspense: I can't send it. Your mother's cakes
are very good, and one of them serves me for a breakfast,
and so I'll go sleep like a good boy.

26. I have got a cruel cold, and stayed within all this day
in my nightgown, and dined on sixpennyworth of victuals,
and read and writ, and was denied to everybody. Dr.
Raymond[1] called often, and I was denied; and at last,
when I was weary, I let him come up, and asked him, without consequence, how Patrick denied me, and whether he
had the art of it? So by this means he shall be used to have
me denied to him; otherwise he would be a plaguy trouble
and hindrance to me: he has sat with me two hours, and
drank a pint of ale cost me fivepence, and smoked his pipe,
and it is now past eleven that he is just gone. Well, my
eighth is with you now, young women; and your seventh to
me is somewhere in a post-boy's bag; and so go to your
gang of deans, and Stoytes, and Walls, and lose your money;
go, sauceboxes: and so good-night, and be happy, dear
rogues. Oh, but your box was sent to Dr. Hawkshaw by
Sterne, and you will have it with Hawkshaw, and spectacles,
etc. etc.

27. To-day Mr. Harley met me in the Court of Requests,[2]

in the real assembly; which was at length explained by a discovery that the
Scottish peers whose votes were sometimes decisive of a question had but few
representatives in the convocation of lacqueys. The sable attendant mentioned
by Swift, being an appendage of the brother of Mrs. Masham, the reigning
favourite, had a title to the chair, the Court and Tory interest being exerted in
his favour" (Scott). Steele alludes to the "Footmen's Parliament" in No. 88
of the *Spectator*.

[1] See p. 1.
[2] A Court of Equity abolished in the reign of Charles I. It met in the
Camera Alba, or Whitehall, and the room appears to have retained the name
of the old Court.

and whispered me to dine with him. At dinner I told him
what those bishops had done, and the difficulty I was under.
He bid me never trouble myself; he would tell the Duke of
Ormond the business was done, and that he need not concern
himself about it. So now I am easy, and they may hang
themselves for a parcel of insolent, ungrateful rascals. I
suppose I told you in my last, how they sent an address to
the Duke of Ormond, and a letter to Southwell, to call on
me for the papers, after the thing was over; but they had
not received my letter, though the Archbishop might, by
what I writ to him, have expected it would be done. Well,
there is an end of that; and in a little time the Queen
will send them notice, etc. And so the methods will be
settled; and then I shall think of returning, although the
baseness of those bishops makes me love Ireland less than
I did.

28. Lord Halifax sent to invite me to dinner; where I
stayed till six, and crossed him in all his Whig talk, and made
him often come over to me. I know he makes court to the
new men, although he affects to talk like a Whig. I had a
letter to-day from the Bishop of Clogher; but I writ to him
lately, that I would obey his commands to the Duke of
Ormond. He says I bid him read the London "Shaver," and
that you both swore it was "Shaver," and not "Shower."[1]
You all lie, and you are puppies, and can't read Presto's hand.
The Bishop is out entirely in his conjectures of my share in
the *Tatlers*.—I have other things to mind, and of much
greater importance;[2] else I have little to do to be acquainted
with a new Ministry, who consider me a little more than
Irish bishops do.

29. Now for your saucy, good dear letter: let me see, what
does it say? come then. I dined to-day with Ford, and
went home early; he debauched[3] me to his chamber again

[1] See p. 34.
[2] Swift's first contribution to the *Examiner* (No. 13) is dated Nov. 2,
1710.
[3] Seduced, induced. Dryden (*Spanish Friar*) has "To debauch a king to
break his laws."

with a bottle of wine till twelve: so good-night. I cannot
write an answer now, you rogues.

30. To-day I have been visiting, which I had long
neglected; and I dined with Mrs. Barton alone; and
sauntered at the Coffee-house till past eight, and have been
busy till eleven, and now I'll answer your letter, saucebox.
Well, let me see now again. My wax candle's almost out,
but however I'll begin. Well then, do not be so tedious,
Mr. Presto; what can you say to MD's letter? Make haste,
have done with your preambles—Why, I say I am glad you
are so often abroad; your mother thinks it is want of exercise
hurts you, and so do I. (She called here to-night, but I was
not within, that's by the bye.) Sure you do not deceive me,
Stella, when you say you are in better health than you were
these three weeks; for Dr. Raymond told me yesterday, that
Smyth of the Blind Quay had been telling Mr. Leigh that
he left you extremely ill; and in short, spoke so, that he
almost put poor Leigh into tears, and would have made me
run distracted; though your letter is dated the 11th instant,
and I saw Smyth in the city above a fortnight ago, as I passed
by in a coach. Pray, pray, don't write, Stella, until you are
mighty, mighty, mighty, mighty, well in your eyes, and are
sure it won't do you the least hurt. Or come, I'll tell you
what; you, Mistress Stella, shall write your share at five or
six sittings, one sitting a day; and then comes Dingley all
together, and then Stella a little crumb towards the end, to
let us see she remembers Presto; and then conclude with
something handsome and genteel, as your most humblecum-
dumble, or, etc. O Lord! does Patrick write word of my
not coming till spring? Insolent man! he know my secrets?
No; as my Lord Mayor said, No; if I thought my shirt knew,
etc. Faith, I will come as soon as it is any way proper for
me to come; but, to say the truth, I am at present a little
involved with the present Ministry in some certain things
(which I tell you as a secret); and soon as ever I can clear my
hands, I will stay no longer; for I hope the First-Fruit business
will be soon over in all its forms. But, to say the truth, the

present Ministry have a difficult task, and want me, etc.   Perhaps they may be just as grateful as others : but, according to the best judgment I have, they are pursuing the true interest of the public ; and therefore I am glad to contribute what is in my power.   For God's sake, not a word of this to any alive.—Your Chancellor ?[1]   Why, madam, I can tell you he has been dead this fortnight.   Faith, I could hardly forbear our little language about a nasty dead Chancellor, as you may see by the blot.[2]   Ploughing ?   A pox plough them ; they'll plough me to nothing.   But have you got your money, both the ten pounds ?   How durst he pay you the second so soon ?   Pray be good huswifes.   Ay, well, and Joe, why, I had a letter lately from Joe, desiring I would take some care of their poor town,[3] who, he says, will lose their liberties. To which I desired Dr. Raymond would return answer, that the town had behaved themselves so ill to me, so little regarded the advice I gave them, and disagreed so much among themselves, that I was resolved never to have more to do with them ; but that whatever personal kindness I could do to Joe, should be done.   Pray, when you happen to see Joe, tell him this, lest Raymond should have blundered or forgotten—Poor Mrs. Wesley !—Why these poligyes[4] for being abroad ?   Why should you be at home at all, until Stella is quite well ?—So, here is Mistress Stella again, with her two eggs, etc.   My " Shower " admired with you ; why, the Bishop of Clogher says, he has seen something of mine of the same sort, better than the "Shower."   I suppose he means "The Morning " ;[5] but it is not half so good.   I want your judgment of things, and not your country's.   How does MD like it ?

[1] Freeman (see p. 69).
[2] " To make this intelligible, it is necessary to observe, that the words *this fortnight*, in the preceding sentence, were first written in what he calls their little language, and afterwards scratched out and written plain.   It must be confessed this little language, which passed current between Swift and Stella, has occasioned infinite trouble in the revisal of these papers " (Deane Swift).
[3] Trim.   An attack upon the liberties of this corporation is among the political offences of Wharton's Lieutenancy of Ireland set forth in Swift's *Short Character of the Earl of Wharton*.
[4] Apologies.
[5] "A Description of the Morning," in No. 9 of the *Tatler*.

and do they taste it *all*? etc. I am glad Dean Bolton[1] has paid the twenty pounds. Why should not I chide the Bishop of Clogher for writing to the Archbishop of Cashel,[2] without sending the letter first to me? It does not signify a ——; for he has no credit at Court. Stuff—they are all puppies. I will break your head in good earnest, young woman, for your nasty jest about Mrs. Barton.[3] Unlucky sluttikin, what a word is there! Faith, I was thinking yesterday, when I was with her, whether she could break them or no, and it quite spoilt my imagination. "Mrs. Walls, does Stella win as she pretends?" "No indeed, Doctor; she loses always, and will play so *ventersomely*, how can she win?" See here now; an't you an impudent lying slut? Do, open Domville's letter; what does it signify, if you have a mind? Yes, faith, you write smartly with your eyes shut; all was well but the *w*. See how I can do it; *Madam Stella, your humble servant.*[4] O, but one may look whether one goes crooked or no, and so write on. I will tell you what you may do; you may write with your eyes half shut, just as when one is going to sleep: I have done so for two or three lines now; it is but just seeing enough to go straight.—Now, Madam Dingley, I think I bid you tell Mr. Walls that, in case there be occasion, I will serve his friend as far as I can; but I hope there will be none. Yet I believe you will have a new Parliament; but I care not whether you have or no a better. You are mistaken in all your conjectures about the *Tatlers*. I have given him one or two hints, and you have heard me talk about the Shilling.[5] Faith, these answering letters are very long ones: you have taken up almost the room of a week in journals; and I will tell you what, I saw fellows wearing crosses to-day,[6] and I wondered what was the matter; but just this minute I recollect it is little Presto's birthday; and I was resolved

---

[1] See p. 38.   [2] William Palliser (died 1726).   [3] See p. 20.
[4] " Here he writ with his eyes shut; and the writing is somewhat crooked, although as well in other respects as if his eyes had been open" (Deane Swift).
[5] *Tatler*, No. 249; cf. p. 93. During this visit to London Swift contributed to only three *Tatlers*, viz. Nos. 230, 238, and 258.
[6] St. Andrew's Day.

6

these three days to remember it when it came, but could not. Pray, drink my health to-day at dinner; do, you rogues. Do you like "Sid Hamet's Rod"? Do you understand it all? Well, now at last I have done with your letter, and so I will lay me down to sleep, and about, fair maids; and I hope merry maids all.

Dec. 1. Morning. I wish Smyth were hanged. I was dreaming the most melancholy things in the world of poor Stella, and was grieving and crying all night.—Pshah, it is foolish: I will rise and divert myself; so good-morrow; and God of His infinite mercy keep and protect you! The Bishop of Clogher's letter is dated Nov. 21. He says you thought of going with him to Clogher. I am heartily glad of it, and wish you would ride there, and Dingley go in a coach. I have had no fit since my first, although sometimes my head is not quite in good order.—At night. I was this morning to visit Mr. Pratt, who is come over with poor, sick Lord Shelburne: they made me dine with them; and there I stayed, like a booby, till eight, looking over them at ombre, and then came home. Lord Shelburne's giddiness is turned into a colic, and he looks miserably.

2. Steele, the rogue, has done the imprudentest thing in the world: he said something in a *Tatler*,[1] that we ought to use the word Great Britain, and not England, in common conversation, as, "The finest lady in Great Britain," etc. Upon this, Rowe, Prior, and I sent him a letter, turning this into ridicule. He has to-day printed the letter,[2] and signed it J. S., M. P., and N. R., the first letters of all our names. Congreve told me to-day, he smoked it immediately. Congreve and I, and Sir Charles Wager, dined to-day at Delaval's, the Portugal Envoy; and I stayed there till eight, and came home, and am now writing to you before I do business, because that dog Patrick is not at home, and the fire is not made, and I am not in my gear. Pox take him!—I was looking by chance at the top of this side, and find I make plaguy mistakes in words; so that you must fence against that as well as bad

---

[1] No. 241.   [2] *Tatler*, No. 258.

writing. Faith, I can't nor won't read what I have written.
(Pox of this puppy!) Well, I'll leave you till I am got to
bed, and then I will say a word or two.—Well, 'tis now
almost twelve, and I have been busy ever since, by a fire too
(I have my coals by half a bushel at a time, I'll assure you),
and now I am got to bed. Well, and what have you to say
to Presto now he is abed? Come now, let us hear your
speeches. No, 'tis a lie; I an't sleepy yet. Let us sit up a
little longer, and talk. Well, where have you been to-day,
that you are but just this minute come home in a coach?
What have you lost? Pay the coachman, Stella. No, faith,
not I, he'll grumble.—What new acquaintance have you got?
come, let us hear. I have made Delaval promise to send me
some Brazil tobacco from Portugal for you, Madam Dingley.
I hope you will have your chocolate and spectacles before
this comes to you.

3. Pshaw, I must be writing to these dear saucy brats every
night, whether I will or no, let me have what business I will,
or come home ever so late, or be ever so sleepy; but an old
saying, and a true one,

> " Be you lords, or be you earls,
> You must write to naughty girls."

I was to-day at Court, and saw Raymond among the Beef-
eaters, staying to see the Queen: so I put him in a better
station, made two or three dozen of bows, and went to
church, and then to Court again, to pick up a dinner, as I
did with Sir John Stanley; and then we went to visit Lord
Mountjoy, and just now left him; and 'tis near eleven at
night, young women; and methinks this letter comes pretty
near to the bottom, and 'tis but eight days since the date,
and don't think I'll write on the other side, I thank you
for nothing. Faith, if I would use you to letters on sheets
as broad as this room, you would always expect them from
me.   O, faith, I know you well enough; but an old
saying, etc.,

> "Two sides in a sheet,
> And one in a street."

I think that's but a silly old saying; and so I'll go to sleep, and do you so too.

4. I dined to-day with Mrs. Vanhomrigh, and then came home, and studied till eleven.   No adventure at all to-day.

5. So I went to the Court of Requests (we have had the Devil and all of rain by the bye) to pick up a dinner; and Henley made me go dine with him and one Colonel Bragg [1] at a tavern; cost me money, faith.   Congreve was to be there, but came not.   I came with Henley to the Coffee - house, where Lord Salisbury [2] seemed mighty desirous to talk with me; and, while he was wriggling himself into my favour, that dog Henley asked me aloud, whether I would go to see Lord Somers as I had promised (which was a lie); and all to vex poor Lord Salisbury, who is a high Tory.   He played two or three other such tricks; and I was forced to leave my lord, and I came home at seven, and have been writing ever since, and will now go to bed.   The other day I saw Jack Temple [3] in the Court of Requests: it was the first time of seeing him; so we talked two or three careless words, and parted.   Is it true that your Recorder and Mayor, and fanatic aldermen, a month or two ago, at a solemn feast, drank Mr. Harley's, Lord Rochester's, [4] and other Tory healths?   Let me know; it was confidently said here.—The scoundrels! It shan't do, Tom.

6. When is this letter to go, I wonder? harkee, young women, tell me that.   Saturday next for certain, and not before: then it will be just a fortnight; time enough for naughty girls, and long enough for two letters, faith. Congreve and Delaval have at last prevailed on Sir Godfrey Kneller to entreat me to let him draw my picture for nothing; but I know not yet when I shall sit. [5]—It is such monstrous rainy weather, that there is no doing with it. Secretary St. John sent to me this morning, that my dining

---

[1] Lieutenant-General Philip Bragg, Colonel of the 28th Regiment of Foot, and M. P. for Armagh, died in 1759.
[2] James Cecil, fifth Earl of Salisbury, who died in 1728.
[3] See p. 5.   [4] See p. 60.
[5] Kneller seems never to have painted Swift's portrait.

with him to-day was put off till to-morrow; so I peaceably
sat with my neighbour Ford, dined with him, and came
home at six, and am now in bed as usual; and now it is time
to have another letter from MD, yet I would not have it till
this goes; for that would look like two letters for one. Is
it not whimsical that the Dean has never once written to me?
And I find the Archbishop very silent to that letter I sent
him with an account that the business was done. I believe
he knows not what to write or say; and I have since written
twice to him, both times with a vengeance.[1] Well, go to
bed, sirrahs, and so will I. But have you lost to-day? Three
shillings! O fie, O fie!

7. No, I won't send this letter to-day, nor till Saturday,
faith; and I am so afraid of one from MD between this and
that; if it comes, I will just say I received a letter, and that
is all. I dined to-day with Mr. Secretary St. John, where
were Lord Anglesea,[2] Sir Thomas Hanmer, Prior, Freind,
etc., and then made a debauch after nine at Prior's house,
and have eaten cold pie, and I hate the thoughts of it, and
I am full, and I don't like it, and I will go to bed, and it is
late, and so good-night.

8. To-day I dined with Mr. Harley and Prior; but Mr.
St. John did not come, though he promised: he chid me
for not seeing him oftener. Here is a damned, libellous
pamphlet come out against Lord Wharton, giving the
character first, and then telling some of his actions: the
character is very well, but the facts indifferent.[3] It has been
sent by dozens to several gentlemen's lodgings, and I had one
or two of them; but nobody knows the author or printer.
We are terribly afraid of the plague; they say it is at

[1] On Nov. 25 and 28.

[2] Arthur Annesley, M.P. for Cambridge University, had recently become
fifth Earl of Anglesea, on the death of his brother (see p. 13). Under George I.
he was Joint Treasurer of Ireland, and Treasurer at War.

[3] A Short Character of the Earl of Wharton, by Swift himself, though
the authorship was not suspected at the time. "Archbishop King," says
Scott, "would have hardly otherwise ventured to mention it to Swift in his
letter of Jan. 9, 1710, as 'a wound given in the dark.'" Elsewhere, however,
in a note, Swift hints that Archbishop King was really aware of the authorship of the pamphlet.

Newcastle.[1] I begged Mr. Harley for the love of God to take some care about it, or we are all ruined. There have been orders for all ships from the Baltic to pass their quarantine before they land; but they neglect it. You remember I have been afraid these two years.

9. O, faith, you are a saucy rogue. I have had your sixth letter just now, before this is gone; but I will not answer a word of it, only that I never was giddy since my first fit; but I have had a cold just a fortnight, and cough with it still morning and evening; but it will go off. It is, however, such abominable weather that no creature can walk. They say here three of your Commissioners will be turned out, Ogle, South, and St. Quintin;[2] and that Dick Stewart[3] and Ludlow will be two of the new ones. I am a little soliciting for another: it is poor Lord Abercorn,[4] but that is a secret; I mean, that I befriend him is a secret; but I believe it is too late, by his own fault and ill fortune. I dined with him to-day. I am heartily sorry you do not go to Clogher, faith, I am; and so God Almighty protect poor, dear, dear, dear, dearest MD. Farewell till to-night. I'll begin my eleventh to-night; so I am always writing to little MD.

LETTER XI

LONDON, *Dec.* 9, 1710.

SO, young women, I have just sent my tenth to the post-office, and, as I told you, have received your seventh (faith, I am afraid I mistook, and said your sixth, and then we shall be all in confusion this month). Well, I told you I dined with Lord Abercorn to-day; and that is enough till

---

[1] A false report : see p. 88 below.
[2] None of these Commissioners of Revenue lost their places at this time. Samuel Ogle was Commissioner from 1699 to 1714; John South from 1696 until his death in 1711 ; and Sir William St. Quintin, Bart., from 1706 to 1713. Stephen Ludlow succeeded South in September 1711.
[3] See p. 53.
[4] James Hamilton, sixth Earl of Abercorn (1656–1734), a Scotch peer who had strongly supported the Union of 1706.

by and bye; for I must go write idle things, and twittle twattle.[1] What's here to do with your little MD's? and so I put this by for a while. 'Tis now late, and I can only say MD is a dear, saucy rogue, and what then? Presto loves them the better.

10. This son of a b—— Patrick is out of the way, and I can do nothing; am forced to borrow coals: 'tis now six o'clock, and I am come home after a pure walk in the park; delicate weather, begun only to-day. A terrible storm last night: we hear one of your packet-boats is cast away, and young Beau Swift[2] in it, and General Sankey:[3] I know not the truth; you will before me. Raymond talks of leaving the town in a few days, and going in a month to Ireland, for fear his wife should be too far gone, and forced to be brought to bed here. I think he is in the right; but perhaps this packet-boat will fright him. He has no relish for London; and I do not wonder at it. He has got some Templars from Ireland that show him the town. I do not let him see me above twice a week, and that only while I am dressing in the morning.—So, now the puppy's come in, and I have got my own ink, but a new pen; and so now you are rogues and sauceboxes till I go to bed; for I must go study, sirrahs. Now I think of it, tell the Bishop of Clogher, he shall not cheat me of one inch of my bell metal. You know it is nothing but to save the town money; and Enniskillen can afford it better than Laracor: he shall have but one thousand five hundred weight. I have been reading, etc., as usual, and am now going to bed; and I find this day's article is long enough: so get you gone till to-morrow, and then. I dined with Sir Matthew Dudley.

11. I am come home again as yesterday, and the puppy had again locked up my ink, notwithstanding all I said to

---

[1] L'Estrange speaks of "insipid twittle twattles." Johnson calls this "a vile word."

[2] A cousin of Swift's; probably a son of William Swift.

[3] Nicholas Sankey (died 1722) succeeded Lord Lovelace as Colonel of a Regiment of Foot in Ireland in 1689. He became Brigadier-General in 1704, Major-General 1707, and Lieutenant-General 1710. He served in Spain, and was taken prisoner at the battle of the Caya in 1709.

him yesterday; but he came home a little after me, so all is well: they are lighting my fire, and I'll go study. The fair weather is gone again, and it has rained all day. I do not like this open weather, though some say it is healthy. They say it is a false report about the plague at Newcastle.[1] I have no news to-day: I dined with Mrs. Vanhomrigh, to desire them to buy me a scarf; and Lady Abercorn[2] is to buy me another, to see who does best: mine is all in rags. I saw the Duke of Richmond[3] yesterday at Court again, but would not speak to him: I believe we are fallen out. I am now in bed; and it has rained all this evening, like wild-fire: have you so much rain in your town? Raymond was in a fright, as I expected, upon the news of this shipwreck; but I persuaded him, and he leaves this town in a week. I got him acquainted with Sir Robert Raymond,[4] the Solicitor-General, who owns him to be of his family; and I believe it may do him a kindness, by being recommended to your new Lord Chancellor.—I had a letter from Mrs. Long, that has quite turned my stomach against her: no less than two nasty jests in it, with dashes to suppose them. She is corrupted in that country town[5] with vile conversation.—I will not answer your letter till I have leisure: so let this go on as it will, what care I? what cares saucy Presto?

12. I was to-day at the Secretary's office with Lewis, and in came Lord Rivers;[6] who took Lewis out and whispered

---

[1] See p. 86.

[2] The Earl of Abercorn (see p. 86) married, in 1686, Elizabeth, only child of Sir Robert Reading, Bart., of Dublin, by Jane, Dowager Countess of Mountrath. Lady Abercorn survived her husband twenty years, dying in 1754, aged eighty-six.

[3] Charles Lennox, first Duke of Richmond and Gordon (1672–1723), was the illegitimate son of Charles II. by Madame de Querouaille.

[4] Sir Robert Raymond, afterwards Lord Raymond (1673–1733), M.P. for Bishop's Castle, Shropshire, was appointed Solicitor-General in May 1710, and was knighted in October. He was removed from office on the accession of George I., but was made Attorney-General in 1720, and in 1724 became a Judge of the King's Bench. In the following year he was made Lord Chief-Justice, and was distinguished both for his learning and his impartiality.

[5] Lynn-Regis.

[6] Richard Savage, fourth Earl Rivers, the father of Richard Savage, the poet. Under the Whigs Lord Rivers was Envoy to Hanover; and after his conversion by Harley, he was Constable of the Tower under the Tories. He died in 1712.

him; and then came up to me to desire my acquaintance, etc., so we bowed and complimented a while, and parted: and I dined with Phil. Savage[1] and his Irish Club, at their boarding-place; and, passing an evening scurvily enough, did not come home till eight. Mr. Addison and I hardly meet once a fortnight; his Parliament and my different friendships keep us asunder. Sir Matthew Dudley turned away his butler yesterday morning; and at night the poor fellow died suddenly in the streets: was not it an odd event? But what care you? But then I knew the butler.—Why, it seems your packet-boat is not lost: psha, how silly that is, when I had already gone through the forms, and said it was a sad thing, and that I was sorry for it! But when must I answer this letter of our MD's? Here it is, it lies between this paper on t'other side of the leaf: one of these odd-come-shortly's I'll consider, and so good-night.

13. Morning. I am to go trapesing with Lady Kerry[2] and Mrs. Pratt[3] to see sights all this day: they engaged me yesterday morning at tea. You hear the havoc making in the army: Meredith, Maccartney, and Colonel Honeywood[4] are obliged to sell their commands at half-value, and leave

[1] Chancellor of the Exchequer in Ireland from 1695 until his death in 1717.

[2] Lord Shelburne's clever sister, Anne, only daughter of Sir William Petty, and wife of Thomas Fitzmaurice, Lord of Kerry, afterwards created first Earl of Kerry.

[3] Mrs. Pratt, an Irish friend of Lady Kerry, lodged at Lord Shelburne's during her visit to London. The reference to Clements (see p. 73), Pratt's relative, in the *Journal* for April 14, 1711, makes it clear that Mrs. Pratt was the wife of the Deputy Vice-Treasurer of Ireland, to whom Swift often alludes (see p. 9).

[4] Lieutenant-General Thomas Meredith, Major-General Maccartney, and Brigadier Philip Honeywood. They alleged that their offence only amounted to drinking a health to the Duke of Marlborough, and confusion to his enemies. But the Government said that an example must be made, because various officers had dropped dangerous expressions about standing by their General, Marlborough, who was believed to be aiming at being made Captain-General for life. For Maccartney see the *Journal* for Nov. 15, 1712, *seq.* Meredith, who was appointed Adjutant-General of the Forces in 1701, was made a Lieutenant-General in 1708. He saw much service under William III. and Marlborough, and was elected M.P. for Midhurst in 1709. He died in 1719 (Dalton's *Army Lists*, iii. 181). Honeywood entered the army in 1694; was at Namur; and was made a Brigadier-General before 1711. After the accession of George I. he became Colonel of a Regiment of Dragoons, and commanded a division at Dettingen. At his death in 1752 he was acting as Governor of Portsmouth, with the rank of General (Dalton, iv. 30).

the army, for drinking destruction to the present Ministry, and dressing up a hat on a stick, and calling it Harley; then drinking a glass with one hand, and discharging a pistol with the other at the maukin,[1] wishing it were Harley himself; and a hundred other such pretty tricks, as inflaming their soldiers, and foreign Ministers, against the late changes at Court. Cadogan[2] has had a little paring: his mother[3] told me yesterday he had lost the place of Envoy; but I hope they will go no further with him, for he was not at those mutinous meetings.—Well, these saucy jades take up so much of my time with writing to them in a morning; but, faith, I am glad to see you whenever I can: a little snap and away; and so hold your tongue, for I must rise: not a word, for your life. How nowww? So, very well; stay till I come home, and then, perhaps, you may hear further from me. And where will you go to-day, for I can't be with you for these ladies? It is a rainy, ugly day. I'd have you send for Walls, and go to the Dean's; but don't play small games when you lose. You'll be ruined by Manilio, Basto, the queen, and two small trumps, in red.[4] I confess 'tis a good hand against the player: but then there are Spadilio, Punto, the king, strong trumps, against you, which, with one trump more, are three tricks ten ace: for, suppose you play your Manilio—Oh, silly, how I prate, and can't get away from this MD in a morning! Go, get you gone, dear naughty girls, and let me rise. There, Patrick locked up my ink again the third time last night: the rogue gets the better of me; but I will rise in spite of you, sirrahs.—At night. Lady Kerry, Mrs. Pratt, Mrs. Cadogan,[5] and I, in one coach; Lady Kerry's

---

[1] Or "malkin"; a counterfeit, or scarecrow.
[2] William Cadogan, Lieutenant-General and afterwards Earl Cadogan (1675-1726), a great friend of Marlborough, was Envoy to the United Provinces and Spanish Flanders. Cadogan retained the post of Lieutenant to the Tower until 1715.
[3] Earl Cadogan's father, Henry Cadogan, barrister, married Bridget, daughter of Sir Hardresse Waller, and sister of Elizabeth, Baroness Shelburne in her own right.
[4] See p. 28.
[5] Cadogan married Margaretta, daughter of William Munter, Counsellor of the Court of Holland.

son[1] and his governor, and two gentlemen, in another; maids, and misses and little master (Lord Shelburne's[2] children), in a third, all hackneys, set out at ten o'clock this morning from Lord Shelburne's house in Piccadilly to the Tower, and saw all the sights, lions,[3] etc.; then to Bedlam;[4] then dined at the chop-house behind the Exchange; then to Gresham College[5] (but the keeper was not at home); and concluded the night at the Puppet-show,[6] whence we came home safe at eight, and I left them. The ladies were all in mobs[7] (how do you call it?), undrest; and it was the rainiest day that ever dripped; and I am weary; and it is now past eleven.

14. Stay, I'll answer some of your letter this morning in bed: let me see; come and appear, little letter. Here I am, says he: and what say you to Mrs. MD this morning fresh and fasting? Who dares think MD negligent? I allow them a fortnight; and they give it me. I could fill a letter in a week; but it is longer every day; and so I keep it a fortnight, and then 'tis cheaper by one half. I have never been giddy, dear Stella, since that morning: I have taken a whole box of pills, and kecked[8] at them every night, and drank a pint of brandy at mornings.—Oh then,

[1] Presumably the eldest son, William, who succeeded his father as second Earl of Kerry in 1741, and died in 1747. He was at Eton and Christ Church, Oxford, and was afterwards a Colonel in the Coldstream Guards.

[2] Henry Petty, third Lord Shelburne, who became Earl of Shelburne in 1719. His son predeceased him, without issue, and on Lord Shelburne's death, in 1751, his honours became extinct. His daughter Anne also died without issue.

[3] The menagerie, which had been one of the sights of London, was removed from the Tower in 1834. In his account of the Tory Fox Hunter in No. 47 of the *Freeholder*, Addison says, "Our first visit was to the lions."

[4] Bethlehem Hospital, for lunatics, in Moorfields, was a popular "sight" in the eighteenth century. Cf. the *Tatler*, No. 30: "On Tuesday last I took three lads, who are under my guardianship, a rambling, in a hackney coach, to show them the town: as the lions, the tombs, Bedlam."

[5] The Royal Society met at Gresham College from 1660 to 1710. The professors of the College lectured on divinity, civil law, astronomy, music, geometry, rhetoric, and physic.

[6] The most important of the puppet-shows was Powell's, in the Little Piazza, Covent Garden, which is frequently mentioned in the *Tatler*.

[7] The precise nature of this negligent costume is not known, but it is always decried by popular writers of the time.

[8] Retched. Bacon has "Patients must not keck at them at the first."

you kept Presto's little birthday :[1] would to God I had been
with you! I forgot it, as I told you before. Rediculous,
madam? I suppose you mean ridiculous : let me have no
more of that; 'tis the author of the *Atalantis's*[2] spelling.
I have mended it in your letter. And can Stella read this
writing without hurting her dear eyes? O, faith, I am
afraid not. Have a care of those eyes, pray, pray, pretty
Stella.—'Tis well enough what you observe, that, if I writ
better, perhaps you would not read so well, being used to
this manner; 'tis an alphabet you are used to: you know
such a pot-hook makes a letter; and you know what letter,
and so and so.—I'll swear he told me so, and that they
were long letters too; but I told him it was a gasconnade
of yours, etc. I am talking of the Bishop of Clogher, how
he forgot. Turn over.[3] I had not room on t'other side
to say that, so I did it on this : I fancy that's a good Irish
blunder. Ah, why do not you go down to Clogher, nauti-
nautinautideargirls; I dare not say *nauti* without *dear*: O,
faith, you govern me. But, seriously, I'm sorry you don't
go, as far as I can judge at this distance. No, we would
get you another horse; I will make Parvisol get you one.
I always doubted that horse of yours : prythee sell him, and
let it be a present to me. My heart aches when I think you
ride him. Order Parvisol to sell him, and that you are to
return me the money : I shall never be easy until he is out
of your hands. Faith, I have dreamt five or six times of
horses stumbling since I had your letter. If he can't sell

[1] Swift was born on November 30.

[2] Mrs. De la Rivière Manley, daughter of Sir Roger Manley, and cousin of
John Manley, M.P., and Isaac Manley (see pp. 7, 24), wrote poems and
plays, but is best known for her *Secret Memoirs and Manners of Several
Persons of Quality, of both sexes. From the New Atalantis*, 1709, a book
abounding in scandalous references to her contemporaries. She was arrested
in October, but was discharged in Feb. 1710. In May 1710 she brought out
a continuation of the *New Atalantis*, called *Memoirs of Europe towards the
Close of the Eighth Century*. In June 1711 she became editress of the Tory
Examiner, and wrote political pamphlets with Swift's assistance. Afterwards
she lived with Alderman Barber, the printer, at whose office she died in 1724.
In her will she mentioned her "much honoured friend, the Dean of St. Patrick,
Dr. Swift."

[3] "He seems to have written these words in a whim, for the sake of what
follows" (Deane Swift).

him, let him run this winter. Faith, if I was near you, I
would whip your — to some tune, for your grave, saucy
answer about the Dean and *Johnsonibus*; I would, young
women. And did the Dean preach for me?[1] Very well.
Why, would they have me stand here and preach to them?
No, the *Tatler* of the Shilling[2] was not mine, more than the
hint, and two or three general heads for it. I have much
more important business on my hands; and, besides, the
Ministry hate to think that I should help him, and have
made reproaches on it; and I frankly told them I would
do it no more. This is a secret though, Madam Stella.
You win eight shillings? you win eight fiddlesticks. Faith,
you say nothing of what you lose, young women.—I hope
Manley is in no great danger; for Ned Southwell is his
friend, and so is Sir Thomas Frankland; and his brother
John Manley stands up heartily for him. On t'other side,
all the gentlemen of Ireland here are furiously against him.
Now, Mistress Dingley, an't you an impudent slut, to expect
a letter next packet from Presto, when you confess yourself
that you had so lately two letters in four days? Unreasonable baggage! No, little Dingley, I am always in bed by
twelve; I mean my candle is out by twelve, and I take
great care of myself. Pray let everybody know, upon occasion, that Mr. Harley got the First-Fruits from the Queen
for the clergy of Ireland, and that nothing remains but the
forms, etc. So you say the Dean and you dined at Stoyte's,
and Mrs. Stoyte was in raptures that I remembered her.
I must do it but seldom, or it will take off her rapture.—
But what now, you saucy sluts? all this written in a morning,
and I must rise and go abroad. Pray stay till night: do not
think I will squander mornings upon you, pray, good madam.
Faith, if I go on longer in this trick of writing in the
morning, I shall be afraid of leaving it off, and think you
expect it, and be in awe. Good-morrow, sirrahs, I will rise.
—At night. I went to-day to the Court of Requests (I will
not answer the rest of your letter yet, that by the way), in

[1] See p. 62.   [2] No. 249 (see p. 81).

hopes to dine with Mr. Harley: but Lord Dupplin,[1] his son-in-law, told me he did not dine at home; so I was at a loss, until I met with Mr. Secretary St. John, and went home and dined with him, where he told me of a good bite.[2] Lord Rivers told me two days ago, that he was resolved to come Sunday fortnight next to hear me preach before the Queen. I assured him the day was not yet fixed, and I knew nothing of it. To-day the Secretary told me that his father, Sir Harry St. John,[3] and Lord Rivers were to be at St. James's Church, to hear me preach there; and were assured I was to preach: so there will be another bite; for I know nothing of the matter, but that Mr. Harley and St. John are resolved I must preach before the Queen; and the Secretary of State has told me he will give me three weeks' warning; but I desired to be excused, which he will not. St. John, "You shall not be excused": however, I hope they will forget it; for if it should happen, all the puppies hereabouts will throng to hear me, and expect something wonderful, and be plaguily baulked; for I shall preach plain honest stuff. I stayed with St. John till eight, and then came home; and Patrick desired leave to go abroad, and by and by comes up the girl to tell me, a gentleman was below in a coach, who had a bill to pay me; so I let him come up, and who should it be but Mr. Addison and Sam Dopping, to haul me out to supper, where I stayed till twelve. If Patrick had been at home, I should have 'scaped this; for I have taught him to deny me almost as well as Mr. Harley's porter.—Where did I leave off in MD's letter? let me see. So, now I have it. You are pleased to say, Madam

---

[1] See p. 30.

[2] In a letter to the Rev. Dr. Tisdall, of Dec. 16, 1703, Swift said: "I'll teach you a way to outwit Mrs. Johnson: it is a new-fashioned way of being witty, and they call it a *bite*. You must ask a bantering question, or tell some damned lie in a serious manner, and then she will answer or speak as if you were in earnest; and then cry you, 'Madam, there's a *bite*!' I would not have you undervalue this, for it is the constant amusement in Court, and everywhere else among the great people." See, too, the *Tatler*, No. 12, and *Spectator*, Nos. 47, 504: "In a word, a Biter is one who thinks you a fool, because you do not think him a knave."

[3] See p. 66.

Dingley, that those who go for England can never tell when to come back. Do you mean this as a reflection upon Presto, madam? Sauceboxes, I will come back as soon as I can, as hope saved,[1] and I hope with some advantage, unless all Ministries be alike, as perhaps they may. I hope Hawkshaw is in Dublin before now, and that you have your things, and like your spectacles: if you do not, you shall have better. I hope Dingley's tobacco did not spoil Stella's chocolate, and that all is safe: pray let me know. Mr. Addison and I are different as black and white, and I believe our friendship will go off, by this damned business of party: he cannot bear seeing me fall in so with this Ministry: but I love him still as well as ever, though we seldom meet.—Hussy, Stella, you jest about poor Congreve's eyes;[2] you do so, hussy; but I'll bang your bones, faith. —Yes, Steele was a little while in prison, or at least in a spunging-house, some time before I came, but not since.[3] —Pox on your convocations, and your Lamberts;[4] they write with a vengeance! I suppose you think it a piece of affectation in me to wish your Irish folks would not like my "Shower"; but you are mistaken. I should be glad to have the general applause there as I have here (though I say it); but I have only that of one or two, and therefore I would have none at all, but let you all be in the wrong. I don't know, this is not what I would say; but I am so tosticated with supper and stuff, that I can't express myself. —What you say of "Sid Hamet" is well enough; that an enemy should like it, and a friend not; and that telling the author would make both change their opinions. Why did you not tell Griffyth [5] that you fancied there was something

---

[1] "As I hope to be saved;" a favourite phrase in the *Journal.*

[2] See p. 48.

[3] This statement receives some confirmation from a pamphlet published in September 1710, called *A Condoling Letter to the Tatler: On Account of the Misfortunes of Isaac Bickerstaff, Esq., a Prisoner in the —— on Suspicion of Debt.*

[4] Dr. Lambert, chaplain to Lord Wharton, was censured in Convocation for being the author of a libellous letter.

[5] Probably the same person as Dr. Griffith, spoken of in the *Journal* for March 3, 1713,—when he was ill,—as having been "very tender of" Stella.

in it of my manner; but first spur up his commendation to
the height, as we served my poor uncle about the sconce
that I mended? Well, I desired you to give what I
intended for an answer to Mrs. Fenton,[1] to save her postage,
and myself trouble; and I hope I have done it, if you
han't.

15. Lord, what a long day's writing was yesterday's answer
to your letter, sirrahs! I dined to-day with Lewis and Ford,
whom I have brought acquainted. Lewis told me a pure
thing. I had been hankering with Mr. Harley to save
Steele his other employment, and have a little mercy on
him; and I had been saying the same thing to Lewis, who
is Mr. Harley's chief favourite. Lewis tells Mr. Harley how
kindly I should take it, if he would be reconciled to Steele,
etc. Mr. Harley, on my account, falls in with it, and
appoints Steele a time to let him attend him, which Steele
accepts with great submission, but never comes, nor sends
any excuse. Whether it was blundering, sullenness, insolence, or rancour of party, I cannot tell; but I shall
trouble myself no more about him. I believe Addison
hindered him out of mere spite, being grated[2] to the soul
to think he should ever want my help to save his friend;
yet now he is soliciting me to make another of his friends
Queen's Secretary at Geneva; and I'll do it if I can; it is
poor Pastoral Philips.[3]

16. O, why did you leave my picture behind you at
t'other lodgings? Forgot it? Well; but pray remember
it now, and don't roll it up, d'ye hear; but hang it carefully
in some part of your room, where chairs and candles and
mop-sticks won't spoil it, sirrahs. No, truly, I will not be

---

[1] See p. 74, note 1.
[2] Vexed, offended. Elsewhere Swift wrote, "I am apt to grate the ears of
more than I could wish."
[3] Ambrose Philips, whose *Pastorals* had been published in the same volume
of Tonson's *Miscellany* as Pope's. Two years later Swift wrote, "I should
certainly have provided for him had he not run party mad." In 1712
his play, *The Distrest Mother*, received flattering notice in the *Spectator*,
and in 1713, to Pope's annoyance, Philips' *Pastorals* were praised in the
Guardian. His pretty poems to children led Henry Carey to nickname him
"Namby Pamby."

godfather to Goody Walls this bout, and I hope she will have no more. There will be no quiet nor cards for this child. I hope it will die the day after the christening. Mr. Harley gave me a paper, with an account of the sentence you speak of against the lads that defaced the statue,[1] and that Ingoldsby[2] reprieved that part of it of standing before the statue. I hope it was never executed. We have got your Broderick out;[3] Doyne[4] is to succeed him, and Cox[5] Doyne. And so there's an end of your letter; 'tis all answered; and now I must go on upon my own stock. Go on, did I say? Why, I have written enough; but this is too soon to send it yet, young women; faith, I dare not use you to it, you'll always expect it; what remains shall be only short journals of a day, and so I'll rise for this morning.—At night. I dined with my opposite neighbour, Darteneuf; and I was soliciting this day to present the Bishop of Clogher Vice-Chancellor;[6] but it won't do; they are all set against him, and the Duke of Ormond, they say, has resolved to dispose of it somewhere else. Well; little saucy rogues, do not stay out too late to-night, because it is Saturday night, and young women should come home soon then.

17. I went to Court to seek a dinner: but the Queen was not at church, she has got a touch of the gout; so the Court

[1] An equestrian statue of William III., in College Green, Dublin. It was common, in the days of party, for students of the University of Dublin to play tricks with this statue.

[2] Lieutenant-General Richard Ingoldsby (died 1712) was Commander of the Forces in Ireland, and one of the Lords Justices in the absence of the Lord Lieutenant.

[3] This seems to have been a mistake; cf. *Journal* for July 13, 1711. Alan Brodrick, afterwards Viscount Midleton, a Whig politician and lawyer, was made Chief Justice of the Queen's Bench in Ireland in 1709, but was removed from office in June 1711, when Sir Richard Cox succeeded him. On the accession of George I. he was appointed Lord Chancellor for Ireland. Afterwards he declined to accept the dedication to him of Swift's *Drapier's Letters*, and supported the prosecution of the author. He died in 1728.

[4] Robert Doyne was appointed Chief Baron of the Exchequer in Ireland in 1695, and Chief Justice of the Common Pleas in 1703. This appointment was revoked on the accession of George I.

[5] See p. 69.

[6] Of the University of Dublin.

7

was thin, and I went to the Coffee-house; and Sir Thomas
Frankland and his eldest son and I went and dined with his
son William.[1]   I talked a great deal to Sir Thomas about
Manley; and find he is his good friend, and so has Ned
Southwell been, and I hope he will be safe, though all the
Irish folks here are his mortal enemies.   There was a devilish
bite to-day.   They had it, I know not how, that I was to
preach this morning at St. James's Church; an abundance
went, among the rest Lord Radnor, who never is abroad
till three in the afternoon.   I walked all the way home
from Hatton Garden at six, by moonlight, a delicate
night.   Raymond called at nine, but I was denied; and
now I am in bed between eleven and twelve, just going
to sleep, and dream of my own dear roguish impudent
pretty MD.

18. You will now have short days' works, just a few lines
to tell you where I am, and what I am doing; only I will
keep room for the last day to tell you news, if there be any
worth sending.   I have been sometimes like to do it at the
top of my letter, until I remark it would be old before it
reached you.   I was hunting to dine with Mr. Harley to-day,
but could not find him; and so I dined with honest Dr.
Cockburn, and came home at six, and was taken out to
next door by Dopping and Ford, to drink bad claret and
oranges; and we let Raymond come to us, who talks of
leaving the town to-morrow, but I believe will stay a day
or two longer.   It is now late, and I will say no more, but
end this line with bidding my own dear saucy MD good-
night, etc.

19. I am come down proud stomach in one instance, for I
went to-day to see the Duke of Buckingham,[2] but came too
late: then I visited Mrs. Barton,[3] and thought to have dined
with some of the Ministry; but it rained, and Mrs. Vanhomrigh

---

[1] See pp. 6, 7. Sir Thomas Frankland's eldest son, Thomas, who afterwards succeeded to the baronetcy, acquired a fortune with his first wife,
Dinah, daughter of Francis Topham, of Agelthorpe, Yorkshire. He died in
1747.
[2] See p. 60.   [3] See p. 20.

was nigh, and I took the opportunity of paying her for a scarf she bought me, and dined there; at four I went to congratulate with Lord Shelburne, for the death of poor Lady Shelburne dowager;[1] he was at his country house, and returned while I was there, and had not heard of it, and he took it very well. I am now come home before six, and find a packet from the Bishop of Clogher, with one enclosed to the Duke of Ormond, which is ten days earlier dated than another I had from Parvisol; however, 'tis no matter, for the Duke has already disposed of the Vice-Chancellorship to the Archbishop of Tuam,[2] and I could not help it, for it is a thing wholly you know in the Duke's power; and I find the Bishop has enemies about the Duke. I write this while Patrick is folding up my scarf, and doing up the fire (for I keep a fire, it costs me twelvepence a week); and so be quiet till I am gone to bed, and then sit down by me a little, and we will talk a few words more. Well; now MD is at my bedside; and now what shall we say? How does Mrs. Stoyte? What had the Dean for supper? How much did Mrs. Walls win? Poor Lady Shelburne: well, go get you to bed, sirrahs.

20. Morning. I was up this morning early, and shaved by candlelight, and write this by the fireside. Poor Raymond just came in and took his leave of me; he is summoned by high order from his wife, but pretends he has had enough of London. I was a little melancholy to part with him; he goes to Bristol, where they are to be with his merchant brother, and now thinks of staying till May; so she must be brought to bed in England. He was so easy and manageable, that I almost repent I suffered him to see me so seldom. But he is gone, and will save Patrick some lies in a week; Patrick is grown admirable at it, and will make his fortune.

---

[1] Mary, daughter of Sir John Williams, Bart., and widow of Charles Petty, second Lord Shelburne, who died in 1696. She had married, as her second husband, Major-General Conyngham, and, as her third husband, Colonel Dallway.

[2] Dr. John Vesey became Bishop of Limerick in 1672, and Archbishop of Tuam in 1678. He died in 1716.

How now, sirrah, must I write in a morning to your
impudence?

> Stay till night,
> And then I'll write,
> In black and white,
> By candlelight,
> Of wax so bright,
> It helps the sight—
> A bite, a bite!

Marry come up, Mistress Boldface.—At night. Dr. Raymond came back, and goes to-morrow. I did not come
home till eleven, and found him here to take leave of
me. I went to the Court of Requests, thinking to find Mr.
Harley and dine with him, and refused Henley, and
everybody, and at last knew not where to go, and met
Jemmy Leigh by chance, and he was just in the same
way, so I dined at his lodgings on a beef-steak, and drank
your health; then left him and went to the tavern with
Ben Tooke and Portlack, the Duke of Ormond's secretary,
drinking nasty white wine till eleven. I am sick, and
ashamed of it, etc.

21. I met that beast Ferris, Lord Berkeley's [1] steward
formerly; I walked with him a turn in the Park, and that
scoundrel dog is as happy as an emperor, has married a wife
with a considerable estate in land and houses about this
town, and lives at his ease at Hammersmith. See your
confounded sect! [2] Well; I had the same luck to-day with
Mr. Harley; 'twas a lovely day, and went by water into the
City, and dined with Stratford at a merchant's house, and
walked home with as great a dunce as Ferris, I mean honest
Colonel Caulfeild,[3] and came home by eight, and now am in
bed, and going to sleep for a wager, and will send this letter
on Saturday, and so; but first I will wish you a merry

---

[1] See p. 14.   [2] Sex.
[3] Toby Caulfeild, third son of the fifth Lord Charlemont. In 1689 he was
Colonel in the Earl of Drogheda's Regiment of Foot, and about 1705 he
succeeded to the command of Lord Skerrin's Regiment of Foot. After
serving in Spain his regiment was reduced, having lost most of its men
(Luttrell, vi. 158).

Christmas and a happy New Year, and pray God we may never keep them asunder again.

22. Morning. I am going now to Mr. Harley's levee on purpose to vex him; I will say I had no other way of seeing him, etc. Patrick says it is a dark morning, and that the Duke of Argyle[1] is to be knighted to-day; the booby means installed at Windsor. But I must rise, for this is a shaving-day, and Patrick says there is a good fire; I wish MD were by it, or I by MD's.—At night. I forgot to tell you, Madam Dingley, that I paid nine shillings for your glass and spectacles, of which three were for the Bishop's case: I am sorry I did not buy you such another case; but if you like it, I will bring one over with me; pray tell me: the glass to read was four shillings, the spectacles two. And have you had your chocolate? Leigh says he sent the petticoat by one Mr. Spencer. Pray have you no further commissions for me? I paid the glass-man but last night, and he would have made me a present of the microscope worth thirty shillings, and would have sent it home along with me; I thought the deuce was in the man: he said I could do him more service than that was worth, etc. I refused his present, but promised him all service I could do him; and so now I am obliged in honour to recommend him to everybody.—At night. I went to Mr. Harley's levee; he came and asked me what I had to do there, and bid me come and dine with him on a family dinner; which I did, and it was the first time I ever saw his lady[2] and daughter;[3] at five my Lord Keeper[4] came in: I

[1] John Campbell, second Duke of Argyle (1680–1743), was installed a Knight of the Garter in December 1710, after he had successfully opposed a vote of thanks to Marlborough, with whom he had quarrelled. It was of this noble-man that Pope wrote—

" Argyle, the State's whole thunder born to wield,
And shake alike the senate and the field."

In a note to Macky's *Memoirs*, Swift describes the Duke as an "ambitious, covetous, cunning Scot, who had no principle but his own interests and greatness."

[2] Harley's second wife, Sarah, daughter of Simon Middleton, of Edmonton, and sister of Sir Hugh Middleton, Bart. She died, without issue, in 1737.

[3] Elizabeth Harley, then unmarried, the daughter of Harley's first wife, Elizabeth, daughter of Thomas Foley, of Whitley Court, Worcestershire. She subsequently married the Marquis of Caermarthen, afterwards Duke of Leeds.

[4] Harcourt (see p. 11).

told Mr. Harley, he had formerly presented me to Sir Simon Harcourt, but now must to my Lord Keeper; so he laughed, etc.

23. Morning. This letter goes to-night without fail; I hope there is none from you yet at the Coffee-house; I will send and see by and by, and let you know, and so and so. Patrick goes to see for a letter: what will you lay, is there one from MD or no? No, I say; done for sixpence. Why has the Dean never once written to me? I won sixpence; I won sixpence; there is not one letter to Presto. Good-morrow, dear sirrahs: Stratford and I dine to-day with Lord Mountjoy. God Almighty preserve and bless you; farewell, etc.

I have been dining at Lord Mountjoy's; and am come to study; our news from Spain this post takes off some of our fears. The Parliament is prorogued to-day, or adjourned rather till after the holidays. Bank Stock is 105, so I may get 12l. for my bargain already. Patrick, the puppy, is abroad, and how shall I send this letter? Good-night, little dears both, and be happy; and remember your poor Presto, that wants you sadly, as hope saved. Let me go study, naughty girls, and don't keep me at the bottom of the paper. O, faith, if you knew what lies on my hands constantly, you would wonder to see how I could write such long letters; but we'll talk of that some other time. Good-night again, and God bless dear MD with His best blessings, yes, yes, and Dingley and Stella and me too, etc.

Ask the Bishop of Clogher about the pun I sent him of Lord Stawel's brother;[1] it will be a pure bite. This letter has 199 lines in it, beside all postscripts; I had a curiosity to reckon.

There is a long letter for you.

It is longer than a sermon, faith.

I had another letter from Mrs. Fenton, who says you were

---

[1] William Stawel, the third baron, who succeeded to the title in 1692, was half-brother to the second Baron Stawel. The brother here referred to was Edward, who succeeded to the title as fourth baron in 1742.

with her; I hope you did not go on purpose. I will answer her letter soon; it is about some money in Lady Giffard's hands.

They say you have had eight packets due to you; so pray, madams, do not blame Presto, but the wind.

My humble service to Mrs. Walls and Mrs. Stoyte; I missed the former a good while.

LETTER XII

LONDON, *Dec.* 23, 1710.

I HAVE sent my 11th to-night as usual, and begin the dozenth, and I told you I dined with Stratford at Lord Mountjoy's, and I will tell tell you no more at present, guess for why; because I am going to mind things, and mighty affairs, not your nasty First-Fruits—I let them alone till Mr. Harley gets the Queen's letter—but other things of greater moment, that you shall know one day, when the ducks have eaten up all the dirt. So sit still a while just by me, while I am studying, and don't say a word, I charge you, and when I am going to bed, I will take you along, and talk with you a little while, so there, sit there.—Come then, let us see what we have to say to these saucy brats, that will not let us go sleep at past eleven. Why, I am a little impatient to know how you do; but that I take it for a standing maxim, that when you are silent, all is pretty well, because that is the way I will deal with you; and if there was anything you ought to know now, I would write by the first post, although I had written but the day before. Remember this, young women; and God Almighty preserve you both, and make us happy together; and tell me how accompts stand between us, that you may be paid long before it is due, not to want. I will return no more money while I stay, so that you need not be in pain to be paid; but let me know at least a month before you can want. Observe this, d'ye hear, little dear sirrahs, and love Presto, as Presto loves MD, etc.

24. You will have a merrier Christmas Eve than we here. I went up to Court before church ; and in one of the rooms, there being but little company, a fellow in a red coat without a sword came up to me, and, after words of course, asked me how the ladies did ? I asked, "What ladies ? " He said, " Mrs. Dingley and Mrs. Johnson." "Very well," said I, " when I heard from them last : and pray when came you from thence, sir ? " He said, " I never was in Ireland "; and just at that word Lord Winchelsea [1] comes up to me, and the man went off : as I went out I saw him again, and recollected him, it was Vedeau [2] with a pox : I then went and made my apologies, that my head was full of something I had to say to Lord Winchelsea, etc., and I asked after his wife, and so all was well ; and he inquired after my lodging, because he had some favour to desire of me in Ireland, to recommend somebody to somebody, I know not what it is. When I came from church, I went up to Court again, where Sir Edmond Bacon [3] told me the bad news from Spain, [4] which you will hear before this reaches you ; as we have it now, we are undone there, and it was odd to see the whole countenances of the Court changed so in two hours. Lady Mountjoy [5] carried me home to dinner, where I stayed not long after, and came home early, and now am got into bed, for you must always write to your MD's in bed, that is a maxim.

> Mr. White and Mr. Red,
> Write to MD when abed ;
> Mr. Black and Mr. Brown,
> Write to MD when you're down ;
> Mr. Oak and Mr. Willow,
> Write to MD on your pillow.—

---

[1] Charles Finch, third Earl of Winchelsea, son of Lord Maidstone, and grandson of Heneage, second Earl of Winchelsea. On his death in 1712 Swift spoke of him as "a worthy honest gentleman, and particular friend of mine."

[2] Vedeau was a shopkeeper, who abandoned his trade for the army (*Journal*, March 28, April 4, 1711). Swift calls him "a lieutenant, who is now broke, and upon half pay" (*Journal*, Nov. 18, 1712).

[3] Sir Edmund Bacon, Bart. (died 1721), of Herringflat, Suffolk, succeeded his father in the baronetcy in 1686.

[4] The reverse at Brihuega.

[5] See p. 57.

What is this? faith, I smell fire; what can it be? this house has a thousand stinks in it. I think to leave it on Thursday, and lodge over the way. Faith, I must rise, and look at my chimney, for the smell grows stronger, stay—I have been up, and in my room, and found all safe, only a mouse within the fender to warm himself, which I could not catch. I smelt nothing there, but now in my bed-chamber I smell it again; I believe I have singed the woollen curtain, and that is all, though I cannot smoke it. Presto is plaguy silly to-night, an't he? Yes, and so he be. Ay, but if I should wake and see fire. Well; I will venture; so good-night, etc.

25. Pray, young women, if I write so much as this every day, how will this paper hold a fortnight's work, and answer one of yours into the bargain? You never think of this, but let me go on like a simpleton. I wish you a merry Christmas, and many, many a one with poor Presto at some pretty place. I was at church to-day by eight, and received the Sacrament, and came home by ten; then went to Court at two: it was a Collar-day, that is, when the Knights of the Garter wear their collars; but the Queen stayed so late at Sacrament, that I came back, and dined with my neighbour Ford, because all people dine at home on this day. This is likewise a Collar-day all over England in every house, at least where there is *brawn*: that's very well.—I tell you a good pun; a fellow hard by pretends to cure agues, and has set out a sign, and spells it *egoes*; a gentleman and I observing it, he said, " How does that fellow pretend to cure *agues* ? " I said I did not know; but I was sure it was not by a *spell*. That is admirable. And so you asked the Bishop about that pun of Lord Stawel's brother. Bite! Have I caught you, young women? Must you pretend to ask after roguish puns, and Latin ones too? Oh but you smoked me, and did not ask the Bishop. Oh but you are a fool, and you did. I met Vedeau again at Court to-day, and I observed he had a sword on; I fancy he was broke, and has got a commission, but I never asked him. Vedeau I think his name is, yet Parvisol's man is Vedel, that is true. Bank Stock will fall like stock-fish by this bad news,

and two days ago I could have got twelve pounds by my bargain; but I do not intend to sell, and in time it will rise. It is odd that my Lord Peterborow foretold this loss two months ago, one night at Mr. Harley's, when I was there; he bid us count upon it, that Stanhope would lose Spain before Christmas; that he would venture his head upon it, and gave us reasons; and though Mr. Harley argued the contrary, he still held to his opinion. I was telling my Lord Angelsea this at Court this morning; and a gentleman by said he had heard my Lord Peterborow affirm the same thing. I have heard wise folks say, "An ill tongue may do much." And 'tis an odd saying,

> "Once I guessed right,
> And I got credit by't;
> Thrice I guessed wrong,
> And I kept my credit on."

No, it is you are sorry, not I.

26. By the Lord Harry, I shall be undone here with Christmas boxes. The rogues of the Coffee-house have raised their tax, everyone giving a crown; and I gave mine for shame, besides a great many half-crowns to great men's porters, etc. I went to-day by water into the city, and dined with no less a man than the City Printer.[1] There is an intimacy between us, built upon reasons that you shall know when I see you; but the rain caught me within twelvepenny length of home. I called at Mr. Harley's, who was not within, dropped my half-crown with his porter, drove to the Coffee-house, where the rain kept me till nine. I had letters to-day from the Archbishop of Dublin and Mr. Bernage;[2] the latter sends me a melancholy account of Lady Shelburne's[3]

---

[1] John Barber, a printer, became Lord Mayor of London in 1732, and died in 1741. Mrs. Manley was his mistress, and died at his printing office. Swift speaks of Barber as his "very good and old friend."

[2] Bernage was an officer serving under Colonel Fielding. In August 1710 a difficulty arose through Arbuthnot trying to get his brother George made Captain over Bernage's head; but ultimately Arbuthnot waived the business, because he would not wrong a friend of Swift's.

[3] See p. 99.

death, and his own disappointments, and would gladly be a
captain; if I can help him, I will.

27. Morning. I bespoke a lodging over the way for to-
morrow, and the dog let it yesterday to another; I gave him
no earnest, so it seems he could do it; Patrick would have had
me give him earnest to bind him; but I would not. So I must
go saunter to-day for a lodging somewhere else. Did you
ever see so open a winter in England? We have not had
two frosty days; but it pays it off in rain: we have not had
three fair days these six weeks. O, faith, I dreamt mightily
of MD last night; but so confused, I cannot tell a word. I
have made Ford acquainted with Lewis; and to-day we dined
together: in the evening I called at one or two neighbours,
hoping to spend a Christmas evening; but none were at
home, they were all gone to be merry with others. I have
often observed this, that in merry times everybody is abroad;
where the deuce are they? So I went to the Coffee-house,
and talked with Mr. Addison an hour, who at last remembered
to give me two letters, which I cannot answer to-night, nor
to-morrow neither, I can assure you, young women, count
upon that. I have other things to do than to answer naughty
girls, an old saying and true,

> Letters from MD's
> Must not be answered in ten days:

it is but bad rhyme, etc.

28. To-day I had a message from Sir Thomas Hanmer, to
dine with him; the famous Dr. Smalridge [1] was of the
company, and we sat till six; and I came home to my new
lodgings in St. Albans Street, [2] where I pay the same rent
(eight shillings a week) for an apartment two pair of stairs;
but I have the use of the parlour to receive persons of quality,
and I am got into my new bed, etc.

---

[1] George Smalridge (1663-1719), the High Church divine and popular
preacher, was made Dean of Carlisle in 1711, and Bishop of Bristol in 1714.
Steele spoke of him in the *Tatler* (Nos. 73, 114) as "abounding in that sort
of virtue and knowledge which makes religion beautiful."

[2] St. Albans Street, Pall Mall, was removed in 1815 to make way for
Waterloo Place. It was named after Henry Jermyn, Earl of St. Albans.

29. Sir Andrew Fountaine has been very ill this week; and sent to me early this morning to have prayers, which you know is the last thing. I found the doctors and all in despair about him. I read prayers to him, found he had settled all things; and, when I came out, the nurse asked me whether I thought it possible he could live; for the doctors thought not. I said, I believed he would live; for I found the seeds of life in him, which I observe seldom fail (and I found them in poor, dearest Stella, when she was ill many years ago); and to-night I was with him again, and he was mightily recovered, and I hope he will do well, and the doctor approved my reasons; but, if he should die, I should come off scurvily. The Secretary of State (Mr. St. John) sent to me to dine with him; Mr. Harley and Lord Peterborow dined there too; and at night came Lord Rivers. Lord Peterborow goes to Vienna in a day or two: he has promised to make me write to him. Mr. Harley went away at six; but we stayed till seven. I took the Secretary aside, and complained to him of Mr. Harley, that he had got the Queen to grant the First-Fruits, promised to bring me to her, and get her letter to the bishops of Ireland; but the last part he had not done in six weeks, and I was in danger to lose reputation, etc. He took the matter right, desired me to be with him on Sunday morning, and promises me to finish the affair in four days; so I shall know in a little time what I have to trust to.—It is nine o'clock, and I must go study, you little rogues; and so good-night, etc.

30. Morning. The weather grows cold, you sauceboxes. Sir Andrew Fountaine, they bring me word, is better. I will go rise, for my hands are starving while I write in bed.— Night. Now Sir Andrew Fountaine is recovering, he desires to be at ease; for I called in the morning to read prayers, but he had given orders not to be disturbed. I have lost a legacy by his living; for he told me he had left me a picture and some books, etc. I called to see my quondam neighbour Ford (do you know what *quondam* is, though?), and he engaged me to dine with him; for he always dines at home on Opera-days. I came home at six, writ to the Archbishop,

then studied till past eleven, and stole to bed, to write to
MD these few lines, to let you know I am in good health at
the present writing hereof, and hope in God MD is so too.
I wonder I never write politics to you: I could make you the
profoundest politician in all the lane.—Well, but when shall
we answer this letter, No. 8 of MD's? Not till next year,
faith. O Lord—bo—but that will be a Monday next. Cod's-
so, is it? and so it is: never saw the like.—I made a pun
t'other day to Ben Portlack [1] about a pair of drawers. Poh,
said he, that's mine a— all over. Pray, pray, Dingley, let
me go sleep; pray, pray, Stella, let me go slumber; and put
out my wax-candle.

31. Morning. It is now seven, and I have got a fire, but
am writing abed in my bed-chamber. 'Tis not shaving-day,
so I shall be ready early to go before church to Mr. St.
John; and to-morrow I will answer our MD's letter.

> Would you answer MD's letter,
> On New Year's Day you'll do it better;
> For, when the year with MD 'gins,
> It without MD never lins.

(These proverbs have always old words in them; *lins* is
leave off.)

> But, if on New Year you write nones,
> MD then will bang your bones.

But Patrick says I must rise. — Night. I was early this
morning with Secretary St. John, and gave him a memorial
to get the Queen's letter for the First - Fruits, who has
promised to do it in a very few days. He told me he had
been with the Duke of Marlborough, who was lamenting his
former wrong steps in joining with the Whigs, and said he
was worn out with age, fatigues, and misfortunes. I swear it
pitied me; and I really think they will not do well in too
much mortifying that man, although indeed it is his own
fault. He is covetous as hell, and ambitious as the Prince
of it: he would fain have been General for life, and has
broken all endeavours for peace, to keep his greatness and

[1] See p. 100.

get money. He told the Queen he was neither covetous nor ambitious. She said if she could have conveniently turned about, she would have laughed, and could hardly forbear it in his face. He fell in with all the abominable measures of the late Ministry, because they gratified him for their own designs. Yet he has been a successful General, and I hope he will continue his command. O Lord, smoke the politics to MD! Well; but, if you like them, I will scatter a little now and then, and mine are all fresh from the chief hands. Well, I dined with Mr. Harley, and came away at six: there was much company, and I was not merry at all. Mr. Harley made me read a paper of verses of Prior's. I read them plain, without any fine manner; and Prior swore, I should never read any of his again; but he would be revenged, and read some of mine as bad. I excused myself, and said I was famous for reading verses the worst in the world; and that everybody snatched them from me when I offered to begin. So we laughed.—Sir Andrew Fountaine still continues ill. He is plagued with some sort of bile.

Jan. 1. Morning. I wish my dearest, pretty Dingley and Stella a happy New Year, and health, and mirth, and good stomachs, and Fr's company. Faith, I did not know how to write Fr. I wondered what was the matter; but now I remember I always write Pdfr. Patrick wishes me a happy New Year, and desires I would rise, for it is a good fire, and faith 'tis cold. I was so politic last night with MD, never saw the like. Get the *Examiners*, and read them; the last nine or ten are full of the reasons for the late change, and of the abuses of the last Ministry; and the great men assure me they are all true. They are written by their encouragement and direction. I must rise and go see Sir Andrew Fountaine; but perhaps to-night I may answer MD's letter: so good-morrow, my mistresses all, good-morrow.

> I wish you both a merry New Year,
> Roast beef, minced pies, and good strong beer,
> And me a share of your good cheer,
> That I was there, or you were here ;
> And you're a little saucy dear.

Good-morrow again, dear sirrahs; one cannot rise for your play.—At night. I went this morning to visit Lady Kerry and Lord Shelburne; and they made me dine with them. Sir Andrew Fountaine is better. And now let us come and see what this saucy, dear letter of MD says. Come out, letter, come out from between the sheets; here it is underneath, and it will not come out. Come out again, I say: so there. Here it is. What says Presto to me, pray? says it. Come, and let me answer for you to your ladies. Hold up your head then, like a good letter. There. Pray, how have you got up with Presto, Madam Stella? You write your eighth when you receive mine: now I write my twelfth when I receive your eighth. Do not you allow for what are upon the road, simpleton? What say you to that? And so you kept Presto's little birthday, I warrant: would to God I had been at the health rather than here, where I have no manner of pleasure, nothing but eternal business upon my hands. I shall grow wise in time; but no more of that: only I say Amen with my heart and vitals, that we may never be asunder again ten days together while poor Presto lives.————————————————

————————————I can't be merry so near any splenetic talk; so I made that long line, and now all's well again. Yes, you are a pretending slut, indeed, with your fourth and fifth in the margin, and your journal, and everything. Wind— we saw no wind here, nothing at all extraordinary at any time. We had it once when you had it not. But an old saying and a true:

> "I hate all wind,
> Before and behind,
> From cheeks with eyes,
> Or from blind.—"

Your chimney fall down! God preserve you. I suppose you only mean a brick or two: but that's a d—ned lie of your chimney being carried to the next house with the wind. Don't put such things upon us; those matters will not pass

here: keep a little to possibilities.   My Lord Hertford [1]
would have been ashamed of such a stretch.   You should
take care of what company you converse with: when one
gets that faculty, 'tis hard to break one's self of it.   Jemmy
Leigh talks of going over; but *quando?*   I do not know
when he will go.   Oh, now you have had my ninth, now you
are come up with me; marry come up with you, indeed.   I
know all that business of Lady S———.[2]   Will nobody cut
that D———y's throat?   Five hundred pounds do you call
poor pay for living three months the life of a king?   They
say she died with grief, partly, being forced to appear as a
witness in court about some squabble among their servants.
—The Bishop of Clogher showed you a pamphlet.[3]   Well,
but you must not give your mind to believe those things;
people will say anything.   The *Character* is here reckoned
admirable, but most of the facts are trifles.   It was first
printed privately here; and then some bold cur ventured to do
it publicly, and sold two thousand in two days: who the
author is must remain uncertain.   Do you pretend to know,
impudence?   How durst you think so?   Pox on your
Parliaments: the Archbishop has told me of it; but we do
not vouchsafe to know anything of it here.   No, no, no
more of your giddiness yet; thank you, Stella, for asking
after it; thank you; God Almighty bless you for your kindness to poor Presto.   You write to Lady Giffard and your
mother upon what I advise when it is too late.   But yet I
fancy this bad news will bring down stocks so low, that one
might buy to great advantage.   I design to venture going to
see your mother some day when Lady Giffard is abroad.
Well, keep your Rathburn [4] and stuff.   I thought he was to
pay in your money upon his houses to be flung down about the
what do you call it.—Well, Madam Dingley, I sent your enclosed

---

[1] Algernon Seymour, Earl of Hertford (1684–1750), only son of Charles
Seymour, Duke of Somerset.   Lord Hertford succeeded to the dukedom in
1748.   From 1708 to 1722 he was M.P. for Northumberland, and from 1708
to 1713 he took an active part in the war in Flanders.
[2] See p. 17.
[3] *A Short Character of the Earl of Wharton* (see p. 85).
[4] See p. 69.

to Bristol, but have not heard from Raymond since he went. Come, come, young women, I keep a good fire; it costs me twelvepence a week, and I fear something more; vex me, and I will have one in my bed-chamber too. No, did not I tell you but just now, we have no high winds here? Have you forgot already?—Now you're at it again, silly Stella; why does your mother say my candles are scandalous? They are good sixes in the pound, and she said I was extravagant enough to burn them by daylight. I never burn fewer at a time than one. What would people have? The D——burst Hawkshaw. He told me he had not the box; and the next day Sterne told me he had sent it a fortnight ago. Patrick could not find him t'other day, but he shall to-morrow. Dear life and heart, do you tease me? does Stella tease Presto? That palsy-water was in the box; it was too big for a packet, and I was afraid of its breaking. Leigh was not in town then; or I would not have trusted it to Sterne, whom yet I have befriended enough to do me more kindness than that. I'll never rest till you have it, or till it is in a way for you to have it. Poor dear rogue, naughty to think it teases me; how could I ever forgive myself for neglecting anything that related to your health? Sure I were a Devil if I did.————————————————See how far I am forced to stand from Stella, because I am afraid she thinks poor Presto has not been careful about her little things; I am sure I bought them immediately according to order, and packed them up with my own hands, and sent them to Sterne, and was six times with him about sending them away. I am glad you are pleased with your glasses. I have got another velvet cap; a new one Lord Herbert[1] bought and presented me one morning I was at breakfast with him, where he was as merry and easy as ever I saw him, yet had received a challenge half an hour before, and half an hour after fought a duel. It was about ten days ago. You

---

[1] Henry Herbert, the last Baron Herbert of Cherbury, succeeded to the peerage in 1709, and soon afterwards married a sister of the Earl of Portsmouth. A ruined man, he committed suicide in 1738.

are mistaken in your guesses about *Tatlers*: I did neither write that on Noses nor Religion,[1] nor do I send him of late any hints at all.—Indeed, Stella, when I read your letter, I was not uneasy at all; but when I came to answer the particulars, and found that you had not received your box, it grated me to the heart, because I thought, through your little words, that you imagined I had not taken the care I ought. But there has been some blunder in this matter, which I will know to-morrow, and write to Sterne, for fear he should not be within. — And pray, pray, Presto, pray now do. — No, Raymond was not above four times with me while he stayed, and then only while I was dressing. Mrs. Fenton has written me another letter about some money of hers in Lady Giffard's hands, that is entrusted to me by my mother, not to come to her husband. I send my letters constantly every fortnight, and, if you will have them oftener, you may, but then they will be the shorter. Pray, let Parvisol sell the horse. I think I spoke to you of it in a former letter: I am glad you are rid of him, and was in pain while I thought you rode him; but, if he would buy you another, or anybody else, and that you could be often able to ride, why do not you do it?

2. I went this morning early to the Secretary of State, Mr. St. John; and he told me from Mr. Harley that the warrant was now drawn, in order for a patent for the First-Fruits: it must pass through several offices, and take up some time, because in things the Queen gives they are always considerate; but that, he assures me, 'tis granted and done, and past all dispute, and desires I will not be in any pain at all. I will write again to the Archbishop to-morrow, and tell him this, and I desire you will say it on occasion. From the Secretary I went to Mr. Sterne, who said he would write to you to-night; and that the box must be at Chester; and that some friend of his goes very soon, and will carry it over. I dined with Mr. Secretary St. John, and at six went to Darteneuf's house to drink punch with

[1] Nos. 257, 260.

him, and Mr. Addison, and little Harrison,[1] a young poet, whose fortune I am making. Steele was to have been there, but came not, nor never did twice, since I knew him, to any appointment. I stayed till past eleven, and am now in bed. Steele's last *Tatler* came out to-day. You will see it before this comes to you, and how he takes leave of the world. He never told so much as Mr. Addison of it, who was surprised as much as I; but, to say the truth, it was time, for he grew cruel dull and dry. To my knowledge he had several good hints to go upon; but he was so lazy and weary of the work that he would not improve them. I think I will send this after[2] to-morrow: shall I before 'tis full, Dingley?

3. Lord Peterborow yesterday called me into a barber's shop, and there we talked deep politics: he desired me to dine with him to-day at the Globe in the Strand; he said he would show me so clearly how to get Spain, that I could not possibly doubt it. I went to-day accordingly, and saw him among half a dozen lawyers and attorneys and hang-dogs, signing of deeds and stuff before his journey; for he goes to-morrow to Vienna. I sat among that scurvy company till after four, but heard nothing of Spain; only I find, by what he told me before, that he fears he shall do no good in his present journey.[3] We are to be mighty constant correspondents. So I took my leave of him, and called at Sir Andrew Fountaine's, who mends much. I came home, an 't please you, at six, and have been studying till now past eleven.

4. Morning. Morrow, little dears. O, faith, I have been dreaming; I was to be put in prison. I do not know why, and I was so afraid of a black dungeon; and then all I had

---

[1] See p. 36.

[2] "*After* is interlined" (Deane Swift).

[3] With this account may be compared what Pope says, as recorded in Spence's *Anecdotes*, p. 223: "Lord Peterborough could dictate letters to nine amanuenses together, as I was assured by a gentleman who saw him do it when Ambassador at Turin. He walked round the room, and told each of them in his turn what he was to write. One perhaps was a letter to the emperor, another to an old friend, a third to a mistress, a fourth to a statesman, and so on: yet he carried so many and so different connections in his head, all at the same time."

been inquiring yesterday of Sir Andrew Fountaine's sickness I thought was of poor Stella. The worst of dreams is, that one wakes just in the humour they leave one. Shall I send this to-day? With all my heart: it is two days within the fortnight; but may be MD are in haste to have a round dozen: and then how are you come up to me with your eighth, young women? But you indeed ought to write twice slower than I, because there are two of you; I own that.— Well then, I will seal up this letter by my morning candle, and carry it into the city with me, where I go to dine, and put it into the post-office with my own fair hands. So, let me see whether I have any news to tell MD. They say they will very soon make some inquiries into the corruptions of the late Ministry; and they must do it, to justify their turning them out. Atterbury,[1] we think, is to be Dean of Christ Church in Oxford; but the College would rather have Smalridge—What's all this to you? What care you for Atterburys and Smalridges? No, you care for nothing but Presto, faith. So I will rise, and bid you farewell; yet I am loth to do so, because there is a great bit of paper yet to talk upon; but Dingley will have it so: "Yes," says she, "make your journals shorter, and send them oftener;" and so I will. And I have cheated you another way too; for this is clipped paper, and holds at least six lines less than the former ones. I will tell you a good thing I said to my Lord Carteret.[2] "So," says he, "my Lord —— came up to me, and asked me," etc. "No," said I, "my Lord —— never did, nor ever can *come up* to you." We all pun here sometimes. Lord Carteret set down Prior t'other day in his chariot; and Prior

[1] Francis Atterbury, Dean of Carlisle, had taken an active part in the defence of Dr. Sacheverell. After a long period of suspense he received the appointment of Dean of Christ Church, and in 1713 he was made Bishop of Rochester and Dean of Westminster. Atterbury was on intimate terms with Swift, Pope, and other writers on the Tory side, and Addison—at whose funeral the Bishop officiated—described him as "one of the greatest geniuses of his age."

[2] John Carteret, second Baron Carteret, afterwards to be well known as a statesman, succeeded to the peerage in 1695, and became Earl Granville and Viscount Carteret on the death of his brother in 1744. He died in 1763. In October 1710, when twenty years of age, he had married Frances, only daughter of Sir Robert Worsley, Bart., of Appuldercombe Isle of Wight.

thanked him for his *charity*; that was fit for Dilly.[1] I do not remember I heard one good one from the Ministry; which is really a shame. Henley is gone to the country for Christmas. The puppy comes here without his wife,[2] and keeps no house, and would have me dine with him at eating-houses; but I have only done it once, and will do it no more. He had not seen me for some time in the Coffee-house, and asking after me, desired Lord Herbert to tell me I was a beast for ever, after the order of Melchisedec. Did you ever read the Scripture?[3] It is only changing the word priest to beast.—I think I am bewitched, to write so much in a morning to you, little MD. Let me go, will you? and I'll come again to-night in a fine clean sheet of paper; but I can nor will stay no longer now; no, I won't, for all your wheedling: no, no, look off, do not smile at me, and say, "Pray, pray, Presto, write a little more." Ah! you are a wheedling slut, you be so. Nay, but prithee turn about, and let me go, do; 'tis a good girl, and do. O, faith, my morning candle is just out, and I must go now in spite of my teeth; for my bed-chamber is dark with curtains, and I am at the wrong side. So farewell, etc. etc.

I am in the dark almost: I must have another candle, when I am up, to seal this; but I will fold it up in the dark, and make what you can of this, for I can only see this paper I am writing upon. Service to Mrs. Walls and Mrs. Stoyte.

God Almighty bless you, etc. What I am doing I can't see; but I will fold it up, and not look on it again.

[1] Dillon Ashe, D.D., Vicar of Finglas, and brother of the Bishop of Clogher. In 1704 he was made Archdeacon of Clogher, and in 1706 Chancellor of Armagh. He seems to have been too fond of drink.
[2] Henley (see p. 37) married Mary, daughter of Peregrine Bertie, the second son of Montagu, Earl of Lindsey, and with her obtained a fortune of £30,000. After Henley's death his widow married her relative, Henry Bertie, third son of James, Earl of Abingdon.
[3] Hebrews v. 6.

LETTER XIII

LONDON, *Jan.* 4, 1710–11.

I WAS going into the City (where I dined) and put my 12th, with my own fair hands, into the post-office as I came back, which was not till nine this night.   I dined with people that you never heard of, nor is it worth your while to know ; an authoress and a printer.[1]   I walked home for exercise, and at eleven got to bed ; and, all the while I was undressing myself, there was I speaking monkey things in air, just as if MD had been by, and did not recollect myself till I got into bed.   I writ last night to the Archbishop, and told him the warrant was drawn for the First-Fruits ; and I told him Lord Peterborow was set out for his journey to Vienna ; but it seems the Lords have addressed to have him stay, to be examined about Spanish affairs, upon this defeat there, and to know where the fault lay, etc.   So I writ to the Archbishop a lie ; but I think it was not a sin.

5. Mr. Secretary St. John sent for me this morning so early, that I was forced to go without shaving, which put me quite out of method.   I called at Mr. Ford's, and desired him to lend me a shaving ; and so made a shift to get into order again.   Lord ! here is an impertinence : Sir Andrew Fountaine's mother and sister[2] are come above a hundred miles, from Worcester, to see him before he died.   They got here but yesterday ; and he must have been past hopes, or past fears, before they could reach him.   I fell a scolding when I heard they were coming ; and the people about him wondered at me, and said what a mighty content it would be on both sides to die when they were with him !   I knew the mother ; she is the greatest Overdo[3] upon earth ; and the sister, they say, is worse ; the poor man will relapse again

---

[1] Probably Mrs. Manley and John Barber (see pp. 92, 106).
[2] Sir Andrew Fountaine's (see p. 28) father, Andrew Fountaine, M.P., married Sarah, daughter of Sir Thomas Chicheley, Master of the Ordnance. Sir Andrew's sister, Elizabeth, married Colonel Edward Clent.   The "scoundrel brother," Brig, died in 1746, aged sixty-four (Blomefield's *Norfolk*, vi. 233–36).
[3] Dame Overdo, the Justice's wife in Ben Jonson's *Bartholomew Fair*.

among them. Here was the scoundrel brother always crying in the outer room till Sir Andrew was in danger; and the dog was to have all his estate if he died; and it is an ignorant, worthless, scoundrel - rake : and the nurses were comforting him, and desiring he would not take on so. I dined to-day the first time with Ophy Butler [1] and his wife; and you supped with the Dean, and lost two-and-twenty pence at cards. And so Mrs. Walls is brought to bed of a girl, who died two days after it was christened; and, betwixt you and me, she is not very sorry: she loves her ease and diversions too well to be troubled with children. I will go to bed.

6. Morning. I went last night to put some coals on my fire after Patrick was gone to bed; and there I saw in a closet a poor linnet he has bought to bring over to Dingley: it cost him sixpence, and is as tame as a dormouse. I believe he does not know he is a bird : where you put him, there he stands, and seems to have neither hope nor fear; I suppose in a week he will die of the spleen. Patrick advised with me before he bought him. I laid fairly before him the greatness of the sum, and the rashness of the attempt; showed how impossible it was to carry him safe over the salt sea : but he would not take my counsel; and he will repent it. 'Tis very cold this morning in bed; and I hear there is a good fire in the room without (what do you call it?), the dining-room. I hope it will be good weather, and so let me rise, sirrahs, do so.—At night. I was this morning to visit the Dean,[2] or Mr. Prolocutor, I think you call him, don't you? Why should not I go to the Dean's as well as you? A little, black man, of pretty near fifty? Ay, the same. A good, pleasant man? Ay, the same. Cunning enough? Yes. One that understands his own interests? As well as anybody. How comes it MD and I don't meet there sometimes? A very good face, and abundance of wit? Do

[1] See p. 7.
[2] Atterbury, who had recently been elected Prolocutor to the Lower House of Convocation.

you know his lady? O Lord! whom do you mean?[1] I mean
Dr. Atterbury, Dean of Carlisle and Prolocutor. Pshaw,
Presto, you are a fool: I thought you had meant our Dean
of St. Patrick's.—Silly, silly, silly, you are silly, both are silly,
every kind of thing is silly. As I walked into the city I was
stopped with clusters of boys and wenches buzzing about the
cake-shops like flies.[2] There had the fools let out their shops
two yards forward into the streets, all spread with great
cakes frothed with sugar, and stuck with streamers of tinsel.
And then I went to Bateman's the bookseller, and laid out
eight - and - forty shillings for books. I bought three little
volumes of Lucian in French for our Stella, and so and so.
Then I went to Garraway's[3] to meet Stratford and dine with
him; but it was an idle day with the merchants, and he was
gone to our end of the town: so I dined with Sir Thomas
Frankland at the Post Office, and we drank your Manley's
health. It was in a newspaper that he was turned out; but
Secretary St. John told me it was false: only that news-
writer is a plaguy Tory. I have not seen one bit of Christmas
merriment.

7. Morning. Your new Lord Chancellor[4] sets out to-morrow
for Ireland: I never saw him. He carries over one Trapp[5]
a parson as his chaplain, a sort of pretender to wit, a second-
rate pamphleteer for the cause, whom they pay by sending
him to Ireland. I never saw Trapp neither. I met Tighe[6]

---

[1] Dr. Sterne, Dean of St. Patrick's, was not married.

[2] January 6 was Twelfth-night.

[3] Garraway's Coffee-house, in Change Alley, was founded by Thomas
Garway, the first coffee-man who sold and retailed tea. A room upstairs was
used for sales of wine "by the candle."

[4] Sir Constantine Phipps, who had taken an active part in Sacheverell's
defence. Phipps' interference in elections in the Tory interest made him very
unpopular in Dublin, and he was recalled on the death of Queen Anne.

[5] Joseph Trapp, one of the seven poets alluded to in the distich :—

"Alma novem genuit celebres Rhedycina poetas,
  Bubb, Stubb, Grubb, Crabb, Trapp, Young, Carey, Tickell, Evans."

Trapp wrote a tragedy in 1704, and in 1708 was chosen the first Professor of
Poetry at Oxford. In 1710 he published pamphlets on behalf of Sacheverell,
and in 1712 Swift secured for him the post of chaplain to Bolingbroke.
During his latter years he held several good livings. Elsewhere Swift calls him
a "coxcomb."

[6] See p. 50.

and your Smyth of Lovet's yesterday by the Exchange.
Tighe and I took no notice of each other; but I stopped
Smyth, and told him of the box that lies for you at Chester,
because he says he goes very soon to Ireland, I think this
week: and I will send this morning to Sterne, to take
measures with Smyth; so good-morrow, sirrahs, and let me
rise, pray. I took up this paper when I came in at evening,
I mean this minute, and then said I, "No, no, indeed, MD,
you must stay"; and then was laying it aside, but could not
for my heart, though I am very busy, till I just ask you how
you do since morning; by and by we shall talk more, so
let me leave you: softly down, little paper, till then; so
there—now to business; there, I say, get you gone; no, I
will not push you neither, but hand you on one side—So—
Now I am got into bed, I'll talk with you. Mr. Secretary St.
John sent for me this morning in all haste; but I would not
lose my shaving, for fear of missing church. I went to Court,
which is of late always very full; and young Manley and I
dined at Sir Matthew Dudley's.—I must talk politics. I
protest I am afraid we shall all be embroiled with parties.
The Whigs, now they are fallen, are the most malicious toads
in the world. We have had now a second misfortune, the
loss of several Virginia ships. I fear people will begin to
think that nothing thrives under this Ministry: and if the
Ministry can once be rendered odious to the people, the
Parliament may be chosen Whig or Tory as the Queen pleases.
Then I think our friends press a little too hard on the Duke
of Marlborough. The country members [1] are violent to have
past faults inquired into, and they have reason; but I do not
observe the Ministry to be very fond of it. In my opinion
we have nothing to save us but a Peace; and I am sure we
cannot have such a one as we hoped; and then the Whigs
will bawl what they would have done had they continued in
power. I tell the Ministry this as much as I dare; and shall
venture to say a little more to them, especially about the
Duke of Marlborough, who, as the Whigs give out, will lay

[1] The extreme Tories, who afterwards formed the October Club.

down his command; and I question whether ever any wise State laid aside a general who had been successful nine years together, whom the enemy so much dread, and his own soldiers cannot but believe must always conquer; and you know that in war opinion is nine parts in ten. The Ministry hear me always with appearance of regard, and much kindness; but I doubt they let personal quarrels mingle too much with their proceedings. Meantime, they seem to value all this as nothing, and are as easy and merry as if they had nothing in their hearts or upon their shoulders; like physicians, who endeavour to cure, but feel no grief, whatever the patient suffers.—Pshaw, what is all this? Do you know one thing, that I find I can write politics to you much easier than to anybody alive? But I swear my head is full; and I wish I were at Laracor, with dear, charming MD, etc.

8. Morning. Methinks, young women, I have made a great progress in four days, at the bottom of this side already, and no letter yet come from MD (that word interlined is morning). I find I have been writing State affairs to MD. How do they relish it? Why, anything that comes from Presto is welcome; though really, to confess the truth, if they had their choice, not to disguise the matter, they had rather, etc. Now, Presto, I must tell you, you grow silly, says Stella. That is but one body's opinion, madam. I promised to be with Mr. Secretary St. John this morning; but I am lazy, and will not go, because I had a letter from him yesterday, to desire I would dine there to-day. I shall be chid; but what care I?—Here has been Mrs. South with me, just come from Sir Andrew Fountaine, and going to market. He is still in a fever, and may live or die. His mother and sister are now come up, and in the house; so there is a lurry.[1] I gave Mrs. South half a pistole for a New Year's gift. So good-morrow, dears both, till anon. — At night. Lord! I have been with Mr. Secretary from dinner till eight; and,

[1] Crowd. A Jacobean writer speaks of "the lurry of lawyers," and "a lurry and rabble of poor friars."

though I drank wine and water, I am so hot! Lady Stanley[1]
came to visit Mrs. St. John,[2] and sent up for me to make up
a quarrel with Mrs. St. John, whom I never yet saw; and do
you think that devil of a Secretary would let me go, but kept
me by main force, though I told him I was in love with his
lady, and it was a shame to keep back a lover, etc.? But
all would not do; so at last I was forced to break away, but
never went up, it was then too late; and here I am, and
have a great deal to do to-night, though it be nine o'clock;
but one must say something to these naughty MD's, else there
will be no quiet.

9. To-day Ford and I set apart to go into the City to buy
books; but we only had a scurvy dinner at an alehouse; and
he made me go to the tavern and drink Florence, four and sixpence a flask; damned wine! so I spent my money, which I
seldom do, and passed an insipid day, and saw nobody, and it
is now ten o'clock, and I have nothing to say, but that 'tis a
fortnight to-morrow since I had a letter from MD; but if I
have it time enough to answer here, 'tis well enough, otherwise woe betide you, faith. I will go to the toyman's, here
just in Pall Mall, and he sells great hugeous battoons;[3] yes,
faith, and so he does. Does not he, Dingley? Yes, faith.
Don't lose your money this Christmas.

10. I must go this morning to Mr. Secretary St. John. I
promised yesterday, but failed, so can't write any more till
night to poor, dear MD. — At night. O, faith, Dingley. I
had company in the morning, and could not go where I

---

[1] See p. 24, note 3.

[2] St. John's first wife was Frances, daughter and co-heiress of Sir Henry
Winchcombe, Bart., of Berkshire, and in her right St. John enjoyed the estates
of Bucklebury, which on her death in 1718 passed to her sister. In April
1711 Swift said that "poor Mrs. St. John" was growing a great favourite of
his; she was going to Bath owing to ill-health, and begged him to take care
of her husband. She "said she had none to trust but me, and the poor creature's tears came fresh in her eyes." Though the marriage was, naturally
enough, unhappy, she did not leave St. John's house until 1713, and she
returned to him when he fell from power. There are letters from her to
Swift as late as 1716, not only doing her best to defend his honour, but speaking of him with tenderness.

[3] "Battoon" means (1) a truncheon; (2) a staff of office. Luttrell, in 1704,
speaks of "a battoon set with diamonds sent him from the French king."

designed; and I had a basket from Raymond at Bristol, with six bottles of wine and a pound of chocolate, and some tobacco to snuff; and he writ under, the carriage was paid; but he lied, or I am cheated, or there is a mistake; and he has written to me so confusedly about some things, that Lucifer could not understand him. This wine is to be drunk with Harley's brother [1] and Sir Robert Raymond, Solicitor-General, in order to recommend the Doctor to your new Lord Chancellor, who left this place on Monday; and Raymond says he is hasting to Chester, to go with him.—I suppose he leaves his wife behind; for when he left London he had no thoughts of stirring till summer. So I suppose he will be with you before this. Ford came and desired I would dine with him, because it was Opera-day; which I did, and sent excuses to Lord Shelburne, who had invited me.

11. I am setting up a new Tatler, little Harrison,[2] whom I have mentioned to you. Others have put him on it, and I encourage him; and he was with me this morning and evening, showing me his first, which comes out on Saturday. I doubt he will not succeed, for I do not much approve his manner; but the scheme is Mr. Secretary St. John's and mine, and would have done well enough in good hands. I recommended him to a printer,[3] whom I sent for, and settled the matter between them this evening. Harrison has just left me, and I am tired with correcting his trash.

12. I was this morning upon some business with Mr. Secretary St. John, and he made me promise to dine with him; which otherwise I would have done with Mr. Harley, whom I have not been with these ten days. I cannot but think they have mighty difficulties upon them; yet I always

[1] Edward Harley, second son of Sir Edward Harley, was M.P. for Leominster and Recorder of the same town. In 1702 he was appointed Auditor of the Imposts, a post which he held until his death in 1735. His wife, Sarah, daughter of Thomas Foley, was a sister of Robert Harley's wife, and his eldest son eventually became third Earl of Oxford. Harley published several books on biblical subjects.

[2] See p. 36. The last number of Steele's *Tatler* appeared on Jan. 2, 1711; Harrison's paper reached to fifty-two numbers.

[3] Dryden Leach (see p. 51).

find them as easy and disengaged as schoolboys on a holiday. Harley has the procuring of five or six millions on his shoulders, and the Whigs will not lend a groat;[1] which is the only reason of the fall of stocks : for they are like Quakers and fanatics, that will only deal among themselves, while all others deal indifferently with them. Lady Marlborough offers, if they will let her keep her employments, never to come into the Queen's presence. The Whigs say the Duke of Marlborough will serve no more; but I hope and think otherwise. I would to Heaven I were this minute with MD at Dublin; for I am weary of politics, that give me such melancholy prospects.

13. O, faith, I had an ugly giddy fit last night in my chamber, and I have got a new box of pills to take, and hope I shall have no more this good while. I would not tell you before, because it would vex you, little rogues; but now it is over. I dined to-day with Lord Shelburne; and to-day little Harrison's new *Tatler* came out : there is not much in it, but I hope he will mend. You must understand that, upon Steele's leaving off, there were two or three scrub *Tatlers*[2] came out, and one of them holds on still, and to-day it advertised against Harrison's; and so there must be disputes which are genuine, like the strops for razors.[3] I am afraid the little toad has not the true vein for it. I will tell you a copy of verses. When Mr. St. John was turned out from being Secretary at War, three years ago, he retired to the country : there he was talking of something he would have written over his summer-house, and a gentleman gave him these verses—

> From business and the noisy world retired,
> Nor vexed by love, nor by ambition fired;
> Gently I wait the call of Charon's boat,
> Still drinking like a fish, and—like a stoat.

---

[1] Cf. p. 53.
[2] Published by John Baker and John Morphew. See Aitken's *Life of Steele*, i. 299-301.
[3] In No. 224 of the *Tatler*, Addison, speaking of polemical advertisements, says : "The inventors of Strops for Razors have written against one another

He swore to me he could hardly bear the jest; for he pretended to retire like a philosopher, though he was but twenty-eight years old: and I believe the thing was true: for he had been a thorough rake.   I think the three grave lines do introduce the last well enough.   Od so, but I will go sleep; I sleep early now.

14. O, faith, young women, I want a letter from MD; 'tis now nineteen days since I had the last: and where have I room to answer it, pray? I hope I shall send this away without any answer at all; for I'll hasten it, and away it goes on Tuesday, by which time this side will be full.   I will send it two days sooner on purpose out of spite; and the very next day after, you must know, your letter will come, and then 'tis too late, and I will so laugh, never saw the like! 'Tis spring with us already.   I ate asparagus t'other day. Did you ever see such a frostless winter?   Sir Andrew Fountaine lies still extremely ill; it costs him ten guineas a day to doctors, surgeons, and apothecaries, and has done so these three weeks.   I dined to-day with Mr. Ford; he sometimes chooses to dine at home, and I am content to dine with him; and at night I called at the Coffee-house, where I had not been in a week, and talked coldly a while with Mr. Addison.   All our friendship and dearness are off: we are civil acquaintance, talk words of course, of when we shall meet, and that is all.   I have not been at any house with him these six weeks: t'other day we were to have dined together at the Comptroller's;[1] but I sent my excuses, being engaged to the Secretary of State.   Is not it odd?   But I think he has used me ill; and I have used him too well, at least his friend Steele.

15. It has cost me three guineas to-day for a periwig.[2]   I

this way for several years, and that with great bitterness."   See also *Spectator*, Nos. 428, 509, and the *Postman* for March 23, 1703: "The so much famed strops for setting razors, etc., are only to be had at Jacob's Coffee-house. . . . Beware of counterfeits, for such are abroad."

    [1] Sir John Holland (see p. 11).

    [2] Addison speaks of a fine flaxen long wig costing thirty guineas (*Guardian*, No. 97), and Duumvir's fair wig, which Phillis threw into the fire, cost forty guineas (*Tatler*, No. 54).

am undone! It was made by a Leicester lad, who married Mr. Worrall's daughter, where my mother lodged;[1] so I thought it would be cheap, and especially since he lives in the city. Well, London lickpenny:[2] I find it true. I have given Harrison hints for another *Tatler* to-morrow. The jackanapes wants a right taste : I doubt he won't do. I dined with my friend Lewis of the Secretary's office, and am got home early, because I have much business to do; but before I begin, I must needs say something to MD, faith—No, faith, I lie, it is but nineteen days to-day since my last from MD. I have got Mr. Harley to promise that whatever changes are made in the Council, the Bishop of Clogher shall not be removed, and he has got a memorial accordingly. I will let the Bishop know so much in a post or two. This is a secret; but I know he has enemies, and they shall not be gratified, if they designed any such thing, which perhaps they might; for some changes there will be made. So drink up your claret, and be quiet, and do not lose your money.

16. Morning. Faith, I will send this letter to-day to shame you, if I han't one from MD before night, that's certain. Won't you grumble for want of the third side, pray now? Yes, I warrant you; yes, yes, you shall have the third, you shall so, when you can catch it, some other time; when you be writing girls. — O, faith, I think I won't stay till night, but seal up this just now, and carry it in my pocket, and whip it into the post-office as I come home at evening. I am going out early this morning. —Patrick's bills for coals and candles, etc., come sometimes to three shillings a week; I keep very good fires, though the weather be warm. Ireland will never be happy till you get

---

[1] Swift's mother, Abigail Erick, was of a Leicestershire family, and after her husband's death she spent much of her time with her friends near her old home. Mr. Worrall, vicar of St. Patrick's, with whom Swift was on terms of intimacy in 1728-29, was evidently a relative of the Worralls where Mrs. Swift had lodged, and we may reasonably suppose that he owed the living to Swift's interest in the family.

[2] The title of a humorous poem by Lydgate. A "lickpenny" is a greedy or grasping person.

small coal[1] likewise; nothing so easy, so convenient, so
cheap, so pretty, for lighting a fire.   My service to Mrs.
Stoyte and Walls; has she a boy or a girl?   A girl, hum;
and died in a week, humm; and was poor Stella forced
to stand for godmother? — Let me know how accompts
stand, that you may have your money betimes.   There's four
months for my lodging, that must be thought on too:
and so go dine with Manley, and lose your money, do,
extravagant sluttikin, but don't fret.—It will be just three
weeks when I have the next letter, that's to-morrow.   Farewell, dearest beloved MD; and love poor, poor Presto, who
has not had one happy day since he left you, as hope saved.
—It is the last sally I will ever make, but I hope it will turn
to some account.   I have done more for these,[2] and I think
they are more honest than the last; however, I will not be
disappointed.   I would make MD and me easy; and I never
desired more.—Farewell, etc. etc.

LETTER XIV

LONDON, *Jan.* 16, 1710–11.

O FAITH, young women, I have sent my letter N. 13
without one crumb of an answer to any of MD's,
there's for you now; and yet Presto ben't angry, faith, not
a bit, only he will begin to be in pain next Irish post, except
he sees MD's little handwriting in the glass-frame at the
bar of St. James's Coffee-house, where Presto would never go
but for that purpose.   Presto is at home, God help him,
every night from six till bed-time, and has as little enjoy-

---

[1] Small wooden blocks used for lighting fires.   See Swift ("Description of
the Morning"),

> "The small-coal man was heard with cadence deep,
> Till drowned in shriller notes of chimney-sweep;"

and Gay (*Trivia*, ii. 35),

> "When small-coal murmurs in the hoarser throat,
> From smutty dangers guard thy threatened coat."

[2] The Tory Ministers.

ment or pleasure in life at present as anybody in the world, although in full favour with all the Ministry. As hope saved, nothing gives Presto any sort of dream of happiness but a letter now and then from his own dearest MD. I love the expectation of it; and when it does not come, I comfort myself that I have it yet to be happy with. Yes, faith, and when I write to MD, I am happy too; it is just as if methinks you were here, and I prating to you, and telling you where I have been: "Well," says you, "Presto, come, where have you been to-day? come, let's hear now." And so then I answer: "Ford and I were visiting Mr. Lewis and Mr. Prior; and Prior has given me a fine Plautus; and then Ford would have had me dine at his lodgings, and so I would not; and so I dined with him at an eating-house, which I have not done five times since I came here; and so I came home, after visiting Sir Andrew Fountaine's mother and sister, and Sir Andrew Fountaine is mending, though slowly."

17. I was making, this morning, some general visits, and at twelve I called at the Coffee-house for a letter from MD; so the man said he had given it to Patrick. Then I went to the Court of Requests and Treasury, to find Mr. Harley, and, after some time spent in mutual reproaches, I promised to dine with him. I stayed there till seven, then called at Sterne's and Leigh's to talk about your box, and to have it sent by Smyth. Sterne says he has been making inquiries, and will set things right as soon as possible. I suppose it lies at Chester, at least I hope so, and only wants a lift over to you. Here has little Harrison been to complain that the printer I recommended to him for his *Tatler* is a coxcomb; and yet to see how things will happen; for this very printer is my cousin, his name is Dryden Leach;[1] did you never hear of Dryden Leach, he that prints the *Postman*? He acted Oroonoko;[2] he's in love with Miss Cross.[3]—Well, so I came

---

[1] See p. 51.

[2] Thomas Southerne's play of *Oroonoko*, based on Mrs. Aphra Behn's novel of the same name, was first acted in 1696.

[3] "Mrs." Cross created the part of Mrs. Clerimont in Steele's *Tender Husband* in 1705.

home to read my letter from Stella, but the dog Patrick was abroad; at last he came, and I got my letter. I found another hand had superscribed it; when I opened it, I found it written all in French, and subscribed Bernage:[1] faith, I was ready to fling it at Patrick's head. Bernage tells me he had been to desire your recommendation to me, to make him a captain; and your cautious[answer, that he had as much power with me as you, was a notable one; if you were here, I would present you to the Ministry as a person of ability. Bernage should let me know where to write to him; this is the second letter I have had without any direction; however, I beg I may not have a third, but that you will ask him, and send me how I shall direct to him. In the meantime, tell him that if regiments are to be raised here, as he says, I will speak to George Granville,[2] Secretary at War, to make him a captain; and use what other interest I conveniently can. I think that is enough, and so tell him, and do not trouble me with his letters, when I expect them from MD; do you hear, young women? write to Presto.

18. I was this morning with Mr. Secretary St. John, and we were to dine at Mr. Harley's alone, about some business of importance; but there were two or three gentlemen there. Mr. Secretary and I went together from his office to Mr. Harley's, and thought to have been very wise; but the deuce a bit, the company stayed, and more came, and Harley went away at seven, and the Secretary and I stayed with the rest of the company till eleven; I would then have had him come away; but he was in for 't; and though he swore he would come away at that flask, there I left him. I wonder at the civility of these people; when he saw I would drink no more, he would always pass the bottle by me, and yet I could not keep the toad from drinking himself, nor he would not let

---

[1] See p. 106.

[2] George Granville, afterwards Lord Lansdowne, was M. P. for Cornwall, and Secretary at War. In December 1711 he was raised to the peerage, and in 1712 was appointed Comptroller of the Household. He died in 1735, when the title became extinct. Granville wrote plays and poems, and was a patron of both Dryden and Pope. Pope called him "Granville the polite." His *Works in Verse and Prose* appeared in 1732.

me go neither, nor Masham,[1] who was with us. When I got home, I found a parcel directed to me; and opening it, I found a pamphlet written entirely against myself, not by name, but against something I writ:[2] it is pretty civil, and affects to be so, and I think I will take no notice of it; 'tis against something written very lately; and indeed I know not what to say, nor do I care. And so you are a saucy rogue for losing your money to-day at Stoyte's; to let that bungler beat you, fie, Stella, an't you ashamed? Well, I forgive you this once, never do so again; no, noooo. Kiss and be friends, sirrah.—Come, let me go sleep, I go earlier to bed than formerly; and have not been out so late these two months; but the Secretary was in a drinking humour. So good-night, myownlittledearsaucyinsolentrogues.

19. Then you read that long word in the last line; no,[3] faith, han't you. Well, when will this letter come from our MD? to-morrow or next day without fail; yes, faith, and so it is coming. This was an insipid snowy day, no walking day, and I dined gravely with Mrs. Vanhomrigh, and came home, and am now got to bed a little after ten; I remember old Culpepper's maxim:

" Would you have a settled head,
You must early go to bed :
I tell you, and I tell 't again,
You must be in bed at ten."

20. And so I went to-day with my new wig, o hoao, to

---

[1] Samuel Masham, son of Sir Francis Masham, Bart., had been a page to the Queen while Princess of Denmark, and an equerry and gentleman of the bed-chamber to Prince George. He married Abigail Hill (see p. 149), daughter of Francis Hill, a Turkey merchant, and sister of General John Hill, and through that lady's influence with the Queen he was raised to the peerage as Baron Masham, in January 1712. Under George I. he was Remembrancer of the Exchequer. He died in 1758.

[2] A roughly printed pamphlet, *The Honourable Descent, Life, and True Character of the . . . Earl of Wharton*, appeared early in 1711, in reply to Swift's *Short Character*; but that can hardly be the pamphlet referred to here, because it is directed against libellers and backbiters, and cannot be described as " pretty civil."

[3] " In that word (the seven last words of the sentence huddled into one) there were some puzzling characters " (Deane Swift).

visit Lady Worsley,[1] whom I had not seen before, although she was near a month in town. Then I walked in the Park to find Mr. Ford, whom I had promised to meet; and coming down the Mall, who should come towards me but Patrick, and gives me five letters out of his pocket. I read the super-scription of the first, "Pshoh," said I; of the second, "Pshoh" again; of the third, "Pshah, pshah, pshah"; of the fourth, "A gad, a gad, a gad, I'm in a rage"; of the fifth and last, "O hoooa; ay marry this is something, this is our MD"; so truly we opened it, I think immediately, and it began the most impudently in the world, thus: "Dear Presto, We are even thus far." "Now we are even," quoth Stephen, when he gave his wife six blows for one. I received your ninth four days after I had sent my thirteenth. But I'll reckon with you anon about that, young women. Why did not you recant at the end of your letter, when you got my eleventh, tell me that, huzzies base? were we even then, were we, sirrah? But I won't answer your letter now, I'll keep it for another time. We had a great deal of snow to-day, and 'tis terrible cold. I dined with Ford, because it was his Opera-day and snowed, so I did not care to stir farther. I will send to-morrow to Smyth.

21. Morning. It has snowed terribly all night, and is vengeance cold. I am not yet up, but cannot write long; my hands will freeze. "Is there a good fire, Patrick?" "Yes, sir." "Then I will rise; come, take away the candle." You must know I write on the dark side of my bed-chamber, and am forced to have a candle till I rise, for the bed stands between me and the window, and I keep the curtains shut this cold weather. So pray let me rise; and Patrick, here, take away the candle.—At night. We are now here in

---

[1] Sir Robert Worsley, Bart., married, in 1690, Frances, only daughter of the first Viscount Weymouth. Their daughter Frances married Lord Carteret (see p. 116) in 1710. In a letter to Colonel Hunter in March 1709 Swift spoke of Lady (then Mrs.) Worsley as one of the principal beauties in town. See, too, Swift's letter to her of April 19, 1730: "My Lady Carteret has been the best queen we have known in Ireland these many years; yet is she mortally hated by all the young girls, because (and it is your fault) she is handsomer than all of them together."

high frost and snow, the largest fire can hardly keep us
warm. It is very ugly walking; a baker's boy broke his
thigh yesterday. I walk slow, make short steps, and never
tread on my heel. 'Tis a good proverb the Devonshire
people have:

> " Walk fast in snow,
> In frost walk slow ;
> And still as you go,
> Tread on your toe.
> When frost and snow are both together,
> Sit by the fire, and spare shoe-leather."

I dined to-day with Dr. Cockburn,[1] but will not do so again
in haste, he has generally such a parcel of Scots with him.

22. Morning. Starving, starving, uth, uth, uth, uth, uth.
—Don't you remember I used to come into your chamber,
and turn Stella out of her chair, and rake up the fire in a
cold morning, and cry Uth, uth, uth? etc. O, faith, I must
rise, my hand is so cold I can write no more. So good-
morrow, sirrahs.—At night. I went this morning to Lady
Giffard's house, and saw your mother, and made her give me
a pint bottle of palsy-water,[2] which I brought home in my
pocket; and sealed and tied up in a paper, and sent it to
Mr. Smyth, who goes to-morrow for Ireland, and sent a letter
to him to desire his care of it, and that he would inquire at
Chester about the box. He was not within: so the bottle
and letter were left for him at his lodgings, with strict orders
to give them to him; and I will send Patrick in a day or
two, to know whether it was given, etc. Dr. Stratford[3] and
I dined to-day with Mr. Stratford[4] in the City, by appointment; but I chose to walk there, for exercise in the frost.
But the weather had given a little, as you women call it, so
it was something slobbery. I did not get home till nine.

> And now I'm in bed,
> To break your head.

---

[1] See p. 7.   [2] See p. 25.
[3] William Stratford, son of Nicholas Stratford, Bishop of Chester, was
Archdeacon of Richmond and Canon of Christ Church, Oxford, until his
death in 1729.
[4] See p. 10.

23. Morning. They tell me it freezes again, but it is not so cold as yesterday : so now I will answer a bit of your letter. —At night. O, faith, I was just going to answer some of our MD's letter this morning, when a printer came in about some business, and stayed an hour; so I rose, and then came in Ben Tooke, and then I shaved and scribbled; and it was such a terrible day, I could not stir out till one, and then I called at Mrs. Barton's, and we went to Lady Worsley's, where we were to dine by appointment. The Earl of Berkeley[1] is going to be married to Lady Louisa Lennox, the Duke of Richmond's daughter. I writ this night to Dean Sterne, and bid him tell you all about the bottle of palsy-water by Smyth; and to-morrow morning I will say something to your letter.

24. Morning. Come now to your letter. As for your being even with me, I have spoken to that already. So now, my dearly beloved, let us proceed to the next. You are always grumbling that you han't letters fast enough; "surely we shall have your tenth;" and yet, before you end your letter, you own you have my eleventh.——And why did not MD go into the country with the Bishop of Clogher? faith, such a journey would have done you good; Stella should have rode, and Dingley gone in the coach. The Bishop of Kilmore[2] I know nothing of; he is old, and may die; he lives in some obscure corner, for I never heard of him. As for my old friends, if you mean the Whigs, I never see them, as you may find by my journals, except Lord Halifax, and him very seldom; Lord Somers never since the first visit, for he has been a false, deceitful rascal.[3] My new friends are very kind, and I have promises enough, but I do not count

[1] James, third Earl of Berkeley (1680–1736), whom Swift calls a "young rake" (see p. 151). The young Countess of Berkeley was only sixteen on her marriage. In 1714 she was appointed a lady of the bed-chamber to Caroline, Princess of Wales, and she died of smallpox in 1717, aged twenty-two. The Earl was an Admiral, and saw much service between 1701 and 1710; under George I. he was First Lord of the Admiralty.

[2] Edward Wettenhall was Bishop of Kilmore from 1699 to 1713.

[3] In the Dedication to *The Tale of a Tub* Swift had addressed Somers in very different terms: "There is no virtue, either in public or private life, which some circumstances of your own have not often produced upon the stage of the world."

upon them, and besides my pretences are very young to them. However, we will see what may be done; and if nothing at all, I shall not be disappointed; although perhaps poor MD may, and then I shall be sorrier for their sakes than my own.—Talk of a merry Christmas (why do you write it so then, young women? sauce for the. goose is sauce for the gander), I have wished you all that two or three letters ago. Good lack; and your news, that Mr. St. John is going to Holland; he has no such thoughts, to quit the great station he is in; nor, if he had, could I be spared to go with him. So, faith, politic Madam Stella, you come with your two eggs a penny, etc. Well, Madam Dingley, and so Mrs. Stoyte invites you, and so you stay at Donnybrook, and so you could not write. You are plaguy exact in your journals, from Dec. 25 to Jan. 4. Well, Smyth and the palsy-water I have handled already, and he does not lodge (or rather did not, for, poor man, now he is gone) at Mr. Jesse's, and all that stuff; but we found his lodging, and I went to Stella's mother on my own head, for I never remembered it was in the letter to desire another bottle; but I was so fretted, so tosticated, and so impatient that Stella should have her water (I mean decently, do not be rogues), and so vexed with Sterne's carelessness.—Pray God, Stella's illness may not return! If they come seldom, they begin to be weary; I judge by myself; for when I seldom visit, I grow weary of my acquaintance.—Leave a good deal of my tenth unanswered!—Impudent slut, when did you ever answer my tenth, or ninth, or any other number? or who desires you to answer, provided you write? I defy the D—— to answer my letters : sometimes there may be one or two things I should be glad you would answer; but I forget them, and you never think of them. I shall never love answering letters again, if you talk of answering. Answering, quotha! pretty answerers truly.— As for the pamphlet you speak of, and call it scandalous, and that one Mr. Presto is said to write it, hear my answer. Fie, child, you must not mind what every idle body tells you—I believe you lie, and that the dogs were not crying it when you said so; come, tell truth.   I am sorry you go to St. Mary's[1] so soon, you will be as poor as rats; that place will drain you with a vengeance: besides, I would have you think of being in the country in summer.   Indeed, Stella, pippins produced plentifully; Parvisol could not send from Laracor: there were about half. a score, I would be glad to know whether they were good for anything.—Mrs. Walls at Donny-brook with you; why is not she brought to bed?   Well, well, well, Dingley, pray be satisfied; you talk as if you were angry about the Bishop's not offering you conveniences for the journey; and so he should.—What sort of Christmas? Why, I have had no Christmas at all; and has it really been Christmas of late?   I never once thought of it.   My service to Mrs. Stoyte, and Catherine; and let Catherine get the coffee ready against I come, and not have so much care on her countenance; for all will go well.—Mr. Bernage, Mr. Bernage, Mr. Fiddlenage, I have had three letters from him now successively; he sends no directions, and how the D—— shall I write to him?   I would have burnt his last, if I had not seen Stella's hand at the bottom: his request is all nonsense.   How can I assist him in buying? and if he be ordered to go to Spain, go he must, or else sell, and I believe one can hardly sell in such a juncture.   If he had stayed, and new regiments raised, I would have used my endeavour to have had him removed; although I have no credit that way, or very little: but, if the regiment goes, he ought to go too; he has had great indulgence, and opportunities of saving; and I have urged him to it a hundred times.   What can I do? whenever it lies in my power to do him a good office, I will do it.   Pray draw up this into a handsome speech, and represent it to him from me, and that I would write, if I knew where to direct to him; and so I have told you, and desired you would tell him, fifty times.   Yes, Madam Stella, I think I can read your long concluding word, but you can't read mine after bidding you good-night.   And yet methinks, I mend extremely in my writing; but when Stella's eyes are

[1] Their lodgings, opposite to St. Mary's Church in Stafford Street, Dublin.

well, I hope to write as bad as ever.—So now I have answered your letter, and mine is an answer; for I lay yours before me, and I look and write, and write and look, and look and write again.—So good-morrow, madams both, and I will go rise, for I must rise; for I take pills at night, and so I must rise early, I don't know why.

25. Morning. I did not tell you how I passed my time yesterday, nor bid you good-night, and there was good reason. I went in the morning to Secretary St. John about some business; he had got a great Whig with him; a creature of the Duke of Marlborough, who is a go-between to make peace between the Duke and the Ministry: so he came out of his closet, and, after a few words, desired I would dine with him at three; but Mr. Lewis stayed till six before he came; and there we sat talking, and the time slipped so, that at last, when I was positive to go, it was past two o'clock; so I came home, and went straight to bed. He would never let me look at his watch, and I could not imagine it above twelve when we went away. So I bid you good-night for last night, and now I bid you good-morrow, and I am still in bed, though it be near ten, but I must rise.

26, 27, 28, 29, 30. I have been so lazy and negligent these last four days that I could not write to MD. My head is not in order, and yet is not absolutely ill, but giddyish, and makes me listless; I walk every day, and take drops of Dr. Cockburn, and I have just done a box of pills; and to-day Lady Kerry sent me some of her bitter drink, which I design to take twice a day, and hope I shall grow better. I wish I were with MD; I long for spring and good weather, and then I will come over. My riding in Ireland keeps me well. I am very temperate, and eat of the easiest meats as I am directed, and hope the malignity will go off; but one fit shakes me a long time. I dined to-day with Lord Mountjoy, yesterday at Mr. Stone's in the City, on Sunday at Vanhomrigh's, Saturday with Ford, and Friday I think at Vanhomrigh's; and that is all the journal I can send MD, for I was so lazy while I was well, that I could not write. I thought to have sent this to-night, but 'tis ten, and I'll go to bed, and write on t'other side to Parvisol to-morrow, and send it on Thursday ; and so good-night, my dears ; and love Presto, and be healthy, and Presto will be so too, etc.

Cut off these notes handsomely, d'ye hear, sirrahs, and give Mrs. Brent hers, and keep yours till you see Parvisol, and then make up the letter to him, and send it him by the first opportunity ; and so God Almighty bless you both, here and ever, and poor Presto.

What, I warrant you thought at first that these last lines were another letter.

Dingley, Pray pay Stella six fishes, and place them to the account of your humble servant, Presto.

Stella, Pray pay Dingley six fishes, and place them to the account of your humble servant, Presto.

There are bills of exchange for you.

LETTER XV

LONDON, *Jan.* 31, 1710–11.

I AM to send you my fourteenth to-morrow ; but my head, having some little disorders, confounds all my journals. I was early this morning with Mr. Secretary St. John about some business, so I could not scribble my morning lines to MD. They are here intending to tax all little printed penny papers a halfpenny every half-sheet, which will utterly ruin Grub Street, and I am endeavouring to prevent it.[1] Besides, I was forwarding an impeachment against a certain great person ; that was two of my businesses with the Secretary, were they not worthy ones ? It was Ford's birthday, and I refused the Secretary, and dined with Ford. We are here in as smart a frost for the time as I have seen ; delicate walking weather, and the Canal and Rosamond's Pond[2] full of the

[1] The Stamp Act was not passed until June 1712 : see the *Journal* for Aug. 7, 1712.
[2] Both in St. James's Park. The Canal was formed by Charles II. from several small ponds, and Rosamond's Pond was a sheet of water in the south-

rabble sliding and with skates, if you know what those are. Patrick's bird's water freezes in the gallipot, and my hands in bed.

Feb. 1. I was this morning with poor Lady Kerry, who is much worse in her head than I. She sends me bottles of her bitter; and we are so fond of one another, because our ailments are the same; don't you know that, Madam Stella? Han't I seen you conning ailments with Joe's wife,[1] and some others, sirrah? I walked into the City to dine, because of the walk, for we must take care of Presto's health, you know, because of poor little MD. But I walked plaguy carefully, for fear of sliding against my will; but I am very busy.

2. This morning Mr. Ford came to me to walk into the City, where he had business, and then to buy books at Bateman's; and I laid out one pound five shillings for a Strabo and Aristophanes, and I have now got books enough to make me another shelf, and I will have more, or it shall cost me a fall; and so as we came back, we drank a flask of right French wine at Ben Tooke's chamber; and when I got home, Mrs. Vanhomrigh sent me word her eldest daughter[2] was taken suddenly very ill, and desired I would come and see her. I went, and found it was a silly trick of Mrs. Armstrong,[3] Lady Lucy's sister, who, with Moll Stanhope, was visiting there: however, I rattled off the daughter.

3. To-day I went and dined at Lady Lucy's, where you know I have not been this long time. They are plaguy Whigs, especially the sister Armstrong, the most insupportable of all women, pretending to wit, without any taste. She was running down the last *Examiner*,[4] the prettiest I had read, with a character of the present Ministry.—I left them at five, and came home. But I forgot to tell you, that this morning

west corner of the Park, "long consecrated," as Warburton said, "to disastrous love and elegiac poetry." It is often mentioned as a place of assignation in Restoration plays. Evelyn (*Diary*, Dec. 1, 1662) describes the "scheets" used on the Canal.

[1] Mrs. Beaumont.

[2] The first direct mention of Hester Vanhomrigh. She is referred to only in two other places in the *Journal* (Feb. 14, 1710–11, and Aug. 14, 1711).

[3] See p. 10.

[4] No. 27, by Swift himself.

my cousin Dryden Leach, the printer, came to me with a heavy complaint, that Harrison the new Tatler had turned him off, and taken the last Tatler's printers again. He vowed revenge; I answered gravely, and so he left me, and I have ordered Patrick to deny me to him from henceforth: and at night comes a letter from Harrison, telling me the same thing, and excused his doing it without my notice, because he would bear all the blame; and in his *Tatler* of this day [1] he tells you the story, how he has taken his old officers, and there is a most humble letter from Morphew and Lillie to beg his pardon, etc.[2] And lastly, this morning Ford sent me two letters from the Coffee-house (where I hardly ever go), one from the Archbishop of Dublin, and t'other from— Who do you think t'other was from?—I'll tell you, because you are friends; why, then it was, faith, it was from my own dear little MD, N. 10. Oh, but will not answer it now, no, noooooh, I'll keep it between the two sheets; here it is, just under; oh, I lifted up the sheet and saw it there: lie still, you shan't be answered yet, little letter; for I must go to bed, and take care of my head.

4. I avoid going to church yet, for fear of my head, though it has been much better these last five or six days, since I have taken Lady Kerry's bitter. Our frost holds like a dragon. I went to Mr. Addison's, and dined with him at his lodgings; I had not seen him these three weeks, we are grown common acquaintance; yet what have not I done for his friend Steele? Mr. Harley reproached me the last time I saw him, that to please me he would be reconciled to Steele, and had promised and appointed to see him, and that Steele never came. Harrison, whom Mr. Addison recommended to me, I have introduced to the Secretary of State, who has promised me to take care of him; and I have represented Addison himself so to the Ministry, that they think and talk in his favour, though they hated him before.—Well, he is now in my debt, and there's an end; and I never had the least obligation to him, and there's

[1] No. 7 of Harrison's series.   [2] The printers of the original *Tatler*.

another end. This evening I had a message from Mr. Harley, desiring to know whether I was alive, and that I would dine with him to-morrow. They dine so late, that since my head has been wrong I have avoided being with them.—Patrick has been out of favour these ten days; I talk dry and cross to him, and have called him "friend" three or four times. But, sirrahs, get you gone.

5. Morning. I am going 'this morning to see Prior, who dines with me at Mr. Harley's; so I can't stay fiddling and talking with dear little brats in a morning, and 'tis still terribly cold.—I wish my cold hand was in the warmest place about you, young women, I'd give ten guineas upon that account with all my heart, faith; oh, it starves my thigh; so I'll rise and bid you good-morrow, my ladies both, good-morrow. Come, stand away, let me rise : Patrick, take away the candle. Is there a good fire?—So—up-a-dazy.— At night. Mr. Harley did not sit down till six, and I stayed till eleven; henceforth I will choose to visit him in the evenings, and dine with him no more if I can help it. It breaks all my measures, and hurts my health; my head is disorderly, but not ill, and I hope it will mend.

6. Here has been such a hurry with the Queen's Birthday, so much fine clothes, and the Court so crowded that I did not go there. All the frost is gone. It thawed on Sunday, and so continues, yet ice is still on the Canal (I did not mean that of Laracor, but St. James's Park) and boys sliding on it. Mr. Ford pressed me to dine with him in his chamber.—Did not I tell you Patrick has got a bird, a linnet, to carry over to Dingley? It was very tame at first, and 'tis now the wildest I ever saw. He keeps it in a closet, where it makes a terrible litter; but I say nothing : I am as tame as a clout. When must we answer our MD's letter? One of these odd-come-shortlies. This is a week old, you see, and no farther yet. Mr. Harley desired I would dine with him again to-day; but I refused him, for I fell out with him yesterday,[1]

---

[1] Harley had forwarded to Swift a banknote for £50 (see *Journal*, March 7, 1710-11).

and will not see him again till he makes me amends : and so I go to bed.

7. I was this morning early with Mr. Lewis of the Secretary's office, and saw a letter Mr. Harley had sent to him, desiring to be reconciled ; but I was deaf to all entreaties, and have desired Lewis to go to him, and let him know I expect further satisfaction. If we let these great Ministers pretend too much, there will be no governing them. He promises to make me easy, if I will but come and see him ; but I won't, and he shall do it by message, or I will cast him off. I'll tell you the cause of our quarrel when I see you, and refer it to yourselves. In that he did something, which he intended for a favour ; and I have taken it quite otherwise, disliking both the thing and the manner, and it has heartily vexed me, and all I have said is truth, though it looks like jest ; and I absolutely refused to submit to his intended favour, and expect further satisfaction. Mr. Ford and I dined with Mr. Lewis. We have a monstrous deal of snow, and it has cost me two shillings to-day in chair and coach, and walked till I was dirty besides. I know not what it is now to read or write after I am in bed. The last thing I do up is to write something to our MD, and then get into bed, and put out my candle, and so go sleep as fast as ever I can. But in the mornings I do write sometimes in bed, as you know.

8. Morning. *I have desired Apronia to be always careful, especially about the legs.* Pray, do you see any such great wit in that sentence ? I must freely own that I do not. But party carries everything nowadays, and what a splutter have I heard about the wit of that saying, repeated with admiration above a hundred times in half an hour ! Pray read it over again this moment, and consider it. I think the word is *advised*, and not *desired*. I should not have remembered it if I had not heard it so often. Why—ay— You must know I dreamed it just now, and waked with it in my mouth. Are you bit, or are you not, sirrahs ? I met Mr. Harley in the Court of Requests, and he asked me

how long I had learnt the trick of writing to myself? He
had seen your letter through the glass case at the Coffee-
house, and would swear it was my hand; and Mr. Ford, who
took and sent it me, was of the same mind. I remember
others have formerly said so too. I think I was little MD's
writing-master.[1]—But come, what is here to do, writing to
young women in a morning? I have other fish to fry; so
good - morrow, my ladies all, good - morrow. Perhaps I'll
answer your letter to-night, perhaps I won't; that's as
saucy little Presto takes the humour.—At night. I walked
in the Park to-day in spite of the weather, as I do always
when it does not actually rain. Do you know what it
has gone and done? We had a thaw for three days, then a
monstrous dirt and snow, and now it freezes, like a pot-lid,
upon our snow. I dined with Lady Betty Germaine, the
first time since I came for England; and there did I sit, like
a booby, till eight, looking over her and another lady at
piquet, when I had other business enough to do. It was
the coldest day I felt this year.

9. Morning. After I had been abed an hour last night,
I was forced to rise and call to the landlady and maid to
have the fire removed in a chimney below stairs, which
made my bed-chamber smoke, though I had no fire in it.
I have been twice served so. I never lay so miserable an
hour in my life. Is it not plaguy vexatious?—It has snowed
all night, and rains this morning. — Come, where's MD's
letter? Come, Mrs. Letter, make your appearance. Here
am I, says she, answer me to my face. — O, faith, I am
sorry you had my twelfth so soon; I doubt you will stay
longer for the rest. I'm so 'fraid you have got my fourteenth while I am writing this; and I would always have
one letter from Presto reading, one travelling, and one
writing. As for the box, I now believe it lost. It is
directed for Mr. Curry, at his house in Capel Street, etc.
I had a letter yesterday from Dr. Raymond in Chester, who
says he sent his man everywhere, and cannot find it; and

[1] At Moor Park.

God knows whether Mr. Smyth will have better success. Sterne spoke to him, and I writ to him with the bottle of palsy-water; that bottle, I hope, will not miscarry: I long to hear you have it. O, faith, you have too good an opinion of Presto's care. I am negligent enough of everything but MD, and I should not have trusted Sterne.—But it shall not go so: I will have one more tug for it.—As to what you say of Goodman Peasly and Isaac,[1] I answer as I did before. Fie, child, you must not give yourself the way to believe any such thing: and afterwards, only for curiosity, you may tell me how these things are approved, and how you like them; and whether they instruct you in the present course of affairs, and whether they are printed in your town, or only sent from hence.—Sir Andrew Fountaine is recovered; so take your sorrow again, but don't keep it, fling it to the dogs. And does little MD walk indeed?—I'm glad of it at heart.—Yes, we have done with the plague here: it was very saucy in you to pretend to have it before your betters. Your intelligence that the story is false about the officers forced to sell,[2] is admirable. You may see them all three here every day, no more in the army than you. Twelve shillings for mending the strong box; that is, for putting a farthing's worth of iron on a hinge, and gilding it; give him six shillings, and I'll pay it, and never employ him or his again.—No indeed, I put off preaching as much as I can. I am upon another foot: nobody doubts here whether I can preach, and you are fools.—The account you give of that weekly paper[3] agrees with us here. Mr. Prior was like to be insulted in the street for being supposed the author of it; but one of the last papers cleared him. Nobody knows who it is, but those few in the secret, I suppose the Ministry and the printer. — Poor Stella's eyes! God bless them, and send them better. Pray spare them, and write not above two lines a day in broad daylight. How

---

[1] Scott says that Swift here alludes to some unidentified pamphlet of which he was the real or supposed author.
[2] See p. 89.   [3] The *Examiner*.

does Stella look, Madam Dingley? Pretty well, a handsome
young woman still. Will she pass in a crowd? Will she
make a figure in a country church?—Stay a little, fair
ladies. I this minute sent Patrick to Sterne: he brings
back word that your box is very safe with one Mr. Earl's
sister in Chester, and that Colonel Edgworth's widow [1]
goes for Ireland on Monday next, and will receive the box
at Chester, and deliver it you safe: so there are some hopes
now.—Well, let us go on to your letter. — The warrant is
passed for the First-Fruits. The Queen does not send a
letter; but a patent will be drawn here, and that will take
up time. Mr. Harley of late has said nothing of presenting
me to the Queen: I was overseen [2] when I mentioned it to
you. He has such a weight of affairs on him, that he cannot
mind all; but he talked of it three or four times to me,
long before I dropped it to you. What, is not Mrs. Walls'
business over yet? I had hopes she was up and well, and
the child dead before this time.—You did right, at last, to
send me your accompts; but I did not stay for them, I
thank you. I hope you have your bill sent in my last, and
there will be eight pounds' interest soon due from Hawkshaw: pray look at his bond. I hope you are good
managers; and that, when I say so, Stella won't think I
intend she should grudge herself wine. But going to those
expensive lodgings requires some fund. I wish you had
stayed till I came over, for some reasons. That Frenchwoman [3] will be grumbling again in a little time: and if
you are invited anywhere to the country, it will vex you to
pay in absence; and the country may be necessary for poor
Stella's health: but do as you like, and do not blame
Presto.—Oh, but you are telling your reasons.—Well, I
have read them; do as you please.—Yes, Raymond says he
must stay longer than he thought, because he cannot settle
his affairs. M—— is in the country at some friend's, comes

---

[1] See p. 43. [2] Mistaken.
[3] Mrs. De Caudres, "over against St. Mary's Church, near Capel Street,
where Stella now lodged.

to town in spring, and then goes to settle in Herefordshire. Her husband is a surly, ill-natured brute, and cares not she should see anybody. O Lord, see how I blundered, and left two lines short; it was that ugly score in the paper[1] that made me mistake. — I believe you lie about the story of the fire, only to make it more odd. Bernage must go to Spain; and I will see to recommend him to the Duke of Argyle, his General, when I see the Duke next: but the officers tell me it would be dishonourable in the last degree for him to sell now, and he would never be preferred in the army; so that, unless he designs to leave it for good and all, he must go. Tell him so, and that I would write if I knew where to direct to him; which I have said fourscore times already. I had rather anything almost than that you should strain yourselves to send a letter when it is inconvenient; we have settled that matter already. I'll write when I can, and so shall MD; and upon occasions extraordinary I will write, though it be a line; and when we have not letters soon, we agree that all things are well; and so that's settled for ever, and so hold your tongue.—Well, you shall have your pins; but for candles' ends, I cannot promise, because I burn them to the stumps; besides, I remember what Stella told Dingley about them many years ago, and she may think the same thing of me.—And Dingley shall have her hinged spectacles.—Poor dear Stella, how durst you write those two lines by candlelight? bang your bones! Faith, this letter shall go to-morrow, I think, and that will be in ten days from the last, young women; that's too soon of all conscience: but answering yours has filled it up so quick, and I do not design to use you to three pages in folio, no, nooooh. All this is one morning's work in bed; —and so good-morrow, little sirrahs; that's for the rhyme.[2] You want politics: faith, I can't think of any; but may be at night I may tell you a passage. Come, sit off the bed,

---

[1] "A crease in the sheet" (Deane Swift).

[2] "In the original it was, *good mallows, little sollahs*. But in these words, and many others, he writes constantly *ll* for *rr*" (Deane Swift).

and let me rise, will you? — At night. I dined to-day with my neighbour Vanhomrigh; it was such dismal weather I could not stir further. I have had some threatenings with my head, but no fits. I still drink Dr. Radcliffe's [1] bitter, and will continue it.

10. I was this morning to see the Secretary of State, and have engaged him to give a memorial from me to the Duke of Argyle in behalf of Bernage. The Duke is a man that distinguishes people of merit, and I will speak to him myself; but the Secretary backing it will be very effectual, and I will take care to have it done to purpose. Pray tell Bernage so, and that I think nothing can be luckier for him, and that I would have him go by all means. I will order it that the Duke shall send for him when they are in Spain; or, if he fails, that he shall receive him kindly when he goes to wait on him. Can I do more? Is not this a great deal?—I now send away this letter, that you may not stay.—I dined with Ford upon his Opera-day, and am now come home, and am going to study; do not you presume to guess, sirrahs, impudent saucy dear boxes. Towards the end of a letter I could not say saucy boxes without putting dear between. An't that right now? Farewell. *This* should *be* longer, *but* that *I* send *it* to-*night*.[2]

O silly, silly loggerhead!

I send a letter this post to one Mr. Staunton, and I direct it to Mr. Acton's in St. Michael's Lane. He formerly lodged there, but he has not told me where to direct. Pray send to that Acton, whether [3] the letter is come there, and whether he has sent it to Staunton.

If Bernage designs to sell his commission and stay at home, pray let him tell me so, that my recommendation to the Duke of Argyle may not be in vain.

---

[1] See p. 21.

[2] "Those letters which are in italics in the original are of a monstrous size, which occasioned his calling himself a loggerhead" (Deane Swift).

[3] *I.e.*, to ask whether.

LETTER XVI

LONDON, *Feb.* 10, 1710–11.

I HAVE just despatched my fifteenth to the post; I tell
you how things will be, after I have got a letter from
MD. I am in furious haste to finish mine, for fear of having
two of MD's to answer in one of Presto's, which would be
such a disgrace, never saw the like; but, before you write to
me, I write at my leisure, like a gentleman, a little every
day, just to let you know how matters go, and so and so;
and I hope before this comes to you, you'll have got your
box and chocolate, and Presto will take more care another
time.

11. Morning. I must rise and go see my Lord Keeper,[1]
which will cost me two shillings in coach-hire. Don't you
call them two thirteens?[2]—At night. It has rained all day,
and there was no walking. I read prayers to Sir Andrew
Fountaine in the forenoon, and I dined with three Irishmen,
at one Mr. Cope's[3] lodgings; the other two were one Morris
an archdeacon,[4] and Mr. Ford. When I came home this
evening, I expected that little jackanapes Harrison would
have come to get help about his *Tatler* for Tuesday: I have
fixed two evenings in the week which I allow him to come.
The toad never came, and I expecting him fell a reading,
and left off other business.—Come, what are you doing?
How do you pass your time this ugly weather? Gaming
and drinking, I suppose: fine diversions for young ladies,
truly! I wish you had some of our Seville oranges, and we
some of your wine. We have the finest oranges for twopence
apiece, and the basest wine for six shillings a bottle. They
tell me wine grows cheap with you. I am resolved to have
half a hogshead when I get to Ireland, if it be good and

---

[1] Harcourt.
[2] "A shilling passes for thirteenpence in Ireland" (Deane Swift).
[3] Robert Cope, a gentleman of learning with whom Swift corresponded.
[4] Archdeacon Morris is not mentioned in Cotton's *Fasti Ecclesiæ Hiber-niæ.*

cheap, as it used to be ; and I will treat MD at my table in an evening, oh hoa, and laugh at great Ministers of State.

12. The days are grown fine and long, —— be thanked. O, faith, you forget all our little sayings, and I am angry. I dined to-day with Mr. Secretary St. John : I went to the Court of Requests at noon, and sent Mr. Harley into the House to call the Secretary, to let him know I would not dine with him if he dined late. By good luck the Duke of Argyle was at the lobby of the House too, and I kept him in talk till the Secretary came out; then told them I was glad to meet them together, and that I had a request to the Duke, which the Secretary must second, and his Grace must grant. The Duke said he was sure it was something in- significant, and wished it was ten times greater. At the Secretary's house I writ a memorial, and gave it to the Secretary to give the Duke, and shall see that he does it. It is, that his Grace will please to take Mr. Bernage into his protection ; and if he finds Bernage answers my character, to give him all encouragement. Colonel Masham [1] and Colonel Hill [2] (Mrs. Masham's [3] brother) tell me my request is reasonable, and they will second it heartily to the Duke too : so I reckon Bernage is on a very good foot when he goes to Spain. Pray tell him this, though perhaps I will write to him before he goes ; yet where shall I direct ? for I suppose he has left Connolly's. [4]

13. I have left off Lady Kerry's bitter, and got another box of pills. I have no fits of giddiness, but only some little disorders towards it ; and I walk as much as I can. Lady Kerry is just as I am, only a great deal worse : I dined

---

[1] See p. 131. [2] See p. 76.

[3] Abigail Hill, afterwards Lady Masham, had been introduced into the Queen's service as bed-chamber woman by the Duchess of Marlborough. Her High Church and Tory views recommended her to Queen Anne, and in 1707 she was privately married to Mr. Samuel Masham, a gentleman in the service of Prince George (see p. 131). The Duchess of Marlborough discovered that Mrs. Masham's cousin, Harley, was using her influence to further his own interests with the Queen ; and in spite of her violence the Duchess found herself gradually supplanted. From 1710 Mrs. Masham's only rival in the royal favour was the Duchess of Somerset. Afterwards she quarrelled with Harley and joined the Bolingbroke faction.

[4] See p. 20.

to-day at Lord Shelburne's, where she is, and we con
ailments, which makes us very fond of each other. I have
taken Mr. Harley into favour again, and called to see him,
but he was not within; I will use to visit him after dinner,
for he dines too late for my head: then I went to visit poor
Congreve, who is just getting out of a severe fit of the gout;
and I sat with him till near nine o'clock. He gave me a
Tatler[1] he had written out, as blind as he is, for little
Harrison. It is about a scoundrel that was grown rich, and
went and bought a coat of arms at the Herald's, and a set
of ancestors at Fleet Ditch; 'tis well enough, and shall be
printed in two or three days, and if you read those kind of
things, this will divert you. It is now between ten and
eleven, and I am going to bed.

14. This was Mrs. Vanhomrigh's daughter's[2] birthday, and
Mr. Ford and I were invited to dinner to keep it, and we
spent the evening there, drinking punch. That was our way
of beginning Lent; and in the morning Lord Shelburne,
Lady Kerry, Mrs. Pratt, and I, went to Hyde Park, instead
of going to church; for, till my head is a little settled, I
think it better not to go; it would be so silly and troublesome to go out sick. Dr. Duke[3] died suddenly two or three
nights ago; he was one of the wits when we were children,
but turned parson, and left it, and never writ farther than a
prologue or recommendatory copy of verses. He had a fine
living given him by the Bishop of Winchester[4] about three
months ago; he got his living suddenly, and he got his dying
so too.

15. I walked purely to-day about the Park, the rain being
just over, of which we have had a great deal, mixed with little
short frosts. I went to the Court of Requests, thinking, if
Mr. Harley dined early, to go with him. But meeting Leigh

[1] No. 14 of Harrison's series.   [2] See p. 139.
[3] Richard Duke, a minor poet and friend of Dryden's, entered the Church
about 1685. In July 1710 he was presented by the Bishop of Winchester to
the living of Witney, Oxfordshire, which was worth £700 a year.
[4] Sir Jonathan Trelawney, one of the seven bishops committed to the Tower
in 1688, was translated to Winchester in 1707, when he appointed Duke to be
his chaplain.

and Sterne, they invited me to dine with them, and away we
went. When we got into his room, one H——, a worthless
Irish fellow, was there, ready to dine with us ; so I stepped out,
and whispered them, that I would not dine with that fellow :
they made excuses, and begged me to stay ; but away I went
to Mr. Harley's, and he did not dine at home ; and at last I
dined at Sir John Germaine's,[1] and found Lady Betty but
just recovered of a miscarriage. I am writing an inscription
for Lord Berkeley's[2] tomb ; you know the young rake his
son, the new Earl, is married to the Duke of Richmond's
daughter,[3] at the Duke's country house, and are now coming
to town. She will be fluxed in two months, and they'll be
parted in a year. You ladies are brave, bold, venturesome
folks ; and the chit is but seventeen, and is ill-natured,
covetous, vicious, and proud in extremes. And so get you
gone to Stoyte to-morrow.

16. Faith, this letter goes on but slow ; 'tis a week old,
and the first side not written. I went to-day into the City
for a walk, but the person I designed to dine with was not
at home ; so I came back, and called at Congreve's, and
dined with him and Estcourt,[4] and laughed till six ; then
went to Mr. Harley's, who was not gone to dinner ; there I
stayed till nine, and we made up our quarrel, and he has
invited me to dinner to-morrow, which is the day of the
week (Saturday) that Lord Keeper and Secretary St. John
dine with him privately, and at last they have consented to
let me among them on that day. Atterbury and Prior went
to bury poor Dr. Duke. Congreve's nasty white wine has
given me the heart-burn.

17. I took some good walks in the Park to-day, and then
went to Mr. Harley. Lord Rivers was got there before me,
and I chid him for presuming to come on a day when only
Lord Keeper and the Secretary and I were to be there ; but
he regarded me not ; so we all dined together, and sat down
at four ; and the Secretary has invited me to dine with him
to-morrow. I told them I had no hopes they could ever

[1] See p. 17.   [2] See p. 14.   [3] See p. 134.   [4] See p. 52.

keep in, but that I saw they loved one another so well, as indeed they seem to do.   They call me nothing but Jonathan; and I said I believed they would leave me Jonathan as they found me; and that I never knew a Ministry do anything for those whom they make companions of their pleasures; and I believe you will find it so; but I care not.   I am upon a project of getting five hundred pounds,[1] without being obliged to any-body; but that is a secret, till I see my dearest MD; and so hold your tongue, and do not talk, sirrahs, for I am now about it.

18. My head has no fits, but a little disordered before dinner; yet I walk stoutly, and take pills, and hope to mend. Secretary St. John would needs have me dine with him to-day; and there I found three persons I never saw, two I had no acquaintance with, and one I did not care for: so I left them early and came home, it being no day to walk, but scurvy rain and wind.   The Secretary tells me he has put a cheat on me; for Lord Peterborow sent him twelve dozen flasks of burgundy, on condition that I should have my share; but he never was quiet till they were all gone, so I reckon he owes me thirty-six pounds.   Lord Peterborow is now got to Vienna, and I must write to him to-morrow.   I begin now to be towards looking for a letter from some certain ladies of Presto's acquaintance, that live at St. Mary's,[2] and are called in a certain language, our little MD.   No, stay, I don't expect one these six days, that will be just three weeks; an't I a reasonable creature?   We are plagued here with an October Club, that is, a set of above a hundred Parliament men of the country, who drink October beer at home, and meet every evening at a tavern near the Parlia-ment to consult affairs, and drive things on to extremes against the Whigs, to call the old Ministry to account, and get off five or six heads.[3]   The Ministry seem not to regard them; yet one of them in confidence told me that there

[1] Cf. p. 155.
[2] Esther Johnson lodged opposite St. Mary's in Dublin.
[3] This famous Tory club began with the meeting together of a few extreme Tories at the Bell in Westminster.   The password to the Club—"October"—was one easy of remembrance to a country gentleman who loved his ale.

must be something thought on, to settle things better. I'll tell you one great State secret: the Queen, sensible how much she was governed by the late Ministry, runs a little into t'other extreme, and is jealous in that point, even of those who got her out of the others' hands. The Ministry is for gentler measures, and the other Tories for more violent. Lord Rivers, talking to me the other day, cursed the paper called the *Examiner*, for speaking civilly of the Duke of Marlborough; this I happened to talk of to the Secretary, who blamed the warmth of that lord and some others, and swore that if their advice were followed they would be blown up in twenty-four hours. And I have reason to think that they will endeavour to prevail on the Queen to put her affairs more in the hands of a Ministry than she does at present; and there are, I believe, two men thought on, one of them you have often met the name of in my letters. But so much for politics.

19. This proved a terrible rainy day, which prevented my walk into the City, and I was only able to run and dine with my neighbour Vanhomrigh, where Sir Andrew Fountaine dined too, who has just began to sally out, and has shipped his mother and sister, who were his nurses, back to the country. This evening was fair, and I walked a little in the Park, till Prior made me go with him to the Smyrna Coffee-house, where I sat a while, and saw four or five Irish persons, who are very handsome, genteel fellows; but I know not their names. I came away at seven, and got home. Two days ago I writ to Bernage, and told him what I had done, and directed the letter to Mr. Curry's, to be left with Dingley. Brigadiers Hill and Masham, brother and husband to Mrs. Masham, the Queen's favourite, Colonel Disney,[1] and

---

[1] "Duke" Disney, "not an old man, but an old rake," died in 1731. Gay calls him "facetious Disney," and Swift says that all the members of the Club "love him mightily." Lady M. W. Montagu speaks of his

"Broad plump face, pert eyes, and ruddy skin,
Which showed the stupid joke which lurked within."

Disney was a French Huguenot refugee, and his real name was Desaulnais. He commanded an Irish regiment, and took part in General Hill's expedition

I, have recommended Bernage to the Duke of Argyle; and
Secretary St. John has given the Duke my memorial; and,
besides, Hill tells me, that Bernage's colonel, Fielding,[1]
designs to make him his captain-lieutenant: but I believe I
said this to you before, and in this letter; but I will not
look.

20. Morning. It snows terribly again; and 'tis mistaken,
for I now want a little good weather. I bid you good-
morrow; and, if it clear up, get you gone to poor Mrs. Walls,
who has had a hard time of it, but is now pretty well again.
I am sorry it is a girl: the poor Archdeacon too, see how
simply he looked when they told him: what did it cost Stella
to be gossip? I'll rise; so, d'ye hear, let me see you at
night; and do not stay late out, and catch cold, sirrahs.—At
night. It grew good weather, and I got a good walk, and
dined with Ford upon his Opera-day; but, now all his wine
is gone, I shall dine with him no more. I hope to send this
letter before I hear from MD, methinks there is—something
great in doing so, only I can't express where it lies; and,
faith, this shall go by Saturday, as sure as you're a rogue.
Mrs. Edgworth was to set out but last Monday; so you won't
have your box so soon perhaps as this letter; but Sterne told
me since that it is safe at Chester, and that she will take
care of it. I'd give a guinea you had it.

21. Morning. Faith, I hope it will be fair for me to walk
into the City; for I take all occasions of walking.—I should
be plaguy busy at Laracor if I were there now, cutting down
willows, planting others, scouring my canal, and every kind
of thing. If Raymond goes over this summer, you must
submit, and make them a visit, that we may have another eel
and trout fishing; and that Stella may ride by, and see

to Canada in 1711 (Kingsford's *Canada*, ii. 465). By his will (*Wentworth
Papers*, 109) he "left nothing to his poor relations, but very handsome to his
bottle companions."

[1] There were several Colonel Fieldings in the first half of the eighteenth
century, and it is not clear which is the one referred to by Swift. Possibly he
was the Edmund Fielding—grandson of the first Earl of Denbigh—who died a
Lieutenant-General in 1741, at the age of sixty-three, but is best known as the
father of Henry Fielding, the novelist.

Presto in his morning-gown in the garden, and so go up with
Joe to the Hill of Bree, and round by Scurlock's Town. O
Lord, how I remember names! faith, it gives me short sighs;
therefore no more of that, if you love me. Good-morrow, I
will go rise like a gentleman; my pills say I must.—At
night. Lady Kerry sent to desire me to engage some lords
about an affair she has in their house here: I called to see
her, but found she had already engaged every lord I knew,
and that there was no great difficulty in the matter; and it
rained like a dog; so I took coach, for want of better
exercise, and dined privately with a hang-dog in the City,
and walked back in the evening. The days are now long
enough to walk in the Park after dinner; and so I do whenever it is fair. This walking is a strange remedy: Mr. Prior
walks, to make himself fat, and I to bring myself down; he
has generally a cough, which he only calls a cold; we often
walk round the Park together. So I'll go sleep.

22. It snowed all this morning prodigiously, and was some
inches thick in three or four hours. I dined with Mr. Lewis
of the Secretary's office at his lodgings: the chairmen that
carried me squeezed a great fellow against a wall, who wisely
turned his back, and broke one of the side-glasses in a
thousand pieces. I fell a scolding, pretended I was like to
be cut to pieces, and made them set down the chair in the
Park, while they picked out the bits of glasses; and, when
I paid them, I quarrelled still; so they dared not grumble,
and I came off for my fare; but I was plaguily afraid they
would have said, "God bless your honour, won't you give
us something for our glass?" Lewis and I were forming
a project how I might get three or four hundred pounds,[1]
which I suppose may come to nothing. I hope Smyth has
brought you your palsy-drops. How does Stella do? I
begin more and more to desire to know. The three weeks
since I had your last is over within two days, and I will
allow three for accidents.

23. The snow is gone every bit, except the remainder of

[1] Cf. p. 152.

some great balls made by the boys. Mr. Sterne was with me this morning about an affair he has before the Treasury. That drab Mrs. Edgworth is not yet set out, but will infallibly next Monday: and this is the third infallible Monday, and pox take her! So you will have this letter first; and this shall go to-morrow; and, if I have one from MD in that time, I will not answer it till my next; only I will say, "Madam, I received your letter, and so, and so." I dined to-day with my Mistress Butler,[1] who grows very disagreeable.

24. Morning. This letter certainly goes this evening, sure as you're alive, young women, and then you will be so shamed that I have had none from you; and, if I was to reckon like you, I would say, I were six letters before you, for this is N. 16, and I have had your N. 10. But I reckon you have received but fourteen, and have sent eleven. I think to go to-day a Minister-of-State-hunting in the Court of Requests; for I have something to say to Mr. Harley. And it is fine, cold, sunshiny weather; I wish dear MD would walk this morning in your Stephen's Green; 'tis as good as our Park, but not so large.[2] Faith, this summer we'll take a coach for sixpence[3] to the Green Well, the two walks, and thence all the way to Stoyte's.[4] My hearty service to Goody Stoyte and Catherine; and I hope Mrs. Walls had a good time. How inconstant I am! I can't imagine I was ever in love with her. Well, I'm going; what have you to say? *I do not care how I write now.*[5] I don't design to write on this side; these few lines are but so much more than your due; so I will write *large* or small as I please. O, faith, my hands are starving in bed; I believe it is a hard frost. I must rise, and bid you good-bye, for I'll seal this letter

---

[1] See p. 14.

[2] "It is a measured mile round the outer wall; and far beyond any the finest square in London" (Deane Swift).

[3] "The common fare for a set-down in Dublin" (*ib.*).

[4] "Mrs. Stoyte lived at Donnybrook, the road to which from Stephen's Green ran into the country about a mile from the south-east corner" (*ib.*).

[5] "Those words in italics are written in a very large hand, and so is the word *large*" (*ib.*).

immediately, and carry it in my pocket, and put it into the post-office with my own fair hands. Farewell.

This letter is just a fortnight's journal to-day. Yes, and so it is, I'm sure, says you, with your two eggs a penny.

Lele, lele, lele.[1]

O Lord, I am saying lele, lele, to myself, in all our little keys : and, now you talk of keys, that dog Patrick broke the key-general of the chest of drawers with six locks, and I have been so plagued to get a new one, besides my good two shillings !

LETTER XVII

LONDON, *Feb.* 24, 1710-11.

NOW, young women, I gave in my sixteenth this evening. I dined with Ford (it was his Opera-day) as usual ; it is very convenient to me to do so, for coming home early after a walk in the Park, which now the days will allow. I called on the Secretary at his office, and he had forgot to give the memorial about Bernage to the Duke of Argyle ; but, two days ago, I met the Duke, who desired I would give it him myself, which should have more power with him than all the Ministry together, as he protested solemnly, repeated it two or three times, and bid me count upon it. So that I verily believe Bernage will be in a very good way to establish himself. I think I can do no more for him at present, and there's an end of that ; and so get you gone to bed, for it is late.

25. The three weeks are out yesterday since I had your last, and so now I will be expecting every day a pretty dear letter from my own MD, and hope to hear that Stella has been much better in her head and eyes : my head continues as it was, no fits, but a little disorder every day, which I can easily bear, if it will not grow worse. I dined to-day with Mr.

---

[1] Deane Swift alters "lele" to "there," but in a note states how he here altered Swift's "cypher way of writing." No doubt "lele" and other favourite words occurred frequently in the MS., as they do in the later letters.

Secretary St. John, on condition I might choose my company,
which were Lord Rivers, Lord Carteret, Sir Thomas Mansel,[1]
and Mr. Lewis; I invited Masham, Hill, Sir John Stanley,
and George Granville, but they were engaged; and I did it
in revenge of his having such bad company when I dined
with him before; so we laughed, etc.   And I ventured to go
to church to-day, which I have not done this month before.
Can you send me such a good account of Stella's health, pray
now? Yes, I hope, and better too.   We dined (says you) at
the Dean's, and played at cards till twelve, and there came in
Mr. French, and Dr. Travors, and Dr. Whittingham, and Mr.
(I forget his name, that I always tell Mrs. Walls of) the
banker's son, a pox on him.   And we were so merry; I vow
they are pure good company.   But I lost a crown; for you
must know I had always hands tempting me to go out,
but never took in anything, and often two black aces without a manilio; was not that hard, Presto?   Hold your
tongue, etc.

26. I was this morning with Mr. Secretary about some
business, and he tells me that Colonel Fielding is now going
to make Bernage his captain-lieutenant, that is, a captain by
commission, and the perquisites of the company; but not
captain's pay, only the first step to it.   I suppose he will like
it; and the recommendation to the Duke of Argyle goes on.
And so trouble me no more about your Bernage; the jackanapes understands what fair solicitors he has got, I warrant
you.   Sir Andrew Fountaine and I dined, by invitation, with
Mrs. Vanhomrigh.   You say they are of no consequence:
why, they keep as good female company as I do male; I see
all the drabs of quality at this end of the town with them:
I saw two Lady Bettys[2] there this afternoon; the beauty of
one, the good-breeding and nature of t'other, and the wit of
neither, would have made a fine woman.   Rare walking in

---

[1] Sir Thomas Mansel, Bart., Comptroller of the Household to Queen Anne,
and a Lord of the Treasury, was raised to the peerage in December 1711 as
Baron Mansel of Margam.   He died in 1723.
[2] Lady Betty Butler and Lady Betty Germaine (see pp. 14, 17).

the Park now: why don't you walk in the Green of St. Stephen? The walks there are finer gravelled than the Mall. What beasts the Irish women are, never to walk!

27. Darteneuf and I, and little Harrison the new Tatler, and Jervas the painter, dined to-day with James,[1] I know not his other name, but it is one of Darteneuf's dining-places, who is a true epicure. James is clerk of the kitchen to the Queen, and has a little snug house at St. James's; and we had the Queen's wine, and such very fine victuals that I could not eat it. Three weeks and three days since my last letter from MD; rare doings! why, truly we were so busy with poor Mrs. Walls, that indeed, Presto, we could not write, we were afraid the poor woman would have died; and it pitied us to see the Archdeacon, how concerned he was. The Dean never came to see her but once; but now she is up again, and we go and sit with her in the evenings. The child died the next day after it was born; and I believe, between friends, she is not very sorry for it.—Indeed, Presto, you are plaguy silly to-night, and han't guessed one word right; for she and the child are both well, and it is a fine girl, likely to live; and the Dean was godfather, and Mrs. Catherine and I were godmothers; I was going to say Stoyte, but I think I have heard they don't put maids and married women together; though I know not why I think so, nor I don't care; what care I? but I must prate, etc.

28. I walked to-day into the City for my health, and there dined; which I always do when the weather is fair, and business permits, that I may be under a necessity of taking a good walk, which is the best thing I can do at present for my health. Some bookseller has raked up everything I writ, and published it t'other day in one volume; but I know nothing of it, 'twas without my knowledge or consent: it makes a

---

[1] James Eckershall, "second clerk of the Queen's Privy Kitchen." Chamberlayne (*Magnæ Britanniæ Notitia*, 1710, p. 536) says that his wages were £11, 8s. 1½d., and board-wages £138, 11s. 10½d., making £150 in all. Afterwards Eckershall was gentleman usher to Queen Anne; he died at Drayton in 1753, aged seventy-four. Pope was in correspondence with him in 1720 on the subject of contemplated speculations in South Sea and other stocks.

four-shilling book, and is called *Miscellanies in Prose and Verse*.[1] Tooke pretends he knows nothing of it; but I doubt he is at the bottom.   One must have patience with these things; the best of it is, I shall be plagued no more.   However, I will bring a couple of them over with me for MD; perhaps you may desire to see them.   I hear they sell mightily.

March 1. Morning.   I have been calling to Patrick to look in his almanac for the day of the month; I did not know but it might be leap-year.   The almanac says 'tis the third after leap-year;" and I always thought till now, that every third year was leap-year.   I am glad they come so seldom; but I'm sure 'twas otherwise when I was a young man; I see times are mightily changed since then.—Write to me, sirrahs; be sure do by the time this side is done, and I'll keep t'other side for the answer: so I'll go write to the Bishop of Clogher; good-morrow, sirrahs.—Night.   I dined to-day at Mrs. Vanhomrigh's, being a rainy day; and Lady Betty Butler, knowing it, sent to let me know she expected my company in the evening, where the Vans (so we call them) were to be.   The Duchess[2] and they do not go over this summer with the Duke; so I go to bed.

2. This rainy weather undoes me in coaches and chairs. I was traipsing to-day with your Mr. Sterne, to go along with them to Moore,[3] and recommend his business to the Treasury.   Sterne tells me his dependence is wholly on me; but I have absolutely refused to recommend it to Mr. Harley, because I have troubled him lately so much with other folks' affairs; and besides, to tell the truth, Mr. Harley told me he did not like Sterne's business: however, I will serve him, because I suppose MD would have me.   But, in saying

[1] In October 1710 (see p. 43) Swift wrote as if he knew about the preparation of these *Miscellanies*.   The volume was published by Morphew instead of Tooke, and it is frequently referred to in the *Journal*.

[2] In 1685 the Duke of Ormond (see p. 5) married, as his second wife, Lady Mary Somerset, eldest surviving daughter of Henry, first Duke of Beaufort.

[3] Arthur Moore, M.P., was a Commissioner of Trade and Plantations from 1710 until his death in 1730.   Gay calls him "grave," and Pope ("Prologue to the Satires," 23) says that Moore blamed him for the way in which his "giddy son," James Moore Smythe, neglected the law.

his dependence lies wholly on me, he lies, and is a fool. I dined with Lord Abercorn, whose son Peasley[1] will be married at Easter to ten thousand pounds.

3. I forgot to tell you that yesterday morning I was at Mr. Harley's levee: he swore I came in spite, to see him among a parcel of fools. My business was to desire I might let the Duke of Ormond know how the affair stood of the First-Fruits. He promised to let him know it, and engaged me to dine with him to-day. Every Saturday, Lord Keeper, Secretary St. John, and I dine with him, and sometimes Lord Rivers; and they let in none else. Patrick brought me some letters into the Park; among which one was from Walls; and t'other, yes, faith, t'other was from our little MD, N. 11. I read the rest in the Park, and MD's in a chair as I went from St. James's to Mr. Harley; and glad enough I was, faith, to read it, and see all right. Oh, but I won't answer it these three or four days at least, or may be sooner. An't I silly? faith, your letters would make a dog silly, if I had a dog to be silly, but it must be a little dog.—I stayed with Mr. Harley till past nine, where we had much discourse together after the rest were gone; and I gave him very truly my opinion where he desired it. He complained he was not very well, and has engaged me to dine with him again on Monday. So I came home afoot, like a fine gentleman, to tell you all this.

4. I dined to-day with Mr. Secretary St. John; and after dinner he had a note from Mr. Harley, that he was much out of order.[2] Pray God preserve his health! everything depends upon it. The Parliament at present cannot go a step without him, nor the Queen neither. I long to be in Ireland; but the Ministry beg me to stay: however, when this Parliament lurry[3] is over, I will endeavour to steal away; by which time I hope the First-Fruit business will be done. This kingdom is certainly ruined as much as was ever any bankrupt

---

[1] James, Lord Paisley, who succeeded his father (see p. 86) as seventh Earl of Abercorn in 1734, married, in 1711, Anne, eldest daughter of Colonel John Plumer, of Blakesware, Herts.
[2] Harley's ill-health was partly due to his drinking habits.
[3] Crowd or confusion.

11

merchant. We must have peace, let it be a bad or a good one, though nobody dares talk of it. The nearer I look upon things, the worse I like them. I believe the confederacy will soon break to pieces, and our factions at home increase. The Ministry is upon a very narrow bottom, and stand like an isthmus, between the Whigs on one side, and violent Tories on the other. They are able seamen; but the tempest is too great, the ship too rotten, and the crew all against them. Lord Somers has been twice in the Queen's closet, once very lately; and your Duchess of Somerset,[1] who now has the key, is a most insinuating woman; and I believe they will endeavour to play the same game that has been played against them.—I have told them of all this, which they know already, but they cannot help it. They have cautioned the Queen so much against being governed, that she observes it too much. I could talk till to-morrow upon these things, but they make me melancholy. I could not but observe that lately, after much conversation with Mr. Harley, though he is the most fearless man alive, and the least apt to despond, he confessed to me that uttering his mind to me gave him ease.

5. Mr. Harley continues out of order, yet his affairs force him abroad: he is subject to a sore throat, and was cupped last night: I sent and called two or three times. I hear he is better this evening. I dined to-day in the City with Dr. Freind at a third body's house, where I was to pass for somebody else; and there was a plaguy silly jest carried on, that made me sick of it. Our weather grows fine, and I will walk like camomile. And pray walk you to your Dean's, or your Stoyte's, or your Manley's, or your Walls'. But your new lodgings make you so proud, you will walk less than ever. Come, let me go to bed, sirrahs.

6. Mr. Harley's going out yesterday has put him a little backwards. I called twice, and sent, for I am in pain for

---

[1] The first wife of Charles Seymour, sixth Duke of Somerset, was Lady Elizabeth Percy, only daughter of Joscelyn, eleventh Earl of Northumberland, and heiress of the house of Percy. She married the Duke, her third husband, at the age of eighteen.

him. Ford caught me, and made me dine with him on his
Opera-day; so I brought Mr. Lewis with me, and sat with
him till six. I have not seen Mr. Addison these three weeks;
all our friendship is over. I go to no Coffee-house. I presented a parson of the Bishop of Clogher's, one Richardson,[1]
to the Duke of Ormond to-day: he is translating prayers and
sermons into Irish, and has a project about instructing the
Irish in the Protestant religion.

7. Morning. Faith, a little would make me, I could find
in my heart, if it were not for one thing, I have a good mind,
if I had not something else to do, I would answer your dear
saucy letter. O, Lord, I am going awry with writing in
bed. O, faith, but I must answer it, or I shan't have room,
for it must go on Saturday; and don't think I will fill the
third side, I an't come to that yet, young women. Well then,
as for your Bernage, I have said enough: I writ to him last
week.—Turn over that leaf. Now, what says MD to the
world to come? I tell you, Madam Stella, my head is a great
deal better, and I hope will keep so. How came yours to be
fifteen days coming, and you had my fifteenth in seven?
Answer me that, rogues. Your being with Goody Walls is
excuse enough: I find I was mistaken in the sex, 'tis a boy.[2]
Yes, I understand your cypher, and Stella guesses right, as
she always does. He[3] gave me al bsadnuk lboinlpl dfaonr
ufainf btoy dpionufnad,[4] which I sent him again by Mr.
Lewis, to whom I writ a very complaining letter that was
showed him; and so the matter ended. He told me he
had a quarrel with me; I said I had another with him,
and we returned to our friendship, and I should think he

---

[1] John Richardson, D.D., rector of Armagh, Cavan, and afterwards chaplain
to the Duke of Ormond. In 1711 he published a *Proposal for the Conversion
of the Popish Natives of Ireland to the Established Religion*, and in 1712 a
Short History of the Attempts to Convert the Popish Natives of Ireland. In
1709 the Lower House of Convocation in Ireland had passed resolutions for
printing the Bible and liturgy in Irish, providing Irish preachers, etc. In
1711 Thomas Parnell, the poet, headed a deputation to the Queen on the
subject, when an address was presented; but nothing came of the proposals,
owing to fears that the English interest in Ireland might be injured. In 1731
Richardson was given the small deanery of Kilmacluagh.

[2] See p. 159.   [3] Harley.

[4] "Bank bill for fifty pound," taking the alternate letters (see pp. 141, 150).

loves me as well as a great Minister can love a man in so
short a time. Did not I do right? I am glad at heart you
have got your palsy-water;[1] pray God Almighty it may do
my dearest little Stella good! I suppose Mrs. Edgworth set
out last Monday se'ennight. Yes, I do read the *Examiners*,
and they are written very finely, as you judge. I do not
think they are too severe on the Duke;[2] they only tax him
of avarice, and his avarice has ruined us. You may count
upon all things in them to be true. The author has said it
is not Prior, but perhaps it may be Atterbury.—Now, Madam
Dingley, says she, 'tis fine weather, says she; yes, says she,
and we have got to our new lodgings. I compute you ought
to save eight pounds by being in the others five months; and
you have no more done it than eight thousand. I am glad
you are rid of that squinting, blinking Frenchman. I will
give you a bill on Parvisol for five pounds for the half-year.
And must I go on at four shillings a week, and neither eat
nor drink for it? Who the Devil said Atterbury and your
Dean were alike? I never saw your Chancellor, nor his
chaplain. The latter has a good deal of learning, and is a
well-wisher to be an author: your Chancellor is an excellent
man. As for Patrick's bird, he bought him for his tameness,
and is grown the wildest I ever saw. His wings have been
quilled thrice, and are now up again: he will be able to fly
after us to Ireland, if he be willing.—Yes, Mrs. Stella, Dingley
writes more like Presto than you; for all you superscribed
the letter, as who should say, Why should not I write like
our Presto as well as Dingley? You with your awkward SS;[3]
cannot you write them thus, SS? No, but always SSS.
Spiteful sluts, to affront Presto's writing; as that when you
shut your eyes you write most like Presto. I know the time
when I did not write to you half so plain as I do now; but
I take pity on you both. I am very much concerned for Mrs.
Walls's eyes. Walls says nothing of it to me in his letter

---

[1] See p. 25.   [2] See Nos. 27 and 29, by Swift himself.
[3] " Print cannot do justice to whims of this kind, as they depend wholly upon
the awkward shape of the letters " (Deane Swift).

dated after yours. You say, "If she recovers, she may lose her sight." I hope she is in no danger of her life. Yes, Ford is as sober as I please : I use him to walk with me as an easy companion, always ready for what I please, when I am weary of business and Ministers. I don't go to a Coffee-house twice a month. I am very regular in going to sleep before eleven.—And so you say that Stella is a pretty girl; and so she be, and methinks I see her just now as handsome as the day is long. Do you know what? when I am writing in our language, I make up my mouth just as if I was speaking it. I caught myself at it just now. And I suppose Dingley is so fair and so fresh as a lass in May, and has her health, and no spleen.—In your account you sent do you reckon as usual from the 1st of November[1] was twelvemonth? Poor Stella, will not Dingley leave her a little daylight to write to Presto? Well, well, we'll have daylight shortly, spite of her teeth; and zoo[2] must cly Lele and Hele, and Hele aden. Must loo mimitate Pdfr, pay? Iss, and so la shall. And so lele's fol ee rettle. Dood-mollow.—At night. Mrs. Barton sent this morning to invite me to dinner; and there I dined, just in that genteel manner that MD used when they would treat some better sort of body than usual.

8. O dear MD, my heart is almost broken. You will hear the thing before this comes to you. I writ a full account of it this night to the Archbishop of Dublin; and the Dean may tell you the particulars from the Archbishop. I was in a sorry way to write, but thought it might be proper to send a true account of the fact; for you will hear a thousand lying circumstances. It is of Mr. Harley's being stabbed this afternoon, at three o'clock, at a Committee of the Council.

---

[1] See p. 54.
[2] "Here is just one specimen given of his way of writing to Stella in these journals. The reader, I hope, will excuse my omitting it in all other places where it occurs. The meaning of this pretty language is: 'And you must cry There, and Here, and Here again. Must you imitate Presto, pray? Yes, and so you shall. And so there's for your letter. Good-morrow'" (Deane Swift). What Swift really wrote was probably as follows: "Oo must cly Lele and Lele and Lele aden. Must oo mimitate Pdfr, pay? Iss, and so oo sall. And so lele's fol oo rettle. Dood-mollow."

I was playing Lady Catharine Morris's[1] cards, where I dined, when young Arundel[2] came in with the story. I ran away immediately to the Secretary, which was in my way: no one was at home. I met Mrs. St. John in her chair; she had heard it imperfectly. I took a chair to Mr. Harley, who was asleep, and they hope in no danger; but he has been out of order, and was so when he came abroad to-day, and it may put him in a fever: I am in mortal pain for him. That desperate French villain, Marquis de Guiscard,[3] stabbed Mr. Harley. Guiscard was taken up by Mr. Secretary St. John's warrant for high treason, and brought before the Lords to be examined; there he stabbed Mr. Harley. I have told all the particulars already to the Archbishop. I have now, at nine, sent again, and they tell me he is in a fair way. Pray pardon my distraction; I now think of all his kindness to me.—The poor creature now lies stabbed in his bed by a desperate French Popish villain. Good-night, and God preserve you both, and pity me; I want it.

9. Morning; seven, in bed. Patrick is just come from Mr. Harley's. He slept well till four; the surgeon sat[4] up with him: he is asleep again: he felt a pain in his wound when he waked: they apprehend him in no danger. This account

[1] Lady Catherine Morice (died 1716) was the eldest daughter of Thomas Herbert, Earl of Pembroke, and wife of Sir Nicholas Morice, Bart., M.P. for Newport.

[2] Perhaps Henry Arundell, who succeeded his father as fifth Baron Arundell of Wardour in 1712, and died in 1726.

[3] Antoine, Abbé de Bourlie and Marquis de Guiscard, was a cadet of a distinguished family of the south of France. He joined the Church, but having been driven from France in consequence of his licentious excesses, he came to England, after many adventures in Europe, with a recommendation from the Duke of Savoy. Godolphin gave him the command of a regiment of refugees, and employed him in projects for effecting a landing in France. These schemes proving abortive, Guiscard's regiment was disbanded, and he was discharged with a pension of £500 a year. Soon after the Tories came to power Guiscard came to the conclusion that there was no hope of employment for him, and little chance of receiving his pension; and he began a treacherous correspondence with the French. When this was detected he was brought before the Privy Council, and finding that everything was known, and wishing a better death than hanging, he stabbed Harley in the breast. Mrs. Manley, under Swift's directions, wrote a *Narrative of Guiscard's Examination*, and the incident greatly added to the security of Harley's position, and to the strength of the Government.

[4] Harley's surgeon, Mr. Green.

the surgeon left with the porter, to tell people that send. Pray God preserve him. I am rising, and going to Mr. Secretary St. John. They say Guiscard will die with the wounds Mr. St. John and the rest gave him. I shall tell you more at night.—Night. Mr. Harley still continues on the mending hand; but he rested ill last night, and felt pain. I was early with the Secretary this morning, and I dined with him, and he told me several particularities of this accident, too long to relate now. Mr. Harley is still mending this evening, but not at all out of danger; and till then I can have no peace. Good-night, etc., and pity Presto.

10. Mr. Harley was restless last night; but he has no fever, and the hopes of his mending increase. I had a letter from Mr. Walls, and one from Mr. Bernage. I will answer them here, not having time to write. Mr. Walls writes about three things. First, about a hundred pounds from Dr. Raymond, of which I hear nothing, and it is now too late. Secondly, about Mr. Clements:[1] I can do nothing in it, because I am not to mention Mr. Pratt; and I cannot recommend without knowing Mr. Pratt's objections, whose relation Clements is, and who brought him into the place. The third is about my being godfather to the child:[2] that is in my power, and (since there is no remedy) will submit. I wish you could hinder it; but if it can't be helped, pay what you think proper, and get the Provost to stand for me, and let his Christian name be Harley, in honour of my friend, now lying stabbed and doubtful of his life. As for Bernage, he writes me word that his colonel has offered to make him captain-lieutenant for a hundred pounds. He was such a fool to offer him money without writing to me till it was done, though I have had a dozen letters from him; and then he desires I would say nothing of this, for fear his colonel should be angry. People are mad. What can I do? I engaged Colonel Disney, who was one of his solicitors to the Secretary, and then told him the story. He assured me that Fielding (Bernage's colonel) said he might have got that sum; but, on account

[1] See p. 73.   [2] Mrs. Walls' baby (see p. 185).

of those great recommendations he had, would give it him for nothing: and I would have Bernage write him a letter of thanks, as of a thing given him for nothing, upon recommendations, etc. Disney tells me he will again speak to Fielding, and clear up this matter; then I will write to Bernage. A pox on him for promising money till I had it promised to me; and then making it such a ticklish point, that one cannot expostulate with the colonel upon it: but let him do as I say, and there is an end. I engaged the Secretary of State in it; and am sure it was meant a kindness to me, and that no money should be given, and a hundred pounds is too much in a Smithfield bargain,[1] as a major-general told me, whose opinion I asked. I am now hurried, and can say no more. Farewell, etc. etc.

How shall I superscribe to your new lodgings, pray, madams? Tell me but that, impudence and saucy-face.

Are not you sauceboxes to write "lele"[2] like Presto?

O poor Presto!

Mr. Harley is better to-night, that makes me so pert, you saucy Gog and Magog.

LETTER XVIII

LONDON, *March* 10, 1710-11,

PRETTY little MD must expect little from me till Mr. Harley is out of danger. We hope he is so now; but I am subject to fear for my friends. He has a head full of the whole business of the nation, was out of order when the villain stabbed him, and had a cruel contusion by the second blow. But all goes on well yet. Mr. Ford and I dined with Mr. Lewis, and we hope the best.

11. This morning Mr. Secretary and I met at Court, where

---

[1] The phrase had its origin in the sharp practices in the horse and cattle markets. Writing to Arbuthnot in 1727, Swift said that Gay "had made a pretty good bargain (that is a Smithfield) for a little place in the Custom House."

[2] "There."

he went to the Queen, who is out of order, and aguish: I doubt the worse for this accident to Mr. Harley. We went together to his house, and his wound looks well, and he is not feverish at all, and I think it is foolish in me to be so much in pain as I am. I had the penknife in my hand, which is broken within a quarter of an inch of the handle. I have a mind to write and publish an account of all the particularities of this fact [1]: it will be very curious, and I would do it when Mr. Harley is past danger.

12. We have been in terrible pain to-day about Mr. Harley, who never slept last night, and has been very feverish. But this evening I called there; and young Mr. Harley (his only son) tells me he is now much better, and was then asleep. They let nobody see him, and that is perfectly right. The Parliament cannot go on till he is well, and are forced to adjourn their money businesses, which none but he can help them in. Pray God preserve him.

13. Mr. Harley is better to-day, slept well all night, and we are a little out of our fears. I send and call three or four times every day. I went into the City for a walk, and dined there with a private man; and coming home this evening, broke my shin in the Strand over a tub of sand left just in the way. I got home dirty enough, and went straight to bed, where I have been cooking it with gold-beater's skin, and have been peevish enough with Patrick, who was near an hour bringing a rag from next door. It is my right shin, where never any humour fell when t'other used to swell; so I apprehend it less: however, I shall not stir till 'tis well, which I reckon will be in a week. I am very careful in these sort of things; but I wish I had Mrs. J——'s water: [2] she is out of town, and I must make a shift with alum. I will dine with Mrs. Vanhomrigh till I am well, who lives but five doors off; and that I may venture.

14. My journals are like to be very diverting, now I cannot

---

[1] See Swift's paper in the *Examiner*, No. 32, and Mrs. Manley's pamphlet, already mentioned.

[2] Presumably Mrs. Johnson's palsy-water (see p. 25).

stir abroad, between accounts of Mr. Harley's mending, and
of my broken shin. I just walked to my neighbour Vanhomrigh at two, and came away at six, when little Harrison
the Tatler came to me, and begged me to dictate a paper to
him, which I was forced in charity to do. Mr. Harley still
mends; and I hope in a day or two to trouble you no more
with him, nor with my shin. Go to bed and sleep, sirrahs,
that you may rise to-morrow and walk to Donnybrook, and
lose your money with Stoyte and the Dean; do so, dear little
rogues, and drink Presto's health. O pray, don't you drink
Presto's health sometimes with your deans, and your Stoytes,
and your Walls, and your Manleys, and your everybodies,
pray now? I drink MD's to myself a hundred thousand times.

15. I was this morning at Mr. Secretary St. John's for all
my shin; and he has given me for young Harrison the Tatler
the prettiest employment in Europe; secretary to my Lord
Raby,[1] who is to be Ambassador Extraordinary at the Hague,
where all the great affairs will be concerted; so we shall lose
the *Tatlers* in a fortnight. I will send Harrison to-morrow
morning to thank the Secretary. Poor Biddy Floyd[2] has got
the smallpox. I called this morning to see Lady Betty
Germaine, and when she told me so, I fairly took my leave.
I have the luck of it;[3] for about ten days ago I was to see
Lord Carteret;[4] and my lady was entertaining me with
telling of a young lady, a cousin, who was then ill in the
house of the smallpox, and is since dead: it was near Lady
Betty's, and I fancy Biddy took the fright by it. I dined

---

[1] Thomas Wentworth, Baron Raby (1672-1739), was created Viscount
Wentworth and Earl of Strafford in June 1711. Lord Raby was Envoy and
Ambassador at Berlin for some years, and was appointed Ambassador at the
Hague in March 1711. In November he was nominated as Joint Plenipotentiary with the Bishop of Bristol to negotiate the terms of peace. He objected to
Prior as a colleague; Swift says he was "as proud as hell." In 1715 it was
proposed to impeach Strafford, but the proceedings were dropped. In his
later years he was, according to Lord Hervey, a loquacious and illiterate, but
constant, speaker in the House of Lords.
[2] A beauty, to whom Swift addressed verses in 1708. During the frost of
January 1709 Swift wrote: "Mrs. Floyd looked out with both her eyes, and we
had one day's thaw; but she drew in her head, and it now freezes as hard as
ever." She was a great friend of Lady Betty Germaine's.
[3] Swift never had the smallpox. [4] See p. 116.

with Mr. Secretary; and a physician came in just from Guiscard, who tells us he is dying of his wounds, and can hardly live till to-morrow. A poor wench that Guiscard kept, sent him a bottle of sack; but the keeper would not let him touch it, for fear it was poison. He had two quarts of old clotted blood come out of his side to-day, and is delirious. I am sorry he is dying; for they had found out a way to hang him. He certainly had an intention to murder the Queen.

16. I have made but little progress in this letter for so many days, thanks to Guiscard and Mr. Harley; and it would be endless to tell you all the particulars of that odious fact. I do not yet hear that Guiscard is dead, but they say 'tis impossible he should recover. I walked too much yesterday for a man with a broken shin; to-day I rested, and went no farther than Mrs. Vanhomrigh's, where I dined; and Lady Betty Butler coming in about six, I was forced in good manners to sit with her till nine; then I came home, and Mr. Ford came in to visit my shin, and sat with me till eleven: so I have been very idle and naughty. It vexes me to the pluck[1] that I should lose walking this delicious day. Have you seen the *Spectator*[2] yet, a paper that comes out every day? 'Tis written by Mr. Steele, who seems to have gathered new life, and have a new fund of wit; it is in the same nature as his *Tatlers*, and they have all of them had something pretty. I believe Addison and he club. I never see them; and I plainly told Mr. Harley and Mr. St. John, ten days ago, before my Lord Keeper and Lord Rivers, that I had been foolish enough to spend my credit with them in favour of Addison and Steele; but that I would engage and promise never to say one word in their behalf, having been used so ill for what I had already done.—So, now I am got into the way of prating again, there will be no quiet for me.

> When Presto begins to prate,
> Give him a rap upon the pate.

O Lord, how I blot! it is time to leave off, etc.

---

[1] Heart.
[2] The first number of the *Spectator* appeared on March 1, 1711.

17. Guiscard died this morning at two; and the coroner's inquest have found that he was killed by bruises received from a messenger, so to clear the Cabinet Councillors from whom he received his wounds. I had a letter from Raymond, who cannot hear of your box; but I hope you have it before this comes to your hands. I dined to-day with Mr. Lewis of the Secretary's office. Mr. Harley has abundance of extravasated blood comes from his breast out of his wound, and will not be well so soon as we expected. I had something to say, but cannot call it to mind. (What was it?)

18. I was to-day at Court to look for the Duke of Argyle, and gave him the memorial about Bernage. The Duke goes with the first fair wind. I could not find him, but I have given the memorial to another to give him; and, however, it shall be sent after him. Bernage has made a blunder in offering money to his colonel without my advice; however, he is made captain-lieutenant, only he must recruit the company, which will cost him forty pounds, and that is cheaper than an hundred. I dined to-day with Mr. Secretary St. John, and stayed till seven, but would not drink his champagne and burgundy, for fear of the gout. My shin mends, but is not well. I hope it will by the time I send this letter, next Saturday.

19. I went to-day into the City, but in a coach, and sossed [1] up my leg on the seat; and as I came home, I went to see poor Charles Barnard's [2] books, which are to be sold by auction, and I itch to lay out nine or ten pounds for some fine editions of fine authors. But 'tis too far, and I shall let it slip, as I usually do all such opportunities. I dined in a coffee-house with Stratford upon chops and some of his wine. Where did MD dine? Why, poor MD dined at home to-day, because of the Archbishop, and they could not go abroad, and had a breast of mutton and a pint of wine. I hope Mrs. Walls mends; and pray give me an account what sort of godfather I made, and whether I behaved myself handsomely.

[1] In one of his poems Swift speaks of Stella "sossing in an easy-chair."
[2] See p. 21.

The Duke of Argyle is gone; and whether he has my memorial, I know not, till I see Dr. Arbuthnot,[1] to whom I gave it. That hard name belongs to a Scotch doctor, an acquaintance of the Duke's and me; Stella can't pronounce it. Oh that we were at Laracor this fine day! the willows begin to peep, and the quicks to bud. My dream is out: I was a-dreamed last night that I ate ripe cherries.—And now they begin to catch the pikes, and will shortly the trouts (pox on these Ministers!)—and I would fain know whether the floods were ever so high as to get over the holly bank or the river walk; if so, then all my pikes are gone; but I hope not. Why don't you ask Parvisol these things, sirrahs? And then my canal, and trouts, and whether the bottom be fine and clear? But harkee, ought not Parvisol to pay in my last year's rents and arrears out of his hands? I am thinking, if either of you have heads to take his accounts, it should be paid in to you; otherwise to Mr. Walls. I will write an order on t'other side; and do as you will. Here's a world of business; but I must go sleep, I'm drowsy; and so good-night, etc.

20. This sore shin ruins me in coach-hire; no less than two shillings to-day going and coming from the City, where I dined with one you never heard of, and passed an insipid day. I writ this post to Bernage, with the account I told you above. I hope he will like it; 'tis his own fault, or it would have been better. I reckon your next letter will be full of Mr. Harley's stabbing. He still mends, but abundance of extravasated blood has come out of the wound: he keeps his bed, and sees nobody. The Speaker's eldest son[2] is just dead of the smallpox, and the House is adjourned a week, to

---

[1] "It is reasonable to suppose that Swift's acquaintance with Arbuthnot commenced just about this time; for in the original letter Swift misspells his name, and writes it Arthbuthnet, in a clear large hand, that MD might not mistake any of the letters" (Deane Swift). Dr. John Arbuthnot had been made Physician in Ordinary to the Queen; he was one of Swift's dearest friends.

[2] Clobery Bromley, M.P. for Coventry, son of William Bromley, M.P. (see p. 76), died on March 20, 1711, and Boyer (*Political State*, i. 255) says that the House, "out of respect to the father, and to give him time, both to perform the funeral rites and to indulge his just affliction," adjourned until the 26th.

give him time to wipe off his tears. I think it very handsomely done; but I believe one reason is, that they want Mr. Harley so much. Biddy Floyd is like to do well: and so go to your Dean's, and roast his oranges, and lose your money, do so, you saucy sluts. Stella, you lost three shillings and fourpence t'other night at Stoyte's, yes, you did, and Presto stood in a corner, and saw you all the while, and then stole away. I dream very often I am in Ireland, and that I have left my clothes and things behind me, and have not taken leave of anybody; and that the Ministry expect me tomorrow, and such nonsense.

21. I would not for a guinea have a letter from you till this goes; and go it shall on Saturday, faith. I dined with Mrs. Vanhomrigh, to save my shin, and then went on some business to the Secretary, and he was not at home.

22. Yesterday was a short day's journal: but what care I? what cares saucy Presto? Darteneuf[1] invited me to dinner to-day. Do not you know Darteneuf? That's the man that knows everything, and that everybody knows; and that knows where a knot of rabble are going on a holiday, and when they were there last: and then I went to the Coffee-house. My shin mends, but is not quite healed: I ought to keep it up, but I don't; I e'en let it go as it comes. Pox take Parvisol and his watch! If I do not receive the ten-pound bill I am to get towards it, I will neither receive watch nor chain; so let Parvisol know.

23. I this day appointed the Duke of Ormond to meet him at Ned Southwell's, about an affair of printing Irish Prayer-Books, etc.,[2] but the Duke never came. There Southwell had letters that two packets are taken; so if MD writ then, the letters are gone; for they are packets coming hither. Mr. Harley is not yet well, but his extravasated blood continues, and I doubt he will not be quite well in a good while: I find you have heard of the fact by Southwell's letters from Ireland: what do you think of it? I dined with

[1] See p. 23. [2] See p. 163.

Sir John Perceval,[1] and saw his lady sitting in the bed, in the forms of a lying-in woman; and coming home my sore shin itched, and I forgot what it was, and rubbed off the scab, and blood came; but I am now got into bed, and have put on alum curd, and it is almost well. Lord Rivers told me yesterday a piece of bad news, as a secret, that the Pretender is going to be married to the Duke of Savoy's daughter.[2] 'Tis very bad if it be true. We were walking in the Mall with some Scotch lords, and he could not tell it until they were gone, and he bade me tell it to none but the Secretary of State and MD. This goes tomorrow, and I have no room but to bid my dearest little MD good-night.

24. I will now seal up this letter, and send it; for I reckon to have none from you ('tis morning now) between this and night; and I will put it in the post with my own hands. I am going out in great haste; so farewell, etc.

LETTER XIX

LONDON, *March* 24, 1710-11.

IT was a little cross in Presto not to send to-day to the Coffee-house to see whether there was a letter from MD before I sent away mine; but, faith, I did it on purpose, because I would scorn to answer two letters of yours successively. This way of journal is the worst in the world for writing of news, unless one does it the last day; and so I will observe henceforward, if there be any politics or stuff worth sending. My shin mends in spite of the scratching last night. I dined to-day at Ned Southwell's with the

[1] Sir John Perceval, Bart. (died 1748), was created Baron Perceval 1715, Viscount Perceval 1722, and Earl of Egmont 1733, all in the Irish peerage. He married, in 1710, Catherine, eldest daughter of Sir Philip Parker A'Morley, Bart., of Erwarton, Suffolk; and his son (born Feb. 27, 1710-11) was made Baron Perceval and Holland, in the English peerage, in 1762.

[2] This report was false. The Old Pretender did not marry until 1718, when he was united to the Princess Clementina Maria, daughter of Prince James Sobieski.

Bishop of Ossory[1] and a parcel of Irish gentlemen. Have
you yet seen any of the *Spectators*? Just three weeks to-day
since I had your last, N. 11. I am afraid I have lost one by
the packet that was taken; that will vex me, considering
the pains MD take to write, especially poor pretty Stella, and
her weak eyes. God bless them and the owner, and send
them well, and little me together, I hope ere long. This
illness of Mr. Harley puts everything backwards, and he is
still down, and like to be so, by that extravasated blood
which comes from his breast to the wound: it was by the
second blow Guiscard gave him after the penknife was
broken. I am shocked at that villainy whenever I think of
it. Biddy Floyd is past danger, but will lose all her beauty:
she had them mighty thick, especially about her nose.

25. Morning. I wish you a merry New Year; this is the
first day of the year, you know, with us, and 'tis Lady-day.
I must rise and go to my Lord Keeper: it is not shaving-day
to-day, so I shall be early. I am to dine with Mr. Secretary
St. John. Good-morrow, my mistresses both, good-morrow.
Stella will be peeping out of her room at Mrs. De Caudres'[2]
down upon the folks as they come from church; and there
comes Mrs. Proby,[3] and that is my Lady Southwell,[4] and
there is Lady Betty Rochfort.[5] I long to hear how you are

---

[1] John Hartstonge, D.D. (died 1717), was Bishop of Ossory from 1693 to
1714, when he was translated to Derry.

[2] See p. 145.

[3] Thomas Proby was Chirurgeon-General in Ireland from 1699 until his death
in 1761. In his *Short Character of Thomas, Earl of Wharton*, Swift speaks of
him as "a person universally esteemed," who had been badly treated by Lord
Wharton. In 1724 Proby's son, a captain in the army, was accused of
popery, and Swift wrote to Lord Carteret that the charge was generally
believed to be false: "The father is the most universally beloved of any man I
ever knew in his station. . . . You cannot do any personal thing more acceptable
to the people of Ireland than in inclining towards lenity to Mr. Proby and his
family." Proby was probably a near relative of Sir Thomas Proby, Bart.,
M.P., of Elton, Hunts, at whose death in 1689 the baronetcy expired. Mrs.
Proby seems to have been a Miss Spencer.

[4] Meliora, daughter of Thomas Coningsby, Baron of Clanbrassil and Earl
of Coningsby, and wife of Sir Thomas Southwell, afterwards Baron Southwell,
one of the Commissioners of Revenue in Ireland, and a member of the Irish
Privy Council. Lady Southwell died in 1736.

[5] Lady Betty Rochfort was the daughter of Henry Moore, third Earl of
Drogheda. Her husband, George Rochfort, M.P. for Westmeath, was son of

settled in your new lodgings. I wish I were rid of my old ones, and that Mrs. Brent could contrive to put up my books in boxes, and lodge them in some safe place, and you keep my papers of importance. But I must rise, I tell you.—At night. So I visited and dined as I told you, and what of that? We have let Guiscard be buried at last, after showing him pickled in a trough this fortnight for twopence apiece: and the fellow that showed would point to his body, and, "See, gentlemen, this is the wound that was given him by his Grace the Duke of Ormond; and this is the wound," etc., and then the show was over, and another set of rabble came in. 'Tis hard our laws would not suffer us to hang his body in chains, because he was not tried; and in the eye of our law every man is innocent till then.—Mr. Harley is still very weak, and never out of bed.

26. This was a most delicious day; and my shin being past danger, I walked like lightning above two hours in the Park. We have generally one fair day, and then a great deal of rain for three or four days together. All things are at a stop in Parliament for want of Mr. Harley; they cannot stir an inch without him in their most material affairs: and we fear, by the caprice of Radcliffe, who will admit none but his own surgeon,[1] he has not been well looked after. I dined at an alehouse with Mr. Lewis, but had his wine. Don't you begin to see the flowers and blossoms of the field? How busy should I be now at Laracor! No news of your box? I hope you have it, and are this minute drinking the chocolate, and that the smell of the Brazil tobacco has not affected it. I would be glad to know whether you like it, because I would send you more by people that are now every day thinking of going to Ireland; therefore pray tell me, and tell me soon: and I will have the strong box.

27. A rainy, wretched, scurvy day from morning till night:

Robert Rochfort, an Irish judge, and brother of Robert Rochfort, M.P., to whose wife Swift addressed his *Advice to a very Young Lady on her Marriage*. Lady Betty's son Robert was created Earl of Belvedere in 1757.

[1] See p. 166. Mr. Bussière, of Suffolk Street, had been called in directly after the outrage, but Radcliffe would not consult with him.

12

and my neighbour Vanhomrigh invited me to dine with them: and this evening I passed at Mr. Prior's with Dr. Freind; and 'tis now past twelve, so I must go sleep.

28. Morning.　O, faith, you're an impudent saucy couple of sluttikins for presuming to write so soon, said I to myself this morning; who knows but there may be a letter from MD at the Coffee-house? Well, you must know, and so, I just now sent Patrick, and he brought me three letters, but not one from MD, no indeed, for I read all the superscriptions; and not one from MD.　One I opened, it was from the Archbishop;[1] t'other I opened, it was from Staunton;[2] the third I took, and looked at the hand.　Whose hand is this? says I; yes, says I, whose hand is this?　Then there was wax between the folds; then I began to suspect; then I peeped; faith, it was Walls's hand after all: then I opened it in a rage, and then it was little MD's hand, dear, little, pretty, charming MD's sweet hand again.　O Lord, an't here a clutter and a stir, and a bustle? never saw the like.　Faith, I believe yours lay some days at the post-office, and that it came before my eighteenth went, but that I did not expect it, and I hardly ever go there.　Well, and so you think I'll answer this letter now; no, faith, and so I won't.　I'll make you wait, young women; but I'll inquire immediately about poor Dingley's exchequer trangum.[3]　What, is that Vedel again a soldier? was he broke? I'll put it in Ben Tooke's hand. I hope Vedel could not sell it.—At night.　Vedel, Vedel, poh, pox, I think it is Vedeau;[4] ay, Vedeau, now I have it; let me see, do you name him in yours? Yes, Mr. John Vedeau is the brother; but where does this brother live? I'll inquire.　This was a fast-day for the public; so I dined late with Sir Matthew Dudley, whom I have not been with a

---

[1] The letter from Dr. King dated March 17, 1711, commenting on Guiscard's attack upon Harley.

[2] See p. 147.

[3] The word "trangram" or "tangram" ordinarily means a toy or gimcrack, or trumpery article. Cf. Wycherley (*Plain Dealer*, iii. 1), "But go, thou trangram, and carry back those trangrams which thou hast stolen or purloined." Apparently "trangum" here means a tally.

[4] See p. 104.

great while. He is one of those that must lose his employment whenever the great shake comes; and I can't contribute
to keep him in, though I have dropped words in his favour
to the Ministry; but he is too violent a Whig, and friend to
the Lord Treasurer,[1] to stay in. 'Tis odd to think how long
they let those people keep their places; but the reason is,
they have not enough to satisfy all expecters, and so they
keep them all in hopes, that they may be good boys in the
meantime; and thus the old ones hold in still. The Comptroller[2] told me that there are eight people expect his staff.
I walked after dinner to-day round the Park. What, do I
write politics to little young women? Hold your tongue, and
go to your Dean's.

29. Morning. If this be a fine day, I will walk into the
City, and see Charles Barnard's library. What care I for your
letter, saucy N. 12? I will say nothing to it yet: faith, I
believe this will be full before its time, and then go it must.
I will always write once a fortnight; and if it goes sooner by
filling sooner, why, then there is so much clear gain. Morrow,
morrow, rogues and lasses both, I can't lie scribbling here in
bed for your play; I must rise, and so morrow again.—At
night. Your friend Montgomery and his sister are here, as I
am told by Patrick. I have seen him often, but take no
notice of him: he is grown very ugly and pimpled. They
tell me he is a gamester, and wins money.—How could I
help it, pray? Patrick snuffed the candle too short, and the
grease ran down upon the paper.[3] It an't my fault, 'tis
Patrick's fault; pray now don't blame Presto. I walked to-
day in the City, and dined at a private house, and went to
see the auction of poor Charles Barnard's books; they were
in the middle of the physic books, so I bought none; and
they are so dear, I believe I shall buy none, and there is an
end; and go to Stoyte's, and I'll go sleep.

---

[1] Swift means Godolphin, the late Lord Treasurer.
[2] Sir John Holland (see p. 11).
[3] "It caused a violent daub on the paper, which still continues much dis-
coloured in the original" (Deane Swift).

30. Morning. This is Good Friday, you must know; and I must rise and go to Mr. Secretary about some business, and Mrs. Vanhomrigh desires me to breakfast with her, because she is to intercede for Patrick, who is so often drunk and quarrelsome in the house, that I was resolved to send him over; but he knows all the places where I send, and is so used to my ways, that it would be inconvenient to me; but when I come to Ireland, I will discharge him.[1] Sir Thomas Mansel,[2] one of the Lords of the Treasury, setting me down at my door to-day, saw Patrick, and swore he was a Teague-lander.[3] I am so used to his face, I never observed it, but thought him a pretty fellow. Sir Andrew Fountaine and I supped this fast - day with Mrs. Vanhomrigh. We were afraid Mr. Harley's wound would turn to a fistula; but we think the danger is now past. He rises every day, and walks about his room, and we hope he will be out in a fortnight. Prior showed me a handsome paper of verses he has writ on Mr. Harley's accident:[4] they are not out; I will send them to you, if he will give me a copy.

31. Morning. What shall we do to make April fools this year, now it happens on Sunday? Patrick brings word that Mr. Harley still mends, and is up every day. I design to see him in a few days: and he brings me word too that he has found out Vedeau's brother's shop: I shall call there in a day or two. It seems the wife lodges next door to the brother. I doubt the scoundrel was broke, and got a commission, or perhaps is a volunteer gentleman, and expects to get one by his valour. Morrow, sirrahs, let me rise.—At night. I dined to-day with Sir Thomas Mansel. We were walking in the Park, and Mr. Lewis came to us. Mansel asked where we dined. We said, "Together." He said, we should dine

---

[1] "He forgot here to say, 'At night.' See what goes before" (Deane Swift).
[2] See p. 158.
[3] Irishman. "Teague" was a term of contempt for an Irishman.
[4] *To Mr. Harley, wounded by Guiscard.* In this piece Prior said, "Britain with tears shall bathe thy glorious wound," a wound which could not have been inflicted by any but a stranger to our land.

with him, only his wife[1] desired him to bring nobody, because she had only a leg of mutton. I said I would dine with him to choose; but he would send a servant to order a plate or two: yet this man has ten thousand pounds a year in land, and is a Lord of the Treasury, and is not covetous neither, but runs out merely by slattering[2] and negligence. The worst dinner I ever saw at the Dean's was better: but so it is with abundance of people here. I called at night at Mr. Harley's, who begins to walk in his room with a stick, but is mighty weak.—See how much I have lost with that ugly grease.[3] 'Tis your fault, pray; and I'll go to bed.

April 1. The Duke of Buckingham's house fell down last night with an earthquake, and is half swallowed up; won't you go and see it?—An April fool, an April fool, oh ho, young women. Well, don't be angry. I will make you an April fool no more till the next time; we had no sport here, because it is Sunday, and Easter Sunday. I dined with the Secretary, who seemed terribly down and melancholy, which Mr. Prior and Lewis observed as well as I: perhaps something is gone wrong; perhaps there is nothing in it. God bless my own dearest MD, and all is well.

2. We have such windy weather, 'tis troublesome walking, yet all the rabble have got into our Park these Easter holidays. I am plagued with one Richardson, an Irish parson, and his project of printing Irish Bibles, etc., to make you Christians in that country: I befriend him what I can, on account of the Archbishop and Bishop of Clogher.—But what business have I to meddle, etc. Do not you remember that, sirrah Stella? what was that about, when you thought I was meddling with something that was not my business? O, faith, you are an impudent slut, I remember your doings, I'll never forget you as long as I live. Lewis and I dined together at his lodgings. But where's the answer to this

[1] Sir Thomas Mansel married Martha, daughter and heiress of Francis Millington, a London merchant.
[2] Slatterning, consuming carelessly.
[3] "The candle grease mentioned before, which soaked through, deformed this part of the paper on the second page" (Deane Swift).

letter of MD's?   O, faith, Presto, you must think of that.
Time enough, says saucy Presto.

3. I was this morning to see Mrs. Barton: I love her better
than anybody here, and see her seldomer.   Why, really now,
so it often happens in the world, that where one loves a body
best—pshah, pshah, you are so silly with your moral observations.   Well, but she told me a very good story.   An old
gentlewoman died here two months ago, and left in her will,
to have eight men and eight maids bearers, who should have
two guineas apiece, ten guineas to the parson for a sermon,
and two guineas to the clerk.   But bearers, parson, and clerk
must be all true virgins; and not to be admitted till they
took their oaths of virginity: so the poor woman still lies
unburied, and so must do till the general resurrection.—I
called at Mr. Secretary's, to see what the D—— ailed him on
Sunday. I made him a very proper speech; told him I
observed he was much out of temper; that I did not expect
he would tell me the cause, but would be glad to see he was
in better; and one thing I warned him of, never to appear
cold to me, for I would not be treated like a schoolboy;
that I had felt too much of that in my life already (meaning
from Sir William Temple); that I expected every great
Minister who honoured me with his acquaintance, if he heard
or saw anything to my disadvantage, would let me know it
in plain words, and not put me in pain to guess by the change
or coldness of his countenance or behaviour; for it was what
I would hardly bear from a crowned head, and I thought no
subject's favour was worth it; and that I designed to let my
Lord Keeper[1] and Mr. Harley know the same thing, that they
might use me accordingly. He took all right; said I had reason;
vowed nothing ailed him but sitting up whole nights at business,
and one night at drinking; would have had me dine with him
and Mrs. Masham's brother, to make up matters; but I would
not. I don't know, but I would not. But indeed I was engaged
with my old friend Rollinson;[2] you never heard of him before.

[1] Harcourt.
[2] William Rollinson, formerly a wine merchant, settled afterwards in

4. I sometimes look a line or two back, and see plaguy mistakes of the pen; how do you get over them? You are puzzled sometimes. Why, I think what I said to Mr. Secretary was right. Don't you remember how I used to be in pain when Sir William Temple would look cold and out of humour for three or four days, and I used to suspect a hundred reasons? I have plucked up my spirit since then, faith; he spoilt a fine gentleman. I dined with my neighbour Vanhomrigh, and MD, poor MD, at home on a loin of mutton and half a pint of wine, and the mutton was raw, poor Stella could not eat, poor dear rogue, and Dingley was so vexed; but we will dine at Stoyte's to-morrow. Mr. Harley promised to see me in a day or two, so I called this evening; but his son and others were abroad, and he asleep, so I came away, and found out Mrs. Vedeau. She drew out a letter from Dingley, and said she would get a friend to receive the money. I told her I would employ Mr. Tooke in it henceforward. Her husband bought a lieutenancy of foot, and is gone to Portugal. He sold his share of the shop to his brother, and put out the money to maintain her, all but what bought the commission. She lodges within two doors of her brother. She told me it made her very melancholy to change her manner of life thus, but trade was dead, etc. She says she will write to you soon. I design to engage Ben Tooke, and then receive the parchment from her.—I gave Mr. Dopping a copy of Prior's verses on Mr. Harley; he sent them yesterday to Ireland, so go look for them, for I won't be at the trouble to transcribe them here. They will be printed in a day or two. Give my hearty service to Stoyte and Catherine: upon my word I love them dearly, and desire you will tell them so: pray desire Goody Stoyte not to let Mrs. Walls and Mrs. Johnson cheat her of her money at ombre, but assure her from me that she is a bungler. Dine with her to-day, and tell her so, and drink my health, and good voyage, and speedy return, and so you're a rogue.

Oxfordshire, where he died at a great age. He was a friend of Pope, Bolingbroke, and Gay.

5. Morning. Now let us proceed to examine a saucy letter
from one Madam MD.—God Almighty bless poor dear Stella,
and send her a great many birthdays, all happy, and healthy,
and wealthy, and with me ever together, and never asunder
again, unless by chance. When I find you are happy or
merry there, it makes me so here, and I can hardly imagine
you absent when I am reading your letter, or writing to you.
No, faith, you are just here upon this little paper, and therefore I see and talk with you every evening constantly, and
sometimes in the morning, but not always in the morning,
because that is not so modest to young ladies.—What, you
would fain palm a letter on me more than you sent: and I,
like a fool, must look over all yours, to see whether this was
really N. 12, or more. [Patrick has this moment brought me
letters from the Bishop of Clogher and Parvisol; my heart
was at my mouth for fear of one from MD; what a disgrace
would it be to have two of yours to answer together! But,
faith, this shall go to-night, for fear; and then come when it
will, I defy it.] No, you are not naughty at all, write when
you are disposed. And so the Dean told you the story of Mr.
Harley from the Archbishop; I warrant it never spoiled your
supper, or broke off your game. Nor yet, have not you the
box? I wish Mrs. Edgworth had the ———. But you have it
now, I suppose; and is the chocolate good, or has the tobacco
spoilt it? Leigh stays till Sterne has done his business, no
longer; and when that will be, God knows: I befriend him
as much as I can, but Harley's accident stops that as well as
all things else. You guess, Madam Dingley, that I shall
stay a round twelvemonth; as hope saved, I would come over,
if I could, this minute; but we will talk of that by and by.—
Your affair of Vedeau I have told you of already; now to the
next, turn over the leaf. Mrs. Dobbins lies, I have no more
provision here or in Ireland than I had. I am pleased that
Stella the conjurer approves what I did with Mr. Harley;[1]
but your generosity makes me mad; I know you repine
inwardly at Presto's absence; you think he has broken his

[1] In relation to the banknote (see p. 163).

word of coming in three months, and that this is always his
trick; and now Stella says she does not see possibly how I
can come away in haste, and that MD is satisfied, etc. An't
you a rogue to overpower me thus? I did not expect to find
such friends as I have done. They may indeed deceive me
too. But there are important reasons [Pox on this grease,
this candle tallow!] why they should not.[1] I have been used
barbarously by the late Ministry; I am a little piqued in
honour to let people see I am not to be despised. The
assurances they give me, without any scruple or provocation,
are such as are usually believed in the world; they may come
to nothing, but the first opportunity that offers, and is
neglected, I shall depend no more, but come away. I could
say a thousand things on this head, if I were with you. I
am thinking why Stella should not go to the Bath, if she be
told it will do her good. I will make Parvisol get up fifty
pounds, and pay it you; and you may be good housewives,
and live cheap there some months, and return in autumn,
or visit London, as you please: pray think of it. I writ to
Bernage, directed to Curry's; I wish he had the letter. I
will send the bohea tea, if I can. The Bishop of Kilmore,[2] I
don't keep such company; an old dying fool whom I never
was with in my life. So I am no godfather;[3] all the better.
Pray, Stella, explain those two words of yours to me, what
you mean by *villian* and *dainger*;[4] and you, Madam Dingley,
what is *christianing*? — Lay your letter *this way, this way,*
and the devil a bit of difference between this way and the
other way. No; I will show you, lay them *this way, this
way,* and not *that way, that way.*[5] — You shall have your
aprons; and I will put all your commissions as they come, in
a paper together, and do not think I will forget MD's orders,
because they are friends; I will be as careful as if they were

[1] "Swift was, at this time, their great support and champion" (Deane Swift).
[2] See p. 134.　　　　　　　　　　[3] See p. 167.
[4] "Stella, with all her wit and good sense, spelled very ill; and Dr. Swift
insisted greatly upon women spelling well" (Deane Swift).
[5] "The slope of the letters in the words *this way, this way,* is to the left hand,
but the slope of the words *that way, that way,* is to the right hand" (Deane
Swift).

strangers. I knew not what to do about this Clements,[1] Walls will not let me say anything as if Mr. Pratt was against him; and now the Bishop of Clogher has written to me in his behalf. This thing does not rightly fall in my way, and that people never consider: I always give my good offices where they are proper, and that I am judge of; however, I will do what I can. But, if he has the name of a Whig, it will be hard, considering my Lord Anglesea and Hyde[2] are very much otherwise, and you know they have the employment of Deputy Treasurer. If the frolic should take you of going to the Bath, I here send you a note on Parvisol; if not, you may tear it, and there's an end. Farewell.

If you have an imagination that the Bath will do you good, I say again, I would have you go; if not, or it be inconvenient, burn this note. Or, if you would go, and not take so much money, take thirty pounds, and I will return you twenty from hence. Do|as you please, sirrahs. I suppose it will not be too late for the first season; if it be, I would have you resolve however to go the second season, if the doctors say it will do you good, and you fancy so.

LETTER XX

LONDON, *April* 5, 1711.

I PUT my nineteenth in the post-office just now myself, as I came out of the City, where I dined. This rain ruins me in coach-hire; I walked away sixpennyworth, and came within a shilling length, and then took a coach,[3] and got a lift back for nothing; and am now busy.

6. Mr. Secretary desired I would see him this morning; said he had several things to say to me, and said not one; and the Duke of Ormond sent to desire I would meet him at

---

[1] See p. 167.   [2] See pp. 24, 85.
[3] By the Act 9 Anne, cap. 23, the number of hackney coaches was increased to 800, and it was provided that they were to go a mile and a half for one shilling, two miles for one shilling and sixpence, and so on.

Mr. Southwell's by ten this morning too, which I did, thinking it was some particular matter. All the Irish in town were there, to consult upon preventing a Bill for laying a duty on Irish yarn; so we talked a while, and then all went to the lobby of the House of Commons, to solicit our friends, and the Duke came among the rest; and Lord Anglesea solicited admirably, and I did wonders. But, after all, the matter was put off till Monday, and then we are to be at it again. I dined with Lord Mountjoy, and looked over him at chess, which put me in mind of Stella and Griffyth.[1] I came home, and that dog Patrick was not within; so I fretted, and fretted, and what good did that do me?

> And so get you gone to your deans,
> You couple of queans.

I cannot find rhyme to Walls and Stoyte.—Yes, yes,

> You expect Mrs. Walls,
> Be dressed when she calls,
> To carry you to Stoyte,
> Or else *honi soit*.

Henley told me that the Tories were insup-port-able people, because they are for bringing in French claret, and will not *sup-port*. Mr. Harley will hardly get abroad this week or ten days yet. I reckon, when I send away this letter, he will be just got into the House of Commons. My last letter went in twelve days, and so perhaps may this. No it won't, for those letters that go under a fortnight are answers to one of yours, otherwise you must take the days as they happen, some dry, some wet, some barren, some fruitful, some merry, some insipid; some, etc.—I will write you word exactly the first day I see young gooseberries, and pray observe how much later you are. We have not had five fine days this five weeks, but rain or wind. 'Tis a late spring they say here.—Go to bed, you two dear saucy brats, and don't keep me up all night.

7. Ford has been at Epsom, to avoid Good Friday and

---

[1] See p. 95.

Easter Sunday. He forced me to-day to dine with him; and tells me there are letters from Ireland, giving an account of a great indiscretion in the Archbishop of Dublin, who applied a story out of Tacitus very reflectingly on Mr. Harley, and that twenty people have written of it; I do not believe it yet.[1] I called this evening to see Mr. Secretary, who has been very ill with the gravel and pain in his back, by burgundy and champagne, added to the sitting up all night at business; I found him drinking tea while the rest were at champagne, and was very glad of it. I have chid him so severely that I hardly knew whether he would take it well: then I went and sat an hour with Mrs. St. John, who is growing a great favourite of mine; she goes to the Bath on Wednesday, for she is much out of health, and has begged me to take care of the Secretary.

8. I dined to-day with Mr. Secretary St. John; he gave me a letter to read, which was from the publisher of the newspaper called the *Postboy*;[2] in it there was a long copy of a letter from Dublin, giving an account of what the Whigs said upon Mr. Harley's being stabbed, and how much they abuse him and Mr. Secretary St. John; and at the end there were half a dozen lines, telling the story of the Archbishop of Dublin, and abusing him horribly; this was to be printed on Tuesday. I told the Secretary I would not suffer that about the Archbishop to be printed, and so I crossed it out; and afterwards, to prevent all danger, I made him give me the letter, and, upon further thought, would let none of it be published: and I sent for the printer, and told him so, and ordered him, in the Secretary's name, to print

---

[1] In a letter to Swift, of March 17, 1711, King said that it might have been thought that Guiscard's attack would have convinced the world that Harley was not in the French interest; but it did not have that effect with all, for some whispered the case of Fenius Rufus and Scevinus in the 15th book of Tacitus: "Accensis indicibus ad prodendum Fenium Rufum, quem eundem conscium et inquisitorem non tolerabant." Next month Swift told King that it was reported that the Archbishop had applied this passage in a speech made to his clergy, and explained at some length the steps he had taken to prevent the story being published in the *Postboy*. King thanked Swift for this action, explaining that he had been arguing on Harley's behalf when someone instanced the story of Rufus.

[2] A Tory paper, published thrice weekly by Abel Roper.

nothing reflecting on anybody in Ireland till he had showed it me. Thus I have prevented a terrible scandal to the Archbishop, by a piece of perfect good fortune. I will let him know it by next post; and pray, if you pick it out, let me know, and whether he is thankful for it; but say nothing.

9. I was to-day at the House of Commons again about their yarn, at Lord Anglesea's desire; but the business is again put off till Monday. I dined with Sir John Stanley, by an assignation I had made with Mr. St. John, and George Granville, the Secretary at War; but they let in other company, some ladies, and so we were not so easy as I intended. My head is pretty tolerable, but every day I feel some little disorders; I have left off snuff since Sunday, finding myself much worse after taking a good deal at the Secretary's. I would not let him drink one drop of champagne or burgundy without water, and in compliment I did so myself. He is much better; but when he is well, he is like Stella, and will not be governed. So go to your Stoyte's, and I'll go sleep.

10. I have been visiting Lady Worsley and Mrs. Barton to-day, and dined soberly with my friend Lewis. The Dauphin is dead of an apoplexy; I wish he had lived till the finishing of this letter, that it might be news to you. Duncombe,[1] the rich alderman, died to-day, and I hear has left the Duke of Argyle, who married his niece, two hundred thousand pounds; I hope it is true, for I love that Duke mightily. I writ this evening to the Archbishop of Dublin, about what I told you; and then went to take leave of poor Mrs. St. John, who gave me strict charge to take care of the Secretary in her absence; said she had none to trust but me; and the poor creature's tears came fresh in her eyes. Before we took leave, I was drawn in by the other ladies and Sir John Stanley to raffle for a fan, with a pox; it was four guineas, and we put in

[1] Sir Charles Duncombe, banker, died on April 9, 1711. The first wife of the Duke of Argyle (see p. 101) was Duncombe's niece, Mary Browne, daughter of Ursula Duncombe and Thomas Browne, of St. Margaret's, Westminster. Duncombe was elected Lord Mayor in 1700, and was the richest commoner in England.

seven shillings apiece, several raffling for absent people; but
I lost, and so missed an opportunity of showing my gallantry to
Mrs. St. John, whom I designed to have presented it to if I
had won.   Is Dilly[1] gone to the Bath?   His face will whizz
in the water; I suppose he will write to us from thence, and
will take London in his way back.—The rabble will say,
"There goes a drunken parson"; and, which is worse, they
will say true.   Oh, but you must know I carried Ford to dine
with Mr. St. John last Sunday, that he may brag, when he
goes back, of dining with a Secretary of State.   The Secretary
and I went away early, and left him drinking with the rest,
and he told me that two or three of them were drunk.   They
talk of great promotions to be made; that Mr. Harley is to
be Lord Treasurer, and Lord Poulett[2] Master of the Horse, etc.,
but they are only conjecture.   The Speaker is to make Mr.
Harley a compliment the first time he comes into the House,
which I hope will be in a week.   He has had an ill surgeon,
by the caprice of that puppy Dr. Radcliffe, which has kept
him back so long; and yesterday he got a cold, but is better
to-day.—What! I think I am stark mad, to write so much in
one day to little saucy MD; here is a deal of stuff, indeed!
can't you bid those little dear rogues good-night, and let
them go sleep, Mr. Presto?   When your tongue runs there's
no ho with you, pray.

11. Again at the lobby (like a lobcock)[3] of the House of
Commons, about your Irish yarn, and again put off till Friday;
and I and Patrick went into the City by water, where I dined,
and then I went to the auction of Charles Barnard's books;
but the good ones were so monstrous dear, I could not reach
them, so I laid out one pound seven shillings but very
indifferently, and came away, and will go there no more.
Henley would fain engage me to go with Steele and Rowe,

---

[1] The Rev. Dillon Ashe (see p. 117).
[2] John, fourth Baron Poulett, was created Earl Poulett in 1706, after serving
as one of the Commissioners for the Treaty of Union with Scotland.   From
August 1710 to May 1711 he was First Lord of the Treasury, and from June
1711 to August 1714 he was Lord Steward of the Household.
[3] Lost or stupid person.

etc., to an invitation at Sir William Read's.[1] Surely you have heard of him. He has been a mountebank, and is the Queen's oculist; he makes admirable punch, and treats you in gold vessels. But I am engaged, and will not go, neither indeed am I fond of the jaunt. So good-night, and go sleep.

12. I went about noon to the Secretary, who is very ill with a cold, and sometimes of the gravel, with his champagne, etc. I scolded him like a dog, and he promises faithfully more care for the future. To-day my Lord Anglesea, and Sir Thomas Hanmer, and Prior, and I dined, by appointment, with Lieutenant-General Webb.[2] My lord and I stayed till ten o'clock; but we drank soberly, and I always with water. There was with us one Mr. Campain,[3] one of the October Club, if you know what that is; a Club of country members, who think the Ministers are too backward in punishing and turning out the Whigs. I found my lord and the rest thought I had more credit with the Ministry than I pretend to have, and would have engaged me to put them upon something that would satisfy their desires, and indeed I think they have some reason to complain; however, I will not burn my fingers. I will remember Stella's chiding, "What had you to do with what did not belong to you?" etc. However, you will give me leave to tell the Ministry my thoughts when they ask them, and other people's thoughts sometimes when they do not ask; so thinks Dingley.

13. I called this morning at Mrs. Vedeau's again, who has employed a friend to get the money; it will be done in a

---

[1] Sir William Read, a quack who advertised largely in the *Tatler* and other papers. He was satirised in No. 547 of the *Spectator*. In 1705 he was knighted for his services in curing many seamen and soldiers of blindness gratis, and he was appointed Oculist in Ordinary to the Queen. Read died in 1715, but his business was continued by his widow.

[2] General John Webb was not on good terms with Marlborough. He was a Tory, and had gained distinction in the war at Wynendale (1708), though the Duke's secretary gave the credit, in the despatch, to Cadogan. There is a well-known account of Webb in Thackeray's *Esmond*. He was severely wounded at Malplaquet in 1709, and in 1710 was given the governorship of the Isle of Wight. He died in 1724.

[3] Henry Campion, M.P. for Penryn, is mentioned in the *Political State* for February 1712 as one of the leading men of the October Club. Campion seems to have been Member, not for Penryn, but for Bossiney.

fortnight, and then she will deliver me up the parchment.   I
went then to see Mr. Harley, who I hope will be out in a few
days; he was in excellent good humour, only complained to
me of the neglect of Guiscard's cure, how glad he would have
been to have had him live.   Mr. Secretary came in to us, and
we were very merry till Lord Chamberlain (Duke of Shrewsbury)[1] came up; then Colonel Masham and I went off, after
I had been presented to the Duke, and that we made two or
three silly compliments suitable to the occasion.   Then I
attended at the House of Commons about your yarn, and it
is again put off.   Then Ford drew me to dine at a tavern; it
happened to be the day and the house where the October
Club dine.   After we had dined, coming down we called to
inquire whether our yarn business had been over that day,
and I sent into the room for Sir George Beaumont.[2]   But I
had like to be drawn into a difficulty; for in two minutes out
comes Mr. Finch,[3] Lord Guernsey's son, to let me know that
my Lord Compton,[4] the steward of this feast, desired, in the
name of the Club, that I would do them the honour to dine
with them.   I sent my excuses, adorned with about thirty
compliments, and got off as fast as I could.   It would have
been a most improper thing for me to dine there, considering
my friendship with the Ministry.   The Club is about a hundred
and fifty, and near eighty of them were then going to dinner
at two long tables in a great ground-room.   At evening I
went to the auction of Barnard's books, and laid out three
pounds three shillings, but I'll go there no more; and so I
said once before, but now I'll keep to it.   I forgot to tell
that when I dined at Webb's with Lord Anglesea, I spoke to
him of Clements, as one recommended for a very honest

[1] See p. 12.
[2] Sir George Beaumont, Bart., M.P. for Leicester, and an acquaintance of
Swift's mother, was made a Commissioner of the Privy Seal in 1712, and one
of the Lords of the Admiralty in 1714.   He died in 1737.
[3] Heneage Finch, afterwards second Earl of Aylesford, was the son of
Heneage Finch, the chief counsel for the seven bishops, who was created Baron
Guernsey in 1703, and Earl of Aylesford in 1714.
[4] James, Lord Compton, afterwards fifth Earl of Northampton, was the
eldest son of George, the fourth Earl.   He was summoned to the House of
Lords in December 1711, and died in 1754.

gentleman and good officer, and hoped he would keep him. He said he had not thought otherwise, and that he should certainly hold his place while he continued to deserve it; and I could not find there had been any intentions from his lordship against him. But I tell you, hunny, the impropriety of this. A great man will do a favour for me, or for my friend; but why should he do it for my friend's friend? Recommendations should stop before they come to that. Let any friend of mine recommend one of his to me for a thing in my power, I will do it for his sake; but to speak to another for my friend's friend is against all reason; and I desire you will understand this, and discourage any such troubles given me.—I hope this may do some good to Clements, it can do him no hurt; and I find by Mrs. Pratt,[1] that her husband is his friend; and the Bishop of Clogher says Clements's danger is not from Pratt, but from some other enemies, that think him a Whig.

14. I was so busy this morning that I did not go out till late. I writ to-day to the Duke of Argyle, but said nothing of Bernage, who, I believe, will not see him till Spain is conquered, and that is, not at all. I was to-day at Lord Shelburne's, and spoke to Mrs. Pratt again about Clements; her husband himself wants some good offices, and I have done him very good ones lately, and told Mrs. Pratt I expected her husband should stand by Clements in return. Sir Andrew Fountaine and I dined with neighbour Vanhomrigh; he is mighty ill of an asthma, and apprehends himself in much danger; 'tis his own fault, that will rake and drink, when he is but just crawled out of his grave. I will send this letter just now, because I think my half-year is out for my lodging; and, if you please, I would be glad it were paid off, and some deal boxes made for my books, and kept in some safe place. I would give something for their keeping: but I doubt that lodging will not serve me when I come back; I would have a larger place for books, and a stable, if possible. So pray be so kind to pay the lodging, and all accounts about it; and

[1] See p. 89.

13

get Mrs. Brent to put up my things.   I would have no books put in that trunk where my papers are.   If you do not think of going to the Bath, I here send you a bill on Parvisol for twenty pounds Irish, out of which you will pay for the lodging, and score the rest to me.   Do as you please, and love poor Presto, that loves MD better than his life a thousand millions of times.   Farewell, MD, etc. etc.

LETTER XXI

LONDON, *April* 14, 1711.

REMEMBER, sirrahs, that there are but nine days between the dates of my two former letters.   I sent away my twentieth this moment, and now am writing on like a fish, as if nothing was done.   But there was a cause for my hasting away the last, for fear it should not come time enough before a new quarter began.   I told you where I dined to-day; but forgot to tell you what I believe, that Mr. Harley will be Lord Treasurer in a short time, and other great removes and promotions made.   This is my thought, etc.

15. I was this morning with Mr. Secretary, and he is grown pretty well.   I dined with him to-day, and drank some of that wine which the Duke of Tuscany used to send to Sir William Temple: [1] he always sends some to the chief Ministers.   I liked it mightily, but he does not; and he ordered his butler to send me a chest of it to-morrow. Would to God MD had it!   The Queen is well again, and was at chapel to-day, etc.

16. I went with Ford into the City to-day, and dined with Stratford, and drank Tokay, and then we went to the auction; but I did not lay out above twelve shillings.   My head is a little out of order to-night, though no formal fit.   My Lord Keeper has sent to invite me to dinner to-morrow, and you'll dine better with the Dean; and God bless you.   I forgot to

[1] In 1670 Temple thanked the Grand Duke of Tuscany for "an entire vintage of the finest wines of Italy" (Temple's *Works*, 1814, ii. 155-56).

tell you that yesterday was sent me a *Narrative* printed, with all the circumstances of Mr. Harley's stabbing. I had not time to do it myself; so I sent my hints to the author of the *Atalantis*,[1] and she has cooked it into a sixpenny pamphlet, in her own style, only the first page is left as I was beginning it. But I was afraid of disobliging Mr. Harley or Mr. St. John in one critical point about it, and so would not do it myself. It is worth your reading, for the circumstances are all true. My chest of Florence was sent me this morning, and cost me seven and sixpence to two servants. I would give two guineas you had it, etc.

17. I was so out of order with my head this morning, that I was going to send my excuses to my Lord Keeper; but however I got up at eleven, and walked there after two, and stayed till eight. There was Sir Thomas Mansel, Prior, George Granville, and Mr. Cæsar,[2] and we were very merry. My head is still wrong, but I have had no formal fit, only I totter a little. I have left off snuff altogether. I have a noble roll of tobacco for grating, very good. Shall I send it to MD, if she likes that sort? My Lord Keeper and our this day's company are to dine on Saturday with George Granville, and to-morrow I dine with Lord Anglesea.

18. Did you ever see such a blundering goosecap as Presto? I saw the number 21 at top, and so I went on as if it were the day of the month, whereas this is but Wednesday the 18th. How shall I do to blot and alter them? I have made a shift to do it behind, but it is a great botch. I dined with Lord Anglesea to-day, but did not go to the House of Commons about the yarn; my head was not well enough. I know not what is the matter; it has never been thus before: two days together giddy from morning till night, but not with any violence or pain; and I totter a little, but can make shift to walk. I doubt I must fall to my pills again: I think of going into the country a little way. I tell you what you

---

1 Mrs. Manley (see p. 166).
2 Charles Cæsar, M.P. for Hertford, was appointed Treasurer of the Navy in June 1711, in the room of Robert Walpole.

must do henceforward : you must enclose your letter in a fair
half-sheet of paper, and direct the outside "To Erasmus
Lewis, Esquire, at my Lord Dartmouth's office at Whitehall " :
for I never go to the Coffee-house, and they will grudge to
take in my letters.   I forgot to tell you that your mother
was to see me this morning, and brought me a flask of sweet-
water for a present, admirable for my head ; but I shall not
smell to it.   She is going to Sheen, with Lady Giffard : she
would fain send your papers over to you, or give them to me.
Say what you would have done, and it shall be done ; because
I love Stella, and she is a good daughter, they say, and so is
Dingley.

19. This morning General Webb was to give me a visit :
he goes with a crutch and stick, yet was forced to come up
two pair of stairs.   I promised to dine with him, but afterwards sent my excuses, and dined privately in my friend
Lewis's lodgings at Whitehall, with whom I had much
business to talk of, relating to the public and myself.   Little
Harrison the Tatler goes to-morrow to the secretaryship I
got him at the Hague, and Mr. St. John has made him a
present of fifty guineas to bear his charges.   An't I a good
friend ?   Why are not you a young fellow, that I might
prefer you ?   I had a letter from Bernage from Kinsale : he
tells me his commission for captain-lieutenant was ready for
him at his arrival : so there are two jackanapeses I have done
with.   My head is something better this evening, though not
well.

20. I was this morning with Mr. Secretary, whose packets
were just come in, and among them a letter from Lord
Peterborow to me : he writes so well, I have no mind to
answer him, and so kind, that I must answer him.   The
Emperor's[1] death must, I think, cause great alterations in
Europe, and, I believe, will hasten a peace.   We reckon our
King Charles will be chosen Emperor, and the Duke of Savoy
set up for Spain ; but I believe he will make nothing of it.

[1] Joseph I.   His successor was his brother Charles, the King of Spain
recognised by England.

Dr. Freind and I dined in the City at a printer's, and it has cost me two shillings in coach-hire, and a great deal more this week and month, which has been almost all rain, with now and then sunshine, and is the truest April that I have known these many years. The lime-trees in the Park are all out in leaves, though not large leaves yet. Wise people are going into the country; but many think the Parliament can hardly be up these six weeks. Mr. Harley was with the Queen on Tuesday. I believe certainly he will be Lord Treasurer: I have not seen him this week.

21. Morning. Lord Keeper, and I, and Prior, and Sir Thomas Mansel, have appointed to dine this day with George Granville. My head, I thank God, is better; but to be giddyish three or four days together mortified me. I take no snuff, and I will be very regular in eating little and the gentlest meats. How does poor Stella just now, with her deans and her Stoytes? Do they give you health for the money you lose at ombre, sirrah? What say you to that? Poor Dingley frets to see Stella lose that four and eleven-pence, the other night. Let us rise. Morrow, sirrahs. I will rise, spite of your little teeth; good - morrow. — At night. O, faith, you are little dear saucyboxes. I was just going in the morning to tell you that I began to want a letter from MD, and in four minutes after Mr. Ford sends me one that he had picked up at St. James's Coffee-house; for I go to no coffee-house at all. And, faith, I was glad at heart to see it, and to see Stella so brisk. O Lord, what pretending? Well, but I will not answer it yet; I'll keep it for t'other side. Well, we dined to-day according to appointment: Lord Keeper went away at near eight, I at eight, and I believe the rest will be fairly fuddled; for young Harcourt,[1] Lord Keeper's son, began to prattle before I came away. It will not do with Prior's lean carcass. I drink

---

[1] Simon Harcourt, M.P. for Wallingford. He married Elizabeth, sister of Sir John Evelyn, Bart., and died in 1720, aged thirty-five, before his father. He was secretary to the society of "Brothers," wrote verses, and was a friend of the poets. His son Simon was created Earl Harcourt in 1749, and was Lord Lieutenant of Ireland.

little, miss my glass often, put water in my wine, and go
away before the rest, which I take to be a good receipt
for sobriety.   Let us put it into rhyme, and so make a
proverb—

> Drink little at a time ;
> Put water with your wine ;
> Miss your glass when you can ;
> And go off the first man.

God be thanked, I am much better than I was, though something of a totterer.   I ate but little to-day, and of the gentlest
meat.   I refused ham and pigeons, pease-soup, stewed beef,
cold salmon, because they were too strong.   I take no snuff
at all, but some herb snuff prescribed by Dr. Radcliffe.

> Go to your deans,
> You couple of queans.

I believe I said that already.   What care I ? what cares
Presto ?

22. Morning.   I must rise and go to the Secretary's.   Mr.
Harley has been out of town this week to refresh himself
before he comes into Parliament.   Oh, but I must rise, so
there is no more to be said ; and so morrow, sirrahs both.—
Night.   I dined to-day with the Secretary, who has engaged
me for every Sunday ; and I was an hour with him this
morning deep in politics, where I told him the objections
of the October Club, and he answered all except one, that
no inquiries are made into past mismanagement.   But indeed
I believe they are not yet able to make any : the late Ministry
were too cunning in their rogueries, and fenced themselves
with an Act of general pardon.   I believe Mr. Harley must
be Lord Treasurer ; yet he makes one difficulty which is
hard to answer : he must be made a lord, and his estate is
not large enough, and he is too generous to make it larger ;
and if the Ministry should change soon by any accident, he
will be left in the suds.   Another difficulty is, that if he be
made a peer, they will want him prodigiously in the House
of Commons, of which he is the great mover, and after him

the Secretary, and hardly any else of weight. Two shillings more to-day for coach and chair. I shall be ruined.

23. So you expect an answer to your letter, do you so? Yes, yes, you shall have an answer, you shall, young women. I made a good pun on Saturday to my Lord Keeper. After dinner we had coarse Doiley napkins,[1] fringed at each end, upon the table, to drink with : my Lord Keeper spread one of them between him and Mr. Prior; I told him I was glad to see there was such a fringeship [friendship] between Mr. Prior and his lordship. Prior swore it was the worst he ever heard : I said I thought so too; but at the same time I thought it was most like one of Stella's that ever I heard. I dined to-day with Lord Mountjoy, and this evening saw the Venetian Ambassador[2] coming from his first public audience. His coach was the most monstrous, huge, fine, rich gilt thing that ever I saw. I loitered this evening, and came home late.

24. I was this morning to visit the Duchess of Ormond,[3] who has long desired it, or threatened she would not let me visit her daughters. I sat an hour with her, and we were good company, when in came the Countess of Bellamont,[4] with a pox. I went out, and we did not know one another; yet hearing me named, she asked, "What, is that Dr. Swift?" said she and I were very well acquainted, and fell a railing at me without mercy, as a lady told me that was there; yet I never was but once in the company of that drab of a Countess. Sir Andrew Fountaine and I dined with my neighbour Van. I design in two days, if possible, to go lodge at Chelsea for the air, and put myself under a necessity of walking to and from London every day. I writ this post to the Bishop of Clogher a long politic letter, to entertain

[1] Doiley, a seventeenth-century linen-draper,—probably "Thomas Doyley, at the Nun, in Henrietta Street, Covent Garden,"—invented stuffs which "might at once be cheap and genteel" (*Spectator*, No. 283).
[2] A special envoy. The Resident from Venice in 1710 was Signor Bianchi.
[3] See p. 160.
[4] Nanfan Coote, second Earl of Bellamont, who died in 1708, married, in 1705, Lucia Anna, daughter of Henry de Nassau, Lord of Auverquerque, and sister of Henry, first Earl of Grantham. She died in 1744.

him. I am to buy statues and harnese[1] for them, with a vengeance. I have packed and sealed up MD's twelve letters against I go to Chelsea. I have put the last commissions of MD in my account-book; but if there be any former ones, I have forgot them. I have Dingley's pocket-book down, and Stella's green silk apron, and the pound of tea; pray send me word if you have any other, and down they shall go. I will not answer your letter yet, saucy boxes. You are with the Dean just now, Madam Stella, losing your money. Why do not you name what number you have received? You say you have received my letters, but do not tell the number.

25. I was this day dining in the City with very insignificant, low, and scurvy company. I had a letter from the Archbishop of Dublin, with a long denial of the report raised on him,[2] which yet has been since assured to me from those who say they have it from the first hand; but I cannot believe them. I will show it to the Secretary to-morrow. I will not answer yours till I get to Chelsea.

26. Chelsea. I have sent two boxes of lumber to my friend Darteneuf's house, and my chest of Florence and other things to Mrs. Vanhomrigh, where I dined to-day. I was this morning with the Secretary, and showed him the Archbishop's letter, and convinced him of his Grace's innocence, and I will do the same to Mr. Harley. I got here in the stage-coach with Patrick and my portmanteau for sixpence, and pay six shillings a week for one silly room with confounded coarse sheets.[3] We have had such a horrible deal of rain, that there is no walking to London, and I must go as I came until it mends; and besides the whelp has taken my lodging as far from London as this town

---

[1] "Farnese" (Deane Swift).   [2] See p. 188.

[3] Swift's changes of residence during the period covered by the *Journal* were numerous. On Sept. 20, 1710, he moved from Pall Mall to Bury Street, "where I suppose I shall continue while in London." But on Dec. 28 he went to new lodgings in St. Albans Street, Haymarket. On April 26, 1711, he moved to Chelsea, and from there to Suffolk Street, to be near the Vanhomrighs. He next moved to St. Martin's Street, Leicester Fields; and a month later to Panton Street, Haymarket. In 1712 he lodged for a time at Kensington Gravel Pits.

could afford, at least half a mile farther than he need; but
I must be content. The best is, I lodge just over against
Dr. Atterbury's house, and yet perhaps I shall not like the
place the better for that. Well, I will stay till to-morrow
before I answer your letter; and you must suppose me
always writing at Chelsea from henceforward, till I alter, and
say London. This letter goes on Saturday, which will be
just a fortnight; so go and cheat Goody Stoyte, etc.

27. Do you know that I fear my whole chest of Florence
is turned sour, at least the two first flasks were so, and
hardly drinkable. How plaguy unfortunate am I! and the
Secretary's own is the best I ever tasted; and I must not tell
him, but be as thankful as if it were the best in Christendom.
I went to town in the sixpenny stage to-day; and hearing
Mr. Harley was not at home, I went to see him, because I
knew by the message of his lying porter that he was at
home. He was very well, and just going out, but made
me promise to dine with him; and betwixt that and indeed
strolling about, I lost four pound seven shillings at play—
with a———a—a—bookseller, and got but about half a
dozen books.[1] I will buy no more books now, that's certain.
Well, I dined at Mr. Harley's, came away at six, shifted my
gown, cassock, and periwig, and walked hither to Chelsea,
as I always design to do when it is fair. I am heartily sorry
to find my friend the Secretary stand a little ticklish with
the rest of the Ministry; there have been one or two disobliging things that have happened, too long to tell: and
t'other day in Parliament, upon a debate of about thirty-five
millions that have not been duly accounted for, Mr. Secretary,
in his warmth of speech, and zeal for his friend Mr. Brydges,[2]
on whom part of the blame was falling, said he did not know
that either Mr. Brydges or the late Ministry were at all to
blame in this matter; which was very desperately spoken,
and giving up the whole cause: for the chief quarrel against

---

[1] At raffling for books.
[2] James Brydges, Paymaster-General, and afterwards Duke of Chandos
(see p. 12).

the late Ministry was the ill management of the treasure, and was more than all the rest together. I had heard of this matter: but Mr. Foley[1] beginning to discourse to-day at table, without naming Mr. St. John, I turned to Mr. Harley, and said if the late Ministry were not to blame in that article, he (Mr. Harley) ought to lose his head for putting the Queen upon changing them. He made it a jest; but by some words dropped, I easily saw that they take things ill of Mr. St. John; and by some hints given me from another hand that I deal with, I am afraid the Secretary will not stand long. This is the fate of Courts. I will, if I meet Mr. St. John alone on Sunday, tell him my opinion, and beg him to set himself right, else the consequences may be very bad; for I see not how they can well want him neither, and he would make a troublesome enemy. But enough of politics.

28. Morning. I forgot to tell you that Mr. Harley asked me yesterday how he came to disoblige the Archbishop of Dublin. Upon which (having not his letter about me) I told him what the Bishop had written to me on that subject,[2] and desired I might read him the letter some other time. But after all, from what I have heard from other hands, I am afraid the Archbishop is a little guilty. Here is one Brent Spencer, a brother of Mr. Proby's,[3] who affirms it, and says he has leave to do so from Charles Dering,[4] who heard the words; and that Ingoldsby[5] abused the Archbishop, etc. Well, but now for your saucy letter: I have no room to answer it; O yes, enough on t'other side. Are you no sicker? Stella jeers Presto for not coming over by Christmas; but indeed Stella does not jeer, but reproach, poor poor Presto. And how can I come away and the First-Fruits not finished? I am of opinion the Duke of Ormond will do

---

[1] Thomas Foley, M.P. for Worcestershire, was created Baron Foley in December 1711, and died in 1733.
[2] See pp. 188, 200.   [3] See p. 176.
[4] Charles Dering, second son of Sir Edward Dering, Bart., M.P. for Kent, was Auditor of the Exchequer in Ireland, and M.P. for Carlingford.
[5] See p. 97.

nothing in them before he goes, which will be in a fortnight, they say; and then they must fall to me to be done in his absence. No, indeed, I have nothing to print: you know they have printed the *Miscellanies*[1] already. Are they on your side yet? If you have my snuff-box, I will have your strong box. Hi, does Stella take snuff again? or is it only because it is a fine box? Not the *Meddle*, but the *Medley*,[2] you fool. Yes, yes, a wretched thing, because it is against you Tories: now I think it very fine, and the *Examiner* a wretched thing. — Twist your mouth, sirrah. Guiscard, and what you will read in the *Narrative*,[3] I ordered to be written, and nothing else. /The *Spectator* is written by Steele, with Addison's help: it is often very pretty. Yesterday it was made of a noble hint I gave him long ago for his *Tatlers*, about an Indian supposed to write his Travels into England.[4] I repent he ever had it. I intended to have written a book on that subject. I believe he has spent it all in one paper, and all the under-hints there are mine too; but I never see him or Addison. / The Queen is well, but I fear will be no long liver; for I am told she has sometimes the gout in her bowels (I hate the word *bowels*). My ears have been, these three months past, much better than any time these two years; but now they begin to be a little out of order again. My head is better, though not right; but I trust to air and walking. You have got my letter, but what number? I suppose 18. Well, my shin has been well this month. No, Mrs. Westley[5] came away without her husband's knowledge, while she was in the country: she has written to me for some tea. They lie; Mr. Harley's wound was very terrible: he had convulsions, and very narrowly escaped. The bruise was nine times worse than the wound: he is weak still. Well, Brooks married; I know all that. I am sorry

---

[1] See pp. 43, 160.
[2] A Whig paper, for the most part by Mainwaring and Oldmixon, in opposition to the *Examiner*. It appeared weekly from October 1710 to August 1711.
[3] See p. 166. [4] See *Spectator*, No. 50, by Addison.
[5] In all probability a mistake for "Wesley" (see p. 2).

for Mrs. Walls's eye: I hope 'tis better. O yes, you are
great walkers: but I have heard them say, "Much talkers,
little walkers": and I believe I may apply the old proverb
to you—

> If you talked no more than you walked,
> Those that think you wits would be baulked.

Yes, Stella shall have a large printed Bible: I have put it
down among my commissions for MD. I am glad to hear
you have taken the fancy of intending to read the Bible.
Pox take the box; is not it come yet? This is trusting to
your young fellows, young women; 'tis your fault: I thought
you had such power with Sterne that he would fly over
Mount Atlas to serve you. You say you are not splenetic;
but if you be, faith, you will break poor Presto's—I will not
say the rest; but I vow to God, if I could decently come
over now, I would, and leave all schemes of politics and
ambition for ever. I have not the opportunities here of
preserving my health by riding, etc., that I have in Ireland;
and the want of health is a great cooler of making one's
court. You guess right about my being bit with a direction
from Walls, and the letter from MD: I believe I described
it in one of my last. This goes to-night; and I must now
rise and walk to town, and walk back in the evening. God
Almighty bless and preserve poor MD. Farewell.

O, faith, don't think, saucy noses, that I'll fill this third
side: I can't stay a letter above a fortnight: it must go
then; and you would rather see a short one like this, than
want it a week longer.

My humble service to the Dean, and Mrs. Walls, and good,
kind, hearty Mrs. Stoyte, and honest Catherine.

LETTER XXII

CHELSEA, *April* 28, 1711.

A T night. I say at night, because I finished my twenty-first this morning here, and put it into the post-office my own self, like a good boy. I think I am a little before you now, young women: I am writing my twenty-second, and have received your thirteenth. I got to town between twelve and one, and put on my new gown and periwig, and dined with Lord Abercorn, where I had not been since the marriage of his son Lord Peasley,[1] who has got ten thousand pounds with a wife. I am now a country gentleman. I walked home as I went, and am a little weary, and am got into bed: I hope in God the air and exercise will do me a little good. I have been inquiring about statues for Mrs. Ashe: I made Lady Abercorn[2] go with me; and will send them word next post to Clogher. I hate to buy for her: I am sure she will maunder. I am going to study.

29. I had a charming walk to and from town to-day: I washed, shaved and all, and changed gown and periwig, by half an hour after nine, and went to the Secretary, who told me how he had differed with his friends in Parliament: I apprehended this division, and told him a great deal of it. I went to Court, and there several mentioned it to me as what they much disliked. I dined with the Secretary; and we proposed doing some business of importance in the afternoon, which he broke to me first, and said how he and Mr. Harley were convinced of the necessity of it; yet he suffered one of his under-secretaries to come upon us after dinner, who stayed till six, and so nothing was done: and what care I? he shall send to me the next time, and ask twice. To-morrow I go to the election at Westminster School, where lads are chosen for the University: they say it is a sight, and a great trial of wits. Our Expedition Fleet is but just sailed: I believe it will come to nothing. Mr.

---

[1] Lord Paisley (see p. 161).   [2] See p. 88.

Secretary frets at their tediousness, but hopes great things from it, though he owns four or five princes are in the secret; and, for that reason, I fear it is no secret to France. There are eight regiments; and the Admiral[1] is your Walker's brother the midwife.

30. Morn. I am here in a pretty pickle: it rains hard; and the cunning natives of Chelsea have outwitted me, and taken up all the three stage coaches. What shall I do? I must go to town: this is your fault. I cannot walk: I will borrow a coat. This is the blind side of my lodging out of town; I must expect such inconveniences as these. Faith, I'll walk in the rain. Morrow. — At night. I got a gentleman's chaise by chance, and so went to town for a shilling, and lie this night in town. I was at the election of lads at Westminster to-day, and a very silly thing it is; but they say there will be fine doings to-morrow. I dined with Dr. Freind,[2] the second master of the school, with a dozen parsons and others: Prior would make me stay. Mr. Harley is to hear the election to-morrow; and we are all to dine with tickets, and hear fine speeches. 'Tis terrible rainy weather again: I lie at a friend's in the City.

May 1. I wish you a merry May Day, and a thousand more. I was baulked at Westminster; I came too late: I heard no speeches nor verses. They would not let me in to their dining-place for want of a ticket; and I would not send in for one, because Mr. Harley excused his coming, and Atterbury was not there; and I cared not for the rest: and so my friend Lewis and I dined with Kitt Musgrave,[3] if you know such a man: and, the weather mending, I walked gravely home

---

[1] Sir Hovenden Walker. The "man midwife" was Sir Chamberlen Walker, his younger brother. The "secret expedition" against Quebec conveyed upwards of 5000 soldiers, under the command of General John Hill (see p. 76), but owing to the want of due preparations and the severe weather encountered, the fleet was compelled to return to England without accomplishing anything.

[2] Robert Freind, elder brother of John Freind, M.D. (see p. 66), became headmaster of Westminster School in 1711, and held the appointment until 1733. He was Rector of Witney, and afterwards Canon of Windsor, Prebendary of Westminster, and Canon of Christ Church. He died in 1751, aged eighty-four.

[3] Christopher Musgrave was Clerk of the Ordnance.

this evening; and so I design to walk and walk till I am well: I fancy myself a little better already. How does poor Stella? Dingley is well enough. Go, get you gone, naughty girl, you are well enough. O dear MD, contrive to have some share of the country this spring: go to Finglas, or Donnybrook, or Clogher, or Killala, or Lowth. Have you got your box yet? Yes, yes. Do not write to me again till this letter goes: I must make haste, that I may write two for one. Go to the Bath: I hope you are now at the Bath, if you had a mind to go; or go to Wexford: do something for your living. Have you given up my lodging, according to order? I have had just now a compliment from Dean Atterbury's lady,[1] to command the garden and library, and whatever the house affords. I lodge just over against them; but the Dean is in town with his Convocation: so I have my Dean and Prolocutor as well as you, young women, though he has not so good wine, nor so much meat.

2. A fine day, but begins to grow a little warm; and that makes your little fat Presto sweat in the forehead. Pray, are not the fine buns sold here in our town; was it not *Rrrrrrrrrare Chelsea buns?*[2] I bought one to-day in my walk; it cost me a penny; it was stale, and I did not like it, as the man said, etc. Sir Andrew Fountaine and I dined at Mrs. Vanhomrigh's, and had a flask of my Florence, which lies in their cellar; and so I came home gravely, and saw nobody of consequence to-day. I am very easy here, nobody plaguing me in a morning; and Patrick saves many a score lies. I sent over to Mrs Atterbury to know whether I might wait on her; but she is gone a visiting: we have exchanged some compliments, but I have not seen her yet. We have no news in our town.

3. I did not go to town to-day, it was so terrible rainy;

---

[1] Atterbury's wife, Katherine Osborn, has been described as "the inspiration of his youth and the solace of his riper years."
[2] The original Chelsea Bun House, in Jew's Row, was pulled down in 1839. Sir R. Philips, writing in 1817, said, "Those buns have afforded a competency, and even wealth, to four generations of the same family; and it is singular that their delicate flavour, lightness, and richness have never been successfully imitated."

nor have I stirred out of my room till eight this evening,
when I crossed the way to see Mrs. Atterbury, and thank
her for her civilities. She would needs send me some veal,
and small beer, and ale, to-day at dinner; and I have lived
a scurvy, dull, splenetic day, for want of MD: I often
thought how happy I could have been, had it rained eight
thousand times more, if MD had been with a body. My
Lord Rochester[1] is dead this morning; they say at one
o'clock; and I hear he died suddenly. To-morrow I shall
know more. He is a great loss to us: I cannot think who
will succeed him as Lord President. I have been writing a
long letter to Lord Peterborow, and am dull.

4. I dined to-day at Lord Shelburne's, where Lady
Kerry[2] made me a present of four India handkerchiefs,
which I have a mind to keep for little MD, only that I had
rather, etc. I have been a mighty handkerchief-monger,
and have bought abundance of snuff ones since I have left
off taking snuff. And I am resolved, when I come over,
MD shall be acquainted with Lady Kerry: we have struck
up a mighty friendship; and she has much better sense
than any other lady of your country. We are almost in
love with one another: but she is most egregiously ugly;
but perfectly well-bred, and governable as I please. I am
resolved, when I come, to keep no company but MD: you
know I kept my resolution last time; and, except Mr.
Addison, conversed with none but you and your club of
deans and Stoytes. 'Tis three weeks, young women, since
I had a letter from you; and yet, methinks, I would not
have another for five pounds till this is gone; and yet I
send every day to the Coffee-house, and I would fain have
a letter, and not have a letter: and I do not know what,
nor I do not know how, and this goes on very slow; it is a
week to-morrow since I began it. I am a poor country

---

[1] See p. 60. King wrote to Swift (May 15, 1711), "The death of the Earl
of Rochester is a great blow to all good men, and even his enemies cannot but
do justice to his character. What influence it will have on public affairs God
only knows."

[2] See p. 89.

gentleman, and do not know how the world passes. Do
you know that every syllable I write I hold my lips just
for all the world as if I were talking in our own little
language to MD? Faith, I am very silly; but I cannot
help it for my life. I got home early to - night. My
solicitors, that used to ply me every morning, knew not
where to find me; and I am so happy not to hear "Patrick,
Patrick," called a hundred times every morning. But I
looked backward, and find I have said this before. What
care I? Go to the Dean, and roast the oranges.

5. I dined to-day with my friend Lewis, and we were
deep in politics how to save the present Ministry; for I
am afraid of Mr. Secretary, as I believe I told you. I went
in the evening to see Mr. Harley; and, upon my word, I
was in perfect joy. Mr. Secretary was just going out of
the door; but I made him come back, and there was the
old Saturday Club, Lord Keeper, Lord Rivers, Mr. Secretary,
Mr. Harley, and I; the first time since his stabbing. Mr.
Secretary went away; but I stayed till nine, and made Mr.
Harley show me his breast, and tell all the story; and I
showed him the Archbishop of Dublin's letter, and defended
him effectually. We were all in mighty good humour.
Lord Keeper and I left them together, and I walked here
after nine two miles, and I found a parson drunk fighting
with a seaman, and Patrick and I were so wise to part
them, but the seaman followed him to Chelsea, cursing at
him, and the parson slipped into a house, and I know no
more. It mortified me to see a man in my coat so over-
taken. A pretty scene for one that just came from sitting
with the Prime Ministers! I had no money in my pocket,
and so could not be robbed. However, nothing but Mr.
Harley shall make me take such a journey again. We
don't yet know who will be President in Lord Rochester's
room. I measured, and found that the penknife would have
killed Mr. Harley if it had gone but half the breadth of
my thumb-nail lower, so near was he to death. I was so
curious as to ask him what were his thoughts while they

14

were carrying him home in the chair. He said he concluded himself a dead man. He will not allow that Guiscard gave him the second stab; though my Lord Keeper, who is blind, and I that was not there, are positive in it. He wears a plaster still as broad as half a crown. Smoke how wide the lines are, but, faith, I don't do it on purpose : but I have changed my side in this new Chelsea bed, and I do not know how, methinks, but it is so unfit, and so awkward, never saw the like.

6. You must remember to enclose your letters in a fair paper, and direct the outside thus : "To Erasmus Lewis, Esq.; at my Lord Dartmouth's office at Whitehall." I said so before, but it may miscarry, you know, yet I think none of my letters did ever miscarry; faith, I think never one; among all the privateers and the storms. O, faith, my letters are too good to be lost. MD's letters may tarry, but never miscarry, as the old woman used to say. And indeed, how should they miscarry, when they never come before their time ? It was a terrible rainy day; yet I made a shift to steal fair weather overhead enough to go and come in. I was early with the Secretary, and dined with him afterwards. In the morning I began to chide him, and tell him my fears of his proceedings. But Arthur Moore[1] came up and relieved him. But I forgot, for you never heard of Arthur Moore. But when I get Mr. Harley alone, I will know the bottom. You will have Dr. Raymond over before this letter, and what care you ?

7. I hope and believe my walks every day do me good. I was busy at home, and set out late this morning, and dined with Mrs. Vanhomrigh, at whose lodgings I always change my gown and periwig. I visited this afternoon, and among others, poor Biddy Floyd,[2] who is very red, but I believe won't be much marked. As I was coming home, I met Sir George Beaumont[3] in the Pall Mall, who would needs walk with me as far as Buckingham House. I was telling him of my head; he said he had been ill of the

---

[1] See p. 160.   [2] See p. 170.   [3] See p. 192.

same disorder, and by all means forbid me bohea tea, which, he said, always gave it him; and that Dr. Radcliffe said it was very bad. Now I had observed the same thing, and have left it off this month, having found myself ill after it several times; and I mention it that Stella may consider it for her own poor little head: a pound lies ready packed up and directed for Mrs. Walls, to be sent by the first convenience. Mr. Secretary told me yesterday that Mr. Harley would this week be Lord Treasurer and a peer; so I expect it every day; yet perhaps it may not be till Parliament is up, which will be in a fortnight.

8. I was to-day with the Duke of Ormond, and recommended to him the care of poor Joe Beaumont, who promises me to do him all justice and favour, and give him encouragement; and desired I would give a memorial to Ned Southwell about it, which I will, and so tell Joe when you see him, though he knows it already by a letter I writ to Mr. Warburton.[1] It was bloody hot walking to-day. I dined in the City, and went and came by water; and it rained so this evening again, that I thought I should hardly be able to get a dry hour to walk home in. I will send to-morrow to the Coffee-house for a letter from MD; but I would not have one methinks till this is gone, as it shall on Saturday. I visited the Duchess of Ormond this morning; she does not go over with the Duke. I spoke to her to get a lad touched for the evil,[2] the son of a grocer in Capel Street, one Bell; the ladies have bought sugar and plums of him. Mrs. Mary used to go there often. This is Patrick's account; and the poor fellow has been here some months with his boy. But the Queen has not been able to touch, and it now grows so warm, I fear she will not at all. Go, go, go to the Dean's, and let him carry you to Donnybrook, and cut asparagus. Has Parvisol sent you any this year? I cannot sleep in the beginnings

---

[1] Swift's curate at Laracor.
[2] Queen Anne was the last sovereign who exercised the supposed royal gift of healing by touch. Dr. Johnson was touched by her, but without effect.

of the nights, the heat or something hinders me, and I am drowsy in the mornings.

9. Dr. Freind came this morning to visit Atterbury's lady and children as physician, and persuaded me to go with him to town in his chariot. He told me he had been an hour before with Sir Cholmley Dering, Charles Dering's nephew, and head of that family in Kent, for which he is Knight of the shire. He said he left him dying of a pistol-shot quite through the body, by one Mr. Thornhill.[1] They fought at sword and pistol this morning in Tuttle Fields,[2] their pistols so near that the muzzles touched. Thornhill discharged first; and Dering, having received the shot, discharged his pistol as he was falling, so it went into the air. The story of this quarrel is long. Thornhill had lost seven teeth by a kick in the mouth from Dering, who had first knocked him down; this was above a fortnight ago. Dering was next week to be married to a fine young lady. This makes a noise here, but you will not value it. Well, Mr. Harley, Lord Keeper, and one or two more, are to be made lords immediately; their patents are now passing, and I read the preamble to Mr. Harley's, full of his praises. Lewis and I dined with Ford: I found the wine; two flasks of my Florence, and two bottles of six that Dr. Raymond sent me of French wine; he sent it to me to drink with Sir Robert Raymond and Mr. Harley's brother,[3] whom I had introduced him to; but they never could find time to come; and now I have left the town, and it is too late. Raymond will think it a cheat. What care I, sirrah?

10. Pshaw, pshaw. Patrick brought me four letters to-

[1] Richard Thornhill was tried at the Old Bailey on May 18, 1711, for the murder of Sir Cholmley Dering, M.P. for Kent, and found guilty of manslaughter only; but he was shortly afterwards assassinated (see *Journal* for Aug. 21, 1711; *Spectator*, No. 84). The quarrel began on April 27, when they fell to blows, and Thornhill being knocked down, had some teeth struck out by Sir C. Dering stamping on him. The spectators then interfered, and Dering expressed himself as ready to beg pardon; but Thornhill not thinking this was sufficient satisfaction, gave Dering the lie, and on May 9 sent him a challenge.

[2] Tothill Fields, Westminster, was a favourite place for duels in the seventeenth century.

[3] See p. 124.

day: from Dilly at Bath; Joe; Parvisol; and what was
the fourth, who can tell? Stand away, who'll guess?
Who can it be? You old man with a stick, can you tell
who the fourth is from? Iss, an please your honour, it is
from one Madam MD, Number Fourteen. Well; but I
can't send this away now, because it was here, and I was
in town; but it shall go on Saturday, and this is Thursday
night, and it will be time enough for Wexford. Take my
method: I write here to Parvisol to lend Stella twenty
pounds, and to take her note promissory to pay it in half
a year, etc. You shall see, and if you want more, let me
know afterwards; and be sure my money shall be always
paid constantly too. Have you been good or ill housewives,
pray?

11. Joe has written me to get him a collector's place,
nothing less; he says all the world knows of my great
intimacy with Mr. Harley, and that the smallest word to
him will do. This is the constant cant of puppies who are
at a distance, and strangers to Courts and Ministers. My
answer is this, which pray send: that I am ready to serve
Joe as far as I can; that I have spoken to the Duke of
Ormond about his money, as I writ to Warburton; that for
the particular he mentions, it is a work of time, which I
cannot think of at present; but, if accidents and opportunities should happen hereafter, I would not be wanting;
that I know best how far my credit goes; that he is at a
distance, and cannot judge; that I would be glad to do him
good, and if fortune throws an opportunity in my way I
shall not be wanting. This is my answer, which you may
send or read to him. Pray contrive that Parvisol may not
run away with my two hundred pounds; but get Burton's[1]
note, and let the money be returned me by bill. Don't
laugh, for I will be suspicious. Teach Parvisol to enclose,
and direct the outside to Mr. Lewis. I will answer your
letter in my next, only what I take notice of here excepted.

[1] Benjamin Burton, a Dublin banker, and brother-in-law of Swift's friend
Stratford (see p. 10). Swift says he hated this "rogue."

I forgot to tell you that at the Court of Requests to-day I could not find a dinner I liked, and it grew late, and I dined with Mrs. Vanhomrigh, etc.

12. Morning. I will finish this letter before I go to town, because I shall be busy, and have neither time nor place there. Farewell, etc. etc.

LETTER XXIII

CHELSEA, *May 12, 1711.*

I SENT you my twenty-second this afternoon in town. I dined with Mr. Harley and the old Club, Lord Rivers, Lord Keeper, and Mr. Secretary. They rallied me last week, and said I must have Mr. St. John's leave; so I writ to him yesterday, that foreseeing I should never dine again with Sir Simon Harcourt, Knight, and Robert Harley, Esq., I was resolved to do it to-day. The jest is, that before Saturday[1] next we expect they will be lords; for Mr. Harley's patent is drawing, to be Earl of Oxford. Mr. Secretary and I came away at seven, and he brought me to our town's end in his coach; so I lost my walk. St. John read my letter to the company, which was all raillery, and passed purely.

13. It rained all last night and this morning as heavy as lead; but I just got fair weather to walk to town before church. The roads are all over in deep puddle. The hay of our town is almost fit to be mowed. I went to Court after church (as I always do on Sundays), and then dined with Mr. Secretary, who has engaged me for every Sunday; and poor MD dined at home upon a bit of veal and a pint of wine. Is it not plaguy insipid to tell you every day where I dine? yet now I have got into the way of it, I cannot forbear it neither. Indeed, Mr. Presto, you had better go answer MD's letter, N. 14. I will answer it when I please, Mr. Doctor.

[1] The day on which the Club met. See letter from Swift to St. John, May 11, 1711.

What is that you say? The Court was very full this morning, expecting Mr. Harley would be declared Earl of Oxford and have the Treasurer's staff. Mr. Harley never comes to Court at all; somebody there asked me the reason. "Why," said I, "the Lord of Oxford knows." He always goes to the Queen by the back stairs. I was told for certain, you jackanapes, Lord Santry[1] was dead, Captain Cammock[2] assured me so; and now he's alive again, they say; but that shan't do: he shall be dead to me as long as he lives. Dick Tighe[3] and I meet, and never stir our hats. I am resolved to mistake him for Witherington, the little nasty lawyer that came up to me so sternly at the Castle the day I left Ireland. I'll ask the gentleman I saw walking with him how long Witherington has been in town.

14. I went to town to-day by water. The hail quite discouraged me from walking, and there is no shade in the greatest part of the way. I took the first boat, and had a footman my companion; then I went again by water, and dined in the City with a printer, to whom I carried a pamphlet in manuscript, that Mr. Secretary gave me. The printer sent it to the Secretary for his approbation, and he desired me to look it over, which I did, and found it a very scurvy piece. The reason I tell you so, is because it was done by your parson Slap, Scrap, Flap (what d'ye call him), Trapp,[4] your Chancellor's chaplain. 'Tis called *A Character of the Present Set of Whigs*, and is going to be printed, and no

[1] Henry Barry, fourth Lord Barry of Santry (1680–1734), was an Irish Privy Councillor, and Governor of Derry. In 1702 he married Bridget, daughter of Sir Thomas Domville, Bart., and in an undated letter (about 1735) to Lady Santry Swift spoke of his esteem for her, "although I had hardly the least acquaintance with your lord, nor was at all desirous to cultivate it, because I did not at all approve of his conduct." Lord Santry's only son and heir, who was born in 1710, was condemned to death for the murder of a footman in 1739, when the barony became extinct by forfeiture. See B. W. Adams's *History of Santry*.

[2] Probably Captain Cammock, of the *Speedwell*, of 28 guns and 125 men (Luttrell, vi. 331), who met on July 13, 1708, off Scotland, two French privateers, one of 16, the other of 18 guns, and fought them several hours. The first privateer got off, much shattered; the other was brought into Carrickfergus.

[3] See p. 50.   [4] See p. 120.

doubt the author will take care to produce it in Ireland. Dr. Freind was with me, and pulled out a twopenny pamphlet just published, called *The State of Wit*,[1] giving a character of all the papers that have come out of late. The author seems to be a Whig, yet he speaks very highly of a paper called the *Examiner*, and says the supposed author of it is Dr. Swift. But above all things he praises the *Tatlers* and *Spectators*; and I believe Steele and Addison were privy to the printing of it. Thus is one treated by these impudent dogs. And that villain Curll[2] has scraped up some trash, and calls it Dr. Swift's *Miscellanies*, with the name at large : and I can get no satisfaction of him. Nay, Mr. Harley told me he had read it, and only laughed at me before Lord Keeper and the rest. Since I came home, I have been sitting with the Prolocutor, Dean Atterbury, who is my neighbour over the way, but generally keeps in town with his Convocation. 'Tis late, etc.

15. My walk to town to-day was after ten, and prodigiously hot. I dined with Lord Shelburne, and have desired Mrs. Pratt, who lodges there, to carry over Mrs. Walls's tea; I hope she will do it, and they talk of going in a fortnight. My way is this : I leave my best gown and periwig at Mrs. Vanhomrigh's, then walk up the Pall Mall, through the Park, out at Buckingham House, and so to Chelsea a little beyond the church : I set out about sunset, and get here in something less than an hour; it is two good miles, and just five thousand seven hundred and forty-eight steps; so there is four miles a day walking, without reckoning what I walk while I stay in town. When I pass the Mall in the evening, it is prodigious to see the number of ladies walking there; and I always cry shame at the ladies of Ireland, who never walk at all, as if their legs were of no use, but to be laid aside. I have been now almost three weeks here, and I

---

[1] This valuable pamphlet is signed " J. G.," and is believed to be by John Gay.

[2] Edmund Curll's collection of Swift's *Miscellanies*, published in 1711, was an expansion of a pamphlet of 1710, *A Meditation upon a Broomstick, and somewhat beside, of the same Author's.*

thank God, am much better in my head, if it does but continue. I tell you what, if I was with you, when we went to Stoyte at Donnybrook, we would only take a coach to the hither end of Stephen's Green, and from thence go every step on foot, yes, faith, every step; it would do DD[1] good as well as Presto.[2] Everybody tells me I look better already; for, faith, I looked sadly, that is certain. My breakfast is milk porridge: I do not love it; faith, I hate it, but it is cheap and wholesome; and I hate to be obliged to either of those qualities for anything.[3]

16. I wonder why Presto will be so tedious in answering MD's letters; because he would keep the best to the last, I suppose. Well, Presto must be humoured, it must be as he will have it, or there will be an old to do.[4] Dead with heat; are not you very hot? My walks make my forehead sweat rarely; sometimes my morning journey is by water, as it was to-day with one Parson Richardson,[5] who came to see me, on his going to Ireland; and with him I send Mrs. Walls's tea, and three books[6] I got from the Lords of the Treasury for the College. I dined with Lord Shelburne to-day; Lady Kerry and Mrs. Pratt are going likewise for Ireland.—Lord! I forgot, I dined with Mr. Prior to-day, at his house, with Dean Atterbury and others; and came home pretty late, and I think I'm in a fuzz, and don't know what I say, never saw the like.

17. Sterne came here by water to see me this morning, and I went back with him to his boat. He tells me that Mrs. Edgworth[7] married a fellow in her journey to Chester; so I believe she little thought of anybody's box but her own. I desired Sterne to give me directions where to get the box in Chester, which he says he will to-morrow; and I will write

---

[1] " In this passage DD signifies both Dingley and Stella" (Deane Swift).
[2] Sir Henry Craik's reading. The old editions have, "It would do: DD goes as well as Presto," which is obviously corrupt.
[3] Cf. *Journal*, June 17, 1712.
[4] Cf. "old doings" (p. 73). [5] See p. 163.
[6] Rymer's *Fœdera*, in three volumes, which Swift obtained for Trinity College, Dublin.
[7] See pp. 43, 145.

to Richardson to get it up there as he goes by, and whip it
over. It is directed to Mrs. Curry: you must caution her of
it, and desire her to send it you when it comes. Sterne says
Jemmy Leigh loves London mightily; that makes him stay
so long, I believe, and not Sterne's business, which Mr.
Harley's accident has put much backward. We expect now
every day that he will be Earl of Oxford and Lord Treasurer.
His patent is passing; but, they say, Lord Keeper's not yet;
at least his son, young Harcourt, told me so t'other day. I
dined to-day privately with my friend Lewis at his lodgings
at Whitehall. T'other day at Whitehall I met a lady of my
acquaintance, whom I had not seen before since I came to
England; we were mighty glad to see each other, and she
has engaged me to visit her, as I design to do. It is one
Mrs. Colledge: she has lodgings at Whitehall, having been
seamstress to King William, worth three hundred a year.
Her father was a fanatic joiner,[1] hanged for treason in
Shaftesbury's plot. This noble person and I were brought
acquainted, some years ago, by Lady Berkeley.[2] I love
good creditable acquaintance: I love to be the worst of the
company: I am not of those that say, "For want of company,
welcome trumpery." I was this evening with Lady Kerry
and Mrs. Pratt at Vauxhall, to hear the nightingales; but
they are almost past singing.

18. I was hunting the Secretary to-day in vain about some
business, and dined with Colonel Crowe, late Governor of
Barbados,[3] and your friend Sterne was the third: he is very
kind to Sterne, and helps him in his business, which lies
asleep till Mr. Harley is Lord Treasurer, because nothing of
moment is now done in the Treasury, the change being

[1] Stephen Colledge, "the Protestant joiner," was hanged in 1681. He had
published attacks on the Roman Catholics, and had advocated resistance to
Charles II.
[2] See p. 14.
[3] Mitford Crowe was appointed Governor of Barbados in 1706, and before
his departure for that island went to Spain, "to settle the accounts of our
army there, of which he is paymaster" (Luttrell, vi. 104). In 1710 charges of
bribery brought against him by merchants were inquired into by the Privy
Council, but he seems to have cleared himself, for in June 1711 Swift speaks of
him as Governor of Jamaica. He died in 1719.

expected every day. I sat with Dean Atterbury till one o'clock after I came home; so 'tis late, etc.

19. Do you know that about our town we are mowing already and making hay, and it smells so sweet as we walk through the flowery meads; but the hay-making nymphs are perfect drabs, nothing so clean and pretty as farther in the country. There is a mighty increase of dirty wenches in straw hats since I knew London. I stayed at home till five o'clock, and dined with Dean Atterbury; then went by water to Mr. Harley's, where the Saturday Club was met, with the addition of the Duke of Shrewsbury. I whispered Lord Rivers that I did not like to see a stranger among us; and the rogue told it aloud: but Mr. Secretary said the Duke writ to have leave; so I appeared satisfied, and so we laughed. Mr. Secretary told me the Duke of Buckingham [1] had been talking to him much about me, and desired my acquaintance. I answered it could not be, for he had not made sufficient advances. Then the Duke of Shrewsbury said he thought that Duke was not used to make advances. I said I could not help that; for I always expected advances in proportion to men's quality, and more from a duke than any other man. The Duke replied that he did not mean anything of his quality; which was handsomely said enough; for he meant his pride: and I have invented a notion to believe that nobody is proud. At ten all the company went away; and from ten to twelve Mr. Harley and I sat together, where we talked through a great deal of matters I had a mind to settle with him; and then walked in a fine moonshine night to Chelsea, where I got by one. Lord Rivers conjured me not to walk so late; but I would, because I had no other way; but I had no money to lose.

20. By what the Lord Keeper told me last night, I find he will not be made a peer so soon; but Mr. Harley's patent for Earl of Oxford is now drawing, and will be done in three days. We made him own it, which he did scurvily, and

[1] See p. 60.

then talked of it like the rest.   Mr. Secretary had too much
company with him to-day; so I came away soon after dinner.
I give no man liberty to swear or talk b——dy, and I found
some of them were in constraint, so I left them to themselves.
I wish you a merry Whitsuntide, and pray tell me how you
pass away your time; but, faith, you are going to Wexford,
and I fear this letter is too late; it shall go on Thursday,
and sooner it cannot, I have so much business to hinder me
answering yours.   Where must I direct in your absence?   Do
you quit your lodgings?

21. Going to town this morning, I met in the Pall Mall a
clergyman of Ireland, whom I love very well and was glad
to see, and with him a little jackanapes, of Ireland too, who
married Nanny Swift, Uncle Adam's[1] daughter, one Perry;
perhaps you may have heard of him.   His wife has sent him
here, to get a place from Lowndes;[2] because my uncle and
Lowndes married two sisters, and Lowndes is a great man
here in the Treasury; but by good luck I have no acquaintance with him: however, he expected I should be his friend
to Lowndes, and one word of mine, etc., the old cant.   But
I will not go two yards to help him.   I dined with Mrs.
Vanhomrigh, where I keep my best gown and periwig, to put
on when I come to town and be a spark.

22. I dined to-day in the City, and coming home this
evening, I met Sir Thomas Mansel and Mr. Lewis in the
Park.   Lewis whispered me that Mr. Harley's patent for
the Earl of Oxford was passed in Mr. Secretary St. John's
office; so to-morrow or next day, I suppose, he will be
declared Earl of Oxford, and have the staff.[3]   This man has
grown by persecutions, turnings out, and stabbing.   What
waiting, and crowding, and bowing will be at his levee! yet,
if human nature be capable of so much constancy, I should

[1] Swift's uncle Adam "lived and died in Ireland," and left no son.   Another
daughter of his became Mrs. Whiteway.
[2] William Lowndes, M.P., secretary to the Treasury, whom Walpole called
"as able and honest a servant as ever the Crown had."
[3] The Lord Treasurer's staff: since the dismissal of Godolphin, the Treasurer-
ship had been held in commission.

believe he will be the same man still, bating the necessary forms of grandeur he must keep up. 'Tis late, sirrahs, and I'll go sleep.

23. Morning. I sat up late last night, and waked late to-day; but will now answer your letter in bed before I go to town, and I will send it to-morrow; for perhaps you mayn't go so soon to Wexford.—No, you are not out in your number; the last was Number 14, and so I told you twice or thrice; will you never be satisfied? What shall we do for poor Stella? Go to Wexford, for God's sake: I wish you were to walk there by three miles a day, with a good lodging at every mile's end. Walking has done me so much good, that I cannot but prescribe it often to poor Stella. Parvisol has sent me a bill for fifty pounds, which I am sorry for, having not written to him for it, only mentioned it two months ago; but I hope he will be able to pay you what I have drawn upon him for: he never sent me any sum before, but one bill of twenty pounds half a year ago. You are welcome as my blood to every farthing I have in the world; and all that grieves me is, I am not richer, for MD's sake, as hope saved.[1] I suppose you give up your lodgings when you go to Wexford; yet that will be inconvenient too: yet I wish again you were under a necessity of rambling the country until Michaelmas, faith. No, let them keep the shelves, with a pox; yet they are exacting people about those four weeks; or Mrs. Brent may have the shelves, if she please. I am obliged to your Dean for his kind offer of lending me money. Will that be enough to say? A hundred people would lend me money, or to any man who has not the reputation of a squanderer. O, faith, I should be glad to be in the same kingdom with MD, however, although you are at Wexford. But I am kept here by a most capricious fate, which I would break through, if I could do it with decency or honour. — To return without some mark of distinction would look extremely little; and I would likewise gladly be somewhat richer than I am. I will say no more, but beg you

---

[1] "As I hope to be saved."

to be easy till Fortune take her course, and to believe that MD's felicity is the great end I aim at in all my pursuits. And so let us talk no more on this subject, which makes me melancholy, and that I would fain divert. Believe me, no man breathing at present has less share of happiness in life than I : I do not say I am unhappy at all, but that everything here is tasteless to me for want of being as I would be. And so, a short sigh, and no more of this. Well, come and let's see what's next, young women. Pox take Mrs. Edgworth and Sterne ! I will take some methods about that box. What orders would you have me give about the picture? Can't you do with it as if it were your own? No, I hope Manley will keep his place ; for I hear nothing of Sir Thomas Frankland's losing his. *I* Send nothing under cover to Mr. Addison, but "To Erasmus Lewis, Esq.; at my Lord Dartmouth's office at Whitehall."*/* Direct your outside so.— Poor dear Stella, don't write in the dark, nor in the light neither, but dictate to Dingley ; she is a naughty, healthy girl, and may drudge for both. Are you good company together? and don't you quarrel too often? Pray love one another, and kiss one another just now, as Dingley is reading this ; for you quarrelled this morning just after Mrs. Marget [1] had poured water on Stella's head : I heard the little bird say so. Well, I have answered everything in your letter that required it, and yet the second side is not full. I'll come home at night, and say more ; and to-morrow this goes for certain. Go, get you gone to your own chambers, and let Presto rise like a modest gentleman, and walk to town. I fancy I begin to sweat less in the forehead by constant walking than I used to do ; but then I shall be so sunburnt, the ladies will not like me. Come, let me rise, sirrahs. Morrow.—At night. I dined with Ford to-day at his lodgings, and I found wine out of my own cellar, some of my own chest of the great Duke's wine : it begins to turn. They say wine with you in Ireland is half a crown a bottle. 'Tis as Stella says ; nothing that once grows dear in Ireland ever

[1] Stella's maid.

grows cheap again, except corn, with a pox, to ruin the
parson. I had a letter to-day from the Archbishop of
Dublin, giving me further thanks about vindicating him to
Mr. Harley and Mr. St. John, and telling me a long story
about your Mayor's election,[1] wherein I find he has had a
finger, and given way to further talk about him; but we
know nothing of it here yet. This walking to and fro, and
dressing myself, takes up so much of my time that I cannot
go among company so much as formerly; yet what must a
body do? I thank God I yet continue much better since
I left the town; I know not how long it may last. I am
sure it has done me some good for the present. I do not
totter as I did, but walk firm as a cock, only once or twice
for a minute, I do not know how; but it went off, and I
never followed it. Does Dingley read my hand as well as
ever? do you, sirrah? Poor Stella must not read Presto's
ugly small hand.

> Preserve your eyes,
> If you be wise.

Your friend Walls's tea will go in a day or two towards
Chester by one Parson Richardson. My humble service to
her, and to good Mrs. Stoyte, and Catherine; and pray walk
while you continue in Dublin. I expect your next but one
will be from Wexford. God bless dearest MD.

24. Morning. Mr. Secretary has sent his groom hither,
to invite me to dinner to-day, etc. God Almighty for ever
bless and preserve you both, and give you health, etc. Amen.
Farewell, etc.

Do not I often say the same thing two or three times in
the same letter, sirrah?

Great wits, they say, have but short memories; that's good
vile conversation.

[1] See letter from King to Swift, May 15, 1711. Alderman Constantine, a
High Churchman, indignant at being passed over by a junior in the contest for
the mayoralty, brought the matter before the Council Board, and produced
an old by-law by which aldermen, according to their ancientry, were required
to keep their mayoralty. King took the side of the city, but the majority
was for the by-law, and disapproved of the election; whereupon the citizens
repealed the by-law and re-elected the same alderman as before.

LETTER XXIV

CHELSEA, *May 24, 1711.*

MORNING. Once in my life the number of my letters and of the day of the month is the same; that's lucky, boys; that's a sign that things will meet, and that we shall make a figure together. What, will you still have the impudence to say London, England, because I say Dublin, Ireland? Is there no difference between London and Dublin, saucyboxes? I have sealed up my letter, and am going to town. Morrow, sirrahs.—At night. I dined with the Secretary to-day; we sat down between five and six. Mr. Harley's patent passed this morning: he is now Earl of Oxford, Earl Mortimer, and Lord Harley of Wigmore Castle. My letter was sealed, or I would have told you this yesterday; but the public news may tell it you. The Queen, for all her favour, has kept a rod[1] for him in her closet this week; I suppose he will take it from her, though, in a day or two. At eight o'clock this evening it rained prodigiously, as it did from five; however, I set out, and in half-way the rain lessened, and I got home, but tolerably wet; and this is the first wet walk I have had in a month's time that I am here: but, however, I got to bed, after a short visit to Atterbury.

25. It rained this morning, and I went to town by water; and Ford and I dined with Mr. Lewis by appointment. I ordered Patrick to bring my gown and periwig to Mr. Lewis, because I designed to go to see Lord Oxford, and so I told the dog; but he never came, though I stayed an hour longer than I appointed; so I went in my old gown, and sat with him two hours, but could not talk over some business I had with him; so he has desired me to dine with him on Sunday, and I must disappoint the Secretary. My lord set me down at a coffee-house, where I waited for the Dean of Carlisle's chariot to bring me to Chelsea; for it has rained prodigiously all this afternoon. The Dean did not come himself, but sent

[1] The Lord Treasurer's staff.

me his chariot, which has cost me two shillings to the coachman; and so I am got home, and Lord knows what is become of Patrick. I think I must send him over to you; for he is an intolerable rascal. If I had come without a gown, he would have served me so, though my life and preferment should have lain upon it: and I am making a livery for him will cost me four pounds; but I will order the tailor to-morrow to stop till further orders. My Lord Oxford can't yet abide to be called "my lord"; and when I called him "my lord," he called me "Dr. Thomas Swift,"[1] which he always does when he has a mind to tease me. By a second hand, he proposed my being his chaplain, which I by a second hand excused; but we had no talk of it to-day: but I will be no man's chaplain alive. But I must go and be busy.

26. I never saw Patrick till this morning, and that only once, for I dressed myself without him; and when I went to town he was out of the way. I immediately sent for the tailor, and ordered him to stop his hand in Patrick's clothes till further orders. Oh, if it were in Ireland, I should have turned him off ten times ago; and it is no regard to him, but myself, that has made me keep him so long. Now I am afraid to give the rogue his clothes. What shall I do? I wish MD were here to entreat for him, just here at the bed's side. Lady Ashburnham[2] has been engaging me this long time to dine with her, and I set to-day apart for it; and whatever was the mistake, she sent me word she was at dinner and undressed, but would be glad to see me in the afternoon: so I dined with Mrs. Vanhomrigh, and would not go to see her at all, in a huff. My fine Florence is turning sour with a vengeance, and I have not drunk half of it. As I was coming home to-night, Sir Thomas Mansel and Tom Harley[3] met me

[1] Swift's "little parson cousin," the resident chaplain at Moor Park. He pretended to have had some part in *The Tale of a Tub*, and Swift always professed great contempt for him. Thomas Swift was son of an Oxford uncle of Swift's, of the same name, and was at school and college with Swift. He became Rector of Puttenham, Surrey, and died in 1752, aged eighty-seven.
[2] The Duke of Ormond's daughter, Lady Mary Butler (see p. 44).
[3] Thomas Harley, the Lord Treasurer's cousin, was secretary to the Treasury.

15

in the Park, and made me walk with them till nine, like
unreasonable whelps ; so I got not here till ten : but it was a
fine evening, and the foot-path clean enough already after this
hard rain.

27. Going this morning to town, I saw two old lame fellows,
walking to a brandy-shop, and when they got to the door,
stood a long time complimenting who should go in first.
Though this be no jest to tell, it was an admirable one to see.
I dined to-day with my Lord Oxford and the ladies, the new
Countess, and Lady Betty,[1] who has been these three days a
lady born. My lord left us at seven, and I had no time to
speak to him about some affairs ; but he promises in a day or
two we shall dine alone ; which is mighty likely, considering we expect every moment that the Queen will give him
the staff, and then he will be so crowded he will be good
for nothing : for aught I know he may have it to-night at
Council.

28. I had a petition sent me t'other day from one
Stephen Gernon, setting forth that he formerly lived with
Harry Tenison,[2] who gave him an employment of gauger,
and that he was turned out after Harry's death, and came
for England, and is now starving, or, as he expresses it, *that
the staff of life has been of late a stranger to his appetite.* To-
day the poor fellow called, and I knew him very well, a young
slender fellow with freckles in his face : you must remember
him ; he waited at table as a better sort of servant. I gave
him a crown, and promised to do what I could to help him
to a service, which I did for Harry Tenison's memory. It
was bloody hot walking to-day, and I was so lazy I dined
where my new gown was, at Mrs. Vanhomrigh's, and came
back like a fool, and the Dean of Carlisle has sat with me till
eleven. Lord Oxford has not the staff yet.

[1] Lord Oxford's daughter Elizabeth married, in 1712, the Marquis of
Caermarthen.
[2] Henry Tenison, M.P. for County Louth, was one of the Commissioners of
the Revenue in Ireland from 1704 until his death in 1709 (Luttrell, v. 381,
vi. 523). Probably he was related to Dr. Tenison, Bishop of Meath, who died
in 1705.

29. I was this morning in town by ten, though it was shaving-day, and went to the Secretary about some affairs, then visited the Duke and Duchess of Ormond; but the latter was dressing to go out, and I could not see her. My Lord Oxford had the staff given him this morning; so now I must call him Lord Oxford no more, but Lord Treasurer: I hope he will stick there: this is twice he has changed his name this week; and I heard to-day in the City (where I dined) that he will very soon have the Garter.—Pr'ythee, do not you observe how strangely I have changed my company and manner of living? I I never go to a coffee-house; you hear no more of Addison, Steele, Henley, Lady Lucy, Mrs. Finch,[1] Lord Somers, Lord Halifax, etc. I think I have altered for the better. Did I tell you the Archbishop of Dublin has writ me a long letter of a squabble in your town about choosing a Mayor, and that he apprehended some censure for the share he had in it?[2] I have not heard anything of it here; but I shall not be always able to defend him. We hear your Bishop Hickman is dead;[3] but nobody here will do anything for me in Ireland; so they may die as fast or slow as they please.—Well, you are constant to your deans, and your Stoyte, and your Walls. Walls will have her tea soon; Parson Richardson is either going or gone to Ireland, and has it with him. I hear Mr. Lewis has two letters for me: I could not call for them to-day, but will to-morrow; and perhaps one of them may be from our little MD, who knows, man? who can tell? Many a more unlikely thing has happened.—Pshaw, I write so plaguy little, I can hardly see it myself. *Write bigger, sirrah*[4] Presto. No, but I won't. Oh, you are a saucy rogue, Mr. Presto, you are so impudent.

---

[1] Anne Finch (died 1720), daughter of Sir William Kingsmill, and wife of Heneage Finch, who became fourth Earl of Winchelsea in 1712. Lady Winchelsea published a volume of poems in 1713, and was a friend of Pope and Rowe. Wordsworth recognised the advance in the growth of attention to "external nature" shown in her writings.

[2] See pp. 223, 297.

[3] This was a mistake. Charles Hickman, D.D., Bishop of Derry, died in November 1713.

[4] "These words in italics are written in a large round hand" (Deane Swift).

Come, dear rogues, let Presto go to sleep; I have been with the Dean, and 'tis near twelve.

30. I am so hot and lazy after my morning's walk, that I loitered at Mrs. Vanhomrigh's, where my best gown and periwig are, and out of mere listlessness dine there very often; so I did to-day; but I got little MD's letter, N. 15 (you see, sirrahs, I remember to tell the number), from Mr. Lewis, and I read it in a closet they lend me at Mrs. Van's; and I find Stella is a saucy rogue and a great writer, and can write finely still when her hand is in, and her pen good. When I came here to-night, I had a mighty mind to go swim after I was cool, for my lodging is just by the river; and I went down with only my nightgown and slippers on at eleven, but came up again; however, one of these nights I will venture.

31. I was so hot this morning with my walk, that I resolve to do so no more during this violent burning weather. It is comical that now we happen to have such heat to ripen the fruit there has been the greatest blast that was ever known, and almost all the fruit is despaired of. I dined with Lord Shelburne: Lady Kerry and Mrs. Pratt are going to Ireland. I went this evening to Lord Treasurer, and sat about two hours with him in mixed company; he left us, and went to Court, and carried two staves with him, so I suppose we shall have a new Lord Steward or Comptroller to-morrow; I smoked that State secret out by that accident. I will not answer your letter yet, sirrahs; no I won't, madam.

June 1. I wish you a merry month of June. I dined again with the Vans and Sir Andrew Fountaine. I always give them a flask of my Florence, which now begins to spoil, but it is near an end. I went this afternoon to Mrs. Vedeau's, and brought away Madam Dingley's parchment and letter of attorney. Mrs. Vedeau tells me she has sent the bill a fortnight ago. I will give the parchment to Ben Tooke, and you shall send him a letter of attorney at your leisure, enclosed to Mr. Presto. Yes, I now think your mackerel is full as good as ours, which I did not think formerly. I was bit about two staves, for there is no new officer made to-day. This

letter will find you still in Dublin, I suppose, or at Donnybrook, or losing your money at Walls' (how does she do?).

2. I missed this day by a blunder and dining in the City.[1]

3. No boats on Sunday, never: so I was forced to walk,
and so hot by the time I got to Ford's lodging that I was
quite spent; I think the weather is mad. I could not go to
church. I dined with the Secretary as usual, and old Colonel
Graham[2] that lived at Bagshot Heath, and they said it was
Colonel Graham's house. Pshaw, I remember it very well,
when I used to go for a walk to London from Moor Park.
What, I warrant you do not remember the Golden Farmer[3]
neither, figgarkick soley?[4]

4. When must we answer this letter, this N. 15 of our
little MD? Heat and laziness, and Sir Andrew Fountaine,
made me dine to-day again at Mrs. Van's; and, in short, this
weather is unsupportable: how is it with you? Lady Betty
Butler and Lady Ashburnham sat with me two or three hours
this evening in my closet at Mrs. Van's. They are very good
girls; and if Lady Betty went to Ireland, you should let her
be acquainted with you. How does Dingley do this hot
weather? Stella, I think, never complains of it; she loves
hot weather. There has not been a drop of rain since Friday
se'ennight. Yes, you do love hot weather, naughty Stella,
you do so; and Presto can't abide it. Be a good girl then,
and I will love you; and love one another, and don't be
quarrelling girls.

5. I dined in the City to-day, and went from hence early
to town, and visited the Duke of Ormond and Mr. Secretary.
They say my Lord Treasurer has a dead warrant in his

---

[1] "This entry is interlined in the original" (Deane Swift).

[2] Colonel James Graham (1649-1730) held various offices under James II.,
and was granted a lease of a lodge in Bagshot Park. Like his brother,
Viscount Preston, he was suspected of treasonable practices in 1691, and he
was arrested in 1692 and 1696. Under Queen Anne and George I. Colonel
Graham was M.P. for Appleby and Westmorland.

[3] Mr. Leslie Stephen has pointed out that this is the name of an inn (now
the Jolly Farmer) near Frimley, on the hill between Bagshot and Farnborough.
This inn is still called the Golden Farmer on the Ordnance map.

[4] "Soley" is probably a misreading for "sollah," a form often used by
Swift for "sirrah," and "figgarkick" may be "pilgarlick" (a poor creature)
in Swift's "little language" (cf. p. 317).

pocket; they mean a list of those who are to be turned out
of employment; and we every day now expect those changes.
I passed by the Treasury to-day, and saw vast crowds waiting
to give Lord Treasurer petitions as he passes by. He is now
at the top of power and favour: he keeps no levees yet. I
am cruel thirsty this hot weather.—I am just this minute
going to swim. I take Patrick down with me, to hold my
nightgown, shirt, and slippers, and borrow a napkin of my
landlady for a cap. So farewell till I come up; but there is
no danger, don't be frighted.—I have been swimming this
half-hour and more; and when I was coming out I dived, to
make my head and all through wet, like a cold bath; but, as
I dived, the napkin fell off and is lost, and I have that to
pay for. O, faith, the great stones were so sharp, I could
hardly set my feet on them as I came out. It was pure and
warm. I got to bed, and will now go sleep.

6. Morning. This letter shall go to-morrow; so I will
answer yours when I come home to-night. I feel no hurt
from last night's swimming. I lie with nothing but the sheet
over me, and my feet quite bare. I must rise and go to town
before the tide is against me. Morrow, sirrahs; dear sirrahs,
morrow.—At night. I never felt so hot a day as this since I
was born. I dined with Lady Betty Germaine, and there was
the young Earl of Berkeley [1] and his fine lady. I never saw
her before, nor think her near so handsome as she passes
for.—After dinner, Mr. Bertue [2] would not let me put ice
in my wine, but said my Lord Dorchester [3] got the bloody
flux with it, and that it was the worst thing in the world.
Thus are we plagued, thus are we plagued; yet I have done
it five or six times this summer, and was but the drier and the
hotter for it. Nothing makes me so excessively peevish as
hot weather. Lady Berkeley after dinner clapped my hat on

[1] See p. 134.

[2] Probably a misprint for " Bertie." This Mr. Bertie may have been the
Hon. James Bertie, second son of the first Earl of Abingdon, and M.P. for
Middlesex.

[3] Evelyn Pierrepont, fifth Earl of Kingston, was made Marquis of Dorchester
in 1706. He became Duke of Kingston-upon-Hull in 1715, and died in 1726,
Lady Mary Wortley Montagu was his daughter.

another lady's head, and she in roguery put it upon the rails.
I minded them not; but in two minutes they called me to
the window, and Lady Carteret[1] showed me my hat out of
her window five doors off, where I was forced to walk to it,
and pay her and old Lady Weymouth[2] a visit, with some more
beldames. Then I went and drank coffee, and made one or
two puns, with Lord Pembroke,[3] and designed to go to Lord
Treasurer; but it was too late, and beside I was half broiled,
and broiled without butter; for I never sweat after dinner, if
I drink any wine. Then I sat an hour with Lady Betty
Butler at tea, and everything made me hotter and drier.
Then I walked home, and was here by ten, so miserably hot,
that I was in as perfect a passion as ever I was in my life
at the greatest affront or provocation. Then I sat an hour,
till I was quite dry and cool enough to go swim; which I did,
but with so much vexation that I think I have given it over :
for I was every moment disturbed by boats, rot them; and
that puppy Patrick, standing ashore, would let them come
within a yard or two, and then call sneakingly to them. The
only comfort I proposed here in hot weather is gone; for
there is no jesting with those boats after it is dark : I had
none last night. I dived to dip my head, and held my cap
on with both my hands, for fear of losing it. Pox take the
boats! Amen. 'Tis near twelve, and so I'll answer your
letter (it strikes twelve now) to-morrow morning.

7. Morning. Well, now let us answer MD's letter, N. 15,
15, 15, 15. Now have I told you the number? 15, 15; there,
impudence, to call names in the beginning of your letter,
before you say, How do you do, Mr. Presto? There is
your breeding! Where is your manners, sirrah, to a gentleman? Get you gone, you couple of jades.—No, I never sit
up late now; but this abominable hot weather will force me
to eat or drink something that will do me hurt. I do venture

[1] See p. 116.
[2] Sir Thomas Thynne, first Viscount Weymouth, who died in 1714, aged
seventy-four, married Frances, daughter of Heneage Finch, second Earl of
Winchelsea.
[3] See p. 52.

to eat a few strawberries.—Why then, do you know in Ireland that Mr. St. John talked so in Parliament?[1] Your Whigs are plaguily bit; for he is entirely for their being all out.—And are you as vicious in snuff as ever? I believe, as you say, it does neither hurt nor good; but I have left it off, and when anybody offers me their box, I take about a tenth part of what I used to do, and then just smell to it, and privately fling the rest away. I keep to my tobacco still,[2] as you say; but even much less of that than formerly, only mornings and evenings, and very seldom in the day.—As for Joe,[3] I have recommended his case heartily to my Lord Lieutenant; and, by his direction, given a memorial of it to Mr. Southwell, to whom I have recommended it likewise. I can do no more, if he were my brother. His business will be to apply himself to Southwell. And you must desire Raymond, if Price of Galway comes to town, to desire him to wait on Mr. South-well, as recommended by me for one of the Duke's chaplains, which was all I could do for him; and he must be presented to the Duke, and make his court, and ply about, and find out some vacancy, and solicit early for it. The bustle about your Mayor I had before, as I told you, from the Archbishop of Dublin. Was Raymond not come till May 18? So he says fine things of me? Certainly he lies. I am sure I used him indifferently enough; and we never once dined together, or walked, or were in any third place; only he came some-times to my lodgings, and even there was oftener denied than admitted.—What an odd bill is that you sent of Raymond's! A bill upon one Murry in Chester, which depends entirely not only upon Raymond's honesty, but his discretion; and in money matters he is the last man I would depend on. Why should Sir Alexander Cairnes[4] in London pay me a bill, drawn

---

[1] Swift is referring to St. John's defence of Brydges (see p. 201).

[2] " He does not mean smoking, which he never practised, but snuffing up cut-and-dry tobacco, which sometimes was just coloured with Spanish snuff; and this he used all his life, but would not own that he took snuff" (Deane Swift).

[3] Beaumont (see p. 1).

[4] Sir Alexander Cairnes, M.P. for Monaghan, a banker, was created a baronet in 1706, and died in 1732.

by God knows who, upon Murry in Chester? I was at
Cairnes's, and they can do no such thing. I went among
some friends, who are merchants, and I find the bill must be
sent to Murry, accepted by him, and then returned back, and
then Cairnes may accept or refuse it as he pleases. Accordingly I gave Sir Thomas Frankland the bill, who has sent it
to Chester, and ordered the postmaster there to get it
accepted, and then send it back, and in a day or two I shall
have an answer; and therefore this letter must stay a day
or two longer than I intended, and see what answer I get.
Raymond should have written to Murry at the same time, to
desire Sir Alexander Cairnes to have answered such a bill, if
it come. But Cairnes's clerks (himself was not at home) said
they had received no notice of it, and could do nothing;
and advised me to send to Murry.—I have been six weeks
to-day at Chelsea, and you know it but just now. And so
Dean —— thinks I write the *Medley*. Pox of his judgment!
It is equal to his honesty. Then you han't seen the *Miscellany* yet?[1] Why, 'tis a four-shilling book: has nobody
carried it over?—No, I believe Manley[2] will not lose his
place; for his friend[3] in England is so far from being out
that he has taken a new patent since the Post Office Act;
and his brother Jack Manley[4] here takes his part firmly; and
I have often spoken to Southwell in his behalf, and he seems
very well inclined to him. But the Irish folks here in general
are horribly violent against him. Besides, he must consider
he could not send Stella wine if he were put out. And so he
is very kind, and sends you a dozen bottles of wine *at a time*,
and you win eight shillings *at a time*; and how much do you
lose? No, no, never one syllable about that, I warrant
you.—Why, this same Stella is so unmerciful a writer, she
has hardly left any room for Dingley. If you have such
summer there as here, sure the Wexford waters are good
by this time. I forgot what weather we had May 6th; go
look in my journal. We had terrible rain the 24th and

[1] See pp. 43, 160.
[2] Isaac Manley (see p. 7).
[3] Sir Thomas Frankland.
[4] See p. 24.

25th, and never a drop since. Yes, yes, I remember
Berested's bridge; the coach sosses up and down as one
goes that way, just as at Hockley-in-the-Hole.[1] I never
impute any illness or health I have to good or ill weather,
but to want of exercise, or ill air, or something I have
eaten, or hard study, or sitting up; and so I fence against
those as well as I can: but who a deuce can help the
weather|? Will Seymour,[2] the General, was excessively hot
with the sun shining full upon him; so he turns to the
sun, and says, "Harkee, friend, you had better go and ripen
cucumbers than plague me at this rate," etc. Another time,
fretting at the heat, a gentleman by said it was such weather
as pleased God: Seymour said, "Perhaps it may; but I am
sure it pleases nobody else." Why, Madam Dingley, the
First-Fruits are done. Southwell told me they went to
inquire about them, and Lord Treasurer said they were done,
and had been done long ago. And I'll tell you a secret you
must not mention, that the Duke of Ormond is ordered to
take notice of them in his speech in your Parliament: and
I desire you will take care to say on occasion that my Lord
Treasurer Harley did it many months ago, before the Duke
was Lord Lieutenant. And yet I cannot possibly come over
yet: so get you gone to Wexford, and make Stella well.—
Yes, yes, I take care not to walk late; I never did but once,
and there are five hundred people on the way as I walk.—
Tisdall is a puppy, and I will excuse him the half-hour he
would talk with me. As for the *Examiner*, I have heard a
whisper that after that of this day,[3] which tells us what this
Parliament has done, you will hardly find them so good. I
prophesy they will be trash for the future; and methinks in
this day's *Examiner* the author talks doubtfully, as if he would

---

[1] Hockley-in-the-Hole, Clerkenwell, a place of public diversion, was famous
for its bear and bull baitings.
[2] Sir William Seymour, second son of Sir Edward Seymour, Bart., of Berry
Pomeroy, retired from the army in 1717, and died in 1728 (Dalton's *Army
Lists*). He was wounded at Landen and Vigo, and saw much service between
his appointment as a Captain of Fusiliers in 1686 and his promotion to the rank
of Lieutenant-General in 1707.
[3] No. 45.

write no more.[1] Observe whether the change be discovered in Dublin, only for your own curiosity, that's all. Make a mouth there. Mrs. Vedeau's business I have answered, and I hope the bill is not lost. Morrow. 'Tis stewing hot, but I must rise and go to town between fire and water. Morrow, sirrahs both, morrow.—At night. I dined to-day with Colonel Crowe, Governor of Jamaica, and your friend Sterne. I presented Sterne to my Lord Treasurer's brother,[2] and gave him his case, and engaged him in his favour. At dinner there fell the swingingest long shower, and the most grateful to me, that ever I saw: it thundered fifty times at least, and the air is so cool that a body is able to live; and I walked home to-night with comfort, and without dirt. I went this evening to Lord Treasurer, and sat with him two hours, and we were in very good humour, and he abused me, and called me Dr. Thomas Swift fifty times: I have told you he does that when he has mind to make me mad.[3] Sir Thomas Frankland gave me to-day a letter from Murry, accepting my bill; so all is well: only, by a letter from Parvisol, I find there are some perplexities.—Joe has likewise written to me, to thank me for what I have done for him; and desires I would write to the Bishop of Clogher, that Tom Ashe[4] may not hinder his father[5] from being portreve. I have written and sent to Joe several times, that I will not trouble myself at all about Trim. I wish them their liberty, but they do not deserve it: so tell Joe, and send to him. I am mighty happy with this rain: I was at the end of my patience, but now I live again. This cannot go till Saturday; and perhaps I may go out of town with Lord Shelburne and Lady Kerry to-morrow for two or

---

[1] "And now I conceive the main design I had in writing these papers is fully executed. A great majority of the nation is at length thoroughly convinced that the Queen proceeded with the highest wisdom, in changing her Ministry and Parliament" (*Examiner*, No. 45).

[2] Edward Harley (see p. 124). [3] See p. 225.

[4] Tom Ashe was an elder brother of the Bishop of Clogher. He had an estate of more than £1000 a year in County Meath, and Nichols describes him as of droll appearance, thick and short in person: "a facetious, pleasant companion, but the most eternal unwearied punster that ever lived."

[5] "Even Joseph Beaumont, the son, was at this time an old man, whose grey locks were venerable; yet his father lived until about 1719" (Deane Swift).

three days. Lady Kerry has written to desire it; but to-morrow I shall know further.—O this dear rain, I cannot forbear praising it : I never felt myself to be revived so in my life. It lasted from three till five, hard as a horn, and mixed with hail.

8. Morning. I am going to town, and will just finish this there, if I go into the country with Lady Kerry and Lord Shelburne : so morrow, till an hour or two hence.—In town. I met Cairnes, who, I suppose, will pay me the money; though he says I must send him the bill first, and I will get it done in absence. Farewell, etc. etc.

LETTER XXV

CHELSEA, *June* 9, 10, 11, 12, 13, 14, 15, 16, 17, 18, 19, 20.

I HAVE been all this time at Wycombe, between Oxford and London, with Lord Shelburne, who has the squire's house at the town's end, and an estate there in a delicious country. Lady Kerry and Mrs. Pratt were with us, and we passed our time well enough; and there I wholly disengaged myself from all public thoughts, and everything but MD, who had the impudence to send me a letter there; but I'll be revenged: I will answer it. This day, the 20th, I came from Wycombe with Lady Kerry after dinner, lighted at Hyde Park Corner, and walked : it was twenty-seven miles, and we came it in about five hours.

21. I went at noon to see Mr. Secretary at his office, and there was Lord Treasurer : so I killed two birds, etc., and we were glad to see one another, and so forth. And the Secretary and I dined at Sir William Wyndham's,[1] who married Lady Catharine Seymour, your acquaintance, I

---

[1] Sir William Wyndham, Bart. (1687–1740), was M.P. for Somerset. He was a close partisan of Bolingbroke's, and in 1713 introduced the Schism Bill, which drove Oxford from office. Wyndham became Chancellor of the Exchequer, and was afterwards a leading opponent of Walpole. His wife, Lady Catherine Seymour (died 1713), was the second daughter of Charles, Duke of Somerset (see p. 270).

suppose. There were ten of us at dinner. It seems, in my absence, they had erected a Club,[1] and made me one; and we made some laws to-day, which I am to digest and add to, against next meeting. Our meetings are to be every Thursday. We are yet but twelve : Lord Keeper and Lord Treasurer were proposed; but I was against them, and so was Mr. Secretary, though their sons are of it, and so they are excluded; but we design to admit the Duke of Shrewsbury. The end of our Club is, to advance conversation and friendship, and to reward deserving persons with our interest and recommendation. We take in none but men of wit or men of interest; and if we go on as we begin, no other Club in this town will be worth talking of. The Solicitor-General, Sir Robert Raymond, is one of our Club; and I ordered him immediately to write to your Lord Chancellor in favour of Dr. Raymond : so tell Raymond, if you see him; but I believe this will find you at Wexford. This letter will come three weeks after the last, so there is a week lost; but that is owing to my being out of town; yet I think it is right, because it goes enclosed to Mr. Reading :[2] and why should he know how often Presto writes to MD, pray ?—I sat this evening with Lady Betty Butler and Lady Ashburnham, and then came home by eleven, and had a good cool walk; for we have had no extreme hot weather this fortnight, but a great deal of rain at times, and a body can live and breathe. I hope it will hold so. We had peaches to-day.

22. I went late to-day to town, and dined with my friend Lewis. I saw Will Congreve attending at the Treasury, by order, with his brethren, the Commissioners of the Wine Licences. I had often mentioned him with kindness to Lord Treasurer; and Congreve told me that, after they had answered to what they were sent for, my lord called him privately, and spoke to him with great kindness, promising his protection, etc. The poor man said he had been used so

---

[1] Swift was afterwards President of this Club, which is better known as " the Society."

[2] Perhaps Daniel Reading, M.P. for Newcastle, Co. Dublin.

ill of late years that he was quite astonished at my lord's goodness, etc., and desired me to tell my lord so; which I did this evening, and recommended him heartily. My lord assured me he esteemed him very much, and would be always kind to him; that what he said was to make Congreve easy, because he knew people talked as if his lordship designed to turn everybody out, and particularly Congreve: which indeed was true, for the poor man told me he apprehended it. As I left my Lord Treasurer, I called on Congreve (knowing where he dined), and told him what had passed between my lord and me; so I have made a worthy man easy, and that is a good day's work.[1] I am proposing to my lord to erect a society or academy for correcting and settling our language, that we may not perpetually be changing as we do. He enters mightily into it, so does the Dean of Carlisle;[2] and I design to write a letter to Lord Treasurer with the proposals of it, and publish it;[3] and so I told my lord, and he approves it. Yesterday's[4] was a sad *Examiner*, and last week was very indifferent, though some little scraps of the old spirit, as if he had given some hints; but yesterday's is all trash. It is plain the hand is changed.

23. I have not been in London to-day: for Dr. Gastrell[5] and I dined, by invitation, with the Dean of Carlisle, my neighbour; so I know not what they are doing in the world, a mere country gentleman. And are not you ashamed both to go into the country just when I did, and stay ten days, just as I did, saucy monkeys? But I never rode; I had no horses, and our coach was out of order, and we went and came in a hired one. Do you keep your lodgings when you

[1] Afterwards Congreve formed a friendship with the Whigs; or, as Swift put it,

> "Took proper principles to thrive,
> And so might every dunce alive."

[2] Atterbury.
[3] This pamphlet, published in February 1712, was called *A Proposal for Correcting, Improving, and Ascertaining the English Tongue, in a Letter to the . . . Lord High Treasurer.*
[4] No. 47.
[5] Francis Gastrell, Canon of Christ Church, was made Bishop of Chester in 1713. His valuable *Notitia Cestriensis* was published in 1845–50.

go to Wexford? I suppose you do; for you will hardly stay above two months. I have been walking about our town to-night, and it is a very scurvy place for walking. I am thinking to leave it, and return to town, now the Irish folks are gone. Ford goes in three days. How does Dingley divert herself while Stella is riding? work, or read, or walk? Does Dingley ever read to you? Had you ever a book with you in the country? Is all that left off? Confess. Well, I'll go sleep; 'tis past eleven, and I go early to sleep: I write nothing at night but to MD.

24. Stratford and I, and Pastoral Philips (just come from Denmark) dined at Ford's to-day, who paid his way, and goes for Ireland on Tuesday. The Earl of Peterborow is returned from Vienna without one servant: he left them scattered in several towns of Germany. I had a letter from him, four days ago, from Hanover, where he desires I would immediately send him an answer to his house at Parson's Green,[1] about five miles off. I wondered what he meant, till I heard he was come. He sent expresses, and got here before them. He is above fifty, and as active as one of five-and-twenty. I have not seen him yet, nor know when I shall, or where to find him.

25. Poor Duke of Shrewsbury has been very ill of a fever: we were all in a fright about him: I thank God, he is better. I dined to-day at Lord Ashburnham's, with his lady, for he was not at home: she is a very good girl, and always a great favourite of mine. Sterne tells me he has desired a friend to receive your box in Chester, and carry it over. I fear he will miscarry in his business, which was sent to the Treasury before he was recommended; for I was positive only to second his recommendations, and all his other friends failed him. However, on your account I will do what I can for him to-morrow with the secretary of the Treasury.

26. We had much company to-day at dinner at Lord Treasurer's. Prior never fails: he is a much better courtier than I; and we expect every day that he will be a Com-

[1] Near Fulham.

missioner of the Customs, and that in a short time a great many more will be turned out. They blame Lord Treasurer for his slowness in turning people out; but I suppose he has his reasons. They still keep my neighbour Atterbury in suspense about the deanery of Christ Church,[1] which has been above six months vacant, and he is heartily angry. I reckon you are now preparing for your Wexford expedition; and poor Dingley is full of carking and caring, scolding. How long will you stay? Shall I be in Dublin before you return? Don't fall and hurt yourselves, nor overturn the coach. Love one another, and be good girls; and drink Presto's health in water, Madam Stella; and in good ale, Madam Dingley.

27. The Secretary appointed me to dine with him to-day, and we were to do a world of business: he came at four, and brought Prior with him, and had forgot the appointment, and no business was done. I left him at eight, and went to change my gown at Mrs. Vanhomrigh's; and there was Sir Andrew Fountaine at ombre with Lady Ashburnham and Lady Frederic Schomberg, and Lady Mary Schomberg,[2] and Lady Betty Butler, and others, talking; and it put me in mind of the Dean and Stoyte, and Walls, and Stella at play, and Dingley and I looking on. I stayed with them till ten, like a fool. Lady Ashburnham is something like Stella; so I helped her, and wished her good cards. It is late, etc.

28. Well, but I must answer this letter of our MD's. Saturday approaches, and I han't written down this side. O, faith, Presto has been a sort of a lazy fellow: but Presto will remove to town this day se'ennight; the Secretary has commanded me to do so; and I believe he and I shall go for some days to Windsor, where he will have leisure to mind some business we have together. To-day, our Society (it must not be called a Club) dined at Mr. Secretary's: we were but eight; the rest sent excuses, or were out of town.

[1] See p. 116.
[2] The daughters of Meinhardt Schomberg, Duke of Leinster, in Ireland, and third Duke of Schomberg. Lady Mary married Count Dagenfeldt, and Lady Frederica married, first, the Earl of Holderness, and, secondly, Earl Fitz Walter.

We sat till eight, and made some laws and settlements; and then I went to take leave of Lady Ashburnham, who goes out of town to-morrow, as a great many of my acquaintance are already, and left the town very thin. I shall make but short journeys this summer, and not be long out of London. The days are grown sensibly short already, all our fruit blasted. Your Duke of Ormond is still at Chester; and perhaps this letter will be with you as soon as he. Sterne's business is quite blown up: they stand to it to send him back to the Commissioners of the Revenue in Ireland for a reference, and all my credit could not alter it, though I almost fell out with the secretary of the Treasury,[1] who is my Lord Treasurer's cousin-germain, and my very good friend. It seems every step he has hitherto taken hath been wrong; at least they say so, and that is the same thing. I am heartily sorry for it; and I really think they are in the wrong, and use him hardly; but I can do no more.

29. Steele has had the assurance to write to me that I would engage my Lord Treasurer to keep a friend of his in an employment: I believe I told you how he and Addison served me for my good offices in Steele's behalf; and I promised Lord Treasurer never to speak for either of them again. Sir Andrew Fountaine and I dined to-day at Mrs. Vanhomrigh's. Dilly Ashe has been in town this fortnight: I saw him twice; he was four days at Lord Pembroke's in the country, punning with him; his face is very well. I was this evening two or three hours at Lord Treasurer's, who called me Dr. Thomas Swift twenty times; that's his way of teasing. I left him at nine, and got home here by ten, like a gentleman; and to-morrow morning I'll answer your little letter, sirrahs.

30. Morning. I am terribly sleepy always in a morning; I believe it is my walk over-night that disposes me to sleep: faith, 'tis now striking eight, and I am but just awake. Patrick comes early, and wakes me five or six times; but I have excuses, though I am three parts asleep. I tell him I

---

[1] Thomas Harley.

sat up late, or slept ill in the night, and often it is a lie.   I
have now got little MD's letter before me, N. 16, no more,
nor no less, no mistake.   Dingley says, "This letter won't be
above six lines"; and I was afraid it was true, though I saw
it filled on both sides.   The Bishop of Clogher writ me word
you were in the country, and that he heard you were well: I
am glad at heart MD rides, and rides, and rides.   Our hot
weather ended in May, and all this month has been
moderate: it was then so hot I was not able to endure it; I
was miserable every moment, and found myself disposed to
be peevish and quarrelsome: I believe a very hot country
would make me stark mad.—Yes, my head continues pretty
tolerable, and I impute it all to walking.   Does Stella eat
fruit?   I eat a little; but I always repent, and resolve against
it.   No, in very hot weather I always go to town by water;
but I constantly walk back, for then the sun is down.   And
so Mrs. Proby [1] goes with you to Wexford: she's admirable
company; you'll grow plaguy wise with those you frequent.
Mrs. Taylor and Mrs. Proby! take care of infection.   I
believe my two hundred pounds will be paid, but that Sir
Alexander Cairnes is a scrupulous puppy: I left the bill with
Mr. Stratford, who is to have the money.   Now, Madam Stella,
what say you? you ride every day; I know that already,
sirrah; and, if you rid every day for a twelvemonth, you
would be still better and better.   No, I hope Parvisol will
not have the impudence to make you stay an hour for the
money; if he does, I'll *un-parvisol* him; pray let me know.
O Lord, how hasty we are!   Stella can't stay writing and
writing; she must write and go a cock-horse, pray now.
Well, but the horses are not come to the door; the fellow
can't find the bridle; your stirrup is broken; where did you
put the whips, Dingley?   Marget, where have you laid Mrs.
Johnson's ribbon to tie about her? reach me my mask: sup
up this before you go.   So, so, a gallop, a gallop: sit fast,
sirrah, and don't ride hard upon the stones.—Well, now
Stella is gone, tell me, Dingley, is she a good girl? and what

[1] See p. 176.

news is that you are to tell me?—No, I believe the box is
not lost: Sterne says it is not.—No, faith, you must go to
Wexford without seeing your Duke of Ormond, unless you
stay on purpose; perhaps you may be so wise.—I tell you
this is your sixteenth letter; will you never be satisfied?
No, no, I will walk late no more; I ought less to venture it
than other people, and so I was told: but I will return to
lodge in town next Thursday. When you come from
Wexford, I would have you send a letter of attorney to Mr.
Benjamin Tooke, bookseller, in London, directed to me; and
he shall manage your affair. I have your parchment safely
locked up in London.—O, Madam Stella, welcome home; was
it pleasant riding? did your horse stumble? how often did
the man light to settle your stirrup? ride nine miles! faith,
you have galloped indeed. Well, but where is the fine thing
you promised me? I have been a good boy, ask Dingley
else. I believe you did not meet the fine-thing-man: faith,
you are a cheat. So you will see Raymond and his wife in
town. Faith, that riding to Laracor gives me short sighs, as
well as you. All the days I have passed here have been dirt
to those. I have been gaining enemies by the scores, and
friends by the couples; which is against the rules of wisdom,
because they say one enemy can do more hurt than ten
friends can do good. But I have had my revenge at least, if
I get nothing else. And so let Fate govern.—Now I think
your letter is answered; and mine will be shorter than
ordinary, because it must go to-day. We have had a great
deal of scattering rain for some days past, yet it hardly keeps
down the dust.—We have plays acted in our town; and
Patrick was at one of them, oh oh. He was damnably
mauled one day when he was drunk; he was at cuffs with a
brother-footman, who dragged him along the floor upon his
face, which looked for a week after as if he had the leprosy;
and I was glad enough to see it. I have been ten times
sending him over to you; yet now he has new clothes, and a
laced hat, which the hatter brought by his orders, and he
offered to pay for the lace out of his wages.—I am to dine

to-day with Dilly at Sir Andrew Fountaine's, who has bought
a new house, and will be weary of it in half a year. I must
rise and shave, and walk to town, unless I go with the Dean
in his chariot at twelve, which is too late: and I have not
seen that Lord Peterborow yet. The Duke of Shrewsbury is
almost well again, and will be abroad in a day or two: what
care you? There it is now: you do not care for my friends.
Farewell, my dearest lives and delights; I love you better
than ever, if possible, as hope saved, I do, and ever will.
God Almighty bless you ever, and make us happy together!
I pray for this twice every day; and I hope God will hear
my poor hearty prayers.—Remember, if I am used ill and
ungratefully, as I have formerly been, 'tis what I am
prepared for, and shall not wonder at it. Yet I am now
envied, and thought in high favour, and have every day
numbers of considerable men teasing me to solicit for them.
And the Ministry all use me perfectly well; and all that
know them say they love me. Yet I can count upon
nothing, nor will, but upon MD's love and kindness.—They
think me useful; they pretended they were afraid of none
but me, and that they resolved to have me; they have often
confessed this: yet all makes little impression on me.—Pox
of these speculations! they give me the spleen; and that is
a disease I was not born to. Let me alone, sirrahs, and be
satisfied: I am, as long as MD and Presto are well.

> Little wealth,
> And much health,
> And a life by stealth:

that is all we want; and so farewell, dearest MD; Stella,
Dingley, Presto, all together, now and for ever all together.
Farewell again and again.

LETTER XXVI

CHELSEA, *June* 30, 1711.

SEE what large paper I am forced to take, to write to MD; Patrick has brought me none clipped; but, faith, the next shall be smaller. I dined to-day, as I told you, with Dilly at Sir Andrew Fountaine's: there were we wretchedly punning, and writing together to Lord Pembroke. Dilly is just such a puppy as ever; and it is so uncouth, after so long an inter-mission. My twenty-fifth is gone this evening to the post. I think I will direct my next (which is this) to Mr. Curry's, and let them send it to Wexford; and then the next enclosed to Reading. Instruct me how I shall do. I long to hear from you from Wexford, and what sort of place it is. The town grows very empty and dull. This evening I have had a letter from Mr. Philips, the pastoral poet, to get him a certain employment from Lord Treasurer. I have now had almost all the Whig poets my solicitors; and I have been useful to Congreve, Steele, and Harrison: but I will do nothing for Philips; I find he is more a puppy than ever, so don't solicit for him. Besides, I will not trouble Lord Treasurer, unless upon some very extraordinary occasion.

July 1. Dilly lies conveniently for me when I come to town from Chelsea of a Sunday, and go to the Secretary's; so I called at his lodgings this morning, and sent for my gown, and dressed myself there. He had a letter from the Bishop, with an account that you were set out for Wexford the morning he writ, which was June 26, and he had the letter the 30th; that was very quick: the Bishop says you design to stay there two months or more. Dilly had also a letter from Tom Ashe, full of Irish news; that your Lady Lyndon [1] is dead, and I know not what besides of Dr. Coghill [2] losing

---

[1] The widow of Sir John Lyndon, who was appointed a Justice of the Court of King's Bench in Ireland in 1682, and died in 1699.

[2] "Marmaduke Coghill, LL.D., was Judge of the Prerogative Court in Ireland. About this time he courted a lady, and was soon to have been married to her; but unfortunately a cause was brought to trial before him,

his drab, etc. The Secretary was gone to Windsor, and I dined with Mrs. Vanhomrigh. Lord Treasurer is at Windsor too; they will be going and coming all summer, while the Queen is there, and the town is empty, and I fear I shall be sometimes forced to stoop beneath my dignity, and send to the ale-house for a dinner. Well, sirrahs, had you a good journey to Wexford? did you drink ale by the way? were you never overturned? how many things did you forget? do you lie on straw in your new town where you are? Cudshoe,[1] the next letter to Presto will be dated from Wexford. What fine company have you there? what new acquaintance have you got? You are to write constantly to Mrs. Walls and Mrs. Stoyte: and the Dean said, "Shall we never hear from you?" "Yes, Mr. Dean, we'll make bold to trouble you with a letter." Then at Wexford; when you meet a lady, "Did your waters pass well this morning, madam?" Will Dingley drink them too? Yes, I warrant; to get her a stomach. I suppose you are all gamesters at Wexford. Do not lose your money, sirrah, far from home. I believe I shall go to Windsor in a few days; at least, the Secretary tells me so. He has a small house there, with just room enough for him and me; and I would be satisfied to pass a few days there sometimes. Sirrahs, let me go to sleep, it is past twelve in our town.

2. Sterne came to me this morning, and tells me he has yet some hopes of compassing his business: he was with Tom Harley, the secretary of the Treasury, and made him doubt a little he was in the wrong; the poor man tells me it will almost undo him if he fails. I called this morning to see Will Congreve, who lives much by himself, is forced to read

wherein a man was sued for beating his wife. When the matter was agitated, the Doctor gave his opinion, 'That although a man had no right to beat his wife unmercifully, yet that, with such a little cane or switch as he then held in his hand, a husband was at liberty, and was invested with a power, to give his wife moderate correction'; which opinion determined the lady against having the Doctor. He died an old man and a bachelor" (Deane Swift). See also Lascelles, *Liber Muner. Hibern.*, part ii. p. 80.

[1] This was a common exclamation of the time, but the spelling varies in different writers. It seems to be a corruption of "God so," or "God ho," but there may have been a confusion with "cat-so," derived from the Italian "cazzo."

for amusement, and cannot do it without a magnifying-glass.
I have set him very well with the Ministry, and I hope he is
in no danger of losing his place. I dined in the City with
Dr. Freind, not among my merchants, but with a scrub
instrument of mischief of mine, whom I never mentioned to
you, nor am like to do. You two little saucy Wexfordians,
you are now drinking waters. You drink waters! you go
fiddlestick. Pray God send them to do you good; if not,
faith, next summer you shall come to the Bath.

3. Lord Peterborow desired to see me this morning at
nine; I had not seen him before since he came home. I
met Mrs. Manley [1] there, who was soliciting him to get some
pension or reward for her service in the cause, by writing her
Atalantis, and prosecution, etc., upon it. I seconded her,
and hope they will do something for the poor woman. My
lord kept me two hours upon politics: he comes home very
sanguine; he has certainly done great things at Savoy and
Vienna, by his negotiations: he is violent against a peace,
and finds true what I writ to him, that the Ministry seems
for it. He reasons well; yet I am for a peace. I took leave
of Lady Kerry, who goes to-morrow for Ireland; she picks
up Lord Shelburne and Mrs. Pratt at Lord Shelburne's house.
I was this evening with Lord Treasurer: Tom Harley was
there, and whispered me that he began to doubt about
Sterne's business; I told him he would find he was in the
wrong. I sat two or three hours at Lord Treasurer's; he
rallied me sufficiently upon my refusing to take him into our
Club, and told a judge who was with us that my name was
Thomas Swift. I had a mind to prevent Sir H. Belasyse [2]

[1] See p. 92. Mrs. Manley was now editing the *Examiner.*
[2] Sir Henry Belasyse was sent to Spain as Commissioner to inquire into the
state of the English forces in that country. The son of Sir Richard Belasyse,
Knight of Ludworth, Durham, Sir Henry finished a chequered career in
1717, when he was buried in Westminster Abbey (Dalton's *Army Lists,* ii. 228).
In his earlier years he served under the United Provinces, and after the accession of William was made a Brigadier-General in the English army, and
in 1694, Lieutenant-General. In 1702 he was second in command of the
expedition to Cadiz, but he was dismissed the service in consequence of the
looting of Port St. Mary. Subsequently he was elected M.P. for Durham,
and in 1713 was appointed Governor of Berwick.

going to Spain, who is a most covetous cur, and I fell a
railing against avarice, and turned it so that he smoked me,
and named Belasyse. I went on, and said it was a shame to
send him; to which he agreed, but desired I would name
some who understood business, and do not love money, for
he could not find them. I said there was something in a
Treasurer different from other men; that we ought not to
make a man a Bishop who does not love divinity, or a General
who does not love war; and I wondered why the Queen
would make a man Lord Treasurer who does not love money.
He was mightily pleased with what I said. He was talking
of the First-Fruits of England, and I took occasion to tell
him that I would not for a thousand pounds anybody but
he had got them for Ireland, who got them for England too.
He bid me consider what a thousand pounds was; I said I
would have him to know I valued a thousand pounds as little
as he valued a million.—Is it not silly to write all this? but
it gives you an idea what our conversation is with mixed
company. I have taken a lodging in Suffolk Street, and go
to it on Thursday; and design to walk the Park and the
town, to supply my walking here: yet I will walk here
sometimes too, in a visit now and then to the Dean.[1] When
I was almost at home, Patrick told me he had two letters for
me, and gave them to me in the dark, yet I could see one
of them was from saucy MD. I went to visit the Dean for
half an hour; and then came home, and first read the other
letter, which was from the Bishop of Clogher, who tells me
the Archbishop of Dublin mentioned in a full assembly of the
clergy the Queen's granting the First-Fruits, said it was
done by the Lord Treasurer, and talked much of my merit
in it: but reading yours I find nothing of that: perhaps the
Bishop lies, out of a desire to please me. I dined with Mrs.
Vanhomrigh. Well, sirrahs, you are gone to Wexford; but
I'll follow you.

4. Sterne came to me again this morning, to advise about
reasons and memorials he is drawing up; and we went to

[1] Atterbury.

town by water together; and having nothing to do, I stole
into the City to an instrument of mine, and then went to see
poor Patty Rolt,[1] who has been in town these two months
with a cousin of hers. Her life passes with boarding in some
country town as cheap as she can, and, when she runs out,
shifting to some cheaper place, or coming to town for a
month. If I were rich, I would ease her, which a little
thing would do. Some months ago I sent her a guinea, and
it patched up twenty circumstances. She is now going to
Berkhamstead in Hertfordshire. It has rained and hailed
prodigiously to-day, with some thunder. This is the last
night I lie at Chelsea; and I got home early, and sat two
hours with the Dean, and ate victuals, having had a very
scurvy dinner. I'll answer your letter when I come to live
in town. You shall have a fine London answer: but first I
will go sleep, and dream of MD.

London, July 5. This day I left Chelsea for good (that's
a genteel phrase), and am got into Suffolk Street. I dined
to-day at our Society, and we are adjourned for a month,
because most of us go into the country: we dined at Lord
Keeper's with young Harcourt, and Lord Keeper was forced
to sneak off, and dine with Lord Treasurer, who had invited
the Secretary and me to dine with him; but we scorned to
leave our company, as George Granville did, whom we have
threatened to expel: however, in the evening I went to Lord
Treasurer, and, among other company, found a couple of
judges with him; one of them, Judge Powell,[2] an old fellow
with grey hairs, was the merriest old gentleman I ever saw,
spoke pleasant things, and laughed and chuckled till he cried
again. I stayed till eleven, because I was not now to walk to
Chelsea.

6. An ugly rainy day. I was to visit Mrs. Barton, then
called at Mrs. Vanhomrigh's, where Sir Andrew Fountaine
and the rain kept me to dinner; and there did I loiter all

---

[1] See p. 10.
[2] Sir John Powell, a Judge of the Queen's Bench, died in 1713, aged sixty-
eight. He was a kindly as well as able judge.

the afternoon, like a fool, out of perfect laziness, and the weather not permitting me to walk: but I'll do so no more. Are your waters at Wexford good in this rain? I long to hear how you are established there, how and whom you visit, what is your lodging, what are your entertainments. You are got far southwards; but I think you must eat no fruit while you drink the waters. I ate some Kentish cherries t'other day, and I repent it already; I have felt my head a little disordered. We had not a hot day all June, or since, which I reckon a mighty happiness. Have you left a direction with Reading for Wexford? I will, as I said, direct this to Curry's, and the next to Reading; or suppose I send this at a venture straight to Wexford? It would vex me to have it miscarry. I had a letter to-night from Parvisol, that White has paid me most of my remaining money; and another from Joe, that they have had their election at Trim, but not a word of who is chosen portreeve.[1] Poor Joe is full of complaints, says he has enemies, and fears he will never get his two hundred pounds; and I fear so too, although I have done what I could. — I'll answer your letter when I think fit, when saucy Presto thinks fit, sirrahs. I am not at leisure yet; when I have nothing to do, perhaps I may vouchsafe. —O Lord, the two Wexford ladies; I'll go dream of you both.

7. It was the dismallest rainy day I ever saw: I went to the Secretary in the morning, and he was gone to Windsor. Then it began raining, and I struck in to Mrs. Vanhomrigh's, and dined, and stayed till night very dull and insipid. I hate this town in summer; I'll leave it for a while, if I can have time.

8. I have a fellow of your town, one Tisdall,[2] lodges in the

---

[1] See p. 235.
[2] This Tisdall has been described as a Dublin merchant; but in all probability he was Richard Tisdall, Registrar of the Irish Court of Chancery, and M.P. for Dundalk (1707-1713) and County Louth (1713-1727). He married Marian, daughter of Richard Boyle, M.P., and died in 1742. Richard Tisdall was a relative of Stella's suitor, the Rev. William Tisdall, and years afterwards Swift took an interest in his son Philip, who became a Secretary of State and Leader of the Irish House of Commons.

same house with me. Patrick told me Squire Tisdall and
his lady lodged here. I pretended I never heard of him;
but I knew his ugly face, and saw him at church in the next
pew to me, and he often looked for a bow, but it would not
do. I think he lives in Capel Street, and has an ugly fine
wife in a fine coach. Dr. Freind and I dined in the City by
invitation, and I drank punch, very good, but it makes me
hot. People here are troubled with agues by this continuance of wet, cold weather; but I am glad to find the season
so temperate. I was this evening to see Will Congreve, who
is a very agreeable companion.

9. I was to-day in the City, and dined with Mr. Stratford,
who tells me Sir Alexander Cairnes makes difficulties about
paying my bill; so that I cannot give order yet to Parvisol
to deliver up the bond to Dr. Raymond. To-morrow I shall
have a positive answer: that Cairnes is a shuffling scoundrel;
and several merchants have told me so: what can one expect
from a Scot and a fanatic? I was at Bateman's the bookseller's, to see a fine old library he has bought; and my
fingers itched, as yours would do at a china-shop; but I
resisted, and found everything too dear, and I have fooled
away too much money that way already. So go and drink
your waters, saucy rogue, and make yourself well; and pray
walk while you are there: I have a notion there is never a
good walk in Ireland.[1] Do you find all places without trees?
Pray observe the inhabitants about Wexford; they are old
English; see what they have particular in their manners,
names, and language: magpies have been always there, and
nowhere else in Ireland, till of late years. They say the
cocks and dogs go to sleep at noon, and so do the people.
Write your travels, and bring home good eyes and health.

10. I dined to-day with Lord Treasurer: we did not sit
down till four. I despatched three businesses with him, and
forgot a fourth. I think I have got a friend an employment;
and besides I made him consent to let me bring Congreve to

[1] " In Ireland there are not public paths from place to place, as in England "
(Deane Swift).

dine with him. You must understand I have a mind to do a small thing, only turn out all the Queen's physicians; for in my conscience they will soon kill her among them. And I must talk over that matter with some people. My Lord Treasurer told me the Queen and he between them have lost the paper about the First-Fruits, but desires I will let the bishops know it shall be done with the first opportunity.

11. I dined to-day with neighbour Van, and walked pretty well in the Park this evening. Stella, hussy, don't you remember, sirrah, you used to reproach me about meddling in other folk's affairs? I have enough of it now: two people came to me to-night in the Park to engage to speak to Lord Treasurer in their behalf, and I believe they make up fifty who have asked me the same favour. I am hardened, and resolve to trouble him, or any other Minister, less than ever. And I observe those who have ten times more credit than I will not speak a word for anybody. I met yesterday the poor lad I told you of, who lived with Mr. Tenison,[1] who has been ill of an ague ever since I saw him. He looked wretchedly, and was exceeding thankful for half a crown I gave him. He had a crown from me before.

12. I dined to-day with young Manley[2] in the City, who is to get me out a box of books and a hamper of wine from Hamburg. I inquired of Mr. Stratford, who tells me that Cairnes has not yet paid my two hundred pounds, but shams and delays from day to day. Young Manley's wife is a very indifferent person of a young woman, goggle-eyed, and looks like a fool: yet he is a handsome fellow, and married her for love after long courtship, and she refused him until he got his last employment.—I believe I shall not be so good a boy for writing as I was during your stay at Wexford, unless I may send my letters every second time to Curry's; pray let me know. This, I think, shall go there: or why not to Wexford itself? That is right, and so it shall this next Tuesday, although it costs you tenpence. What care I?

[1] See p. 226.
[2] Probably a son of John Manley, M.P. (see p. 24).

JULY 1711] JOURNAL TO STELLA 253

13. This toad of a Secretary is come from Windsor, and I cannot find him; and he goes back on Sunday, and I can't see him to-morrow. I dined scurvily to-day with Mr. Lewis and a parson; and then went to see Lord Treasurer, and met him coming from his house in his coach: he smiled, and I shrugged, and we smoked each other; and so my visit is paid. I now confine myself to see him only twice a week: he has invited me to Windsor, and betwixt two stools, etc. I will go live at Windsor, if possible, that's pozzz. I have always the luck to pass my summer in London. I called this evening to see poor Sir Matthew Dudley, a Commissioner of the Customs; I know he is to be out for certain: he is in hopes of continuing: I would not tell him bad news, but advised him to prepare for the worst. Dilly was with me this morning, to invite me to dine at Kensington on Sunday with Lord Mountjoy, who goes soon for Ireland. Your late Chief-Justice Broderick[1] is here, and they say violent as a tiger. How is party among you at Wexford? Are the majority of ladies for the late or present Ministry? Write me Wexford news, and love Presto, because he is a good boy.

14. Although it was shaving-day, I walked to Chelsea, and was there by nine this morning; and the Dean of Carlisle and I crossed the water to Battersea, and went in his chariot to Greenwich, where we dined at Dr. Gastrell's, and passed the afternoon at Lewisham, at the Dean of Canterbury's;[2] and there I saw Moll Stanhope,[3] who is grown monstrously tall, but not so handsome as formerly. It is the first little rambling journey I have had this summer about London, and they are the agreeablest pastimes one can have, in a friend's coach, and to good company. Bank Stock is fallen three or four per cent. by the whispers about the town of the Queen's being ill, who is however very well.

15. How many books have you carried with you to

---

[1] See p. 97.
[2] Dr. George Stanhope, who was Vicar of Lewisham as well as of Deptford. He was a popular preacher and a translator of Thomas à Kempis and other religious writers.
[3] See p. 10.

Wexford? What, not one single book? Oh, but your time will be so taken up; and you can borrow of the parson. I dined to-day with Sir Andrew Fountaine and Dilly at Kensington with Lord Mountjoy; and in the afternoon Stratford came there, and told me my two hundred pounds were paid at last; so that business is over, and I am at ease about it; and I wish all your money was in the Bank too. I will have my other hundred pounds there, that is in Hawkshaw's hands. Have you had the interest of it paid yet? I ordered Parvisol to do it. What makes Presto write so crooked? I will answer your letter to-morrow, and send it on Tuesday. Here's hot weather come again, yesterday and to-day: fine drinking waters now. We had a sad pert dull parson at Kensington to-day. I almost repent my coming to town; I want the walks I had.

16. I dined in the City to-day with a hedge [1] acquaintance, and the day passed without any consequence. I will answer your letter to-morrow.

17. Morning. I have put your letter before me, and am going to answer it. Hold your tongue: stand by. Your weather and ours were not alike; we had not a bit of hot weather in June, yet you complain of it on the 19th day. What, you used to love hot weather then? I could never endure it: I detest and abominate it. I would not live in a hot country, to be king of it. What a splutter you keep about my bonds with Raymond, and all to affront Presto! Presto will be suspicious of everything but MD, in spite of your little nose. Soft and fair, Madam Stella, how you gallop away, in your spleen and your rage, about repenting my journey, and preferment here, and sixpence a dozen, and nasty England, and Laracor all my life. Hey-dazy, will you never have done? I had no offers of any living. Lord Keeper told me some months ago he would give me one when I pleased; but I told him I would not take any from him; and the Secretary told me t'other day he had

[1] A favourite word with Swift, when he wished to indicate anything obscure or humble.

refused a very good one for me, but it was in a place he did
not like; and I know nothing of getting anything here,
and, if they would give me leave, I would come over just
now. Addison, I hear, has changed his mind about going
over; but\ I have not seen him these four months./—Oh
ay, that's true, Dingley; that's like herself: millions of
businesses to do before she goes. Yes, my head has been
pretty well, but threatening within these two or three days,
which I impute to some fruit I ate; but I will eat no more:
not a bit of any sort. I suppose you had a journey without
dust, and that was happy. I long for a Wexford letter, but
must not think of it yet: your last was finished but three
weeks ago. It is d——d news you tell me of Mrs. F——; it
makes me love England less a great deal. I know nothing
of the trunk being left or taken; so 'tis odd enough, if the
things in it were mine; and I think I was told that there
are some things for me that my mother left particularly to
me. I am really sorry for ——; that scoundrel —— will have
his estate after his mother's death. Let me know if Mrs.
Walls has got her tea: I hope Richardson [1] stayed in Dublin
till it came. Mrs. Walls needed not have that blemish in
her eye; for I am not in love with her at all. No, I do not
like anything in the *Examiner* after the 45th, except the
first part of the 46th; [2] all the rest is trash; and if you like
them, especially the 47th, your judgment is spoiled by ill
company and want of reading, which I am more sorry for
than you think: and I have spent fourteen years in
improving you to little purpose. (Mr. Tooke is come here,
and I must stop.)—At night. I dined with Lord Treasurer
to-day, and he kept me till nine; so I cannot send this
to-night, as I intended, nor write some other letters. Green,[3]
his surgeon, was there, and dressed his breast; that is, put
on a plaster, which is still requisite: and I took an opportunity to speak to him of the Queen; but he cut me short
with this saying, "*Laissez faire à Don Antoine*," which is a
French proverb, expressing, "Leave that to me." I find he is

[1] See p. 163. [2] See pp. 234-5. [3] See p. 166.

against her taking much physic; and I doubt he cannot persuade her to take Dr. Radcliffe. However, she is very well now, and all the story of her illness, except the first day or two, was a lie. We had some business, that company hindered us from doing, though he is earnest for it, yet would not appoint me a certain day, but bids me come at all times till we can have leisure. This takes up a great deal of my time, and I can do nothing I would do for them. I was with the Secretary this morning, and we both think to go to Windsor for some days, to despatch an affair, if we can have leisure. Sterne met me just now in the street by his lodgings, and I went in for an hour to Jemmy Leigh, who loves London dearly: he asked after you with great respect and friendship.—To return to your letter. Your Bishop Mills [1] hates me mortally: I wonder he should speak well of me, having abused me in all places where he went. So you pay your way. Cudsho: you had a fine supper, I warrant; two pullets, and a bottle of wine, and some currants.—It is just three weeks to-day since you set out to Wexford; you were three days going, and I do not expect a letter these ten days yet, or rather this fortnight. I got a grant of the *Gazette* [2] for Ben Tooke this morning from Mr. Secretary: it will be worth to him a hundred pounds a year.

18. To-day I took leave of Mrs. Barton, who is going into the country; and I dined with Sir John Stanley,[3] where I have not been this great while. There dined with us Lord Rochester, and his fine daughter, Lady Jane,[4] just growing a top-toast. I have been endeavouring to save Sir Matthew

---

[1] Thomas Mills (1671–1740) was made Bishop of Waterford and Lismore in 1708. A man of learning and a liberal contributor to the cost of church restorations, he is charged by Archbishop King with giving all the valuable livings in his gift to his non-resident relatives.

[2] Tooke was appointed printer of the *London Gazette* in 1711 (see p. 8).

[3] See p. 24.

[4] Lady Jane Hyde, the elder daughter of Henry Hyde, Earl of Rochester (see p. 24), married William Capel, third Earl of Essex. Her daughter Charlotte's husband, the son of the Earl of Jersey, was created Earl of Clarendon in 1776. Lady Jane's younger sister, Catherine, who became the famous Duchess of Queensberry, Gay's patroness, is represented by Prior, in *The Female Phaeton*, as jealous, when a young girl, of her sister, "Lady Jenny," who went to balls, and "brought home hearts by dozens."

Dudley,[1] but fear I cannot. I walked the Mall six times to-night for exercise, and would have done more; but, as empty as the town is, a fool got hold of me, and so I came home, to tell you this shall go to-morrow, without fail, and follow you to Wexford, like a dog.

19. Dean Atterbury sent to me to dine with him at Chelsea. I refused his coach, and walked, and am come back by seven, because I would finish this letter, and some others I am writing. Patrick tells me the maid says one Mr. Walls, a clergyman, a tall man, was here to visit me. Is it your Irish Archdeacon? I shall be sorry for it; but I shall make shift to see him seldom enough, as I do Dilly. What can he do here? or is it somebody else? The Duke of Newcastle [2] is dead by the fall he had from his horse. God send poor Stella her health, and keep MD happy! Farewell, and love Presto, who loves MD above all things ten million of times. God bless the dear Wexford girls. Farewell again, etc. etc.

LETTER XXVII

LONDON, *July* 19, 1711.

I HAVE just sent my 26th, and have nothing to say, because I have other letters to write (pshaw, I began too high); but I must lay the beginning like a nest-egg: to-morrow I will say more, and fetch up this line to be straight. This is enough at present for two dear saucy naughty girls.

20. Have I told you that Walls has been with me, and leaves the town in three days? He has brought no gown with him. Dilly carried him to a play. He has come upon a foolish errand, and goes back as he comes. I was this day

---

[1] See p. 7.
[2] John Holles, Duke of Newcastle, had held the Privy Seal from 1705, and was regarded by the Ministers as a possible plenipotentiary in the event of their negotiations for a peace being successful. He married Lady Margaret Cavendish, daughter and co-heiress of Henry Cavendish, second Duke of Newcastle, and was one of the richest nobles in England. His death, on July 15, 1711, was the result of a fall while stag-hunting. The Duke's only daughter married, in 1713, Edward, Lord Harley, the Earl of Oxford's son.

17

with Lord Peterborow, who is going another ramble: I
believe I told you so. I dined with Lord Treasurer, but
cannot get him to do his own business with me; he has put
me off till to-morrow.

21, 22. I dined yesterday with Lord Treasurer, who would
needs take me along with him to Windsor, although I refused
him several times, having no linen, etc. I had just time to
desire Lord Forbes [1] to call at my lodging and order my man
to send my things to-day to Windsor by his servant. I lay
last night at the Secretary's lodgings at Windsor, and borrowed
one of his shirts to go to Court in. The Queen is very well.
I dined with Mr. Masham; and not hearing anything of my
things, I got Lord Winchelsea to bring me to town. Here I
found that Patrick had broke open the closet to get my linen
and nightgown, and sent them to Windsor, and there they
are; and he, not thinking I would return so soon, is gone
upon his rambles: so here I am left destitute, and forced to
borrow a nightgown of my landlady, and have not a rag to
put on to-morrow: faith, it gives me the spleen.

23. Morning. It is a terrible rainy day, and rained prodigiously on Saturday night. Patrick lay out last night,
and is not yet returned: faith, poor Presto is a desolate
creature; neither servant, nor linen, nor anything.—Night.
Lord Forbes's man has brought back my portmantua, and
Patrick is come; so I am in Christian circumstances: I shall
hardly commit such a frolic again. I just crept out to Mrs.
Van's, and dined, and stayed there the afternoon: it has
rained all this day. Windsor is a delicious place: I never
saw it before, except for an hour about seventeen years ago.
Walls has been here in my absence, I suppose, to take his
leave; for he designed not to stay above five days in London.
He says he and his wife will come here for some months next
year; and, in short, he dares not stay now for fear of her.

24. I dined to-day with a hedge [2] friend in the City; and

---

[1] Alexander Forbes, fourth Lord Forbes, who was afterwards attainted for
his share in the Rebellion of 1745.
[2] Obscure (cf. p. 52).

Walls overtook me in the street, and told me he was just getting on horseback for Chester. He has as much curiosity as a cow: he lodged with his horse in Aldersgate Street: he has bought his wife a silk gown, and himself a hat. And what are you doing? what is poor MD doing now? how do you pass your time at Wexford? how do the waters agree with you? Let Presto know soon; for Presto longs to know, and must know. Is not Madam Proby curious company? I am afraid this rainy weather will spoil your waters. We have had a great deal of wet these three days. Tell me all the particulars of Wexford: the place, the company, the diversions, the victuals, the wants, the vexations. Poor Dingley never saw such a place in her life; sent all over the town for a little parsley to a boiled chicken, and it was not to be had; the butter is stark naught, except an old English woman's; and it is such a favour to get a pound from her now and then! I am glad you carried down your sheets with you, else you must have lain in sackcloth. O Lord!

25. I was this forenoon with Mr. Secretary at his office, and helped to hinder a man of his pardon, who is condemned for a rape. The Under Secretary was willing to save him, upon an old notion that a woman cannot be ravished; but I told the Secretary he could not pardon him without a favourable report from the judge; besides, he was a fiddler, and consequently a rogue, and deserved hanging for something else; and so he shall swing. What, I must stand up for the honour of the fair sex! 'Tis true the fellow had lain with her a hundred times before, but what care I for that! What, must a woman be ravished because she is a whore?— The Secretary and I go on Saturday to Windsor for a week. I dined with Lord Treasurer, and stayed with him till past ten. I was to-day at his levee, where I went against my custom, because I had a mind to do a good office for a gentleman: so I talked with him before my lord, that he might see me, and then found occasion to recommend him this afternoon. I was forced to excuse my coming to the levee,

that I did it to see the sight; for he was going to chide me away: I had never been there but once, and that was long before he was Treasurer. The rooms were all full, and as many Whigs as Tories. He whispered me a jest or two, and bid me come to dinner. I left him but just now; and 'tis late.

26. Mr. Addison and I have at last met again. I dined with him and Steele to-day at young Jacob Tonson's. The two Jacobs [1] think it is I who have made the Secretary take from them the printing of the *Gazette*, which they are going to lose, and Ben Tooke and another [2] are to have it. Jacob came to me the other day, to make his court; but I told him it was too late, and that it was not my doing. I reckon they will lose it in a week or two. Mr. Addison and I talked as usual, and as if we had seen one another yesterday; and Steele and I were very easy, though I writ him lately a biting letter, in answer to one of his, where he desired me to recommend a friend of his to Lord Treasurer. Go, get you gone to your waters, sirrah. Do they give you a stomach? Do you eat heartily?—We have had much rain to-day and yesterday.

27. I dined to-day in the City, and saw poor Patty Rolt, and gave her a pistole to help her a little forward against she goes to board in the country. She has but eighteen pounds a year to live on, and is forced to seek out for cheap places. Sometimes they raise their price, and sometimes they starve her, and then she is forced to shift. Patrick the puppy put too much ink in my standish,[3] and, carrying too many things together, I spilled it on my paper and floor. The town is dull, wet, and empty; Wexford is worth two of it; I hope so at least, and that poor little MD finds it so. I reckon upon

---

[1] Jacob Tonson the elder, who died in 1736, outlived his nephew, Jacob Tonson the younger, by a few months. The elder Tonson, the secretary of the Kit-Cat Club, published many of Dryden's works, and the firm continued to be the chief publishers of the time during the greater part of the eighteenth century.

[2] John Barber.

[3] By his will Swift left to Deane Swift his "large silver standish, consisting of a large silver plate, an ink-pot, and a sand-box."

going to Windsor to-morrow with Mr. Secretary, unless he changes his mind, or some other business prevents him. I shall stay there a week, I hope.

28. Morning. Mr. Secretary sent me word he will call at my lodgings by two this afternoon, to take me to Windsor; so I must dine nowhere; and I promised Lord Treasurer to dine with him to-day; but I suppose we shall dine at Windsor at five, for we make but three hours there.[1] I am going abroad, but have left Patrick to put up my things, and to be sure to be at home half an hour before two.—Windsor, at night. We did not leave London till three, and dined here between six and seven; at nine I left the company, and went to see Lord Treasurer, who is just come. I chid him for coming so late; he chid me for not dining with him; said he stayed an hour for me. Then I went and sat with Mr. Lewis till just now, and it is past eleven. I lie in the same house with the Secretary, one of the Prebendary's houses. The Secretary is not come from his apartment in the Castle. Do you think that abominable dog Patrick was out after two to-day, and I in a fright every moment, for fear the chariot should come; and when he came in, he had not put up one rag of my things! I never was in a greater passion, and would certainly have cropped one of his ears, if I had not looked every moment for the Secretary, who sent his equipage to my lodging before, and came in a chair from Whitehall to me, and happened to stay half an hour later than he intended. One of Lord Treasurer's servants gave me a letter to-night: I found it was from ——, with an offer of fifty pounds, to be paid me in what manner I pleased; because, he said, he desired to be well with me. I was in a rage;[2] but my friend Lewis cooled me, and said it is what the best men sometimes meet with; and I have been not seldom served in the like manner, although not so grossly. In these cases I never demur a moment, nor ever found the least inclination to take anything. Well, I will go try to sleep in my new bed, and to

[1] *I.e.*, we are only three hours in getting there.
[2] Cf. p. 141.

dream of poor Wexford MD, and Stella that drinks water, and Dingley that drinks ale.

29. I was at Court and church to-day, as I was this day se'ennight: I generally am acquainted with about thirty in the drawing-room, and I am so proud I make all the lords come up to me: one passes half an hour pleasant enough. We had a dunce to preach before the Queen to-day, which often happens. Windsor is a delicious situation, but the town is scoundrel. I have this morning got the *Gazette* for Ben Tooke and one Barber a printer; it will be about three hundred pounds a year between them. The other fellow was printer of the *Examiner*, which is now laid down.[1] I dined with the Secretary: we were a dozen in all, three Scotch lords, and Lord Peterborow. The Duke of Hamilton[2] would needs be witty, and hold up my train as I walked upstairs. It is an ill circumstance that on Sundays much company always meet at the great tables. Lord Treasurer told at Court what I said to Mr. Secretary on this occasion. The Secretary showed me his bill of fare, to encourage me to dine with him. "Poh," said I, "show me a bill of company, for I value not your dinner." See how this is all blotted,[3] I can write no more here, but to tell you I love MD dearly, and God bless them.

30. In my conscience, I fear I shall have the gout. I sometimes feel pains about my feet and toes: I never drank till within these two years, and I did it to cure my head. I often sit evenings with some of these people, and drink in my turn; but I am now resolved to drink ten times less than before; but they advise me to let what I drink be all wine, and not to put water to it. Tooke and the printer stayed to-day to

---

[1] The *Examiner* was revived in December 1711, under Oldisworth's editorship, and was continued by him until 1714.
[2] James Douglas, fourth Duke of Hamilton, was created Duke of Brandon in the English peerage in September 1711, and was killed by Lord Mohun in a duel in 1712. Swift calls him "a worthy good-natured person, very generous, but of a middle understanding." He married, in 1698, as his second wife, Elizabeth, daughter and heiress of Digby, Lord Gerard, a lady to whom Swift often refers in the *Journal.* She outlived the Duke thirty-two years.
[3] See p. 260.

finish their affair, and treated me and two of the Under
Secretaries upon their getting the *Gazette*.   Then I went to
see Lord Treasurer, and chid him for not taking notice of me
at Windsor.   He said he kept a place for me yesterday at
dinner, and expected me there; but I was glad I did not go,
because the Duke of Buckingham was there, and that would
have made us acquainted; which I have no mind to.   However, we appointed to sup at Mr. Masham's, and there stayed
till past one o'clock; and that is late, sirrahs : and I have
much business.

31. I have sent a noble haunch of venison this afternoon to
Mrs. Vanhomrigh : I wish you had it, sirrahs.   I dined gravely
with my landlord the Secretary.   The Queen was abroad
to-day in order to hunt; but, finding it disposed to rain, she
kept in her coach; she hunts in a chaise with one horse,
which she drives herself, and drives furiously, like Jehu, and
is a mighty hunter, like Nimrod.   Dingley has heard of
Nimrod, but not Stella, for it is in the Bible.   I was to-day at
Eton, which is but just cross the bridge, to see my Lord Kerry's
son,[1] who is at school there.   Mr. Secretary has given me a
warrant for a buck; I can't send it to MD.   It is a sad thing,
faith, considering how Presto loves MD, and how MD would
love Presto's venison for Presto's sake.   God bless the two
dear Wexford girls !

Aug. 1. We had for dinner the fellow of that haunch of
venison I sent to London; 'twas mighty fat and good, and
eight people at dinner; that was bad.   The Queen and I
were going to take the air this afternoon, but not together;
and were both hindered by a sudden rain.   Her coaches and
chaises all went back, and the guards too; and I scoured into
the market-place for shelter.   I intended to have walked up
the finest avenue I ever saw, two miles long, with two rows
of elms on each side.   I walked in the evening a little upon
the terrace, and came home at eight : Mr. Secretary came
soon after, and we were engaging in deep discourse, and I was
endeavouring to settle some points of the greatest consequence,

---

[1] William Fitzmaurice (see p. 91).

and had wormed myself pretty well into him, when his Under Secretary came in (who lodges in the same house with us) and interrupted all my scheme. I have just left him: it is late, etc.

2. I have been now five days at Windsor, and Patrick has been drunk three times that I have seen, and oftener I believe. He has lately had clothes that have cost me five pounds, and the dog thinks he has the whip-hand of me: he begins to master me; so now I am resolved to part with him, and will use him without the least pity. The Secretary and I have been walking three or four hours to-day. The Duchess of Shrewsbury [1] asked him, was not that Dr.—Dr.— and she could not say my name in English, but said Dr. Presto, which is Italian for Swift. Whimsical enough, as Billy Swift [2] says. I go to-morrow with the Secretary to his house at Bucklebury, twenty-five miles from hence, and return early on Sunday morning. I will leave this letter behind me locked up, and give you an account of my journey when I return. I had a letter yesterday from the Bishop of Clogher, who is coming up to his Parliament. Have you any correspondence with him to Wexford? Methinks, I now long for a letter from you, dated Wexford, July 24, etc. O Lord, that would be so pretending; [3] and then, says you, Stella can't write much, because it is bad to write when one drinks the waters; and I think, says you, I find myself better already, but I cannot tell yet whether it be the journey or the waters. Presto is so silly to-night; yes he be; but Presto loves MD dearly, as hope saved.

3. Morning. I am to go this day at noon, as I told you, to Bucklebury: we dine at twelve, and expect to be there in

---

[1] The Duke of Shrewsbury (see p. 12) married an Italian lady, Adelhida, daughter of the Marquis of Paliotti, of Bologna, descended maternally from Robert Dudley, Earl of Leicester, Queen Elizabeth's favourite. Lady Cowper (*Diary*, pp. 8, 9) says that the Duchess " had a wonderful art of entertaining and diverting people, though she would sometimes exceed the bounds of decency ; . . . but then, with all her prate and noise, she was the most cunning, designing woman alive, obliging to people in prosperity, and a great party-woman." As regards the name " Presto," see p. 5, note 3.

[2] Probably a cousin.

[3] Presumptuous : claiming much.

four hours. I cannot bid you good-night now, because I shall be twenty-five miles from this paper to-night, and so my journal must have a break ; so good-morrow, etc.

4, 5. I dined yesterday at Bucklebury, where we lay two ·nights, and set out this morning at eight, and were here at twelve ; in four hours we went twenty-six miles. Mr. Secretary was a perfect country gentleman at Bucklebury : he smoked tobacco with one or two neighbours ; he inquired after the wheat in such a field ; he went to visit his hounds, and knew all their names ; he and his lady saw me to my chamber just in the country fashion. His house is in the midst of near three thousand pounds a year he had by his lady,[1] who is descended from Jack Newbury, of whom books and ballads are written ; and there is an old picture of him in the house. She is a great favourite of mine. I lost church to-day ; but I dressed and shaved, and went to Court, and would not dine with the Secretary, but engaged myself to a private dinner with Mr. Lewis, and one friend more. We go to London to-morrow ; for Lord Dartmouth, the other Secretary, is come, and they are here their weeks by turns.

6. Lord Treasurer comes every Saturday to Windsor, and goes away on Monday or Tuesday. I was with him this morning at his levee, for one cannot see him otherwise here, he is so hurried : we had some talk ; and I told him I would stay this week at Windsor by myself, where I can have more leisure to do some business that concerns them. Lord Treasurer and the Secretary thought to mortify me ; for they told me they had been talking a great deal of me to-day to the Queen, and she said she had never heard of me. I told them that was their fault, and not hers, etc., and so we laughed. I dined with the Secretary, and let him go to London at five without me ; and here am I alone in the Prebendary's house, which Mr. Secretary has taken ; only Mr. Lewis is in my neighbourhood, and we shall be good company.

---

[1] See p. 123. John Winchcombe, a weaver of Newbury, marched with a hundred of his workmen, at his own expenses, against the Scots in 1513.

The Vice-Chamberlain,[1] and Mr. Masham, and the Green
Cloth,[2] have promised me dinners. I shall want but four till
Mr. Secretary returns. We have a music-meeting in our
town to-night. I went to the rehearsal of it, and there was
Margarita,[3] and her sister, and another drab, and a parcel of
fiddlers: I was weary, and would not go to the meeting,
which I am sorry for, because I heard it was a great assembly.
Mr. Lewis came from it, and sat with me till just now; and
'tis late.

7. I can do no business, I fear, because Mr. Lewis, who has
nothing or little to do here, sticks close to me. I dined to-
day with the gentlemen ushers, among scurvy company; but
the Queen was hunting the stag till four this afternoon, and
she drove in her chaise above forty miles, and it was five
before we went to dinner. Here are fine walks about this
town. I sometimes walk up the avenue.

8. There was a Drawing-room to-day at Court; but so few
company, that the Queen sent for us into her bed-chamber,
where we made our bows, and stood about twenty of us round
the room, while she looked at us round with her fan in her
mouth, and once a minute said about three words to some
that were nearest her, and then she was told dinner was
ready, and went out. I dined at the Green Cloth, by Mr.
Scarborow's[4] invitation, who is in waiting. It is much the
best table in England, and costs the Queen a thousand pounds
a month while she is at Windsor or Hampton Court, and is
the only mark of magnificence or hospitality I can see in the

---

[1] Thomas Coke, M.P., of Derbyshire, was appointed a Teller of the
Exchequer in 1704, and Vice-Chamberlain to the Queen in 1706. In 1706 he
married—as his second wife—Mrs. Hale, one of the maids of honour (Luttrell,
v. 411, 423; vi. 113, 462; Lady Cowper's *Diary*, 15, 16), a lady whose
" piercing " beauty it was, apparently, that Steele described under the name of
Chloe, in No. 4 of the *Tatler*. Jervas painted her as a country girl, "with a
liveliness that shows she is conscious, but not affected, of her perfections."
Coke was the Sir Plume of Pope's *Rape of the Lock*.
[2] The committee of management of the Royal household.
[3] Francesca Margherita de l'Epine, the famous singer, and principal rival of
Mrs. Tofts, came to England in 1692, and constantly sang in opera until her
retirement in 1718, when she married Dr. Pepusch. She died in 1746. Her
sister, Maria Gallia, also a singer, did not attain the same popularity.
[4] Charles Scarborow and Sir William Foster were the Clerks of the Board
of Green Cloth.

Queen's family: it is designed to entertain foreign Ministers, and people of quality, who come to see the Queen, and have no place to dine at.

9. Mr. Coke, the Vice-Chamberlain, made me a long visit this morning, and invited me to dinner; but the toast, his lady,[1] was unfortunately engaged to Lady Sunderland.[2] Lord Treasurer stole here last night, but did not lie at his lodgings in the Castle; and, after seeing the Queen, went back again. I just drank a dish of chocolate with him. I fancy I shall have reason to be angry with him very soon; but what care I? I believe I shall die with Ministries in my debt.—This night I received a certain letter from a place called Wexford, from two dear naughty girls of my acquaintance; but, faith, I will not answer it here, no in troth. I will send this to Mr. Reading, supposing it will find you returned; and I hope better for the waters.

10. Mr. Vice-Chamberlain lent me his horses to ride about and see the country this morning. Dr. Arbuthnot, the Queen's physician and favourite, went out with me to show me the places: we went a little after the Queen, and over-took Miss Forester,[3] a maid of honour, on her palfrey, taking the air; we made her go along with us. We saw a place they have made for a famous horse-race to-morrow, where the Queen will come. We met the Queen coming back, and Miss Forester stood, like us, with her hat off while the Queen went by. The Doctor and I left the lady where we found her, but under other conductors; and we dined at a little

---

[1] See note on Thomas Coke, p. 266.

[2] The Earl of Sunderland's second wife, Lady Anne Churchill, who died in 1716, aged twenty-eight. She was the favourite daughter of the Duke of Marlborough, and was called "the little Whig." Verses were written in honour of her beauty and talent by Charles Montagu, Earl of Halifax, Dr. Watts and others, and her portrait was painted by Lely and Kneller.

[3] Mary, daughter of Sir William Forester, of Dothill, Shropshire. In 1700, at the age of thirteen, she had been secretly married to her cousin, George Downing, a lad of fifteen. Three years later, Downing, on his return from abroad, refused to acknowledge his wife, and in 1715 both parties petitioned the House of Lords for leave to bring in a Bill declaring the marriage to be void; but leave was refused (Lords' *Journals*, xx. 41, 45). Downing had become Sir George Downing, Bart., in 1711, and had been elected M. P. for Dunwich; he died without issue in 1749, and was the founder of Downing College, Cambridge.

place he has taken, about a mile off.—When I came back I found Mr. Scarborow had sent all about to invite me to the Green Cloth, and lessened his company on purpose to make me easy. It is very obliging, and will cost me thanks. Much company is come to town this evening, to see to-morrow's race. I was tired with riding a trotting mettlesome horse a dozen miles, having not been on horseback this twelvemonth. And Miss Forester did not make it easier; she is a silly true maid of honour, and I did not like her, although she be a toast, and was dressed like a man.[1]

11. I will send this letter to-day. I expect the Secretary by noon. I will not go to the race unless I can get room in some coach. It is now morning. I must rise, and fold up and seal my letter. Farewell, and God preserve dearest MD.

I believe I shall leave this town on Monday.

LETTER XXVIII

WINDSOR, *Aug.* 11, 1711.

I SENT away my twenty-seventh this morning in an express to London, and directed to Mr. Reading : this shall go to your lodgings, where I reckon you will be returned before it reaches you. I intended to go to the race[2] to-day, but was hindered by a visit : I believe I told you so in my last. I dined to-day at the Green Cloth, where everybody had been at the race but myself, and we were twenty in all, and very noisy company; but I made the Vice-Chamberlain and two friends more sit at a side table, to be a little quiet. At six I went to see the Secretary, who is returned; but Lord Keeper sent to desire I would sup with him, where I stayed till just

---

[1] In a discussion upon what would be the result if beards became the fashion, Budgell (*Spectator*, No. 331) says, " Besides, we are not certain that the ladies would not come into the mode, when they take the air on horseback. They already appear in hats and feathers, coats and periwigs."

[2] Horse-racing was much encouraged by Charles II., who, as Strutt tells us, appointed races to be made in Datchet Mead, when he was residing at Windsor. By Queen Anne's time horse-racing was becoming a regular institution : see *Spectator*, No. 173.

now : Lord Treasurer and Secretary were to come to us, but both failed. 'Tis late, etc.

12. I was this morning to visit Lord Keeper, who made me reproaches that I had never visited him at Windsor. He had a present sent him of delicious peaches, and he was champing and champing, but I durst not eat one; I wished Dingley had some of them, for poor Stella can no more eat fruit than Presto. Dilly Ashe is come to Windsor; and after church I carried him up to the drawing-room, and talked to the Keeper and Treasurer, on purpose to show them to him; and he saw the Queen and several great lords, and the Duchess of Montagu;[1] he was mighty happy, and resolves to fill a letter to the Bishop.[2] My friend Lewis and I dined soberly with Dr. Adams,[3] the only neighbour prebendary. One of the prebendaries here is lately a peer, by the death of his father. He is now Lord Willoughby of Broke,[4] and will sit in the House of Lords with his gown. I supped to-night at Masham's with Lord Treasurer, Mr. Secretary, and Prior. The Treasurer made us stay till twelve, before he came from the Queen, and 'tis now past two.

13. I reckoned upon going to London to-day; but by an accident the Cabinet Council did not sit last night, and sat to-day, so we go to-morrow at six in the morning. I missed the race to-day by coming out too late, when everybody's coach was gone, and ride I would not : I felt my last riding three days after. We had a dinner to-day at the Secretary's lodgings without him : Mr. Hare,[5] his Under Secretary, Mr. Lewis, Brigadier Sutton,[6] and I, dined together; and I made

[1] John Montagu, second Duke of Montagu, married Lady Mary Churchill, youngest daughter of the Duke of Marlborough.
[2] Of Clogher.
[3] John Adams, Prebendary of Canterbury and Canon of Windsor. He was made Provost of King's College, Cambridge, in 1712, and died in 1720.
[4] The Hon. and Rev. George Verney, Canon of Windsor (died 1728), became fourth Lord Willoughby de Broke on the death of his father (Sir Richard Verney, the third Baron), in July 1711. Lord Willoughby became Dean of Windsor in 1713.
[5] Thomas Hare, Under Secretary of State in Bolingbroke's office.
[6] Richard Sutton was the second son of Robert Sutton, the nephew of the Robert Sutton who was created Viscount Lexington by Charles I. Sutton served under William III. and Marlborough in Flanders, and was made a

the Vice-Chamberlain take a snap with us, rather than stay till five for his lady, who was gone to the race. The reason why the Cabinet Council was not held last night was because Mr. Secretary St. John would not sit with your Duke of Somerset.[1] So to-day the Duke was forced to go to the race while the Cabinet was held. We have music-meetings in our town, and I was at the rehearsal t'other day; but I did not value it, nor would go to the meeting. Did I tell you this before?

London, 14. We came to town this day in two hours and forty minutes: twenty miles are nothing here. I found a letter from the Archbishop of Dublin, sent me the Lord knows how. He says some of the bishops will hardly believe that Lord Treasurer got the Queen to remit the First-Fruits before the Duke of Ormond was declared Lord Lieutenant, and that the bishops have written a letter to Lord Treasurer to thank him. He has sent me the address of the Convocation, ascribing, in good part, that affair to the Duke, who had less share in it than MD; for if it had not been for MD, I should not have been so good a solicitor. I dined to-day in the City, about a little bit of mischief, with a printer.—I found Mrs. Vanhomrigh all in combustion, squabbling with her rogue of a landlord; she has left her house, and gone out of our neighbourhood a good way. Her eldest daughter is come of age, and going to Ireland to look after her fortune, and get it in her own hands.[2]

15. I dined to-day with Mrs. Van, who goes to-night to her new lodgings. I went at six to see Lord Treasurer; but his company was gone, contrary to custom, and he was busy,

Brigadier - General in 1710, in which year also he was elected M.P. for Newark. In 1711 he was appointed Governor of Hull, and he died, a Lieutenant-General, in 1737 (Dalton's *Army Lists*, iii. 153).

[1] Charles Seymour, sixth Duke of Somerset (1662–1748), known as "the proud Duke of Somerset." Through the influence which his wife—afterwards Mistress of the Robes (see p. 162)—had obtained over the Queen, he bore no small part in bringing about the changes of 1710. His intrigues during this period were, however, mainly actuated by jealousy of Marlborough, and he had really no sympathies with the Tories. His intrigues with the Whigs caused the utmost alarm to St. John and to Swift.

[2] The third and last reference to Vanessa in the *Journal*.

and I was forced to stay some time before I could see him. We were together hardly an hour, and he went away, being in haste. He desired me to dine with him on Friday, because there would be a friend of his that I must see: my Lord Harley told me, when he was gone, that it was Mrs. Masham his father meant, who is come to town to lie-in, and whom I never saw, though her husband is one of our Society. God send her a good time! her death would be a terrible thing.[1]—Do you know that I have ventured all my credit with these great Ministers, to clear some misunderstandings betwixt them; and if there be no breach, I ought to have the merit of it. 'Tis a plaguy ticklish piece of work, and a man hazards losing both sides. It is a pity the world does not know my virtue.—I thought the clergy in Convocation in Ireland would have given me thanks for being their solicitor; but I hear of no such thing. Pray talk occasionally on that subject, and let me know what you hear. Do you know the greatness of my spirit, that I value their thanks not a rush, but at my return shall freely let all people know that it was my Lord Treasurer's action, wherein the Duke of Ormond had no more share than a cat? And so they may go whistle, and I'll go sleep.

16. I was this day in the City, and dined at Pontack's[2] with Stratford, and two other merchants. Pontack told us, although his wine was so good, he sold it cheaper than others; he took but seven shillings a flask. Are not these pretty rates? The books he sent for from Hamburg are come, but not yet got out of the custom-house. My library will be at least double when I come back. I shall go to Windsor again on Saturday, to meet our Society, who are

---

[1] "Pray God preserve her life, which is of great importance" (Swift to Archbishop King, Aug. 15, 1711). St. John was at this moment very anxious to conciliate Mrs. Masham, as he felt that she was the only person capable of counteracting the intrigues of the Duchess of Somerset with the Queen.

[2] Pontack, of Abchurch Lane, son of Arnaud de Pontac, President of the Parliament of Bordeaux, was proprietor of the most fashionable eating-house in London. There the Royal Society met annually at dinner until 1746. Several writers speak of the dinners at a guinea a head and upwards served at Pontack's, and Swift comments on the price of the wine.

to sup at Mr. Secretary's; but I believe I shall return on Monday, and then I will answer your letter, that lies here safe underneath;—I see it; lie still: I will answer you when the ducks have eaten up the dirt.

17. I dined to-day at Lord Treasurer's with Mrs. Masham, and she is extremely like one Mrs. Malolly, that was once my landlady in Trim. She was used with mighty kindness and respect, like a favourite. It signifies nothing going to this Lord Treasurer about business, although it be his own. He was in haste, and desires I will come again, and dine with him to-morrow. His famous lying porter is fallen sick, and they think he will die: I wish I had all my half-crowns again. I believe I have told you he is an old Scotch fanatic, and the damn'dest liar in his office alive.[1] I have a mind to recommend Patrick to succeed him: I have trained him up pretty well. I reckon for certain you are now in town. The weather now begins to alter to rain.

Windsor, 18. I dined to-day with Lord Treasurer, and he would make me go with him to Windsor, although I was engaged to the Secretary, to whom I made my excuses: we had in the coach besides, his son and son-in-law, Lord Harley and Lord Dupplin, who are two of our Society, and seven of us met by appointment, and supped this night with the Secretary. It was past nine before we got here, but a fine moonshiny night. I shall go back, I believe, on Monday. 'Tis very late.

19. The Queen did not stir out to-day, she is in a little fit of the gout. I dined at Mr. Masham's; we had none but our Society members, six in all, and I supped with Lord Treasurer. The Queen has ordered twenty thousand pounds to go on with the building at Blenheim, which has been starved till now, since the change of the Ministry.[2]   I

---

[1] "His name was Read" (Scott).

[2] Up to the end of 1709 the warrants for the payment of the works at Blenheim had been regularly issued by Godolphin and paid at the Treasury; over £200,000 was expended in this manner. But after the dismissal of the Whigs the Queen drew tight the purse-strings. The £20,000 mentioned by Swift was paid in 1711, but on June 1, 1712, Anne gave positive orders that nothing further should be allowed for Blenheim, though £12,000 remained due to the contractors.

suppose it is to reward his last action of getting into the French lines.[1] Lord Treasurer kept me till past twelve.

London, 20. It rained terribly every step of our journey to-day: I returned with the Secretary after a dinner of cold meat, and went to Mrs. Van's, where I sat the evening. I grow very idle, because I have a great deal of business. Tell me how you passed your time at Wexford; and are not you glad at heart you have got home safe to your lodgings at St. Mary's, pray? And so your friends come to visit you; and Mrs. Walls is much better of her eye; and the Dean is just as he used to be: and what does Walls say of London? 'tis a reasoning coxcomb. And Goody Stoyte, and Hannah what d'ye call her; no, her name an't Hannah, Catherine I mean; they were so glad to see the ladies again! and Mrs. Manley wanted a companion at ombre.

21. I writ to-day to the Archbishop of Dublin, and enclosed a long politic paper by itself. You know the bishops are all angry (smoke the wax-candle drop at the bottom of this paper) I have let the world know the First-Fruits were got by Lord Treasurer before the Duke of Ormond was Governor. I told Lord Treasurer all this, and he is very angry; but I pacified him again by telling him they were fools, and knew nothing of what passed here; but thought all was well enough if they complimented the Duke of Ormond. Lord Treasurer gave me t'other day a letter of thanks he received from the bishops of Ireland, signed by seventeen; and says he will write them an answer. The Dean of Carlisle sat with me to-day till three; and I went to dine with Lord Treasurer, who dined abroad, so did the Secretary, and I was left in the suds. 'Twas almost four, and I got to Sir Matthew Dudley, who had half dined. Thornhill, who killed Sir Cholmley Dering,[2] was murdered by two men, on Turnham Green, last Monday night: as they stabbed him,

---

[1] The piercing of the lines before Bouchain, which Villars had declared to be the *non plus ultra* of the Allies, one of the most striking proofs of Marlborough's military genius.

[2] See p. 212.

18

they bid him remember Sir Cholmley Dering. They had
quarrelled at Hampton Court, and followed and stabbed him
on horseback. We have only a Grub Street paper of it, but
I believe it is true. I went myself through Turnham Green
the same night, which was yesterday.

22. We have had terrible rains these two or three days. I
intended to dine at Lord Treasurer's, but went to see Lady
Abercorn, who is come to town, and my lord; and I dined
with them, and visited Lord Treasurer this evening. His
porter is mending. I sat with my lord about three hours,
and am come home early to be busy. Passing by White's
Chocolate-house,[1] my brother Masham called me, and told
me his wife was brought to bed of a boy, and both very
well. (Our Society, you must know, are all brothers.) Dr.
Garth told us that Mr. Henley[2] is dead of an apoplexy.
His brother-in-law, Earl Poulett, is gone down to the
Grange, to take care of his funeral. The Earl of Danby,[3]
the Duke of Leeds's eldest grandson, a very hopeful young
man of about twenty, is dead at Utrecht of the smallpox.—
I long to know whether you begin to have any good effect by
your waters.—Methinks this letter goes on slowly; 'twill be a
fortnight next Saturday since it was begun, and one side not
filled. O fie fors hame, Presto! Faith, I'm so tosticated to
and from Windsor, that I know not what to say; but, faith,
I'll go to Windsor again on Saturday, if they ask me, not else.
So lose your money again, now you are come home; do, sirrah.

Take your magnifying-glass, Madam Dingley.

You shan't read this, sirrah Stella; don't read it for your
life, for fear of your dearest eyes.

[1] A fashionable gaming-house in St. James's Street.
[2] See p. 37. The Grange, near Arlesford, Hampshire, was Henley's seat.
His wife (see p. 117) was the daughter of Peregrine Bertie, son of Montagu
Bertie, second Earl of Lindsey; and Earl Poulett (see p. 190) married Bridget,
an elder daughter of Bertie's.
[3] William Henry Hyde, Earl of Danby, grandson of the first Duke of Leeds
(see p. 60), and eldest son of Peregrine Osborne, Baron Osborne and Viscount
Dunblane, who succeeded to the dukedom in 1712. Owing to this young
man's death (at the age of twenty-one), his brother, Peregrine Hyde, Marquis of
Caermarthen, who married Harley's daughter Elizabeth, afterwards became
third Duke of Leeds.

There's enough for this side; these Ministers hinder me.

Pretty, dear, little, naughty, saucy MD.

Silly, impudent, loggerhead Presto.

23. Dilly and I dined to-day with Lord Abercorn, and had a fine fat haunch of venison, that smelt rarely on one side: and after dinner Dilly won half a crown of me at back-gammon at his lodgings, to his great content. It is a scurvy empty town this melancholy season of the year; but I think our weather begins to mend. The roads are as deep as in winter. The grapes are sad things; but the peaches are pretty good, and there are some figs. I sometimes venture to eat one, but always repent it. You say nothing of the box sent half a year ago. I wish you would pay me for Mrs. Walls's tea. Your mother is in the country, I suppose. Pray send me the account of MD, Madam Dingley, as it stands since November,[1] that is to say, for this year (excluding the twenty pounds lent Stella for Wexford), for I cannot look in your letters. I think I ordered that Hawkshaw's interest should be paid to you. When you think proper, I will let Parvisol know you have paid that twenty pounds, or part of it; and so go play with the Dean, and I will answer your letter to-morrow. Good-night, sirrahs, and love Presto, and be good girls.

24. I dined to-day with Lord Treasurer, who chid me for not dining with him yesterday, for it seems I did not under-stand his invitation; and their Club of the Ministry dined together, and expected me. Lord Radnor[2] and I were walking the Mall this evening; and Mr. Secretary met us, and took a turn or two, and then stole away, and we both believed it was to pick up some wench; and to-morrow he will be at the Cabinet with the Queen: so goes the world! Prior has been out of town these two months, nobody knows where, and is lately returned. People confidently affirm he has been in France, and I half believe it. It is said he was sent by the Ministry, and for some overtures towards a peace. The Secretary pretends he knows nothing of it. I believe

<hr>

[1] See p. 54.   [2] See p. 8.

your Parliament will be dissolved. I have been talking about the quarrel between your Lords and Commons with Lord Treasurer, and did, at the request of some people, desire that the Queen's answer to the Commons' address might express a dislike of some principles, etc.; but was answered dubiously.—And so now to your letter, fair ladies. I know drinking is bad; I mean writing is bad in drinking the waters; and was angry to see so much in Stella's hand. But why Dingley drinks them, I cannot imagine; but truly she'll drink waters as well as Stella: why not? I hope you now find the benefit of them since you are returned; pray let me know particularly. I am glad you are forced upon exercise, which, I believe, is as good as the waters for the heart of them. 'Tis now past the middle of August; so by your reckoning you are in Dublin. It would vex me to the dogs that letters should miscarry between Dublin and Wexford, after 'scaping the salt seas. I will write no more to that nasty town in haste again, I warrant you. I have been four Sundays together at Windsor, of which a fortnight together; but I believe I shall not go to-morrow, for I will not, unless the Secretary asks me. I know all your news about the Mayor: it makes no noise here at all, but the quarrel of your Parliament does; it is so very extraordinary, and the language of the Commons so very pretty. The *Examiner* has been down this month, and was very silly the five or six last papers; but there is a pamphlet come out, in answer to a letter to the seven Lords who examined Gregg.[1] The Answer[2] is by the real author of the *Examiner*, as I believe; for it is very well written. We had Trapp's poem on the Duke of Ormond[3] printed here, and the printer

[1] William Gregg was a clerk in Harley's office when the latter was Secretary of State under the Whig Administration. In 1707-8 he was in treasonable correspondence with M. de Chamillart, the French Secretary of State. When he was detected he was tried for high treason, and hanged on April 28. The Lords who examined Gregg did their utmost to establish Harley's complicity, which Gregg, however, with his dying breath solemnly denied.

[2] By Swift himself. The title was, *Some Remarks upon a Pamphlet entitled, A Letter to the Seven Lords of the Committee appointed to examine Gregg.*

[3] See p. 120. There is no copy in the British Museum.

sold just eleven of them. 'Tis a dull piece, not half so good as Stella's; and she is very modest to compare herself with such a poetaster. I am heartily sorry for poor Mrs. Parnell's [1] death; she seemed to be an excellent good-natured young woman, and I believe the poor lad is much afflicted; they appeared to live perfectly well together. Dilly is not tired at all with England, but intends to continue here a good while: he is mighty easy to be at distance from his two sisters-in-law. He finds some sort of scrub acquaintance; goes now and then in disguise to a play; smokes his pipe; reads now and then a little trash, and what else the Lord knows. I see him now and then; for he calls here, and the town being thin, I am less pestered with company than usual. I have got rid of many of my solicitors, by doing nothing for them: I have not above eight or nine left, and I'll be as kind to them. Did I tell you of a knight who desired me to speak to Lord Treasurer to give him two thousand pounds, or five hundred pounds a year, until he could get something better? I honestly delivered my message to the Treasurer, adding, the knight was a puppy, whom I would not give a groat to save from the gallows. Cole Reading's father-in-law has been two or three times at me, to recommend his lights to the Ministry, assuring me that a word of mine would, etc. Did not that dog use to speak ill of me, and profess to hate me? He knows not where I lodge, for I told him I lived in the country; and I have ordered Patrick to deny me constantly to him.—Did the Bishop of London [2] die in Wexford? poor gentleman! Did he drink the waters? were you at his burial? was it a great funeral? so far from his

[1] Thomas Parnell, the poet, married, in 1706, Anne, daughter of Thomas Minchin, of Tipperary. In 1711 Parnell was thirty-two years of age, and was Archdeacon of Clogher and Vicar of Clontibret. Swift took much trouble to obtain for Parnell the friendship of Bolingbroke and other persons of note, and Parnell became a member of the Scriblerus Club. In 1716 he was made Vicar of Finglas, and after his death in 1718 Pope prepared an edition of his poems. The fits of depression to which Parnell was liable became more marked after his wife's death, and he seems to have to some extent given way to drink. His sincerity and charm of manner made him welcome with men of both parties.

[2] Dr. Henry Compton had been Bishop of London since 1675. He was dangerously ill early in 1711, but he lived until 1713, when he was eighty-one.

friends! But he was very old: we shall all follow. And yet it was a pity, if God pleased. He was a good man; not very learned: I believe he died but poor. Did he leave any charity legacies? who held up his pall? was there a great sight of clergy? do they design a tomb for him?—Are you sure it was the Bishop of London? because there is an elderly gentleman here that we give the same title to: or did you fancy all this in your water, as others do strange things in their wine? They say these waters trouble the head, and make people imagine what never came to pass. Do you make no more of killing a Bishop? are these your Whiggish tricks?—Yes, yes, I see you are in a fret. O, faith, says you, saucy Presto, I'll break your head; what, can't one report what one hears, without being made a jest and a laughing-stock? Are these your English tricks, with a murrain? And Sacheverell will be the next Bishop? He would be glad of an addition of two hundred pounds a year to what he has, and that is more than they will give him, for aught I see. He hates the new Ministry mortally, and they hate him, and pretend to despise him too. They will not allow him to have been the occasion of the late change; at least some of them will not: but my Lord Keeper owned it to me the other day. No, Mr. Addison does not go to Ireland this year: he pretended he would; but he is gone to Bath with Pastoral Philips, for his eyes.—So now I have run over your letter; and I think this shall go to-morrow, which will be just a fortnight from the last, and bring things to the old form again, after your rambles to Wexford, and mine to Windsor. Are there not many literal faults in my letters? I never read them over, and I fancy there are. What do you do then? do you guess my meaning, or are you acquainted with my manner of mistaking? I lost my handkerchief in the Mall to-night with Lord Radnor; but I made him walk with me to find it, and find it I did not. Tisdall [1] (that lodges with me) and I have had no conversation, nor do we pull off our hats in the streets. There is a

[1] See p. 250.

cousin of his (I suppose), a young parson, that lodges in the house too; a handsome, genteel fellow. Dick Tighe[1] and his wife lodged over against us; and he has been seen, out of our upper windows, beating her two or three times: they are both gone to Ireland, but not together; and he solemnly vows never to live with her. Neighbours do not stick to say that she has a tongue: in short, I am told she is the most urging, provoking devil that ever was born; and he a hot, whiffling[2] puppy, very apt to resent. I'll keep this bottom till to-morrow: I'm sleepy.

25. I was with the Secretary this morning, who was in a mighty hurry, and went to Windsor in a chariot with Lord Keeper; so I was not invited, and am forced to stay at home, but not at all against my will; for I could have gone, and would not. I dined in the City with one of my printers, for whom I got the *Gazette*, and am come home early; and have nothing to say to you more, but finish this letter, and not send it by the bellman. Days grow short, and the weather grows bad, and the town is splenetic, and things are so oddly contrived that I cannot be absent; otherwise I would go for a few days to Oxford, as I promised.—They say it is certain that Prior has been in France,[3] nobody doubts it: I had not time to ask the Secretary, he was in such haste. Well, I will take my leave of dearest MD for a while; for I must begin my next letter to-night: consider that, young women; and pray be merry, and good girls, and love Presto. There

---

[1] See p. 50.

[2] L'Estrange speaks of "a whiffling fop"; and Swift says, "Every whiffler in a laced coat, who frequents the chocolate-house, shall talk of the Constitution."

[3] Prior's first visit to France with a view to the secret negotiations with that country which the Ministers were now bent on carrying through, had been made in July, when he and Gaultier reached Calais in a fishing-boat and proceeded to Fontainbleau under assumed names. He returned to England in August, but was recognised at Dover, whence the news spread all over London, to the great annoyance of the Ministers. The officer who recognised Prior was John Macky, reputed author of those *Characters* upon which Swift wrote comments. Formerly a secret service agent under William III., Macky had been given the direction of the Ostend mail packets by Marlborough, to whom he communicated the news of Prior's journey. Bolingbroke threatened to hang Macky, and he was thrown into prison; but the accession of George I. again brought him favour and employment.

is now but one business the Ministry want me for, and when that is done, I will take my leave of them. I never got a penny from them, nor expect it. In my opinion, some things stand very ticklish; I dare say nothing at this distance. Farewell, dear sirrahs, dearest lives: there is peace and quiet with MD, and nowhere else. They have not leisure here to think of small things, which may ruin them; and I have been forward enough. Farewell again, dearest rogues; I am never happy but when I write or think of MD. I have enough of Courts and Ministries, and wish I were at Laracor; and if I could with honour come away this moment, I would. Bernage[1] came to see me to-day; he is just landed from Portugal, and come to raise recruits; he looks very well, and seems pleased with his station and manner of life. He never saw London nor England before; he is ravished with Kent, which was his first prospect when he landed. Farewell again, etc. etc.

LETTER XXIX

LONDON, *Aug.* 25, 1711.

I HAVE got a pretty small gilt sheet of paper, to write to MD. I have this moment sent my 28th by Patrick, who tells me he has put it in the post-office; 'tis directed to your lodgings: if it wants more particular direction, you must set me right. It is now a solar month and two days since the date of your last, N. 18; and I reckon you are now quiet at home, and thinking to begin your 19th, which will be full of your quarrel between the two Houses, all which I know already. Where shall I dine to-morrow? can you tell? Mrs. Vanhomrigh boards now, and cannot invite one; and there I used to dine when I was at a loss: and all my friends are gone out of town, and your town is now at the fullest, with your Parliament and Convocation. But let me alone, sirrahs; for Presto is going to be very busy; not Presto, but the other I.

1 See p. 106.

26. People have so left the town that I am at a loss for a dinner. It is a long time since I have been at London upon a Sunday; and the Ministers are all at Windsor. It cost me eighteenpence in coach-hire before I could find a place to dine in. I went to Frankland's,[1] and he was abroad, and the drab his wife looked out at window, and bowed to me without inviting me up: so I dined with Mr. Coote,[2] my Lord Mountrath's brother; my lord is with you in Ireland. This morning at five my Lord Jersey[3] died of the gout in his stomach, or apoplexy, or both: he was abroad yesterday, and his death was sudden. He was Chamberlain to King William, and a great favourite, turned out by the Queen as a Tory, and stood now fair to be Privy Seal; and by his death will, I suppose, make that matter easier, which has been a very stubborn business at Court, as I have been informed. I never remember so many people of quality to have died in so short a time.

27. I went to-day into the City, to thank Stratford for my books, and dine with him, and settle my affairs of my money in the Bank, and receive a bill for Mrs. Wesley for some things I am to buy for her; and the d—— a one of all these could I do. The merchants were all out of town, and I was forced to go to a little hedge place for my dinner. May my enemies live here in summer! and yet I am so unlucky that I cannot possibly be out of the way at this juncture. People leave the town so late in summer, and return so late in winter, that they have almost inverted the seasons. It is autumn this good while in St. James's Park; the limes have been losing their leaves, and those remaining on the trees are all parched: I hate this season, where everything grows worse and worse. The only good thing of it is the fruit, and

---

[1] See p. 7.   [2] See p. 34.

[3] Edward Villiers (1656-1711), created Viscount Villiers in 1691, was made Earl of Jersey in 1697. Under William III. he was Lord Chamberlain and Secretary of State, but he was dismissed from office in 1704. When he died he had been nominated as a plenipotentiary at the Congress of Utrecht, and was about to receive the appointment of Lord Privy Seal. Lord Jersey married, in 1681, when she was eighteen, Barbara, daughter of William Chiffinch, closet-keeper to Charles II.; she died in 1735.

that I dare not eat. Had you any fruit at Wexford? A few cherries, and durst not eat them. I do not hear we have yet got a new Privy Seal. The Whigs whisper that our new Ministry differ among themselves, and they begin to talk out Mr. Secretary: they have some reasons for their whispers, although I thought it was a greater secret. I do not much like the posture of things; I always apprehended that any falling out would ruin them, and so I have told them several times. The Whigs are mighty full of hopes at present; and whatever is the matter, all kind of stocks fall. I have not yet talked with the Secretary about Prior's journey. I should be apt to think it may foretell a peace, and that is all we have to preserve us. The Secretary is not come from Windsor, but I expect him to-morrow. Burn all politics!

28. We begin to have fine weather, and I walked to-day to Chelsea, and dined with the Dean of Carlisle, who is laid up with the gout. It is now fixed that he is to be Dean of Christ Church in Oxford. I was advising him to use his interest to prevent any misunderstanding between our Ministers; but he is too wise to meddle, though he fears the thing and the consequences as much as I. He will get into his own warm, quiet deanery, and leave them to themselves; and he is in the right.—When I came home to-night, I found a letter from Mr. Lewis, who is now at Windsor; and in it, forsooth, another which looked like Presto's hand; and what should it be but a 19th from MD? O, faith, I 'scaped narrowly, for I sent my 28th but on Saturday; and what should I have done if I had two letters to answer at once? I did not expect another from Wexford, that is certain. Well, I must be contented; but you are dear saucy girls, for all that, to write so soon again, faith; an't you?

29. I dined to-day with Lord Abercorn, and took my leave of them: they set out to-morrow for Chester, and, I believe, will now fix in Ireland. They have made a pretty good journey of it: his eldest son[1] is married to a lady with ten

[1] Lord Paisley was the Earl of Abercorn's eldest surviving son (see p. 161).

thousand pounds; and his second son[1] has, t'other day, got
a prize in the lottery of four thousand pounds, beside two
small ones of two hundred pounds each: nay, the family was
so fortunate, that my lord bestowing one ticket, which is a
hundred pounds, to one of his servants, who had been his
page, the young fellow got a prize, which has made it
another hundred. I went in the evening to Lord Treasurer,
who desires I will dine with him to-morrow, when he will
show me the answer he designs to return to the letter of
thanks from your bishops in Ireland. The Archbishop of
Dublin desired me to get myself mentioned in the answer
which my lord would send; but I sent him word I would
not open my lips to my lord upon it. He says it would
convince the bishops of what I have affirmed, that the First-
Fruits were granted before the Duke of Ormond was declared
Governor; and I writ to him that I would not give a
farthing to convince them. My Lord Treasurer began a
health to my Lord Privy Seal: Prior punned, and said it
was so *privy*, he knew not who it was; but I fancy they have
fixed it all, and we shall know to-morrow. But what care
you who is Privy Seal, saucy sluttikins?

30. When I went out this morning, I was surprised with
the news that the Bishop of Bristol is made Lord Privy Seal.
You know his name is Robinson,[2] and that he was many years
Envoy in Sweden. All the friends of the present Ministry
are extremely glad, and the clergy above the rest. The
Whigs will fret to death to see a civil employment given to
a clergyman. It was a very handsome thing in my Lord
Treasurer, and will bind the Church to him for ever. I
dined with him to-day, but he had not written his letter;[3]

---

[1] The Hon. John Hamilton, the Earl's second surviving son, died in 1714.

[2] Dr. John Robinson (1650-1723) had gone out as chaplain to the Embassy
at the Court of Sweden in 1682, and had returned in 1708 with the double
reputation of being a thorough Churchman and a sound diplomatist. He was
soon made Dean of Windsor, and afterwards Bishop of Bristol. He was now
introduced to the Council Board, and it was made known to those in the
confidence of Ministers that he would be one of the English plenipotentiaries
at the coming Peace Congress. In 1713 Dr. Robinson was made Bishop of
London.

[3] To the Irish bishops: see above.

but told me he would not offer to send it without showing it to me: he thought that would not be just, since I was so deeply concerned in the affair. We had much company: Lord Rivers, Mar,[1] and Kinnoull,[2] Mr. Secretary, George Granville, and Masham: the last has invited me to the christening of his son to-morrow se'ennight; and on Saturday I go to Windsor with Mr. Secretary.

31. Dilly and I walked to-day to Kensington to Lady Mountjoy, who invited us to dinner. He returned soon, to go to a play, it being the last that will be acted for some time: he dresses himself like a beau, and no doubt makes a fine figure. I went to visit some people at Kensington: Ophy Butler's wife[3] there lies very ill of an ague, which is a very common disease here, and little known in Ireland.— I am apt to think we shall soon have a peace, by the little words I hear thrown out by the Ministry. I have just thought of a project to bite the town. I have told you that it is now known that Mr. Prior has been lately in France. I will make a printer of my own sit by me one day, and I will dictate to him a formal relation of Prior's journey,[4] with several particulars, all pure invention; and I doubt not but it will take.

Sept. 1. Morning. I go to-day to Windsor with Mr. Secretary; and Lord Treasurer has promised to bring me back. The weather has been fine for some time, and I believe we shall have a great deal of dust. — At night. Windsor. The Secretary and I dined to-day at Parson's Green, at my Lord Peterborow's house, who has left it and his gardens to the Secretary during his absence. It is the finest garden I have ever seen about this town; and abund-

[1] John Erskine, Earl of Mar (1675-1732), who was attainted for his part in the Rebellion of 1715. His first wife, Lady Margaret Hay, was a daughter of Lord Kinnoull.

[2] Thomas Hay, sixth Earl of Kinnoull (died 1719), a Commissioner for the Treaty of Union between England and Scotland, and one of the Scotch representative peers in the first Parliament of Great Britain. His son and heir, Viscount Dupplin, afterwards Baron Hay (see p. 30), who married Harley's daughter Abigail, is often mentioned in the *Journal*.

[3] See p. 7.

[4] The title of the pamphlet was, *A New Journey to Paris, together with some Secret Transactions between the French King and an English Gentleman. By the Sieur du Baudrier. Translated from the French.*

ance of hot walls for grapes, where they are in great plenty, and ripening fast. I durst not eat any fruit but one fig; but I brought a basket full to my friend Lewis here at Windsor. Does Stella never eat any? what, no apricots at Donny-brook! nothing but claret and ombre! I envy people maunching and maunching peaches and grapes, and I not daring to eat a bit. My head is pretty well, only a sudden turn any time makes me giddy for a moment, and sometimes it feels very stuffed; but if it grows no worse, I can bear it very well. I take all opportunities of walking; and we have a delicious park here just joining to the Castle, and an avenue in the great park very wide and two miles long, set with a double row of elms on each side. Were you ever at Windsor? I was once, a great while ago; but had quite forgotten it.

2. The Queen has the gout, and did not come to chapel, nor stir out from her chamber, but received the sacrament there, as she always does the first Sunday in the month. Yet we had a great Court; and, among others, I saw your Ingoldsby,[1] who, seeing me talk very familiarly with the Keeper, Treasurer, etc., came up and saluted me, and began a very impertinent discourse about the siege of Bouchain. I told him I could not answer his questions, but I would bring him one that should; so I went and fetched Sutton (who brought over the express about a month ago), and delivered him to the General, and bid him answer his questions; and so I left them together. Sutton after some time comes back in a rage, finds me with Lord Rivers and Masham, and there complains of the trick I had played him, and swore he had been plagued to death with Ingoldsby's talk. But he told me Ingoldsby asked him what I meant by bringing him; so, I suppose, he smoked me a little. So we laughed, etc. My Lord Willoughby,[2] who is one of the chaplains, and Prebendary of Windsor, read prayers last night to the family; and the Bishop of Bristol, who is Dean of Windsor, officiated last night at the Cathedral. This they do to be popular; and it pleases mightily. I dined with Mr.

[1] See p. 97.   [2] See p. 269.

Masham, because he lets me have a select company: for the Court here have got by the end a good thing I said to the Secretary some weeks ago. He showed me his bill of fare, to tempt me to dine with him. "Poh," said I, "I value not your bill of fare; give me your bill of company." Lord Treasurer was mightily pleased, and told it everybody as a notable thing. I reckon upon returning to-morrow: they say the Bishop will then have the Privy Seal delivered him at a great Council.

3. Windsor still. The Council was held so late to-day that I do not go back to town till to-morrow. The Bishop was sworn Privy Councillor, and had the Privy Seal given him: and now the patents are passed for those who were this long time to be made lords or earls. Lord Raby,[1] who is Earl of Strafford, is on Thursday to marry a namesake of Stella's; the daughter of Sir H. Johnson in the City; he has three-score thousand pounds with her, ready money; besides the rest at the father's death. I have got my friend Stratford to be one of the directors of the South Sea Company, who were named to-day. My Lord Treasurer did it for me a month ago; and one of those whom I got to be printer of the *Gazette* I am recommending to be printer to the same company. He treated Mr. Lewis and me to-day at dinner. I supped last night and this with Lord Treasurer, Keeper, etc., and took occasion to mention the printer. I said it was the same printer whom my Lord Treasurer has appointed to print for the South Sea Company. He denied, and I insisted on it; and I got the laugh on my side.

London, 4. I came as far as Brentford in Lord Rivers's chariot, who had business with Lord Treasurer; then I went into Lord Treasurer's. We stopped at Kensington, where Lord Treasurer went to see Mrs. Masham, who is now what they call in the straw. We got to town by three, and

---

[1] The Earl of Strafford (see p. 170) married, on Sept. 6, 1711, Anne, only daughter and heiress of Sir Henry Johnson, of Bradenham, Buckinghamshire, a wealthy shipbuilder. Many of Lady Strafford's letters to her husband are given in the *Wentworth Papers*, 1883.

I lighted at Lord Treasurer's, who commanded me not to stir: but I was not well; and when he went up, I begged the young lord to excuse me, and so went into the City by water, where I could be easier, and dined with the printer, and dictated to him some part of Prior's *Journey to France*. I walked from the City, for I take all occasions of exercise. Our journey was horridly dusty.

5. When I went out to-day, I found it had rained mightily in the night, and the streets were as dirty as winter: it is very refreshing after ten days dry.—I went into the City, and dined with Stratford, thanked him for his books, gave him joy of his being director, of which he had the first notice by a letter from me. I ate sturgeon, and it lies on my stomach. I almost finished Prior's *Journey* at the printer's; and came home pretty late, with Patrick at my heels.

7. Morning. But what shall we do about this letter of MD's, N. 19? Not a word answered yet, and so much paper spent! I cannot do anything in it, sweethearts, till night. —At night. O Lord, O Lord! the greatest disgrace that ever was has happened to Presto. What do you think? but, when I was going out this forenoon a letter came from MD, N. 20, dated Dublin. O dear, O dear! O sad, O sad!— Now I have two letters together to answer: here they are, lying together. But I will only answer the first; for I came in late. I dined with my friend Lewis at his lodgings, and walked at six to Kensington to Mrs. Masham's son's christening. It was very private; nobody there but my Lord Treasurer, his son and son-in-law, that is to say, Lord Harley and Lord Dupplin, and Lord Rivers and I. The Dean of Rochester[1] christened the child, but soon went away. Lord Treasurer and Lord Rivers were godfathers; and Mrs. Hill,[2] Mrs. Masham's sister, godmother. The child roared like a bull, and I gave Mrs. Masham joy of it; and she charged me to take care of my nephew, because, Mr. Masham being a brother of our Society, his son, you know,

[1] Samuel Pratt, who was also Clerk of the Closet.
[2] Alice Hill, woman of the bed-chamber to the Queen, died in 1762.

is consequently a nephew. Mrs. Masham sat up dressed in bed, but not, as they do in Ireland, with all smooth about her, as if she was cut off in the middle; for you might see the counterpane (what d'ye call it?) rise about her hips and body. There is another name of the counterpane; and you will laugh now, sirrahs. George Granville came in at supper, and we stayed till eleven; and Lord Treasurer set me down at my lodging in Suffolk Street. Did I ever tell you that Lord Treasurer hears ill with the left ear, just as I do? He always turns the right, and his servants whisper him at that only. I dare not tell him that I am so too, for fear he should think I counterfeited, to make my court.

6. You must read this before the other; for I mistook, and forgot to write yesterday's journal, it was so insignificant. I dined with Dr. Cockburn, and sat the evening with Lord Treasurer till ten o'clock. On Thursdays he has always a large select company, and expects me. So good-night for last night, etc.

8. Morning. I go to Windsor with Lord Treasurer to-day, and will leave this behind me, to be sent to the post. And now let us hear what says the first letter, N. 19. You are still at Wexford, as you say, Madam Dingley. I think no letter from me ever yet miscarried. And so Inish-Corthy,[1] and the river Slainy; fine words those in a lady's mouth. Your hand like Dingley's, you scambling,[2] scattering sluttikin! *Yes, mighty like indeed, is not it?*[3] Pisshh, do not talk of writing or reading till your eyes are well, and long well; only I would have Dingley read sometimes to you, that you may not lose the desire of it. God be thanked, that the ugly numbing is gone! Pray use exercise when you go to town. What game is that ombra which Dr. Elwood[4] and you play at? is it the Spanish game ombre? Your card-purse? you a card-purse! you a fiddlestick. You have luck

---

[1] Enniscorthy, the name of a town in the county of Wexford.
[2] Scrambling.
[3] " These words in italics are written in strange, misshapen letters, inclining to the right hand, in imitation of Stella's writing " (Deane Swift).
[4] Senior Fellow of Trinity College, Dublin.

indeed; and luck in a bag. What a devil! is that eight-shilling tea-kettle copper, or tin japanned? It is like your Irish politeness, raffling for tea-kettles. What a splutter you keep, to convince me that Walls has no taste! My head continues pretty well. Why do you write, dear sirrah Stella, when you find your eyes so weak that you cannot see? what comfort is there in reading what you write, when one knows that? So Dingley cannot write, because of the clutter of new company come to Wexford! I suppose the noise of their hundred horses disturbs you; or do you lie in one gallery, as in an hospital? What! you are afraid of losing in Dublin the acquaintance you have got in Wexford, and chiefly the Bishop of Raphoe,[1] an old, doting, perverse coxcomb? Twenty at a time at breakfast. That is like five pounds at a time, when it was never but once. I doubt, Madam Dingley, you are apt to lie in your travels, though not so bad as Stella; she tells thumpers, as I shall prove in my next, if I find this receives encouragement.—So Dr. Elwood says there are a world of pretty things in my works. A pox on his praises! an enemy here would say more. The Duke of Buckingham would say as much, though he and I are terribly fallen out; and the great men are perpetually inflaming me against him: they bring me all he says of me, and, I believe, make it worse out of roguery.—No, 'tis not your pen is bewitched, Madam Stella, but your old *scrawling, splay-foot pot-hooks, s, s,*[2] ay that's it: there the s, s, s, there, there, that's exact. Farewell, etc.

Our fine weather is gone; and I doubt we shall have a rainy journey to-day. Faith, 'tis shaving-day, and I have much to do.

When Stella says her pen was bewitched, it was only because there was a hair in it. You know, the fellow they call God-help-it had the same thoughts of his wife, and for the same reason. I think this is very well observed, and I unfolded the letter to tell you it.

[1] John Pooley, appointed Bishop of Raphoe in 1702.
[2] "These words in italics are miserably scrawled, in imitation of Stella's hand (Deane Swift).

19

Cut off those two notes above; and see the nine pounds indorsed, and receive the other; and send me word how my accounts stand, that they may be adjusted by Nov. 1.[1] Pray be very particular; but the twenty pounds I lend you is not to be included: so make no blunder. I won't wrong you, nor you shan't wrong me; that is the short. O Lord, how stout Presto is of late! But he loves MD more than his life a thousand times, for all his stoutness; tell them that; and that I'll swear it, as hope saved, ten millions of times, etc. etc.

I open my letter once more, to tell Stella that if she does not use exercise after her waters, it will lose all the effects of them: I should not live if I did not take all opportunities of walking. Pray, pray, do this, to oblige poor Presto.

LETTER XXX

WINDSOR, *Sept.* 8, 1711.

I MADE the coachman stop, and put in my twenty-ninth at the post-office at two o'clock to-day, as I was going to Lord Treasurer, with whom I dined, and came here by a quarter-past eight; but the moon shone, and so we were not in much danger of overturning; which, however, he values not a straw, and only laughs when I chide at him for it. There was nobody but he and I, and we supped together, with Mr. Masham, and Dr. Arbuthnot, the Queen's favourite physician, a Scotchman. I could not keep myself awake after supper, but did all I was able to disguise it, and thought I came off clear; but, at parting, he told me I had got my nap already. It is now one o'clock; but he loves sitting up late.

9. The Queen is still in the gout, but recovering: she saw company in her bed-chamber after church; but the crowd was so great, I could not see her. I dined with my brother Sir William Wyndham,[2] and some others of our Society, to avoid the great tables on Sunday at Windsor, which I hate.

[1] See p. 54.   [2] See p. 236.

The usual company supped to-night at Lord Treasurer's, which was Lord Keeper, Mr. Secretary, George Granville, Masham, Arbuthnot, and I. But showers have hindered me from walking to-day, and that I do not love.—Noble fruit, and I dare not eat a bit. I ate one fig to-day, and sometimes a few mulberries, because it is said they are wholesome, and you know a good name does much. I shall return to town to-morrow, though I thought to have stayed a week, to be at leisure for something I am doing. But I have put it off till next; for I shall come here again on Saturday, when our Society are to meet at supper at Mr. Secretary's. My life is very regular here: on Sunday morning I constantly visit Lord Keeper, and sup at Lord Treasurer's with the same set of company. I was not sleepy to-night; I resolved I would not; yet it is past midnight at this present writing.

London, 10. Lord Treasurer and Masham and I left Windsor at three this afternoon: we dropped Masham at Kensington with his lady, and got home by six. It was seven before we sat down to dinner, and I stayed till past eleven. Patrick came home with the Secretary: I am more plagued with Patrick and my portmantua than with myself. I forgot to tell you that when I went to Windsor on Saturday I over-took Lady Giffard and Mrs. Fenton[1] in a chariot, going, I suppose, to Sheen. I was then in a chariot too, of Lord Treasurer's brother, who had business with the Treasurer; and my lord came after, and overtook me at Turnham Green, four miles from London; and then the brother went back, and I went in the coach with Lord Treasurer: so it happened that those people saw me, and not with Lord Treasurer. Mrs. F. was to see me about a week ago; and desired I would get her son into the Charter-house.

11. This morning the printer sent me an account of Prior's Journey;[2] it makes a twopenny pamphlet. I suppose you will see it, for I dare engage it will run; 'tis a formal, grave lie, from the beginning to the end. I writ all but about the last page; that I dictated, and the printer writ.

[1] See p. 74.   [2] See p. 284.

Mr. Secretary sent to me to dine where he did; it was at Prior's: when I came in, Prior showed me the pamphlet, seemed to be angry, and said, "Here is our English liberty!" I read some of it, and said I liked it mightily, and envied the rogue the thought; for, had it come into my head, I should have certainly done it myself. We stayed at Prior's till past ten; and then the Secretary received a packet with the news of Bouchain being taken, for which the guns will go off to-morrow. Prior owned his having been in France, for it was past denying: it seems he was discovered by a rascal at Dover, who had positive orders to let him pass. I believe we shall have a peace.

12. It is terrible rainy weather, and has cost me three shillings in coaches and chairs to-day, yet I was dirty into the bargain. I was three hours this morning with the Secretary about some business of moment, and then went into the City to dine. The printer tells me he sold yesterday a thousand of Prior's *Journey*, and had printed five hundred more. It will do rarely, I believe, and is a pure bite. And what is MD doing all this while? got again to their cards, their Walls, their deans, their Stoytes, and their claret? Pray present my service to Mr. Stoyte and Catherine. Tell Goody Stoyte she owes me a world of dinners, and I will shortly come over and demand them.—Did I tell you of the Archbishop of Dublin's last letter? He had been saying, in several of his former, that he would shortly write to me something about myself; and it looked as if he intended something for me: at last out it comes, and consists of two parts. First, he advises me to strike in for some preferment now I have friends; and secondly, he advises me, since I have parts, and learning, and a happy pen, to think of some new subject in divinity not handled by others, which I should manage better than anybody. A rare spark this, with a pox! but I shall answer him as rarely. Methinks he should have invited me over, and given me some hopes or promises. But hang him! and so good-night, etc.

13. It rained most furiously all this morning till about

twelve, and sometimes thundered; I trembled for my shillings, but it cleared up, and I made a shift to get a walk in the Park, and then went with the Secretary to dine with Lord Treasurer. Upon Thursdays there is always a select company: we had the Duke of Shrewsbury, Lord Rivers, the two Secretaries, Mr. Granville, and Mr. Prior. Half of them went to Council at six; but Rivers, Granville, Prior, and I, stayed till eight. Prior was often affecting to be angry at the account of his journey to Paris; and indeed the two last pages, which the printer got somebody to add,[1] are so romantic, they spoil all the rest. Dilly Ashe pretended to me that he was only going to Oxford and Cambridge for a fortnight, and then would come back. I could not see him as I appointed t'other day; but some of his friends tell me he took leave of them as going to Ireland; and so they say at his lodging. I believe the rogue was ashamed to tell me so, because I advised him to stay the winter, and he said he would. I find he had got into a good set of scrub acquaintance, and I thought passed his time very merrily; but I suppose he languished after Balderig, and the claret of Dublin; and, after all, I think he is in the right; for he can eat, drink, and converse better there than here. Bernage was with me this morning: he calls now and then; he is in terrible fear of a peace. He said he never had his health so well as in Portugal. He is a favourite of his Colonel.

14. I was mortified enough to-day, not knowing where in the world to dine, the town is so empty. I met H. Coote,[2] and thought he would invite me, but he did not: Sir John Stanley did not come into my head; so I took up with Mrs. Van, and dined with her and her damned landlady, who, I believe, by her eyebrows, is a bawd. This evening I met Addison and Pastoral Philips in the Park, and supped with them at Addison's lodgings: we were very good company, and I yet know no man half so agreeable to me as he is. I sat with them till twelve, so you may think it is late, young women; however, I would have some little conversation with

---

[1] Cf. the entry on the 11th (p. 291).   [2] See p. 34.

MD before your Presto goes to bed, because it makes me sleep, and dream, and so forth. Faith, this letter goes on slowly enough, sirrahs; but I cannot write much at a time till you are quite settled after your journey, you know, and have gone all your visits, and lost your money at ombre. You never play at chess now, Stella. That puts me in mind of Dick Tighe; I fancy I told you he used to beat his wife here; and she deserved it; and he resolves to part with her; and they went to Ireland in different coaches. O Lord, I said all this before, I am sure. Go to bed, sirrahs.

Windsor, 15. I made the Secretary stop at Brentford, because we set out at two this afternoon, and fasting would not agree with me. I only designed to eat a bit of bread-and-butter; but he would light, and we ate roast beef like dragons. And he made me treat him and two more gentlemen; faith, it cost me a guinea. I do not like such jesting, yet I was mightily pleased with it too. To-night our Society met at the Secretary's: there were nine of us; and we have chosen a new member, the Earl of Jersey,[1] whose father died lately. 'Tis past one, and I have stolen away.

16. I design to stay here this week by myself, about some business that lies on my hands, and will take up a great deal of time. Dr. Adams,[2] one of the canons, invited me to-day to dinner. The tables are so full here on Sunday that it is hard to dine with a few, and Dr. Adams knows I love to do so; which is very obliging. The Queen saw company in her bed-chamber; she looks very well, but she sat down. I supped with Lord Treasurer as usual, and stayed till past one as usual, and with our usual company, except Lord Keeper, who did not come this time to Windsor. I hate these suppers mortally, but I seldom eat anything.

---

[1] William, Lord Villiers, second Earl of Jersey (died 1721), a strong Jacobite, had been M.P. for Kent before his father's death. He married, in 1704, Judith, only daughter of a City merchant, Frederick Herne, son of Sir Nathaniel Herne, Alderman; she died in 1735. Lord Jersey, one of "the prettiest young peers in England," was a companion of Bolingbroke, and stories in the *Wentworth Papers* (pp. 149, 230, 395, 445), show that he had a bad reputation.
[2] See p. 269.

17. Lord Treasurer and Mr. Secretary stay here till to-morrow; some business keeps them, and I am sorry for it, for they hinder me a day. Mr. Lewis and I were going to dine soberly with a little Court friend at one. But Lord Harley and Lord Dupplin kept me by force, and said we should dine at Lord Treasurer's, who intended to go at four to London. I stayed like a fool, and went with the two young lords to Lord Treasurer, who very fairly turned us all three out of doors. They both were invited to the Duke of Somerset, but he was gone to a horse-race, and would not come till five; so we were forced to go to a tavern, and sent for wine from Lord Treasurer's, who at last, we were told, did not go to town till the morrow, and at Lord Treasurer's we supped again; and I desired him to let me add four shillings to the bill I gave him. We sat up till two, yet I must write to little MD.

18. They are all gone early this morning, and I am alone to seek my fortune; but Dr. Arbuthnot engages me for my dinners; and he yesterday gave me my choice of place, person, and victuals for to-day. So I chose to dine with Mrs. Hill, who is one of the dressers, and Mrs. Masham's sister, no company but us three, and to have a shoulder of mutton, a small one; which was exactly, only there was too much victuals besides; and the Doctor's wife [1] was of the company. And to-morrow Mrs. Hill and I are to dine with the Doctor. I have seen a fellow often about Court whom I thought I knew. I asked who he was, and they told me it was the gentleman porter; then I called him to mind; he was Killy's acquaintance (I won't say yours); I think his name is Lovet,[2] or Lovel, or something like it. I believe he does not know me, and in my present posture I shall not be fond of renewing old acquaintance; I believe I used to see him with the Bradleys; and, by the way, I have not seen Mrs. Bradley since I came to England. I left your letter in London, like a fool; and cannot answer it till I go back,

[1] The name of Arbuthnot's wife is not known: she died in 1730.
[2] James Lovet, one of the "Yeomen Porters" at Court.

which will not be until Monday next; so this will be above a fortnight from my last; but I will fetch it up in my next; so go and walk to the Dean's for your health this fine weather.

19. The Queen designs to have cards and dancing here next week, which makes us think she will stay here longer than we believed. Mrs. Masham is not well after her lying-in: I doubt she got some cold; she is lame in one of her legs with a rheumatic pain. Dr. Arbuthnot and Mrs. Hill go to-morrow to Kensington to see her, and return the same night. Mrs. Hill and I dined wth the Doctor to-day. I rode out this morning with the Doctor to see Cranburn, a house of Lord Ranelagh's,[1] and the Duchess of Marlborough's lodge, and the Park; the finest places they are, for nature and plantations, that ever I saw; and the finest riding upon artificial roads, made on purpose for the Queen. Arbuthnot made me draw up a sham subscription for a book, called *A History of the Maids of Honour since Harry the Eighth,* showing they make the best wives, with a list of all the maids of honour since, etc.; to pay a crown in hand, and the other crown upon delivery of the book; and all in common forms of those things. We got a gentleman to write it fair, because my hand is known; and we sent it to the maids of honour, when they came to supper. If they bite at it, it will be a very good Court jest; and the Queen will certainly have it: we did not tell Mrs. Hill.

20. To-day I was invited to the Green Cloth by Colonel Godfrey, who married the Duke of Marlborough's sister,[2] mother to the Duke of Berwick by King James: I must tell you those things that happened before you were born. But I made my excuses, and young Harcourt (Lord Keeper's son)

---

[1] Richard Jones, Earl of Ranelagh, who died without male issue in January 1712. Writing to Archbishop King on Jan. 8, Swift said, "Lord Ranelagh died on Sunday morning; he was very poor and needy, and could hardly support himself for want of a pension which used to be paid him."

[2] Arabella Churchill, maid of honour to the Duchess of York, and mistress of James II., afterwards married Colonel Charles Godfrey, Clerk Comptroller of the Green Cloth and Master of the Jewel Office. Her second son by James II. was created Duke of Albemarle.

and I dined with my next neighbour, Dr Adams.[1] Mrs. Masham is better, and will be here in three or four days. She had need; for the Duchess of Somerset is thought to gain ground daily.—We have not sent you over all your bills; and I think we have altered your money-bill. The Duke of Ormond is censured here, by those in power, for very wrong management in the affair of the mayoralty.[2] He is governed by fools, and has usually much more sense than his advisers, but never proceeds by it. I must know how your health continues after Wexford. Walk and use exercise, sirrahs both; and get somebody to play at shuttlecock with you, Madam Stella, and walk to the Dean's and Donnybrook.

21. Colonel Godfrey sent to me again to-day; so I dined at the Green Cloth, and we had but eleven at dinner, which is a small number there, the Court being always thin of company till Saturday night.—This new ink and pen make a strange figure; *I must write larger, yes I must, or Stella will not be able to read this.*[3] S. S. S., there is your S's for you, Stella. The maids of honour are bit, and have all contributed their crowns, and are teasing others to subscribe for the book. I will tell Lord Keeper and Lord Treasurer to-morrow; and I believe the Queen will have it. After a little walk this evening, I squandered away the rest of it in sitting at Lewis's lodging, while he and Dr. Arbuthnot played at picquet. I have that foolish pleasure, which I believe nobody has beside me, except old Lady Berkeley.[4] But I fretted when I came away: I will loiter so no more, for I have a plaguy deal of business upon my hands, and very little time to do it. The pamphleteers begin to be very busy against the Ministry: I have begged Mr. Secretary to make examples of

---

[1] See p. 269.

[2] The Lord Mayor and Sheriffs of Dublin, elected in August 1711, "not being approved of by the Government, the City was obliged to proceed to another election, which occasioned a great ferment among the vulgar sort" (Boyer, *Political State*, 1711, p. 500). After two other persons had been elected and disapproved of, Alderman Gore was elected Lord Mayor, and approved (*ib.* pp. 612–17).

[3] "These words in italics are written enormously large" (Deane Swift).

[4] See p. 14.

one or two of them, and he assures me he will. They are very bold and abusive.

22. This being the day the Ministry come to Windsor, I ate a bit or two at Mr. Lewis's lodgings, because I must sup with Lord Treasurer; and at half an hour after one, I led Mr. Lewis a walk up the avenue, which is two miles long. We walked in all about five miles; but I was so tired with his slow walking, that I left him here, and walked two miles towards London, hoping to meet Lord Treasurer, and return with him; but it grew darkish, and I was forced to walk back, so I walked nine miles in all; and Lord Treasurer did not come till after eight; which is very wrong, for there was no moon, and I often tell him how ill he does to expose himself so; but he only makes a jest of it. I supped with him, and stayed till now, when it is half an hour after two. He is as merry and careless and disengaged as a young heir at one-and-twenty. 'Tis late indeed.

23. The Secretary did not come last night, but at three this afternoon. I have not seen him yet, but I verily think they are contriving a peace as fast as they can, without which it will be impossible to subsist. The Queen was at church to-day, but was carried in a chair. I and Mr. Lewis dined privately with Mr. Lowman,[1] Clerk of the Kitchen. I was to see Lord Keeper this morning, and told him the jest of the maids of honour; and Lord Treasurer had it last night. That rogue Arbuthnot puts it all upon me. The Court was very full to-day. I expected Lord Treasurer would have invited me to supper; but he only bowed to me; and we had no discourse in the drawing-room. It is now seven at night, and I am at home; and I hope Lord Treasurer will not send for me to supper: if he does not, I will reproach him; and he will pretend to chide me for not coming.—So farewell till I go to bed, for I am going to be busy.—It is now past ten, and I went down to ask the servants about Mr. Secretary: they tell me the Queen is yet at Council, and that she went to supper, and came out to the Council afterwards. It is

---

[1] Henry Lowman, First Clerk of the Kitchen.

certain they are managing a peace.   I will go to bed, and
there is an end.—It is now eleven, and a messenger is come
from Lord Treasurer to sup with them ; but I have excused
myself, and am glad I am in bed ; for else I should sit up
till two, and drink till I was hot.   Now I'll go sleep.

London, 24.   I came to town by six with Lord Treasurer,
and have stayed till ten.   That of the Queen's going out to
sup, and coming in again, is a lie, as the Secretary told
me this morning ; but I find the Ministry are very busy
with Mr. Prior, and I believe he will go again to France.
I am told so much, that we shall certainly have a peace
very soon.   I had charming weather all last week at
Windsor ; but we have had a little rain to-day, and
yesterday was windy.   Prior's *Journey* sells still ; they
have sold two thousand, although the town is empty.   I
found a letter from Mrs. Fenton here, desiring me, in Lady
Giffard's name, to come and pass a week at Sheen, while she
is at Moor Park.   I will answer it with a vengeance : and now
you talk of answering, there is MD's N. 20 is yet to be
answered : I had put it up so safe, I could hardly find it ;
but here it is, faith, and I am afraid I cannot send this till
Thursday ; for I must see the Secretary to-morrow morning,
and be in some other place in the evening.

25.   Stella writes like an emperor, and gives such an
account of her journey, never saw the like.   Let me see ;
stand away, let us compute ; you stayed four days at Inish-
Corthy, two nights at Mrs. Proby's mother's, and yet was
but six days in journey ; for your words are, " We left
Wexford this day se'ennight, and came here last night."
I have heard them say that " travellers may lie by authority."
Make up this, if you can.   How far is it from Wexford to
Dublin ? how many miles did you travel in a day ?[1]   Let me
see—thirty pounds in two months is nine score pounds a year ;

---

[1] " The Doctor was always a bad reckoner, either of money or anything else ;
and this is one of his rapid computations.   For, as Stella was seven days in
journey, although Dr. Swift says only six, she might well have spent four days
at Inish-Corthy, and two nights at Mrs. Proby's mother's, the distance from
Wexford to Dublin being but two easy days' journey " (Deane Swift).

a matter of nothing in Stella's purse! I dreamed Billy
Swift was alive, and that I told him you writ me word he
was dead, and that you had been at his funeral; and I
admired at your impudence, and was in mighty haste to run
and let you know what lying rogues you were. Poor lad!
he is dead of his mother's former folly and fondness; and
yet now I believe, as you say, that her grief will soon wear
off.—O yes, Madam Dingley, mightily tired of the company,
no doubt of it, at Wexford! And your description of it is
excellent; clean sheets, but bare walls; I suppose then you
lay upon the walls.—Mrs. Walls has got her tea; but who
pays me the money? Come, I shall never get it; so I make
a present of it, to stop some gaps, etc. Where's the thanks
of the house? So, that's well; why, it cost four-and-thirty
shillings English—you must adjust that with Mrs. Walls;
I think that is so many pence more with you.—No, Leigh
and Sterne, I suppose, were not at the water-side: I fear
Sterne's business will not be done; I have not seen him this
good while. I hate him, for the management of that box;
and I was the greatest fool in nature for trusting to such a
young jackanapes; I will speak to him once more about it,
when I see him. Mr. Addison and I met once more since,
and I supped with him; I believe I told you so somewhere in
this letter. The Archbishop chose an admirable messenger
in Walls, to send to me; yet I think him fitter for a
messenger than anything.—The D—— she has! I did not
observe her looks. Will she rot out of modesty with Lady
Giffard? I pity poor Jenny [1]—but her husband is a dunce,
and with respect to him she loses little by her deafness. I
believe, Madam Stella, in your accounts you mistook one
liquor for another, and it was an hundred and forty quarts of
wine, and thirty-two of water.—This is all written in the
morning before I go to the Secretary, as I am now doing.
I have answered your letter a little shorter than ordinary;
but I have a mind it should go to-day, and I will give you
my journal at night in my next; for I'm so afraid of another

[1] Mrs. Fenton.

letter before this goes: I will never have two together again unanswered.—What care I for Dr. Tisdall and Dr. Raymond, or how many children they have! I wish they had a hundred apiece.—Lord Treasurer promises me to answer the bishops' letter to-morrow, and show it me; and I believe it will confirm all I said, and mortify those that threw the merit on the Duke of Ormond; for I have made him jealous of it; and t'other day, talking of the matter, he said, "I am your witness, you got it for them before the Duke was Lord Lieutenant." My humble service to Mrs. Walls, Mrs. Stoyte, and Catherine. Farewell, etc.

What do you do when you see any literal mistakes in my letters? how do you set them right? for I never read them over to correct them. Farewell, again.

Pray send this note to Mrs. Brent, to get the money when Parvisol comes to town, or she can send to him.

LETTER XXXI

LONDON, *Sept.* 25, 1711.

I DINED in the City to-day, and at my return I put my 30th into the post-office; and when I got home I found for me one of the noblest letters I ever read: it was from ——, three sides and a half in folio, on a large sheet of paper; the two first pages made up of satire upon London, and crowds and hurry, stolen from some of his own school-boy's exercises: the side and a half remaining is spent in desiring me to recommend Mrs. South, your Commissioner's widow,[1] to my Lord Treasurer for a pension. He is the prettiest, discreetest fellow that ever my eyes beheld, or that ever dipped pen into ink. I know not what to say to him. A pox on him, I have too many such customers on this side already. I think I will send him word that I never saw my Lord Treasurer in my life: I am sure I industriously avoided the name of any great person when I saw him, for fear of his

[1] See p. 86.

reporting it in Ireland. And this recommendation must be a secret too, for fear the Duke of Bolton [1] should know it, and think it was too mean. I never read so d——d a letter in my life: a little would make me send it over to you.—I must send you a pattern, the first place I cast my eyes on, I will not pick and choose. *In this place* (meaning the Exchange in London), *which is the compendium of old Troynovant, as that is of the whole busy world, I got such a surfeit, that I grew sick of mankind, and resolved for ever after to bury myself in the shady retreat of* ——. You must know that London has been called by some Troynovant, or New Troy. Will you have any more? Yes, one little bit for Stella, because she'll be fond of it. *This wondrous theatre* (meaning London) *was no more to me than a desert, and I should less complain of solitude in a Connaught shipwreck, or even the great bog of Allen.* A little scrap for Mrs. Marget,[2] and then I have done. *Their royal fanum, wherein the idol Pecunia is daily worshipped, seemed to me to be just like a hive of bees working and labouring under huge weights of cares.* Fanum is a temple, but he means the Exchange; and Pecunia is money: so now Mrs. Marget will understand her part. One more paragraph, and I— Well, come, don't be in such a rage, you shall have no more. Pray, Stella, be satisfied; 'tis very pretty: and that I must be acquainted with such a dog as this!—Our peace goes on fast. Prior was with the Secretary two hours this morning: I was there a little after he went away, and was told it. I believe he will soon be despatched again to France; and I will put somebody to write an account of his second journey: I hope you have seen the other. This latter has taken up my time with storming at it.

26. Bernage has been with me these two days; yesterday I sent for him to let him know that Dr. Arbuthnot is putting in strongly to have his brother made a captain over

---

[1] Charles Paulet, second Duke of Bolton, was appointed Lord Lieutenant of Ireland in 1717, and died in 1722. In a note on Macky's character of the Duke, Swift calls him "a great booby"; and Lady Cowper (*Diary*, p. 154) says that he was generally to be seen with his tongue lolling out of his mouth.
[2] Stella's maid.

Bernage's [1] head. Arbuthnot's brother is but an ensign, but the Doctor has great power with the Queen: yet he told me he would not do anything hard to a gentleman who is my friend; and I have engaged the Secretary and his Colonel [2] for him. To-day he told me very melancholy, that the other had written from Windsor (where he went to solicit) that he has got the company; and Bernage is full of the spleen. I made the Secretary write yesterday a letter to the Colonel in Bernage's behalf. I hope it will do yet; and I have written to Dr. Arbuthnot to Windsor, not to insist on doing such a hardship. I dined in the City at Pontack's, with Stratford; it cost me seven shillings: he would have treated, but I did not let him. I have removed my money from the Bank to another fund. I desire Parvisol may speak to Hawkshaw to pay in my money when he can, for I will put it in the funds; and, in the meantime, borrow so much of Mr. Secretary, who offers to lend it me. Go to the Dean's, sirrahs.

27. Bernage was with me again to-day, and is in great fear, and so was I; but this afternoon, at Lord Treasurer's, where I dined, my brother, George Granville, Secretary at War, after keeping me a while in suspense, told me that Dr. Arbuthnot had waived the business, because he would not wrong a friend of mine; that his brother is to be a lieutenant, and Bernage is made a captain. I called at his lodging, and the soldier's coffee-house, to put him out of pain, but cannot find him; so I have left word, and shall see him to-morrow morning, I suppose. Bernage is now easy; he has ten shillings a day, beside lawful cheating. However, he gives a private sum to his Colonel, but it is very cheap: his Colonel loves him well, but is surprised to see him have so many friends. So he is now quite off my hands. I left the company early to-night, at Lord Treasurer's; but the Secretary followed me, to desire I would go with him to W——. Mr. Lewis's man came in before I could finish that word beginning with a W, which ought to be Windsor, and brought me a very handsome rallying letter from Dr.

1 See p. 106. 2 Colonel Fielding (see p. 154).

Arbuthnot, to tell me he had, in compliance to me, given up his brother's pretensions in favour of Bernage, this very morning; that the Queen had spoken to Mr. Granville to make the company easy in the other's having the captainship. Whether they have done it to oblige me or no, I must own it so. He says he this very morning begged Her Majesty to give Mr. Bernage the company. I am mighty well pleased to have succeeded so well; but you will think me tedious, although you like the man, as I think.

Windsor, 28. I came here a day sooner than ordinary, at Mr. Secretary's desire, and supped with him and Prior, and two private Ministers from France, and a French priest.[1] I know not the two Ministers' names; but they are come about the peace. The names the Secretary called them, I suppose, were feigned; they were good rational men. We have already settled all things with France, and very much to the honour and advantage of England; and the Queen is in mighty good humour. All this news is a mighty secret; the people in general know that a peace is forwarding. The Earl of Strafford[2] is to go soon to Holland, and let them know what we have been doing: and then there will be the devil and all to pay; but we'll make them swallow it with a pox. The French Ministers stayed with us till one, and the Secretary and I sat up talking till two; so 'you will own 'tis late, sirrahs, and time for your little saucy Presto to go to bed and sleep adazy; and God bless poor little MD: I hope they are now fast asleep, and dreaming of Presto.

29. Lord Treasurer came to-night, as usual, at half an hour after eight, as dark as pitch. I am weary of chiding him; so I commended him for observing his friend's advice, and coming so early, etc. I was two hours with Lady Oglethorpe[3]

---

[1] The envoys were Ménager and the Abbé du Bois; the priest was the Abbé Gaultier.

[2] See p. 170.

[3] Sir Theophilus Oglethorpe, General, who died in 1702, married Eleanor, daughter of Richard Wall, of Rogane, Tipperary. She died in 1732, and Swift described her as so "cunning a devil that she had great influence as a reconciler of the differences at Court." One of her sons was General James Oglethorpe, the philanthropist, a d friend of Dr. Johnson.

to-night, and then supped with Lord Treasurer, after dining at the Green Cloth: I stayed till two; this is the effect of Lord Treasurer's being here; I must sup with him, and he keeps cursed hours. Lord Keeper and the Secretary were absent; they cannot sit up with him. This long sitting up makes the periods in my letters so short. I design to stay here all the next week, to be at leisure by myself, to finish something of weight I have upon my hands, and which must soon be done. I shall then think of returning to Ireland, if these people will let me; and I know nothing else they have for me to do. I gave Dr. Arbuthnot my thanks for his kindness to Bernage, whose commission is now signed. Methinks I long to know something of Stella's health, how it continues after Wexford waters.

30. The Queen was not at chapel to-day, and all for the better, for we had a dunce to preach: she has a little of the gout. I dined with my brother Masham, and a moderate company, and would not go to Lord Treasurer's till after supper at eleven o'clock, and pretended I had mistaken the hour; so I ate nothing: and a little after twelve the company broke up, the Keeper and Secretary refusing to stay; so I saved this night's debauch. Prior went away yesterday with his Frenchmen, and a thousand reports are raised in this town. Some said they knew one to be the Abbé de Polignac: others swore it was the Abbé du Bois. The Whigs are in a rage about the peace; but we'll wherret[1] them, I warrant, boys. Go, go, go to the Dean's and don't mind politics, young women, they are not good after the waters; they are stark naught: they strike up into the head. Go, get two black aces, and fish for a manilio.

Oct. 1. Sir John Walter,[2] an honest drunken fellow, is now in waiting, and invited me to the Green Cloth to-day, that he might not be behindhand with Colonel Godfrey, who is a Whig. I was engaged to the Mayor's feast with

---

[1] " Worrit," trouble, tease.
[2] Sir John Walter, Bart. (died 1722), was M.P. for the city of Oxford. He and Charles Godfrey (see p. 296) were the Clerks Comptrollers of the Green Cloth.

20

Mr. Masham; but waiting to take leave of Lord Treasurer, I came too late, and so returned sneaking to the Green Cloth, and did not see my Lord Treasurer neither; but was resolved not to lose two dinners for him. I took leave to-day of my friend and solicitor Lord Rivers, who is commanded by the Queen to set out for Hanover on Thursday. The Secretary does not go to town till to-morrow; he and I, and two friends more, drank a sober bottle of wine here at home, and parted at twelve; he goes by seven to-morrow morning, so I shall not see him. I have power over his cellar in his absence, and make little use of it. Lord Dartmouth and my friend Lewis stay here this week; but I can never work out a dinner from Dartmouth. Masham has promised to provide for me: I squired his lady out of her chaise to-day, and must visit her in a day or two. So you have had a long fit of the finest weather in the world; but I am every day in pain that it will go off. I have done no business to-day; I am very idle.

2. My friend Lewis and I, to avoid over much eating and great tables, dined with honest Jemmy Eckershall,[1] Clerk of the Kitchen, now in waiting, and I bespoke my dinner: but the cur had your acquaintance Lovet, the gentleman porter, to be our company. Lovet, towards the end of dinner, after twenty wrigglings, said he had the honour to see me formerly at Moor Park, and thought he remembered my face. I said I thought I remembered him, and was glad to see him, etc., and I escaped for that much, for he was very pert. It has rained all this day, and I doubt our good weather is gone. I have been very idle this afternoon, playing at twelvepenny picquet with Lewis: I won seven shillings, which is the only money I won this year: I have not played above four times, and I think always at Windsor. Cards are very dear: there is a duty on them of sixpence a pack, which spoils small gamesters.

3. Mr. Masham sent this morning to desire I would ride out with him, the weather growing again very fine. I was

[1] See p. 159.

very busy, and sent my excuses; but desired he would
provide me a dinner. I dined with him, his lady, and her
sister, Mrs. Hill, who invites us to-morrow to dine with her,
and we are to ride out in the morning. I sat with Lady
Oglethorpe till eight this evening, then was going home to
write; looked about for the woman that keeps the key of
the house: she told me Patrick had it. I cooled my heels in
the cloisters till nine, then went in to the music-meeting,
where I had been often desired to go; but was weary in half
an hour of their fine stuff, and stole out so privately that
everybody saw me; and cooled my heels in the cloisters again
till after ten: then came in Patrick. I went up, shut the
chamber door, and gave him two or three swinging cuffs on
the ear, and I have strained the thumb of my left hand with
pulling him, which I did not feel until he was gone. He
was plaguily afraid and humbled.

4. It was the finest day in the world, and we got out
before eleven, a noble caravan of us. The Duchess of
Shrewsbury in her own chaise with one horse, and Miss
Touchet [1] with her, Mrs. Masham and Mrs. Scarborow, one of
the dressers, in one of the Queen's chaises; Miss Forester
and Miss Scarborow,[2] two maids of honour, and Mrs. Hill on
horseback. The Duke of Shrewsbury, Mr. Masham, George
Fielding,[3] Arbuthnot, and I, on horseback too. Mrs. Hill's
horse was hired for Miss Scarborow, but she took it in
civility; her own horse was galled and could not be rid, but
kicked and winced: the hired horse was not worth eighteenpence. I borrowed coat, boots, and horse, and in short we
had all the difficulties, and more than we used to have in
making a party from Trim to Longfield's.[4] My coat was
light camlet, faced with red velvet, and silver buttons. We

---

[1] No doubt one of the daughters of Mervyn Tuchet, fourth Earl of Castle-
haven, who died in 1686.
[2] Henrietta Maria, daughter of Charles Scarborow (see p. 266). She
married, in 1712, Sir Robert Jenkinson, Bart., M.P. for Oxfordshire, who died
without issue in 1717. See *Wentworth Papers*, 244.
[3] In July 1712 a Commission passed empowering Conyers Darcy and George
Fielding (an equerry to the Queen) to execute the office of Master of the Horse.
[4] At Killibride, about four miles from Trim.

rode in the great park and the forest about a dozen miles, and the Duchess and I had much conversation : we got home by two, and Mr. Masham, his lady, Arbuthnot and I, dined with Mrs. Hill. Arbuthnot made us all melancholy, by some symptoms of bloody u——e : he expects a cruel fit of the stone in twelve hours ; he says he is never mistaken, and he appears like a man that was to be racked to-morrow. I cannot but hope it will not be so bad ; he is a perfectly honest man, and one I have much obligation to. It rained a little this afternoon, and grew fair again. Lady Oglethorpe sent to speak to me, and it was to let me know that Lady Rochester [1] desires she and I may be better acquainted. 'Tis a little too late ; for I am not now in love with Lady Rochester : they shame me out of her, because she is old. Arbuthnot says he hopes my strained thumb is not the gout ; for he has often found people so mistaken. I do not remember the particular thing that gave it me, only I had it just after beating Patrick, and now it is better ; so I believe he is mistaken.

5. The Duchess of Shrewsbury sent to invite me to dinner ; but I was abroad last night when her servant came, and this morning I sent my excuses, because I was engaged, which I was sorry for. Mrs. Forester taxed me yesterday about the *History of the Maids of Honour* ; [2] but I told her fairly it was no jest of mine ; for I found they did not relish it altogether well ; and I have enough already of a quarrel with that brute Sir John Walter, who has been railing at me in all companies ever since I dined with him ; that I abused the Queen's meat and drink, and said nothing at the table was good, and all a d——d lie ; for after dinner, commending the wine, I said I thought it was something small. You would wonder how all my friends laugh at this quarrel. It will be such a jest for the Keeper, Treasurer, and Secretary. — I dined with honest Colonel Godfrey, took a good walk of an

[1] Swift's " mistress," Lady Hyde (see p. 24), whose husband had become Earl of Rochester in May 1711. She was forty-one in 1711.
[2] See p. 296.

hour on the terrace, and then came up to study; but it grows bloody cold, and I have no waistcoat here.

6. I never dined with the chaplains till to-day; but my friend Gastrell and the Dean of Rochester [1] had often invited me, and I happened to be disengaged: it is the worst provided table at Court. We ate on pewter: every chaplain, when he is made a dean, gives a piece of plate, and so they have got a little, some of it very old. One who was made Dean of Peterborough (a small deanery) said he would give no plate; he was only Dean of Pewterborough. The news of Mr. Hill's miscarriage in his expedition [2] came to-day, and I went to visit Mrs. Masham and Mrs. Hill, his two sisters, to condole with them. I advised them by all means to go to the music-meeting to-night, to show they were not cast down, etc., and they thought my advice was right, and went. I doubt Mr. Hill and his admiral made wrong steps; however, we lay it all to a storm, etc. I sat with the Secretary at supper; then we both went to Lord Treasurer's supper, and sat till twelve. The Secretary is much mortified about Hill, because this expedition was of his contriving, and he counted much upon it; but Lord Treasurer was just as merry as usual, and old laughing at Sir John Walter and me falling out. I said nothing grieved me but that they would take example, and perhaps presume upon it, and get out of my government; but that I thought I was not obliged to govern bears, though I governed men. They promise to be as obedient as ever, and so we laughed; and so I go to bed; for it is colder still, and you have a fire now, and are at cards at home.

7. Lord Harley and I dined privately to-day with Mrs. Masham and Mrs. Hill, and my brother Masham. I saw Lord Halifax at Court, and we joined and talked; and the Duchess of Shrewsbury came up and reproached me for not dining with her. I said that was not so soon done, for I expected more advances from ladies, especially duchesses: she promised to comply with any demands I pleased; and I agreed to dine with her to-morrow, if I did not go to London

[1] See p. 287. [2] See p. 206.

too soon, as I believe I shall before dinner.   Lady Oglethorpe brought me and the Duchess of Hamilton [1] together to-day in the drawing-room, and I have given her some encouragement, but not much.   Everybody has been teasing Walter.   He told Lord Treasurer that he took his company from him that were to dine with him : my lord said, "I will send you Dr. Swift:" Lord Keeper bid him take care what he did; "for," said he, "Dr. Swift is not only all our favourite, but our governor."   The old company supped with Lord Treasurer, and got away by twelve.

London, 8.   I believe I shall go no more to Windsor, for we expect the Queen will come in ten days to Hampton Court.   It was frost last night, and cruel cold to-day.   I could not dine with the Duchess, for I left Windsor half an hour after one with Lord Treasurer, and we called at Kensington, where Mrs. Masham was got to see her children for two days.   I dined, or rather supped, with Lord Treasurer, and stayed till after ten.   Tisdall [2] and his family are gone from hence, upon some wrangle with the family.   Yesterday I had two letters brought me to Mr. Masham's; one from Ford, and t'other from our little MD, N. 21.   I would not tell you till to-day, because I would not.   I won't answer it till the next, because I have slipped two days by being at Windsor, which I must recover here.   Well, sirrahs, I must go to sleep.   The roads were as dry as at midsummer to-day.   This letter shall go to-morrow.

9. Morning.   It rains hard this morning.   I suppose our fair weather is now at an end.   I think I'll put on my waistcoat to-day : shall I ?   Well, I will then, to please MD.   I think of dining at home to-day upon a chop and a pot.   The town continues yet very thin.   Lord Strafford is gone to Holland, to tell them what we have done here toward a peace.   We shall soon hear what the Dutch say, and how they take it.   My humble service to Mrs. Walls, Mrs. Stoyte, and Catherine.—Morrow, dearest sirrahs, and farewell ; and God Almighty bless MD, poor little dear MD, for so I mean,

---

[1] See p. 262, note 2.   [2] See p. 250.

and Presto too. I'll write to you again to-night, that is, I'll begin my next letter. Farewell, etc.

This little bit belongs to MD; we must always write on the margin :[1] you are saucy rogues.

LETTER XXXII

LONDON, *Oct.* 9, 1711.

I WAS forced to lie down at twelve to-day, and mend my night's sleep: I slept till after two, and then sent for a bit of mutton and pot of ale from the next cook's shop, and had no stomach. I went out at four, and called to see Biddy Floyd, which I had not done these three months: she is something marked, but has recovered her complexion quite, and looks very well. Then I sat the evening with Mrs. Vanhomrigh, and drank coffee, and ate an egg. I likewise took a new lodging to-day, not liking a ground-floor, nor the ill smell, and other circumstances. I lodge, or shall lodge, by Leicester Fields, and pay ten shillings a week ; that won't hold out long, faith. I shall lie here but one night more. It rained terribly till one o'clock to-day. I lie, for I shall lie here two nights, till Thursday, and then remove. Did I tell you that my friend Mrs. Barton has a brother [2] drowned, that went on the expedition with Jack Hill ? He was a lieutenant-colonel, and a coxcomb ; and she keeps her chamber in form, and the servants say she receives no messages. — Answer MD's letter, Presto, d'ye hear? No, says Presto, I won't yet, I'm busy ; you're a saucy rogue. Who talks ?

10. It cost me two shillings in coach-hire to dine in the City with a printer. I have sent, and caused to be sent, three pamphlets out in a fortnight. I will ply the rogues warm ; and whenever anything of theirs makes a noise, it shall have an answer. I have instructed an under spur-leather to write

[1] "This happens to be the only single line written upon the margin of any of his journals. By some accident there was a margin about as broad as the back of a razor, and therefore he made this use of it" (Deane Swift).
[2] Lieutenant-Colonel Barton, of Colonel Kane's regiment.

so, that it is taken for mine. A rogue that writes a newspaper, called *The Protestant Postboy*, has reflected on me in one of his papers; but the Secretary has taken him up, and he shall have a squeeze extraordinary. He says that an ambitious tantivy,[1] missing of his towering hopes of preferment in Ireland, is come over to vent his spleen on the late Ministry, etc. I'll tantivy him with a vengeance. I sat the evening at home, and am very busy, and can hardly find time to write, unless it were to MD. I am in furious haste.

11. I dined to-day with Lord Treasurer. Thursdays are now his days when his choice company comes, but we are too much multiplied. George Granville sent his excuses upon being ill; I hear he apprehends the apoplexy, which would grieve me much. Lord Treasurer calls Prior nothing but Monsieur Baudrier, which was the feigned name of the Frenchman that writ his *Journey to Paris*.[2] They pretend to suspect me, so I talk freely of it, and put them out of their play. Lord Treasurer calls me now Dr. Martin, because martin[3] is a sort of a swallow, and so is a swift. When he and I came last Monday from Windsor, we were reading all the signs on the road.[4] He is a pure trifler; tell the Bishop of Clogher so. I made him make two lines in verse for the Bell and Dragon, and they were rare bad ones. I suppose Dilly is with you by this time: what could his reason be of leaving London, and not owning it? 'Twas plaguy silly. I believe his natural inconstancy made him weary. I think he is the king of inconstancy. I stayed with Lord Treasurer till ten; we had five lords and three commoners. Go to ombre, sirrahs.

12. Mrs. Vanhomrigh has changed her lodging as well as I. She found she had got with a bawd, and removed. I

---

[1] A nickname for the High Church party.   [2] See p. 284.
[3] "From this pleasantry of my Lord Oxford, the appellative Martinus Scriblerus took its rise" (Deane Swift).
[4] Cf. the *Imitation of the Sixth Satire of the Second Book of Horace*, 1714, where Swift says that, during their drives together, Harley would

> "gravely try to read the lines
> Writ underneath the country signs."

dined with her to-day; for though she boards, her landlady does not dine with her. I am grown a mighty lover of herrings; but they are much smaller here than with you. In the afternoon I visited an old major-general, and ate six oysters; then sat an hour with Mrs. Colledge,[1] the joiner's daughter that was hanged; it was the joiner was hanged, and not his daughter; with Thompson's wife, a magistrate. There was the famous Mrs. Floyd of Chester, who, I think, is the handsomest woman (except MD) that ever I saw. She told me that twenty people had sent her the verses upon Biddy,[2] as meant to her: and, indeed, in point of handsomeness, she deserves them much better. I will not go to Windsor to-morrow, and so I told the Secretary to-day. I hate the thoughts of Saturday and Sunday suppers with Lord Treasurer. Jack Hill is come home from his unfortunate expedition, and is, I think, now at Windsor: I have not yet seen him. He is privately blamed by his own friends for want of conduct. He called a council of war, and therein it was determined to come back. But they say a general should not do that, because the officers will always give their opinion for returning, since the blame will not lie upon them, but the general. I pity him heartily. Bernage received his commission to-day.

13. I dined to-day with Colonel Crowe,[3] late Governor of Barbadoes; he is a great acquaintance of your friend Sterne, to whom I trusted the box. Lord Treasurer has refused Sterne's business, and I doubt he is a rake; Jemmy Leigh stays for him, and nobody knows where to find him. I am so busy now I have hardly time to spare to write to our little MD, but in a fortnight I hope it will be over. I am going now to be busy, etc.

14. I was going to dine with Dr. Cockburn, but Sir Andrew Fountaine met me, and carried me to Mrs. Van's, where I drank the last bottle of Raymond's wine, admirable good, better than any I get among the Ministry. I must pick up time to answer this letter of MD's; I'll do it in a day or two

---

[1] See p. 218.   [2] See p. 170.   [3] See p. 218.

for certain.—I am glad I am not at Windsor, for it is very cold, and I won't have a fire till November. I am contriving how to stop up my grate with bricks. Patrick was drunk last night; but did not come to me, else I should have given him t'other cuff. I sat this evening with Mrs. Barton; it is the first day of her seeing company; but I made her merry enough, and we were three hours disputing upon Whig and Tory. She grieved for her brother only for form, and he was a sad dog. Is Stella well enough to go to church, pray? no numbings left? no darkness in your eyes? do you walk and exercise? Your exercise is ombre.—People are coming up to town: the Queen will be at Hampton Court in a week. Lady Betty Germaine, I hear, is come; and Lord Pembroke is coming: his wife [1] is as big with child as she can tumble.

15. I sat at home till four this afternoon to-day writing, and ate a roll and butter; then visited Will Congreve an hour or two, and supped with Lord Treasurer, who came from Windsor to-day, and brought Prior with him. The Queen has thanked Prior for his good service in France, and promised to make him a Commissioner of the Customs. Several of that Commission are to be out; among the rest, my friend Sir Matthew Dudley. I can do nothing for him, he is so hated by the Ministry. Lord Treasurer kept me till twelve, so I need not tell you it is now late.

16. I dined to-day with Mr. Secretary at Dr. Coatesworth's,[2] where he now lodges till his house be got ready in Golden Square. One Boyer,[3] a French dog, has abused me in a pamphlet, and I have got him up in a messenger's hands:

---

[1] Lord Pembroke (see p. 52) married, in 1708, as his second wife, Barbara, Dowager Baroness Arundell of Trerice, formerly widow of Sir Richard Mauleverer, and daughter of Sir Thomas Slingsby. She died in 1722.

[2] Caleb Coatesworth, who died in 1741, leaving a large fortune.

[3] Abel Boyer, Whig journalist and historian, attacked Swift in his pamphlet, *An Account of the State and Progress of the Present Negotiations for Peace.* Boyer says that he was released from custody by Harley; and in the *Political State* for 1711 (p. 646) he speaks of Swift as "a shameless and most contemptible ecclesiastical turncoat, whose tongue is as *swift* to revile as his mind is *swift* to change." The *Postboy* said that Boyer would "be prosecuted with the utmost severity of the law" for this attack.

the Secretary promises me to swinge him. Lord Treasurer
told me last night that he had the honour to be abused with
me in a pamphlet. I must make that rogue an example, for
warning to others. I was to see Jack Hill this morning,
who made that unfortunate expedition; and there is still
more misfortune; for that ship, which was admiral of his
fleet,[1] is blown up in the Thames, by an accident and carelessness of some rogue, who was going, as they think, to steal
some gunpowder: five hundred men are lost. We don't yet
know the particulars. I am got home by seven, and am
going to be busy, and you are going to play and supper; you
live ten times happier than I; but I should live ten times
happier than you if I were with MD. I saw Jemmy Leigh
to-day in the street, who tells me that Sterne has not lain
above once these three weeks in his lodgings, and he doubts
he takes ill courses; he stays only till he can find Sterne to
go along with him, and he cannot hear of him. I begged
him to inquire about the box when he comes to Chester,
which he promises.

17. The Secretary and I dined to-day with Brigadier
Britton,[2] a great friend of his. The lady of the house is
very gallant, about thirty-five; she is said to have a great
deal of wit; but I see nothing among any of them that
equals MD by a bar's length, as hope saved. My Lord
Treasurer is much out of order; he has a sore throat, and
the gravel, and a pain in his breast where the wound was:
pray God preserve him. The Queen comes to Hampton
Court on Tuesday next; people are coming fast to town,
and I must answer MD's letter, which I can hardly find
time to do, though I am at home the greatest part of the
day. Lady Betty Germaine and I were disputing Whig and
Tory to death this morning. She is grown very fat, and

---

[1] The "Edgar." Four hundred men were killed.
[2] William Bretton, or Britton, was made Lieutenant-Colonel in 1702, Colonel
of a new Regiment of Foot 1705, Brigadier-General 1710, and Colonel of
the King's Own Borderers in April 1711 (Dalton, *Army Lists*, iii. 238). In
December 1711 he was appointed Envoy Extraordinary to the King of
Prussia (*Postboy*, Jan. 1, 1712), and he died in December 1714 or January 1715.

looks mighty well. Biddy Floyd was there, and she is, I think, very much spoiled with the smallpox.

18. Lord Treasurer is still out of order, and that breaks our method of dining there to-day. He is often subject to a sore throat, and some time or other it will kill him, unless he takes more care than he is apt to do. It was said about the town that poor Lord Peterborow was dead at Frankfort; but he is something better, and the Queen is sending him to Italy, where I hope the warm climate will recover him: he has abundance of excellent qualities, and we love one another mightily. I was this afternoon in the City, ate a bit of meat, and settled some things with a printer. I will answer your letter on Saturday, if possible, and then send away this; so to fetch up the odd days I lost at Windsor, and keep constant to my fortnight. Ombre time is now coming on, and we shall have nothing but Manley, and Walls, and Stoytes, and the Dean. Have you got no new acquaintance? Poor girls; nobody knows MD's good qualities.—'Tis very cold; but I will not have a fire till November, that's pozz.—Well, but coming home to-night, I found on my table a letter from MD; faith, I was angry, that is, with myself; and I was afraid too to see MD's hand so soon, for fear of something, I don't know what: at last I opened it, and it was over well, and a bill for the two hundred guineas. However, 'tis a sad thing that this letter is not gone, nor your twenty-first answered yet.

19. I was invited to-day to dine with Mrs. Van, with some company who did not come; but I ate nothing but herrings; you must know I hardly ever eat of above one thing, and that the plainest ordinary meat at table; I love it best, and believe it wholesomest. You love rarities; yes you do; I wish you had all that I ever see where I go. I was coming home early, and met the Secretary in his chair, who persuaded me to go with him to Britton's; for he said he had been all day at business, and had eaten nothing. So I went, and the time pased so, that we stayed till two, so you may believe 'tis late enough.

20. This day has gone all wrong, by sitting up so late last night. Lord Treasurer is not yet well, and can't go to Windsor. I dined with Sir Matthew Dudley, and took occasion to hint to him that he would lose his employment, for which I am very sorry. Lord Pembroke and his family are all come to town. I was kept so long at a friend's this evening that I cannot send this to-night. When I knocked at my lodgings, a fellow asked me where lodged Dr. Swift? I told him I was the person: he gave me a letter he brought from the Secretary's office, and I gave him a shilling: when I came up, I saw Dingley's hand: faith, I was afraid, I do not know what. At last it was a formal letter from Dingley about her exchequer business. Well, I'll do it on Monday, and settle it with Tooke. And now, boys, for your letter, I mean the first, N. 21. Let's see; come out, little letter. I never had the letter from the Bishop that Raymond mentions; but I have written to Ned Southwell, to desire the Duke of Ormond to speak to his reverence, that he may leave off his impertinence. What a pox can they think I am doing for the Archbishop here? You have a pretty notion of me in Ireland, to make me an agent for the Archbishop of Dublin.—Why! do you think I value your people's ingratitude about my part in serving them? I remit them their first-fruits of ingratitude, as freely as I got the other remitted to them. The Lord Treasurer defers writing his letter to them, or else they would be plaguily confounded by this time. For he designs to give the merit of it wholly to the Queen and me, and to let them know it was done before the Duke of Ormond was Lord Lieutenant. You visit, you dine abroad, you see friends; you pilgarlick;[1] you walk from Finglas, you a cat's foot. O Lord—Lady Gore[2] hung her child by the *waist*;

---

[1] See p. 229, note 4.
[2] It is not clear which of several Lady Gores is here referred to. It may be (1) the wife of Sir William Gore, Bart., of Manor Gore, and Custos Rotulorum, County Leitrim, who married Hannah, eldest daughter and co-heir of James Hamilton, Esq., son of Sir Frederick Hamilton, and niece of Gustavus Hamilton, created Viscount Boyne. She died 1733. Or (2) the wife of Sir Ralph Gore, Bart. (died 1732), M.P. for County Donegal, and afterwards

what is that waist?[1] I don't understand that word; he
must hang on till you explain or spell it.—I don't believe he
was pretty, that's a liiii.—Pish! burn your First-Fruits; again
at it. Stella has made twenty false spellings in her writing;
I'll send them to you all back again on the other side of this
letter, to mend them; I won't miss one. Why, I think
there were seventeen bishops' names to the letter Lord
Oxford received.—I will send you some pamphlets by Leigh;
put me in mind of it on Monday, for I shall go then to the
printer; yes, and the *Miscellany*.[2] I am mightily obliged to
Walls, but I don't deserve it by any usage of him here,
having seen him but twice, and once *en passant*. Mrs.
Manley forsworn ombre! What! and no blazing star
appear? no monsters born? no whale thrown up? have you
not found out some evasion for her? She had no such
regard to oaths in her younger days. I got the books for
nothing, Madam Dingley; but the wine I got not; it was
but a promise.—Yes, my head is pretty well in the main,
only now and then a little threatening or so.—You talk of
my reconciling some great folks. I tell you what. The
Secretary told me last night that he had found the reason
why the Queen was cold to him for some months past; that
a friend had told it him yesterday; and it was, that they
suspected he was at the bottom with the Duke of
Marlborough. Then he said he had reflected upon all
I had spoken to him long ago, but he thought it had only
been my suspicion, and my zeal and kindness for him. I
said I had reason to take that very ill, to imagine I knew so
little of the world as to talk at a venture to a great Minister;
that I had gone between him and Lord Treasurer often, and
told each of them what I had said to the other, and that I

Speaker of the Irish House of Commons. He married Miss Colville, daughter
of Sir Robert Colville, of Newtown, Leitrim, and, as his second wife, Elizabeth,
only daughter of Dr. Ashe, Bishop of Clogher. Or (3) the wife of Sir Arthur
Gore, Bart. (died 1727), of Newtown Gore, Mayo, who married Eleanor,
daughter of Sir George St. George, Bart., of Carrick, Leitrim, and was
ancestor of the Earls of Arran.

[1] " Modern usage has sanctioned Stella's spelling " (Scott). Swift's spelling
was " wast."

had informed him so before. He said all that you may imagine to excuse himself, and approve my conduct. I told him I knew all along that this proceeding of mine was the surest way to send me back to my willows in Ireland, but that I regarded it not, provided I could do the kingdom service in keeping them well together. I minded him how often I had told Lord Treasurer, Lord Keeper, and him together, that all things depended on their union, and that my comfort was to see them love one another; and I had told them all singly that I had not said this by chance, etc. He was in a rage to be thus suspected; swears he will be upon a better foot, or none at all; and I do not see how they can well want him in this juncture. I hope to find a way of settling this matter. I act an honest part, that will bring me neither honour nor praise. MD must think the better of me for it: nobody else shall ever know of it. Here's politics enough for once; but Madam DD gave me occasion for it. I think I told you I have got into lodgings that don't smell ill—O Lord! the spectacles: well, I'll do that on Monday too; although it goes against me to be employed for folks that neither you nor I care a groat for. Is the eight pounds from Hawkshaw included in the thirty-nine pounds five shillings and twopence? How do I know by this how my account stands? Can't you write five or six lines to cast it up? Mine is forty-four pounds *per annum*, and eight pounds from Hawkshaw makes fifty-two pounds. Pray set it right, and let me know; you had best.—And so now I have answered N. 21, and 'tis late, and I will answer N. 22 in my next: this cannot go to-night, but shall on Tuesday: and so go to your play, and lose your money, with your two eggs a penny; silly jade; you witty? very pretty.

21. Mrs. Van would have me dine with her again to-day, and so I did, though Lady Mountjoy has sent two or three times to have me see and dine with her, and she is a little body I love very well. My head has ached a little in the evenings these three or four days, but it is not of the

giddy sort, so I do not much value it. I was to see Lord
Harley to-day, but Lord Treasurer took physic, and I could
not see him. He has voided much gravel, and is better,
but not well: he talks of going on Tuesday to see the Queen
at Hampton Court; I wish he may be able. I never saw
so fine a summer day as this was: how is it with you, pray?
and can't you remember, naughty packs? I han't seen
Lord Pembroke yet. He will be sorry to miss Dilly: I
wonder you say nothing of Dilly's being got to Ireland;
if he be not there soon, I shall have some certain odd
thoughts: guess them if you can.

22. I dined in the City to-day with Dr. Freind, at one of
my printers: I inquired for Leigh, but could not find him:
I have forgot what sort of apron you want. I must rout
among your letters, a needle in a bottle of hay. I gave
Sterne directions, but where to find him Lord knows. I
have bespoken the spectacles; got a set of *Examiners*, and
five pamphlets, which I have either written or contributed
to, except the best, which is the *Vindication of the Duke
of Marlborough*, and is entirely of the author of the
Atalantis.[1] I have settled Dingley's affair with Tooke,
who has undertaken it, and understands it. I have bespoken
a *Miscellany*: what would you have me do more? It cost
me a shilling coming home; it rains terribly, and did so in
the morning. Lord Treasurer has had an ill day, in much
pain. He writes and does business in his chamber now he
is ill: the man is bewitched: he desires to see me, and I'll
maul him, but he will not value it a rush. I am half weary
of them all. I often burst out into these thoughts, and will
certainly steal away as soon as I decently can. I have many
friends, and many enemies; and the last are more constant
in their nature. I have no shuddering at all to think of
retiring to my old circumstances, if you can be easy; but I
will always live in Ireland as I did the last time; I will not
hunt for dinners there, nor converse with more than a very
few.

[1] Mrs. Manley.

23. Morning. This goes to-day, and shall be sealed by and by. Lord Treasurer takes physic again to - day: I believe I shall dine with Lord Dupplin. Mr. Tooke brought me a letter directed for me at Morphew's the bookseller. I suppose, by the postage, it came from Ireland. It is a woman's hand, and seems false spelt on purpose: it is in such sort of verse as Harris's petition;[1] rallies me for writing merry things, and not upon divinity; and is like the subject of the Archbishop's last letter, as I told you. Can you guess whom it came from? It is not ill written; pray find it out. There is a Latin verse at the end of it all rightly spelt; yet the English, as I think, affectedly wrong in many places. My plaguing time is coming. A young fellow brought me a letter from Judge Coote,[2] with recommendation to be lieutenant of a man-of-war. He is the son of one Echlin,[3] who was minister of Belfast before Tisdall, and I have got some other new customers; but I shall trouble my friends as little as possible. Saucy Stella used to jeer me for meddling with other folks' affairs; but now I am punished for it.—Patrick has brought the candle, and I have no more room. Farewell, etc. etc.

Here is a full and true account of Stella's new spelling :—

Plaguely,	.	.	Plaguily.[4]
Dineing,	.	.	Dining.
Straingers,	.	.	Strangers.
Chais,	.	.	Chase.
Waist,	.	.	Wast.
Houer,	.	.	Hour.
Immagin,	.	.	Imagine.
A bout,	.	.	About.

[1] Swift's own lines, " Mrs. Frances Harris's Petition."
[2] Thomas Coote was a Justice of the Court of Queen's Bench, in Ireland, from 1692 until his removal in 1715.
[3] Probably a relative of Robert Echlin, Dean of Tuam, who was killed by some of his own servants in April 1712, at the age of seventy-three. His son John became Prebendary and Vicar-General of Tuam, and died in 1764, aged eighty-three. In August 1731 Bolingbroke sent Swift a letter by the hands of "Mr. Echlin," who would, he said, tell Swift of the general state of things in England.
[4] " This column of words, as they are corrected, is in Stella's hand" (Deane Swift).

21

Intellegence,	.	.	.	Intelligence.
Aboundance,	.	.	.	Abundance.
Merrit,	.	.	.	Merit.
Secreet,	.	.	.	Secret.
Phamphlets,	.	.	.	Pamphlets.
Bussiness,		.	.	Business.

Tell me truly, sirrah, how many of these are mistakes of the pen, and how many are you to answer for as real ill spelling? There are but fourteen; I said twenty by guess. You must not be angry, for I will have you spell right, let the world go how it will. Though, after all, there is but a mistake of one letter in any of these words. I allow you henceforth but six false spellings in every letter you send me.

LETTER XXXIII

LONDON, *Oct.* 23, 1711.

I DINED with Lord Dupplin as I told you I would, and put my thirty-second into the post-office my own self; and I believe there has not been one moment since we parted wherein a letter was not upon the road going or coming to or from PMD. If the Queen knew it, she would give us a pension; for it is we bring good luck to their post-boys and their packets; else they would break their necks and sink. But, an old saying and a true one:

Be it snow, or storm, or hail,
PMD's letters never fail;
Cross winds may sometimes make them tarry,
But PMD's letters can't miscarry.

Terrible rain to-day, but it cleared up at night enough to save my twelvepence coming home. Lord Treasurer is much better this evening. I hate to have him ill, he is so confoundedly careless. I won't answer your letter yet, so be satisfied.

24. I called at Lord Treasurer's to-day at noon: he was eating some broth in his bed-chamber, undressed, with a

thousand papers about him. He has a little fever upon him, and his eye terribly bloodshot; yet he dressed himself and went out to the Treasury. He told me he had a letter from a lady with a complaint against me; it was from Mrs. Cutts, a sister of Lord Cutts, who writ to him that I had abused her brother: [1] you remember the "Salamander," it is printed in the *Miscellany*. I told my lord that I would never regard complaints, and that I expected, whenever he received any against me, he would immediately put them into the fire, and forget them, else I should have no quiet. I had a little turn in my head this morning; which, though it did not last above a moment, yet being of the true sort, has made me as weak as a dog all this day. 'Tis the first I have had this half-year. I shall take my pills if I hear of it again. I dined at Lady Mountjoy's with Harry Coote,[2] and went to see Lord Pembroke upon his coming to town.—The Whig party are furious against a peace, and every day some ballad comes out reflecting on the Ministry on that account. The Secretary St. John has seized on a dozen booksellers and publishers into his messengers' hands.[3] Some of the foreign Ministers have published the preliminaries agreed on here between France and England; and people rail at them as insufficient to treat a peace upon; but the secret is, that the French have agreed to articles much more important, which our Ministers have not communicated, and the people, who think they know all, are discontented that there is no more. This was an inconvenience I foretold to the Secretary, but we could contrive no way to fence against it. So there's politics for you.

25. The Queen is at Hampton Court: she went on Tuesday in that terrible rain. I dined with Lewis at his

---

[1] Swift's verses, " The Description of a Salamander," are a scurrilous attack on John, Lord Cutts (died 1707), who was famous for his bravery. Joanna Cutts, the sister who complained of Swift's abuse, died unmarried.

[2] See p. 34.

[3] Fourteen printers or publishers were arrested, under warrants signed by St. John, for publishing pamphlets directed against the Government. They appeared at the Court of Queen's Bench on Oct. 23, and were continued on their own recognisances till the end of the term.

lodgings, to despatch some business we had. I sent this morning and evening to Lord Treasurer, and he is much worse by going out; I am in pain about evening. He has sent for Dr. Radcliffe; pray God preserve him. The Chancellor of the Exchequer[1] showed me to-day a ballad[2] in manuscript against Lord Treasurer and his South Sea project; it is very sharply written: if it be not printed, I will send it you. If it be, it shall go in your packet of pamphlets. — I found out your letter about directions for the apron, and have ordered to be bought a cheap green silk work apron; I have it by heart. I sat this evening with Mrs. Barton, who is my near neighbour. It was a delicious day, and I got my walk, and was thinking whether MD was walking too just at that time that Presto was.— This paper does not cost me a farthing, I have it from the Secretary's office. I long till to-morrow to know how my Lord Treasurer sleeps this night, and to hear he mends: we are all undone without him; so pray for him, sirrahs, and don't stay too late at the Dean's.

26. I dined with Mrs. Van; for the weather is so bad, and I am so busy, that I can't dine with great folks: and besides I dare eat but little, to keep my head in order, which is better. Lord Treasurer is very ill, but I hope in no danger. We have no quiet with the Whigs, they are so violent against a peace; but I'll cool them, with a vengeance, very soon. I have not heard from the Bishop of Clogher, whether he has got his statues.[3] I writ to him six weeks ago; he's so busy with his Parliament. I won't answer your letter yet, say what you will, saucy girls.

27. I forgot to go about some business this morning, which cost me double the time; and I was forced to be at the Secretary's office till four, and lose my dinner; so I went to Mrs. Van's, and made them get me three herrings, which I am very fond of, and they are a light victuals: besides, I was

[1] Robert Benson (see p. 41).
[2] "The South Sea Whim," printed in Scott's *Swift*, ii. 398.
[3] See pp. 200, 205, 340.

to have supped at Lady Ashburnham's; but the drab did not
call for us in her coach, as she promised, but sent for us, and
so I sent my excuses. It has been a terrible rainy day, but
so flattering in the morning, that I would needs go out in my
new hat. I met Leigh and Sterne as I was going into the
Park. Leigh says he will go to Ireland in ten days, if he can
get Sterne to go with him; so I will send him the things for
MD, and I have desired him to inquire about the box. I hate
that Sterne for his carelessness about it; but it was my fault.

29. I was all this terrible rainy day with my friend Lewis
upon business of importance; and I dined with him, and
came home about seven, and thought I would amuse myself
a little, after the pains I had taken. I saw a volume of
Congreve's plays in my room, that Patrick had taken to read;
and I looked into it, and in mere loitering read in it till
twelve, like an owl and a fool: if ever I do so again; never
saw the like. Count Gallas,[1] the Emperor's Envoy, you will
hear, is in disgrace with us: the Queen has ordered her
Ministers to have no more commerce with him; the reason
is, the fool writ a rude letter to Lord Dartmouth, Secretary
of State, complaining of our proceedings about a peace; and
he is always in close confidence with Lord Wharton and
Sunderland, and others of the late Ministry. I believe you
begin to think there will be no peace; the Whigs here are
sure it cannot be, and stocks are fallen again. But I am
confident there will, unless France plays us tricks; and you
may venture a wager with any of your Whig acquaintance
that we shall not have another campaign. You will get
more by it than by ombre, sirrah.—I let slip telling you
yesterday's journal, which I thought to have done this
morning, but blundered. I dined yesterday at Harry Coote's,
with Lord Hatton,[2] Mr. Finch, a son of Lord Nottingham,

---

[1] Count Gallas was dismissed with a message that he might depart from the
kingdom when he thought fit. He published the preliminaries of peace in the
Daily Courant.

[2] William, second Viscount Hatton, who died without issue in 1760. His
half-sister Anne married Daniel Finch, second Earl of Nottingham, and Lord
Hatton was therefore uncle to his fellow-guest, Mr. Finch.

and Sir Andrew Fountaine. I left them soon, but hear they stayed till two in the morning, and were all drunk: and so good-night for last night, and good-night for to-night. You blundering goosecap, an't you ashamed to blunder to young ladies? I shall have a fire in three or four days now, oh ho.

30. I was to-day in the City concerting some things with a printer, and am to be to-morrow all day busy with Mr. Secretary about the same. I won't tell you now; but the Ministers reckon it will do abundance of good, and open the eyes of the nation, who are half bewitched against a peace. Few of this generation can remember anything but war and taxes, and they think it is as it should be; whereas 'tis certain we are the most undone people in Europe, as I am afraid I shall make appear beyond all contradiction. But I forgot; I won't tell you what I will do, nor what I will not do: so let me alone, and go to Stoyte, and give Goody Stoyte and Catherine my humble service; I love Goody Stoyte better than Goody Walls. Who'll pay me for this green apron? I will have the money; it cost ten shillings and sixpence. I think it plaguy dear for a cheap thing; but they said that English silk would cockle,[1] and I know not what. You have the making into the bargain. 'Tis right Italian: I have sent it and the pamphlets to Leigh, and will send the *Miscellanies* and spectacles in a day or two. I would send more; but, faith, I'm plaguy poor at present.

31. The devil's in this Secretary: when I went this morning he had people with him; but says he, "we are to dine with Prior to-day, and then will do all our business in the afternoon": at two, Prior sends word he is otherwise engaged; then the Secretary and I go and dine with Brigadier Britton, sit till eight, grow merry, no business done; he is in haste to see Lady Jersey;[2] we part, and appoint no time to meet

---

[1] Crinkle or contract. Gay writes: "Showers soon drench the camblet's cockled grain."

[2] The Countess of Jersey (see p. 294), like her husband, was a friend of Bolingbroke's. Lady Strafford speaks of her having lately (November 1711) "been in pickle for her sins," at which she was not surprised. Before the Earl succeeded

again. This is the fault of all the present Ministers, teasing me to death for my assistance, laying the whole weight of their affairs upon it, yet slipping opportunities. Lord Treasurer mends every day, though slowly: I hope he will take care of himself. Pray, will you send to Parvisol to send me a bill of twenty pounds as soon as he can, for I want money. I must have money; I will have money, sirrahs.

Nov. 1. I went to-day into the City to settle some business with Stratford, and to dine with him; but he was engaged, and I was so angry I would not dine with any other merchant, but went to my printer, and ate a bit, and did business of mischief with him, and I shall have the spectacles and *Miscellany* to-morrow, and leave them with Leigh. A fine day always makes me go into the City, if I can spare time, because it is exercise; and that does me more good than anything. I have heard nothing since of my head, but a little, I don't know how, sometimes: but I am very temperate, especially now the Treasurer is ill, and the Ministers often at Hampton Court, and the Secretary not yet fixed in his house, and I hate dining with many of my old acquaintance. Here has been a fellow discovered going out of the East India House with sixteen thousand pounds in money and bills; he would have escaped, if he had not been so uneasy with thirst, that he stole out before his time, and was caught. But what is that to MD? I wish we had the money, provided the East India Company was never the worse; you know we must not covet, etc. Our weather, for this fortnight past, is chequered, a fair and a rainy day: this was very fine, and I have walked four miles; wish MD would do so, lazy sluttikins.

2. It has rained all day with a *continuendo*, and I went in a chair to dine with Mrs. Van; always there in a very rainy day. But I made a shift to come back afoot. I live a very retired life, pay very few visits, and keep but very little

to the title, Lady Wentworth wrote to her son: "It's said Lord Villors Lady was worth fower scoar thoussand pd; you might have got her, as wel as Lord Villors . . . . He [Lord Jersey] has not don well by his son, the young lady is not yoused well as I hear amongst them, which in my openion is not well."— *Wentworth Papers* (pp. 214, 234).

company; I read no newspapers. I am sorry I sent you the *Examiner*, for the printer is going to print them in a small volume: it seems the author is too proud to have them printed by subscription, though his friends offered, they say, to make it worth five hundred pounds to him. The *Spectators* are likewise printing in a larger and a smaller volume, so I believe they are going to leave them off, and indeed people grow weary of them, though they are often prettily written. We have had no news for me to send you now towards the end of my letter. The Queen has the gout a little: I hoped the Lord Treasurer would have had it too, but Radcliffe told me yesterday it was the rheumatism in his knee and foot; however, he mends, and I hope will be abroad in a short time. I am told they design giving away several employments before the Parliament sits, which will be the thirteenth instant. I either do not like, or not understand this policy; and if Lord Treasurer does not mend soon, they must give them just before the session. But he is the greatest procrastinator in the world.

3. A fine day this, and I walked a pretty deal. I stuffed the Secretary's pockets with papers, which he must read and settle at Hampton Court, where he went to-day, and stays some time. They have no lodgings for me there, so I can't go, for the town is small, chargeable, and inconvenient. Lord Treasurer had a very ill night last night, with much pain in his knee and foot, but is easier to-day.—And so I went to visit Prior about some business, and so he was not within, and so Sir Andrew Fountaine made me dine to-day again with Mrs. Van, and I came home soon, remembering this must go to-night, and that I had a letter of MD's to answer. O Lord, where is it? let me see; so, so, here it is. You grudge writing so soon. Pox on that bill! the woman would have me manage that money for her. I do not know what to do with it now I have it: I am like the unprofitable steward in the Gospel: I laid it up in a napkin; there thou hast what is thine own, etc. Well, well, I know of your new Mayor. (I'll tell you a pun: a fishmonger owed a man two

crowns; so he sent him a piece of bad ling and a tench, and then said he was paid: how is that now? find it out; for I won't tell it you: which of you finds it out?) Well, but as I was saying, what care I for your Mayor? I fancy Ford may tell Forbes right about my returning to Ireland before Christmas, or soon after. I'm sorry you did not go on with your story about Pray God you be John; I never heard it in my life, and wonder what it can be.—Ah, Stella, faith, you leaned upon your Bible to think what to say when you writ that. Yes, that story of the Secretary's making me an example is true; "never heard it before;" why, how could you hear it? is it possible to tell you the hundredth part of what passes in our companies here? The Secretary is as easy with me as Mr. Addison was. I have often thought what a splutter Sir William Temple makes about being Secretary of State:[1] I think Mr. St. John the greatest young man I ever knew; wit, capacity, beauty, quickness or apprehension, good learning, and an excellent taste; the best orator in the House of Commons, admirable conversation, good nature, and good manners; generous, and a despiser of money. His only fault is talking to his friends in way of complaint of too great a load of business, which looks a little like affectation; and he endeavours too much to mix the fine gentleman and man of pleasure with the man of business. What truth and sincerity he may have I know not: he is now but thirty-two, and has been Secretary above a year. Is not all this extraordinary? how he stands with the Queen and Lord Treasurer I have told you before. This is his character; and I believe you will be diverted by knowing it. I writ to the Archbishop of Dublin, Bishop of Cloyne[2] and of Clogher together, five weeks ago from Windsor: I hope they had my letters; pray know if Clogher had his.—Fig for your physician and his advice, Madam Dingley: if I grow worse, I will; otherwise I will trust to temperance and exercise: your fall of the leaf; what care I when the leaves fall? I am sorry to see them fall with all

[1] Cf. p. 66.   [2] Charles Crow, appointed Bishop of Cloyne in 1702.

my heart; but why should I take physic because leaves fall
off from trees? that won't hinder them from falling. If a
man falls from a horse, must I take physic for that?—This
arguing makes you mad; but it is true right reason, not to be
disproved.—I am glad at heart to hear poor Stella is better;
use exercise and walk, spend pattens and spare potions, wear
out clogs and waste claret. Have you found out my pun of
the fishmonger? don't read a word more till you have got it.
And Stella is handsome again, you say? and is she fat? I
have sent to Leigh the set of *Examiners*: the first thirteen
were written by several hands, some good, some bad; the
next three-and-thirty were all by one hand, that makes forty-
six: then that author,[1] whoever he was, laid it down on purpose to confound guessers; and the last six were written by
a woman.[2] Then there is an account of Guiscard by the same
woman, but the facts sent by Presto. Then an answer to the
letter to the Lords about Gregg by Presto; Prior's *Journey* by
Presto; *Vindication of the Duke of Marlborough*, entirely by
the same woman; *Comment on Hare's Sermon* by the same
woman, only hints sent to the printer from Presto to give
her.[3] Then there's the *Miscellany*, an apron for Stella, a
pound of chocolate, without sugar, for Stella, a fine snuff-rasp
of ivory, given me by Mrs. St. John for Dingley, and a large roll
of tobacco, which she must hide or cut shorter out of modesty,
and four pair of spectacles for the Lord knows who. There's
the cargo, I hope it will come safe. Oh, Mrs. Masham and I
are very well; we write to one another, but it is upon
business; I believe I told you so before: pray pardon my
forgetfulness in these cases; poor Presto can't help it. MD
shall have the money as soon as Tooke gets it. And so I
think I have answered all, and the paper is out, and now I
have fetched up my week, and will send you another this

---

[1] Swift.   [2] Mrs. Manley.
[3] The titles of these pamphlets are as follows:—(1) *A True Narrative of
. . . the Examination of the Marquis de Guiscard;* (2) *Some Remarks upon
a Pamphlet entitled, A Letter to the Seven Lords;* (3) *A New Journey to
Paris;* (4) *The Duke of Marlborough's Vindication;* (5) *A Learned Comment
on Dr. Hare's Sermon.*

day fortnight.—Why, you rogues, two crowns make *tench-ill-ling*:[1] you are so dull you could never have found it out. Farewell, etc. etc.

LETTER XXXIV

LONDON, *Nov.* 3, 1711.

MY thirty-third lies now before me just finished, and I am going to seal and send it, so let me know whether you would have me add anything: I gave you my journal of this day; and it is now nine at night, and I am going to be busy for an hour or two.

4. I left a friend's house to-day where I was invited, just when dinner was setting on, and pretended I was engaged, because I saw some fellows I did not know; and went to Sir Matthew Dudley's, where I had the same inconvenience, but he would not let me go; otherwise I would have gone home, and sent for a slice of mutton and a pot of ale, rather than dine with persons unknown, as bad, for aught I know, as your deans, parsons, and curates. Bad slabby weather to-day.— Now methinks I write at ease, when I have no letter of MD's to answer. But I mistook, and have got the large paper. The Queen is laid up with the gout at Hampton Court: she is now seldom without it any long time together; I fear it will wear her out in a very few years. I plainly find I have less twitchings about my toes since these Ministers are sick and out of town, and that I don't dine with them. I would compound for a light easy gout to be perfectly well in my head.—Pray walk when the frost comes, young ladies go a frost-biting. It comes into my head, that, from the very time you first went to Ireland, I have been always plying you to walk and read. The young fellows here have begun a kind of fashion to walk, and many of them have got swinge-ing strong shoes on purpose; it has got as far as several young lords; if it hold, it would be a very good thing. Lady

[1] See the pun on p. 329.

Lucy[1] and I are fallen out; she rails at me, and I have left visiting her.

5. MD was very troublesome to me last night in my sleep; I was a dreamed, methought, that Stella was here. I asked her after Dingley, and she said she had left her in Ireland, because she designed her stay to be short, and such stuff.— Monsieur Pontchartain, the Secretary of State in France, and Monsieur Fontenelle, the Secretary of the Royal Academy there (who writ the *Dialogues des Morts*, etc.), have sent letters to Lord Pembroke that the Academy have, with the King's consent, chosen him one of their members in the room of one who is lately dead. But the cautious gentleman has given me the letters to show my Lord Dartmouth and Mr. St. John, our two Secretaries, and let them see there is no treason in them; which I will do on Wednesday, when they come from Hampton Court. The letters are very handsome, and it is a very great mark of honour and distinction to Lord Pembroke. I hear the two French Ministers are come over again about the peace; but I have seen nobody of consequence to know the truth. I dined to-day with a lady of my acquaintance, who was sick, in her bed-chamber, upon three herrings and a chicken: the dinner was my bespeaking. We begin now to have chestnuts and Seville oranges; have you the latter yet? 'Twas a terrible windy day, and we had processions in carts of the Pope and the Devil, and the butchers rang their cleavers. You know this is the Fifth of November, Popery and gunpowder.

6. Since I am used to this way of writing, I fancy I could hardly make out a long letter to MD without it. I think I ought to allow for every line taken up by telling you where I dined; but that will not be above seven lines in all, half a line to a dinner. Your Ingoldsby[2] is going over, and they say here he is to be made a lord.—Here was I staying in my room till two this afternoon for that puppy Sir Andrew Fountaine, who was to go with me into the City, and never came; and if I had not shot a dinner flying, with one Mr.

Murray, I might have fasted, or gone to an alehouse.—You never said one word of Goody Stoyte in your letter; but I suppose these winter nights we shall hear more of her. Does the Provost[1] laugh as much as he used to do? We reckon him here a good-for-nothing fellow.—I design to write to your Dean one of these days, but I can never find time, nor what to say.—I will think of something: but if DD[2] were not in Ireland I believe seriously I should not think of the place twice a year. Nothing there ever makes the subject of talk in any company where I am.

7. I went to-day to the City on business; but stopped at a printer's, and stayed there: it was a most delicious day. I hear the Parliament is to be prorogued for a fortnight longer; I suppose, either because the Queen has the gout, or that Lord Treasurer is not well, or that they would do something more towards a peace. I called at Lord Treasurer's at noon, and sat a while with Lord Harley, but his father was asleep. A bookseller has reprinted or new-titled a sermon of Tom Swift's,[3] printed last year, and publishes an advertisement calling it *Dr. Swift's Sermon*. Some friend of Lord Galway[4] has, by his directions, published a four-shilling book about his conduct in Spain, to defend him; I have but just seen it. But what care you for books, except Presto's *Miscellanies?* Leigh promised to call and see me, but has not yet; I hope he will take care of his cargo, and get your Chester box. A murrain take that box! everything is spoiled that is in it. How does the strong box do? You say nothing of Raymond: is his wife brought to bed again; or how? has he finished his house; paid his debts; and put out the rest of the money to use? I am glad to hear poor Joe is like to get his two hundred pounds. I suppose Trim is now reduced to slavery again. I am glad of it; the people were as great rascals as

---

[1] Pratt (see p. 5). [2] Stella and Dingley.
[3] *Noah's Dove, an Exhortation to Peace, set forth in a Sermon preached on the Seventh of November, 1710, a Thanksgiving Day, by Thomas Swift, A.M., formerly Chaplain to Sir William Temple, now Rector of Puttenham in Surrey.* Thomas Swift was Swift's "little parson cousin" (see p. 225).
[4] See p. 36. The book referred to is, apparently, *An Impartial Enquiry into the Management of the War in Spain*, post-dated 1712.

the gentlemen. But I must go to bed, sirrahs: the Secretary is still at Hampton Court with my papers, or is come only to-night. They plague me with attending them.

8. I was with the Secretary this morning, and we dined with Prior, and did business this afternoon till about eight; and I must alter and undo, and a clutter. I am glad the Parliament is prorogued. I stayed with Prior till eleven; the Secretary left us at eight. Prior, I believe, will be one of those employed to make the peace, when a Congress is opened. Lord Ashburnham told to-day at the Coffee-house that Lord Harley[1] was yesterday morning married to the Duke of Newcastle's daughter, the great heiress, and it got about all the town. But I saw Lord Harley yesterday at noon in his nightgown, and he dined in the City with Prior and others; so it is not true; but I hope it will be so; for I know it has been privately managing this long time:[2] the lady will not have half her father's estate; for the Duke left Lord Pelham's son his heir.[3] The widow Duchess will not stand to the will, and she is now at law with Pelham. However, at worst, the girl will have about ten thousand pounds a year to support the honour; for Lord Treasurer will never save a groat for himself. Lord Harley is a very valuable young gentleman; and they say the girl is handsome, and has good sense, but red hair.

9. I designed a jaunt into the City to-day to be merry, but was disappointed; so one always is in this life; and I could not see Lord Dartmouth to-day, with whom I had some business. Business and pleasure both disappointed. You can go to your Dean, and for want of him, Goody Stoyte, or Walls, or Manley, and meet everywhere with cards and

[1] Lord Harley (afterwards second Earl of Oxford) (see p. 30) married, on Oct. 31, 1713, Lady Henrietta Cavendish Holles, only daughter of John Holles, last Duke of Newcastle of that family (see p. 257).

[2] Bolingbroke afterwards said that the great aim (at length accomplished) of Harley's administration was to marry his son to this young lady. Swift wrote a poetical address to Lord Harley on his marriage.

[3] Thomas Pelham, first Baron Pelham, married, as his second wife, Lady Grace Holles, daughter of the Earl of Clare and sister of the Duke of Newcastle. Their eldest son, Thomas, who succeeded to the barony in 1712, was afterwards created Earl of Clare and Duke of Newcastle.

claret. I dined privately with a friend on a herring and chicken, and half a flask of bad Florence. I begin to have fires now, when the mornings are cold. I have got some loose bricks at the back of my grate for good husbandry. Fine weather. Patrick tells me my caps are wearing out. I know not how to get others. I want a necessary woman strangely. I am as helpless as an elephant.—I had three packets from the Archbishop of Dublin, cost me four shillings, all about Higgins,[1] printed stuff, and two long letters. His people forgot to enclose them to Lewis; and they were only directed to Doctor Swift, without naming London or anything else. I wonder how they reached me, unless the postmaster directed them. I have read all the trash, and am weary.

10. Why, if you must have it out, something is to be published of great moment,[2] and three or four great people are to see there are no mistakes in point of fact: and 'tis so troublesome to send it among them, and get their corrections, that I am weary as a dog. I dined to-day with the printer, and was there all the afternoon; and it plagues me, and there's an end, and what would you have? Lady Dupplin, Lord Treasurer's daughter,[3] is brought to bed of a son. Lord Treasurer has had an ugly return of his gravel. 'Tis good for us to live in gravel pits,[4] but not for gravel pits to live in us; a man in this case should leave no stone unturned. Lord Treasurer's sickness, the Queen's gout, the forwarding the peace, occasion putting off the Parliament a fortnight longer. My head has had no ill returns. I had good walking to-day in the City, and take all opportunities of it

[1] Francis Higgins, Rector of Baldruddery, called "the Sacheverell of Ireland," was an extreme High Churchman, who had been charged with sedition on account of sermons preached in London in 1707. In 1711 he was again prosecuted as "a disloyal subject and disturber of the public peace." At that time he was Prebendary of Christ Church, Dublin; in 1725 he was made Archdeacon of Cashel.

[2] Swift's pamphlet, *The Conduct of the Allies*.

[3] Lord Oxford's daughter Abigail married, in 1709, Viscount Dupplin, afterwards seventh Earl of Kinnoull (see p. 30). She died in 1750, and her husband in 1758, when the eldest son, Thomas, became Earl. The second son, Robert, was made Archbishop of York in 1761.

[4] Kensington Gravel Pits was then a famous health resort.

on purpose for my health; but I can't walk in the Park, because that is only for walking's sake, and loses time, so I mix it with business. I wish MD walked half as much as Presto. If I was with you, I'd make you walk; I would walk behind or before you, and you should have masks on, and be tucked up like anything; and Stella is naturally a stout walker, and carries herself firm; methinks I see her strut, and step clever over a kennel; and Dingley would do well enough if her petticoats were pinned up; but she is so embroiled, and so fearful, and then Stella scolds, and Dingley stumbles, and is so daggled.[1] Have you got the whalebone petticoats among you yet? I hate them; a woman here may hide a moderate gallant under them. Pshaw, what's all this I'm saying? Methinks I am talking to MD face to face.

11. Did I tell you that old Frowde,[2] the old fool, is selling his estate at Pepperhara, and is skulking about the town nobody knows where? and who do you think manages all this for him, but that rogue Child,[3] the double squire of Farnham? I have put Mrs. Masham, the Queen's favourite, upon buying it, but that is yet a great secret; and I have employed Lady Oglethorpe to inquire about it. I was with Lady Oglethorpe to-day, who is come to town for a week or two, and to-morrow I will see to hunt out the old fool: he is utterly ruined, and at this present in some blind alley with some dirty wench. He has two sons that must starve, and he never gives them a farthing. If Mrs. Masham buys the land, I will desire her to get the Queen to give some pension to the old fool, to keep him from absolutely starving. What do you meddle with other people's affairs for? says Stella. Oh, but Mr.

[1] Draggled. Pope has, "A puppy, daggled through the town."
[2] Writing of Peperharrow, Manning and Bray state (Surrey, ii. 32, 47) that Oxenford Grange was conveyed to Philip Froud (died 1736) in 1700, and was sold by him in 1713 to Alan Broderick, afterwards Viscount Midleton. This Froud (Swift's "old Frowde") had been Deputy Postmaster-General; he was son of Sir Philip Frowde, who was knighted in 1665 (Le Neve's Knights, Harleian Society, p. 190), and his son Philip was Addison's friend (see p. 58).
[3] Probably the Charles Child, Esq., of Farnham, whose death is recorded in the Gentleman's Magazine for 1754.

Masham and his wife are very urgent with me, since I first put them in the head of it. I dined with Sir Matthew Dudley, who, I doubt, will soon lose his employment.

12. Morning. I am going to hunt out old Frowde, and to do some business in the City. I have not yet called to Patrick to know whether it be fair. — It has been past dropping these two days. Rainy weather hurts my pate and my purse. He tells me 'tis very windy, and begins to look dark; woe be to my shillings! an old saying and a true,

> Few fillings,
> Many shillings.

If the day be dark, my purse will be light.

> To my enemies be this curse,
> A dark day and a light purse.

And so I'll rise, and go to my fire, for Patrick tells me I have a fire; yet it is not shaving-day, nor is the weather cold; this is too extravagant. What is become of Dilly? I suppose you have him with you. Stella is just now showing a white leg, and putting it into the slipper. Present my service to her, and tell her I am engaged to the Dean, and desire she will come too: or, Dingley, can't you write a note? This is Stella's morning dialogue, no, morning speech I mean.—Morrow, sirrahs, and let me rise as well as you; but I promise you Walls can't dine with the Dean to-day, for she is to be at Mrs. Proby's just after dinner, and to go with Gracy Spencer [1] to the shops to buy a yard of muslin, and a silver lace for an under petticoat. Morrow again, sirrahs.— At night. I dined with Stratford in the City, but could not finish my affairs with him; but now I am resolved to buy five hundred pounds South Sea Stock, which will cost me three hundred and eighty ready money; and I will make use of the bill of a hundred pounds you sent me, and transfer Mrs. Walls over to Hawkshaw; or if she dislikes it, I will borrow a hundred pounds of the Secretary, and repay her. Three shillings coach-hire to-day. I have spoken to Frowde's

---

[1] Grace Spencer was probably Mrs. Proby's sister (see pp. 176, 202).

22

brother to get me the lowest price of the estate, to tell Mrs. Masham.

13. I dined privately with a friend to-day in the neighbourhood. Last Saturday night I came home, and the drab had just washed my room, and my bed-chamber was all, wet, and I was forced to go to bed in my own defence, and no fire: I was sick on Sunday, and now have got a swingeing cold. I scolded like a dog at Patrick, although he was out with me: I detest washing of rooms; can't they wash them in a morning, and make a fire, and leave open the windows? I slept not a wink last night for hawking [1] and spitting: and now everybody has colds. Here's a clutter: I'll go to bed and sleep if I can.

14. Lady Mountjoy sent to me two days ago, so I dined with her to-day, and in the evening went to see Lord Treasurer. I found Patrick had been just there with a how d'ye,[2] and my lord had returned answer that he desired to see me. Mrs. Masham was with him when I came, and they are never disturbed: 'tis well she is not very handsome; they sit alone together settling the nation. I sat with Lady Oxford, and stopped Mrs. Masham as she came out, and told her what progress I had made, etc., and then went to Lord Treasurer: he is very well, only uneasy at rising or sitting, with some rheumatic pain in his thigh, and a foot weak. He showed me a small paper, sent by an unknown hand to one Mr. Cook, who sent it to my lord: it was written in plain large letters thus:

> "Though G——d's knife did not succeed,
> A F——n's yet may do the deed."

And a little below: "*Burn this, you dog.*" My lord has

---

[1] Cf. Shakespeare, *As You Like It*, v. 3: "Shall we clap into 't roundly, without hawking or spitting, which are the only prologues to a bad voice?"
[2] In the "Verses on his own Death," 1731, Swift says:
"When daily howd'y's come of course,
And servants answer, 'Worse and worse!'"
Cf. Steele (*Tatler*, No. 109), "After so many howdies, you proceed to visit or not, as you like the run of each other's reputation or fortune," and (*Spectator*, No. 143), "the howd'ye servants of our women."

frequently such letters as these: once he showed me one, which was a vision describing a certain man, his dress, his sword, and his countenance, who was to murder my lord. And he told me he saw a fellow in the chapel at Windsor with a dress very like it. They often send him letters signed, " Your humble servant, The Devil," and such stuff. I sat with him till after ten, and have business to do.

15. The Secretary came yesterday to town from Hampton Court, so I went to him early this morning; but he went back last night again: and coming home to-night I found a letter from him to tell me that he was just come from Hampton Court, and just returning, and will not be here till Saturday night. A pox take him! he stops all my business. I'll beg leave to come back when I have got over this, and hope to see MD in Ireland soon after Christmas.—I'm weary of Courts, and want my journeys to Laracor; they did me more good than all the Ministries these twenty years. I dined to-day in the City, but did no business as I designed. Lady Mountjoy tells me that Dilly is got to Ireland, and that the Archbishop of Dublin was the cause of his returning so soon. The Parliament was prorogued two days ago for a fortnight, which, with the Queen's absence, makes the town very dull and empty. They tell me the Duke of Ormond brings all the world away with him from Ireland. London has nothing so bad in it in winter as your knots of Irish folks; but I go to no coffee-house, and so I seldom see them. This letter shall go on Saturday; and then I am even with the world again. I have lent money, and cannot get it, and am forced to borrow for myself.

16. My man made a blunder this morning, and let up a visitor, when I had ordered to see nobody; so I was forced to hurry a hang-dog instrument of mine into my bed-chamber, and keep him cooling his heels there above an hour.—I am going on fairly in the common forms of a great cold; I believe it will last me about ten days in all.—I should have told you, that in those two verses sent to Lord Treasurer, G——d stands for Guiscard; that is easy; but we differed

about F——n; I thought it was for Frenchman, because he hates them, and they him: and so it would be, That although Guiscard's knife missed its design, the knife of a Frenchman might yet do it. My lord thinks it stands for Felton, the name of him that stabbed the first Duke of Buckingham.—Sir Andrew Fountaine and I dined with the Vans to-day, and my cold made me loiter all the evening. Stay, young women, don't you begin to owe me a letter? just a month to-day since I had your N. 22. I'll stay a week longer, and then I'll expect like agog; till then you may play at ombre, and so forth, as you please. The Whigs are still crying down our peace, but we will have it, I hope, in spite of them: the Emperor comes now with his two eggs a penny, and promises wonders to continue the war; but it is too late; only I hope the fear of it will serve to spur on the French to be easy and sincere. Night, sirrahs; I'll go early to bed.

17. Morning. This goes to-night; I will put it myself in the post-office. I had just now a long letter from the Archbishop of Dublin, giving me an account of the ending your session, how it ended in a storm; which storm, by the time it arrives here, will be only half nature. I can't help it, I won't hide. I often advised the dissolution of that Parliament, although I did not think the scoundrels had so much courage; but they have it only in the wrong, like a bully that will fight for a whore, and run away in an army. I believe, by several things the Archbishop says, he is not very well either with the Government or clergy.—See how luckily my paper ends with a fortnight.—God Almighty bless and preserve dearest little MD.—I suppose your Lord Lieutenant is now setting out for England. I wonder the Bishop of Clogher does not write to me, or let me know of his statues, and how he likes them: I will write to him again, as soon as I have leisure. Farewell, dearest MD, and love Presto, who loves MD infinitely above all earthly things, and who will.—My service to Mrs. Stoyte and Catherine. I'm sitting in my bed, but will rise to seal this. Morrow, dear rogues. Farewell again, dearest MD, etc.

LETTER XXXV

LONDON, *Nov.* 17, 1711.

I PUT my last this evening in the post-office. I dined with Dr. Cockburn. This being Queen Elizabeth's birthday, we have the D—— and all to do among us. I just heard of the stir as my letter was sealed this morning, and was so cross I would not open it to tell you. I have been visiting Lady Oglethorpe [1] and Lady Worsley; [2] the latter is lately come to town for the winter, and with child, and what care you? This is Queen Elizabeth's birthday, usually kept in this town by apprentices, etc.; but the Whigs designed a mighty procession by midnight, and had laid out a thousand pounds to dress up the Pope, Devil, cardinals, Sacheverell, etc., and carry them with torches about, and burn them. They did it by contribution. Garth gave five guineas; Dr. Garth I mean, if ever you heard of him. But they were seized last night, by order from the Secretary: you will have an account of it, for they bawl it about the streets already. [3] They had some very foolish and mischievous designs; and it was thought they would have put the rabble upon assaulting my Lord Treasurer's house and the Secretary's, and other violences. The militia was raised to prevent it, and now, I suppose, all will be quiet. The figures are now at the Secretary's office at Whitehall. I design to see them if I can.

18. I was this morning with Mr. Secretary, who just came from Hampton Court. He was telling me more particulars about this business of burning the Pope. It cost a great deal of money, and had it gone on, would have cost three times as much; but the town is full of it, and half a dozen

---

[1] See p. 304.   [2] See p. 132.

[3] The Tories alleged that the Duke of Marlborough, the Duke of Montagu, Steele, etc., were to take part in the procession (cf. *Spectator*, No. 269). Swift admits that the images seized were worth less than £40, and not £1000, as he had said, and that the Devil was not like Harley; yet he employed someone to write a lying pamphlet, *A True Relation of the Several Facts and Circumstances of the Intended Riot and Tumult*, etc.

Grub Street papers already. The Secretary and I dined at Brigadier Britton's, but I left them at six, upon an appointment with some sober company of men and ladies, to drink punch at Sir Andrew Fountaine's. We were not very merry; and I don't love rack punch, I love it better with brandy; are you of my opinion? Why then, twelvepenny weather; sirrahs, why don't you play at shuttlecock? I have thought of it a hundred times; faith, Presto will come over after Christmas, and will play with Stella before the cold weather is gone. Do you read the *Spectators*? I never do; they never come in my way; I go to no coffee-houses. They say abundance of them are very pretty; they are going to be printed in small volumes; I'll bring them over with me. I shall be out of my hurry in a week, and if Leigh be not gone over, I will send you by him what I am now finishing. I don't know where Leigh is; I have not seen him this good while, though he promised to call: I shall send to him. The Queen comes to town on Thursday for good and all.

19. I was this morning at Lord Dartmouth's office, and sent out for him from the Committee of Council, about some business. I was asking him more concerning this bustle about the figures in wax-work of the Pope, and Devil, etc. He was not at leisure, or he would have seen them. I hear the owners are so impudent, that they design to replevin them by law. I am assured that the figure of the Devil is made as like Lord Treasurer as they could. Why, I dined with a friend in St. James's Street. Lord Treasurer, I am told, was abroad to-day; I will know to-morrow how he does after it. The Duke of Marlborough is come, and was yesterday at Hampton Court with the Queen; no, it was t'other day; no, it was yesterday; for to-day I remember Mr. Secretary was going to see him, when I was there, not at the Duke of Marlborough's, but at the Secretary's; the Duke is not so fond of me. What care I? I won seven shillings to-night at picquet: I play twice a year or so.

20. I have been so teased with Whiggish discourse by

Mrs. Barton and Lady Betty Germaine, never saw the like. They turn all this affair of the Pope-burning into ridicule; and, indeed, they have made too great a clutter about it, if they had no real reason to apprehend some tumults. I dined with Lady Betty. I hear Prior's commission is passed to be Ambassador Extraordinary and Plenipotentiary for the peace; my Lord Privy Seal, who you know is Bishop of Bristol, is the other; and Lord Strafford, already Ambassador at The Hague, the third: I am forced to tell you, ignorant sluts, who is who. I was punning scurvily with Sir Andrew Fountaine and Lord Pembroke this evening: do you ever pun now? Sometimes with the Dean, or Tom Leigh.[1] Prior puns very well. Odso, I must go see His Excellency, 'tis a noble advancement: but they could do no less, after sending him to France. Lord Strafford is as proud as Hell, and how he will bear one of Prior's mean birth on an equal character with him, I know not. And so I go to my business, and bid you good-night.

21. I was this morning busy with my printer: I gave him the fifth sheet,[2] and then I went and dined with him in the City, to correct something, and alter, etc., and I walked home in the dusk, and the rain overtook me: and I found a letter here from Mr. Lewis; well, and so I opened it; and he says the peace is past danger, etc. Well, and so there was another letter enclosed in his: well, and so I looked on the outside of this t'other letter. Well, and so who do you think this t'other letter was from? Well, and so I'll tell you; it was from little MD, N. 23, 23, 23, 23. I tell you it is no more, I have told you so before: but I just looked again to satisfy you. Hie, Stella, you write like an emperor, a great deal together; a very good hand, and but four false spellings in all. Shall I send them to you? I am glad you did not take my correction ill. Well, but I won't answer your letter now, sirrah saucyboxes, no, no; not yet; just a

[1] A brother of Jemmy Leigh (see p. 6), and one of Stella's card-playing acquaintances.
[2] Of *The Conduct of the Allies* (see pp. 335, 345).

month and three days from the last, which is just five weeks:
you see it comes just when I begin to grumble.

22. Morning. Tooke has just brought me Dingley's
money. I will give you a note for it at the end of this
letter. There was half a crown for entering the letter of
attorney; but I swore to stop that. I'll spend your money
bravely here. Morrow, dear sirrahs. — At night. I dined
to-day with Sir Thomas Hanmer; his wife, the Duchess of
Grafton,[1] dined with us: she wears a great high head-dress,
such as was in fashion fifteen years ago, and looks like a mad
woman in it; yet she has great remains of beauty. I was
this evening to see Lord Harley, and thought to have sat
with Lord Treasurer, but he was taken up with the Dutch
Envoy and such folks; and I would not stay. One particular
in life here, different from what I have in Dublin, is, that
whenever I come home I expect to find some letter for me,
and seldom miss; and never any worth a farthing, but often
to vex me. The Queen does not come to town till Saturday.
Prior is not yet declared; but these Ministers being at
Hampton Court, I know nothing; and if I write news from
common hands, it is always lies. You will think it affectation;
but nothing has vexed me more for some months past, than
people I never saw pretending to be acquainted with me,
and yet speak ill of me too; at least some of them. An old
crooked Scotch countess, whom I never heard of in my life,
told the Duchess of Hamilton[2] t'other day that I often
visited her. People of worth never do that; so that a man
only gets the scandal of having scurvy acquaintance. Three
ladies were railing against me some time ago, and said they
were very well acquainted with me; two of which I had never
heard of, and the third I had only seen twice where I
happened to visit. A man who has once seen me in a coffee-
house will ask me how I do, when he sees me talking at

[1] Sir Thomas Hanmer (see p. 69) married, in 1698, Isabella, widow of the
first Duke of Grafton, and only daughter and heiress of Henry, Earl of
Arlington. She died in 1723.
[2] James, Duke of Hamilton (see p. 262), married, in 1698, as his second wife,
Elizabeth, daughter and sole heir of Digby, Lord Gerard. She died in 1744.

Court with a Minister of State; who is sure to ask me how
I came acquainted with that scoundrel. But come, sirrahs,
this is all stuff to you, so I'll say no more on this side the
paper, but turn over.

23. My printer invited Mr. Lewis and me to dine at a
tavern to-day, which I have not done five times since I came
to England; I never will call it Britain, pray don't call it
Britain. My week is not out, and one side of this paper is
out, and I have a letter to answer of MD's into the bargain:
must I write on the third side? faith, that will give you an
ill habit. I saw Leigh last night: he gives a terrible account
of Sterne; he reckons he is seduced by some wench; he is
over head and ears in debt, and has pawned several things.
Leigh says he goes on Monday next for Ireland, but believes
Sterne will not go with him; Sterne has kept him these
three months. Leigh has got the apron and things, and
promises to call for the box at Chester; but I despair of it.
Good-night, sirrahs; I have been late abroad.

24. I have finished my pamphlet [1] to-day, which has cost
me so much time and trouble: it will be published in three
or four days, when the Parliament begins sitting. I suppose
the Queen is come to town, but know nothing, having been
in the City finishing and correcting with the printer. When
I came home, I found letters on my table as usual, and one
from your mother, to tell me that you desire your writings
and a picture should be sent to me, to be sent over to you.
I have just answered her letter, and promised to take care of
them if they be sent to me. She is at Farnham: it is too
late to send them by Leigh; besides, I will wait your orders,
Madam Stella. I am going to finish a letter to Lord Treasurer
about reforming our language; [2] but first I must put an end
to a ballad; and go you to your cards, sirrahs, this is card
season.

25. I was early with the Secretary to-day, but he was gone
to his devotions, and to receive the sacrament: several rakes
did the same; it was not for piety, but employments; accord-

---

[1] *The Conduct of the Allies.*   [2] See p. 238.

ing to Act of Parliament. I dined with Lady Mary Dudley;[1] and passed my time since insipidly, only I was at Court at noon, and saw fifty acquaintance I had not met this long time : that is the advantage of a Court, and I fancy I am better known than any man that goes there. Sir John Walter's[2] quarrel with me has entertained the town ever since; and yet we never had a word, only he railed at me behind my back. The Parliament is again to be prorogued for eight or nine days, for the Whigs are too strong in the House of Lords : other reasons are pretended, but that is the truth. The prorogation is not yet known, but will be to-morrow.

26. Mr. Lewis and I dined with a friend of his, and un- expectedly there dined with us an Irish knight, one Sir John St. Leger,[3] who follows the law here, but at a great distance : he was so pert, I was forced to take him down more than once. I saw to-day the Pope, and Devil, and the other figures of cardinals, etc., fifteen in all, which have made such a noise. I have put an under-strapper upon writing a two- penny pamphlet[4] to give an account of the whole design. My large pamphlet[5] will be published to-morrow ; copies are sent to the great men this night. Domville[6] is come home from his travels ; I am vexed at it : I have not seen him yet ; I design to present him to all the great men.

27. Domville came to me this morning, and we dined at Pontack's, and were all day together, till six this evening : he is perfectly as fine a gentleman as I know ; he set me down at Lord Treasurer's, with whom I stayed about an hour, till Monsieur Buys, the Dutch Envoy, came to him about business. My Lord Treasurer is pretty well, but stiff in the

[1] Sir Matthew Dudley (see p. 7) married Lady Mary O'Bryen, youngest daughter of Henry, Earl of Thomond.
[2] See p. 305.
[3] Sir John St. Leger (died 1743) was M.P. for Doneraile and a Baron of the Exchequer in Ireland from 1714 to 1741. His elder brother, Arthur, was created Viscount Doneraile in 1703.
[4] *Relation of the Facts and Circumstances of the Intended Riot on Queen Elizabeth's Birthday.*
[5] *The Conduct of the Allies.*   [6] See p. 73.

hips with the remains of the rheumatism. I am to bring
Domville to my Lord Harley in a day or two. It was the
dirtiest rainy day that ever I saw. The pamphlet is published;
Lord Treasurer had it by him on the table, and was asking
me about the mottoes in the title-page; he gave me one of
them himself.[1] I must send you the pamphlet, if I can.

28. Mrs. Van sent to me to dine with her to-day, because
some ladies of my acquaintance were to be there; and there
I dined. I was this morning to return Domville his visit,
and went to visit Mrs. Masham, who was not within. I am
turned out of my lodging by my landlady: it seems her
husband and her son are coming home; but I have taken
another lodging hard by, in Leicester Fields. I presented
Mr. Domville to Mr. Lewis and Mr. Prior this morning. Prior
and I are called the two Sosias,[2] in a Whig newspaper. Sosias,
can you read it? The pamphlet begins to make a noise:
I was asked by several whether I had seen it, and they
advised me to read it, for it was something very extraordinary.
I shall be suspected; and it will have several paltry answers.
It must take its fate, as Savage[3] said of his sermon that he
preached at Farnham on Sir William Temple's death. Domville saw Savage in Italy, and says he is a coxcomb, and half
mad: he goes in red, and with yellow waistcoats, and was at
ceremony kneeling to the Pope on a Palm Sunday, which is
much more than kissing his toe; and I believe it will ruin him
here when 'tis told. I'll answer your letter in my new lodgings:
I have hardly room; I must borrow from the other side.

29. New lodgings. My printer came this morning to tell
me he must immediately print a second edition,[4] and Lord
Treasurer made one or two small additions: they must work
day and night to have it out on Saturday; they sold a

---

[1] The first motto was " Partem tibi Gallia nostri eripuit," etc. (Horace, 2 Od.
17–24).
[2] See Plautus's *Amphitrus*, or Dryden's *Amphitryon*.
[3] It is not known whether or no this was Dr. William Savage, Master of
Emmanuel College, Cambridge. No copy of the sermon—if it was printed—.
has been found. See Courtenay's *Memoirs of Sir William Temple*.
[4] Of *The Conduct of the Allies*, a pamphlet which had a very wide circulation. See a paper by Edward Solly in the *Antiquarian Magazine*, March 1885.

thousand in two days. Our Society met to-day; nine of us were present: we dined at our brother Bathurst's.[1] We made several regulations, and have chosen three new members, Lord Orrery,[2] Jack Hill, who is Mrs. Masham's brother, he that lately miscarried in the expedition to Quebec, and one Colonel Disney.[3]—We have taken a room in a house near St. James's to meet in. I left them early about correcting the pamphlet, etc., and am now got home, etc.

30. This morning I carried Domville to see my Lord Harley, and I did some business with Lord Treasurer, and have been all this afternoon with the printer, adding something to the second edition. I dined with the printer: the pamphlet makes a world of noise, and will do a great deal of good; it tells abundance of most important facts which were not at all known. I'll answer your letter to-morrow morning; or suppose I answer it just now, though it is pretty late. Come then.—You say you are busy with Parliaments, etc.; that's more than ever I will be when I come back; but you will have none these two years. Lord Santry, etc., yes, I have had enough on't.[4] I am glad Dilly is mended; does not he thank me for showing him the Court and the great people's faces? He had his glass out at the Queen and the rest. 'Tis right what Dilly says: I depend upon nothing from my friends, but to go back as I came. Never fear Laracor, 'twill mend with a peace, or surely they'll give me the Dublin parish. Stella is in the right: the Bishop of Ossory[5] is the silliest, best-natured wretch breathing, of as little consequence as an egg-shell. Well, the spelling I have mentioned before; only the next time say *at least,* and not

[1] Allen Bathurst, M.P. (1684-1775), created Baron Bathurst in December 1711, and Earl Bathurst in 1772. His second and eldest surviving son was appointed Lord Chancellor in the year preceding the father's death. Writing to her son in January 1711 (*Wentworth Papers*, 173), Lady Wentworth said of Bathurst, "He is, next to you, the finest gentleman and the best young man I know; I love him dearly."
[2] See p. 72. [3] See p. 153.
[4] Swift is alluding to the quarrel between Lord Santry (see p. 215) and Francis Higgins (see p. 335), which led to Higgins's prosecution. The matter is described at length in Boyer's *Political State*, 1711, pp. 617 *seq.*
[5] See p. 176.

at lest. Pox on your Newbury![1] what can I do for him?
I'll give his case (I am glad it is not a woman's) to what
members I know; that's all I can do. Lord Treasurer's
lameness goes off daily. Pray God preserve poor good Mrs.
Stoyte; she would be a great loss to us all: pray give her my
service, and tell her she has my heartiest prayers. I pity
poor Mrs. Manley; but I think the child is happy to die,
considering how little provision it would have had.—Poh,
every pamphlet abuses me, and for things that I never writ.
Joe[2] should have written me thanks for his two hundred
pounds: I reckon he got it by my means; and I must thank
the Duke of Ormond, who I dare swear will say he did it
on my account. Are they golden pippins, those seven
apples? We have had much rain every day as well as you.
£7, 17s. 8d., old blunderer, not 18s: I have reckoned it
eighteen times. Hawkshaw's eight pounds is not reckoned:
and if it be secure, it may lie where it is, unless they desire
to pay it: so Parvisol may let it drop till further orders;
for I have put Mrs. Wesley's money into the Bank, and will
pay her with Hawkshaw's. — I mean that Hawkshaw's
money goes for an addition to MD, you know; but be good
housewives. Bernage never comes now to see me; he has
no more to ask; but I hear he has been ill.—A pox on Mrs.
South's[3] affair; I can do nothing in it, but by way of
assisting anybody else that solicits it, by dropping a
favourable word, if it comes in my way. Tell Walls I do no
more for anybody with my Lord Treasurer, especially a thing
of this kind. Tell him I have spent all my discretion, and
have no more to use.—And so I have answered your letter
fully and plainly.—And so I have got to the third side of my
paper, which is more than belongs to you, young women.

> It goes to-morrow,
> To nobody's sorrow.

You are silly, not I; I'm a poet, if I had but, etc.—Who's
silly now? rogues and lasses, tinderboxes and buzzards. O

[1] No doubt the same as Colonel Newburgh (see *Journal*, March 5, 1711-12).
[2] Beaumont (see pp. 1, 250).   [3] See p. 301.

Lord, I am in a high vein of silliness; methought I was speaking to dearest little MD face to face. There; so, lads, enough for to-night; to cards with the blackguards. Goodnight, my delight, etc.

Dec. 1. Pish, sirrahs, put a date always at the bottom of your letter, as well as the top, that I may know when you send it; your last is of November 3, yet I had others at the same time, written a fortnight after. Whenever you would have any money, send me word three weeks before, and in that time you will certainly have an answer, with a bill on Parvisol: pray do this; for my head is full, and it will ease my memory. Why, I think I quoted to you some of ———'s letter, so you may imagine how witty the rest was; for it was all of a bunch, as Goodman Peesley [1] says. Pray let us have no more *bussiness*, but *busyness*: the deuce take me if I know how to spell it; your wrong spelling, Madam Stella, has put me out: it does not look right; let me see, *bussiness, busyness, business, bisyness, bisness, bysness*; faith, I know not which is right, I think the second; I believe I never writ the word in my life before; yes, sure I must, though; *business, busyness, bisyness.* — I have perplexed myself, and can't do it. Prithee ask Walls. *Business*, I fancy that's right. Yes it is; I looked in my own pamphlet, and found it twice in ten lines, to convince you that I never writ it before. Oh, now I see it as plain as can be; so yours is only an *s* too much. The Parliament will certainly meet on Friday next: the Whigs will have a great majority in the House of Lords, no care is taken to prevent it; there is too much neglect; they are warned of it, and that signifies nothing: it was feared there would be some peevish address from the Lords against a peace. 'Tis said about the town that several of the Allies begin now to be content that a peace should be treated. This is all the news I have. The Queen is pretty well: and so now I bid poor dearest MD farewell till to-night; then I will talk with them again.

The fifteen images that I saw were not worth forty

[1] Cf. p. 144.

pounds, so I stretched a little when I said a thousand. The Grub Street account of that tumult is published. The Devil is not like Lord Treasurer: they were all in your odd antic masks, bought in common shops.[1] I fear Prior will not be one of the plenipotentiaries.

I was looking over this letter, and find I make many mistakes of leaving out words; so 'tis impossible to find my meaning, unless you be conjurers. I will take more care for the future, and read over every day just what I have written that day, which will take up no time to speak of.

LETTER XXXVI

LONDON, *Dec.* 1, 1711.

MY last was put in this evening. I intended to dine with Mr. Masham to-day, and called at White's chocolate-house to see if he was there. Lord Wharton saw me at the door, and I saw him, but took no notice, and was going away, but he came through the crowd, called after me, and asked me how I did, etc. This was pretty; and I believe he wished every word he spoke was a halter to hang me. Masham did not dine at home, so I ate with a friend in the neighbour-hood. The printer has not sent me the second edition; I know not the reason, for it certainly came out to-day; perhaps they are glutted with it already. I found a letter from Lord Harley on my table, to tell me that his father desires I would make two small alterations. I am going to be busy, etc.

2. Morning. See the blunder; I was making it the 37th day of the month, from the number above. Well, but I am staying here for old Frowde, who appointed to call this morning: I am ready dressed to go to church: I suppose he dare not stir out but on Sundays.[2] The printer called early this morning, told me the second edition went off yesterday in five hours, and he must have a third ready to-morrow, for they might have sold half another: his men are all at work with it, though it be Sunday. This

---

[1] See p. 341. [2] See p. 336. Debtors could not be arrested on Sunday.

old fool will not come, and I shall miss church. Morrow, sirrahs.—At night. I was at Court to-day: the Queen is well, and walked through part of the rooms. I dined with the Secretary, and despatched some business. He tells me the Dutch Envoy designs to complain of that pamphlet. The noise it makes is extraordinary. It is fit it should answer the pains I have been at about it. I suppose it will be printed in Ireland. Some lay it to Prior, others to Mr. Secretary St. John, but I am always the first they lay everything to. I'll go sleep, etc.

3. I have ordered Patrick not to let any odd fellow come up to me; and a fellow would needs speak with me from Sir George Pretyman.[1] I had never heard of him, and would not see the messenger: but at last it proved that this Sir George has sold his estate, and is a beggar. Smithers, the Farnham carrier, brought me this morning a letter from your mother, with three papers enclosed of Lady Giffard's writing; one owning some exchequer business of £100 to be Stella's;[2] another for £100 that she has of yours, which I made over to you for Mariston; and a third for £300; the last is on stamped paper. I think they had better lie in England in some good hand till Lady Giffard dies; and I will think of some such hand before I come over. I was asking Smithers about all the people of Farnham. Mrs. White[3] has left off dressing, is troubled with lameness and swelled legs, and seldom stirs out; but her old hang-dog husband as hearty as ever. I was this morning with Lord Treasurer, about something he would have altered in the pamphlet;[4] but it can't be till the fourth edition, which I believe will be soon; for I dined with the printer, and he tells me they have sold off half the third. Mrs. Perceval[5] and her daughter have been in town

---

[1] Sir George Pretyman, Bart., dissipated the fortune of the family. The title became dormant in 1749.

[2] See the Introduction.

[3] For the Whites of Farnham, see Manning and Bray's *Surrey*, iii. 177.

[4] *The Conduct of the Allies.*

[5] The Percevals were among Swift's principal friends in the neighbourhood of Laracor. In a letter to John Temple in 1706 (Forster's *Life of Swift*, 182)

these three weeks, which I never heard till to-day; and Mrs. Wesley[1] is come to town too, to consult Dr. Radcliffe. The Whigs are resolved to bring that pamphlet into the House of Lords to have it condemned, so I hear. But the printer will stand to it, and not own the author; he must say he had it from the penny-post. Some people talk as if the House of Lords would do some peevish thing, for the Whigs are now a great majority in it; our Ministers are too negligent of such things: I have never slipped giving them warning; some of them are sensible of it; but Lord Treasurer stands too much upon his own legs. I fancy his good fortune will bear him out in everything; but in reason I should think this Ministry to stand very unsteady; if they can carry a peace, they may hold; I believe not else.

4. Mr. Secretary sent to me to-day to dine with him alone; but we had two more with us, which hindered me doing some business. I was this morning with young Harcourt, secretary to our Society, to take a room for our weekly meetings; and the fellow asked us five guineas a week only to have leave to dine once a week; was not that pretty? so we broke off with him, and are to dine next Thursday at Harcourt's (he is Lord Keeper's son). They have sold off above half the third edition, and answers are coming out: the Dutch Envoy refused dining with Dr. Davenant,[2] because he was suspected to write it: I have made some alterations in every edition, and it has cost me more trouble, for the time, since the printing, than before. 'Tis sent over to Ireland, and I suppose you will have it reprinted.

5. They are now printing the fourth edition, which is reckoned very extraordinary, considering 'tis a dear twelve-penny book, and not bought up in numbers by the party to give away, as the Whigs do, but purely upon its own strength.

Swift alludes to Perceval; in spite of different views in politics, "I always loved him," says Swift, "very well as a man of very good understanding and humour." Perceval was related to Sir John Perceval, afterwards Earl of Egmont (see p. 175).

[1] See p. 2.
[2] See p. 58.

23

I have got an under spur-leather to write an *Examiner* again,[1] and the Secretary and I will now and then send hints; but we would have it a little upon the Grub Street, to be a match for their writers. I dined with Lord Treasurer to-day at five: he dined by himself after his family, and drinks no claret yet, for fear of his rheumatism, of which he is almost well. He was very pleasant, as he is always: yet I fancied he was a little touched with the present posture of affairs. The Elector of Hanover's Minister here has given in a violent memorial against the peace, and caused it to be printed. The Whig lords are doing their utmost for a majority against Friday, and design, if they can, to address the Queen against the peace. Lord Nottingham,[2] a famous Tory and speech-maker, is gone over to the Whig side: they toast him daily, and Lord Wharton says, It is Dismal (so they call him from his looks) will save England at last. Lord Treasurer was hinting as if he wished a ballad was made on him, and I will get up one against to-morrow.[3] He gave me a scurrilous printed paper of bad verses on himself, under the name of the English Catiline, and made me read them to the company. It was his birthday, which he would not tell us, but Lord Harley whispered it to me.

6. I was this morning making the ballad, two degrees above Grub Street: at noon I paid a visit to Mrs. Masham, and then went to dine with our Society. Poor Lord Keeper dined below stairs, I suppose, on a bit of mutton. We chose two members: we were eleven met, the greatest meeting we ever had: I am next week to introduce Lord Orrery. The printer came before we parted, and brought the ballad,

[1] The *Examiner* was resumed on Dec. 6, 1711, under Oldisworth's editorship, and was continued by him until July 1714.
[2] Daniel Finch, second Earl of Nottingham, a staunch Tory, had quarrelled with the Government and the Court. On Dec. 7, 1711, he carried, by six votes, an amendment to the Address, to the effect that no peace would be acceptable which left Spain in the possession of the House of Bourbon. Harley's counter-stroke was the creation of twelve new peers. The Whigs rewarded Nottingham by withdrawing their opposition to the Occasional Conformity Bill.
[3] This " Song " begins:

" An orator dismal of Nottinghamshire,
Who had forty years let out his conscience for hire."

which made them laugh very heartily a dozen times. He is going to print the pamphlet [1] in small, a fifth edition, to be taken off by friends, and sent into the country. A sixpenny answer is come out, good for nothing, but guessing me, among others, for the author. To-morrow is the fatal day for the Parliament meeting, and we are full of hopes and fears. We reckon we have a majority of ten on our side in the House of Lords; yet I observed Mrs. Masham a little uneasy: she assures me the Queen is stout. The Duke of Marlborough has not seen the Queen for some days past; Mrs. Masham is glad of it, because she says he tells a hundred lies to his friends of what she says to him: he is one day humble, and the next day on the high ropes. The Duke of Ormond, they say, will be in town to-night by twelve.

7. This being the day the Parliament was to meet, and the great question to be determined, I went with Dr. Freind to dine in the City, on purpose to be out of the way, and we sent our printer to see what was our fate; but he gave us a most melancholy account of things. The Earl of Nottingham began, and spoke against a peace, and desired that in their address they might put in a clause to advise the Queen not to make a peace without Spain; which was debated, and carried by the Whigs by about six voices: and this has happened entirely by my Lord Treasurer's neglect, who did not take timely care to make up all his strength, although every one of us gave him caution enough. Nottingham has certainly been bribed. The question is yet only carried in the Committee of the whole House, and we hope when it is reported to the House to-morrow, we shall have a majority, by some Scotch lords coming to town. However, it is a mighty blow and loss of reputation to Lord Treasurer, and may end in his ruin. I hear the thing only as the printer brought it, who was at the debate; but how the Ministry take it, or what their hopes and fears are, I cannot tell until I see them. I shall be early with the Secretary to-morrow, and then I will tell you more, and shall write a full account to the Bishop

[1] *The Conduct of the Allies.*

of Clogher to-morrow, and to the Archbishop of Dublin, if I
have time. I am horribly down at present. I long to know
how Lord Treasurer bears this, and what remedy he has.
The Duke of Ormond came this day to town, and was there.

8. I was early this morning with the Secretary, and talked
over this matter. He hoped that when it was reported this
day in the House of Lords, they would disagree with their
Committee, and so the matter would go off, only with a little
loss of reputation to the Lord Treasurer. I dined with Mr.
Cockburn, and after, a Scotch member came in, and told us
that the clause was carried against the Court in the House
of Lords almost two to one. I went immediately to Mrs.
Masham, and meeting Dr. Arbuthnot (the Queen's favourite
physician), we went together. She was just come from
waiting at the Queen's dinner, and going to her own. She
had heard nothing of the thing being gone against us. It
seems Lord Treasurer had been so negligent that he was
with the Queen while the question was put in the House : I
immediately told Mrs. Masham that either she and Lord
Treasurer had joined with the Queen to betray us, or that
they two were betrayed by the Queen : she protested
solemnly it was not the former, and I believed her ; but she
gave me some lights to suspect the Queen is changed. For
yesterday, when the Queen was going from the House,
where she sat to hear the debate, the Duke of Shrewsbury, Lord Chamberlain, asked her whether he or the
Great Chamberlain Lindsey[1] ought to lead her out ; she
answered short, "Neither of you," and gave her hand to the
Duke of Somerset, who was louder than any in the House for
the clause against peace. She gave me one or two more
instances of this sort, which convince me that the Queen is
false, or at least very much wavering. Mr. Masham begged
us to stay, because Lord Treasurer would call, and we were
resolved to fall on him about his negligence in securing a

[1] Robert Bertie, Lord Willoughby de Eresby, and fourth Earl of Lindsey,
was created Marquis of Lindsay in 1706, and Duke of Ancaster and Kesteven
in 1715. He died in 1723.

majority. He came, and appeared in good humour as usual, but I thought his countenance was much cast down. I rallied him, and desired him to give me his staff, which he did : I told him, if he would secure it me a week, I would set all right : he asked how ; I said I would immediately turn Lord Marlborough, his two daughters,[1] the Duke and Duchess of Somerset, and Lord Cholmondeley,[2] out of all their employments ; and I believe he had not a friend but was of my opinion. Arbuthnot asked how he came not to secure a majority. He could answer nothing but that he could not help it, if people would lie and forswear. A poor answer for a great Minister. There fell from him a Scripture expression, that "the hearts of kings are unsearchable."[3] I told him it was what I feared, and was from him the worst news he could tell me. I begged him to know what he had to trust to : he stuck a little ; but at last bid me not fear, for all would be well yet. We would fain have had him eat a bit where he was, but he would go home, it was past six : he made me go home with him. There we found his brother and Mr. Secretary. He made his son take a list of all in the House of Commons who had places, and yet voted against the Court, in such a manner as if they should lose their places : I doubt he is not able to compass it. Lord Keeper came in an hour, and they were going upon business. So I left him, and returned to Mrs. Masham ; but she had company with her, and I would not stay.—This is a long journal, and of a day that may produce great alterations, and hazard the ruin of England. The Whigs are all in triumph ; they foretold how all this would be, but we thought it boasting. Nay, they said the Parliament should be dissolved before Christmas, and perhaps it may : this is all your d——d Duchess of

[1] Lady Sunderland (see p. 267) and Lady Rialton, ladies of the bed-chamber to the Queen.

[2] Hugh Cholmondeley (died 1724), the second Viscount, was created Viscount Malpas and Earl of Cholmondeley in 1706, and in 1708 was appointed Treasurer of Her Majesty's Household, an office which he held until 1713, in spite of his Whig sympathies. "Good for nothing, so far as ever I knew," Swift wrote of him.

[3] Prov. xxv. 3.

Somerset's doings. I warned them of it nine months ago, and a hundred times since: the Secretary always dreaded it. I told Lord Treasurer I should have the advantage of him; for he would lose his head, and I should only be hanged, and so carry my body entire to the grave.

9. I was this morning with Mr. Secretary: we are both of opinion that the Queen is false. I told him what I heard, and he confirmed it by other circumstances. I then went to my friend Lewis, who had sent to see me. He talks of nothing but retiring to his estate in Wales. He gave me reasons to believe the whole matter is settled between the Queen and the Whigs; he hears that Lord Somers is to be Treasurer, and believes that, sooner than turn out the Duchess of Somerset, she will dissolve the Parliament, and get a Whiggish one, which may be done by managing elections. Things are now in the crisis, and a day or two will determine. I have desired him to engage Lord Treasurer that as soon as he finds the change is resolved on, he will send me abroad as Queen's Secretary somewhere or other, where I may remain till the new Ministers recall me; and then I will be sick for five or six months, till the storm has spent itself. I hope he will grant me this; for I should hardly trust myself to the mercy of my enemies while their anger is fresh. I dined to-day with the Secretary, who affects mirth, and seems to hope all will yet be well. I took him aside after dinner, told him how I had served them, and had asked no reward, but thought I might ask security; and then desired the same thing of him, to send me abroad before a change. He embraced me, and swore he would take the same care of me as himself, etc., but bid me have courage, for that in two days my Lord Treasurer's wisdom would appear greater than ever; that he suffered all that had happened on purpose, and had taken measures to turn it to advantage. I said, "God send it"; but I do not believe a syllable; and, as far as I can judge, the game is lost. I shall know more soon, and my letters will at least be a good history to show you the steps of this change.

10. I was this morning with Lewis, who thinks they will let the Parliament sit till they have given the money, and then dissolve them in spring, and break the Ministry. He spoke to Lord Treasurer about what I desired him. My lord desired him with great earnestness to assure me that all would be well, and that I should fear nothing. I dined in the City with a friend. This day the Commons went to the Queen with their address, and all the Lords who were for the peace went with them, to show their zeal. I have now some further conviction that the Queen is false, and it begins to be known.

11. I went between two and three to see Mrs. Masham; while I was there she went to her bed-chamber to try a petticoat. Lord Treasurer came in to see her, and seeing me in the outer room, fell a rallying me: says he, "You had better keep company with me, than with such a fellow as Lewis, who has not the soul of a chicken, nor the heart of a mite." Then he went in to Mrs. Masham, and as he came back desired her leave to let me go home with him to dinner. He asked whether I was not afraid to be seen with him. I said I never valued my Lord Treasurer in my life, and therefore should have always the same esteem for Mr. Harley and Lord Oxford. He seemed to talk confidently, as if he reckoned that all this would turn to advantage. I could not forbear hinting that he was not sure of the Queen, and that those scoundrel, starving lords would never have dared to vote against the Court, if Somerset had not assured them that it would please the Queen. He said that was true, and Somerset did so. I stayed till six; then De Buys, the Dutch Envoy, came to him, and I left him. Prior was with us a while after dinner. I see him and all of them cast down, though they make the best of it.

12. Ford is come to town; I saw him last night: he is in no fear, but sanguine, although I have told him the state of things. This change so resembles the last, that I wonder they do not observe it. The Secretary sent for me yesterday to dine with him, but I was abroad; I hope he had something

to say to me. This is morning, and I write in bed. I am going to the Duke of Ormond, whom I have not yet seen. Morrow, sirrahs. — At night. I was to see the Duke of Ormond this morning: he asked me two or three questions after his civil way, and they related to Ireland: at last I told him that, from the time I had seen him, I never once thought of Irish affairs. He whispered me that he hoped I had done some good things here: I said, if everybody else had done half as much, we should not be as we are: then we went aside, and talked over affairs. I told him how all things stood, and advised him what was to be done. I then went and sat an hour with the Duchess; then as long with Lady Oglethorpe,[1] who is so cunning a devil that I believe she could yet find a remedy, if they would take her advice. I dined with a friend at Court.

13. I was this morning with the Secretary: he will needs pretend to talk as if things would be well: " Will you believe it," said he, "if you see these people turned out?" I said, yes, if I saw the Duke and Duchess of Somerset out: he swore if they were not, he would give up his place. Our Society dined to-day at Sir William Wyndham's; we were thirteen present. Lord Orrery and two other members were introduced: I left them at seven. I forgot to tell you that the printer told me yesterday that Morphew, the publisher, was sent for by that Lord Chief-Justice,[2] who was a manager against Sacheverell; he showed him two or three papers and pamphlets; among the rest mine of the *Conduct of the Allies,* threatened him, asked who was the author, and has bound him over to appear next term. He would not have the impudence to do this, if he did not foresee what was coming at Court.

14. Lord Shelburne was with me this morning, to be informed of the state of affairs, and desired I would answer all his objections against a peace, which was soon done, for

---

[1] See p. 304.

[2] Thomas Parker, afterwards created Earl of Macclesfield, was appointed Lord Chief-Justice in March 1710. In September 1711 he declined Harley's offer of the Lord Chancellorship, a post which he accepted under a Whig Government in the next reign.

he would not give me room to put in a word. He is a man of good sense enough; but argues so violently, that he will some day or other put himself into a consumption. He desires that he may not be denied when he comes to see me, which I promised, but will not perform. Leigh and Sterne set out for Ireland on Monday se'nnight: I suppose they will be with you long before this.—I was to-night drinking very good wine in scurvy company, at least some of them; I was drawn in, but will be more cautious for the future; 'tis late, etc.

15. Morning. They say the Occasional Bill[1] is brought to-day into the House of Lords; but I know not. I will now put an end to my letter, and give it into the post-house myself. This will be a memorable letter, and I shall sigh to see it some years hence. Here are the first steps toward the ruin of an excellent Ministry; for I look upon them as certainly ruined; and God knows what may be the consequences. —I now bid my dearest MD farewell; for company is coming, and I must be at Lord Dartmouth's office by noon. Farewell, dearest MD; I wish you a merry Christmas; I believe you will have this about that time. Love Presto, who loves MD above all things a thousand times. Farewell again, dearest MD, etc.

LETTER XXXVII

LONDON, *Dec.* 15, 1711.

I PUT in my letter this evening myself. I was to-day inquiring at the Secretary's office of Mr. Lewis how things went: I there met Prior, who told me he gave all for gone, etc., and was of opinion the whole Ministry would give up their places next week: Lewis thinks they will not till spring, when the session is over; both of them entirely despair. I went to see Mrs. Masham, who invited me to dinner; but I was engaged to Lewis. At four I went to Masham's. He came and whispered me that he had it from a very good hand that all would be well, and I found them both very

[1] The Bill against Occasional Conformity.

cheerful. The company was going to the opera, but desired I would come and sup with them. I did so at ten, and Lord Treasurer was there, and sat with us till past twelve, and was more cheerful than I have seen him these ten days. Mrs. Masham told me he was mightily cast down some days ago, and he could not indeed hide it from me. Arbuthnot is in good hopes that the Queen has not betrayed us, but only has been frightened, and flattered, etc. But I cannot yet be of his opinion, whether my reasons are better, or that my fears are greater. I do resolve, if they give up, or are turned out soon, to retire for some months, and I have pitched upon the place already: but I will take methods for hearing from MD, and writing to them. But I would be out of the way upon the first of the ferment; for they lay all things on me, even some I have never read.

16. I took courage to-day, and went to Court with a very cheerful countenance. It was mightily crowded; both parties coming to observe each other's faces. I have avoided Lord Halifax's bow till he forced it on me; but we did not talk together. I could not make less than fourscore bows, of which about twenty might be to Whigs. The Duke of Somerset is gone to Petworth, and, I hear, the Duchess too, of which I shall be very glad. Prince Eugene,[1] who was expected here some days ago, we are now told, will not come at all. The Whigs designed to have met him with forty thousand horse. Lord Treasurer told me some days ago of his discourse with the Emperor's Resident, that puppy Hoffman, about Prince Eugene's coming; by which I found my lord would hinder it, if he could; and we shall be all glad if he does not come, and think it a good point gained. Sir Andrew Fountaine, Ford, and I dined to-day with Mrs. Van, by invitation.

17. I have mistaken the day of the month, and been forced to mend it thrice. I dined to-day with Mr. Masham

---

[1] The proposed visit to London of Prince Eugene of Savoy, the renowned General, and friend of Marlborough, was viewed by the Government with considerable alarm.

and his lady, by invitation. Lord Treasurer was to be there, but came not. It was to entertain Buys, the Dutch Envoy, who speaks English well enough : he was plaguily politic, telling a thousand lies, of which none passed upon any of us. We are still in the condition of suspense, and I think have little hopes. The Duchess of Somerset is not gone to Petworth ; only the Duke, and that is a poor sacrifice. I believe the Queen certainly designs to change the Ministry, but perhaps may put it off till the session is over : and I think they had better give up now, if she will not deal openly ; and then they need not answer for the consequences of a peace, when it is in other hands, and may yet be broken. They say my Lord Privy Seal sets out for Holland this week : so the peace goes on.

18. It has rained hard from morning till night, and cost me three shillings in coach-hire. We have had abundance of wet weather. I dined in the City, and was with the printer, who has now a fifth edition of the *Conduct*, etc.: it is in small, and sold for sixpence ; they have printed as many as three editions, because they are to be sent in numbers into the country by great men, etc., who subscribe for hundreds. It has been sent a fortnight ago to Ireland : I suppose you will print it there. The Tory Lords and Commons in Parliament argue all from it ; and all agree that never anything of that kind was of so great consequence, or made so many converts. By the time I have sent this letter, I expect to hear from little MD : it will be a month, two days hence, since I had your last, and I will allow ten days for accidents. I cannot get rid of the leavings of a cold I got a month ago, or else it is a new one. I have been writing letters all this evening till I am weary, and I am sending out another little thing, which I hope to finish this week, and design to send to the printer in an unknown hand. There was printed a Grub Street speech of Lord Nottingham ;[1] and he was such an owl to complain of it in the House of Lords, who have

[1] Swift's " An excellent new Song ; being the intended Speech of a famous orator against Peace," a ballad " two degrees above Grub Street " (see p. 354).

taken up the printer for it. I heard at Court that Walpole [1] (a great Whig member) said that I and my whimsical Club writ it at one of our meetings, and that I should pay for it. He will find he lies: and I shall let him know by a third hand my thoughts of him. He is to be Secretary of State, if the Ministry changes; but he has lately had a bribe proved against him in Parliament, while he was Secretary at War. He is one of the Whigs' chief speakers.

19. Sad dismal weather. I went to the Secretary's office, and Lewis made me dine with him. I intended to have dined with Lord Treasurer. I have not seen the Secretary this week. Things do not mend at all. Lord Dartmouth despairs, and is for giving up; Lewis is of the same mind; but Lord Treasurer only says, "Poh, poh, all will be well." I am come home early to finish something I am doing; but I find I want heart and humour, and would read any idle book that came in my way. I have just sent away a penny paper to make a little mischief. Patrick is gone to the burial of an Irish footman, who was Dr. King's [2] servant; he died of a consumption, a fit death for a poor starving wit's footman. The Irish servants always club to bury a countryman.

20. I was with the Secretary this morning, and, for aught I can see, we shall have a languishing death: I can know nothing, nor themselves neither. I dined, you know, with our Society, and that odious Secretary would make me President next week; so I must entertain them this day se'nnight at the Thatched House Tavern,[3] where we dined

---

[1] Robert Walpole was then M.P. for King's Lynn, and Leader of the Opposition in the House of Commons. He had been Secretary at War from February 1708 to September 1710, and the Commissioners of Public Accounts having reported, on Dec. 21, 1711, that he had been guilty of venality and corruption, he was expelled from the House of Commons, and taken to the Tower.

[2] William King, D.C.L., author of the *Journey to London in 1698, Dialogues of the Dead, The Art of Cookery*, and other amusing works, was, at the end of the month, appointed Gazetteer, in succession to Steele, on Swift's recommendation. Writing earlier in the year, Gay said that King deserved better than to "languish out the small remainder of his life in the Fleet Prison." The duties of Gazetteer were too much for his easy-going nature and failing health, and he resigned the post in July 1712. He died in the following December.

[3] At the bottom of St. James's Street, on the west side.

to-day : it will cost me five or six pounds ; yet the Secretary
says he will give me wine. I found a letter when I came
home from the Bishop of Clogher.

21. This is the first time I ever got a new cold before the
old one was going : it came yesterday, and appeared in all due
forms, eyes and nose running, etc., and is now very bad ; and
I cannot tell how I got it. Sir Andrew Fountaine and I
were invited to dine with Mrs. Van. I was this morning
with the Duke of Ormond ; and neither he nor I can think
of anything to comfort us in present affairs. We must certainly fall, if the Duchess of Somerset be not turned out ;
and nobody believes the Queen will ever part with her. The
Duke and I were settling when Mr. Secretary and I should
dine with him, and he fixes upon Tuesday ; and when I came
away I remembered it was Christmas Day. I was to see
Lady ——, who is just up after lying-in ; and the ugliest
sight I have seen, pale, dead, old and yellow, for want of
her paint. She has turned my stomach. But she will soon
be painted, and a beauty again.

22. I find myself disordered with a pain all round the
small of my back, which I imputed to champagne I had
drunk ; but find it to have been only my new cold. It was
a fine frosty day, and I resolved to walk into the City. I
called at Lord Treasurer's at eleven, and stayed some time
with him.—He showed me a letter from a great Presbyterian
parson [1] to him, complaining how their friends had betrayed
them by passing this Conformity Bill ; and he showed me
the answer he had written, which his friends would not let
him send ; but was a very good one. He is very cheerful ;
but gives one no hopes, nor has any to give. I went into
the City, and there I dined.

23. Morning. As I was dressing to go to church, a friend
that was to see me advised me not to stir out ; so I shall
keep at home to-day, and only eat some broth, if I can get
it. It is a terrible cold frost, and snow fell yesterday, which

---

[1] The Rev. John Shower, pastor of the Presbyterian Congregation at
Curriers' Hall, London Wall.

still remains: look there, you may see it from the pent-houses. The Lords made yesterday two or three votes about peace, and Hanover, of a very angry kind to vex the Ministry, and they will meet sooner by a fortnight than the Commons; and they say, are preparing some knocking addresses. Morrow, sirrahs. I'll sit at home, and when I go to bed I will tell you how I am.—I have sat at home all day, and eaten only a mess of broth and a roll. I have written a Prophecy,[1] which I design to print; I did it to-day, and some other verses.

24. I went into the City to-day in a coach, and dined there. My cold is going. It is now bitter hard frost, and has been so these three or four days. My Prophecy is printed, and will be published after Christmas Day; I like it mightily: I don't know how it will pass. You will never understand it at your distance, without help. I believe everybody will guess it |to be mine, because it is somewhat in the same manner with that of "Merlin"[2] in the Miscellanies. My Lord Privy Seal set out this day for Holland: he'll have a cold journey. I gave Patrick half a crown for his Christmas box, on condition he would be good, and he came home drunk at midnight. I have taken a memorandum of it, because I never design to give him a groat more. 'Tis cruel cold.

25. I wish MD a merry Christmas, and many a one; but mine is melancholy: I durst not go to church to-day, finding myself a little out of order, and it snowing prodigiously, and freezing. At noon I went to Mrs. Van, who had this week engaged me to dine there to-day: and there I received the news that poor Mrs. Long[3] died at Lynn in Norfolk on Saturday last, at four in the morning: she was sick but four hours. We suppose it was the asthma, which she was subject to as well as the dropsy, as she sent me word in her last letter,

[1] The Windsor Prophecy, in which the Duchess of Somerset (see p. 162) is attacked as "Carrots from Northumberland."
[2] Merlin's Prophecy, 1709, written in pseudo-mediæval English.
[3] See p. 10.

written about five weeks ago; but then said she was recovered. I never was more afflicted at any death. The poor creature had retired to Lynn two years ago, to live cheap, and pay her debts. In her last letter she told me she hoped to be easy by Christmas; and she kept her word, although she meant it otherwise. She had all sorts of amiable qualities, and no ill ones, but the indiscretion of too much neglecting her own affairs. She had two thousand pounds left her by an old grandmother,[1] with which she intended to pay her debts, and live on an annuity she had of one hundred pounds a year, and Newburg House, which would be about sixty pounds more. That odious grandmother living so long, forced her to retire; for the two thousand pounds was settled on her after the old woman's death, yet her brute of a brother, Sir James Long,[2] would not advance it for her; else she might have paid her debts, and continued here, and lived still: I believe melancholy helped her on to her grave. I have ordered a paragraph to be put in the *Postboy*,[3] giving an account of her death, and making honourable mention of her; which is all I can do to serve her memory: but one reason was spite; for her brother would fain have her death a secret, to save the charge of bringing her up here to bury her, or going into mourning. Pardon all this, for the sake of a poor creature I had so much friendship for.

26. I went to Mr. Secretary this morning, and he would have me dine with him. I called at noon at Mrs. Masham's, who desired me not to let the *Prophecy* be published, for fear of angering the Queen about the Duchess of Somerset; so I writ to the printer to stop them. They have been printed and given about, but not sold. I saw Lord Treasurer there, who had been two hours with the Queen; and Mrs. Masham is in hopes things will do well again.

---

[1] Dorothy, daughter of Sir Edward Leach, of Shipley, Derbyshire.

[2] Sir James Long, Bart. (died 1729), was at this time M.P. for Chippenham.

[3] The number containing this paragraph is not in the British Museum.

I went at night again, and supped at Mr. Masham's, and Lord Treasurer sat with us till one o'clock. So 'tis late, etc.

27. I entertained our Society at the Thatched House Tavern to-day at dinner; but brother Bathurst sent for wine, the house affording none. The printer had not received my letter, and so he brought up dozens apiece of the *Prophecy*; but I ordered him to part with no more. 'Tis an admirable good one, and people are mad for it. The frost still continues violently cold. Mrs. Masham invited me to come to-night and play at cards; but our Society did not part till nine. But I supped with Mrs. Hill, her sister, and there was Mrs. Masham and Lord Treasurer, and we stayed till twelve. He is endeavouring to get a majority against next Wednesday, when the House of Lords is to meet, and the Whigs intend to make some violent addresses against a peace, if not prevented. God knows what will become of us.—It is still prodigiously cold; but so I told you already. We have eggs on the spit, I wish they may not be addled. When I came home to-night I found, forsooth, a letter from MD, N. 24, 24, 24, 24; there, do you know the numbers now? and at the same time one from Joe,[1] full of thanks: let him know I have received it, and am glad of his success, but won't put him to the charge of a letter. I had a letter some time ago from Mr. Warburton,[2] and I beg one of you will copy out what I shall tell you, and send it by some opportunity to Warburton. 'Tis as follows: The Doctor has received Mr. Warburton's letter, and desires he will let the Doctor know where[3] that accident he mentions is like soon to happen, and he will do what he can in it.—And pray, madam, let them know that I do this to save myself the trouble, and them the expense of a letter. And I think that this is enough for one that comes home at twelve from a Lord Treasurer and Mrs. Masham. Oh, I could tell you ten thousand things of our mad politics,

---

[1] Joseph Beaumont (see pp. 1, 250, 349).
[2] See p. 19.
[3] Apparently a misprint for " whether."

upon what small circumstances great affairs have turned. But I will go rest my busy head.

28. I was this morning with brother Bathurst to see the Duke of Ormond. We have given his Grace some hopes to be one of our Society. The Secretary and I and Bathurst are to dine with him on Sunday next. The Duke is not in much hopes, but has been very busy in endeavouring to bring over some lords against next Wednesday. The Duchess caught me as I was going out; she is sadly in fear about things, and blames me for not mending them by my credit with Lord Treasurer; and I blame her. She met me in the street at noon, and engaged me to dine with her, which I did; and we talked an hour after dinner in her closet. If we miscarry on Wednesday, I believe it will be by some strange sort of neglect. They talk of making eight new lords by calling up some peers' eldest sons; but they delay strangely. I saw Judge Coote [1] to-day at the Duke of Ormond's : he desires to come and see me, to justify his principles.

29. Morning. This goes to-day. I will not answer yours, your 24th, till next, which shall begin to-night, as usual. Lord Shelburne has sent to invite me to dinner, but I am engaged with Lewis at Ned Southwell's. Lord Northampton and Lord Aylesbury's sons [2] are both made peers ; but we shall want more. I write this post to your Dean. I owe the Archbishop a letter this long time. All people that come from Ireland complain of him, and scold me for protecting him. Pray, Madam Dingley, let me know what Presto has received for this year, or whether anything is due to him for last : I cannot look over your former letters now. As for Dingley's own account of her exchequer money, I will give it on t'other side. Farewell, my own dearest MD, and love Presto ; and God ever bless dearest MD, etc. etc. I wish you many happy Christmases and new years.

[1] See p. 321.
[2] James Compton, afterwards fifth Earl of Northampton (died 1754), was summoned to the House of Lords as Baron Compton in December 1711. Charles Bruce, who succeeded his father as third Earl of Aylesbury in 1741, was created Lord Bruce, of Whorlton, at the same time.

24

I have owned to the Dean a letter I just had from you, but that I had not one this great while before.

DINGLEY'S ACCOUNT

Received of Mr. Tooke	£6	17	6
Deducted for entering the letter of attorney .	0	2	6
For the three half-crowns it used to cost you, I			
don't know why nor wherefore . . .	0	7	6
For exchange to Ireland	0	10	0
For coach-hire	0	2	6
In all, just £8		0	0

So there's your money, and we are both even : for I'll pay you no more than that eight pounds Irish, and pray be satisfied.

Churchwarden's accounts, boys.

Saturday night. I have broke open my letter, and tore it into the bargain, to let you know that we are all safe : the Queen has made no less than twelve lords,[1] to have a majority ; nine new ones, the other three peers' sons ; and has turned out the Duke of Somerset. She is awaked at last, and so is Lord Treasurer : I want nothing now but to see the Duchess out. But we shall do without her. We are all extremely happy. Give me joy, sirrahs. This is written in a coffee-house. Three of the new lords are of our Society.

[1] James, Lord Compton, eldest son of the Earl of Northampton ; Charles, Lord Bruce, eldest son of the Earl of Aylesbury ; Henry Paget, son of Lord Paget ; George Hay, Viscount Dupplin, the son-in-law of the Lord Treasurer, created Baron Hay ; Viscount Windsor, created Baron Montjoy ; Sir Thomas Mansel, Baron Mansel ; Sir Thomas Willoughby, Baron Middleton ; Sir Thomas Trevor, Baron Trevor ; George Granville, Baron Lansdowne ; Samuel Masham, Baron Masham ; Thomas Foley, Baron Foley ; and Allen Bathurst, Baron Bathurst.

LETTER XXXVIII

LONDON, *Dec.* 29, 1711.

I PUT my letter in this evening, after coming from dinner at Ned Southwell's, where I drank very good Irish wine, and we are in great joy at this happy turn of affairs. The Queen has been at last persuaded to her own interest and security, and I freely think she must have made both herself and kingdom very unhappy, if she had done otherwise. It is still a mighty secret that Masham is to be one of the new lords; they say he does not yet know it himself; but the Queen is to surprise him with it. Mr. Secretary will be a lord at the end of the session; but they want him still in Parliament. After all, it is a strange unhappy necessity of making so many peers together; but the Queen has drawn it upon herself, by her confounded trimming and moderation. Three, as I told you, are of our Society.

30. I writ the Dean and you a lie yesterday; for the Duke of Somerset is not yet turned out. I was to-day at Court, and resolved to be very civil to the Whigs; but saw few there. When I was in the bed-chamber talking to Lord Rochester, he went up to Lady Burlington,[1] who asked him who I was; and Lady Sunderland and she whispered about me: I desired Lord Rochester to tell Lady Sunderland I doubted she was not as much in love with me as I was with her; but he would not deliver my message. The Duchess of Shrewsbury came running up to me, and clapped her fan up to hide us from the company, and we gave one another joy of this change; but sighed when we reflected on the Somerset family not being out. The Secretary and I, and brother Bathurst, and Lord Windsor, dined with the Duke of Ormond. Bathurst and Windsor[2] are to be two of the

---

[1] Juliana, widow of the second Earl of Burlington, and daughter of the Hon. Henry Noel, was Mistress of the Robes to Queen Anne. She died in 1750, aged seventy-eight.

[2] Thomas Windsor, Viscount Windsor (died 1738), an Irish peer, who had served under William III. in Flanders, was created Baron Montjoy, of the Isle

new lords. I desired my Lord Radnor's brother,[1] at Court to-day, to let my lord know I would call on him at six, which I did, and was arguing with him three hours to bring him over to us, and I spoke so closely that I believe he will be tractable; but he is a scoundrel, and though I said I only talked for my love to him, I told a lie; for I did not care if he were hanged: but everyone gained over is of consequence. The Duke of Marlborough was at Court to-day, and nobody hardly took notice of him. Masham's being a lord begins to take wind: nothing at Court can be kept a secret. Wednesday will be a great day: you shall know more.

31. Our frost is broken since yesterday, and it is very slabbery;[2] yet I walked to the City and dined, and ordered some things with the printer. I have settled Dr. King in the Gazette; it will be worth two hundred pounds a year to him. Our new lords' patents are passed: I don't like the expedient, if we could have found any other. I see I have said this before. I hear the Duke of Marlborough is turned out of all his employments: I shall know to-morrow when I am to carry Dr. King to dine with the Secretary.—These are strong remedies; pray God the patient is able to bear them. The last Ministry people are utterly desperate.

Jan. 1. Now I wish my dearest little MD many happy new years; yes, both Dingley and Stella, ay and Presto too, many happy new years. I dined with the Secretary, and it is true that the Duke of Marlborough is turned out of all. The Duke of Ormond has got his regiment of foot-guards, I know not who has the rest. If the Ministry be not sure of a peace, I shall wonder at this step, and do not approve it at best. The Queen and Lord Treasurer mortally hate the Duke of Marlborough, and to that he owes his fall, more

of Wight, in December 1711. He married Charlotte, widow of John, Baron Jeffries, of Wem, and daughter of Philip Herbert, Earl of Pembroke.

[1] The Hon. Russell Robartes, brother of Lord Radnor (see p. 8), was Teller of the Exchequer, and M.P. for Bodmin. His son became third Earl of Radnor in 1723.

[2] Gay (*Trivia*, ii. 92) speaks of "the slabby pavement."

than to his other faults: unless he has been tampering too far with his party, of which I have not heard any particulars; however it be, the world abroad will blame us. I confess my belief that he has not one good quality in the world beside that of a general, and even that I have heard denied by several great soldiers. But we have had constant success in arms while he commanded. Opinion is a mighty matter in war, and I doubt the French think it impossible to conquer an army that he leads, and our soldiers think the same; and how far even this step may encourage the French to play tricks with us, no man knows. I do not love to see personal resentment mix with public affairs.

2. This being the day the Lords meet, and the new peers to be introduced, I went to Westminster to see the sight; but the crowd was too great in the house. So I only went into the robing-room, to give my four brothers joy, and Sir Thomas Mansel,[1] and Lord Windsor; the other six I am not acquainted with. It was apprehended the Whigs would have raised some difficulties, but nothing happened. I went to see Lady Masham at noon, and wish her joy of her new honour, and a happy new year. I found her very well pleased; for peerage will be some sort of protection to her upon any turn of affairs. She engaged me to come at night, and sup with her and Lord Treasurer: I went at nine, and she was not at home, so I would not stay.—No, no, I won't answer your letter yet, young women. I dined with a friend in the neighbourhood. I see nothing here like Christmas, except brawn or mince-pies in places where I dine, and giving away my half-crowns like farthings to great men's porters and butlers. Yesterday I paid seven good guineas to the fellow at the tavern where I treated the Society. I have a great mind to send you the bill. I think I told you some articles. I have not heard whether anything was done in the House of Lords after introducing the new ones. Ford has been sitting with me till peeast tweeleve a clock.

[1] See p. 158.

3. This was our Society day: Lord Dupplin was President; we choose every week; the last President treats and chooses his successor. I believe our dinner cost fifteen pounds beside wine. The Secretary grew brisk, and would not let me go, nor Lord Lansdowne,[1] who would fain have gone home to his lady, being newly married to Lady Mary Thynne. It was near one when we parted, so you must think I cannot write much to-night. The adjourning of the House of Lords yesterday, as the Queen desired, was just carried by the twelve new lords, and one more. Lord Radnor was not there: I hope I have cured him. Did I tell you that I have brought Dr. King in to be Gazetteer? It will be worth above two hundred pounds a year to him: I believe I told you so before, but I am forgetful. Go, get you gone to ombre, and claret, and toasted oranges. I'll go sleep.

4. I cannot get rid of the leavings of my cold. I was in the City to-day, and dined with my printer, and gave him a ballad made by several hands, I know not whom. I believe Lord Treasurer had a finger in it; I added three stanzas; I suppose Dr. Arbuthnot had the greatest share. I had been overseeing some other little prints, and a pamphlet made by one of my under-strappers. Somerset is not out yet. I doubt not but you will have the *Prophecy* in Ireland, although it is not published here, only printed copies given to friends. Tell me, do you understand it? No, faith, not without help. Tell me what you stick at, and I'll explain. We turned out a member of our Society yesterday for gross neglect and non-attendance. I writ to him by order to give him notice of it. It is Tom Harley,[2] secretary to the Treasurer, and cousin-german to Lord Treasurer. He is going to Hanover from the Queen. I am

[1] George Granville (see p. 130), now Baron Lansdowne, married Lady Mary Thynne, widow of Thomas Thynne, and daughter of Edward, Earl of Jersey (see p. 281). In October 1710 Lady Wentworth wrote to her son, " Pray, my dear, why will you let Lady Mary Thynne go? She is young, rich, and not unhandsome, some say she is pretty ; and a virtuous lady, and of the nobility, and why will you not try to get her? " (*Wentworth Papers*, 149).

[2] See p. 225.

JAN. 1711-12] JOURNAL TO STELLA 375

to give the Duke of Ormond notice of his election as soon as
I can see him.

5. I went this morning with a parishioner of mine, one
Nuttal, who came over here for a legacy of one hundred
pounds, and a roguish lawyer had refused to pay him, and
would not believe he was the man. I writ to the lawyer a
sharp letter, that I had taken Nuttal into my protection, and
was resolved to stand by him, and the next news was, that
the lawyer desired I would meet him, and attest he was the
man, which I did, and his money was paid upon the spot. I
then visited Lord Treasurer, who is now right again, and all
well, only that the Somerset family is not out yet. I hate
that; I don't like it, as the man said, by, etc. Then I went
and visited poor Will Congreve, who had a French fellow
tampering with one of his eyes; he is almost blind of both.
I dined with some merchants in the City, but could not see
Stratford, with whom I had business. Presto, leave off your
impertinence, and answer our letter, saith MD. Yes, yes,
one of these days, when I have nothing else to do. O, faith,
this letter is a week written, and not one side done yet.—
These ugly spots are not tobacco, but this is the last gilt
sheet I have of large paper, therefore hold your tongue.
Nuttal was surprised when they gave him bits of paper
instead of money, but I made Ben Tooke put him in his
geers:[1] he could not reckon ten pounds, but was puzzled
with the Irish way. Ben Tooke and my printer have desired
me to make them stationers to the Ordnance, of which Lord
Rivers is Master, instead of the Duke of Marlborough. It
will be a hundred pounds a year apiece to them, if I can get
it. I will try to-morrow.

6. I went this morning to Earl Rivers, gave him joy of his
new employment, and desired him to prefer my printer and
bookseller to be stationers to his office. He immediately
granted it me; but, like an old courtier, told me it was
wholly on my account, but that he heard I had intended to
engage Mr. Secretary to speak to him, and desired I would

[1] Harness.

engage him to do so, but that, however, he did it only for my
sake.   This is a Court trick, to oblige as many as you can at
once.   I read prayers to poor Mrs. Wesley, who is very much
out of order, instead of going to church; and then I went to
Court, which I found very full, in expectation of seeing Prince
Eugene, who landed last night, and lies at Leicester House;
he was not to see the Queen till six this evening.   I hope
and believe he comes too late to do the Whigs any good.   I
refused dining with the Secretary, and was like to lose my
dinner, which was at a private acquaintance's.   I went at six
to see the Prince at Court, but he was gone in to the Queen;
and when he came out, Mr. Secretary, who introduced him,
walked so near him that he quite screened me from him
with his great periwig.   I'll tell you a good passage: as
Prince Eugene was going with Mr. Secretary to Court, he
told the Secretary that Hoffman, the Emperor's Resident,
said to His Highness that it was not proper to go to Court
without a long wig, and his was a tied-up one: "Now," says the
Prince, " I knew not what to do, for I never had a long periwig
in my life; and I have sent to all my valets and footmen, to
see whether any of them have one, that I might borrow it,
but none of them has any."—Was not this spoken very greatly
with some sort of contempt?   But the Secretary said it was
a thing of no consequence, and only observed by gentlemen
ushers.   I supped with Lord Masham, where Lord Treasurer
and Mr. Secretary supped with us : the first left us at twelve,
but the rest did not part till two, yet I have written all this,
because it is fresh : and now I'll go sleep if I can; that is, I
believe I shall, because I have drank a little.

7. I was this morning to give the Duke of Ormond notice
of the honour done him to make him one of our Society, and
to invite him on Thursday next to the Thatched House : he has
accepted it with the gratitude and humility such a preferment
deserves, but cannot come till the next meeting, because
Prince Eugene is to dine with him that day, which I allowed
for a good excuse, and will report accordingly.   I dined with
Lord Masham, and sat there till eight this evening, and came

home, because I was not very well, but a little griped; but
now I am well again, I will not go, at least but very seldom,
to Lord Masham's suppers. Lord Treasurer is generally there,
and that tempts me, but late sitting up does not agree with
me : there's the short and the long, and I won't do it; so
take your answer, dear little young women ; and I have no
more to say to you to-night, because of the Archbishop, for I
am going to write a long letter to him, but not so politely as
formerly : I won't trust him.

8. Well, then, come, let us see this letter; if I must answer
it, I must. What's here now? yes, faith, I lamented my
birthday [1] two days after, and that's all: and you rhyme,
Madam Stella; were those verses made upon my birthday?
faith, when I read them, I had them running in my head all
the day, and said them over a thousand times ; they drank
your health in all their glasses, and wished, etc. I could not
get them out of my head. What? no, I believe it was not;
what do I say upon the eighth of December? Compare, and
see whether I say so. I am glad of Mrs. Stoyte's recovery,
heartily glad ; your Dolly Manley's and Bishop of Cloyne's [2]
child I have no concern about: I am sorry in a civil way,
that's all. Yes, yes, Sir George St. George dead.[3]—Go, cry,
Madam Dingley ; I have written to the Dean. Raymond
will be rich, for he has the building itch. I wish all he has
got may put him out of debt. Poh, I have fires like lightning ;
they cost me twelvepence a week, beside small coal. I have
got four new caps, madam, very fine and convenient, with
striped cambric, instead of muslin ; so Patrick need not mend
them, but take the old ones. Stella snatched Dingley's word
out of her pen; Presto a cold ? Why, all the world here is
dead with them : I never had anything like it in my life ;
'tis not gone in five weeks. I hope Leigh is with you before
this, and has brought your box. How do you like the ivory
rasp ? Stella is angry ; but I'll have a finer thing for her. Is

[1] On his birthday Swift read the third chapter of Job.
[2] See p. 329.
[3] Sir George St. George of Dunmore, Co. Galway, M.P. for Co. Leitrim
from 1661 to 1692, and afterwards for Co. Galway, died in December 1711.

not the apron as good ?   I'm sure I shall never be paid it; so
all's well again.—What ? the quarrel with Sir John Walter? [1]
Why, we had not one word of quarrel; only he railed at me
when I was gone : and Lord Keeper and Treasurer teased me
for a week.   It was nuts to them; a serious thing with a
vengeance.—The Whigs may sell their estates then, or hang
themselves, as they are disposed ; for a peace there will be.
Lord Treasurer told me that Connolly [2] was going to Hanover.
Your Provost [3] is a coxcomb.   Stella is a good girl for not
being angry when I tell her of spelling; I see none wrong in
this.   God Almighty be praised that your disorder lessens ;
it increases my hopes mightily that they will go off.   And
have you been plagued with the fear of the plague? never
mind those reports; I have heard them five hundred times.
Replevi ?   Replevin, simpleton, 'tis Dingley I mean; but it
is a hard word, and so I'll excuse it.   I stated Dingley's
accounts in my last.   I forgot Catherine's sevenpenny dinner.
I hope it was the beef-steaks; I'll call and eat them in spring ;
but Goody Stoyte must give me coffee, or green tea, for I
drink no bohea.   Well, ay, the pamphlet; but there are
some additions to the fourth edition ; the fifth edition was of
four thousand, in a smaller print, sold for sixpence.   Yes, I
had the twenty-pound bill from Parvisol: and what then ?
Pray now eat the Laracor apples; I beg you not to keep
them, but tell me what they are.   You have had Tooke's bill
in my last.   And so there now, your whole letter is answered.
I tell you what I do; I lay your letter before me, and take it
in order, and answer what is necessary; and so and so.   Well,
when I expected we were all undone, I designed to retire
for six months, and then steal over to Laracor; and I had in
my mouth a thousand times two lines of Shakespeare, where
Cardinal Wolsey says,

> " A weak old man, battered with storms of state,
>   Is come to lay his weary bones among you." [4]

I beg your pardon ; I have cheated you all this margin, I did

[1] See pp. 305, 346.   [2] See p. 20.   [3] Dr. Pratt (see p. 5).
[4] *King Henry VIII.*, act iv. sc. 2 : " An old man broken with the storms," etc.

not perceive it; and I went on wider and wider like Stella; awkward sluts; *she writes so so, there* :[1] that's as like as two eggs a penny.—"A weak old man," now I am saying it, and shall till to-morrow.—The Duke of Marlborough says there is nothing he now desires so much as to contrive some way how to soften Dr. Swift. He is mistaken; for those things that have been hardest against him were not written by me. Mr. Secretary told me this from a friend of the Duke's; and I'm sure now he is down, I shall not trample on him; although I love him not, I dislike his being out.—Bernage was to see me this morning, and gave some very indifferent excuses for not calling here so long. I care not twopence. Prince Eugene did not dine with the Duke of Marlborough on Sunday, but was last night at Lady Betty Germaine's assemblée, and a vast number of ladies to see him. Mr. Lewis and I dined with a private friend. I was this morning to see the Duke of Ormond, who appointed me to meet him at the Cockpit at one, but never came. I sat too some time with the Duchess. We don't like things very well yet. I am come home early, and going to be busy. I'll go write.

9. I could not go sleep last night till past two, and was waked before three by a noise of people endeavouring to break open my window. For a while I would not stir, thinking it might be my imagination; but hearing the noise continued, I rose and went to the window, and then it ceased. I went to bed again, and heard it repeated more violently; then I rose and called up the house, and got a candle: the rogues had lifted up the sash a yard; there are great sheds before my windows, although my lodgings be a storey high; and if they get upon the sheds they are almost even with my window. We observed their track, and panes of glass fresh broken. The watchmen told us to-day they saw them, but could not catch them. They attacked others in the neighbourhood about the same time, and actually robbed a house in Suffolk Street, which is the next street but one to us. It is

---

[1] "These words in the manuscript imitate Stella's writing, and are sloped the wrong way" (Deane Swift).

said they are seamen discharged from service. I went up to call my man, and found his bed empty; it seems he often lies abroad. I challenged him this morning as one of the robbers. He is a sad dog; and the minute I come to Ireland I will discard him. I have this day got double iron bars to every window in my dining-room and bed-chamber; and I hide my purse in my thread stocking between the bed's head and the wainscot. Lewis and I dined with an old Scotch friend, who brought the Duke of Douglas [1] and three or four more Scots upon us.

10. This was our Society day, you know; but the Duke of Ormond could not be with us, because he dined with Prince Eugene. It cost me a guinea contribution to a poet, who had made a copy of verses upon monkeys, applying the story to the Duke of Marlborough; the rest gave two guineas, except the two physicians,[2] who followed my example. I don't like this custom: the next time I will give nothing. I sat this evening at Lord Masham's with Lord Treasurer: I don't like his countenance; nor I don't like the posture of things well.

> We cannot be stout,
> Till Somerset's out:

as the old saying is.

11. Mr. Lewis and I dined with the Chancellor of the Exchequer, who eats the most elegantly of any man I know in town. I walked lustily in the Park by moonshine till eight, to shake off my dinner and wine; and then went to sup at Mr. Domville's with Ford, and stayed till twelve. It is told me to-day as a great secret that the Duke of Somerset will be out soon, that the thing is fixed; but what shall we do with the Duchess? They say the Duke will make her leave the Queen out of spite, if he be out. It has stuck upon that fear a good while already. Well, but Lewis gave me a letter from MD, N. 25. O Lord, I did not expect one this fortnight, faith. You are mighty good, that's certain: but I won't

[1] Archibald Douglas, third Marquis of Douglas, was created Duke of Douglas in 1703. He died, without issue, in 1761.
[2] Arbuthnot and Freind.

answer it, because this goes to-morrow, only what you say of the printer being taken up; I value it not; all's safe there; nor do I fear anything, unless the Ministry be changed : I hope that danger is over. However, I shall be in Ireland before such a change; which could not be, I think, till the end of the session, if the Whigs' designs had gone on.—Have not you an apron by Leigh, Madam Stella? have you all I mentioned in a former letter?

12. Morning. This goes to-day as usual. I think of going into the City; but of that at night. 'Tis fine moderate weather these two or three days last. Farewell, etc. etc.

LETTER XXXIX

LONDON, *Jan.* 12, 1711-12.

WHEN I sealed up my letter this morning, I looked upon myself to be not worth a groat in the world. Last night, after Mr. Ford and I left Domville, Ford desired me to go with him for a minute upon earnest business, and then told me that both he and I were ruined; for he had trusted Stratford with five hundred pounds for tickets for the lottery, and he had been with Stratford, who confessed he had lost fifteen thousand pounds by Sir Stephen Evans,[1] who broke last week; that he concluded Stratford must break too; that he could not get his tickets, but Stratford made him several excuses, which seemed very blind ones, etc. And Stratford had near four hundred pounds of mine, to buy me five hundred pounds in the South Sea Company. I came home reflecting a little; nothing concerned me but MD. I called all my philosophy and religion up; and, I thank God, it did not keep me awake beyond my usual time above a quarter of an hour. This morning I sent for Tooke, whom I had employed to buy the stock of Stratford, and settle things with him. He told me I was secure; for Stratford had transferred it to me in form in the South Sea House, and he

[1] Sir Stephen Evance, goldsmith, was knighted in 1690.

had accepted it for me, and all was done on stamped parchment. However, he would be further informed; and at night sent me a note to confirm me. However, I am not yet secure; and, besides, am in pain for Ford, whom I first brought acquainted with Stratford. I dined in the City.

13. Domville and I dined with Ford to-day by appointment: the Lord Mansel told me at Court to-day that I was engaged to him; but Stratford had promised Ford to meet him and me to-night at Ford's lodgings. He did so; said he had hopes to save himself in his affair with Evans. Ford asked him for his tickets: he said he would send them to-morrow; but looking in his pocket-book, said he believed he had some of them about him, and gave him as many as came to two hundred pounds, which rejoiced us much; besides, he talked so frankly, that we might think there is no danger. I asked him, Was there any more to be settled between us in my affair? He said, No; and answered my questions just as Tooke had got them from others; so I hope I am safe. This has been a scurvy affair. I believe Stella would have half laughed at me, to see a suspicious fellow like me over-reached. I saw Prince Eugene to-day at Court: I don't think him an ugly-faced fellow, but well enough, and a good shape.

14. The Parliament was to sit to-day, and met; but were adjourned by the Queen's directions till Thursday. She designs to make some important speech then. She pretended illness; but I believe they were not ready, and they expect some opposition: and the Scotch lords are angry,[1] and must be pacified. I was this morning to invite the Duke of Ormond to our Society on Thursday, where he is then to be introduced. He has appointed me at twelve to-morrow about some business: I would fain have his help to impeach a certain lord; but I doubt we shall make nothing of it. I intended

---

[1] Because of the refusal of the House of Lords to allow the Duke of Hamilton (see p. 262), a Scottish peer who had been raised to the peerage of Great Britain as Duke of Brandon, to sit under that title. The Scottish peers discontinued their attendance at the House until the resolution was partially amended; and the Duke of Hamilton always sat as a representative Scottish peer.

to have dined with Lord Treasurer, but I was told he would
be busy : so I dined with Mrs. Van; and at night I sat with
Lord Masham till one. Lord Treasurer was there, and chid
me for not dining with him : he was in very good humour. I
brought home two flasks of burgundy in my chair : I wish
MD had them. You see it is very late; so I'll go to bed,
and bid MD good night.

15. This morning I presented my printer and bookseller to
Lord Rivers, to be stationers to the Ordnance; stationers,
that's the word; I did not write it plain at first. I believe it
will be worth three hundred pounds a year between them.
This is the third employment I have got for them. Rivers
told them the Doctor commanded him, and he durst not
refuse it. I would have dined with Lord Treasurer to-day
again, but Lord Mansel would not let me, and forced me
home with him. I was very deep with the Duke of Ormond
to-day at the Cockpit, where we met to be private; but I
doubt I cannot do the mischief I intended. My friend Penn
came there, Will Penn the Quaker, at the head of his brethren,
to thank the Duke for his kindness to their people in Ireland.
To see a dozen scoundrels with their hats on, and the Duke
complimenting with his off, was a good sight enough. I sat
this evening with Sir William Robinson,[1] who has mighty
often invited me to a bottle of wine : and it is past twelve.

16. This being fast-day, Dr. Freind and I went into the
City to dine late, like good fasters. My printer and bookseller want me to hook in another employment for them in
the Tower, because it was enjoyed before by a stationer,
although it be to serve the Ordnance with oil, tallow, etc., and
is worth four hundred pounds per annum more : I will try
what I can do. They are resolved to ask several other employments of the same nature to other offices; and I will then
grease fat sows, and see whether it be possible to satisfy them.
Why am not I a stationer? The Parliament sits to-morrow,

[1] Sir William Robinson (1655-1736), created a baronet in 1689, was M.P. for
York from 1697 to 1722. His descendants include the late Earl De Grey and
the Marquis of Ripon.

and Walpole, late Secretary at War, is to be swinged for bribery, and the Queen is to communicate something of great importance to the two Houses, at least they say so. But I must think of answering your letter in a day or two.

17. I went this morning to the Duke of Ormond about some business, and he told me he could not dine with us to-day, being to dine with Prince Eugene. Those of our Society of the House of Commons could not be with us, the House sitting late on Walpole. I left them at nine, and they were not come. We kept some dinner for them. I hope Walpole will be sent to the Tower, and expelled the House; but this afternoon the members I spoke with in the Court of Requests talked dubiously of it. It will be a leading card to maul the Duke of Marlborough for the same crime, or at least to censure him. The Queen's message was only to give them notice of the peace she is treating, and to desire they will make some law to prevent libels against the Government; so farewell to Grub Street.

18. I heard to-day that the commoners of our Society did not leave the Parliament till eleven at night, then went to those I left, and stayed till three in the morning. Walpole is expelled, and sent to the Tower. I was this morning again with Lord Rivers, and have made him give the other employment to my printer and bookseller; 'tis worth a great deal. I dined with my friend Lewis privately, to talk over affairs. We want to have this Duke of Somerset out, and he apprehends it will not be, but I hope better. They are going now at last to change the Commissioners of the Customs; my friend Sir Matthew Dudley will be out, and three more, and Prior will be in. I have made Ford copy out a small pamphlet, and sent it to the press, that I might not be known for author; 'tis *A Letter to the October Club*,[1] if ever you heard of such a thing.—Methinks this letter goes on but slowly for almost a week: I want some little conversation with MD, and to know what they are doing just now. I am

[1] See p. 152. The full title was, *Some Advice humbly offered to the Members of the October Club, in a Letter from a Person of Honour.*

sick of politics. I have not dined with Lord Treasurer these three weeks : he chides me, but I don't care : I don't.

19. I dined to-day with Lord Treasurer : this is his day of choice company, where they sometimes admit me, but pretend to grumble. And to-day they met on some extraordinary business ; the Keeper, Steward, both Secretaries, Lord Rivers, and Lord Anglesea : I left them at seven, and came away, and have been writing to the Bishop of Clogher. I forgot to know where to direct to him since Sir George St. George's death,[1] but I have directed to the same house : you must tell me better, for the letter is sent by the bellman. Don't write to me again till this is gone, I charge you, for I won't answer two letters together. The Duke of Somerset is out, and was with his yellow liveries at Parliament to-day. You know he had the same with the Queen, when he was Master of the Horse : we hope the Duchess will follow, or that he will take her away in spite. Lord Treasurer, I hope, has now saved his head. Has the Dean received my letter? ask him at cards to-night.

20. There was a world of people to-day at Court to see Prince Eugene, but all bit, for he did not come. I saw the Duchess of Somerset talking with the Duke of Buckingham ; she looked a little down, but was extremely courteous. The Queen has the gout, but is not in much pain. Must I fill this line too ?[2] well then, so let it be. The Duke of Beaufort[3] has a mighty mind to come into our Society; shall we let him? I spoke to the Duke of Ormond about it, and he doubts a little whether to let him in or no. They say the Duke of Somerset is advised by his friends to let his wife stay with the Queen; I am sorry for it. I dined with the Secretary

---

[1] See p. 377.
[2] "It is the last of the page, and written close to the edge of the paper" (Deane Swift).
[3] Henry Somerset, second Duke of Beaufort. In September 1711 the Duke —who was then only twenty-seven—married, as his third wife, Mary, youngest daughter of the Duke of Leeds. In the following January Lady Strafford wrote, "The Duke and Duchess of Beaufort are the fondest of one another in the world ; I fear 'tis too hot to hold. . . . I own I fancy people may love one another as well without making so great a rout" (*Wentworth Papers*, 256). The Duke died in 1714, at the age of thirty.

25

to-day, with mixed company; I don't love it. Our Society does not meet till Friday, because Thursday will be a busy day in the House of Commons, for then the Duke of Marlborough's bribery is to be examined into about the pension paid him by those that furnished bread to the army.

21. I have been five times with the Duke of Ormond about a perfect trifle, and he forgets it: I used him like a dog this morning for it. I was asked to-day by several in the Court of Requests whether it was true that the author of the *Examiner* was taken up in an action of twenty thousand pounds by the Duke of Marlborough?[1] I dined in the City, where my printer showed me a pamphlet, called *Advice to the October Club*, which he said was sent him by an unknown hand: I commended it mightily; he never suspected me; 'tis a twopenny pamphlet. I came home and got timely to bed; but about eleven one of the Secretary's servants came to me to let me know that Lord Treasurer would immediately speak to me at Lord Masham's upon earnest business, and that, if I was abed, I should rise and come. I did so: Lord Treasurer was above with the Queen; and when he came down he laughed, and said it was not he that sent for me: the business was of no great importance, only to give me a paper, which might have been done to-morrow. I stayed with them till past one, and then got to bed again. Pize[2] take their frolics. I thought to have answered your letter.

22. Dr. Gastrell was to see me this morning: he is an eminent divine, one of the canons of Christ Church, and one I love very well: he said he was glad to find I was not with James Broad. I asked what he meant. "Why," says he, "have you not seen the Grub Street paper, that says Dr. Swift was taken up as author of the *Examiner*, on 'an action of twenty thousand pounds, and was now at James Broad's?" who, I suppose, is some bailiff. I knew of this; but at the

---

[1] "Upon the 10th and 17th of this month the *Examiner* was very severe upon the Duke of Marlborough, and in consequence of this report pursued him with greater virulence in the following course of his papers" (Deane Swift).
[2] A term of execration. Scott (*Kenilworth*) has, "A pize on it."

Court of Requests twenty people told me they heard I had been taken up. Lord Lansdowne observed to the Secretary and me that the Whigs spread three lies yesterday; that about me; and another, that Maccartney, who was turned out last summer,[1] is again restored to his places in the army; and the third, that Jack Hill's commission for Lieutenant of the Tower is stopped, and that Cadogan is to continue. Lansdowne thinks they have some design by these reports; I cannot guess it. Did I tell you that Sacheverell has desired mightily to come and see me? but I have put it off: he has heard that I have spoken to the Secretary in behalf of a brother whom he maintains, and who desires an employment.[2] T'other day at the Court of Requests Dr. Yalden [3] saluted me by name: Sacheverell, who was just by, came up to me, and made me many acknowledgment and compliments. Last night I desired Lord Treasurer to do something for that brother of Sacheverell's: he said he never knew he had a brother, but thanked me for telling him, and immediately put his name in his table-book.[4] I will let Sacheverell know this, that he may take his measures accordingly, but he shall be none of my acquaintance. I dined to-day privately with the Secretary, left him at six, paid a visit or two, and came home.

23. I dined again to-day with the Secretary, but could not despatch some business I had with him, he has so much besides upon his hands at this juncture, and preparing against the great business to-morrow, which we are top full of. The Minister's design is that the Duke of Marlborough shall be censured as gently as possible, provided his friends will not make head to defend him, but if they do, it may end in some

---

[1] See p. 89.

[2] In a letter to Swift of Jan. 31, 1712, Sacheverell, after expressing his indebtedness to St. John and Harley, said, "For yourself, good Doctor, who was the first spring to move it, I can never sufficiently acknowledge the obligation," and in a postscript he hinted that a place in the Custom House which he heard was vacant might suit his brother.

[3] Thomas Yalden, D.D., (1671-1736), Addison's college friend, succeeded Atterbury as preacher of Bridewell Hospital in 1713. In 1723 he was arrested on suspicion of being involved in the Atterbury plot.

[4] Tablets.

severer votes. A gentleman, who was just now with him, tells me he is much cast down, and fallen away; but he is positive, if he has but ten friends in the House, that they shall defend him to the utmost, and endeavour to prevent the least censure upon him, which I think cannot be, since the bribery is manifest. Sir Solomon Medina [1] paid him six ' thousand pounds a year to have the employment of providing bread for the army, and the Duke owns it in his letter to the Commissioners of Accounts. I was to-night at Lord Masham's: Lord Dupplin took out my new little pamphlet, and the Secretary read a great deal of it to Lord Treasurer: they all commended it to the skies, and so did I, and they began a health to the author. But I doubt Lord Treasurer suspected; for he said, "This is Mr. Davenant's style," which is his cant when he suspects me.[2] But I carried the matter very well. Lord Treasurer put the pamphlet in his pocket to read at home. I'll answer your letter to-morrow.

24. The Secretary made me promise to dine with him to-day, after the Parliament was up: I said I would come; but I dined at my usual time, knowing the House would sit late on this great affair. I dined at a tavern with Mr. Domville and another gentleman; I have not done so before these many months. At ten this evening I went to the Secretary, but he was not come home: I sat with his lady till twelve, then came away; and he just came as I was gone, and he sent to my lodgings, but I would not go back; and so I know not how things have passed, but hope all is well; and I will tell you to-morrow day. It is late, etc.

25. The Secretary sent to me this morning to know whether we should dine together. I went to him, and there I learned that the question went against the Duke of Marlborough, by a majority of a hundred; so the Ministry is mighty well satisfied, and the Duke will now be able to do

---

[1] Sir Solomon de Medina, a Jew, was knighted in 1700.
[2] Davenant had been said to be the writer of papers which Swift contributed to the *Examiner*.

no hurt. The Secretary and I, and Lord Masham, etc., dined with Lieutenant-General Withers,[1] who is just going to look after the army in Flanders: the Secretary and I left them a little after seven, and I am come home, and will now answer your letter, because this goes to-morrow: let me see —The box at Chester; oh, burn that box, and hang that Sterne; I have desired one to inquire for it who went toward Ireland last Monday, but I am in utter despair of it. No, I was not splenetic; you see what plunges the Court has been at to set all right again. And that Duchess is not out yet, and may one day cause more mischief. Somerset shows all about a letter from the Queen, desiring him to let his wife continue with her. Is not that rare! I find Dingley smelled a rat; because the Whigs are *upish*; but if ever I hear that word again, I'll *uppish* you. I am glad you got your rasp safe and sound; does Stella like her apron? Your critics about guarantees of succession are puppies; that's an answer to the objection. The answerers here made the same objection, but it is wholly wrong. I am of your opinion that Lord Marlborough is used too hardly: I have often scratched out passages from papers and pamphlets sent me, before they were printed, because I thought them too severe. But he is certainly a vile man, and has no sort of merit beside the military. The *Examiners* are good for little: I would fain have hindered the severity of the two or three last, but could not. I will either bring your papers over, or leave them with Tooke, for whose honesty I will engage. And I think it is best not to venture them with me at sea. Stella is a prophet, by foretelling so very positively that all would be well. Duke of Ormond speak against peace? No, simpleton, he is one of the staunchest we have for the Ministry. Neither trouble yourself about the printer: he appeared the first day of the term, and is to appear when summoned again; but nothing else will come of it. Lord Chief-Justice [2] is

---

[1] Henry Withers, a friend of "Duke" Disney (see p. 153), was appointed Lieutenant-General in 1707, and Major-General in 1712. On his death in 1729 he was buried in Westminster Abbey. [2] See p. 360.

cooled since this new settlement. No; I will not split my journals in half; I will write but once a fortnight: but you may do as you will; which is, read only half at once, and t'other half next week. So now your letter is answered. (P—— on these blots.) What must I say more? I will set out in March, if there be a fit of fine weather; unless the Ministry desire me to stay till the end of the session, which may be a month longer; but I believe they will not: for I suppose the peace will be made, and they will have no further service for me. I must make my canal fine this summer, as fine as I can. I am afraid I shall see great neglects among my quicksets. I hope the cherry-trees on the river walk are fine things now. But no more of this.

26. I forgot to finish this letter this morning, and am come home so late I must give it to the bellman; but I would have it go to-night, lest you should think there is anything in the story of my being arrested in an action of twenty thousand pounds by Lord Marlborough, which I hear is in Dyer's *Letter*,[1] and, consequently, I suppose, gone to Ireland. Farewell, dearest MD, etc. etc.

LETTER XL

LONDON, *Jan.* 26, 1711-12.

I HAVE no gilt paper left of this size, so you must be content with plain. Our Society dined together to-day, for it was put off, as I told you, upon Lord Marlborough's business on Thursday. The Duke of Ormond dined with us to-day, the first time: we were thirteen at table; and Lord Lansdowne came in after dinner, so that we wanted but three. The Secretary proposed the Duke of Beaufort, who

---

[1] Dyer's *News Letter*, the favourite reading of Sir Roger de Coverley (*Spectator*, No. 127), was the work of John Dyer, a Jacobite journalist. In the *Tatler* (No. 18) Addison says that Dyer was "justly looked upon by all the fox-hunters in the nation as the greatest statesman our country has produced." Lord Chief-Justice Holt referred to the *News Letter* as "a little scandalous paper of a scandalous author" (Howell's *State Trials*, xiv. 1150).

desires to be one of our Society; but I stopped it, because the Duke of Ormond doubts a little about it; and he was gone before it was proposed. I left them at seven, and sat this evening with poor Mrs. Wesley, who has been mightily ill to-day with a fainting fit; she has often convulsions, too: she takes a mixture with asafœtida, which I have now in my nose, and everything smells of it. I never smelt it before; 'tis abominable. We have eight packets, they say, due from Ireland.

27. I could not see Prince Eugene at Court to-day, the crowd was so great. The Whigs contrive to have a crowd always about him, and employ the rabble to give the word, when he sets out from any place. When the Duchess of Hamilton came from the Queen after church, she whispered me that she was going to pay me a visit. I went to Lady Oglethorpe's, the place appointed; for ladies always visit me in third places; and she kept me till near four: she talks too much, is a plaguy detractor, and I believe I shall not much like her. I was engaged to dine with Lord Masham: they stayed as long as they could, yet had almost dined, and were going in anger to pull down the brass peg for my hat, but Lady Masham saved it. At eight I went again to Lord Masham's; Lord Treasurer is generally there at night: we sat up till almost two. Lord Treasurer has engaged me to contrive some way to keep the Archbishop of York[1] from being seduced by Lord Nottingham. I will do what I can in it to-morrow. 'Tis very late, so I must go sleep.

28. Poor Mrs. Manley, the author, is very ill of a dropsy and sore leg: the printer tells me he is afraid she cannot live long. I am heartily sorry for her: she has very generous principles for one of her sort, and a great deal of good sense and invention: she is about forty, very homely, and very fat. Mrs. Van made me dine with her to-day. I was this

---

[1] Dr. John Sharp, made Archbishop of York in 1691, was called by Swift "the harmless tool of others' hate." Swift believed that Sharp, owing to his dislike of *The Tale of a Tub*, assisted in preventing the bishopric of Hereford being offered to him. Sharp was an excellent preacher, with a taste for both poetry and science.

morning with the Duke of Ormond and the Prolocutor about what Lord Treasurer spoke to me yesterday; I know not what will be the issue. There is but a slender majority in the House of Lords, and we want more. We are sadly mortified at the news of the French taking the town in Brazil from the Portuguese. The sixth edition of three thousand of the *Conduct of the Allies* is sold, and the printer talks of a seventh: eleven thousand of them have been sold, which is a most prodigious run. The little twopenny *Letter of Advice to the October Club* does not sell: I know not the reason, for it is finely written, I assure you; and, like a true author, I grow fond of it, because it does not sell: you know that it is usual to writers to condemn the judgment of the world: if I had hinted it to be mine, everybody would have bought it, but it is a great secret.

29. I borrowed one or two idle books of *Contes des Fées*,[1] and have been reading them these two days, although I have much business upon my hands. I loitered till one at home; then went to Mr. Lewis at his office; and the Vice-Chamberlain told me that Lady Rialton[2] had yesterday resigned her employment of lady of the bed-chamber, and that Lady Jane Hyde,[3] Lord Rochester's daughter, a mighty pretty girl, is to succeed. He said, too, that Lady Sunderland would resign in a day or two. I dined with Lewis, and then went to see Mrs. Wesley, who is better to-day. But you must know that Mr. Lewis gave me two letters, one from the Bishop of Cloyne, with an enclosed from Lord Inchiquin[4] to Lord Treasurer, which he desires I would deliver and recommend. I am told that lord was much in with Lord Wharton, and I remember he was to have been one of the Lords Justices by

---

[1] An edition of the Countess d'Aulnoy's *Les Contes des Fées* appeared in 1710, in four volumes.

[2] Francis Godolphin, Viscount Rialton, the eldest son of Sidney, Earl of Godolphin, succeeded his father as second Earl on Sept. 15, 1712. He held various offices, including that of Lord Privy Seal (1735-1740), and died in 1766, aged eighty-eight. He married, in 1698, Lady Henrietta Churchill, who afterwards was Duchess of Marlborough in her own right. She died in 1733.

[3] See p. 256. Ladies of the bed-chamber received £1000 a year.

[4] William O'Brien, third Earl of Inchiquin, succeeded his father in 1691, and died in 1719.

his recommendation; yet the Bishop recommends him as a great friend to the Church, etc. I'll do what I think proper. T'other letter was from little saucy MD, N. 26. O Lord, never saw the like, under a cover, too, and by way of journal; we shall never have done. Sirrahs, how durst you write so soon, sirrahs? I won't answer it yet.

30. I was this morning with the Secretary, who was sick, and out of humour: he would needs drink champagne some days ago, on purpose to spite me, because I advised him against it, and now he pays for it. Stella used to do such tricks formerly; he put me in mind of her. Lady Sunderland has resigned her place too. It is Lady Catherine Hyde [1] that succeeds Lady Rialton, and not Lady Jane. Lady Catherine is the late Earl of Rochester's daughter. I dined with the Secretary, then visited his lady; and sat this evening with Lady Masham: the Secretary came to us; but Lord Treasurer did not; he dined with the Master of the Rolls, [2] and stayed late with him. Our Society does not meet till to-morrow se'nnight, because we think the Parliament will be very busy to-morrow upon the state of the war, and the Secretary, who is to treat as President, must be in the House. I fancy my talking of persons and things here must be very tedious to you, because you know nothing of them, and I talk as if you did. You know Kevin's Street, and Werburgh Street, and (what do you call the street where Mrs. Walls lives?) and Ingoldsby, [3] and Higgins, [4] and Lord Santry; [5] but what care you for Lady Catherine Hyde? Why do you say nothing of your health, sirrah? I hope it is well.

31. Trimnel, Bishop of Norwich, [6] who was with this Lord

---

[1] Lady Catherine Hyde was an unmarried daughter of Laurence Hyde, first Earl of Rochester (see p. 60). Notwithstanding Swift's express statement that the lady to whom he here refers was the late Earl's daughter, and the allusion to her sister, Lady Dalkeith, on p. 514, she has been confused by previous editors with her niece, Lady Catherine Hyde (see p. 256), daughter of the second Earl, and afterwards Duchess of Queensberry. That lady, not long afterwards to be celebrated by Prior, was a child under twelve when Swift wrote.

[2] Sir John Trevor (1637-1717), formerly Speaker of the House of Commons.
[3] See p. 97.   [4] See p. 335.   [5] See p. 215.
[6] Charles Trimnel, made Bishop of Norwich in 1708, and Bishop of Winchester in 1721, was strongly opposed to High Church doctrines.

Sunderland at Moor Park in their travels, preached yesterday before the House of Lords; and to-day the question was put to thank him, and print his sermon; but passed against him; for it was a terrible Whig sermon. The Bill to repeal the Act for naturalising Protestant foreigners passed the House of Lords to-day by a majority of twenty, though the Scotch lords went out, and would vote neither way, in discontent about the Duke of Hamilton's patent, if you know anything of it. A poem is come out to-day inscribed to me, by way of a flirt;[1] for it is a Whiggish poem, and good for nothing. They plagued me with it in the Court of Requests. I dined with Lord Treasurer at five alone, only with one Dutchman. Prior is now a Commissioner of the Customs. I told you so before, I suppose. When I came home to-night, I found a letter from Dr. Sacheverell, thanking me for recommending his brother to Lord Treasurer and Mr. Secretary for a place. Lord Treasurer sent to him about it: so good a solicitor was I, although I once hardly thought I should be a solicitor for Sacheverell.

Feb. 1. Has not your Dean of St. Patrick received my letter? you say nothing of it, although I writ above a month ago. My printer has got the gout, and I was forced to go to him to-day, and there I dined. It was a most delicious day: why don't you observe whether the same days be fine with you? To-night, at six, Dr. Atterbury, and Prior, and I, and Dr. Freind, met at Dr. Robert Freind's[2] house at Westminster, who is master of the school: there we sat till one, and were good enough company. I here take leave to tell politic Dingley that the passage in the *Conduct of the Allies* is so far from being blamable that the Secretary designs to insist upon it in the House of Commons, when the Treaty of Barrier[3] is debated there, as it now shortly will, for they have ordered it to be laid before them. The pamphlet of *Advice to the October Club* begins now to sell; but I believe its fame will hardly reach Ireland: 'tis finely written, I assure you. I long to answer your letter, but won't yet; you know, 'tis late, etc.

---

[1] Jibe or jest.　　　　　　　　　[2] See p. 206.
[3] The treaty concluded with Holland in 1711.

2. This ends Christmas,[1] and what care I ? I have neither seen, nor felt, nor heard any Christmas this year. I passed a lazy dull day. I was this morning with Lord Treasurer, to get some papers from him, which he will remember as much as a cat, although it be his own business. It threatened rain, but did not much; and Prior and I walked an hour in the Park, which quite put me out of my measures. I dined with a friend hard by; and in the evening sat with Lord Masham till twelve. Lord Treasurer did not come; this is an idle dining-day usually with him. We want to hear from Holland how our peace goes on; for we are afraid of those scoundrels the Dutch, lest they should play us tricks. Lord Mar,[2] a Scotch earl, was with us at Lord Masham's: I was arguing with him about the stubbornness and folly of his countrymen; they are so angry about the affair of the Duke of Hamilton, whom the Queen has made a duke of England, and the House of Lords will not admit him. He swears he would vote for us, but dare not, because all Scotland would detest him if he did : he should never be chosen again, nor be able to live there.

3. I was at Court to-day to look for a dinner, but did not like any that were offered me; and I dined with Lord Mountjoy. The Queen has the gout in her knee, and was not at chapel. I hear we have a Dutch mail, but I know not what news, although I was with the Secretary this morning. He showed me a letter from the Hanover Envoy, Mr. Bothmar, complaining that the Barrier Treaty is laid before the House of Commons; and desiring that no infringement may be made in the guarantee of the succession; but the Secretary has written him a peppering answer. I fancy you understand all this, and are able states-girls, since you have read the *Conduct of the Allies*. We are all preparing against the Birthday; I think it is Wednesday next. If the Queen's gout increases, it will spoil sport. Prince Eugene has two fine suits made against it; and the Queen is to give him a sword worth four thousand pounds, the diamonds set transparent.

---

[1] Feb. 2 is the Purification of the Virgin Mary.   [2] See p. 284.

4. I was this morning soliciting at the House of Commons' door for Mr. Vesey, a son of the Archbishop of Tuam,[1] who has petitioned for a Bill to relieve him in some difficulty about his estate : I secured him above fifty members. I dined with Lady Masham. We have no packet from Holland, as I was told yesterday : and this wind will hinder many people from appearing at the Birthday, who expected clothes from Holland. I appointed to meet a gentleman at the Secretary's to-night, and they both failed. The House of Commons have this day made many severe votes about our being abused by our Allies. Those who spoke drew all their arguments from my book, and their votes confirm all I writ; the Court had a majority of a hundred and fifty : all agree that it was my book that spirited them to these resolutions; I long to see them in print. My head has not been as well as I could wish it for some days past, but I have not had any giddy fit, and I hope it will go over.

5. The Secretary turned me out of his room this morning, and showed me fifty guineas rolled up, which he was going to give some French spy. I dined with four Irishmen at a tavern to-day : I thought I had resolved against it before, but I broke it. I played at cards this evening at Lady Masham's, but I only played for her while she was waiting; and I won her a pool, and supped there. Lord Treasurer was with us, but went away before twelve. The ladies and lords have all their clothes ready against to-morrow : I saw several mighty fine, and I hope there will be a great appearance, in spite of that spiteful French fashion of the Whiggish ladies not to come, which they have all resolved to a woman; and I hope it will more spirit the Queen against them for ever.

6. I went to dine at Lord Masham's at three, and met all the company just coming out of Court; a mighty crowd : they stayed long for their coaches : I had an opportunity of seeing several lords and ladies of my acquaintance in their

[1] See p. 99.

fineries. Lady Ashburnham [1] looked the best in my eyes. They say the Court was never fuller nor finer. Lord Treasurer, his lady, and two daughters and Mrs. Hill, dined with Lord and Lady Masham; the five ladies were monstrous fine. The Queen gave Prince Eugene the diamond sword to-day; but nobody was by when she gave it except my Lord Chamberlain. There was an entertainment of opera songs at night, and the Queen was at all the entertainment, and is very well after it. I saw Lady Wharton,[2] as ugly as the devil, coming out in the crowd all in an undress; she has been with the Marlborough daughters[3] and Lady Bridgewater[4] in St. James's, looking out of the window all undressed to see the sight. I do not hear that one Whig lady was there, except those of the bed-chamber. Nothing has made so great a noise as one Kelson's chariot, that cost nine hundred and thirty pounds, the finest was ever seen. The rabble huzzaed him as much as they did Prince Eugene. This is Birthday chat.

7. Our Society met to-day: the Duke of Ormond was not with us; we have lessened our dinners, which were grown so extravagant that Lord Treasurer and everybody else cried shame. I left them at seven, visited for an hour, and then came home, like a good boy. The Queen is much better after yesterday's exercise: her friends wish she would use a little more. I opposed Lord Jersey's[5] election into our Society, and he is refused: I likewise opposed the Duke of Beaufort; but I believe he will be chosen in spite of me: I don't much care; I shall not be with them above two months; for I resolve to set out for Ireland the beginning of April next (before I treat them again), and see my willows.

8. I dined to-day in the City. This morning a scoundrel

---

[1] Lady Mary Butler (see pp. 14, 44), daughter of the Duke of Ormond, who married, in 1710, John, third Lord Ashburnham, afterwards Earl of Ashburnham.
[2] See p. 4.   [3] See p. 357.
[4] Scroop Egerton, fifth Earl and first Duke of Bridgewater, married, in 1703, Lady Elizabeth Churchill, third daughter of the Duke of Marlborough. She died in 1714, aged twenty-six.
[5] See p. 294.

dog, one of the Queen's music, a German, whom I had never seen, got access to me in my chamber by Patrick's folly, and gravely desired me to get an employment in the Customs for a friend of his, who would be very grateful ; and likewise to forward a project of his own, for raising ten thousand pounds a year upon operas : I used him civiller than he deserved ; but it vexed me to the pluck.[1] He was told I had a mighty interest with Lord Treasurer, and one word of mine, etc.— Well ; I got home early on purpose to answer MD's letter, N. 26 ; for this goes to-morrow.—Well ; I never saw such a letter in all my life ; so saucy, so journalish, so sanguine, so pretending, so everything. I satisfied all your fears in my last : all is gone well, as you say ; yet you are an impudent slut to be so positive ; you will swagger so upon your sagacity that we shall never have done. Pray don't mislay your reply ; I would certainly print it, if I had it here : how long is it ? I suppose half a sheet : was the answer written in Ireland ? Yes, yes, you shall have a letter when you come from Ballygall. I need not tell 'you again who's out and who's in : we can never get out the Duchess of Somerset.—So, they say Presto writ the *Conduct*, etc. Do they like it ? I don't care whether they do or no ; but the resolutions printed t'other day in the Votes are almost quotations from it, and would never have passed if that book had not been written. I will not meddle with the Spectator, let him fair-sex it to the world's end. My disorder is over, but blood was not from the p——les.—Well, Madam Dingley, the frost ; why, we had a great frost, but I forget how long ago ; it lasted above a week or ten days : I believe about six weeks ago ; but it did not break so soon with us, I think, as December 29 ; yet I think it was about that time, on second thoughts. MD can have no letter from Presto, says you ; and yet four days before you own you had my thirty-seventh, unreasonable sluts ! The Bishop of Gloucester is not dead,[2] and I am as likely to succeed the Duke of Marlborough as him if he were ; there's

[1] Heart.
[2] Edward Fowler, D.D., appointed Bishop of Gloucester in 1691, died in 1714.

enough for that now. It is not unlikely that the Duke of Shrewsbury will be your Governor; at least I believe the Duke of Ormond will not return.—Well, Stella again: why, really three editions of the *Conduct*, etc., is very much for Ireland; it is a sign you have some honest among you. Well; I will do Mr. Manley [1] all the service I can; but he will ruin himself. What business had he to engage at all about the City? Can't he wish his cause well, and be quiet, when he finds that stirring will do it no good, and himself a great deal of hurt? I cannot imagine who should open my letter: it must be done at your side.—If I hear of any thoughts of turning out Mr. Manley, I will endeavour to prevent it. I have already had all the gentlemen of Ireland here upon my back often, for defending him. So now I have answered your saucy letter. My humble service to Goody Stoyte and Catherine; I will come soon for my dinner.

9. Morning. My cold goes off at last; but I think I have got a small new one. I have no news since last. They say we hear by the way of Calais, that peace is very near concluding. I hope it may be true. I'll go and seal up my letter, and give it myself to-night into the post-office; and so I bid my dearest MD farewell till to-night. I heartily wish myself with them, as hope saved. My willows, and quicksets, and trees, will be finely improved, I hope, this year. It has been fine hard frosty weather yesterday and to-day. Farewell, etc. etc. etc.

LETTER XLI [2]

LONDON, Feb. 9, 1711-12.

WHEN my letter is gone, and I have none of yours to answer, my conscience is so clear, and my shoulder so light, and I go on with such courage to prate upon nothing

---

[1] Isaac Manley (see p. 7).

[2] This letter, the first of the series published by Hawkesworth, of which we have the originals (see Preface), was addressed "To Mrs. Johnson at her Lodgings over against St. Mary's Church, near Capell Street, Dublin, Ireland"; and was endorsed by her "Recd. Mar. 1st."

to deerichar MD, oo would wonder.   I dined with Sir
Matthew Dudley, who is newly turned out of Commission of
the Customs.   He affects a good heart, and talks in the ex-
tremity of Whiggery, which was always his principle, though
he was gentle a little, while he kept in employment.   We
can yet get no packets from Holland.   I have not been
with any of the Ministry these two or three days.   I keep
out of their way on purpose, for a certain reason, for some
time, though I must dine with the Secretary to-morrow, the
choosing of the company being left to me.   I have engaged
Lord Anglesea [1] and Lord Carteret,[2] and have promised to
get three more ; but I have a mind that none else should
be admitted : however, if I like anybody at Court to-morrow,
I may perhaps invite them.   I have got another cold, but not
very bad.   Nite . . . MD.

10. I saw Prince Eugene at Court to-day very plain ; he's
plaguy yellow, and tolerably ugly besides.   The Court was
very full, and people had their Birthday clothes.   I dined with
the Secretary to-day.   I was to invite five, but I only invited
two, Lord Anglesea and Lord Carteret.   Pshaw, I told you
this but yesterday.   We have no packets from Holland yet.
Here are a parcel of drunken Whiggish lords, like your Lord
Santry,[3] who come into chocolate-houses and rail aloud at
the Tories, and have challenges sent them, and the next
morning come and beg pardon.   General Ross [4] was like to
swinge the Marquis of Winchester [5] for this trick t'other
day ; and we have nothing else now to talk of till the Parliament has had another bout with the state of the war,
as they intended in a few days.   They have ordered the
Barrier Treaty to be laid before them ; and it was talked
some time ago, as if there was a design to impeach Lord

---

[1] See p. 85.   [2] See p. 116.   [3] See p. 215.
[4] Charles Ross, son of the eleventh Baron Ross, was Colonel of the Royal
Irish Dragoons from 1695 to 1705.   He was a Lieutenant-General under the
Duke of Ormond in Flanders, and died in 1732 (Dalton, ii. 212, iii. 34).
[5] Charles Paulet, Marquis of Winchester, succeeded his father (see p. 302) as
third Duke of Bolton in 1722.   He married, as his second wife, Lavinia Fenton,
the actress who took the part of Polly Peacham in Gay's *Beggar's Opera* in
1728, and he died in 1754.

Townshend, who made it. I have no more politics now. Nite dee MD.

11. I dined with Lord Anglesea to-day, who had seven Irishmen to be my companions, of which two only were coxcombs ; one I did not know, and t'other was young Blith,[1] who is a puppy of figure here, with a fine chariot. He asked me one day at Court, when I had been just talking with some lords who stood near me, " Doctor, when shall we see you in the county of Meath ? " I whispered him to take care what he said, for the people would think he was some barbarian. He never would speak to me since, till we met to-day. I went to Lady Masham's to-night, and sat with Lord Treasurer and the Secretary there till past two o'clock ; and when I came home, found some letters from Ireland, which I read, but can say nothing of them till to-morrow, 'tis so very late ; but I[2] must always be . . . ,[3] late or early. Nite deelest sollahs.[4]

12. One letter was from the Bishop of Clogher last night, and t'other from Walls, about Mrs. South's[5] salary, and his own pension of £18 for his tithe of the park. I will do nothing in either ; the first I cannot serve in, and the other is a trifle ; only you may tell him I had his letter, and will speak to Ned Southwell about what he desires me. You say nothing of your Dean's receiving my letter. I find Clements,[6] whom I recommended to Lord Anglesea last year, at Walls's desire, or rather the Bishop of Clogher's, is mightily in Lord Anglesea's favour. You may tell the Bishop and Walls so ; I said to Lord Anglesea that I was [glad] I had the good luck to recommend him, etc. I dined in the City with my printer, to consult with him about some papers Lord Treasurer gave

[1] John Blith, or Bligh, son of the Right Hon. Thomas Bligh, M.P. of Rathmore, Co. Meath (see p. 22). In August 1713 he married Lady Theodosia Hyde, daughter of Edward, third Earl of Clarendon. Lord Berkeley of Stratton wrote, "Lady Theodosia Hyde . . . is married to an Irish Mr. Blythe, of a good estate, who will soon have enough of her, if I can give any guess" (*Wentworth Papers*, 353). In 1715 Bligh was made Baron Clifton, of Rathmore, and Earl of Darnley in 1725. He died in 1728.
[2] Obliterated.
[3] Word obliterated ; probably "found." Forster reads "oors, dee MD."
[4] Words obliterated.   [5] See pp. 86, 301.   [6] See pp. 73, 192-3.

me last night, as he always does, too late; however, I will
do something with them. My third cold is a little better;
I never had anything like it before, three colds successively;
I hope I shall have the fourth.[1] Those messengers come from
Holland to-day, and they brought over the six packets that
were due. I know not the particulars yet, for when I was with
the Secretary at noon they were just opening; but one thing
I find, that the Dutch are playing us tricks, and tampering with the French; they are dogs; I shall know more
tomollow . . . MD.[2]

13. I dined to-day privately with my friend Lewis, at his
lodgings, to consult about some observations on the Barrier
Treaty. Our news from Holland is not good. The French
raise difficulties, and make such offers to the Allies as cannot
be accepted. And the Dutch are uneasy that we are likely
to get anything for ourselves; and the Whigs are glad at all
this. I came home early, and have been very busy three
or four hours. I had a letter from Dr. Pratt[3] to-day by a
private hand, recommending the bearer to me, for something
that I shall not trouble myself about. Wesley[4] writ to recommend the same fellow to me. His expression is that,
hearing I am acquainted with my Lord Treasurer, he desires
I would do so and so: a matter of nothing. What puppies
are mankind! I hope I shall be wiser when I have once done
with Courts. I think you han't troubled me much with your
recommendations. I would do you all the saavis[5] I could.
Pray have you got your aplon,[6] maram Ppt? I paid for
it but yesterday; that puts me in mind of it. I writ an
inventory of what things I sent by Leigh in one of my letters;
did you compare it with what you got? I hear nothing of
your cards now; do you never play? Yes, at Ballygall. Go
to bed. Nite, deelest MD.[7]

---

[1] Words obliterated. Forster reads "fourth. Euge, euge, euge."
[2] Words obliterated; one illegible.
[3] See p. 5.   [4] See p. 2.   [5] Service.
[6] "Aplon"—if this is the right word—means, of course, apron—the apron
referred to on p. 389.
[7] Words obliterated.

14. Our Society dined to-day at Mr. Secretary's house. I went there at four; but hearing the House of Commons would sit late upon the Barrier Treaty, I went for an hour to Kensington, to see Lord Masham's children. My young nephew,[1] his son of six months old, has got a swelling in his neck; I fear it is the evil. We did not go to dinner till eight at night, and I left them at ten. The Commons have been very severe on the Barrier Treaty, as you will find by their votes. A Whig member took out the *Conduct of the Allies*, and read that passage about the succession with great resentment; but none seconded him. The Church party carried every vote by a great majority. The A. B.[2] Dublin is so railed at by all who come from Ireland that I can defend him no longer. Lord Anglesea assured me that the story of applying Piso out of Tacitus[3] to Lord Treasurer's being wounded is true. I believe the Duke of Beaufort will be admitted to our Society next meeting. To-day I published the *Fable of Midas*,[4] a poem, printed in a loose half-sheet of paper. I know not how it will sell; but it passed wonderfully at our Society to-night; and Mr. Secretary read it before me the other night to Lord Treasurer, at Lord Masham's, where they equally approved of it. Tell me how it passes with you. I think this paper is larger than ordinary; for here is six days' journal, and no nearer the bottom. I fear these journals are very dull. Nite my deelest lives.

15. Mr. Lewis and I dined by invitation with a Scotch acquaintance, after I had been very busy in my chamber till two afternoon. My third cold is now very troublesome on my breast, especially in the morning. This is a great revolution in my health; colds never used to return so soon with me, or last so long. 'Tis very surprising this news

---

[1] As the son of a "brother" of the Club.
[2] The Archbishop, Dr. King.
[3] See Tacitus, *Annals*, book ii. Cn. Calpurnius Piso, who was said to have poisoned Germanicus, was found with his throat cut.
[4] This satire on Marlborough concludes—

> "And Midas now neglected stands,
> With asses' ears and dirty hands."

to-day of the Dauphin and Dauphiness both dying within
six days. They say the old King is almost heart-broke. He
has had prodigious mortifications in his family. The Dauphin
has left two little sons, of four and two years old; the eldest
is sick. There is a foolish story got about the town that
Lord Strafford, one of our Plenipotentiaries, is in the interests
of France; and it has been a good while said that Lord
Privy Seal [1] and he do not agree very well. They are both
long practised in business, but neither of them of much parts.
Strafford has some life and spirit, but is infinitely proud, and
wholly illiterate. Nite, MD.

16. I dined to-day in the City with my printer, to finish
something I am doing about the Barrier Treaty; [2] but it is not
quite done. I went this evening to Lord Masham's, where
Lord Treasurer sat with us till past twelve. The Lords have
voted an Address to the Queen, to tell her they are not
satisfied with the King of France's offers. The Whigs
brought it in of a sudden; and the Court could not prevent
it, and therefore did not oppose it. The House of Lords is
too strong in Whigs, notwithstanding the new creations; for
they are very diligent, and the Tories as lazy: the side that
is down has always most industry. The Whigs intended to
have made a vote that would reflect on Lord Treasurer; but
their project was not ripe. I hit my face such a rap by
calling the coach to stop to-night, that it is plaguy sore, the
bone beneath the eye. Nite dee logues.

17. The Court was mighty full to-day, and has been these
many Sundays; but the Queen was not at chapel. She has
got a little fit of the gout in her foot. The good of going to
Court is that one sees all one's acquaintance, whom otherwise
I should hardly meet twice a year. Prince Eugene dines
with the Secretary to-day, with about seven or eight General
Officers, or foreign Ministers. They will be all drunk, I am
sure. I never was in company with this Prince: I have
proposed to some lords that we should have a sober meal

---

[1] Dr. Robinson, Bishop of Bristol.
[2] *Some Remarks on the Barrier Treaty.*

with him; but I can't compass it. It is come over in the Dutch news prints that I was arrested on an action of twenty thousand pounds by the Duke of Marlborough. I did not like my Court invitation to-day; so Sir Andrew Fountaine and I went and dined with Mrs. Van. I came home at six, and have been very busy till this minute, and it is past twelve. So I got into bed to write to MD . . .MD.[1] We reckon the Dauphin's death will put forward the peace a good deal. Pray is Dr. Griffith[2] reconciled to me yet? Have I done enough to soften him? . . .[3] Nite deelest logues.

18. Lewis had Guiscard's picture: he bought it, and offered it to Lord Treasurer, who promised to send for it, but never did; so I made Lewis give it me, and I have it in my room; and now Lord Treasurer says he will take it from me: is that fair? He designs to have it at length in the clothes he was when he did the action, and a penknife in his hand; and Kneller is to copy it from this that I have. I intended to dine with Lord Treasurer to-day, but he has put me off till to-morrow; so I dined with Lord Dupplin. You know Lord Dupplin very well; he is a brother of the Society. Well, but I have received a letter from the Bishop of Cloyne, to solicit an affair for him with Lord Treasurer, and with the Parliament, which I will do as soon as fly. I am not near so keen about other people's affairs as . . .[4] Ppt used to reproach me about; it was a judgment on me. Harkee, idle dearees both, meetinks I begin to want a rettle flom[5] MD: faith, and so I do. I doubt you have been in pain about the report of my being arrested. The pamphleteers have let me alone this month, which is a great wonder: only the third part of the *Answer to the Conduct*, which is lately come out. (Did I tell you of it already?) The House of Commons

---

[1] Several words are obliterated. Forster reads "MD MD, for we must always write to MD MD MD, awake or asleep;" but the passage is illegible.
[2] See pp. 95, 517-8.
[3] A long erasure. Forster reads "Go to bed. Help pdfr. Rove pdfr. MD MD. Nite darling rogues."
[4] Word obliterated. Forster reads "saucy."
[5] Letter from.

goes on in mauling the late Ministry and their proceedings. Nite deelest MD.[1]

19. I dined with Lord Treasurer to-day, and sat with him till ten, in spite of my teeth, though my printer waited for me to correct a sheet. I told him of four lines I writ extempore with my pencil, on a bit of paper in his house, while he lay wounded. Some of the servants, I suppose, made waste-paper of them, and he never had heard of them. Shall I tell them you? They were inscribed to Mr. Harley's physician. Thus—

> On Britain Europe's safety lies;[2]
> Britain is lost, if Harley dies.
> Harley depends upon your skill:
> Think what you save, or what you kill.

Are not they well enough to be done off-hand; for that is the meaning of the word extempore, which you did not know, did you? I proposed that some company should dine with him on the 8th of March, which was the day he was wounded, but he says he designs that the Lords of the Cabinet, who then sat with him, should dine that day with him:[3] however, he has invited me too. I am not got rid of my cold; it plagues me in the morning chiefly. Nite, MD.

20. After waiting to catch the Secretary coming out from Sir Thomas Hanmer, for two hours, in vain, about some business, I went into the City to my printer, to correct some sheets of the *Barrier Treaty and Remarks*, which must be finished to-morrow: I have been horrible busy for some days past, with this and some other things; and I wanted some very necessary papers, which the Secretary was to give me, and the pamphlet must now be published without them. But they are all busy too. Sir Thomas Hanmer is Chairman of the Committee for drawing up a Representation of the state of the nation[4] to the Queen, where all the wrong

---

[1] Words partially obliterated.
[2] Swift wrote by mistake, "On Europe Britain's safety lies"; the slip was pointed out by Hawkesworth. All the verse is written in the MSS. as prose.
[3] "Them" (MS.).
[4] See Wyon's *Queen Anne*, ii. 366-7.

steps of the Allies and late Ministry about the war will be mentioned. The Secretary, I suppose, was helping him about it to-day; I believe it will be a pepperer. Nite, deel MD.

21. I have been six hours to-day morning writing nineteen pages of a letter to Lord Treasurer, about forming a Society or Academy to correct and fix the English language.[1] (Is English a speech or a language?) It will not be above five or six more. I will send it to him to-morrow, and will print it, if he desires me. I dined, you know, with our Society to-day: Thursday is our day. We had a new member admitted; it was the Duke of Beaufort. We had thirteen met: brother Ormond was not there, but sent his excuse that Prince Eugene dined with him. I left them at seven, being engaged to go to Sir Thomas Hanmer, who desired I would see him at that hour. His business was that I would *hoenlbp ihainm itavoi dsroanvs ubpl tohne sroeqporaensiepnotlastoiqobn*,[2] which I consented to do; but know not whether I shall succeed, because it is a little out of my way. However, I have taken my share. Nite, MD.

22. I finished the rest of my letter to Lord Treasurer to-day, and sent it to him about one o'clock; and then dined privately with my friend Mr. Lewis, to talk over some affairs of moment. I had gotten the thirteenth volume of Rymer's Collection of the Records of the Tower for the University of Dublin.[3] I have two volumes now. I will write to the Provost, to know how I shall send them to him; no, I won't, for I will bring them myself among my own books. I was with Hanmer this morning, and there were the Secretary and Chancellor of the Exchequer[4] very busy with him, laying their heads together about the representation. I went to Lord Masham's to-night, and Lady Masham made me read to her a pretty twopenny pamphlet, called *The St. Albans*

[1] *A Proposal for Correcting, Improving, and Ascertaining the English Tongue, in a Letter to the Most Honourable Robert, Earl of Oxford*, 1712.
[2] "Help him to draw up the representation" (omitting every other letter).
[3] See p. 217.
[4] Robert Benson.

Ghost.[1]   I thought I had writ it myself; so did they; but I did not. Lord Treasurer came down to us from the Queen, and we stayed till two o'clock. That is the best night-place I have. The usual[2] company are Lord and Lady Masham, Lord Treasurer, Dr. Arbuthnot, and I; sometimes the Secretary, and sometimes Mrs. Hill of the bed-chamber, Lady Masham's sister. I assure oo, it im vely rate now; but zis goes to-morrow: and I must have time to converse with own richar MD. Nite, deelest sollahs.[3]

23. I have no news to tell you this last day, nor do I know where I shall dine. I hear the Secretary is a little out of order; perhaps I may dine there, perhaps not. I sent Hanmer what he wanted from me, I know not how he will approve of it. I was to do more of the same sort; I am going out, and must carry zis in my pottick to give it at some general post-house. I will talk further with oo at night. I suppose in my next I shall answer a let sen from MD that will be sent me. On Tuesday it will be *f* day heks since I had your last, N. 26. This day se'nnight I expect one, for that will be something more than a full month. Farewell, MD . . . deelest . . . MD MD MD . . . ME ME ME . . . logues . . . lele.[4]

LETTER XLII[5]

LONDON, *Feb.* 23, 1711-12.

AFTER having disposed my last letter in the post-office, I am now to begin this with telling MD that I dined with the Secretary to-day, who is much out of order with a cold, and feverish; yet he went to the Cabinet Council to-night at six, against my will. The Secretary is much the

---

[1] *The Story of the St. Albans Ghost,* 1712.
[2] "Usually" (MS.).
[3] These words are partially obliterated.
[4] This sentence is obliterated. Forster reads, " Farewell, mine deelest rife deelest char Ppt, MD MD MD Ppt, FW, Lele MD, ME ME ME ME aden FW MD Lazy ones Lele Lele all a Lele."
[5] Endorsed by Stella " Recd. Mar. 19."

greatest commoner in England, and turns the whole
Parliament, who can do nothing without him; and if he
lives and has his health, will, I believe, be one day at the
head of affairs. I have told him sometimes that, if I were
a dozen years younger, I would cultivate his favour, and
trust my fortune with his. But what care oo for all this?
I am sorry when I came first acquainted with this Ministry
that I did not send you their names and characters, and
then you would have relished what[1] I would have writ,
especially if I had let you into the particulars of affairs:
but enough of this. Nite, deelest logues.

24. I went early this morning to the Secretary, who is
not yet well. Sir Thomas Hanmer and the Chancellor of
the Exchequer came while I was there, and he would not
let me stir; so I did not go to church, but was busy with
them till noon, about the affair I told you in my last. The
other two went away; and I dined with the Secretary, and
found my head very much out of order, but no absolute
fit; and I have not been well all this day. It has shook
me a little. I sometimes sit up very late at Lord
Masham's, and have writ much for several days past: but
I will amend both; for I have now very little business,
and hope I shall have no more, and I am resolved to be a
great rider this summer in Ireland. I was to see Mrs.
Wesley this evening, who has been somewhat better for
this month past, and talks of returning to the Bath in a
few weeks. Our peace goes on but slowly; the Dutch are
playing tricks, and we do not push it strongly as we ought.
The fault of our Court is delay, of which the Queen has a
great deal; and Lord Treasurer is not without his share.
But pay richar MD ret us know a little of your life and
tonvelsasens.[2] Do you play at ombre, or visit the Dean,
and Goody Walls and Stoytes and Manleys, as usual? I
must have a letter from oo, to fill the other side of this
sheet. Let me know what you do. Is my aunt alive yet?
Oh, pray, now I think of it, be so kind to step to my aunt,

---

1 "Would" (MS.).

2 Conversation.

and take notice of my great-grandfather's picture; you know he has a ring on his finger, with a seal of an anchor and dolphin about it; but I think there is besides, at the bottom of the picture, the same coat of arms quartered with another, which I suppose was my great-grandmother's. If this be so, it is a stronger argument than the seal. And pray see whether you think that coat of arms was drawn at the same time with the picture, or whether it be of a later hand; and ask my aunt what she knows about it. But perhaps there is no such coat of arms on the picture, and I only dreamed it. My reason is, because I would ask some herald here, whether I should choose that coat, or one in Guillim's large folio of heraldry,[1] where my uncle Godwin is named with another coat of arms of three stags. This is sad stuff to rite; so nite, MD.

25. I was this morning again with the Secretary, and we were two hours busy; and then went together to the Park, Hyde Park, I mean; and he walked to cure his cold, and we were looking at two Arabian horses sent some time ago to Lord Treasurer.[2] The Duke of Marlborough's coach overtook us, with his Grace and Lord Godolphin in it; but they did not see us, to our great satisfaction; for neither of us desired that either of those two lords should see us together There was half a dozen ladies riding like cavaliers to take the air. My head is better to-day. I dined with the Secretary; but we did no business after dinner, and at six I walked into the fields; the days are grown pure and long; then I went to visit Perceval[3] and his family, whom I had seen but twice since they came to town. They too are going to the Bath next month. Countess Doll of Meath[4] is such an owl that,

---

[1] John Guillim's *Display of Heraldrie* appeared first in 1610. The edition to which Swift refers was probably that of 1679, which is wrongly described as the "fifth edition," instead of the seventh.

[2] "One of the horses here mentioned may have been the celebrated Godolphin Arabian from whom descends all the blue blood of the racecourse, and who was the grandfather of Eclipse" (Larwood's *Story of the London Parks*, 99).

[3] See p. 352.

[4] Dorothea, daughter of James Stopford, of New Hall, County Meath, and sister of Lady Newtown-Butler, was the second wife of Edward, fourth Earl of

wherever I visit, people are asking me whether I know such
an Irish lady, and her figure and her foppery? I came home
early, and have been amusing myself with looking into one
of Rymer's volumes of the Records of the Tower, and am
mighty easy to think I have no urgent business upon my
hands. My third cold is not yet off; I sometimes cough,
and am not right with it in the morning. Did I tell you
that I believe it is Lady Masham's hot room that gives it me?
I never knew such a stove; and in my conscience I believe
both my lord and she, my Lord Treasurer, Mr. Secretary,
and myself have all suffered by it. We have all had colds
together, but I walk home on foot. Nite dee logues.

26. I was again busy with the Secretary.[1] We read over
some papers, and did a good deal of business; and I dined
with him, and we were to do more business after dinner; but
after dinner is after dinner—an old saying and a true, " much
drinking, little thinking." We had company with us, and
nothing could be done, and I am to go there again to-morrow.
I have now nothing to do; and the Parliament, by the
Queen's recommendation, is to take some method for preventing libels, etc., which will include pamphlets, I suppose.
I don't know what method they will take, but it comes on
in a day or two. To-day in the morning I visited upwards:
first I saw the Duke of Ormond below stairs, and gave him
joy of his being declared General in Flanders; then I went
up one pair of stairs, and sat with the Duchess; then I went
up another pair of stairs, and paid a visit to Lady Betty; and
desired her woman to go up to the garret, that I might pass
half an hour with her, but she was young and handsome, and
would not. The Duke is our President this week, and I have
bespoke a small dinner on purpose, for good example. Nite
mi deelest logues.

27. I was again with the Secretary this morning; but we

Meath, who died without issue in 1707. She afterwards married General
Richard Gorges (see *Journal*, April 5, 1713), of Kilbrue, County Meath, and
Swift wrote an epitaph on them—" Doll and Dickey."

[1] Here follow some obliterated words.

only read over some papers with Sir Thomas Hanmer; then I called at Lord Treasurer's; it was his levee-day, but I went up to his bed-chamber, and said what I had to say. I came down and peeped in at the chamber, where a hundred fools were waiting, and two streets were full of coaches. I dined in the City with my printer,[1] and came back at six to Lord Treasurer, who had invited me to dinner, but I refused him. I sat there an hour or two, and then went to Lord Masham's. They were all abroad: so truly I came, and read whatever stuff was next me. I can sit and be idle now, which I have not been above a year past. However, I will stay out the session, to see if they have any further commands for me, and that, I suppose, will end in April. But I may go somewhat before, for I hope all will be ended by then, and we shall have either a certain peace, or certain war. The Ministry is contriving new funds for money by lotteries, and we go on as if the war were to continue, but I believe it will not. 'Tis pretty late now, ung oomens; so I bid oo nite, own dee dallars.

28. I have been packing up some books in a great box I have bought, and must buy another for clothes and luggage. This is a beginning towards a removal. I have sent to Holland for a dozen shirts, and design to buy another new gown and hat. I will come over like a zinkerman,[2] and lay out nothing in clothes in Ireland this good while. I have writ this night to the Provost. Our Society met to-day as usual, and we were fourteen, beside the Earl of Arran,[3] whom his brother, the Duke of Ormond, brought among us against all order. We were mightily shocked; but, after some whispers, it ended in choosing Lord Arran one of our

---

[1] Barber (see p. 106).

[2] " The editors supposed Zinkerman (which they printed in capitals) to mean some outlandish or foreign distinction ; but it is the little language for ' gentleman ' " (Forster).

[3] The Hon. Charles Butler, second son of Thomas, Earl of Ossory, eldest son of James, Duke of Ormond, was elevated to the peerage of Ireland in 1693 as Earl of Arran, and was also created a peer of England, as Baron Butler. He held various offices under William III. and Queen Anne, and died without issue in 1759.

Society, which I opposed to his face, but it was carried by all the rest against me.

29. This is leap year, and this is leap day. Prince George was born on this day. People are mistaken; and some here think it is St. David's Day; but they do not understand the virtue of leap year. I have nothing to do now, boys, and have been reading all this day like Gumdragon; and yet I was dictating some trifles this morning to a printer. I dined with a friend hard by, and the weather was so discouraging I could not walk. I came home early, and have read two hundred pages of Arrian. Alexander the Great is just dead : I do not think he was poisoned; betwixt you and me, all those are but idle stories : it is certain that neither Ptolemy nor Aristobulus thought so, and they were both with him when he[1] died. It is a pity we have not their histories. The Bill for limiting Members of Parliament to have but so many places passed the House of Commons, and will pass the House of Lords, in spite of the Ministry, which you know is a great lessening of the Queen's power. Four of the new lords voted against the Court in this point. It is certainly a good Bill in the reign of an ill prince, but I think things are not settled enough for it at present. And the Court may want a majority upon a pinch. Nite deelest logues. Rove Pdfr.

March 1. I went into the City to inquire after poor Stratford,[2] who has put himself a prisoner into the Queen's Bench, for which his friends blame him much, because his creditors designed to be very easy with him. He grasped at too many things together, and that was his ruin. There is one circumstance relative to Lieutenant-General Meredith[3] that is very melancholy : Meredith was turned out of all his employments last year, and had about £10,000 left to live on. Stratford, upon friendship, desired he might have the management of it for Meredith, to put it into the stocks and funds for the best advantage, and now he has lost it all.— You have heard me often talk of Stratford; we were class-

---

[1] "They" (MS.).   [2] See pp. 10, 381-2.   [3] See p. 89.

fellows at school and university. I dined with some merchants, his friends, to-day, and they said they expected his breaking this good while. I gave him notice of a treaty of peace, while it was a secret, of which he might have made good use, but that helped to ruin him; for he gave money, reckoning there would be actually a peace by this time, and consequently stocks rise high. Ford narrowly 'scaped losing £500 by him, and so did I too. Nite, my two deelest rives MD.

2. Morning. I was wakened at three this morning, my man and the people of the house telling me of a great fire in the Haymarket. I slept again, and two hours after my man came in again, and told me it was my poor brother Sir William Wyndham's[1] house burnt, and that two maids, leaping out of an upper room to avoid the fire, both fell on their heads, one of them upon the iron spikes before the dooi, and both lay dead in the streets. It is supposed to have been some carelessness of one or both those maids. The Duke of Ormond was there helping to put out the fire. Brother Wyndham gave £6000 but a few months ago for that house, as he told me, and it was very richly furnished. I shall know more particulars at night. He married Lady Catherine Seymour, the Duke of Somerset's daughter; you know her, I believe.—At night. Wyndham's young child escaped very narrowly; Lady Catherine escaped barefoot; they all went to Northumberland House. Mr. Brydges's[2] house, at next door, is damaged much, and was like to be burnt. Wyndham has lost above £10,000 by this accident; his lady above a thousand pounds worth of clothes. It

---

[1] Sir William Wyndham, Bart., of Orchard Wyndham, married Lady Catherine Seymour, daughter of the sixth Duke of Somerset (see p. 236). Their eldest son, Charles, succeeded his uncle, the Duke of Somerset, as Earl of Egremont; and the second son, Percy, was afterwards created Earl of Thomond. The Wyndhams' house was in Albemarle Street; the loss was over £20,000; but they were "much more concerned for their servants than for all the other losses" (*Wentworth Papers*, 274). The Duke of Ormond "worked as hard as any of the ordinary men, and gave many guineas about to encourage the men to work hard." The Queen gave the Wyndhams temporary lodgings in "St. James's house."

[2] See p. 12.

was a terrible accident. He was not at Court to-day. I dined with Lord Masham. The Queen was not at church. Nite, MD.

3. Pray tell Walls that I spoke to the Duke of Ormond and Mr. Southwell about his friend's affair, who, I find, needed not me for a solicitor, for they both told me the. thing would be done. I likewise mentioned his own affair to Mr. Southwell, and I hope that will be done too, for Southwell seems to think it reasonable, and I will mind him of it again. Tell him this nakedly. You need not know the particulars. They are secrets: one of them is about Mrs. South having a pension; the other about his salary from the Government for the tithes of the park that lie in his parish, to be put upon the establishment, but oo must not know zees sings, zey are secrets; and we must keep them flom nauty dallars. I dined in the City with my printer, with whom I had some small affair; but I have no large work on my hands now. I was with Lord Treasurer this morning, and hat[1] care oo for zat? Oo dined with the Dean to-day. Monday is parson's holiday, and oo lost oo money at cards and dice; ze Givars[2] device. So I'll go to bed. Nite, my two deelest logues.

4. I sat to-day with poor Mrs. Wesley, who made me dine with her. She is much better than she was. I heartily pray for her health, out of the entire love I bear to her worthy husband. This day has passed very insignificantly. But it is a great comfort to me now that I can come home and read, and have nothing upon my hands to write. I was at Lord Masham's to-night, and stayed there till one. Lord Treasurer was there; but I thought, I thought he looked melancholy, just as he did at the beginning of the session, and he was not so merry as usual. In short, the majority in the House of Lords is a very weak one: and he has much ado to keep it up; and he is not able to make those removes he would, and oblige his friends; and I doubt too[3] he does not take care enough about it, or rather cannot do all himself, and will not

---

[1] What.   [2] Devil's.   [3] "To" (MS.).

employ others: which is his great fault, as I have often told
you. 'Tis late. Nite, MD.

5. I wish you a merry Lent. I hate Lent; I hate different
diets, and furmity and butter, and herb porridge; and sour
devout faces of people who only put on religion for seven
weeks. I was at the Secretary's office this morning; and
there a gentleman brought me two letters, dated last
October; one from the Bishop of Clogher, t'other from
Walls. The gentleman is called Colonel Newburgh.[1]   I
think you mentioned him to me some time ago; he has
business in the House of Lords. I will do him what service
I can. The Representation of the House of Commons is
printed:[2] I have not seen it yet; it is plaguy severe, they
say. I dined with Dr. Arbuthnot, and had a true Lenten
dinner, not in point of victuals, but spleen; for his wife and
a child or two were sick in the house, and that was full as
mortifying as fish. We have had fine mighty cold frosty
weather for some days past. I hope you take the advantage
of it, and walk now and then. You never answer that part
of my letters where I desire you to walk. I must keep my
breath to cool my Lenten porridge. Tell Jemmy Leigh that
his boy that robbed him now appears about the town:
Patrick has seen him once or twice. I knew nothing of his
being robbed till Patrick told me he had seen the boy. I
wish it had been Sterne that had been robbed, to be
revenged for the box that he lost,[3] and be p——xed to him.
Nite, MD.

6. I hear Mr. Prior has suffered by Stratford's breaking.
I was yesterday to see Prior, who is not well, and I thought
he looked melancholy. He can ill afford to lose money. I
walked before dinner in the Mall a good while with Lord
Arran and Lord Dupplin, two of my brothers, and then we
went to dinner, where the Duke of Beaufort was our
President. We were but eleven to-day. We are now in all
nine lords and ten commoners. The Duke of Beaufort had
the confidence to propose his brother-in-law, the Earl of

---

[1] See p. 349.   [2] See p. 406.   [3] See pp. 113-4.

Danby,[1] to be a member; but I opposed it so warmly that it was waived. Danby is not above twenty, and we will have no more boys, and we want but two to make up our number. I stayed till eight, and then we all went away soberly. The Duke of Ormond's treat last week cost £20, though it was only four dishes and four, without a dessert; and I bespoke it in order to be cheap. Yet I could not prevail to change the house. Lord Treasurer is in a rage with us for being so extravagant: and the wine was not reckoned neither; for that is always brought by him that is President. Lord Orrery [2] is to be President next week; and I will see whether it cannot be cheaper; or else we will leave the house. . . .[3] Lord Masham made me go home with him to-night to eat boiled oysters. Take oysters, wash them clean; that is, wash their shells clean; then put your oysters into an earthen pot, with their hollow sides down, then put this pot into a great kettle with water, and so let them boil. Your oysters are boiled in their own liquor, and not mixed water. Lord Treasurer was not with us; he was very ill to-day with a swimming in the head, and is gone home to be cupped, and sent to desire Lady Masham to excuse him to the Queen. Nite, dee MD.

7. I was to-day at the House of Lords about a friend's Bill. Then I crossed the water at Westminster Stairs to Southwark, went through St. George's Fields to the Mint, which is the dominion of the King's [4] Bench Prison, where Stratford lodges in a blind alley, and writ to me to come to him; but he was gone to the 'Change. I thought he had something to say to me about his own affairs. I found him at his usual coffee-house, and went to his own lodgings, and dined with him and his wife, and other company. His business was only to desire I would intercede with the Ministry about his brother-in-law, Ben Burton,[5] of Dublin, the banker, who is likely to come

---

[1] Peregrine Hyde Osborne, Earl of Danby, afterwards Marquis of Caermarthen and third Duke of Leeds (see p. 473). His sister Mary was married to the Duke of Beaufort (see p. 385).

[2] See p. 72.

[3] Several undecipherable words. Forster reads, "Pidy Pdfr, deelest Sollahs."

[4] "K" (MS.). It should, of course, be "Queen's."   [5] See p. 213.

27

into trouble, as we hear, about spreading false Whiggish news.   I hate Burton, and told Stratford so; and I will advise the Duke of Ormond to make use of it, to keep the rogue in awe.   Mrs. Stratford tells me her husband's creditors have consented to give him liberty to get up his debts abroad ; and she hopes he will pay them all.   He was cheerfuller than I have seen him this great while.   I have walked much to-day.—Night, deelest logues.

8. This day twelvemonth Mr. Harley was stabbed; but he is ill, and takes physic to-day, I hear ('tis now morning), and cannot have the Cabinet Council with him, as he intended, nor me to say grace.   I am going to see him.   Pray read the Representation ; 'tis the finest that ever was writ.   Some of it is Pdfr's style, but not very much.   This is the day of the Queen's accession to the Crown ; so it is a great day.   I am going to Court, and will dine with Lord Masham ; but I must go this moment to see the Secretary about some businesses ; so I will seal up this, and put it in the post my own self. Farewell, deelest hearts and souls, MD.   Farewell MD MD MD FW FW FW ME ME Lele Lele Lele Sollahs lele.

LETTER XLIII[1]

LONDON, *March* 8, 1711-12.

I CARRIED my forty-second letter in my pocket till evening, and then put it in the general post.—I went in the morning to see Lord Treasurer, who had taken physic, and was drinking his broth.   I had been with the Secretary before, to recommend a friend, one Dr. Freind,[2] to be Physician-General ; and the Secretary promised to mention it to the Queen.   I can serve everybody but myself.   Then I went to Court, and carried Lord Keeper and the Secretary to dine with Lord Masham, when we drank the Queen and Lord

---

[1] Addressed "To Mrs. Johnson, at her lodgings over against St. Mary's Church, near Capel Street, Dublin, Ireland."   Endorsed "Mar. 30."
[2] See p. 66.

Treasurer with every health, because this was the day of his stabbing.—Then I went and played pools at picquet with Lady Masham and Mrs. Hill; won ten shillings, gave a crown to the box, and came home. I met at my lodgings a letter from Joe, with a bit annexed from Ppt. What Joe asks is entirely out of my way, and I take it for a foolish whim in him. Besides, I know not who is to give a patent: if the Duke of Ormond, I would speak to him; and if it come in my head I will mention it to Ned Southwell. They have no patents that I know of for such things here, but good security is all; and to think that I would speak to Lord Treasurer for any such matter at random is a jest. Did I tell you of a race of rakes, called the Mohocks,[1] that play the devil about this town every night, slit people's noses, and beat them, etc.? Nite, sollahs, and rove Pdfr. Nite, MD.

9. I was at Court to-day, and nobody invited me to dinner, except one or two, whom I did not care to dine with; so I dined with Mrs. Van. Young Davenant[2] was telling us at Court how he was set upon by the Mohocks, and how they ran his chair through with a sword. It is not safe being in the streets at night for them. The Bishop of Salisbury's son[3]

[1] The Mohocks succeeded the Scowrers of William III.'s reign. Gay (*Trivia*, iii. 325) says—
  "Who has not heard the Scowrers' midnight fame?
  Who has not trembled at the Mohocks' name?"
Lady Wentworth (*Wentworth Papers*, 277) says: "They put an old woman into a hogshead, and rolled her down a hill; they cut off some noses, others' hands, and several barbarous tricks, without any provocation. They are said to be young gentlemen; they never take any money from any." See also the *Spectator*, Nos. 324, 332, and 347 (where Budgell alludes to "the late panic fear"), and Defoe's *Review* for March 15, 1712. Swift was in considerable alarm about the Mohocks throughout March, and said that they were all Whigs. The reports that numbers of persons, including men of figure, had joined together to commit assaults in the streets, made many fear to leave their houses at night. A proclamation was issued for the suppressing of riots and the discovery of those guilty of the late outrages; but it seems probable that the disorders were not more frequent than might be expected from time to time in a great city.
[2] Henry Davenant, son of Charles Davenant (see p. 58), was Resident at Frankfort. Macky described him as "very giddy-headed, with some wit," to which Swift added, "He is not worth mentioning."
[3] Thomas Burnet, youngest son of Gilbert Burnet, Bishop of Salisbury, was at this time a young man about town of no good reputation. Afterwards he turned his attention to the law, and was appointed a Judge of the Court of Common Pleas in 1741. He was knighted in 1745, and died in 1753.

is said to be of the gang.   They are all Whigs; and a great
lady sent to me, to speak to her father and to Lord Treasurer,
to have a care of them, and to be careful likewise of myself;
for she heard they had malicious intentions against the
Ministers and their friends.   I know not whether there be
anything in this, though others are of the same opinion.
The weather still continues very fine and frosty.   I walked
in the Park this evening, and came home early to avoid the
Mohocks.   Lord Treasurer is better.   Nite, my own two
deelest MD.

10.   I went this morning again to the Lord Treasurer, who
is quite recovered; and I stayed till he went out.   I dined
with a friend in the City, about a little business of printing;
but not my own.   You must buy a small twopenny pamphlet,
called *Law is a Bottomless Pit.*[1]   'Tis very prettily written,
and there will be a Second Part.   The Commons are very
slow in bringing in their Bill to limit the press, and the
pamphleteers make good use of their time; for there come
out three or four every day.   Well, but is not it time, methinks, to have a letter from MD?   'Tis now six weeks since
I had your Number 26.   I can assure oo I expect one before
this goes; and I'll make shorter day's journals than usual,
'cause I hope to fill up a good deal of t'other side with my
answer.   Our fine weather lasts yet, but grows a little windy.
We shall have rain soon, I dispose.   Go to cards, sollahs, and
I to seep.   Nite, MD.

11.   Lord Treasurer has lent the long letter I writ him[2] to
Prior, and I can't get Prior to return it.   I want to have it
printed, and to make up this Academy for the improvement
of our language.   Faith, we never shall improve it so much
as FW has done; sall we?   No, faith, ourrichar gangridge.[3]
I dined privately with my friend Lewis, and then went to see
Ned Southwell, and talk with him about Walls's business, and

---

[1] By Arbuthnot, written to recommend the peace proposals of the Government.   The full title was, *Law is a Bottomless Pit.   Exemplified in the case of
the Lord Strutt, John Bull, Nicholas Frog, and Lewis Baboon; who spent all
they had in a Law Suit.*

[2] See pp. 238, 407.   [3] Our little language.

Mrs. South's. The latter will be done; but his own not. Southwell tells me that it must be laid before Lord Treasurer, and the nature of it explained, and a great deal of clutter, which is not worth the while; and maybe Lord Treasurer won't do it [at] last; and it is, as Walls says himself, not above forty shillings a year difference. You must tell Walls this, unless he would have the business a secret from you : in that case only say I did all I could with Ned Southwell, and it can't be done; for it must be laid before Lord Treasurer, etc., who will not do it; and besides, it is not worth troubling his lordship. So nite, my two deelest nuntyes nine MD.[1]

12. Here is the D—— and all to do with these Mohocks. Grub Street papers about them fly like lightning, and a list printed of near eighty put into several prisons, and all a lie; and I begin almost to think there is no truth, or very little, in the whole story. He that abused Davenant was a drunken gentleman; none of that gang. My man tells me that one of the lodgers heard in a coffee-house, publicly, that one design of the Mohocks was upon me, if they could catch me; and though I believe nothing of it, I forbear walking late, and they have put me to the charge of some shillings already. I dined to-day with Lord Treasurer and two gentlemen of the Highlands of Scotland, yet very polite men. I sat there till nine, and then went to Lord Masham's, where Lord Treasurer followed me, and we sat till twelve; and I came home in a chair for fear of the Mohocks, and I have given him warning of it too. Little Harrison,[2] whom I sent to Holland, is now actually made Queen's Secretary at The Hague. It will be in the *Gazette* to-morrow. 'Tis worth twelve hundred pounds a year. Here is a young fellow has writ some Sea Eclogues, poems of Mermen, resembling pastorals of shepherds, and they are very pretty, and the thought is new. Mermen are he-mermaids; Tritons, natives of the sea. Do you understand me? I think to recommend

---

[1] Forster reads, "two deelest nauty nown MD."
[2] See p. 36.

him to our Society to-morrow. His name is Diaper.[1] P——
on him, I must do something for him, and get him out of the
way. I hate to have any new wits rise, but when they do
rise I would encourage them; but they tread on our heels
and thrust us off the stage. Nite deelest MD.

13. You would laugh to see our printer constantly attending our Society after dinner, and bringing us whatever new
thing he has printed, which he seldom fails to do. Yet he
had nothing to-day. Lord Lansdowne, one of our Society,
was offended at a passage in this day's *Examiner*, which he
thinks reflects on him, as I believe it does, though in a
mighty civil way. 'Tis only that his underlings cheat; but
that he is a very fine gentleman every way, etc.[2] Lord
Orrery was President to-day; but both our dukes were
absent. Brother Wyndham recommended Diaper to the
Society. I believe we shall make a contribution among ourselves, which I don't like. Lord Treasurer has yet done
nothing for us, but we shall try him soon. The company
parted early, but Freind, and Prior, and I, sat a while longer
and reformed the State, and found fault with the Ministry.
Prior hates his Commission of the Customs, because it spoils
his wit. He says he dreams of nothing but cockets,[3] and
dockets, and drawbacks, and other jargon words of the
custom-house. Our good weather went away yesterday,
and the nights are now dark, and I came home before ten.
Night nown . . . deelest sollahs.

14. I have been plagued this morning with solicitors, and
with nobody more than my brother, Dr. Freind, who must
needs have to get old Dr. Lawrence,[4] the Physician-General,

---

[1] William Diaper, son of Joseph Diaper of Bridgewater, was sent to Balliol
College, Oxford, in 1699, at the age of fourteen. He entered the Church, and
was curate at Brent, Somerset; but he died in 1717, aged twenty-nine.

[2] The *Examiner* (vol. ii. No. 15) complained of general bribery and
oppression on the part of officials and underlings in the public service,
especially in matters connected with the army; but the writer said that the
head (Lord Lansdowne) was just and liberal in his nature, and easy in his
fortune, and a man of honour and virtue.

[3] Sealed documents given to show that a merchant's goods are entered.

[4] Thomas Lawrence, First Physician to Queen Anne, and Physician-General
to the Army, died in 1714 (*Gentleman's Magazine*, 1815, ii. 17). His daughter
Elizabeth was second wife to Lord Mohun.

turned out and himself in. He has argued with me so long upon the reasonableness of it, that I am fully convinced it is very unreasonable; and so I would tell the Secretary, if I had not already made him speak to the Queen. Besides, I know not but my friend Dr. Arbuthnot would be content to have it himself, and I love him ten times better than Freind. What's all this to you? but I must talk of things as they happen in the day, whether you know anything of them or no. I dined in the City, and, coming back, one Parson Richardson[1] of Ireland overtook me. He was here last summer upon a project of converting the Irish and printing Bibles, etc., in that language, and is now returned to pursue it on. He tells me Dr. Coghill[2] came last night [to] town. I will send to see how he does to-morrow. He gave me a letter from Walls about his old business. Nite, deelest MD.

15. I had intended to be early with the Secretary this morning, when my man admitted upstairs one Mr. Newcomb,[3] an officer, who brought me a letter from the Bishop of Clogher, with four lines added by Mrs. Ashe, all about that Newcomb. I think, indeed, his case is hard, but God knows whether I shall be able to do him any service. People will not understand: I am a very good second, but I care not to begin a recommendation, unless it be for an intimate friend. However, I will do what I can. I missed the Secretary, and then walked to Chelsea to dine with the Dean of Christ Church,[4] who was engaged to Lord Orrery with some other Christ Church men. He made me go with him whether I would or not, for they have this long time admitted me a Christ Church man. Lord Orrery, generally every winter, gives his old acquaintance of that college a

---

[1] See p. 163.   [2] See p. 245.
[3] No officer named Newcomb appears in Dalton's *Army Lists*; but the allusion to General Ross, below, adds to the probability that Swift was referring to one of the sons of Sir Thomas Newcomen, Bart., who was killed at the siege of Enniskillen. Beverley Newcomen (Dalton, iii. 52, iv. 60), who was probably Swift's acquaintance, was described in a petition of 1706 as a Lieutenant who had served at Killiecrankie, and had been in Major-General Ross's regiment ever since 1695.
[4] Atterbury.

dinner. There were nine clergymen at table, and four laymen. The Dean and I soon left them, and after a visit or two, I went to Lord Masham's, and Lord Treasurer, Arbuthnot and I sat till twelve. And now I am come home and got to bed. I came afoot, but had my man with me. Lord Treasurer advised me not to go in a chair, because the Mohocks insult chairs more than they do those on foot. They think there is some mischievous design in those villains. Several of them, Lord Treasurer told me, are actually taken up. I heard at dinner that one of them was killed last night. We shall know more in a little time. I don't like them, as the men said.[1] Nite MD.

16. This morning, at the Secretary's, I met General Ross,[2] and recommended Newcomb's case to him, who promises to join with me in working up the Duke of Ormond to do something for him. Lord Winchelsea[3] told me to-day at Court that two of the Mohocks caught a maid of old Lady Winchelsea's,[4] at the door of their house in the Park, where she was with a candle, and had just lighted out somebody. They cut all her face, and beat her without any provocation. I hear my friend Lewis has got a Mohock in one of the messenger's hands. The Queen was at church to-day, but was carried in an open chair. She has got an ugly cough, Arbuthnot, her physician, says. I dined with Crowe,[5] late Governor of Barbados; an acquaintance of Sterne's.[6] After dinner I asked him whether he had heard of Sterne. "Here he is," said he, "at the door in a coach:" and in came Sterne. He has been here this week. He is buying a captainship in his cousin Sterne's[7] regiment. He told me he left Jemmy Leigh playing at cards with you. He is to give 800 guineas for his commission. I suppose you know all this better than

---

[1] Evidently a familiar quotation at the time. Forster reads, incorrectly, "But the more I lite MD."
[2] See p. 400.   [3] See p. 104.
[4] In 1681, Elizabeth, only daughter and heiress of John Ayres, of the City of London, then aged about twenty, became the fourth and last wife of Heneage Finch, Earl of Winchelsea, who died in 1689. She lived until 1745.
[5] See p. 218.   [6] Enoch Sterne (see p. 20).
[7] Lieut.-Col. Robert Sterne was in Col. Frederick Hamilton's Regiment in 1695.

I. How shall I have room to answer oo rettle[1] hen I get it, I have gone so far already? Nite, deelest logues MD.

17. Dr. Sacheverell came this morning to give me thanks for getting his brother an employment. It was but six or seven weeks since I spoke to Lord Treasurer for him. Sacheverell brought Trapp[2] along with him. We dined together at my printer's, and I sat with them till seven. I little thought, and I believe so did he, that ever I should be his solicitor to the present Ministry, when I left Ireland. This is the seventh I have now provided for since I came, and can do nothing for myself. I don't care; I shall have Ministries and other people obliged to me. Trapp is a coxcomb, and the t'other is not very deep; and their judgment in things of wit or sense is miraculous. The Second Part of *Law is a Bottomless Pit*[3] is just now printed, and better, I think, than the first. Night, my two deel saucy dallars.

18. There is a proclamation out against the Mohocks. One of those that are taken is a baronet. I dined with poor Mrs. Wesley, who is returning to the Bath. Mrs. Perceval's[4] young daughter has got the smallpox, but will do well. I walked this evening in the Park, and met Prior, who made me go home with him, where I stayed till past twelve, and could not get a coach, and was alone, and was afraid enough of the Mohocks. I will do so no more, though I got home safe. Prior and I were talking discontentedly of some managements, that no more people are turned out, which get Lord Treasurer many enemies: but whether the fault be in him, or the Queen, I know not; I doubt, in both. Ung omens, it is now seven weeks since I received your last; but I expect one next Irish packet, to fill the rest of this paper; but if it don't come, I'll do without it: so I wish oo good luck at ombre with the Dean. Nite, nuntyes nine.[5]

---

[1] Letter. [2] See p. 120.
[3] The title was, *John Bull in his Senses: being the Second Part of Law is a Bottomless Pit.*
[4] See p. 352.
[5] Cf. p. 421. Forster reads "nnutyas," when the words would mean "as naughty as nine," apparently.

19. Newcomb came to me this morning, and I went to the Duke of Ormond to speak for him; but the Duke was just going out to take the oaths for General. The Duke of Shrewsbury is to be Lord Lieutenant of Ireland. I walked with Domville and Ford to Kensington, where we dined, and it cost me above a crown. I don't like it, as the man said.[1] It was very windy walking. I saw there Lord Masham's children. The youngest, my nephew, I fear, has got the king's evil; the other two are daughters of three and four years old. 'Twas very windy walking. The gardens there are mighty fine. I passed the evening at Lord Masham's with Lord Treasurer and Arbuthnot, as usual, and we stayed till past one; but I had my man to come with me, and at home I found three letters; one from one Fetherston, a parson, with a postscript of Tisdall's to recommend him: and Fetherston, whom I never saw, has been so kind to give me a letter of attorney to recover a debt for him. Another from Lord Abercorn, to get him the dukedom of Chatelherault [2] from the King of France; in which I will do what I can, for his pretensions are very just. The third, I warrant you, from our MD. 'Tis a great stir this, of getting a dukedom from the King of France: but it is only to speak to the Secretary, and get the Duke of Ormond to engage in it, and mention the case to Lord Treasurer, etc., and this I shall do. Nite deelest richar MD.

20. I was with the Duke of Ormond this morning, about Lord Abercorn, Dr. Freind, and Newcomb. Some will do, and some will not do; that's wise, marams.[3] The Duke of Shrewsbury is certainly to be your Governor. I will go in a day or two, and give the Duchess joy, and recommend the

---

[1] See p. 424, note 1.

[2] In 1549, James, second Earl of Arran, was made Duke of Chatelherault by Henry II. of France. His eldest son died without issue; the *second*, John, became first Marquis of Hamilton, and was great-grandfather of Lady Anne Hamilton (Duchess of Hamilton), mother of the Duke of Swift's *Journal*. The Earl of Abercorn, on the other hand, was descended from Claud, *third* son of the Earl of Arran, but in the male line; and his claim was therefore the stronger, according to the French law of inheritance.

[3] Madams.

Archbishop of Dublin to her. I writ to the Archbishop, some months ago, that it would be so, and told him I would speak a good word for him to the Duchess; and he says he has a great respect for her, etc. I made our Society change their house, and we met to-day at the Star and Garter in the Pall Mall. Lord Arran was President. The other dog was so extravagant in his bills, that for four dishes and four, first and second course, without wine or dessert, he charged twenty-one pounds, six shillings, and eightpence, to the Duke of Ormond. We design, when all have been Presidents this turn, to turn it into a reckoning of so much a head; but we shall break up when the session ends. Nite deelest MD.

21. Morning. Now I will answer MD's rettle, N. 27; you that are adding to your number and grumbling, had made it 26, and then altered[1] it to 27. I believe it is above a month since your last; yes, it is above seven weeks since I had your last: but I ought to consider that this was twelve days right,[2] so that makes it pretty even. O, the sirry zade,[3] with her excuses of a fortnight at Ballygall, seeing their friends, and landlord running away. O Rold, hot a cruttle[4] and a bustle!—No—if you will have it—I am not Dean of Wells,[5] nor know anything of being so; nor is there anything in the story; and that's enough. It was not Roper[6] sent that news: Roper is my humble slave.—Yes, I heard of your resolves, and that Burton was embroiled. Stratford spoke to me in his behalf; but I said I hated the rascal. Poor Catherine gone to Wales? But she will come back again, I hope. I would see her in my journey, if she were near the road; and bring her over. Joe[7] is a fool; that sort

---

[1] This word is doubtful. Forster reads "cobbled."
[2] A mistake, apparently, for "writing." The letter was begun on March 8.
[3] Silly jade. [4] O Lord, what a clutter.
[5] On the death of Dr. William Graham, Dean of Wells, it was reported that Swift was to be his successor. Dr. Brailsford, however, received the appointment.
[6] Abel Roper (1665-1726), a Tory journalist, published, thrice weekly, the *Postboy*, to which Swift sometimes sent paragraphs. Boyer (*Political State*, 1711, p. 678) said that Roper was only the tool of a party; " there are men of figure and distinction behind the curtain, who furnish him with such scandalous reflections as they think proper to cast upon their antagonists."
[7] Joe Beaumont.

of business is not at all in my way, pray put him off it.
People laugh when I mention it. Bed ee paadon, Maram;
I'm drad oo rike ee aplon:[1] no harm, I hope. And so . . .
DD wonders she has not a letter at the day; oo'll have it
soon. . . . The D—— he is! married to that vengeance!
Men are not to be believed. I don't think her a fool. Who
would have her? Dilly will be governed like an ass; and she
will govern like a lion. Is not that true, Ppt? Why, Sterne
told me he left you at ombre with Leigh; and yet you never
saw him. I know nothing of his wife being here: it may
cost her a c——[2] (I don't care to write that word plain).
He is a little in doubt about buying his commission. Yes, I
will bring oo over all the little papers I can think on. I
thought I sent you, by Leigh, all that were good at that
time. The author of the *Sea Eclogues* sent books to the
Society yesterday, and we gave him guineas apiece; and,
maybe, will do further from him (for him, I mean). So the
Bishop of Clogher, and lady, were your guests for a night or
two. Why, Ppt, you are grown a great gamester and
company keeper. I did say to myself, when I read those
names, just what you guess; and you clear up the matter
wonderfully. You may converse with those two nymphs if
you please, but the —— take me if ever I do. Iss, fais, it
is delightful to hear that Ppt is every way Ppt now, in
health, and looks, and all. Pray God keep her so, many,
many, many years. I doubt the session will not be over till
the end of April; however, I shall not wait for it, if the
Ministry will let me go sooner. I wish I were just now in
my garden at Laracor. I would set out for Dublin early on
Monday, and bring you an account of my young trees, which
you are better acquainted with than the Ministry, and so am
I. Oh, now you have got Number 41, have you so? Why,
perhaps, I forgot, and kept it to next post in my pocket: I
have done such tricks. My cold is better, but not gone. I
want air and riding. Hold ee tongue, oo Ppt, about colds

---

[1] Beg your pardon, Madams, I'm glad you like your apron (see p. 402).
[2] This word was smudged by Swift.

at Moor Park! the case is quite different. I will do what you desire me for Tisdall, when I next see Lord Anglesea. Pray give him my service. The weather is warm these three or four days, and rainy. I am to dine to-day with Lewis and Darteneuf at Somers's,[1] the Clerk of the Kitchen at Court. Darteneuf loves good bits and good sups. Good mollows richar sollohs.—At night. I dined, as I said; and it cost me a shilling for a chair. It has rained all day, and is very warm. Lady Masham's young son, my nephew, is very ill; and she is out of mind[2] with grief. I pity her mightily. I am got home early, and going to write to the Bishop of Clogher, but have no politics to send him. Nite my own two deelest saucy d[ear] ones.

22. I am going into the City this morning with a friend about some business; so I will immediately seal up this, and keep it in my pottick till evening, and zen put it in the post. The weather continues warm and gloomy. I have heard no news since I went to bed, so can say no more. Pray send . . . that I may have time to write to . . .[3] about it. I have here underneath given order for forty shillings to Mrs. Brent, which you will send to Parvisol. Farewell, deelest deel MD, and rove Pdfr dearly dearly. Farewell, MD, MD, FW, FW, FW, ME, ME, ME, Lele lele lele lele lele lele, and lele aden.

LETTER XLIV[4]

LONDON, *March* 22, 1711-12.

UGLY, nasty weather. I was in the City to-day with Mrs. Wesley and Mrs. Perceval, to get money from a banker for Mrs. Wesley, who goes to Bath on Thursday. I left them there, and dined with a friend, and went to see Lord

---

[1] I cannot find Somers in contemporary lists of officials. Cf. pp. 159, 298.
[2] Obliterated and doubtful.
[3] Words obliterated and illegible. Forster reads, conjecturally, "Pray send Pdfr the ME account that I may have time to write to Parvisol."
[4] Addressed to "Mrs. Dingley," etc. Endorsed "Apr. 14."

Treasurer; but he had people with him I did not know: so I went to Lady Masham's, and lost a crown with her at picquet, and then sat with Lord Masham and Lord Treasurer, etc., there till past one; but I had my man with me, to come home. I gave in my forty-third, and one for the Bishop of Clogher, to the post-office, as I came from the City; and so oo know 'tis late now, and I have nothing to say for this day. Our Mohocks are all vanished; however, I shall take care of my person. Nite my own two deelest nuntyes MD.

23. I was this morning, before church, with the Secretary, about Lord Abercorn's business, and some others. My soliciting season is come, and will last as long as the session. I went late to Court, and the company was almost gone. The Court serves me for a coffee-house; once a week I meet acquaintance there, that I should not otherwise see in a quarter. There is a flying report that the French have offered a cessation of arms, and to give us Dunkirk, and the Dutch Namur, for security, till the peace is made. The Duke of Ormond, they say, goes in a week. Abundance of his equipage is already gone. His[1] friends are afraid the expense of this employment will ruin him, since he must lose the government of Ireland. I dined privately with a friend, and refused all dinners offered me at Court; which, however, were but two, and I did not like either. Did I tell you of a scoundrel about the Court that sells employments to ignorant people, and cheats them of their money? He lately made a bargain for the Vice-Chamberlain's place, for seven thousand pounds, and had received some guineas earnest; but the whole thing was discovered t'other day, and examination taken of it by Lord Dartmouth, and I hope he will be swinged. The Vice-Chamberlain told me several particulars of it last night at Lord Masham's. Can DD play at ombre yet, enough to hold the cards while Ppt steps into the next room? Nite deelest sollahs.[2]

---

[1] "Is" (MS.).

[2] The words after "yet" are partially obliterated.

24. This morning I recommended Newcomb again to the Duke of Ormond, and left Dick Stewart[1] to do it further. Then I went to visit the Duchess of Hamilton, who was not awake. So I went to the Duchess of Shrewsbury, and sat an hour at her toilet. I talked to her about the Duke's being Lord Lieutenant. She said she knew nothing of it; but I rallied her out of that, and she resolves not to stay behind the Duke. I intend to recommend the Bishop of Clogher to her for an acquaintance. He will like her very well : she is, indeed, a most agreeable woman, and a great favourite of mine. I know not whether the ladies in Ireland will like her. I was at the Court of Requests, to get some lords to be at a committee to-morrow, about a friend's Bill: and then the Duke of Beaufort gave me a poem, finely bound in folio, printed at Stamford, and writ by a country squire. Lord Exeter[2] desired the Duke to give it the Queen, because the author is his friend; but the Duke desired I would let him know whether it was good for anything. I brought it home, and will return it to-morrow, as the dullest thing I ever read ; and advise the Duke not to present it. I dined with Domville at his lodgings, by invitation; for he goes in a few days for Ireland. Nite dee MD.

25. There is a mighty feast at a Tory sheriff's to-day in the City: twelve hundred dishes of meat.—Above five lords, and several hundred gentlemen, will be there, and give four or five guineas apiece, according to custom. Dr. Coghill and I dined, by invitation, at Mrs. Van's. It has rained or mizzled all day, as my pockets feel. There are two new answers come out to the *Conduct of the Allies*. The last year's *Examiners*, printed together in a small volume, go off but slowly. The printer over-printed himself by at least a thousand ; so soon out of fashion are party papers, however so well writ. The *Medleys* are coming out in the same volume, and perhaps may sell better. Our news about a cessation of arms begins to flag, and I have not these three days seen anybody in business to ask them about it. We

---

[1] See p. 53.　　　[2] John Cecil, sixth Earl of Exeter (died 1721).

had a terrible fire last night in Drury Lane, or thereabouts, and three or four people destroyed. One of the maids of honour has the smallpox; but the best is, she can lose no beauty; and we have one new handsome maid of honour. Nite MD.

26. I forgot to tell you that on Sunday last, about seven at night, it lightened above fifty times as I walked the Mall, which I think is extraordinary at this time of the year, and the weather was very hot. Had you anything of this in Dublin? I intended to dine with Lord Treasurer to-day; but Lord Mansel and Mr. Lewis made me dine with them at Kit Musgrave's.[1] I sat the evening with Mrs. Wesley, who goes to-morrow morning to the Bath. She is much better than she was. The news of the French desiring a cessation of arms, etc., was but town talk. We shall know in a few days, as I am told, whether there will be a peace or not. The Duke of Ormond will go in a week for Flanders, they say. Our Mohocks go on still, and cut people's faces every night; fais, they shan't cut mine, I like it better as it is. The dogs will cost me at least a crown a week in chairs. I believe the souls of your houghers of cattle have got into them, and now they don't distinguish between a cow and a Christian. I forgot to wish you yesterday a happy New Year. You know the twenty-fifth of March is the first day of the year, and now you must leave off cards, and put out your fire. I'll put out mine the first of April, cold or not cold. I believe I shall lose credit with you by not coming over at the beginning of April; but I hoped the session would be ended, and I must stay till then; yet I would fain be at the beginning of my willows growing. Perceval tells me that the quicksets upon the flat in the garden do not grow so well as those famous ones on the ditch. They want digging about them. The cherry-trees, by the river-side, my heart is set upon. Nite MD.

27. Society day. You know that, I suppose. Dr. Arthburnett[2] was President. His dinner was dressed in the

[1] See p. 206.   [2] Arbuthnot.

Queen's kitchen, and was mighty fine. We ate it at Ozinda's Chocolate-house,[1] just by St. James's. We were never merrier, nor better company, and did not part till after eleven. I did not summon Lord Lansdowne: he and I are fallen out. There was something in an *Examiner* a fortnight ago that he thought reflected on the abuses in his office (he is Secretary at War), and he writ to the Secretary that he heard I had inserted that paragraph. This I resented highly, that he should complain of me before he spoke to me. I sent him a peppering letter, and would not summon him by a note, as I did the rest; nor ever will have anything to say to him, till he begs my pardon. I met Lord Treasurer to-day at Lady Masham's. He would fain have carried me home to dinner, but I begged his pardon. What! upon a Society day! No, no. 'Tis rate, sollahs. I an't dlunk. Nite MD.

28. I was with my friend Lewis to-day, getting materials for a little mischief; and I dined with Lord Treasurer, and three or four fellows I never saw before. I left them at seven, and came home, and have been writing to the Archbishop of Dublin, and cousin Deane,[2] in answer to one of his of four months old, that I spied by chance, routing among my papers. I have a pain these two days exactly upon the top of my left shoulder. I fear it is something rheumatic; it winches[3] now and then. Shall I put flannel to it? Domville is going to Ireland; he came here this morning to take leave of me, but I shall dine with him to-morrow. Does the Bishop of Clogher talk of coming for England this summer? I think Lord Molesworth told me so about two months ago. The weather is bad again; rainy and very cold this evening. Do you know what the longitude is? A projector[4] has been applying himself to me, to recommend him to the

---

[1] A resort of the Tories.
[2] Deane Swift, a son of Swift's uncle Godwin, was a merchant in Lisbon.
[3] Winces. Lyly says, "Rubbe there no more, least I winch."
[4] Probably William Whiston, who was deprived of the Lucasian professorship at Cambridge in 1710 for his heterodox views. Parliament having offered a reward for the discovery of means of finding the longitude, Whiston made several attempts (1714 and 1721).

Ministry, because he pretends to have found out the longitude. I believe he has no more found it out than he has found out mine . . .[1] However, I will gravely hear what he says, and discover him a knave or fool. Nite MD.

29. I am plagued with these pains in my shoulder; I believe it is rheumatic; I will do something for it to-night. Mr. Lewis and I dined with Mr. Domville, to take our leave of him. I drank three or four glasses of champagne by perfect teasing, though it is bad for my pain; but if it continue, I will not drink any wine without water till I am well. The weather is abominably cold and wet. I am got into bed, and have put some old flannel, for want of new, to my shoulder, and rubbed it with Hungary water.[2] It is plaguy hard. I never would drink any wine, if it were not for my head, and drinking has given me this pain. I will try abstemiousness for a while. How does MD do now; how does DD and Ppt? You must know I hate pain, as the old woman said. But I'll try to go seep. My flesh sucks up Hungary water rarely. My man is an awkward rascal, and makes me peevish. Do you know that t'other day he was forced to beg my pardon, that he could not shave my head, his hand shook so? He is drunk every day, and I design to turn him off soon as ever I get to Ireland. I'll write no more now, but go to sleep, and see whether sleep and flannel will cure my shoulder. Nite deelest MD.

30. I was not able to go to church or Court to-day for my shoulder. The pain has left my shoulder, and crept to my neck and collar-bone. It makes me think of poo Ppt's bladebone. Urge, urge, urge; dogs gnawing. I went in a chair at two, and dined with Mrs. Van, where I could be easy, and came back at seven. My Hungary water is gone;

---

[1] Word obliterated.

[2] Distilled water prepared with rosemary flowers. In Fielding's *Joseph Andrews*, a lady gives up to a highway robber, in her fright, a silver bottle which, the ruffian said, contained some of the best brandy he had ever tasted; this she "afterwards assured the company was a mistake of her maid, for that she had ordered her to fill the bottle with Hungary water."

and to-night I use spirits of wine, which my landlady tells
me is very good. It has rained terribly all day long, and is
extremely cold. I am very uneasy, and such cruel twinges
every moment! Nite deelest MD.

31. April 1, 2, 3, 4, 5, 6, 7, 8. All these days I have
been extremely ill, though I twice crawled out a week ago;
but am now recovering, though very weak. The violence
of my pain abated the night before last : I will just tell you
how I was, and then send away this letter, which ought to
have gone Saturday last. The pain increased with mighty
violence in my left shoulder and collar-bone, and that side my
neck. On Thursday morning appeared great red spots in
all those places where my pain was, and the violence of the
pain was confined to my neck behind, a little on the left
side; which was so violent that I had not a minute's ease,
nor hardly a minute's sleep in three days and nights. The
spots increased every day, and bred little pimples, which are
now grown white, and full of corruption, though small. The
red still continues too, and most prodigious hot and inflamed.
The disease is the shingles. I eat nothing but water-gruel;
am very weak; but out of all violent pain. The doctors say
it would have ended in some violent disease if it had not
come out thus. I shall now recover fast. I have been in no
danger of life, but miserable torture. I must not write too
much. So adieu, deelest MD MD MD FW FW, ME ME
ME, Lele. I can say lele yet, oo see. Fais, I don't conceal
a bit, as hope saved.[1]

I [2] must purge and clyster after this; and my next letter
will not be in the old order of journal, till I have done with
physic. An't oo surprised to see a letter want half a side?

[1] As I hope to be saved.
[2] Added on the fourth page, as the letter was folded.

LETTER XLV[1]

LONDON, *April* 24, 1712.

I HAD your twenty-eighth two or three days ago. I can
hardly answer it now. Since my last I have been
extremely ill. 'Tis this day just a month since I felt a small
pain on the tip of my left shoulder, which grew worse, and
spread for six days; then broke all out by my collar and
left side of my neck in monstrous red spots inflamed, and
these grew to small pimples. For four days I had no rest,
nor nights, for a pain in my neck; then I grew a little
better; afterward, where my pains were, a cruel itching
seized me, beyond whatever I could imagine, and kept me
awake several nights. I rubbed it vehemently, but did not
scratch it: then it grew into three or four great sores like
blisters, and run; at last I advised the doctor to use it like a
blister, so I did with melilot[2] plasters, which still run: and
am now in pain enough, but am daily mending. I kept my
chamber a fortnight, then went out a day or two, but then
confined myself again. Two days ago I went to a neighbour
to dine, but yesterday again kept at home. To-day I will
venture abroad a little, and hope to be well in a week or ten
days. I never suffered so much in my life. I have taken my
breeches in above two inches, so I am leaner, which answers
one question in your letter. The weather is mighty fine. I
write in the morning, because I am better then. I will go
and try to walk a little. I will give DD's certificate to Tooke
to-morrow. Farewell, MD MD MD, ME ME, FW FW
ME ME.

[1] Addressed to " Mrs. Johnson," etc.   Endorsed " May 1st."
[2] A kind of clover, used for soothing purposes.

LETTER XLVI[1]

LONDON, *May* 10, 1712.

I HAVE not yet ease or humour enough to go on in my journal method, though I have left my chamber these ten days. My pain continues still in my shoulder and collar: I keep flannel on it, and rub it with brandy, and take a nasty diet drink. I still itch terribly, and have some few pimples; I am weak, and sweat; and then the flannel makes me mad with itching; but I think my pain lessens. A journal, while I was sick, would have been a noble thing, made up of pain and physic, visits, and messages; the two last were almost as troublesome as the two first. One good circumstance is that I am grown much leaner. I believe I told you that I have taken in my breeches two inches. I had your N. 29 last night. In answer to your good opinion of my disease, the doctors said they never saw anything so odd of the kind; they were not properly shingles, but *herpes miliaris*, and twenty other hard names. I can never be sick like other people, but always something out of the common way; and as for your notion of its coming without pain, it neither came, nor stayed, nor went without pain, and the most pain I ever bore in my life. Medemeris[2] is retired in the country, with the beast her husband, long ago. I thank the Bishop of Clogher for his proxy; I will write to him soon. Here is Dilly's wife in town; but I have not seen her yet. No, sinkerton:[3] 'tis not a sign of health, but a sign that, if it had not come out, some terrible fit of sickness would have followed. I was at our Society last Thursday, to receive a new member, the Chancellor of the Exchequer;[4] but I drink nothing above wine and water. We shall have a peace, I hope, soon, or at least entirely broke; but I believe the first. My *Letter to Lord Treasurer*, about the English tongue,[5]

[1] Addressed to "Mrs. Dingley," etc.   Endorsed "May 15."
[2] Madam Ayris.   [3] Simpleton.
[4] Robert Benson (see p. 41).   [5] See pp. 407, 420.

is now printing ; and I suffer my name to be put at the end
of it, which I never did before in my life. *The Appendix to
the Third Part of John Bull*[1] was published yesterday; it is
equal to the rest. I hope you read *John Bull.* It was a
Scotch gentleman,[2] a friend of mine, that writ it; but they
put it upon me. The Parliament will hardly be up till June.
We were like to be undone some days ago with a tack ; but
we carried it bravely, and the Whigs came in to help us.
Poor Lady Masham, I am afraid, will lose her only son, about
a twelvemonth old, with the king's evil. I never would let
Mrs. Fenton see me during my illness, though she often
came ; but she has been once here since I recovered.
Bernage has been twice-to see me of late.   His regiment will
be broke, and he only upon half-pay ; so perhaps he thinks he
will want me again.   I am told here the Bishop of Clogher
and family are coming over, but he says nothing of it himself.   I have been returning the visits of those that sent howdees[3] in my sickness ; particularly the Duchess of Hamilton,
who came and sat with me two hours.   I make bargains with
all people that I dine with, to let me scrub my back against
a chair ; and the Duchess of Ormond[4] was forced to bear it
the other day.   Many of my friends are gone to Kensington,
where the Queen has been removed for some time.   This is
a long letter for a kick[5] body.   I will begin the next in the
journal way, though my journals will be sorry ones.   My left
hand is very weak, and trembles ; but my right side has not
been touched.

> This is a pitiful letter
> For want of a better ;
> But plagued with a tetter,
> My fancy does fetter.

Ah ! my poor willows and quicksets ! Well, but you must
read *John Bull.*   Do you understand it all ?   Did I tell you

---

[1] The title was, *An Appendix to John Bull still in his Senses : or, Law is a
Bottomless Pit.*
[2] Arbuthnot.
[3] Enquiries by servants.
[4] See p. 160.
[5] Sick.

that young Parson Gery [1] is going to be married, and asked my advice when it was too late to break off? He tells me Elwick has purchased forty pounds a year in land adjoining to his living. Ppt does not say one word of her own little health. I am angry almost; but I won't, 'cause see im a dood dallar in odle sings; [2] iss, and so im DD too. God bless MD, and FW, and ME, ay and Pdfr too. Farewell, MD, MD, MD, FW, FW, FW. ME, ME Lele. I can say lele it, ung oomens, iss I tan, well as oo.

LETTER XLVII [3]

LONDON, *May* 31, 1712.

I CANNOT yet arrive to my journal letters, my pains continuing still, though with less violence; but I don't love to write journals while I am in pain; and above all, not journals to MD. But, however, I am so much mended, that I intend my next shall be in the old way; and yet I shall, perhaps, break my resolution when I feel pain. I believe I have lost credit with you, in relation to my coming over; but I protest it is impossible for one who has anything to do with this Ministry to be certain when he fixes any time. There is a business which, till it take some turn or other, I cannot leave this place in prudence or honour. And I never wished so much as now that I had stayed in Ireland; but the die is cast, and is now a spinning, and till it settles, I cannot tell whether it be an ace or a sise. [4] I am confident by what you know yourselves, that you will justify

---

[1] Afterwards Rector of Letcombe, Berks. It was to his house that Swift repaired a few weeks before the Queen's death. On June 8, 1714, he wrote, "I am at a clergyman's house, whom I love very well, but he is such a melancholy, thoughtful man, partly from nature, and partly by a solitary life, that I shall soon catch the spleen from him. His wife has been this month twenty miles off at her father's, and will not return these ten days, and perhaps the house will be worse when she comes." Swift spells the name "Geree"; later on in the *Journal* he mentions two of Mr. Gery's sisters, Betty (Mrs. Elwick) and Moll (Mrs. Wigmore); probably he made the acquaintance of the family when he was living with the Temples at Moor Park (see p. 502).

[2] Because she is a good girl in other things.

[3] Addressed to "Mrs. Dingley," etc. Endorsed "June 5."

[4] Sice, the number six at dice.

me in all this. The moment I am used ill, I will leave them;
but know not how to do it while things are in suspense.—
The session will soon be over (I believe in a fortnight), and
the peace, we hope, will be made in a short time; and there
will be no further occasion for me; nor have I anything to
trust to but Court gratitude, so that I expect to see my
willows[1] a month after the Parliament is up: but I will take
MD in my way, and not go to Laracor like an unmannerly
spraenekich ferrow.[2] Have you seen my *Letter to Lord
Treasurer*? There are two answers come out to it already;[3]
though it is no politics, but a harmless proposal about the
improvement of the English Tongue. I believe if I writ an
essay upon a straw some fool would answer it. About ten
days hence I expect a letter from MD, N. 30.—You are now
writing it, near the end, as I guess.—I have not received
DD's money; but I will give you a note for it on Parvisol,
and bed oo paadon[4] I have not done it before. I am just now
thinking to go lodge at Kensington for the air. Lady
Masham has teased me to do it, but business has hindered
me; but now Lord Treasurer has removed thither. Fifteen
of our Society dined together under a canopy in an arbour
at Parson's Green[5] last Thursday: I never saw anything so
fine and romantic. We got a great victory last Wednesday
in the House of Lords by a majority, I think, of twenty-
eight; and the Whigs had desired their friends to bespeak
places to see Lord Treasurer carried to the Tower.[6] I met
your Higgins[7] here yesterday: he roars at the insolence of
the Whigs in Ireland, talks much of his own sufferings and
expenses in asserting the cause of the Church; and I find he

[1] At Laracor Swift had "a canal and river-walk and willows."
[2] Splenetic fellow.
[3] One of them was by Oldmixon: *Reflections on Dr. Swift's Letter to the
Earl of Oxford.*
[4] Beg your pardon.   [5] See p. 239.
[6] On May 28, Lord Halifax moved an Address to the Queen that the
instructions given to the Duke of Ormond might be laid before the House, and
that further orders might be issued to him to act offensively, in concert with the
Allies. Wharton and Nottingham supported the motion, but it was negatived
by 68 votes against 40. A similar motion in the House of Commons was
defeated by 203 against 73.
[7] See p. 335.

would fain plead merit enough to desire that his fortune should be mended. I believe he designs to make as much noise as he can in order to preferment. Pray let the Provost, when he sees you, give you ten English shillings, and I will give as much here to the man who delivered me Rymer's books:[1] he knows the meaning. Tell him I will not trust him, but that you can order it to be paid me here ; and I will trust you till I see you. Have I told you that the rogue Patrick has left me these two months, to my great satisfaction ? I have got another, who seems to be much better, if he continues it. I am printing a threepenny pamphlet,[2] and shall print another in a fortnight, and then I have done, unless some new occasion starts. Is my curate Warburton married to Mrs. Melthrop in my parish ? so I hear. Or is it a lie ? Has Raymond got to his new house ? Do you see Joe now and then ? What luck have you at ombre ? How stands it with the Dean ? . . . [3] My service to Mrs. Stoyte, and Catherine, if she be come from Wales. I have not yet seen Dilly Ashe's wife. I called once, but she was not at home : I think she is under the doctor's hand. . . . [4] I believe the news of the Duke of Ormond producing letters in the council of war, with orders not to fight, will surprise you in Ireland. Lord Treasurer said in the House of Lords that in a few days the treaty of peace should be laid before them ; and our Court thought it wrong to hazard a battle, and sacrifice many lives in such a juncture. If the peace holds, all will do well, otherwise I know not how we shall weather it. And it was reckoned as a wrong step in politics for Lord Treasurer to open himself so much. The Secretary would not go so far to satisfy the Whigs in the House of Commons ; but there all went swimmingly. I'll say no more to oo to-nite, sellohs, because I must send away the letter, not by the bell,[5] but early : and besides, I have not much more to say at zis

---

[1] See p. 217.
[2] *Some Reasons to prove that no Person is obliged by his Principles, as a Whig, to oppose Her Majesty : in a Letter to a Whig Lord.*
[3] Several words obliterated.   [4] Several words obliterated.
[5] The bellman.

plesent liting.[1] Does MD never read at all now, pee?[2] But oo walk plodigiousry, I suppose; oo make nothing of walking to, to, to, ay, to Donnybrook. I walk too as much as I can, because sweating is good; but I'll walk more if I go to Kensington. I suppose I shall have no apples this year neither, for I dined t'other day with Lord Rivers, who is sick at his country - house, and he showed me all his cherries blasted. Nite deelest sollahs; farewell deelest rives; rove poo poo Pdfr. Farewell deelest richar MD, MD, MD, FW, FW, FW, FW, FW, ME, ME, Lele, ME, Lele, Lele, richar MD.

LETTER XLVIII[3]

KENSINGTON, *June 17, 1712.*

I HAVE been so tosticated about since my last, that I could not go on in my journal manner, though my shoulder is a great deal better; however, I feel constant pain in it, but I think it diminishes, and I have cut off some slices from my flannel. I have lodged here near a fortnight, partly for the air and exercise, partly to be near the Court, where dinners are to be found. I generally get a lift in a coach to town, and in the evening I walk back. On Saturday I dined with the Duchess of Ormond at her lodge near Sheen, and thought to get a boat back as usual. I walked by the bank to Cue [Kew], but no boat, then to Mortlake, but no boat, and it was nine o'clock. At last a little sculler called, full of nasty people. I made him set me down at Hammersmith, so walked two miles to this place, and got here by eleven. Last night I had another such difficulty. I was in the City till past ten at night; it rained hard, but no coach to be had. It gave over a little, and I walked all the way here, and got home by twelve. I love these shabby difficulties when they are over; but I hate them, because they arise from not having a thousand pound a year. I had your N. 30

[1] This present writing.   [2] Please.
[3] Addressed to " Mrs. Rebecca Dingley," etc.   Endorsed " June 23d."

about three days ago, which I will now answer. And first, I did not relapse, but found [1] I came out before I ought; and so, and so, as I have told you in some of my last. The first coming abroad made people think I was quite recovered, and I had no more messages afterwards. Well, but *John Bull* is not writ by the person you imagine, as hope![2] It is too good for another to own. Had it been Grub Street, I would have let people think as they please; and I think that's right: is not it now? so flap ee hand, and make wry mouth oo-self, sauci doxi. Now comes DD. Why sollah, I did write in a fortnight my 47th; and if it did not come in due time, can I help wind and weather? am I a Laplander? am I a witch? can I work miracles? can I make easterly winds? Now I am against Dr. Smith. I drink little water with my wine, yet I believe he is right. Yet Dr. Cockburn told me a little wine would not hurt me; but it is so hot and dry, and water is so dangerous. The worst thing here is my evenings at Lord Masham's, where Lord Treasurer comes, and we sit till after twelve. But it is convenient I should be among them for a while as much as possible. I need not tell oo why. But I hope that will be at an end in a month or two, one way or other, and I am resolved it shall. But I can't go to Tunbridge, or anywhere else out of the way, in this juncture. So Ppt designs for Templeoag (what a name is that!). Whereabouts is that place? I hope not very far from Dublin. Higgins is here, roaring that all is wrong in Ireland, and would have me get him an audience of Lord Treasurer to tell him so; but I will have nothing to do in it, no, not I, faith. We have had no thunder till last night, and till then we were dead for want of rain; but there fell a great deal: no field looked green. I reckon the Queen will go to Windsor in three or four weeks: and if the Secretary takes a house there, I shall be sometimes with him. But how affectedly Ppt talks of my being here all the summer; which I do not intend: nor to stay one minute longer in England than becomes the circumstances I am in. I wish

---

[1] Mr. Ryland reads " second."   [2] As I hope to be saved.

you would go soon into the country, and take a good deal of it; and where better than Trim? Joe will be your humble servant, Parvisol your slave, and Raymond at your command, for he piques himself on good manners. I have seen Dilly's wife—and I have seen once or twice old Bradley[1] here. He is very well, very old, and very wise: I believe I must go see his wife, when I have leisure. I should be glad to see Goody Stoyte and her husband; pray give them my humble service, and to Catherine, and to Mrs. Walls—I am not the least bit in love with Mrs. Walls—I suppose the cares of the husband increase with the fruitfulness of the wife. I am grad at halt[2] to hear of Ppt's good health: pray let her finish it by drinking waters. I hope DD had her bill, and has her money. Remember to write a due time before ME money is wanted, and be good galls, dood dallars, I mean, and no crying dallars. I heard somebody coming upstairs, and forgot I was in the country; and I was afraid of a visitor: that is one advantage of being here, that I am not teased with solicitors. Molt, the chemist, is my acquaintance. My service to Dr. Smith. I sent the question to him about Sir Walter Raleigh's cordial, and the answer he returned is in these words: "It is directly after Mr. Boyle's receipt." That commission is performed; if he wants any of it, Molt shall use him fairly. I suppose Smith is one of your physicians. So, now your letter is fully and impartially answered; not as rascals answer me: I believe, if I writ an essay upon a straw, I should have a shoal of answerers: but no matter for that; you see I can answer without making any reflections, as becomes men of learning. Well, but now for the peace : why, we expect it daily; but the French have the staff in their own hands, and we trust to their honesty. I wish it were otherwise. Things are now in the way of being soon in the extremes of well or ill. I hope and believe the first. Lord Wharton is gone out of town in a rage, and curses himself and friends for ruining themselves in defending Lord Marlborough and Godolphin, and taking Nottingham

[1] See p. 295.   [2] Glad at heart.

into their favour. He swears he will meddle no more during this reign; a pretty speech at sixty-six, and the Queen is near twenty years younger, and now in very good health; for you must know her health is fixed by a certain reason, that she has done with braces (I must use the expression), and nothing ill is happened to her since; so she has a new lease of her life. Read the *Letter to a Whig Lord*.[1] Do you ever read? Why don't you say so? I mean does DD read to Ppt? Do you walk? I think Ppt should walk to[2] DD, as DD reads to Ppt, for Ppt oo must know is a good walker; but not so good as Pdfr. I intend to dine to-day with Mr. Lewis, but it threatens rain; and I shall be too late to get a lift; and I must write to the Bishop of Clogher. 'Tis now ten in the morning; and this is all writ at a heat. Farewell deelest . . . deelest MD, MD, MD, MD, MD, FW, FW, FW, ME, ME, ME, Lele, ME, Lele, ME, Lele, ME, Lele, Lele, Lele, ME.

LETTER XLIX[3]

KENSINGTON, *July* 1, 1712.

I NEVER was in a worse station for writing letters than this, especially for writing to MD, since I left off my journals. For I go to town early; and when I come home at night, I generally go to Lord Masham, where Lord Treasurer comes, and we stay till past twelve. But I am now resolved to write journals again, though my shoulder is not yet well; for I have still a few itching pimples, and a little pain now and then. It is now high cherry-time with us; take notice, is it so soon with you? And we have early apricots, and gooseberries are ripe. On Sunday Archdeacon Parnell came here to see me. It seems he has been ill for grief of his wife's death,[4] and has been two months at the Bath. He has a

---

[1] The threepenny pamphlet mentioned on p. 441.   [2] *I.e.*, for.
[3] Addressed to "Mrs. Dingley." Endorsed "July 8."
[4] See p. 277.

mind to go to Dunkirk with Jack Hill,[1] and I persuade
him to it, and have spoke to Hill to receive him; but I
doubt he won't have spirit to go. I have made Ford[2]
Gazetteer, and got two hundred pounds a year settled on the
employment by the Secretary of State, beside the perquisites.
It is the prettiest employment in England of its bigness; yet
the puppy does not seem satisfied with it. I think people
keep some follies to themselves, till they have occasion to
produce them. He thinks it not genteel enough, and makes
twenty difficulties. 'Tis impossible to make any man easy.
His salary is paid him every week, if he pleases, without
taxes or abatements. He has little to do for it. He has
a pretty office, with coals, candles, papers, etc.; can frank
what letters he will; and his perquisites, if he takes care,
may be worth one hundred pounds more. I hear the Bishop
of Clogher is landing, or landed, in England; and I hope to
see him in a few days. I was to see Mrs. Bradley[3] on
Sunday night. Her youngest son is married to somebody
worth nothing, and her daughter was forced to leave Lady
Giffard, because she was striking up an intrigue with a footman, who played well upon the flute. This is the mother's
account of it. Yesterday the old Bishop of Worcester,[4] who
pretends to be a prophet, went to the Queen, by appointment, to prove to Her Majesty, out of Daniel and the
Revelations, that four years hence there would be a war
of religion; that the King of France would be a Protestant, and fight on their side; that the Popedom would be
destroyed, etc.; and declared that he would be content to
give up his bishopric if it were not true. Lord Treasurer,
who told it me, was by, and some others; and I am told
Lord Treasurer confounded him sadly in his own learning,
which made the old fool very quarrelsome. He is near

---

[1] See p. 76.   [2] See p. 9.   [3] See pp. 295, 444.
[4] Dr. William Lloyd—one of the Seven Bishops of 1688—was eighty-four
years of age at this time; he died five years later. He was a strong anti-
papist, and a great student of the Apocalypse, besides being a hard-working
bishop. A curious letter from him to Lord Oxford about a coming war of
religion is given in the Welbeck Papers (Hist. MSS. Comm.) v. 128.

ninety years old. Old Bradley is fat and lusty, and has lost his palsy. Have you seen *Toland's Invitation to Dismal*?[1] How do you like it? But it is an imitation of Horace, and perhaps you don't understand Horace. Here has been a great sweep of employments, and we expect still more removals. The Court seems resolved to make thorough work. Mr. Hill intended to set out to-morrow for Dunkirk, of which he is appointed Governor; but he tells me to-day that he cannot go till Thursday or Friday. I wish it were over. Mr. Secretary tells me he is [in] no fear at all that France will play tricks with us. If we have Dunkirk once, all is safe. We rail now all against the Dutch, who, indeed, have acted like knaves, fools, and madmen. Mr. Secretary is soon to be made a viscount. He desired I would draw the preamble of his patent; but I excused myself from a work that might lose me a great deal of reputation, and get me very little. We would fain have the Court make him an earl, but it would not be; and therefore he will not take the title of Bullenbrook,[2] which is lately extinct in the elder branch of his family. I have advised him to be called Lord Pomfret; but he thinks that title is already in some other family;[3] and, besides, he objects that it is in Yorkshire, where he has no estate; but there is nothing in that, and I love Pomfret. Don't you love Pomfret? Why? 'Tis in all our histories; they are full of Pomfret Castle. But what's all this to you? You don't care for this. Is Goody Stoyte come to London? I have not heard of her yet. The Dean of St. Patrick's never had the manners to answer my letter. I was t'other day to see Sterne[4] and his wife. She is not half so handsome as when I saw her with you at Dublin.

---

[1] *Toland's Invitation to Dismal to dine with the Calf's Head Club.* The Earl of Nottingham (Dismal) had deserted the Tories, and Swift's imitation of Horace (Epist. I. v.) is an invitation from Toland to dine with "his trusty friends" in celebration of the execution of Charles I. The Calf's Head Club was in the habit of toasting "confusion to the race of kings."

[2] Bolingbroke.

[3] George Fitzroy, Duke of Northumberland (died 1716), a natural son of Charles II., was also Viscount Falmouth and Baron of Pontefract. See *Notes and Queries*, viii. i. 135.

[4] Enoch Sterne.

They design to pass the summer at a house near Lord Somers's, about a dozen miles off. You never told me how my *Letter to Lord Treasurer* passes in Ireland. I suppose you are drinking at this time Temple-something's[1] waters. Steele was arrested the other day for making a lottery directly against an Act of Parliament. He is now under prosecution; but they think it will be dropped out of pity.[2] I believe he will very soon lose his employment, for he has been mighty impertinent of late in his *Spectators*; and I will never offer a word in his behalf. Raymond writes me word that the Bishop of Meath[3] was going to summon me, in order to suspension, for absence, if the Provost had not prevented him. I am prettily rewarded for getting them their First-Fruits, with a p——. We have had very little hot weather during the whole month of June; and for a week past we have had a great deal of rain, though not every day. I am just now told that the Governor of Dunkirk has not orders yet to deliver up the town to Jack Hill and his forces, but expects them daily. This must put off Hill's journey a while, and I don't like these stoppings in such an affair. Go, get oo gone, and drink oo waters, if this rain has not spoiled them, sauci doxi. I have no more to say to oo at plesent; but rove Pdfr, and MD, and ME. And Podefr will rove Pdfr, and MD and ME. I wish you had taken any account when I sent money to Mrs. Brent. I believe I han't done it a great while. And pray send me notice when ME . . . to have it when it is due.[4] Farewell, dearest MD FW FW FW ME ME ME.

---

[1] Templeoag (p. 443).

[2] Swift probably was only repeating an inaccurate rumour, for there is no evidence that Steele was arrested. His gambling scheme was withdrawn directly an information was laid under the new Act of Parliament against gambling (Aitken's *Life of Steele*, i. 347).

[3] Dr. William Moreton (1641-1715), Swift's diocesan, was translated from the see of Kildare to that of Meath in 1705.

[4] Words obliterated. Forster reads conjecturally, "when ME wants me to send. She ought to have it," etc.

LETTER L[1]

KENSINGTON, *July* 17, 1712.

I AM weary of living in this place, and glad to leave it soon. The Queen goes on Tuesday to Windsor, and I shall follow in three or four days after. I can do nothing here, going early to London, and coming late from it, and supping at Lady Masham's. I dined to-day with the Duke of Argyle at Cue [Kew], and would not go to the Court to-night, because of writing to MD. The Bishop of Clogher has been here this fortnight: I see him as often as I can. Poor Master Ashe has a sad redness in his face; it is St. Anthony's fire; his face all swelled, and will break in his cheek, but no danger. Since Dunkirk has been in our hands, Grub Street has been very fruitful. Pdfr has writ five or six Grub Street papers this last week. Have you seen *Toland's Invitation to Dismal*, or *Hue and Cry after Dismal*, or *Ballad on Dunkirk*, or *Argument that Dunkirk is not in our Hands?* Poh! you have seen nothing. I am dead here with the hot weather; yet I walk every night home, and believe it does me good: but my shoulder is not yet right; itchings, and scratchings, and small achings. Did I tell you I had made Ford Gazetteer, with two hundred pounds a year salary, beside perquisites? I had a letter lately from Parvisol, who says my canal looks very finely; I long to see it; but no apples; all blasted again. He tells me there will be a triennial visitation in August. I must send Raymond another proxy. So now I will answer oo rettle N. 33,[2] dated June 17. Ppt writes as well as ever, for all her waters. I wish I had never come here, as often and as heartily as Ppt. What had I to do here? I have heard of the Bishop's making me uneasy, but I did not think it was because I never writ to him. A little would make me write to him, but I don't know what to say.

---

[1] Addressed to "Mrs. Dingley," etc. Endorsed "July 23."
[2] "N. 33" seems a mistake. Letter No. 32 was received after Swift had left Kensington and gone to Windsor; see pp. 452, 456 (Ryland).

I find I am obliged to the Provost for keeping the Bishop [1] from being impertinent. Yes, Maram DD, but oo would not be content with letters flom Pdfr of six lines, or twelve either, fais. I hope Ppt will have done with the waters soon, and find benefit by them. I believe, if they were as far off as Wexford, they would do as much good; for I take the journey to contribute as much as anything. I can assure you the Bishop of Clogher's being here does not in the least affect my staying or going. I never talked to Higgins but once in my life in the street, and I believe he and I shall hardly meet but by chance. What care I whether my *Letter to Lord Treasurer* be commended there or no? Why does not somebody among you answer it, as three or four have done here? (I am now sitting with nothing but my nightgown, for heat.) Ppt shall have a great Bible. I have put it down in my memlandums [2] just now. And DD shall be repaid her t'other book; but patience, all in good time: you are so hasty, a dog would, etc. So Ppt has neither won nor lost. Why, mun, I play sometimes too at picket, that is picquet, I mean; but very seldom.—Out late? why, 'tis only at Lady Masham's, and that is in our town; but I never come late here from London, except once in rain, when I could not get a coach. We have had very little thunder here; none these two months. Why, pray, madam philosopher, how did the rain hinder the thunder from doing any harm? I suppose it ssquenched it. So here comes Ppt aden [3] with her little watery postscript. O Rold, dlunken srut! [4] drink Pdfr's health ten times in a morning! you are a whetter, fais; I sup MD's fifteen times evly molning in milk porridge. Lele's fol oo now—and lele's fol oo rettle, and evly kind of sing [5]—and now I must say something else. You hear Secretary St. John is made Viscount Bullinbrook. [6] I can hardly persuade him to take that title, because the

[1] Dr. Moreton (see p. 448).
[2] Memoranda.
[3] Again.
[4] O Lord, drunken slut.
[5] There's for you now, and there's for your letter, and every kind of thing.
[6] Bolingbroke.

eldest branch of his family had it in an earldom, and it was last year extinct. If he did not take it, I advised him to be Lord Pomfret, which I think is a noble title. You hear of it often in the *Chronicles*, Pomfret Castle : but we believed it was among the titles of some other lord. Jack Hill sent his sister a pattern of a head-dress from Dunkirk; it was like our fashion twenty years ago, only not quite so high, and looked very ugly. I have made Trapp[1] chaplain to Lord Bullinbroke, and he is mighty happy and thankful for it. Mr. Addison returned me my visit this morning. He lives in our town. I shall be mighty retired, and mighty busy for a while at Windsor. Pray why don't MD go to Trim, and see Laracor, and give me an account of the garden, and the river, and the holly and the cherry-trees on the river-walk ?

19. I could not send this letter last post, being called away before I could fold or finish it. I dined yesterday with Lord Treasurer; sat with him till ten at night; yet could not find a minute for some business I had with him. He brought me to Kensington, and Lord Bulingbrook would not let me go away till two; and I am now in bed, very lazy and sleepy at nine. I must shave head and face, and meet Lord Bullinbrook at eleven, and dine again with Lord Treasurer. To-day there will be another Grub,[2] *A Letter from the Pretender to a Whig Lord*. Grub Street has but ten days to live ; then an Act of Parliament takes place that ruins it, by taxing every half-sheet at a halfpenny. We have news just come, but not the particulars, that the Earl of Albemarle,[3] at the head of eight thousand Dutch, is beaten, lost the greatest part of his men, and himself a prisoner. This perhaps may cool their courage, and make them think of a peace. The Duke of Ormond has got abundance of credit by his good conduct of affairs in Flanders. We had a good deal of

---

[1] See p. 120.
[2] Grub Street pamphlet. The title was, *A Supposed Letter from the Pretender to another Whig Lord*.
[3] Arnold Joost Van Keppel, created Earl of Albemarle in 1697. He died in 1718. The action referred to was at Denain, where the Dutch were defeated by Villars.

rain last night, very refreshing. 'Tis late, and I must rise.
Don't play at ombre in your waters, sollah.   Farewell, deelest
MD, MD MD MD FW FW ME ME ME Lele Lele Lele.

LETTER LI [1]

LONDON, *Aug.* 7, 1712.

I HAD your N. 32 at Windsor: I just read it, and immediately sealed it up again, and shall read it no more this
twelvemonth at least.   The reason of my resentment at it is,
because you talk as glibly of a thing as if it were done, which,
for aught I know, is farther from being done than ever, since
I hear not a word of it, though the town is full of it, and the
Court always giving me joy and vexation.   You might be sure
I would have let you know as soon as it was done ; but I believe
you fancied I would affect not to tell it you, but let you learn
it from newspapers and reports.   I remember only there was
something in your letter about ME's money, and that shall be
taken care of on the other side.   I left Windsor on Monday
last, upon Lord Bolingbroke's being gone to France, and somebody's being here that I ought often to consult with in an affair
I am upon: but that person talks of returning to Windsor
again, and I believe I shall follow him.   I am now in a hedge-
lodging very busy, as I am every day till noon: so that this
letter is like to be short, and you are not to blame me these
two months ; for I protest, if I study ever so hard, I cannot in
that time compass what I am upon.   We have a fever both
here and at Windsor, which hardly anybody misses ; but it
lasts not above three or four days, and kills nobody.[2]   The
Queen has forty servants down of it at once.   I dined
yesterday with Treasurer, but could do no business, though
he sent for me, I thought, on purpose ; but he desires I will
dine with him again to-day.   Windsor is a most delightful
place, and at this time abounds in dinners.   My lodgings there

---

[1] Addressed to " Mrs. Dingley," etc.   Endorsed " Aug. 14."
[2] Perhaps this was influenza.

look upon Eton and the Thames. I wish I was owner of
them ; they belong to a prebend. God knows what was in
your letter; and if it be not answered, whose fault is it,
sauci dallars ?—Do you know that Grub Street is dead and
gone last week ? No more ghosts or murders now for love or
money. I plied it pretty close the last fortnight, and published
at least seven penny papers of my own, besides some of
other people's : but now every single half-sheet pays a halfpenny to the Queen.[1] The *Observator* is fallen ; the *Medleys*
are jumbled together with the *Flying Post* ; the *Examiner*
is deadly sick ; the *Spectator* keeps up, and doubles its price ;
I know not how long it will hold. Have you seen the red
stamp the papers are marked with ? Methinks it is worth a
halfpenny, the stamping it. Lord Bolingbroke and Prior set
out for France last Saturday. My lord's business is to hasten
the peace before the Dutch are too much mauled, and hinder
France from carrying the jest of beating them too far. Have
you seen the Fourth Part of *John Bull* ?[2] It is equal to the
rest, and extremely good. The Bishop of Clogher's son has
been ill of St. Anthony's fire, but is now quite well. I was
afraid his face would be spoiled, but it is not. Dilly is just
as he used to be, and puns as plentifully and as bad. The
two brothers see one another; but I think not the two
sisters. Raymond writ to me that he intended to invite you
to Trim. Are you, have you, will you be there? Won't oo
see pool Laratol ?[3] Parvisol says I shall have no fruit. Blasts
have taken away all. Pray observe the cherry-trees on the
river-walk ; but oo are too lazy to take such a journey.
If you have not your letters in due time for two months hence,

---

[1] By the Stamp Act passed on June 10, 1712—which was repealed in 1859—a
duty of one halfpenny was levied on all pamphlets and newspapers contained in
half a sheet or less, and a duty of one penny on those of more than half but
not exceeding a whole sheet. Swift opposed the idea in January 1711 (see p.
138), and Defoe argued against the Bill in the *Review* for April 26, 1712, and
following numbers. Addison, in the *Spectator*, No. 445, spoke of the mortality
among authors resulting from the Stamp Act as "the fall of the leaf."
[2] The title is, *Lewis Baboon turned honest, and John Bull politician. Being
the Fourth Part of Law is a Bottomless Pit.* This pamphlet—really the fifth of
the series—appeared on July 31, 1712.
[3] Poor Laracor.

impute it to my being tosticated between this and Windsor. And pray send me again the state of ME's money ; for I will not look into your letter for it.   Poor Lord Winchelsea [1] is dead, to my great grief.   He was a worthy honest gentleman, and particular friend of mine : and, what is yet worse, my old acquaintance, Mrs. Finch,[2] is now Countess of Winchelsea, the title being fallen to her husband, but without much estate.   I have been poring my eyes all this morning, and it is now past two afternoon, so I shall take a little walk in the Park.   Do you play at ombre still ?   Or is that off by Mr. Stoyte's absence, and Mrs. Manley's grief ?   Somebody was telling me of a strange sister that Mrs. Manley has got in Ireland, who disappointed you all about her being handsome. My service to Mrs. Walls.   Farewell, deelest MD MD MD, FW FW FW, ME ME ME ME ME.   Lele, logues both ; rove poo Pdfr.

LETTER LII [3]

WINDSOR, *Sept.* 15, 1712.

I NEVER was so long without writing to MD as now, since I left them, nor ever will again while I am able to write. I have expected from one week to another that something would be done in my own affairs ; but nothing at all is, nor I don't know when anything will, or whether ever at all, so slow are people at doing favours.   I have been much out of order of late with the old giddiness in my head.   I took a vomit for it two days ago, and will take another about a day or two hence.   I have eat mighty little fruit ; yet I impute my disorder to that little, and shall henceforth wholly forbear it.   I am engaged in a long work, and have done all I can of it, and wait for some papers from the Ministry for

---

[1] See p. 104.
[2] On the death of the third Earl in 1712, the title of Earl of Winchelsea passed to his uncle, Heneage Finch, who had married Anne, daughter of Sir William Kingsmill (see p. 227).
[3] Addressed to "Mrs. Dingley," etc   Endorsed "Oct. 1st.   At Portraune" [Portraine].

materials for the rest; and they delay me, as if it were a
favour I asked of them; so that I have been idle here this
good while, and it happened in a right time, when I was too
much out of order to study.   One is kept constantly out of
humour by a thousand unaccountable things in public proceedings; and when I reason with some friends, we cannot
conceive how affairs can last as they are. God only knows,
but it is a very melancholy subject for those who have any
near concern in it.   I am again endeavouring, as I was last
year, to keep people [1] from breaking to pieces upon a hundred
misunderstandings.   One cannot withhold them from drawing different ways, while the enemy is watching to destroy
both.   See how my style is altered, by living and thinking
and talking among these people, instead of my canal and
river-walk and willows.   I lose all my money here among
the ladies; [2] so that I never play when I can help it, being
sure to lose.   I have lost five pounds the five weeks I have
been here.   I hope Ppt is luckier at picquet with the Dean
and Mrs. Walls.   The Dean never answered my letter,
though.   I have clearly forgot whether I sent a bill for ME
in any of my last letters.   I think I did; pray let me know,
and always give me timely notice.   I wait here but to see
what they will do for me; and whenever preferments are
given from me, as hope saved, I will come over.

18. I have taken a vomit to-day, and hope I shall be
better.   I have been very giddy since I writ what is before,
yet not as I used to be: more frequent, but not so violent.
Yesterday we were alarmed with the Queen's being ill:
she had an aguish and feverish fit; and you never saw such
countenances as we all had, such dismal melancholy.   Her
physicians from town were sent for, but towards night she
grew better; to-day she missed her fit, and was up: we are
not now in any fear; it will be at worst but an ague, and we
hope even that will not return.   Lord Treasurer would not
come here from London, because it would make a noise if
he came before his usual time, which is Saturday, and he

[1] Oxford and Bolingbroke.   [2] Including Hester Vanhomrigh.

goes away on Mondays.   The Whigs have lost a great support in the Earl of Godolphin.[1]   It is a good jest to hear the Ministers talk of him now with humanity and pity, because he is dead, and can do them no more hurt.   Lady Orkney,[2] the late King's mistress (who lives at a fine place, five miles from hence, called Cliffden[3]), and I, are grown mighty acquaintance.   She is the wisest woman I ever saw ; and Lord Treasurer made great use of her advice in the late change of affairs.   I heard Lord Marlborough is growing ill of his diabetes; which, if it be true, may soon carry him off; and then the Ministry will be something more at ease. MD has been a long time without writing to Pdfr, though they have not the same cause : it is seven weeks since your last came to my hands, which was N. 32, that you may not be mistaken.   I hope Ppt has not wanted her health.   You were then drinking waters.   The doctor tells me I must go into a course of steel, though I have not the spleen; for that they can never give me, though I have as much provocation to it as any man alive.   Bernage's[4] regiment is broke ; but he is upon half-pay.   I have not seen him this long time; but I suppose he is overrun with melancholy.   My Lord Shrewsbury is certainly designed to be Governor of Ireland ; and I believe the Duchess will please the people there mightily.   The Irish Whig leaders promise great things to themselves from his government; but care shall be taken, if possible, to prevent them.   Mrs. Fenton[5] has writ to me

---

[1] He died on Sept. 15, 1712.

[2] Elizabeth Villiers, eldest daughter of Sir Edward Villiers, Knight Marischal of England, and sister of the first Earl of Jersey.   In 1695 she married Lord George Hamilton (son of Lord William Douglas, afterwards Duke of Hamilton), who was raised to the peerage of Scotland in 1696 as Earl of Orkney.   William III. gave her an Irish estate worth £26,000 a year. Swift's opinion of her wisdom is confirmed by Lord Lansdowne, who speaks, in his *Progress of Poetry*, of

> " Villiers, for wisdom and deep judgment famed,
>   Of a high race, victorious beauty brings
>   To grace our Courts, and captivate our Kings."

The "beauty" seems a poetic licence ; Swift says the lady squinted "like a dragon."

[3] Cliefden.   [4] See p. 106.

[5] Swift's sister (see p. 74).

that she has been forced to leave Lady Giffard, and come to town, for a rheumatism: that lady does not love to be troubled with sick people. Mrs. Fenton writes to me as one dying, and desires I would think of her son: I have not answered her letter. She is retired [1] to Mrs. Povey's. Is my aunt alive yet? and do you ever see her? I suppose she has forgot the loss of her son. Is Raymond's new house quite finished? and does he squander as he used to do? Has he yet spent all his wife's fortune? I hear there are five or six people putting strongly in for my livings; God help them! But if ever the Court should give me anything, I would recommend Raymond to the Duke of Ormond; not for any particular friendship to him, but because it would be proper for the minister of Trim to have Laracor. You may keep the gold-studded snuff-box now; for my brother Hill, Governor of Dunkirk, has sent me the finest that ever you saw.[2] It is allowed at Court that none in England comes near it, though it did not cost above twenty pounds. And the Duchess of Hamilton has made me pockets for [it] like a woman's, with a belt and buckle (for, you know, I wear no waistcoat in summer), and there are several divisions, and one on purpose for my box, oh ho!—We have had most delightful weather this whole week; but illness and vomiting have hindered me from sharing in a great part of it. Lady Masham made the Queen send to Kensington for some of her preserved ginger for me, which I take in the morning, and hope it will do me good. Mrs. Brent[3] sent me a letter by a young fellow, a printer, desiring I would recommend him here, which you may tell her I have done: but I cannot promise what will come of it, for it is necessary they should be made free here [4] before they can be employed. I remember I put the boy prentice to Brent. I hope Parvisol has set my tithes well this year: he has writ nothing to me about it; pray talk to him of it when you see him, and let him give me an account

---

[1] Forster reads "returned."
[2] See Swift's letter to General Hill of Aug. 12, 1712.
[3] Swift's housekeeper at Laracor.   [4] *I.e.*, be made freemen of the City.

how things are. I suppose the corn is now off the ground. I hope he has sold that great ugly horse. Why don't you sell to him? He keeps me at charges for horses that I never ride: yours is lame, and will never be good for anything. The Queen will stay here about a month longer, I suppose; but Lady Masham will go in ten days to lie in at Kensington. Poor creature, she fell down in the court here t'other day. She would needs walk across it upon some displeasure with her chairmen, and was likely to be spoiled so near her time; but we hope all is over for a black eye and a sore side: though I shall not be at ease till she is brought to bed. I find I can fill up a letter, some way or other, without a journal. If I had not a spirit naturally cheerful, I should be very much discontented at a thousand things. Pray God preserve MD's health, and Pdfr's, and that I may live far from the envy and discontent that attends those who are thought to have more favour at Courts than they really possess. Love Pdfr, who loves MD above all things. Farewell, deelest, ten thousand times deelest, MD MD MD, FW FW, ME ME ME ME. Lele, Lele, Lele, Lele.

LETTER LIII[1]

LONDON, *Oct.* 9, 1712.

I HAVE left Windsor these ten days, and am deep in pills with asafœtida, and a steel bitter drink; and I find my head much better than it was. I was very much discouraged; for I used to be ill for three or four days together, ready to totter as I walked. I take eight pills a day, and have taken, I believe, a hundred and fifty already. The Queen, Lord Treasurer, Lady Masham, and I, were all ill together, but are now all better; only Lady Masham expects every day to lie in at Kensington. There was never such a lump of lies spread about the town together as now. I doubt not but

---

[1] Addressed to "Mrs. Dingley," etc. Endorsed "Octr. 18. At Portraune."

you will have them in Dublin before this comes to you, and
all without the least grounds of truth. I have been mightily
put backward in something I am writing by my illness, but
hope to fetch it up, so as to be ready when the Parliament
meets. Lord Treasurer has had an ugly fit of the rheumatism,
but is now near quite well. I was playing at one-and-thirty
with him and his family t'other night. He gave us all
twelvepence apiece to begin with: it put me in mind of Sir
William Temple.[1] I asked both him and Lady Masham
seriously whether the Queen were at all inclined to a
dropsy, and they positively assured me she was not: so
did her physician Arbuthnot, who always attends her. Yet
these devils have spread that she has holes in her legs, and
runs at her navel, and I know not what. Arbuthnot has
sent me from Windsor a pretty Discourse upon Lying, and I
have ordered the printer to come for it. It is a proposal for
publishing a curious piece, called *The Art of Political Lying*,
in two volumes, etc. And then there is an abstract of the
first volume, just like those pamphlets which they call *The
Works of the Learned*.[2] Pray get it when it comes out. The
Queen has a little of the gout in one of her hands. I believe
she will stay a month still at Windsor. Lord Treasurer
showed me the kindest letter from her in the world, by which
I picked out one secret, that there will be soon made some
Knights of the Garter. You know another is fallen by Lord
Godolphin's death: he will be buried in a day or two at
Westminster Abbey. I saw Tom Leigh [3] in town once. The
Bishop of Clogher has taken his lodging for the winter; they
are all well. I hear there are in town abundance of people
from Ireland; half a dozen bishops at least. The poor old
Bishop of London,[4] at past fourscore, fell down backward
going upstairs, and I think broke or cracked his skull; yet is

---

[1] "Sometimes, when better company was not to be had, he [Swift] was
honoured by being invited to play at cards with his patron; and on such
occasions Sir William was so generous as to give his antagonist a little silver
to begin with" (Macaulay, *History of England*, chap. xix.).

[2] *The History of the Works of the Learned*, a quarto periodical, was published from 1699 to 1711.

[3] See p. 343.   [4] See p. 277.

now recovering. The town is as empty as at midsummer; and if I had not occasion for physic, I would be at Windsor still. Did I tell you of Lord Rivers's will? He has left legacies to about twenty paltry old whores by name, and not a farthing to any friend, dependent, or relation: he has left from his only child, Lady Barrymore,[1] her mother's estate, and given the whole to his heir-male, a popish priest, a second cousin, who is now Earl Rivers, and whom he used in his life like a footman. After him it goes to his chief wench and bastard. Lord Treasurer and Lord Chamberlain are executors of this hopeful will. I loved the man, and detest his memory. We hear nothing of peace yet: I believe verily the Dutch are so wilful, because they are told the Queen cannot live. I had poor MD's letter, N. 3,[2] at Windsor: but I could not answer it then; poor Pdfr was vely kick[3] then: and, besides, it was a very inconvenient place to send letters from. Oo thought to come home the same day, and stayed a month: that was a sign the place was agreeable.[4] I should love such a sort of jaunt. Is that lad Swanton[5] a little more fixed than he used to be? I think you like the girl very well. She has left off her grave airs, I suppose. I am now told Lord Godolphin was buried last night.—O poo Ppt! lay down oo head aden, fais I . . .; I always reckon if oo are ill I shall hear it, and therefore hen oo are silent I reckon all is well.[6] I believe I 'scaped the new fever[7] for the same reason that Ppt did, because I am not well; but why should DD 'scape it, pray? She is

---

[1] Lady Elizabeth Savage, daughter of Richard, fourth Earl Rivers (see p. 88), was the second wife of James Barry, fourth Earl of Barrymore. Of Earl Rivers' illegitimate children, one, Bessy, married (1) Frederick Nassau, third Earl of Rochford, and (2) a clergyman named Carter; while another, Richard Savage, was the poet. Earl Rivers' successor, John Savage, the fifth Earl, was a Roman Catholic priest, the grandson of John, first Earl Rivers. On his death in 1728 the title became extinct.

[2] No. 32.   [3] Very sick.

[4] From "but I" to "agreeable" is partially obliterated.

[5] Mrs. Swanton was the eldest daughter of Willoughby Swift, and therefore Swift's second cousin. In her will Esther Johnson left to Swift "a bond of thirty pounds, due to me by Dr. Russell, in trust for the use of Mrs. Honoria Swanton.'

[6] This sentence is partially obliterated.   [7] See p. 452.

melthigal, oo know, and ought to have the fever; but I
hope it is now too late, and she won't have it at all. Some
physicians here talk very melancholy, and think it foreruns
the plague, which is actually at Hamburg. I hoped Ppt
would have done with her illness; but I think we both have
that faculty never to part with a disorder for ever; we
are very constant. I have had my giddiness twenty-three
years by fits. Will Mrs. Raymond never have done lying-
in? He intends to leave beggars enough; for I dare-
say he has squandered away the best part of his fortune
already, and is not out of debt. I had a letter from him
lately.

Oct. 11. Lord Treasurer sent for me yesterday and the
day before to sit with him, because he is not yet quite well
enough to go abroad; and I could not finish my letter.
How the deuce come I to be so exact in ME money? Just
seventeen shillings and eightpence more than due; I believe
you cheat me. If Hawkshaw does not pay the interest I
will have the principal; pray speak to Parvisol and have
his advice what I should do about it. Service to Mrs.
Stoyte and Catherine and Mrs. Walls. Ppt makes 'a petition
with many apologies. John Danvers, you know, is Lady
Giffard's friend. The rest I never heard of. I tell you
what, as things are at present, I cannot possibly speak to
Lord Treasurer for anybody. I need tell you no more.
Something or nothing will be done in my own affairs: if the
former, I will be a solicitor for your sister;[1] if the latter,
I have done with Courts for ever. Opportunities will often
fall in my way, if I am used well, and I will then make it my
business. It is my delight to do good offices for people who
want and deserve, and a tenfold delight to do it to a relation
of Ppt, whose affairs she has so at heart.[2] I have taken
down his name and his case (not *her* case), and whenever a
proper time comes, I will do all I can; zat's enough to say
when I can do no more; and I beg oo pardon a sousand

[1] See p. 25.
[2] The latter half of this sentence is partially obliterated.

times,[1] that I cannot do better. I hope the Dean of St.
P[atrick's] is well of his fever : he has never writ to me : I am
glad of it; pray don't desire him to write. I have dated
your bill late, because it must not commence, ung oomens,
till the first of November [2] next. O, fais, I must be ise; [3]
iss, fais, must I; else ME will cheat Pdfr. Are you good
housewives and readers? Are you walkers? I know you
are gamesters. Are you drinkers? Are you— O Rold,
I must go no further, for fear of abusing fine radies.[4]
Parvisol has never sent me one word how he set this year's
tithes. Pray ask whether tithes set well or ill this year.
The Bishop of Killaloe [5] tells me wool bears a good rate in
Ireland: but how is corn? I dined yesterday with Lady
Orkney, and we sat alone from two till eleven at night.—You
have heard of her, I suppose. I have twenty letters upon my
hands, and am so lazy and so busy, I cannot answer them,
and they grow upon me for several months. Have I any
apples at Laracor? It is strange every year should blast
them, when I took so much care for shelter. Lord Bolingbroke has been idle at his country - house this fortnight,
which puts me backward in a business I have. I am got
into an ordinary room two pair of stairs, and see nobody, if
I can help it; yet some puppies have found me out, and my
man is not such an artist as Patrick at denying me. Patrick
has been soliciting to come to me again, but in vain. The
printer has been here with some of the new whims printed,
and has taken up my time. I am just going out, and can
only bid oo farewell. Farewell, deelest ickle MD, MD MD
MD FW FW FW FW ME ME ME ME. Lele deel ME
Lele lele lele sollahs bose.[6]

[1] Partly obliterated.   [2] See p. 54.
[3] Wise.   [4] Partly obliterated.
[5] See p. 43.   [6] This sentence is almost obliterated.

LETTER LIV[1]

LONDON, *Oct.* 28, 1712.

I HAVE been in physic this month, and have been better these three weeks. I stop my physic, by the doctor's orders, till he sends me further directions. DD grows politician, and longs to hear the peace is proclaimed. I hope we shall have it soon, for the Dutch are fully humbled; and Prior is just come over from France for a few days; I suppose upon some important affair. I saw him last night, but had no private talk with him. Stocks rise upon his coming. As for my stay in England, it cannot be long now, so tell my friends. The Parliament will not meet till after Christmas, and by that time the work I am doing will be over, and then nothing shall keep me. I am very much discontented at Parvisol, about neglecting to sell my horses, etc.

Lady Masham is not yet brought to bed; but we expect it daily. I dined with her to-day. Lord Bolingbroke returned about two months ago, and Prior about a week; and goes back (Prior I mean) in a few days. Who told you of my snuff-box and pocket? Did I? I had a letter to-day from Dr. Coghill,[2] desiring me to get Raphoe for Dean Sterne, and the deanery for myself. I shall indeed, I have such obligations to Sterne. But however, if I am asked who will make a good bishop, I shall name him before anybody. Then comes another letter, desiring I would recommend a Provost,[3] supposing that Pratt (who has been here about a week) will certainly be promoted; but I believe he will not. I presented Pratt to Lord Treasurer, and truly young Molyneux[4] would have had me present him too; but I directly

---

[1] The MS. of this letter has not been preserved.
[2] See p. 245.
[3] Swift's friend, Dr. Pratt (see p. 5), was then Provost of Trinity College, Dublin.
[4] Samuel Molyneux, then aged twenty-three, was the son of William Molyneux (1656-1698), M.P. for Dublin University, a writer on philosophical and scientific subjects, and the friend of Locke. Samuel Molyneux took his M.A. degree in Dublin in 1710, and in 1712 visited England. He was befriended by

answered him I would not, unless he had business with him.
He is the son of one Mr. Molyneux of Ireland. His father
wrote a book;[1] I suppose you know it. Here is the Duke
of Marlborough going out of England (Lord knows why),
which causes many speculations. Some say he is conscious
of guilt, and dare not stand it. Others think he has a mind
to fling an odium on the Government, as who should say that
one who has done such great services to his country cannot
live quietly in it, by reason of the malice of his enemies. I
have helped to patch up these people[2] together once more.
God knows how long it may last. I was to-day at a trial
between Lord Lansdowne and Lord Carteret, two friends of
mine. It was in the Queen's Bench, for about six thousand
a year (or nine, I think). I sat under Lord Chief-Justice
Parker, and his pen falling down I reached it up. He made
me a low bow; and I was going to whisper him that *I had
done good for evil; for he would have taken mine from me.*[3]
I told it Lord Treasurer and Bolingbroke. Parker would
not have known me, if several lords on the bench, and in
the court, bowing, had not turned everybody's eyes, and
set them a whispering. I owe the dog a spite, and will pay
him in two months at furthest, if I can. So much for that.
But you must have chat, and I must say every sorry thing
that comes into my head. They say the Queen will stay a
month longer at Windsor. These devils of Grub Street
rogues, that write the *Flying Post* and *Medley* in one paper,[4]
will not be quiet. They are always mauling Lord Treasurer,
Lord Bolingbroke, and me. We have the dog under prosecution, but Bolingbroke is not active enough; but I hope to
swinge him. He is a Scotch rogue, one Ridpath.[5] They get

the Duke of Marlborough at Antwerp, and in 1714 was sent by the Duke on a
mission to the Court of Hanover. He held office under George I., but devoted
most of his attention to astronomical research, until his death in 1728.
[1] Probably *The Case of Ireland's being bound by Acts of Parliament in
England stated* (1698).
[2] Oxford and Bolingbroke.   [3] See p. 360.   [4] See p. 453.
[5] George Ridpath (died 1726), a Whig journalist, of whom Pope (*Dunciad*,
i. 208) wrote—
    "To Dulness Ridpath is as dear as Mist."
He edited the *Flying Post* for some years, and also wrote for the *Medley* in

out upon bail, and write on. We take them again, and get fresh bail; so it goes round. They say some learned Dutchman has wrote a book, proving by civil law that we do them wrong by this peace; but I shall show by plain reason that we have suffered the wrong, and not they. I toil like a horse, and have hundreds of letters still to read : and squeeze a line out of each, or at least the seeds of a line. Strafford goes back to Holland in a day or two, and I hope our peace is very near. I have about thirty pages more to write (that is, to be extracted), which will be sixty in print. It is the most troublesome part of all, and I cannot keep myself private, though I stole into a room up two pair of stairs, when I came from Windsor; but my present man has not yet learned his lesson of denying me discreetly.

30. The Duchess of Ormond found me out to-day, and made me dine with her. Lady Masham is still expecting. She has had a cruel cold. I could not finish my letter last post for the soul of me. Lord Bolingbroke has had my papers these six weeks, and done nothing to them. Is Tisdall yet in the world? I propose writing controversies, to get a name with posterity. The Duke of Ormond will not be over these three or four days. I desire to make him join with me in settling all right among our people. I have ordered the Duchess to let me have an hour with the Duke at his first coming, to give him a true state of persons and things. I believe the Duke of Shrewsbury will hardly be declared your Governor yet; at least, I think so now; but resolutions alter very often. The Duke of Hamilton gave me a pound of snuff to-day, admirable good. I wish DD had it, and Ppt too, if she likes it. It cost me a quarter of an hour

1712. In September William Hurt and Ridpath were arrested for libellous and seditious articles, but were released on bail. On October 23 they appeared before the Court of Queen's Bench, and were continued on their recognizances. In February 1713 Ridpath was tried and, in spite of an able defence by leading Whig lawyers, was convicted. Sentence was postponed, and when Ridpath failed to appear, as ordered, in April, his recognizances were escheated, and a reward offered for his discovery ; but he had fled to Scotland, and from thence to Holland.

30

of his politics, which I was forced to hear.   Lady Orkney[1] is
making me a writing-table of her own contrivance, and a bed-
nightgown.   She is perfectly kind, like a mother.   I think
the devil was in it the other day, that I should talk to her of
an ugly squinting cousin of hers, and the poor lady herself,
you know, squints like a dragon.   The other day we had a
long discourse with her about love ; and she told us a saying
of her sister Fitz-Hardinge,[2] which I thought excellent, that
in men, desire begets love, and in women, love begets desire.
We have abundance of our old criers[3] still hereabouts.   I
hear every morning your women with the old satin and
taffeta, etc., the fellow with old coats, suits or cloaks.   Our
weather is abominable of late.   We have not two tolerable
days in twenty.   I have lost money again at ombre, with
Lord Orkney and others ; yet, after all, this year I have lost
but three-and-twenty shillings ; so that, considering card
money, I am no loser.

Our Society hath not yet renewed their meetings.   I hope
we shall continue to do some good this winter ; and Lord
Treasurer promises the Academy for reforming our language
shall soon go forward.   I must now go hunt those dry letters
for materials.   You will see something very notable, I hope.
So much for that.   God Almighty bless you.

LETTER LV[4]

LONDON, *Nov.* 15, 1712.

BEFORE this comes to your hands, you will have heard
of the most terrible accident that hath almost ever
happened.   This morning, at eight, my man brought me
word that the Duke of Hamilton had fought with Lord

---

[1] See p. 456.

[2] Lady Orkney's sister, Barbara Villiers, who married John Berkeley, fourth
Viscount Fitz-Hardinge, had been governess to the Duke of Gloucester, Queen
Anne's son.   She died in 1708, in her fifty-second year ; and on her husband's
death four years later the peerage became extinct.

[3] For the street criers, see the *Spectator*, No. 251.

[4] Addressed to "Mrs. Dingley."   Endorsed "Nov. 26, just come from
Portraine" ; and " The band-box plot—D : Hamilton's murther."

Mohun,[1] and killed him, and was brought home wounded.[2]
I immediately sent him to the Duke's house, in St. James's
Square; but the porter could hardly answer for tears, and a
great rabble was about the house. In short, they fought at
seven this morning. The dog Mohun was killed on the spot;
and while [3] the Duke was over him, Mohun, shortening his
sword, stabbed him in at the shoulder to the heart. The
Duke was helped toward the cake-house by the Ring in Hyde
Park (where they fought), and died on the grass, before he
could reach the house; and was brought home in his coach
by eight, while the poor Duchess [4] was asleep. Maccartney,[5]
and one Hamilton,[6] were the seconds, who fought likewise,
and are both fled. I am told that a footman of Lord Mohun's
stabbed the Duke of Hamilton; and some say Maccartney did
so too. Mohun gave the affront, and yet sent the challenge.
I am infinitely concerned for the poor Duke, who was a frank,
honest, good-natured man. I loved him very well, and I
think he loved me better. He had [7] the greatest mind in
the world to have me go with him to France, but durst not
tell it me; and those he did, said I could not be spared,

[1] Charles Mohun, fifth Baron Mohun, had been twice arraigned of murder,
but acquitted; and during his short but turbulent life he had taken part in
many duels. Even Burnet could say nothing in his favour.
[2] This duel between the Duke of Hamilton (see p. 262) and Lord Mohun,
who had married nieces of Lord Macclesfield, had its origin in a protracted
dispute about some property. The challenge came from Lord Mohun, and
the combatants fought like "enraged lions." Tory writers suggested that
the duel was a Whig conspiracy to get rid of the Duke of Hamilton (*Examiner*,
Nov. 20, 1712). The whole subject is discussed from the Whig point of view
in Boyer's *Political State* for 1712, pp. 297-326.
[3] "Will" (MS.). [4] See p. 262, note 2.
[5] George Maccartney (see pp. 89, 387) fought at Almanza, Malplaquet, and
Douay. After the duel, Maccartney escaped to Holland, but on the accession
of George I. he returned to England, and was tried for murder (June 1716),
when Colonel Hamilton gave evidence against him. Hamilton's evidence was
discredited, and he found it necessary to sell his commission and leave the
country. Maccartney was found guilty as an accessory, and "burnt" in the
hand. Within a month he was given an appointment in the army, and
promoted to be Lieutenant-General. He died in 1730.
[6] Colonel John Hamilton, of the Scots Guards. He surrendered himself,
and was tried at the Old Bailey on Dec. 12, 1712, when he was found guilty of
manslaughter, on two indictments; and on the following day he was "burnt"
in the hand. Hamilton died in October 1716, soon after Maccartney's trial,
from a sudden vomiting of blood.
[7] "That" (MS.).

which was true. They have removed the poor Duchess to a
lodging in the neighbou '.,od, where I have been with her
two hours, and am just come away. I never saw so melancholy
a scene; for indeed all reasons for real grief belong to her;
nor is it possible for anybody to be a greater loser in all
regards. She has moved my very soul. The lodging was
inconvenient, and they would have removed her to another;
but I would not suffer it, because it had no room backward,
and she must have been tortured with the noise of the Grub
Street screamers mention[ing] her husband's murder to her ears.

I believe you have heard the story of my escape, in opening
the bandbox sent to Lord Treasurer.[1] The prints have told a
thousand lies of it; but at last we gave them a true account
of it at length, printed in the evening;[2] only I would not
suffer them to name me, having been so often named before,
and teased to death with questions. I wonder how I came
to have so much presence of mind, which is usually not my
talent; but so it pleased God, and I saved myself and him;
for there was a bullet apiece. A gentleman told me that if
I had been killed, the Whigs would have called it a judgment,
because the barrels were of inkhorns, with which I had done
them so much mischief. There was a pure Grub Street of it,
full of lies and inconsistencies.[3] I do not like these things
at all, and I wish myself more and more among my willows.[4]

[1] The story (as told in the Tory *Postboy* of Nov. 11 to 13) was that on Nov. 4
a bandbox was sent to the Earl of Oxford by post. When he began to open
it he saw a pistol, whereupon a gentleman present [Swift] asked for the
box, and opening it, by the window, found powder, nails, etc., so arranged
that, if opened in the ordinary way, the whole would have been fired, and two
barrels discharged different ways. No doubt a box so packed was received,
but whether anything serious was intended, or whether it was a hoax, cannot
be said with any certainty. The Earl of Oxford is said to have met allusions
to the subject with a smile, and Swift seems to have been annoyed at the
reports which were put into circulation.
[2] "We have received a more particular account relating to the box sent to
the Lord Treasurer, as mentioned in our last, which is as follows," etc.
(*Evening News*, Nov. 11 to 13, 1712).
[3] Either *A Letter to the People, to be left for them at the Booksellers, with a
word or two of the Bandbox Plot* (by T. Burnet), 1712, or *An Account of the
Duel . . ., with Previous Reflections on Sham Plots* (by A. Boyer), 1712.
Swift's connection with the Bandbox Plot was ridiculed in the *Flying Post* for
Nov. 20 to 22.
[4] Cf. p. 154.

There is a devilish spirit among people, and the Ministry must exert themselves, or sink. Nite dee sollahs, I'll go seep.[1]

16. I thought to have finished this yesterday; but was too much disturbed. I sent a letter early this morning to Lady Masham, to beg her to write some comforting words to the poor Duchess. I dined to-[day] with Lady Masham at Kensington, where she is expecting these two months to lie in. She has promised me to get the Queen to write to the Duchess kindly on this occasion; and to-morrow I will beg Lord Treasurer to visit and comfort her. I have been with her two hours again, and find her worse: her violences not so frequent, but her melancholy more formal and settled. She has abundance of wit and spirit; about thirty-three years old; handsome and airy, and seldom spared anybody that gave her the least provocation; by which she had many enemies and few friends. Lady Orkney, her sister-in-law, is come to town on this occasion, and has been to see her, and behaved herself with great humanity. They have been always very ill together, and the poor Duchess could not have patience when people told her I went often to Lady Orkney's. But I am resolved to make them friends; for the Duchess is now no more the object of envy, and must learn humility from the severest master, Affliction. I design to make the Ministry put out a proclamation (if it can be found proper) against that villain Maccartney. What shall we do with these murderers? I cannot end this letter to-night, and there is no occasion; for I cannot send it till Tuesday, and the crowner's inquest on the Duke's body is to be to-morrow, and I shall know more. But what care oo for all this? Iss, poo MD im sorry for poo Pdfr's [2] friends; and this is a very surprising event. 'Tis late, and I'll go to bed. This looks like journals. Nite.

17. I was to-day at noon with the Duchess of Hamilton again, after I had been with Lady Orkney, and charged her

---

[1] This sentence is partially obliterated.
[2] Part of this sentence has been obliterated.

to be kind to her sister in her affliction. The Duchess told me Lady Orkney had been with her, and that she did not treat her as gently as she ought. They hate one another, but I will try to patch it up. I have been drawing up a paragraph for the *Postboy*, to be out to-morrow, and as malicious as possible, and very proper for Abel Roper,[1] the printer of it. I dined at Lord Treasurer's at six in the evening, which is his usual hour of returning from Windsor: he promises to visit the Duchess to-morrow, and says he has a message to her from the Queen. Thank God. I have stayed till past one with him. So nite deelest MD.[2]

18. The Committee of Council is to sit this afternoon upon the affair of the Duke of Hamilton's murder, and I hope a proclamation will be out against Maccartney. I was just now ('tis now noon) with the Duchess, to let her know Lord Treasurer will see her. She is mightily out of order. The jury have not yet brought in their verdict upon the crowner's inquest. We suspect Maccartney stabbed the Duke while he was fighting. The Queen and Lord Treasurer are in great concern at this event. I dine to-day again with Lord Treasurer; but must send this to the post-office before, because else I shall not have time; he usually keeping me so late. Ben Tooke bid me write to DD to send her certificate, for it is high time it should be sent, he says. Pray make Parvisol write to me, and send me a general account of my affairs; and let him know I shall be over in spring, and that by all means he sells the horses. Prior has kissed the Queen's hand, and will return to France in a few days, and Lord Strafford to Holland; and now the King of Spain has renounced his pretensions to France, the peace must follow very soon unavoidably. You must no more call Philip, Duke of Anjou, for we now acknowledge him King of Spain. Dr. Pratt tells me you are all mad in Ireland with your playhouse frolics and prologues, and I know not what. The Bishop of

[1] See p. 427. I have not been able to find a copy of the paper containing Swift's paragraph.
[2] This sentence is partially obliterated.

Clogher and family are well: they have heard from you, or you from them, lately, I have forgot which: I dined there t'other day, but the Bishop came not till after dinner; and our meat and drink was very so so. Mr. Vedeau [1] was with me yesterday, and inquired after you. He was a lieutenant, and is now broke, and upon half-pay. He asked me nothing for himself; but wanted an employment for a friend, who would give a handsome pair of gloves. One Hales sent me up a letter t'other day, which said you lodged in his house, and therefore desired I would get him a civil employment. I would not be within, and have directed my man to give him an answer, that I never open letters brought me by the writers, etc. I was complaining to a lady that I wanted to mend an employment from forty to sixty pounds a year, in the Salt Office, and thought it hard I could not do it. She told me one Mr. Griffin [2] should do it. And afterward I met Griffin at her lodgings; and he was, as I found, one I had been acquainted with. I named Filby [3] to him, and his abode somewhere near Nantwich. He said frankly he had formerly examined the man, and found he understood very little of his business; but if he heard he mended, he would do what I desired. I will let it rest a while, and then resume it; and if Ppt writes to Filby, she may advise him to diligence, etc. I told Griffin positively I would have it done, if the man mended. This is an account of poo Ppt's commission to her most humble servant Pdfr. I have a world of writing to finish, and little time; these toads of Ministers are so slow in their helps. This makes me sometimes steal a week from the exactness I used to write to MD. Farewell, dee logues, deelest MD MD MD, . . . FW FW FW ME ME ME Lele.

Smoke the folding of my letters of late. [4]

[1] See p. 104.
[2] Apparently Humphrey Griffith, who was one of the Commissioners of Salt; but Swift gives the name as "Griffin" throughout.
[3] See pp. 25, 461.
[4] For these shorter letters Swift folded the folio sheet before writing.

LETTER LVI[1]

LONDON, *Dec.* 12, 1712.

HERE is now a stlange ting; a rettle flom MD unanswered: never was before. I am slower, and MD
is faster: but the last was owing to DD's certificate. Why
could it not be sent before, pay now? Is it so hard for DD
to prove she is alive? I protest solemnly I am not able to
write to MD for other business, but I will resume my journal
method next time. I find it is easier, though it contains
nothing but where I dine, and the occurrences of the day.
I will write now but once in three weeks till this business is
off my hands, which must be in six, I think, at farthest. O
Ppt, I remember your reprimanding me for meddling in
other people's affairs: I have enough of it now, with a
wanion.[2] Two women have been here six times apiece; I
never saw them yet. The first I have despatched with a
letter; the other I must see, and tell her I can do nothing
for her: she is wife of one Connor,[3] an old college acquaintance, and comes on a foolish errand, for some old pretensions, that will succeed when I am Lord Treasurer. I am
got [up] two pair of stairs, in a private lodging, and have
ordered all my friends not to discover where I am; yet every
morning two or three sots are plaguing me, and my present
servant has not yet his lesson perfect of denying me. I have
written a hundred and thirty pages in folio, to be printed,
and must write thirty more, which will make a large book of
four shillings.[4] I wish I knew an opportunity of sending you
some snuff. I will watch who goes to Ireland, and do it if
possible. I had a letter from Parvisol, and find he has set
my livings very low. Colonel Hamilton, who was second to
the Duke of Hamilton, is tried to-day. I suppose he is come

[1] Addressed to "Mrs. Dingley," etc.   Endorsed "Decr. 18."
[2] Vengeance.
[3] Charles Connor, scholar of Trinity College, Dublin, who took his B.A.
degree in the same year as Swift (1686), and his M.A. degree in 1691.
[4] *The History of the Peace of Utrecht.*

off, but have not heard.[1] I dined with Lord Treasurer, but
left him by nine, and visited some people. Lady Betty,[2] his[3]
daughter, will be married on Monday next (as I suppose) to
the Marquis of Caermarthen. I did not know your country
place had been Portraine, till you told me so in your last.
Has Swanton taken it of Wallis? That Wallis was a grave,
wise coxcomb. God be thanked that Ppt im better of her
disoddles.[4] Pray God keep her so. The pamphlet of
Political Lying is written by Dr. Arbuthnot, the author of
John Bull; 'tis very pretty, but not so obvious to be understood. Higgins,[5] first chaplain to the Duke of Hamilton?
Why, the Duke of Hamilton never dreamt of a chaplain, nor
I believe ever heard of Higgins. You are glorious news-
mongers in Ireland—Dean Francis,[6] Sir R. Levinge,[7] stuff
stuff: and Pratt, more stuff. We have lost our fine frost
here; and Abel Roper tells us you have had floods in Dublin;
ho, brave[8] you! Oh ho! Swanton seized Portraine, now I
understand oo. Ay, ay, now I see Portraune at the top of
your letter. I never minded it before. Now to your second,
N. 36. So, you read one of the Grub Streets about the bandbox.[9] The Whig papers have abused me about the bandbox.
God help me, what could I do? I fairly ventured my life.
There is a particular account of it in the *Postboy*, and
Evening Post of that day. Lord Treasurer has had the seal
sent him that sealed the box, and directions where to find
the other pistol in a tree in St. James's Park, which Lord
Bolingbroke's messenger found accordingly; but who sent
the present is not yet known. The Duke of Hamilton
avoided the quarrel as much as possible, according to the
foppish rules of honour in practice. What signified your
writing angry to Filby? I hope you said nothing of hearing

[1] See p. 467, note 6.
[2] Lord Oxford's daughter Elizabeth married, on Dec. 16, 1712,
Peregrine Hyde, Marquis of Caermarthen, afterwards third Duke of Leeds
(see pp. 226, 417). She died on Nov. 20, 1713, a few days after the birth of
a son. Swift called her "a friend I extremely loved."
[3] "Is" (MS.). [4] Disorders. [5] See p. 335.
[6] John Francis, Rector of St. Mary's, Dublin, was made Dean of Leighlin in 1705.
[7] See p. 67. [8] Possibly "have." [9] See p. 468.

anything from me. Heigh! do oo write by sandlelight! nauti, nauti, nauti dallar, a hundred times, fol doing so. O, fais, DD, I'll take care of myself! The Queen is in town, and Lady Masham's month of lying-in is within two days of being out. I was at the christening on Monday. I could not get the child named Robin, after Lord Treasurer; it is Samuel, after the father. My brother Ormond sent me some chocolate to-day. I wish you had share of it: but they say 'tis good for me, and I design to drink some in a morning. Our Society meets next Thursday, now the Queen is in town; and Lord Treasurer assures me that the Society for reforming the language shall soon be established. I have given away ten shillings to-day to servants; 'tan't be help if one should cry one's eyes out.[1] Hot a stir is here about your company and visits! Charming company, no doubt; now I keep no company at all, nor have I any desire to keep any. I never go to a coffee-house nor a tavern, nor have I touched a card since I left Windsor. I make few visits, nor go to levees; my only debauching is sitting late where I dine, if I like the company. I have almost dropped the Duchesses of Shrews-bury and Hamilton, and several others. Lord Treasurer, the Duke of Ormond, and Lady Orkney are all that I see very often. Oh yes, and Lady Masham and Lord Bolingbroke, and one or two private friends. I make no figure but at Court, where I affect to turn from a lord to the meanest of my acquaintance, and I love to go there on Sundays to see the world. But, to say the truth, I am growing weary of it. I dislike a million of things in the course of public affairs; and if I were to stay here much longer, I am sure I should ruin my-self with endeavouring to mend them. I am every day invited into schemes of doing this, but I cannot find any that will prob-ably succeed. It is impossible to save people against their own will; and I have been too much engaged in patchwork already. Do you understand all this stuff? No. Well zen, you are now returned to ombre and the Dean, and Christmas; I wish oo a very merry one; and pray don't lose oo money,

---

[1] This clause is omitted by Mr. Ryland.

nor play upon Watt Welch's game.   Nite, sollahs, 'tis rate
I'll go to seep; I don't seep well, and therefore never dare to
drink coffee or tea after dinner: but I am very seepy in a molning.   This is the effect of time and years.   Nite deelest MD.
   13. Morn.   I am so very seepy in the morning that my
man wakens me above ten times; and now I can tell oo no
news of this day.   (Here is a restless dog, crying cabbages
and savoys, plagues me every morning about this time; he
is now at it.   I wish his largest cabbage were sticking in his
throat.)   I lodge over against the house in Little Rider
Street, where DD lodged.   Don't oo lememble, maram?
To-night I must see the Abbé Gaultier,[1] to get some particulars for my History.   It was he who was first employed
by France in the overtures of peace, and I have not had time
this month to see him; he is but a puppy too.   Lady Orkney
has just sent to invite me to dinner; she has not given me
the bed-nightgown;[2] besides, I am come very much off from
writing in bed, though I am doing it this minute; but I stay
till my fire is burnt up.   My grate is very large; two bushels
of coals in a week: but I save it in lodgings.   Lord Abercorn
is come to London, and will plague me, and I can do him
no service.   The Duke of Shrewsbury goes in a day or two
for France, perhaps to-day.   We shall have a peace very
soon; the Dutch are almost entirely agreed, and if they stop
we shall make it without them; that has been long resolved.
One Squire Jones,[3] a scoundrel in my parish, has writ to me
to desire I would engage Joe Beaumont to give him his
interest for Parliament - man for Trim: pray tell Joe this;
and if he designed to vote for him already, then he may tell
Jones that I received his letter, and that I writ to Joe to do
it.   If Joe be engaged for any other, then he may do what
he will: and Parvisol may say he spoke to Joe, but Joe's
engaged, etc.   I received three pair of fine thread stockings
from Joe lately.   Pray thank him when you see him, and
that I say they are very fine and good.   (I never looked at

[1] See p. 304.   [2] See p. 466.
[3] Thomas Jones, Esq., was M.P. for Trim in the Parliament of 1713-4.

them yet, but that's no matter.) This is a fine day. I am ruined with coaches and chairs this twelvepenny weather. I must see my brother Ormond at eleven, and then the Duchess of Hamilton, with whom I doubt I am in disgrace, not having seen her these ten days. I send this to-day, and must finish it now; and perhaps some people may come and hinder me; for it im ten o'clock (but not shaving-day), and I must be abroad at eleven. Abbé Gaultier sends me word I can't see him to-night; pots cake him! I don't value anything but one letter he has of Petecum's,[1] showing the roguery of the Dutch. Did not the *Conduct of the Allies* make you great politicians? Fais, I believe you are not quite so ignorant as I thought you. I am glad to hear oo walked so much in the country. Does DD ever read to you, ung ooman? O, fais! I shall find strange doings hen I turn ole![2] Here is somebody coming that I must see that wants a little place; the son of cousin Rooke's eldest daughter, that died many years ago. He's here. Farewell, deelest MD MD MD ME ME ME FW FW FW, Lele.

LETTER LVII[3]

LONDON, *Dec.* 18, 1712.

OUR Society was to meet to-day; but Lord Harley, who was President this week, could not attend, being gone to Wimbledon with his new brother - in - law, the young Marquis of Caermarthen, who married Lady Betty Harley on Monday last; and Lord Treasurer is at Wimbledon too. However, half a dozen of us met, and I propose our meetings should be once a fortnight; for, between you and me, we do no good. It cost me nineteen shillings to-day for my Club at dinner; I don't like it, fais. We have terrible snowy slobbery weather. Lord Abercorn is come to town, and will see me, whether I will or no. You know he has a pretence

---

[1] A Dutch agent employed in the negotiations with Lewis XIV.
[2] When I come home.
[3] Addressed to " Mrs. Dingley," etc. Endorsed " Jan. 13."

to a dukedom in France, which the Duke of Hamilton was soliciting for; but Abercorn resolves to spoil their title, if they will not allow him a fourth part; and I have advised the Duchess to compound with him, and have made the Ministry of my opinion. Night, dee sollahs, MD, MD.

19. Ay mally zis is sumsing rike,[1] for Pdfr to write journals again! 'Tis as natural as mother's milk, now I am got into it. Lord Treasurer is returned from Wimbledon ('tis not above eight miles off), and sent for me to dine with him at five; but I had the grace to be abroad, and dined with some others, with honest Ben Tooke, by invitation. The Duchess of Ormond promised me her picture, and coming home to-night, I found hers and the Duke's both in my chamber. Was not that a pretty civil surprise? Yes, and they are in fine gilded frames, too. I am writing a letter to thank her, which I will send to-morrow morning. I'll tell her she is such a prude that she will not let so much as her picture be alone in a room with *a man*, unless the Duke's be with it; and so forth.[2] We are full of snow, and dabbling. Lady Masham has come abroad these three days, and seen the Queen. I dined with her t'other day at her sister Hill's. I hope she will remove in a few days to her new lodgings at St. James's from Kensington. Nite, dee logues MD.

20. I lodge [up] two pair of stairs, have but one room, and deny myself to everybody almost, yet I cannot be quiet; and all my mornings are lost with people, who will not take answers below stairs; such as Dilly, and the Bishop, and Provost, etc. Lady Orkney invited me to dinner to-day, which hindered me from dining with Lord Treasurer. This is his day that his chief friends in the Ministry dine with him. However, I went there about six, and sat with them till past nine, when they all went off; but he kept me back,

---

[1] "Ay, marry, this is something like." The earlier editions give, "How agreeable it is in a morning." The words in the MS. are partially obliterated.

[2] In this letter (Dec. 20, 1712) Swift paid many compliments to the Duchess of Ormond (see p. 160): "All the accomplishments of your mind and person are so deeply printed in the heart, and represent you so lively to my imagination, that I should take it for a high affront if you believed it in the power of colours to refresh my memory."

and told me the circumstances of Lady Betty's match.   The young fellow has £60,000 ready money, three great houses furnished, £7000 a year at present, and about five more after his father and mother die.   I think Lady Betty's portion is not above £8000.   I remember either Tisdall writ to me in somebody's letter, or you did it for him, that I should mention him on occasion to Lord Anglesea, with whom, he said, he had some little acquaintance.   Lord Anglesea was with me to-night at Lord Treasurer's; and then I asked him about Tisdall, and described him.   He said he never saw him, but that he had sent him his book.[1]   See what it is to be a puppy.   Pray tell Mr. Walls that Lord Anglesea thanked me for recommending Clements [2] to him; that he says he is £20,000 the better for knowing Clements.   But pray don't let Clements go and write a letter of thanks, and tell my lord that he hears so and so, etc.   Why, 'tis but like an Irish understanding to do so.   Sad weather; two shillings in coaches to-day, and yet I am dirty.   I am now going to read over something and correct it.   So, nite.

21. Puppies have got a new way of plaguing me. . I find letters directed for me at Lord Treasurer's, sometimes with enclosed ones to him, and sometimes with projects, and some-times with libels.   I usually keep them three or four days without opening.   I was at Court to-day, as I always am on Sundays, instead of a coffee-house, to see my acquaintance. This day se'nnight, after I had been talking at Court with Sir William Wyndham, the Spanish Ambassador [3] came to him and said he heard that was Dr. Swift, and desired him to tell me that his master, and the King of France, and the Queen, were more obliged to me than any man in Europe; so we bowed, and shook hands, etc.   I took it very well of him.   I dined with Lord Treasurer, and must again to-morrow, though I had rather not (as DD says); but now the Queen is in town, he does not keep me so late.   I have not had time to see Fanny Manley since she came, but intend it one of these

---

[1] Tisdall's *Conduct of the Dissenters in Ireland* (see p. 517).
[2] See pp. 73, 192-3.   [3] Monteleon.

days. Her uncle, Jack Manley,[1] I hear, cannot live a month, which will be a great loss to her father in Ireland, for I believe he is one of his chief supports. Our peace now will soon be determined ; for Lord Bolingbroke tells me this morning that four provinces of Holland[2] have complied with the Queen, and we expect the rest will do so immediately. Nite MD.

22. Lord Keeper promised me yesterday the first, convenient living to poor Mr. Gery,[3] who is married, and wants some addition to what he has. He is a very worthy creature. I had a letter some weeks ago from Elwick,[4] who married Betty Gery. It seems the poor woman died some time last summer. Elwick grows, rich, and purchases lands. I dined with Lord Treasurer to-day, who has engaged me to come again to - morrow. I gave Lord Bolingbroke a poem of Parnell's.[5] I made Parnell insert some compliments in it to his lordship. He is extremely pleased with it, and read some parts of it to-day to Lord Treasurer, who liked it as much. And indeed he outdoes all our poets here a bar's length. Lord Bolingbroke has ordered me to bring him to dinner on Christmas Day, and I made Lord Treasurer promise to see him ; and it may one day do Parnell a kindness. You know Parnell. I believe I have told you of that poem. Nite, deel MD.

23. This morning I presented one Diaper,[6] a poet, to Lord Bolingbroke, with a new poem, which is a very good one ; and I am to give him a sum of money from my lord ; and I have contrived to make a parson of him, for he is half one already, being in deacon's orders, and serves a small cure in the country ; but has a sword at his a—— here in town. 'Tis a poor little short wretch, but will do best in a gown, and we will make Lord Keeper give him a living. Lord Bolingbroke writ to Lord Treasurer to excuse me to-day ; so I dined with the former, and Monteleon, the Spanish Ambassador, who made me many compliments. I stayed till nine,

---

[1] See pp. 7, 24.
[2] Utrecht, North and South Holland, and West Frieseland.
[3] See p. 439.   [4] See p. 439.
[5] *On Queen Anne's Peace.*
[6] See p. 422. The poem was *Dryades, or the Nymph's Prophecy.*

and now it is past ten, and my man has locked me up, and
I have just called to mind that I shall be in disgrace with
Tom Leigh.[1]   That coxcomb had got into acquaintance with
one Eckershall,[2] Clerk of the Kitchen to the Queen, who was
civil to him at Windsor on my account; for I had done some
service to Eckershall.   Leigh teases me to pass an evening at
his lodgings with Eckershall.   I put it off several times, but
was forced at last to promise I would come to-night; and it
never was in my head till I was locked up, and I have called
and called, but my man is gone to bed; so I will write an
excuse to-morrow.   I detest that Tom Leigh, and am as
formal to him as I can when I happen to meet him in the
Park.   The rogue frets me, if he knew it.   He asked me
why I did not wait on the Bishop of Dromore.[3]   I answered
I had not the honour to be acquainted with him, and would
not presume, etc.   He takes me seriously, and says the
Bishop is no proud man, etc.   He tells me of a judge in
Ireland that has done ill things.   I ask why he is not
out?   Says he, "I think the bishops, and you, and I, and
the rest of the clergy, should meet and consult about it."   I
beg his pardon, and say, "I cannot be serviceable that way."
He answers, "Yes, everybody may help something."—Don't
you see how curiously he contrives to vex me; for the dog
knows that with half a word I could do more than all of them
together.   But he only does it from the pride and envy of his
own heart, and not out of a humorous design of teasing.   He
is one of those that would rather a service should not be done,
than done by a private man, and of his own country.   You
take all this, don't you?   Nite dee sollahs, I'll go seep a dozey.

24.   I dined to-day with the Chancellor of the Exchequer,
in order to look over some of my papers; but nothing was
done.   I have been also mediating between the Hamilton
family and Lord Abercorn, to have them compound with
him; and I believe they will do it.   Lord Selkirk,[4] the late

<hr>

[1] See p. 343.   [2] See p. 159.
[3] Dr. Tobias Pullen (1648–1713) was made Bishop of Dromore in 1695.
[4] Lord Charles Douglas, Earl of Selkirk, died unmarried in 1739.   When his

Duke's brother, is to be in town, in order to go to France, to
make the demands; and the Ministry are of opinion they will
get some satisfaction, and they empowered me to advise the
Hamilton side to agree with Abercorn, who asks a fourth
part, and will go to France and spoil all if they won't yield
it. Nite sollahs.

25. All melly Titmasses—melly Titmasses—I said it first
—I wish it a souzand [times] zoth with halt[1] and soul.[2]   I
carried Parnell to dine at Lord Bolingbroke's, and he behaved
himself very well; and Lord Bolingbroke is mightily pleased
with him.   I was at St. James's Chapel by eight this morning;
and church and sacrament were done by ten.   The Queen
has the gout in her hand, and did not come to church to-
day; and I stayed so long in my chamber that I missed going
to Court.   Did I tell you that the Queen designs to have a
Drawing-room and company every day?   Nite dee logues.

26. I was to wish the Duke of Ormond a happy Christmas,
and give half a crown to his porter.   It will cost me a
dozen half-crowns among such fellows.   I dined with Lord
Treasurer, who chid me for being absent three days.   Mighty
kind, with a p——; less of civility, and more of his interest!
We hear Maccartney is gone over to Ireland.   Was it not
comical for a gentleman to be set upon by highwaymen, and
to tell them he was Maccartney?   Upon which they brought
him to a justice of peace, in hopes of the reward,[3] and the
rogues were sent to gaol.   Was it not great presence of
mind?   But maybe you heard this already; for there was a
Grub Street of it.   Lord Bolingbroke told me I must walk
away to-day when dinner was done, because Lord Treasurer,

father, William, first Earl of Selkirk, married Anne, Duchess of Hamilton, the
Duchess obtained for her husband, in 1660, the title of Duke of Hamilton, for
life.   James II. conferred the Earldom of Selkirk on his Grace's second and
younger sons, primogenitively; and the second son having died without issue,
the third, Charles, became Earl.   The fifth son, George, was created Earl of
Orkney (see p. 456).   The difference between Lord Selkirk and the Earl of
Abercorn (see p. 86) to which Swift alludes was in connection with the claim
to the Dukedom of Chatelherault (see p. 426).
   [1] Heart.   [2] This sentence is almost illegible.
   [3] A reward of £500 was offered by the Crown for Maccartney's apprehension,
and £200 by the Duchess of Hamilton.
   31

and he, and another, were to enter upon business; but I said
it was as fit I should know their business as anybody, for I
was to justify [it].[1] So the rest went, and I stayed, and it
was so important, I was like to sleep over it. I left them at
nine, and it is now twelve. Nite, MD.

27. I dined to-day with General Hill, Governor of Dunkirk.
Lady Masham and Mrs. Hill, his two sisters, were of the
company, and there have I been sitting this evening till
eleven, looking over others at play; for I have left off loving
play myself; and I think Ppt is now a great gamester. I
have a great cold on me, not quite at its height. I have
them seldom, and therefore ought to be patient. I met Mr.
Addison and Pastoral Philips on the Mall to-day, and took
a turn with them; but they both looked terrible dry and
cold. A curse of party! And do you know I have taken
more pains to recommend the Whig wits to the favour and
mercy of the Ministers than any other people. Steele I
have kept in his place. Congreve I have got to be used
kindly, and secured. Rowe I have recommended, and got a
promise of a place. Philips I could certainly have provided
for, if he had not run party mad, and made me withdraw my
recommendation; and I set Addison so right at first that he
might have been employed, and have partly secured him the
place he has; yet I am worse used by that faction than any
man. / Well, go to cards, sollah Ppt, and dress the wine and
olange, sollah MD, and I'll go seep. 'Tis rate. Nite MD.

28. My cold is so bad that I could not go to church to-
day, nor to Court; but I was engaged to Lord Orkney's with
the Duke of Ormond, at dinner; and ventured, because I
could cough and spit there as I pleased. The Duke and
Lord Arran left us, and I have been sitting ever since with
Lord and Lady Orkney till past eleven: and my cold is
worse, and makes me giddy. I hope it is only my cold. Oh,
says Ppt, everybody is giddy with a cold; I hope it is no
more; but I'll go to bed, for the fellow has bawled " Past
twelve." Night, deels.

[1] In the proposed *History of the Peace of Utrecht.*

29. I got out early to-day, and escaped all my duns. I went to see Lord Bolingbroke about some business, and truly he was gone out too. I dined in the City upon the broiled leg of a goose and a bit of brawn, with my printer. Did I tell you that I forbear printing what I have in hand, till the Court decides something about me? I will contract no more enemies, at least I will not embitter worse those I have already, till I have got under shelter; and the Ministers know my resolution, so that you may be disappointed in seeing this thing as soon as you expected. I hear Lord Treasurer is out of order. My cold is very bad. Every [body] has one. Nite two dee logues.

30. I suppose this will be full by Saturday; zen[1] it sall go. Duke of Ormond, Lord Arran, and I, dined privately to-day at an old servant's house of his. The Council made us part at six. One Mrs. Ramsay dined with us; an old lady of about fifty-five, that we are all very fond of. I called this evening at Lord Treasurer's, and sat with him two hours. He has been cupped for a cold, and has been very ill. He cannot dine with Parnell and me at Lord Bolingbroke's to-morrow, but says he will see Parnell some other time. I hoise[2] up Parnell partly to spite the envious Irish folks here, particularly Tom Leigh. I saw the Bishop of Clogher's family to-day; Miss is mighty ill of a cold, coughs incessantly.[3] Nite MD.

31. To-day Parnell and I dined with Lord Bolingbroke, to correct Parnell's poem. I made him show all the places he disliked; and when Parnell has corrected it fully he shall print it. I went this evening to sit with Lord Treasurer. He is better, and will be out in a day or two. I sat with him while the young folks went to supper; and then went down, and there were the young folks merry together, having turned Lady Oxford up to my lord, and I stayed with them till twelve. There was the young couple, Lord and Lady

---

[1] Mr. Ryland's reading. Forster has "Iss." These words are obliterated.
[2] Hoist. Cf. "Hoised up the mainsail" (Acts xxvii. 40).
[3] It was afterwards found that Miss Ashe was suffering from smallpox.

Caermarthen, and Lord and Lady Dupplin, and Lord Harley
and I; and the old folks were together above. It looked
like what I have formerly done so often; stealing together
from the old folks, though indeed it was not from poor
Lord Treasurer, who is as young a fellow as any of us: but
Lady Oxford is a silly mere old woman.[1] My cold is still so
bad that I have not the least smelling. I am just got home,
and 'tis past twelve; and I'll go to bed, and settle my head,
heavy as lead. Nite MD.

Jan. 1, 1712–13. A sousand melly new eels[2] to deelest
richar MD. Pray God Almighty bless you, and send you
ever happy! I forgot to tell you that yesterday Lord
Abercorn was here, teasing me about his French duchy,
and suspecting my partiality to the Hamilton family in such
a whimsical manner that Dr. Pratt, who was by, thought he
was mad. He was no sooner gone but Lord Orkney sent
to know whether he might come and sit with me half an
hour upon some business. I returned answer that I would
wait on him; which I did. We discoursed a while, and he
left me with Lady Orkney; and in came the Earl of Selkirk,
whom I had never seen before. He is another brother of
the Duke of Hamilton, and is going to France, by a power
from his mother, the old Duchess,[3] to negotiate their
pretensions to the duchy of Chatelherault. He teased me
for two hours in spite of my teeth, and held my hand when
I offered to stir; would have had me engage the Ministry to
favour him against Lord Abercorn, and to convince them
that Lord Abercorn had no pretensions; and desired I would
also convince Lord Abercorn himself so; and concluded he
was sorry I was a greater friend to Abercorn than Hamilton.

---

[1] See p. 101. We are told in the *Wentworth Papers*, p. 263, that the
Duchess of Shrewsbury remarked to Lady Oxford, "Madam, I and my Lord
are so weary of talking politics; what are you and your Lord?" whereupon
Lady Oxford sighed and said she knew no Lord but the Lord Jehovah. The
Duchess rejoined, "Oh, dear! Madam, who is that? I believe 'tis one of the
new titles, for I never heard of him before."

[2] A thousand merry new years. The words are much obliterated.

[3] Lady Anne Hamilton, daughter of James, first Duke of Hamilton, became
Duchess on the death of her uncle William, the second Duke, at the battle of
Worcester.

I had no patience, and used him with some plainness. Am not I purely handled between a couple of puppies? Ay, says Ppt, you must be meddling in other folks' affairs. I appeal to the Bishop of Clogher whether Abercorn did not complain that I would not let him see me last year, and that he swore he would take no denial from my servant when he came again. The Ministers gave me leave to tell the Hamilton family it was their opinion that they ought to agree with Abercorn. Lord Anglesea was then by, and told Abercorn; upon which he gravely tells me I was commissioned by the Ministers, and ought to perform my commission, etc.—But I'll have done with them. I have warned Lord Treasurer and Lord Bolingbroke to beware of Selkirk's teasing,——x on him! Yet Abercorn vexes me more. The whelp owes to me all the kind receptions he has had from the Ministry. I dined to-day at Lord Treasurer's with the young folks, and sat with Lord Treasurer till nine, and then was forced to Lady Masham's, and sat there till twelve, talking of affairs, till I am out of humour, as everyone must that knows them inwardly. A thousand things wrong, most of them easy to mend; yet our schemes availing at best but little, and sometimes nothing at all. One evil, which I twice patched up with the hazard of all the credit I had, is now spread more than ever.[1] But burn politics, and send me from Courts and Ministers! Nite deelest richar MD.

2. I sauntered about this morning, and went with Dr. Pratt to a picture auction, where I had like to be drawn in to buy a picture that I was fond of, but, it seems, was good for nothing. Pratt was there to buy some pictures for the Bishop of Clogher, who resolves to lay out ten pounds to furnish his house with curious pieces. We dined with the Bishop, I being by chance disengaged. And this evening I sat with the Bishop of Ossory,[2] who is laid up with the gout. The French Ambassador, Duke d'Aumont,[3] came to town

---

[1] The quarrel between Oxford and Bolingbroke.　　[2] See p. 176.
[3] Burnet (History, iv. 382) says that the Duc d'Aumont was "a good-natured and generous man, of profuse expense, throwing handfuls of money

to-night; and the rabble conducted him home with shouts. I cannot smell yet, though my cold begins to break. It continues cruel hard frosty weather. Go and be melly, . . . sollahs.[1]

3. Lord Dupplin and I went with Lord and Lady Orkney this morning at ten to Wimbledon, six miles off, to see Lord and Lady Caermarthen. It is much the finest place about this town. Did oo never see it? I was once there before, about five years ago. You know Lady Caermarthen is Lord Treasurer's daughter, married about three weeks ago. I hope the young fellow will be a good husband.—I must send this away now. I came back just by nightfall, cruel cold weather; I have no smell yet, but my cold something better. Nite (?) sollahs; I'll take my reeve. I forget how MD's accounts are. Pray let me know always timely before MD wants; and pray give the bill on t'other side to Mrs. Brent as usual. I believe I have not paid her this great while. Go, play cards, and . . . rove Pdfr. Nite richar MD . . . roves Pdfr. FW lele . . . MD MD MD MD MD FW FW FW FW MD MD Lele . . .[2]

The six odd shillings, tell Mrs. Brent, are for her new year's gift.

I[3] am just now told that poor dear Lady Ashburnham,[4] the Duke of Ormond's daughter, died yesterday at her country house. The poor creature was with child. She was my greatest favourite, and I am in excessive concern for her loss. I hardly knew a more valuable person on all accounts. You must have heard me talk of her. I am afraid to see the Duke and Duchess. She was naturally very healthy; I am afraid she has been thrown away for want of

often out of his coach as he went about the streets. He was not thought a man of business, and seemed to employ himself chiefly in maintaining the dignity of his character and making himself acceptable to the nation."
[1] Partially obliterated.
[2] For the most part illegible. Forster reads, "Go, play cards, and be melly, deelest logues, and rove Pdfr. Nite richar MD, FW oo roves Pdfr. FW lele lele ME ME MD MD MD MD MD MD. MD FW FW FW ME ME FW FW FW FW FW ME ME ME."
[3] On the third page of the paper.   [4] See p. 44.

care. Pray condole with me. 'Tis extremely moving. Her lord's a puppy; and I shall never think it worth my while to be troubled with him, now he has lost all that was valuable in his possession; yet I think he used her pretty well. I hate life when I think it exposed to such accidents; and to see so many thousand wretches burdening the earth, while such as her die, makes me think God did never intend life for a blessing. Farewell.

LETTER LVIII[1]

LONDON, *Jan.* 4, 1712-13.

I ENDED my last with the melancholy news of poor Lady Ashburnham's death. The Bishop of Clogher and Dr. Pratt made me dine with them to-day at Lord Mountjoy's, pursuant to an engagement, which I had forgot. Lady Mountjoy told me that Maccartney was got safe out of our clutches, for she had spoke with one who had a letter from him from Holland. Others say the same thing. 'Tis hard such a dog should escape.—As I left Lord Mountjoy's I saw the Duke d'Aumont, the French Ambassador, going from Lord Bolingbroke's, where he dined, to have a private audience of the Queen. I followed, and went up to Court, where there was a great crowd. I was talking with the Duke of Argyle by the fireside in the bed-chamber, when the Ambassador came out from the Queen. Argyle presented me to him, and Lord Bolingbroke and we talked together a while. He is a fine gentleman, something like the Duke of Ormond, and just such an expensive man. After church to-day I showed the Bishop of Clogher, at Court, who was who. Nite my two dee logues, and . . .[2]

5. Our frost is broke, but it is bloody cold. Lord Treasurer is recovered, and went out this evening to the

---

[1] To " Mrs. Dingley," etc. Endorsed " Feb. 4."
[2] This sentence is scribbled over. Forster reads the last word as "lastalls," *i.e.* rascals, but it seems rather to be "ledles."

Queen. I dined with Lady Oxford, and then sat with Lord Treasurer while he went out. He gave me a letter from an unknown hand, relating to Dr. Brown,[1] Bishop of Cork, recommending him to a better bishopric, as a person who opposed Lord Wharton, and was made a bishop on that account, celebrating him for a great politician, etc. : in short, all directly contrary to his character, which I made bold to explain. What dogs there are in the world! I was to see the poor Duke and Duchess of Ormond this morning. The Duke was in his public room, with Mr. Southwell[2] and two more gentlemen. When Southwell and I were alone with him, he talked something of Lord Ashburnham, that he was afraid the Whigs would get him again. He bore up as well as he could, but something falling accidentally in discourse, the tears were just falling out of his eyes, and I looked off to give him an opportunity (which he took) of wiping them with his handkerchief. I never saw anything so moving, nor such a mixture of greatness of mind, and tenderness, and discretion. Nite MD.

6. Lord Bolingbroke and Parnell and I dined, by invitation, with my friend Darteneuf,[3] whom you have heard me talk of. Lord Bolingbroke likes Parnell mightily; and it is pleasant to see that one who hardly passed for anything in Ireland makes his way here with a little friendly forwarding. It is scurvy rainy weather, and I have hardly been abroad to-day, nor know anything that passes.—Lord Treasurer is quite recovered, and I hope will be careful to keep himself well. The Duchess of Marlborough is leaving England to go to her Duke, and makes presents of rings to several friends, they say worth two hundred pounds apiece. I am sure she ought to give me one, though the Duke pretended to think me his greatest enemy, and got people to tell me so, and very mildly to let me know how gladly he would have me softened toward him. I bid a lady of his acquaintance and mine let him know that I had hindered many a bitter

---

[1] Dr. Peter Brown was appointed Bishop of Cork in 1709.
[2] See p. 26.   [3] See p. 23.

thing against him; not for his own sake, but because I
thought it looked base; and I desired everything should be
left him, except power. Nite MD.

7. I dined with Lord and Lady Masham to-day, and this
evening played at ombre with Mrs. Vanhom, merely for
amusement. The Ministers have got my papers, and will
neither read them nor give them to me; and I can hardly
do anything. Very warm slabby weather, but I made a
shift to get a walk; yet I lost half of it, by shaking off Lord
Rochester,[1] who is a good, civil, simple man. The Bishop
of Ossory will not be Bishop of Hereford,[2] to the great grief
of himself and his wife. And hat is MD doing now, I
wonder? Playing at cards with the Dean and Mrs. Walls?
I think it is not certain yet that Maccartney is escaped. I
am plagued with bad authors, verse and prose, who send me
their books and poems, the vilest trash I ever saw; but I
have given their names to my man, never to let them see
me. I have got new ink, and 'tis very white; and I don't
see that it turns black at all. I'll go to seep; 'tis past
twelve.—Nite, MD.

8. Oo must understand that I am in my geers, and have
got a chocolate-pot, a present from Mrs. Ashe of Clogher,
and some chocolate from my brother Ormond, and I treat
folks sometimes. I dined with Lord Treasurer at five o'clock
to-day, and was by while he and Lord Bolingbroke were at
business; for it is fit I should know all that passes now,
because, etc. The Duke of Ormond employed me to speak
to Lord Treasurer to-day about an affair, and I did so; and
the Duke had spoke himself two hours before, which vexed
me, and I will chide the Duke about it. I'll tell you a good
thing; there is not one of the Ministry but what will employ
me as gravely to speak for them to Lord Treasurer as if I
were their brother or his; and I do it as gravely: though I
know they do it only because they will not make themselves

---

[1] See p. 24, note 4.
[2] Dr. H. Humphreys, Bishop of Hereford, died on Nov. 20, 1712. His
successor was Dr. Philip Bisse (1667-1721), Bishop of St. David's (see p. 14).

uneasy, or had rather I should be denied than they. I believe our peace will not be finished these two months; for I think we must have a return from Spain by a messenger, who will not go till Sunday next. Lord Treasurer has invited me to dine with him again to-morrow. Your Commissioner, Keatley,[1] is to be there. Nite dee richar MD.[2]

9. Dr. Pratt drank chocolate with me this morning, and then we walked. I was yesterday with him to see Lady Betty Butler, grieving for her sister Ashburnham. The jade was in bed in form, and she did so cant, she made me sick. I meet Tom Leigh every day in the Park, to preserve his health. He is as ruddy as a rose, and tells me his Bishop of Dromore[3] recovers very much. That Bishop has been very near dying. This day's *Examiner* talks of the play of "What is it like?"[4] and you will think it to be mine, and be bit; for I have no hand in these papers at all. I dined with Lord Treasurer, and shall again to-morrow, which is his day when all the Ministers dine with him. He calls it whipping-day. It is always on Saturday, and we do indeed usually rally him about his faults on that day. I was of the original Club, when only poor Lord Rivers, Lord Keeper, and Lord Bolingbroke came; but now Ormond, Anglesea, Lord Steward,[5] Dartmouth, and other rabble intrude, and I scold at it; but now they pretend as good a title as I; and, indeed, many Saturdays I am not there. The company being too many, I don't love it. Nite MD.

10. At seven this evening, as we sat after dinner at Lord Treasurer's, a servant said Lord Peterborow was at the door. Lord Treasurer and Lord Bolingbroke went out to meet him, and brought him in. He was just returned from abroad,

---

[1] Thomas Keightley, a Commissioner of the Great Seal in Ireland.
[2] Nearly obliterated. Mr. Ryland reads, "deelest MD."
[3] See p. 480.
[4] In the *Examiner* for Jan. 5 to 9, 1712[-13], there is an account of the game of Similitudes. One person thinks of a subject, and the others, not knowing what it is, name similitudes, and when the subject is proclaimed, must make good the comparisons. On the occasion described, the subject chosen was Faction. The prize was given to a Dutchman, who argued that Faction was like butter, because too much fire spoiled its consistency.
[5] Earl Poulett (see p. 190).

where he has been above a year. Soon as he saw me, he left the Duke of Ormond and other lords, and ran and kissed me before he spoke to them; but chid me terribly for not writing to him, which I never did this last time he was abroad, not knowing where he was; and he changed places so often, it was impossible a letter should overtake him. He left England with a bruise, by his coach overturning, that made him spit blood, and was so ill, we expected every post to hear of his death; but he outrode it or outdrank it, or something, and is come home lustier than ever. He is at least sixty, and has more spirits than any young fellow I know in England. He has got the old Oxford regiment of horse, and I believe will have a Garter. I love the hang-dog dearly. Nite dee MD.

11. The Court was crammed to-day to see [1] the French Ambassador; but he did not come. Did I never tell you that I go to Court on Sundays as to a coffee-house, to see acquaintance, whom I should otherwise not see twice a year? The Provost [2] and I dined with Ned Southwell, by appointment, in order to settle your kingdom, if my scheme can be followed; but I doubt our Ministry will be too tedious. You must certainly have a new Parliament; but they would have that a secret yet. Our Parliament here will be prorogued for three weeks. Those puppies the Dutch will not yet come in, though they pretend to submit to the Queen in everything; but they would fain try first how our session begins, in hopes to embroil us in the House of Lords: and if my advice had been taken, the session should have begun, and we would have trusted the Parliament to approve the steps already made toward the peace, and had an Address perhaps from them to conclude without the Dutch, if they would not agree.—Others are of my mind, but it is not reckoned so safe, it seems; yet I doubt whether the peace will be ready so soon as three weeks, but that is a secret. Nite MD.

12. Pratt and I walked into the City to one Bateman's,[3] a

---

[1] "Say" (MS.).   [2] Dr. Pratt.   [3] See p. 120.

famous bookseller, for old books. There I laid out four
pounds like a fool, and we dined at a hedge ale-house, for
two shillings and twopence, like emperors. Let me see, I
bought Plutarch, two volumes, for thirty shillings, etc. Well,
I'll tell you no more; oo don't understand Greek.[1] We have
no news, and I have nothing more to say to-day, and I can't
finish my work. These Ministers will not find time to do
what I would have them. So nite, nown dee dallars.

13. I was to have dined to-day with Lord Keeper, but
would not, because that brute Sir John Walter[2] was to be
one of the company. You may remember he railed at me
last summer was twelvemonth at Windsor, and has never
begged my pardon, though he promised to do it; and Lord
Mansel, who was one of the company, would certainly have
set us together by the ears, out of pure roguish mischief. So
I dined with Lord Treasurer, where there was none but Lord
Bolingbroke. I stayed till eight, and then went to Lady
Orkney's, who has been sick, and sat with her till twelve,
from whence you may consider it is late, sollahs. The
Parliament was prorogued to-day, as I told you, for three
weeks. Our weather is very bad and slobbery, and I shall
spoil my new hat (I have bought a new hat), or empty my
pockets. Does Hawkshaw pay the interest he owes? Lord
Abercorn plagues me to death. I have now not above six
people to provide for, and about as many to do good offices
to; and thrice as many that I will do nothing for; nor can
I if I would. Nite dee MD.

14. To-day I took the circle of morning visits. I went to
the Duchess of Ormond, and there was she, and Lady Betty,
and Lord Ashburnham together: this was the first time the
mother and daughter saw each other since Lady Ashburnham's death. They were both in tears, and I chid them for
being together, and made Lady Betty go to her own chamber;
then sat a while with the Duchess, and went after Lady
Betty, and all was well. There is something of farce in all
these mournings, let them be ever so serious. People will

---

[1] This sentence is partially obliterated.   [2] See pp. 305, 308.

pretend to grieve more than they really do, and that takes off from their true grief. I then went to the Duchess of Hamilton, who never grieved, but raged, and stormed, and railed.[1] She is pretty quiet now, but has a diabolical temper. Lord Keeper and his son, and their two ladies, and I, dined to-day with Mr. Cæsar,[2] Treasurer of the Navy, at his house in the City, where he keeps his office. We happened to talk of Brutus, and I said something in his praise, when it struck me immediately that I had made a blunder in doing so; and, therefore, I recollected myself, and said, "Mr. Cæsar, I beg your pardon." So we laughed, etc. Nite, my own deelest richar logues, MD.

15. I forgot to tell you that last night I had a present sent me (I found it, when I came home, in my chamber) of the finest wild fowl I ever saw, with the vilest letter, and from the vilest poet in the world, who sent it me as a bribe to get him an employment. I knew not where the scoundrel lived, so I could not send them back, and therefore I gave them away as freely as I got them, and have ordered my man never to let up the poet when he comes. The rogue should have kept the wings at least for his muse. One of his fowls was a large capon pheasant, as fat as a pullet. I ate share of it to-day with a friend. We have now a Drawing-room every Wednesday, Thursday, and Saturday at one o'clock. The Queen does not come out; but all her Ministers, foreigners, and persons of quality are at it. I was there to-day; and as Lord Treasurer came towards me, I avoided him, and he hunted me thrice about the room. I affect never to take notice of him at church or Court. He knows it, for I have told him so; and to-night, at Lord Masham's, he gave an account of it to the company; but my reasons are, that people seeing me speak to him causes a great deal of teasing. I tell you what comes into my head, that I never knew whether MD were Whigs or Tories, and I

[1] Cf. the account of Beatrix's feelings on the [death of the Duke in *Esmond*, book iii. chaps. 6 and 7.
[2] See p. 195.

value our conversation the more that it never turned on that subject. I have a fancy that Ppt is a Tory, and a violent one. I don't know why; but methinks she looks like one, and DD a sort of a Trimmer. Am I right? I gave the Examiner a hint about this prorogation, and to praise the Queen for her tenderness to the Dutch in giving them still more time to submit.[1] It fitted the occasions at present. Nite MD.

16. I was busy to-day at the Secretary's office, and stayed till past three. The Duke of Ormond and I were to dine at Lord Orkney's. The Duke was at the Committee, so I thought all was safe. When I went there, they had almost dined; for the Duke had sent to excuse himself, which I never knew. I came home at seven, and began a little whim, which just came into my head; and will make a threepenny pamphlet.[2] It shall be finished and out in a week; and if it succeeds, you shall know what it is; otherwise, not. I cannot send this to-morrow, and will put it off till next Saturday, because I have much business. So my journals shall be short, and Ppt must have patience. So nite, dee sollahs.

17. This rogue Parnell has not yet corrected his poem, and I would fain have it out. I dined to-day with Lord Treasurer, and his Saturday company, nine of us in all. They went away at seven, and Lord Treasurer and I sat talking an hour after. After dinner he was talking to the lords about the speech the Queen must make when the Parliament meets. He asked me how I would make it. I was going to be serious, because it was seriously put; but I turned it to a jest. And because they had been speaking of

---

[1] "Her Majesty is all goodness and tenderness to her people and her Allies. . . . She has now prorogued the best Parliament that ever assembled in her reign and respited her own glory, and the wishes, prayers, and wants of her people, only to give some of her Allies an opportunity to think of the returns they owe her, and try if there be such a thing as gratitude, justice, or humanity in Europe. The conduct of Her Majesty is without parallel. Never was so great a condescension made to the unreasonable clamours of an insolent faction now dwindled to the most contemptible circumstances."—*Examiner*, Jan. 12–16, 1712[-13].

[2] *Mr. Collins's Discourse of Freethinking, put into plain English by way of Abstract, for the use of the Poor*, an ironical pamphlet on Arthur Collins's *Discourse of Freethinking*, 1713.

the Duchess of Marlborough going to Flanders after the
Duke, I said the speech should begin thus : " My Lords
and Gentlemen, In order to my own quiet, and that of my
subjects, I have thought fit to send the Duchess of Marlborough abroad after the Duke." This took well, and turned
off the discourse. I must tell you I do not at all like the
present situation of affairs, and remember I tell you so.
Things must be on another foot, or we are all undone. I
hate this driving always to an inch. Nite MD.

18. We had a mighty full Court to-day. Dilly was with
me at the French church, and edified mightily. The Duke
of Ormond and I dined at Lord Orkney's ; but I left them at
seven, and came home to my whim. I have made a great
progress. My large Treatise [1] stands stock still. Some think
it too dangerous to publish, and would have me print only
what relates to the peace. I cannot tell what I shall do.
—The Bishop of Dromore is dying. They thought yesterday
he could not live two hours ; yet he is still alive, but is utterly
past all hopes. Go to cards, sollahs, and nite.

19. I was this morning to see the Duke and Duchess of
Ormond. The Duke d'Aumont came in while I was with
the Duke of Ormond, and we complimented each other like
dragons. A poor fellow called at the door where I lodge,
with a parcel of oranges for a present for me. I bid my man
know what his name was, and whence he came. He sent word
his name was Bun, and that I knew him very well. I bid
my man tell him I was busy, and he could not speak to me ;
and not to let him leave his oranges. I know no more of it,
but I am sure I never heard the name, and I shall take no
such presents from strangers. Perhaps he might be only
some beggar, who wanted a little money. Perhaps it might
be something worse. Let them keep their poison for their
rats. I don't love it.[2] That blot is a blunder. Nite dee
MD. . . .

---

[1] *The History of the Peace of Utrecht.*
[2] A line here has been erased. Forster imagined that he read, "Nite dear
MD, drowsy drowsy dear."

20. A Committee of our Society dined to-day with the Chancellor of the Exchequer. Our Society does not meet now as usual, for which I am blamed : but till Lord Treasurer will agree to give us money and employments to bestow, I am averse to it ; and he gives us nothing but promises. The Bishop of Dromore is still alive, and that is all. We expect every day he will die, and then Tom Leigh must go back, which is one good thing to the town. I believe Pratt will drive at one of these bishoprics. Our English bishopric[1] is not yet disposed of. I believe the peace will not be ready by the session. Nite MD.

21. I was to-day with my printer, to give him a little pamphlet I have written, but not politics. It will be out by Monday. If it succeeds, I will tell you of it ; otherwise, not. We had a prodigious thaw to-day, as bad as rain ; yet I walked like a good boy all the way. The Bishop of Dromore still draws breath, but cannot live two days longer. My large book lies flat. Some people think a great part of it ought not to be now printed. I believe I told you so before. This letter shall not go till Saturday, which makes up the three weeks exactly; and I allow MD six weeks, which are now almost out ; so oo must know I expect a rettle vely soon, and that MD is vely werr ;[2] and so nite, dee MD.

22. This is one of our Court days, and I was there. I told you there is a Drawing-room, Wednesday, Thursday, and Saturday. The Hamiltons and Abercorns have done teasing me. The latter, I hear, is actually going to France. Lord Treasurer quarrelled with me at Court for being four days without dining with him ; so I dined there to-day, and he has at last fallen in with my project (as he calls it) of coining halfpence and farthings, with devices, like medals, in honour of the Queen, every year changing the device. I wish it may be done. Nite MD.

23. The Duke of Ormond and I appointed to dine with Ned Southwell to-day, to talk of settling your affairs of Parliament in Ireland, but there was a mixture of company, and the

[1] Hereford.   [2] Very well.

Duke of Ormond was in haste, and nothing was done. If your Parliament meets this summer, it must be a new one; but I find some are of opinion there should be none at all these two years. I will trouble myself no more about it. My design was to serve the Duke of Ormond. Dr. Pratt and I sat this evening with the Bishop of Clogher, and played at ombre for threepences. That, I suppose, is but low with you. I found, at coming home, a letter from MD, N. 37. I shall not answer it zis bout, but will the next. I am sorry for poo poo Ppt. Pray walk hen oo can. I have got a terrible new cold before my old one was quite gone, and don't know how. Pay. . . .[1] I shall have DD's money soon from the Exchequer. The Bishop of Dromore is dead now at last. Nite, dee MD.

24. I was at Court to-day, and it was comical to see Lord Abercorn bowing to me, but not speaking, and Lord Selkirk the same.[2] I dined with Lord Treasurer and his Saturday Club, and sat with him two hours after the rest were gone, and spoke freer to him of affairs than I am afraid others do, who might do more good. All his friends repine, and shrug their shoulders; but will not deal with him so freely as they ought. It is an odd business; the Parliament just going to sit, and no employments given. They say they will give them in a few days. There is a new bishop made of Hereford;[3] so Ossory[4] is disappointed. I hinted so to his friends two months ago, to make him leave off deluding himself, and being indiscreet, as he was. I have just time to send this, without giving to the bellman. Nite deelest richar MD. . . . dee MD MD MD FW FW FW ME ME ME Lele Lele Lele.

My second cold is better now. Lele lele lele lele.

[1] Sentence obliterated. Forster professes to read, " Pay can oo walk oftener —oftener still?"
[2] See p. 480.
[3] Dr. Bisse, translated from St. David's.
[4] See pp. 176, 489.

LETTER LIX[1]

LONDON, *Jan.* 25, 1712–1713.

WE had such a terrible storm to-day, that, going to Lord Bolingbroke's, I saw a hundred tiles fallen down; and one swinger fell about forty yards before me, that would have killed a horse: so, after church and Court, I walked through the Park, and took a chair to Lord Treasurer's. Next door to his house, a tin chimneytop had fallen down, with a hundred bricks. It is grown calm this evening. I wonder had you such a wind to-day? I hate it as much as any hog does. Lord Treasurer has engaged me to dine again with him to-morrow. He has those tricks sometimes of inviting me from day to day, which I am forced to break through. My little pamphlet[2] is out: 'tis not politics. If it takes, I say again you shall hear of it. Nite dee logues.

26. This morning I felt a little touch of giddiness, which has disordered and weakened me with its ugly remains all this day. Pity Pdfr. After dinner at Lord Treasurer's, the French Ambassador, Duke d'Aumont, sent Lord Treasurer word that his house was burnt down to the ground. It took fire in the upper rooms, while he was at dinner with Monteleon, the Spanish Ambassador, and other persons; and soon after Lord Bolingbroke came to us with the same story. We are full of speculations upon it, but I believe it was the carelessness of his French rascally servants. 'Tis odd that this very day Lord Somers, Wharton, Sunderland, Halifax, and the whole club of Whig lords, dined at Pontack's[3] in the City, as I received private notice. They have some damned design. I tell you another odd thing; I was observing it to Lord Treasurer, that he was stabbed on the day King William died; and the day I saved his life, by opening the bandbox,[4] was King William's birthday. My friend Mr. Lewis has had a lie spread on him by the mistake

---

[1] To "Mrs. Dingley," etc.   Endorsed "Febr. 26."
[2] See p. 494.   [3] See p. 271.   [4] See p. 468.

of a man, who went to another of his name, to give him thanks for passing his Privy Seal to come from France.[1] That other Lewis spread about that the man brought him thanks from Lord Perth and Lord Melfort (two lords with the Pretender), for his great services, etc. The Lords will examine that t'other Lewis to-morrow in council; and I believe you will hear of it in the prints, for I will make Abel Roper give a relation of it. Pray tell me if it be necessary to write a little plainer; for I looked over a bit of my last letter, and could hardly read it. I'll mend my hand, if oo please: but you are more used to it *nor* I, as Mr. Raymond says. Nite MD.

27. I dined to-day with Lord Treasurer: this makes four days together; and he has invited me again to-morrow, but I absolutely refused him. I was this evening at a christening with him of Lord Dupplin's[2] daughter. He went away at ten; but they kept me and some others till past twelve; so you may be sure 'tis late, as they say. We have now stronger suspicions that the Duke d'Aumont's house was set on fire by malice. I was to-day to see Lord Keeper, who has quite lost his voice with a cold. There Dr. Radcliffe told me that it was the Ambassador's confectioner set the house on fire by boiling sugar, and going down and letting it boil over. Yet others still think differently; so I know not what to judge. Nite my own deelest MD, rove Pdfr.

28. I was to-day at Court, where the Spanish Ambassador talked to me as if he did not suspect any design in burning d'Aumont's house: but Abbé Gaultier, Secretary for France here, said quite otherwise; and that d'Aumont had a letter the very same day to let him know his house should be burnt, and they tell several other circumstances too tedious to write. One is, that a fellow mending the tiles just when the fire broke out, saw a pot with wildfire[3] in the room. I

---

[1] A result of confusion between Erasmus Lewis and Henry Lewis, a Hamburg merchant. See Swift's paper in the *Examiner* of Jan. 30 to Feb. 2, reprinted in his *Works* under the title, "A Complete Refutation of the Falsehoods alleged against Erasmus Lewis, Esq."

[2] Lord Dupplin (see p. 30) had been created Baron Hay in December 1711.

[3] A composition of inflammable materials.

dined with Lord Orkney. Neither Lord Abercorn nor Selkirk will now speak with me. I have disobliged both sides. Nite dear MD.

29. Our Society met to-day, fourteen of us, and at a tavern. We now resolve to meet but once a fortnight, and have a Committee every other week of six or seven, to consult about doing some good. I proposed another message to Lord Treasurer by three principal members, to give a hundred guineas to a certain person, and they are to urge it as well as they can. We also raised sixty guineas upon our own Society; but I made them do it by sessors,[1] and I was one of them, and we fitted our tax to the several estates. The Duke of Ormond pays ten guineas, and I the third part of a guinea; at that rate, they may tax as often as they please. Well, but I must answer oor rettle, ung oomens: not yet; 'tis rate now, and I can't tind it. Nite deelest MD.

30. I have drank Spa waters this two or three days; but they do not pass, and make me very giddy. I an't well; faith, I'll take them no more. I sauntered after church with the Provost to-day to see a library to be sold, and dined at five with Lord Orkney. We still think there was malice in burning d'Aumont's house. I hear little Harrison[2] is come over; it was he I sent to Utrecht. He is now Queen's Secretary to the Embassy, and has brought with him the Barrier Treaty, as it is now corrected by us, and yielded to by the Dutch, which was the greatest difficulty to retard the peace. I hope he will bring over the peace a month hence, for we will send him back as soon as possible. I long to see the little brat, my own creature. His pay is in all a thousand pounds a year, and they have never paid him a groat, though I have teased their hearts out. He must be three or four hundred pounds in debt at least, the brat! Let me go to bed, sollahs.—Nite dee richar MD.

31. Harrison was with me this morning: we talked three hours, and then I carried him to Court. When we went down to the door of my lodging, I found a coach waited for

[1] Assessors.   [2] See p. 36.

him. I chid him for it; but he whispered me it was impossible to do otherwise; and in the coach he told me he had not one farthing in his pocket to pay it; and therefore took the coach for the whole day, and intended to borrow money somewhere or other. So there was the Queen's Minister entrusted in affairs of the greatest importance, without a shilling in his pocket to pay a coach! I paid him while he was with me seven guineas, in part of a dozen of shirts he bought me in Holland. I presented him to the Duke of Ormond, and several lords at Court; and I contrived it so that Lord Treasurer came to me and asked (I had Parnell by me) whether that was Dr. Parnell, and came up and spoke to him with great kindness, and invited him to his house. I value myself upon making the Ministry desire to be acquainted with Parnell, and not Parnell with the Ministry. His poem is almost fully corrected, and shall soon be out. Here's enough for to-day: only to tell you that I was in the City with my printer to alter an *Examiner* about my friend Lewis's story,[1] which will be told with remarks. Nite MD.

Feb. 1. I could do nothing till to-day about the *Examiner*, but the printer came this morning, and I dictated to him what was fit to be said, and then Mr. Lewis came, and corrected it as he would have it; so I was neither at church nor Court. The Duke of Ormond and I dined at Lord Orkney's. I left them at seven, and sat with Sir Andrew Fountaine, who has a very bad sore leg, for which he designs to go to France. Fais, here's a week gone, and one side of this letter not finished. Oh, but I write now but once in three weeks; iss, fais, this shall go sooner. The Parliament is to sit on the third, but will adjourn for three or four days; for the Queen is laid up with the gout, and both Speakers out of order, though one of them, the Lord Keeper, is almost well. I spoke to the Duke of Ormond a good deal about Ireland. We do not altogether agree, nor am I judge enough of Irish affairs; but I will speak to Lord Treasurer

[1] See p. 499.

to-morrow, that we three may settle them some way or other. Nite sollahs both, rove Pdfr.

2. I had a letter some days ago from Moll Gery;[1] her name is now Wigmore, and her husband has turned parson. She desires nothing but that I would get Lord Keeper to give him a living; but I will send her no answer, though she desires it much. She still makes mantuas at Farnham. It rained all this day, and Dilly came to me, and was coaching it into the City; so I went with him for a shaking, because it would not cost me a farthing. There I met my friend Stratford,[2] the merchant, who is going abroad to gather up his debts, and be clear in the world. He begged that I would dine with some merchant friends of ours there, because it was the last time I should see him: so I did, and thought to have seen Lord Treasurer in the evening, but he happened to go out at five; so I visited some friends, and came home. And now I have the greatest part of your letter to answer; and yet I will not do it to-night, say what oo please. The Parliament meets to-morrow, but will be prorogued for a fortnight; which disappointment will, I believe, vex abundance of them, though they are not Whigs; for they are forced to be in town at expense for nothing: but we want an answer from Spain, before we are sure of everything being right for the peace; and God knows whether we can have that answer this month. It is a most ticklish juncture of affairs; we are always driving to an inch: I am weary of it. Nite MD.

3. The Parliament met, and was prorogued, as I said, and I found some cloudy faces, and heard some grumbling. We have got over all our difficulties with France, I think. They have now settled all the articles of commerce between us and them, wherein they were very much disposed to play the rogue if we had not held them to [it]; and this business we wait from Spain is to prevent some other rogueries of the French, who are finding an evasion to trade to the Spanish West Indies; but I hope we shall prevent it. I dined with

[1] See p. 439.   .   [2] See pp. 10, 381, 413.

Lord Treasurer, and he was in good humour enough. I gave him that part of my book in manuscript to read where his character was, and drawn pretty freely. He was reading and correcting it with his pencil, when the Bishop of St. David's [1] (now removing to Hereford) came in and interrupted us. I left him at eight, and sat till twelve with the Provost and Bishop of Clogher at the Provost's. Nite MD.

4. I was to-day at Court, but kept out of Lord Treasurer's way, because I was engaged to the Duke of Ormond, where I dined, and, I think, ate and drank too much. I sat this evening with Lady Masham, and then with Lord Masham and Lord Treasurer at Lord Masham's. It was last year, you may remember, my constant evening place. I saw Lady Jersey [2] with Lady Masham, who has been laying out for my acquaintance, and has forced a promise for me to drink chocolate with her in a day or two, which I know not whether I shall perform (I have just mended my pen, you see), for I do not much like her character; but she is very malicious, and therefore I think I must keep fair with her. I cannot send this letter till Saturday next, I find; so I will answer oors now. I see no different days of the month; yet it is dated January 3: so it was long a coming. I did not write to Dr. Coghill that I would have nothing in Ireland, but that I was soliciting nothing anywhere, and that is true. I have named Dr. Sterne to Lord Treasurer, Lord Bolingbroke, and the Duke of Ormond, for a bishopric, and I did it heartily. I know not what will come of it; but I tell you as a great secret that I have made the Duke of Ormond promise me to recommend nobody till he tells me, and this for some reasons too long to mention. My head is still in no good order. I am heartily sorry for poo Ppt, I'm sure. Her head is good for . . .[3] I'll answer more to-mollow. Nite, dearest MD; nite dee sollahs, MD.[4]

5. I must go on with oo letter. I dined to-day with Sir Andrew Fountaine and the Provost, and I played at ombre

---

[1] Dr. Bisse.
[3] Forster reads, "something."
[2] See p. 326.
[4] Hardly legible.

with him all the afternoon. I won, yet Sir Andrew is an
admirable player. Lord Pembroke[1] came in, and I gave
him three or four scurvy Dilly puns, that begin with an *if.*
Well, but oor letter, well, ret me see.—No; I believe I shall
write no more this good while, nor publish what I have done.
Nauty (?) Ppt oo, are vely tempegant. I did not suspect
oo would tell Filby.[2] Oo are so . . .[3] Turns and
visitations—what are these? I'll preach and visit as much
for Mr. Walls. Pray God mend poopt's[4] health; mine is
but very indifferent. I have left off Spa water; it makes
my leg swell. Nite deelest MD.

6. This is the Queen's Birthday, and I never saw it
celebrated with so much luxury and fine clothes. I went to
Court to see them, and I dined with Lord Keeper, where the
ladies were fine to admiration. I passed the evening at Mrs.
Vanhomrigh's, and came home pretty early, to answer oo
rettle again. Pray God keep the Queen. She was very ill
about ten days ago, and had the gout in her stomach. When
I came from Lord Keeper's, I called at Lord Treasurer's,
because I heard he was very fine, and that was a new thing;
and it was true, for his coat and waistcoat were embroidered.
I have seen the Provost often since, and never spoke to him
to speak to the Temples about Daniel Carr, nor will; I don't
care to do it. I have writ lately to Parvisol. Oo did well
to let him make up his accounts. All things grow dear
in Ireland, but corn to the parsons; for my livings are fallen
much this year by Parvisol's account. Nite dee logues, MD.

7. [8] I was at Court to-day, but saw no Birthday clothes;
the great folks never wear them above once or twice. I
dined with Lord Orkney, and sat the evening with Sir
Andrew Fountaine, whose leg is in a very dubious condition.
Pray let me know when DD's money is near due: always
let me know it beforehand. This, I believe, will hardly go
till Saturday; for I tell you what, being not very well, I dare

---

[1] See p. 52.   [2] Stella's brother-in-law (see pp. 471, 473).
[3] Forster guesses, "Oo are so 'recise; not to oor health."
[4] For "poo Ppt's." Mr. Ryland reads, "people's."

not study much : so I let company come in a morning, and
the afternoon pass in dining and sitting somewhere. Lord
Treasurer is angry if I don't dine with him every second
day, and I cannot part with him till late : he kept me last
night till near twelve. Our weather is constant rain above
these two months, which hinders walking, so that our spring
is not like yours. I have not seen Fanny Manley[1] yet; I
cannot find time. I am in rebellion with all my acquaintance,
but I will mend with my health and the weather. Clogher
make a figure! Clogher make a ——. Colds! why, we
have been all dying with colds; but now they are a little
over, and my second is almost off. I can do nothing for
Swanton indeed. It is a thing impossible, and wholly out
of my way. If he buys, he must buy. So now I have
answered oo rettle; and there's an end of that now; and
I'll say no more, but bid oo nite, dee MD.

8. [9] It was terrible rainy to-day from morning till night.
I intended to have dined with Lord Treasurer, but went to
see Sir Andrew Fountaine, and he kept me to dinner, which
saved coach-hire; and I stayed with him all the afternoon,
and lost thirteen shillings and sixpence at ombre. There
was management! and Lord Treasurer will chide; but I'll
dine with him to-morrow. The Bishop of Clogher's daughter
has been ill some days,[2] and it proves the smallpox. She is
very full; but it comes out well, and they apprehend no
danger. Lady Orkney has given me her picture; a very
fine original of Sir Godfrey Kneller's; it is now a mending.
He has favoured her squint admirably; and you know I
love a cast in the eye. I was to see Lady Worsley[3] to-day,
who is just come to town; she is full of rheumatic pains.
All my acquaintance grow old and sickly. She lodges in
the very house in King Street, between St. James's Street
and St. James's Square, where DD's brother bought the
sweetbread, when I lodged there, and MD came to see me.
Short sighs.[4] Nite MD.

[1] See p. 478. [2] See p. 483. [3] See p. 132.
[4] Obliterated ; Forster's reading.

9. [10] I thought to have dined with Lord Treasurer to-day, but he dined abroad at Tom Harley's; so I dined at Lord Masham's, and was winning all I had lost playing with Lady Masham at crown picquet, when we went to pools, and I lost it again. Lord Treasurer came in to us, and chid me for not following him to Tom Harley's. Miss Ashe is still the same, and they think her not in danger; my man calls there daily after I am gone out, and tells me at night. I was this morning to see Lady Jersey, and we have made twenty parties about dining together, and I shall hardly keep one of them. She is reduced after all her greatness to seven servants, and a small house, and no coach.[1] I like her tolerably as yet. Nite MD.

10. [11] I made visits this morning to the Duke and Duchess of Ormond, and Lady Betty, and the Duchess of Hamilton. (When I was writing this near twelve o'clock, the Duchess of Hamilton sent to have me dine with her to-morrow. I am forced to give my answer through the door, for my man has got the key, and is gone to bed; but I cannot obey her, for our Society meets to-morrow.) I stole away from Lord Treasurer by eight, and intended to have passed the evening with Sir Thomas Clarges[2] and his lady; but met them in another place, and have there sat till now. My head has not been ill to-day. I was at Court, and made Lord Mansel walk with me in the Park before we went to dinner.—Yesterday and to-day have been fair, but yet it rained all last night. I saw Sterne staring at Court to-day. He

---

[1] Writing in October 1713, Lord Berkeley of Stratton told Lord Strafford of "a fine prank of the widow Lady Jersey" (see p. 281). "It is well known her lord died much in debt, and she, after taking upon her the administration, sold everything and made what money she could, and is run away into France without paying a farthing of the debts, with only one servant and unknown to all her friends, and hath taken her youngest son, as 'tis supposed to make herself a merit in breeding him a papist. My Lord Bolingbroke sent after her, but too late, and they say the Queen hath writ a letter with her own hand to the King of France to send back the boy" (*Wentworth Papers*, p. 357). See also p. 538, below. I am not sure whether in the present passage Swift is referring to the widow or the younger Lady Jersey (see p. 326).

[2] Sir Thomas Clarges, Bart. (died 1759), M.P. for Lostwithiel, married Barbara, youngest daughter of John Berkeley, fourth Viscount Fitz-Hardinge, and of Barbara Villiers (see p. 466), daughter of Sir Edward Villiers.

has been often to see me, he says: but my man has not yet let him up. He is in deep mourning; I hope it is not for his wife.[1] I did not ask him. Nite MD.

12.[2] I have reckoned days wrong all this while; for this is the twelfth. I do not know when I lost it. I dined to-day with our Society, the greatest dinner I have ever seen. It was at Jack Hill's, the Governor of Dunkirk. I gave an account of sixty guineas I had collected, and am to give them away to two authors to-morrow; and Lord Treasurer has promised us a hundred pounds to reward some others. I found a letter on my table last night to tell me that poor little Harrison, the Queen's Secretary, that came lately from Utrecht with the Barrier Treaty, was ill, and desired to see me at night; but it was late, and I could not go till to-day. I have often mentioned him in my letters, you may remember. . . . I went in the morning, and found him mighty ill, and got thirty guineas for him from Lord Bolingbroke, and an order for a hundred pounds from the Treasury to be paid him to-morrow; and I have got him removed to Knightsbridge for air. He has a fever and inflammation on his lungs; but I hope will do well. Nite.

13. I was to see a poor poet, one Mr. Diaper,[3] in a nasty garret, very sick. I gave him twenty guineas from Lord Bolingbroke, and disposed the other sixty to two other authors, and desired a friend to receive the hundred pounds for poor Harrison, and will carry it to him to-morrow morning. I sent to see how he did, and he is extremely ill; and I very much afflicted for him, for he is my own creature, and in a very honourable post, and very worthy of it. I dined in the City. I am in much concern for this poor lad. His mother and sister attend him, and he wants nothing. Nite poo dee MD.

14. I took Parnell this morning, and we walked to see

---

[1] See pp. 428, 447.
[2] Altered from "11" in the MS. It is not certain where the error in the dates began; but the entry of the 6th must be correctly dated, because the Feb. 6 was the Queen's Birthday.
[3] See pp. 422, 479.

poor Harrison. I had the hundred pounds in my pocket. I told Parnell I was afraid to knock at the door; my mind misgave me. I knocked, and his man in tears told me his master was dead an hour .before. Think what grief this is to me! I went to his mother, and have been ordering things for his funeral with as little cost as possible, to-morrow at ten at night. Lord Treasurer was much concerned when I told him. I could not dine with Lord Treasurer, nor any- where else; but got a bit of meat toward evening. No loss ever grieved me so much: poor creature! Pray God Almighty bless poor MD. Adieu.

I send this away to-night, and am sorry it must go while I am in so much grief.

LETTER LX [1]

LONDON, *Feb.* 15 [1712-13].

I DINED to-day with Mr. Rowe [2] and a projector, who has been teasing me with twenty schemes to get grants; and I don't like one of them; and, besides, I was out of humour for the loss of poor Harrison. At ten this night I was at his funeral, which I ordered to be as private as possible. We had but one coach with four of us; and when it was carrying us home after the funeral, the braces broke; and we were forced to sit in it, and have it held up, till my man went for chairs,[3] at eleven at night in terrible rain. I am come home very melancholy, and will go to bed. Nite . . . MD.[4]

16. I dined to-day with Lord Dupplin and some company to divert me; but left them early, and have been reading a foolish book for amusement. I shall never have courage again to care for making anybody's fortune. The Parliament meets to-morrow, and will be prorogued another fortnight, at which several of both parties were angry; but it cannot be

---

[1] Addressed to " Mrs. Dingley," etc. Endorsed " Mar. 7."
[2] See p. 27.
[3] Sedan chairs were then comparatively novel (see Gay's *Trivia*).
[4] Some words obliterated. Forster reads, " Nite MD, My own deelest MD."

helped, though everything about the peace is past all danger. I never saw such a continuance of rainy weather. We have not had two fair days together these ten weeks. I have not dined with Lord Treasurer these four days, nor can I till Saturday; for I have several engagements till then, and he will chide me to some purpose. I am perplexed with this hundred pounds of poor Harrison's, what to do with it. I cannot pay his relations till they administer, for he is much in debt;[1] but I will have the staff in my own hands, and venture nothing. Nite poo dee MD.

17. Lady Jersey and I dined by appointment to-day with Lord Bolingbroke. He is sending his brother[2] to succeed Mr.[3] Harrison. It is the prettiest post in Europe for a young gentleman. I lose my money at ombre sadly; I make a thousand blunders. I play but[4] threepenny ombre; but it is what you call running ombre. Lady Clarges,[5] and a drab I hate, won a dozen shillings of me last night. The Parliament was prorogued to-day; and people grumble; and the good of it is the peace cannot be finished by the time they meet, there are so many fiddling things to do. Is Ppt an ombre lady yet? You know all the tricks of it now, I suppose. I reckon you have all your cards from France, for ours pay sixpence a pack taxes, which goes deep to the box. I have given away all my Spa water, and take some nasty steel drops, and my head has been better this week past. I send every day to see how Miss Ashe does: she is very full, they say, but in no danger. I fear she will lose some of her beauty. The son lies out of the house. I wish he had them too, while he is so young.—Nite MD.

[1] Peter Wentworth wrote to Lord Strafford, on Feb. 17, 1713, "Poor Mr. Harrison is very much lamented; he died last Saturday. Dr. Swift told me that he had told him . . . he owed about £300, and the Queen owed him £500, and that if you or some of your people could send an account of his debts, that I might give it to him, he would undertake to solicit Lord Treasurer and get this £500, and give the remainder to his mother and sister" (*Wentworth Papers*, 320).
[2] George St. John (eldest son of Sir Harry St. John by his second marriage) was Secretary to the English Plenipotentiaries at Utrecht. He died at Venice in 1716 (Lady Cowper's *Diary*, 65).
[3] Forster wrongly reads, "poor."
[4] "Putt" (MS.).   [5] See p. 506.

18. The Earl of Abingdon[1] has been teasing me these three months to dine with him; and this day was appointed about a week ago, and I named my company; Lord Stawel,[2] Colonel Disney,[3] and Dr. Arbuthnot; but the two last slipped out their necks, and left Stawell and me to dine there. We did not dine till seven, because it is Ash Wednesday. We had nothing but fish, which Lord Stawell could not eat, and got a broiled leg of a turkey. Our wine was poison; yet the puppy has twelve thousand pound a year. His carps were raw, and his candles tallow. He[4] shall not catch me in haste again, and everybody has laughed at me for dining with him. I was to-day to let Harrison's mother know I could not pay till she administers; which she will do. I believe she is an old bawd,[5] and her daughter a ——. There were more Whigs to-day at Court than Tories. I believe they think the peace must be made, and so come to please the Queen. She is still lame with the gout. Nite MD.

19. I was at Court to-day, to speak to Lord Bolingbroke to look over Parnell's poem since it is corrected; and Parnell and I dined with him, and he has shown him three or four more places to alter a little. Lady Bolingbroke came down to us while we were at dinner, and Parnell stared at her as if she were a goddess. I thought she was like Parnell's wife, and he thought so too. Parnell is much pleased with Lord Bolingbroke's favour to him, and I hope it may one day turn to his advantage. His poem will be printed in a few days. Our weather continues as fresh raining as if it had not rained at all. I sat to-night at Lady Masham's, where Lord Treasurer came and scolded me for not dining with him. I told him I could not till Saturday. I have stayed there till past twelve. So nite dee sollahs, nite.

---

[1] Montagu Bertie, second Earl of Abingdon (died 1743), was a strong Tory.
[2] See p. 102. These friends were together again on an expedition to Bath in 1715, when Jervas wrote to Pope (Aug. 12, 1715) that Arbuthnot, Disney, and he were to meet at Hyde Park Corner, proceed to Mr. Hill's at Egham, meet Pope next day, and then go to Lord Stawell's to lodge the night. Lord Stawell's seat, Aldermaston, was seventeen miles from Binfield.
[3] See p. 153.   [4] " I " (MS.).
[5] Obliterated. Forster reads, " devil," and Mr. Ryland, " bitch."

20. Lady Jersey, Lady Catherine Hyde,[1] the Spanish Ambassador, the Duke d'Atree,[2] another Spaniard, and I, dined to-day by appointment with Lord Bolingbroke; but they fell a drinking so many Spanish healths in champagne that I stole away to the ladies, and drank tea till eight; and then went and lost my money at ombre with Sir Andrew Fountaine, who has a very bad leg. Miss Ashe is past all danger; and her eye, which was lately bad (I suppose one effect of her distemper), is now better. I do not let the Bishop see me, nor shall this good while. Good luck! when I came home, I warrant, I found a letter from MD, No. 38; and oo write so small nowadays, I hope oo poor eyes are better. Well, this shall go to-morrow se'nnight, with a bill for MD. I will speak to Mr. Griffin[3] to-morrow about Ppt's brother Filby, and desire, whether he deserves or no, that his employment may be mended; that is to say, if I can see Griffin; otherwise not; and I'll answer oo rettle hen I Pdfr think fit. Nite MD.

21. Methinks I writ a little saucy last night. I mean the last . . .[4] I saw Griffin at Court. He says he knows nothing of a salt-work at Recton; but that he will give Filby a better employment, and desires Filby will write to him. If I knew how to write to Filby, I would; but pray do you. Bid him make no mention of you; but only let Mr. Griffin know that he has the honour to be recommended by Dr. S——, etc.; that he will endeavour to deserve, etc.; and if you dictated a whole letter for him, it would be better; I hope he can write and spell well. I'll inquire for a direction to Griffin before I finish this. I dined with Lord Treasurer and seven lords to-day. You know Saturday is his great day, but I sat with them alone till eight, and then came home, and have been writing a letter to Mrs. Davis, at York. She took care to have a letter delivered for me at Lord Treasurer's;

[1] See p. 393.
[2] Victor Marie, duc d'Estrées, Marshal of France (died 1727).
[3] See p. 471.
[4] Several words are obliterated. Forster reads, "the last word, God 'give me"; but " 'give me " is certainly wrong.

for I would not own one she sent by post. She reproaches me for not writing to her these four years; and I have honestly told her it was my way never to write to those whom I am never likely to see, unless I can serve them, which I cannot her, etc. Davis the schoolmaster's widow. Nite MD.

22. I dined to-day at Lord Orkney's, with the Duke of Ormond and Sir Thomas Hanmer.[1] Have you ever heard of the latter? He married the Duchess of Grafton in his youth (she dined with us too). He is the most considerable man in the House of Commons. He went last spring to Flanders, with the Duke of Ormond; from thence to France, and was going to Italy; but the Ministry sent for him, and he has been come over about ten days. He is much out of humour with things: he thinks the peace is kept off too long, and is full of fears and doubts. It is thought he is designed for Secretary of State, instead of Lord Dartmouth. We have been acquainted these two years; and I intend, in a day or two, to have an hour's talk with him on affairs. I saw the Bishop of Clogher at Court; Miss is recovering. I know not how much she will be marked. The Queen is slowly mending of her gout, and intends to be brought in a chair to Parliament when it meets, which will be March 3; for I suppose they will prorogue no more; yet the peace will not be signed then, and we apprehend the Tories themselves will many of them be discontented. Nite dee MD.

23. It was ill weather to-day, and I dined with Sir Andrew Fountaine, and in the evening played at ombre with him and the Provost, and won twenty-five shillings; so I have recovered myself pretty well. Dilly has been dunning me to see Fanny Manley; but I have not yet been able to do it. Miss Ashe is now quite out of danger; and hope will not be

---

[1] See p. 69. Sir Thomas Hanmer married, in 1698, at the age of twenty-two, Isabella, Dowager Duchess of Grafton, daughter of Henry, Earl of Arlington, and Countess of Arlington in her own right. Hanmer was not made Secretary of State, but he succeeded Bromley as Speaker of the House of Commons.

much marked. I cannot tell how to direct to Griffin; and think he lives in Bury Street, near St. James's Street, hard by me; but I suppose your brother may direct to him to the Salt Office, and, as I remember, he knows his Christian name, because he sent it me in the list of the Commissioners. Nite dee MD.

24. I walked this morning to Chelsea, to see Dr. Atterbury, Dean of Christ Church. I had business with him about entering Mr. Fitzmaurice,[1] my Lord Kerry's son, into his College; and Lady Kerry[2] is a great favourite of mine. Lord Harley, Lord Dupplin, young Bromley[3] the Speaker's son, and I, dined with Dr. Stratford[4] and some other clergymen; but I left them at seven to go to Lady Jersey, to see Monteleon the Spanish Ambassador play at ombre. Lady Jersey was abroad, and I chid the servants, and made a rattle; but since I came home she sent me a message that I was mistaken, and that the meeting is to be to-morrow. I have a worse memory than when I left you, and every day forget appointments; but here my memory was by chance too good. But I'll go to-morrow; for Lady Catherine Hyde and Lady Bolingbroke are to be there by appointment, and I listed[5] up my periwig, and all, to make a figure. Well, who can help it? Not I, vow to . . .![6] Nite MD.

25. Lord Treasurer met me last night at Lord Masham's, and thanked me for my company in a jeer, because I had not dined with him in three days. He chides me if I stay away but two days together. What will this come to? Nothing. My grandmother used to say, "More of your

---

[1] William Fitzmaurice (see pp. 91, 263) entered Christ Church, Oxford, matriculating on March 10, 1712-13, at the age of eighteen.

[2] See p. 89.

[3] William Bromley, second son of Bromley the Speaker (see p. 76), was a boy of fourteen at this time. In 1727 he was elected M.P. for Warwick, and he died in 1737, shortly after being elected Member for Oxford University.

[4] See p. 133.

[5] Sometimes "list" means to border or edge; at others, to sew together, so as to make a variegated display, or to form a border. Probably it here means the curling of the bottom of the wig.

[6] The last eight words have been much obliterated, and the reading is doubtful.

33

lining, and less of your dining." However, I dined with him, and could hardly leave him at eight, to go to Lady Jersey's, where five or six foreign Ministers were, and as many ladies. Monteleon played like the English, and cried "gacco," and knocked his knuckles for trump, and played at small games like Ppt. Lady Jersey whispered me to stay and sup with the ladies when the fellows were gone; but they played till eleven, and I would not stay. I think this letter must go on Saturday; that's certain; and it is not half full yet. Lady Catherine Hyde had a mighty mind I should be acquainted with Lady Dalkeith,[1] her sister, the Duke of Monmouth's eldest son's widow, who was of the company to-night; but I did not like her; she paints too much. Nite MD.

26. This day our Society met at the Duke of Ormond's, but I had business that called me another way; so I sent my excuses, and dined privately with a friend. Besides, Sir Thomas Hanmer whispered me last night at Lady Jersey's that I must attend Lord Treasurer and Duke of Ormond at supper at his house to-night; which I did at eleven, and stayed till one, so oo may be sure 'tis late enough. There was the Duchess of Grafton, and the Duke her son; nine of us in all. The Duke of Ormond chid me for not being at the Society to-day, and said sixteen were there. I said I never knew sixteen people good company in my life; no, fais, nor eight either. We have no news in this town at all. I wonder why I don't write you news. I know less of what passes than anybody, because I go to[2] no coffee-house, nor see any but Ministers, and such people ; and Ministers never talk politics in conversation. The Whigs are forming great schemes against the meeting of Parliament, which will be next Tuesday, I still think, without fail; and we hope to hear

---

[1] Lady Henrietta Hyde, second daughter of Laurence Hyde, first Earl of Rochester (see p. 60), married James Scott, Earl of Dalkeith, son of the Duke of Monmouth. Lord Dalkeith died in 1705, leaving a son, who succeeded his grandmother (Monmouth's widow) as second Duke of Buccleuch. Lady Catherine Hyde (p. 293) was a younger sister of Lady Dalkeith.
[2] Swift first wrote "I frequent."

by then that the peace is ready to sign. The Queen's gout mends daily. Nite MD.

27. I passed a very insipid day, and dined privately with a friend in the neighbourhood. Did I tell you that I have a very fine picture of Lady Orkney,[1] an original, by Sir Godfrey Kneller, three-quarters length? I have it now at home, with a fine frame. Lord Bolingbroke and Lady Masham have promised to sit for me; but I despair of Lord Treasurer; only I hope he will give me a copy, and then I shall have all the pictures of those I really love here; just half a dozen; only I'll make Lord Keeper give me his print in a frame. This letter must go to-morrow, because of sending ME a bill; else it should not till next week, I assure oo. I have little to do now with my pen; for my grand business stops till they are more pressing, and till something or other happens; and I believe I shall return with disgust to finish it, it is so very laborious. Sir Thomas Hanmer has my papers now. And hat is MD doing now? Oh, at ombre with the Dean always on Friday night, with Mrs. Walls. Pray don't play at small games. I stood by, t'other night, while the Duke d'Atree[2] lost six times with manilio, basto, and three small trumps; and Lady Jersey won above twenty pounds. Nite dee richar[3] MD.

28. I was at Court to-day, when the Abbé Gaultier whispered me that a courier was just come with an account that the French King had consented to all the Queen's demands, and his consent was carried to Utrecht, and the peace will be signed in a few days. I suppose the general peace cannot be so soon ready; but that is no matter. The news presently ran about the Court. I saw the Queen carried out in her chair, to take the air in the garden. I met Griffin at Court, and he told me that orders were sent to examine Filby; and, if he be fit, to make him (I think he called it) an assistant; I don't know what, Supervisor, I think; but it is some employment a good deal better than his own. The Parliament will have another

---

[1] See p. 456.   [2] D'Estrées.   [3] Little (almost illegible).

short prorogation, though it is not known yet. I dined with Lord Treasurer and his Saturday company, and left him at eight to put this in the post-office time enough. And now I must bid oo farewell, deelest richar Ppt. God bless oo ever, and rove Pdfr. Farewell MD MD MD FW FW FW FW ME ME ME Lele Lele.

LETTER LXI[1]

LONDON, *March* 1, 1712-13.

'TIS out of my head whether I answered all your letter in my last yesterday or no. I think I was in haste, and could not: but now I see I answered a good deal of it; no, only about your brother, and ME's bill. I dined with Lady Orkney, and we talked politics till eleven at night; and, as usual, found everything wrong, and put ourselves out of humour. Yes, I have Lady Giffard's picture sent me by your mother. It is boxed up at a place where my other things are. I have goods in two or three places; and when I leave a lodging, I box up the books I get (for I always get some), and come naked into a new lodging; and so on. Talk not to me of deaneries; I know less of that than ever by much. Nite MD.

2. I went to-day into the City to see Pat Rolt,[2] who lodges with a City cousin, a daughter of coz Cleve; (you are much the wiser). I had never been at her house before. My he-coz Thompson the butcher is dead, or dying. I dined with my printer, and walked home, and went to sit with Lady Clarges. I found four of them at whist; Lady Godolphin[3] was one. I sat by her, and talked of her cards, etc., but she would not give me one look, nor say a word to me. She refused some time ago to be acquainted with me. You know she is Lord Marlborough's eldest daughter. She is a fool for her pains, and I'll pull her down. What can I do

---

[1] Addressed to " Mrs. Dingley," etc.   Endorsed " Mar. 27."
[2] See p. 10.   [3] Formerly Lady Rialton (see p. 392).

for Dr. Smith's daughter's husband? I have no personal credit with any of the Commissioners. I'll speak to Keatley;[1] but I believe it will signify nothing. In the Customs people must rise by degrees, and he must at first take what is very low, if he be qualified for that. Ppt mistakes me; I am not angry at your recommending anyone to me, provided you will take my answer. Some things are in my way, and then I serve those I can. But people will not distinguish, but take things ill, when I have no power; but Ppt is wiser. And employments in general are very hard to be got. Nite MD.

3. I dined to-day with Lord Treasurer, who chid me for my absence, which was only from Saturday last. The Parliament was again prorogued for a week, and I suppose the peace will be ready by then, and the Queen will be able to be brought to the House, and make her speech. I saw Dr. Griffith[2] two or three months ago, at a Latin play at Westminster; but did not speak to him. I hope he will not die; I should be sorry for Ppt's sake; he is very tender of her. I have long lost all my colds, and the weather mends a little. I take some steel drops, and my head is pretty well. I walk when I can, but am grown very idle; and, not finishing my thing, I gamble[3] abroad and play at ombre. I shall be more careful in my physic than Mrs. Price: 'tis not a farthing matter her death, I think; and so I say no more to-night, but will read a dull book, and go sleep. Nite dee MD.

4. Mr. Ford has been this half-year inviting me to dine at his lodgings: so I did to-day, and brought the Provost and Dr. Parnell with me, and my friend Lewis was there. Parnell went away, and the other three played at ombre, and I looked on; which I love, and would not play. Tisdall is a pretty fellow, as you say; and when I come back to Ireland with nothing, he will condole with me with abundance of secret pleasure. I believe I told you what he wrote to me, that I have saved England, and he Ireland;[4] but

[1] See p. 490.   [2] See pp. 95, 405.   [3] Pun on "gambol."   [4] See p. 478.

I can bear that. I have learned to hear and see, and say nothing. I was to see the Duchess of Hamilton to-day, and met Blith[1] of Ireland just going out of her house into his coach. I asked her how she came to receive young fellows. It seems he had a ball in the Duke of Hamilton's house when the Duke died ; and the Duchess got an advertisement put in the *Postboy*,[2] reflecting on the ball, because the Marlborough daughters[3] were there ; and Blith came to beg the Duchess's pardon, and clear himself. He's a sad dog. Nite poo dee deelest MD.

5. Lady Masham has miscarried ; but is well almost again. I have many visits to-day. I met Blith at the Duke of Ormond's ; and he begged me to carry him to the Duchess of Hamilton, to beg her pardon again. I did on purpose to see how the blunderbuss behaved himself; but I begged the Duchess to use him mercifully, for she is the devil of a teaser. The good of it is, she ought to beg his pardon, for he meant no harm ; yet she would not allow him to put in an advertisement to clear himself from hers, though hers was all a lie. He appealed to me, and I gravely gave it against him. I was at Court to-day, and the foreign Ministers have got a trick of employing me to speak for them to Lord Treasurer and Lord Bolingbroke; which I do when the case is reasonable. The College[4] need not fear; I will not be their Governor. I dined with Sir Thomas Hanmer and his Duchess.[5] The Duke of Ormond was there, but we parted soon, and I went to visit Lord Pembroke for the first time ; but it was to see some curious books. Lord Cholmondeley[6] came in ; but I would not talk to him, though he made many advances. I hate the scoundrel for all he is your Griffith's friend.—Yes, yes, I am abused enough, if that be all. Nite sollahs.

[1] See p. 401.
[2] "Upon Tuesday last, the house where His Grace the late Duke of Hamilton and Brandon lived was hired for that day, where there was a fine ball and entertainment ; and it is reported in town, that a great lady, lately gone to travel, left one hundred guineas, with orders that it should be spent in that manner, and in that house" (*Postboy*, Feb. 26–28, 1712–13). The "great lady" was, presumably, the Duchess of Marlborough.
[3] See pp. 357, 397.   [4] Trinity College, Dublin.   [5] See p. 512.   [6] See p. 357.

6. I was to-day at an auction of pictures with Pratt,[1] and laid out two pound five shillings for a picture of Titian, and if it were a Titian it would be worth twice as many pounds. If I am cheated, I'll part with it to Lord Masham : if it be a bargain, I'll keep it to myself. That's my conscience. But I made Pratt buy several pictures for Lord Masham. Pratt is a great virtuoso that way. I dined with Lord Treasurer, but made him go to Court at eight. I always tease him to be gone. I thought to have made Parnell dine with him, but he was ill; his head is out of order like mine, but more constant, poor boy!—I was at Lord Treasurer's levee with the Provost, to ask a book for the College.—I never go to his levee, unless to present somebody. For all oor rallying, saucy[2] Ppt, as hope saved, I expected they would have decided about me long ago; and as hope saved, as soon as ever things are given away and I not provided for, I will be gone with the very first opportunity, and put up bag and baggage. But people are slower than can be thought. Nite MD.

7. Yes, I hope Leigh will soon be gone, a p—— on him! I met him once, and he talked gravely to me of not seeing the Irish bishops here, and the Irish gentlemen; but I believe my answers fretted him enough. I would not dine with Lord Treasurer to-day, though it was Saturday (for he has engaged me for to-morrow), but went and dined with Lord Masham, and played at ombre, sixpenny running ombre, for three hours. There were three voles[3] against me, and I was once a great loser, but came off for three shillings and sixpence. One may easily lose five guineas at it. Lady Orkney is gone out of town to-day, and I could not see her for laziness, but writ to her. She has left me some physic. Fais, I never knew MD's politics before, and I think it pretty extraordinary, and a great compliment to you, and I believe never three people conversed so much with so little politics. I avoid all conversation with the other party; it is not to be borne, and I am sorry for it. O yes, things [are] very dear.

[1] Dr. Pratt, Provost of Trinity College.   [2] Obliterated, and doubtful.
[3] A deal at cards, that draws the whole tricks.

DD must come in at last with DD's two eggs a penny. There the proverb was well applied. Parvisol has sent me a bill of fifty pounds, as I ordered him, which, I hope, will serve me, and bring me over. Pray God MD does not be delayed for it; but I have had very little from him this long time. I was not at Court to-day; a wonder! Nite sollahs . . . Pdfr.

8. Oo must know, I give chocolate almost every day to two or three people that I suffer to come to see me in a morning. My man begins to lie pretty well. 'Tis nothing for people to be denied ten times. My man knows all I will see, and denies me to everybody else. This is the day of the Queen's coming to the Crown, and the day Lord Treasurer was stabbed by Guiscard. I was at Court, where everybody had their Birthday clothes on, and I dined with Lord Treasurer, who was very fine. He showed me some of the Queen's speech, which I corrected in several places, and penned the vote of address of thanks for the speech; but I was of opinion the House should not sit on Tuesday next, unless they hear the peace is signed; that is, provided they are sure it will be signed the week after, and so have one scolding for all. Nite MD.

9. Lord Treasurer would have had me dine with him to-day; he desired me last night, but I refused, because he would not keep the day of his stabbing with all the Cabinet, as he intended: so I dined with my friend Lewis; and the Provost and Parnell, and Ford, was with us. I lost sixteen shillings at ombre; I don't like it, as etc. At night Lewis brought us word that the Parliament does not sit to-morrow. I hope they are sure of the peace by next week, and then they are right in my opinion: otherwise I think they have done wrong, and might have sat three weeks ago. People will grumble; but Lord Treasurer cares not a rush. Lord Keeper is suddenly taken ill of a quinsy, and some lords are commissioned, I think Lord Trevor,[1] to prorogue the Parlia-

---

[1] Previous editors have misread "Trevor" as "Treasurer." Thomas Trevor, Chief-Justice of the Common Pleas, was created Baron Trevor, of

ment in his stead. You never saw a town so full of ferment and expectation. Mr. Pope has published a fine poem, called *Windsor Forest*.[1] Read it. Nite.

10. I was early this morning to see Lord Bolingbroke. I find he was of opinion the Parliament should sit; and says they are not sure the peace will be signed next week. The prorogation is to this day se'nnight. I went to look on a library I am going to buy, if we can agree. I have offered a hundred and twenty pounds, and will give ten more. Lord Bolingbroke will lend me the money. I was two hours poring on the books. I will sell some of them, and keep the rest; but I doubt they won't take the money. I dined in the City, and sat an hour in the evening with Lord Treasurer, who was in very good humour; but reproached me for not dining with him yesterday and to-day. What will all this come to? Lord Keeper had a pretty good night, and is better. I was in pain for him. How do oo do sollahs? . . . Nite MD.[2]

11. I was this morning to visit the Duke and Duchess of Ormond, and the Duchess of Hamilton, and went with the Provost to an auction of pictures, and laid out fourteen shillings. I am in for it, if I had money; but I doubt I shall be undone; for Sir Andrew Fountaine invited the Provost and me to dine with him, and play at ombre, when I fairly lost fourteen shillings. Fais, it won't do; and I shall be out of conceit with play this good while. I am come home; and it is late, and my puppy let out my fire, and I am gone to bed and writing there, and it is past twelve a good while. Went out four matadores and a trump in black, and was bested. Vely bad, fais! Nite my deelest logues MD.

12. I was at another auction of pictures to-day, and a great auction it was. I made Lord Masham lay out forty

Bromham, in January 1712. By commission of March 9, 1713, he occupied the woolsack during the illness of the Lord Keeper, Harcourt.

[1] This is the only reference to Pope in the *Journal*. In his *Windsor Forest* the young poet assisted the Tories by his reference to the peace of Utrecht, then awaiting ratification.

[2] Several words have been obliterated. Forster reads, "Rove Pdfr, poo Pdfr, Nite MD MD MD," but this is more than the space would contain.

pounds. There were pictures sold of twice as much value apiece. Our Society met to-day at the Duke of Beaufort's: a prodigious fine dinner, which I hate; but we did some business. Our printer was to attend us, as usual; and the Chancellor of the Exchequer sent the author of the *Examiner* [1] twenty guineas. He is an ingenious fellow, but the most confounded vain coxcomb in the world, so that I dare not let him see me, nor am acquainted with him. I had much discourse with the Duke of Ormond this morning, and am driving some points to secure us all in case of accidents, etc. [2] I left the Society at seven. I can't drink now at all with any pleasure. I love white Portugal wine better than claret, champagne, or burgundy. I have a sad vulgar appetite. I remember Ppt used to maunder, when I came from a great dinner, and DD had but a bit of mutton. I cannot endure above one dish; nor ever could since I was a boy, and loved stuffing. It was a fine day, which is a rarity with us, I assure [you]. Never fair two days together. Nite dee MD.

13. I had a rabble of Irish parsons this morning drinking my chocolate. I cannot remember appointments. I was to have supped last night with the Swedish Envoy at his house, and some other company, but forgot it; and he rallied me to-day at Lord Bolingbroke's, who excused me, saying, the Envoy ought not to be angry, because I serve Lord Treasurer and him the same way. For that reason, I very seldom promise to go anywhere. I dined with Lord Treasurer, who chid me for being absent so long, as he always does if I miss a day. I sat three hours this evening with Lady Jersey; but the first two hours she was at ombre with some company. I left Lord Treasurer at eight: I fancied he was a little thoughtful, for he was playing with an orange by fits, which, I told him, among common men looked like the spleen. This letter shall not go to-morrow; no haste, ung oomens;

---

[1] William Oldisworth (1680–1734), a Tory journalist and pamphleteer, who published various works, including a translation of the *Iliad*. He died in a debtors' prison.

[2] Some words obliterated. The reading is Forster's, and seems to be correct.

nothing that presses. I promised but once in three weeks, and I am better than my word. I wish the peace may be ready, I mean that we have notice it is signed, before Tuesday; otherwise the grumbling will much increase. Nite logues.

14. It was a lovely day this, and I took the advantage of walking a good deal in the Park, before I went to Court. Colonel Disney, one of our Society, is ill of a fever, and, we fear, in great danger. We all love him mightily, and he would be a great loss. I doubt I shall not buy the library; for a roguey bookseller has offered sixty pounds more than I designed to give; so you see I meant to have a good bargain. I dined with Lord Treasurer and his Saturday company; but there were but seven at table. Lord Peterborrow is ill, and spits blood, with a bruise he got before he left England; but, I believe, an Italian lady he has brought over is the cause that his illness returns. You know old Lady Bellasis[1] is dead at last? She has left Lord Berkeley of Stratton[2] one of her executors, and it will be of great advantage to him; they say above ten thousand pounds. I stayed with Lord Treasurer upon business, after the company was gone; but I dare not tell you upon what. My letters would be good memoirs, if I durst venture to say a thousand things that pass; but I hear so much of letters opening at your post-office that I am fearful, etc., and so good-nite, sollahs, rove Pdfr, MD.

15. Lord Treasurer engaged me to dine with him again to-day, and I had ready what he wanted; but he would not see it, but put me off till to-morrow. The Queen goes to chapel now. She is carried in an open chair, and will be well enough to go to Parliament on Tuesday, if the Houses meet, which is not yet certain; neither, indeed, can the

[1] Susan Armine, elder daughter of Sir William Armine, Bart., of Osgodby, Lincolnshire, was created a life peeress in 1674, as Baroness Belasyse of Osgodby. She died March 6, 1713. Her first husband was the Honourable Sir Henry Belasyse, son and heir of John, Baron Belasyse, of Worlaby; and her second, Mr. Fortney, of Chequers.
[2] See p. 48.

Ministers themselves tell; for it depends on winds and weather, and circumstances of negotiation. However, we go on as if it was certainly to meet; and I am to be at Lord Treasurer's to-morrow, upon that supposition, to settle some things relating that way. Ppt[1] may understand me. The doctors tell me that if poor Colonel Disney does not get some sleep to-night, he must die. What care you? Ah! but I do care. He is one of our Society; a fellow of abundance of humour; an old battered rake, but very honest, not an old man, but an old rake. It was he that said of Jenny Kingdom,[2] the maid of honour, who is a little old, that, since she could not get a husband, the Queen should give her a brevet to act as a married woman. You don't understand this. They give brevets to majors and captains to act as colonels in the army. Brevets are commissions. Ask soldiers, dull sollahs. Nite MD.

16. I was at Lord Treasurer's before he came; and, as he entered, he told me the Parliament was prorogued till Thursday se'nnight. They have had some expresses, by which they count that the peace may be signed by that time; at least, that France, Holland, and we, will sign some articles, by which we shall engage to sign the peace when it is ready: but Spain has no Minister there; for Monteleon, who is to be their Ambassador at Utrecht, is not yet gone from hence; and till he is there, the Spaniards can sign no peace: and [of] one thing take notice, that a general peace can hardly be finished these two months, so as to be proclaimed here; for, after signing, it must be ratified; that is, confirmed by the several princes at their Courts, which to Spain will cost a month; for we must have notice that it is ratified in all Courts before we can proclaim it. So be not in too much haste. Nite MD.

---

[1] A word before "Ppt" is illegible. Forster's reading, "yes," does not seem right.

[2] In November 1711 it was reported that Miss Kingdom was privately married to Lord Conway (*Wentworth Papers*, 207), but this was not the case. Lord Conway was a widower in 1713, but he married an Irish lady named Bowden.

17. The Irish folks were disappointed that the Parliament did not meet to-day, because it was St. Patrick's Day; and the Mall was so full of crosses that I thought all the world was Irish. Miss Ashe is almost quite well, and I see the Bishop, but shall not yet go to his house. I dined again with Lord Treasurer; but the Parliament being prorogued, I must keep what I have till next week: for I believe he will not see it till just the evening before the session. He has engaged me to dine with him again to-morrow, though I did all I could to put it off; but I don't care to disoblige him. Nite dee sollahs 'tis late. Nite MD.

18. I have now dined six days successively with Lord Treasurer; but to-night I stole away while he was talking with somebody else, and so am at liberty to-morrow. There was a flying report of a general cessation of arms: everybody had it at Court; but, I believe, there is nothing in it. I asked a certain French Minister how things went. And he whispered me in French, "Your Plenipotentiaries and ours play the fool." None of us, indeed, approve of the conduct of either at this time; but Lord Treasurer was in full good-humour for all that. He had invited a good many of his relations; and, of a dozen at table, they were all of the Harley family but myself. Disney is recovering, though you don't care a straw. Dilly murders us with his *if* puns. You know them. . . .[1] Nite MD.

19. The Bishop of Clogher has made an *if* pun that he is mighty proud of, and designs to send it over to his brother Tom. But Sir Andrew Fountaine has wrote to Tom Ashe last post, and told him the pun, and desired him to send it over to the Bishop as his own; and, if it succeeds, 'twill be a pure bite. The Bishop will tell it us as a wonder that he and his brother should jump so exactly. I'll tell you the pun :—If there was a hackney coach at Mr. Pooley's[2] door, what town in Egypt would it be? Why, it would be Heca-

---

[1] Forster reads, "Nite, my own dee sollahs. Pdfr roves MD"; but the last three words, at least, do not seem to be in the MS.

[2] Probably the Bishop of Raphoe's son (see p. 289).

tompolis; *Hack at Tom Pooley's.* "Sillly," says Ppt. I dined
with a private friend to-day; for our Society, I told you,
meet but once a fortnight. I have not seen Fanny Manley
yet; I can't help it. Lady Orkney is come to town: why,
she was at her country house; hat[1] care you? Nite darling (?)
dee MD.

20. Dilly read me a letter to-day from Ppt. She seems to
have scratched her head when she writ it. 'Tis a sad thing
to write to people without tact. There you say, you hear I
was going to Bath. No such thing; I am pretty well,
I thank God. The town is now sending me to Savoy.[2]
Forty people have given me joy of it, yet there is not the
least truth that I know in it. I was at an auction of pictures,
but bought none. I was so glad of my liberty, that I would
dine nowhere; but, the weather being fine, I sauntered into
the City, and ate a bit about five, and then supped at Mr.
Burke's[3] your Accountant-General, who had been engaging
me this month. The Bishop of Clogher was to have been
there, but was hindered by Lord Paget's[4] funeral. The
Provost and I sat till one o'clock; and, if that be not late, I
don't know what is late. Parnell's poem will be published on
Monday, and to-morrow I design he shall present it to Lord
Treasurer and Lord Bolingbroke at Court. The poor lad is
almost always out of order with his head. Burke's wife is his
sister. She has a little of the pert Irish way. Nite MD.

21. Morning. I will now finish my letter; for company
will come, and a stir, and a clutter; and I'll keep the letter
in my pottick,[5] and give it into the post myself. I must go
to Court, and you know on Saturdays I dine with Lord
Treasurer, of course. Farewell, deelest MD MD MD, FW
FW FW, MD ME ME ME Lele sollahs.[6]

---

[1] What.   [2] As Master of the Savoy.
[3] William Burgh was Comptroller and Accountant-General for Ireland from
1694 to 1717, when his patent was revoked. He was succeeded by Eustace
Budgell.
[4] William Paget, sixth Lord Paget, died in March 1713, aged seventy-six.
He spent a great part of his life as Ambassador at Vienna and Constantinople.
[5] Pocket.
[6] Forster reads, "Lele lele logues"; Mr. Ryland, "Lele lele . . ."

LETTER LXII[1]

LONDON, *March* 21, 1712–13.

I GAVE your letter in this night. I dined with Lord Treasurer to-day, and find he has been at a meeting at Lord Halifax's house, with four principal Whigs; but he is resolved to begin a speech against them when the Parliament sits; and I have begged that the Ministers may have a meeting on purpose to settle that matter, and let us be the attackers; and I believe it will come to something, for the Whigs intend to attack the Ministers: and if, instead of that, the Ministers attack the Whigs, it will be better: and farther, I believe we shall attack them on those very points they intend to attack us. The Parliament will be again prorogued for a fortnight, because of Passion Week. I forgot to tell you that Mr. Griffin has given Ppt's brother[2] a new employment, about ten pounds a year better than his former; but more remote, and consequently cheaper. I wish I could have done better, and hope oo will take what can be done in good part, and that oo brother will not dislike it.—Nite own dear . . . MD.

22. I dined to-day with Lord Steward.[3] There Frank Annesley[4] (a Parliament-man) told me he had heard that I had wrote to my friends in Ireland to keep firm to the Whig interest; for that Lord Treasurer would certainly declare for it after the peace. Annesley said twenty people had told him this. You must know this is what they endeavour to report of Lord Treasurer, that he designs to declare for the Whigs; and a Scotch fellow has wrote the same to Scotland; and his meeting with those lords gives occasion to such reports. Let me henceforth call Lord Treasurer Eltee, because possibly my letters may be opened. Pray remember Eltee.

---

[1] Addressed to "Mrs. Dingley," etc. Endorsed "Apr. 13."
[2] Esther Johnson's brother-in-law, Filby (see p. 471).
[3] Earl Poulett (see p. 190).
[4] Francis Annesley, M.P. for Westbury. His colleague in the representation of that borough was Henry Bertie (third son of James, Earl of Abingdon), who married Earl Poulett's sister-in-law, Anthony Henley's widow (see p. 117).

You know the reason ; L. T. and Eltee pronounced the same way. Stay, 'tis five weeks since I had a letter from MD. I allow you six. You see why I cannot come over the beginning of April ; whoever has to do with this Ministry can fix no time: but as[1] hope saved, it is not Pdfr's fault. Pay don't blame poo Pdfr. Nite deelest logues MD.[2]

23. I dined to-day at Sir Thomas Hanmer's, by an old appointment : there was the Duke of Ormond, and Lord and Lady Orkney. I left them at six. Everybody is as sour as vinegar. I endeavour to keep a firm friendship between the Duke of Ormond and Eltee. (Oo know who Eltee is, or have oo fordot already ?) I have great designs, if I can compass them ; but delay is rooted in Eltee's heart ; yet the fault is not altogether there, that things are no better. Here is the cursedest libel in verse come out that ever was seen, called *The Ambassadress* ;[3] it is very dull, too ; it has been printed three or four different ways, and is handed about, but not sold. It abuses the Queen horribly. The *Examiner* has cleared me to-day of being author of his paper, and done it with great civilities to me.[4] I hope it will stop people's mouths ; if not, they must go on and be hanged, I care not. 'Tis terribly rainy weather, I'll go sleep. Nite deelest MD.

24. It rained all this day, and ruined me in coach-hire. I went to Colonel Disney, who is past danger. Then I visited Lord Keeper, who was at dinner ; but I would not dine with him, but drove to Lord Treasurer (Eltee I mean), paid the coachman, and went in ; but he dined abroad : so I was forced to call the coachman again, and went to Lord Boling-broke's. He dined abroad too ; and at Lord Dupplin's I

---

[1] " Has " (MS.).

[2] A dozen words are erased. The reading is Forster's, and appears to be correct.

[3] *The British Ambassadress's Speech to the French King.* The printer was sent to the pillory and fined.

[4] The *Examiner* (vol. iii. No. 35) said that Swift—" a gentleman of the first character for learning, good sense, wit, and more virtues than even they can set off and illustrate "—was not the author of that periodical. " Out of pure regard to justice, I strip myself of all the honour that lucky untruth did this paper."

alighted, and by good luck got a dinner there, and then went
to the Latin play at Westminster School, acted by the boys;
and Lord Treasurer (Eltee I mean again) honoured them
with his presence. Lady Masham's eldest son, about two
years old, is ill, and I am afraid will not live : she is full
of grief, and I pity and am angry with her. Four shillings
to-day in coach-hire; fais, it won't do. Our peace will
certainly be ready by Thursday fortnight; but our Plenipotentiaries were to blame that it was not done already. They
thought their powers were not full enough to sign the peace,
unless every Prince was ready, which cannot yet be ; for
Spain has no Minister yet at Utrecht; but now ours have
new orders. Nite MD.

25. Weather worse than ever; terrible rain all day, but I
was resolved I would spend no more money. I went to an
auction of pictures with Dr. Pratt, and there met the Duke of
Beaufort, who promised to come with me to Court, but did
not. So a coach I got, and went to Court, and did some
little business there, but was forced to go home ; for oo must
understand I take a little physic over-night, which works me
next day. Lady Orkney is my physician. It is hiera picra,[1]
two spoonfuls, devilish stuff! I thought to have dined with
Eltee, but would not, merely to save a shilling; but I dined
privately with a friend, and played at ombre, and won six
shillings. Here are several people of quality lately dead of
the smallpox. I have not yet seen Miss Ashe, but hear she
is well. The Bishop of Clogher has bought abundance of
pictures, and Dr. Pratt has got him very good pennyworths.[2]
I can get no walks, the weather is so bad. Is it so with oo,
sollahs ? . . .[3]

26. Though it was shaving-day, head and beard, yet I was
out early to see Lord Bolingbroke, and talk over affairs with
him ; and then I went to the Duke of Ormond's, and so to
Court, where the Ministers did not come, because the Parliament was prorogued till this day fortnight. We had terrible

---

[1] A purgative electuary.   [2] Bargains.
[3] Three or four words illegible. Forster reads, " Nite, nite, own MD."

rain and hail to-day.   Our Society met this day, but I left
them before seven, and went to Sir A[ndrew] F[ountaine],
and played at ombre with him and Sir Thomas Clarges, till
ten, and then went to Sir Thomas Hanmer.   His wife, the
Duchess of Grafton, left us after a little while, and I stayed
with him about an hour, upon some affairs, etc.   Lord
Bolingbroke left us at the Society before I went; for there is
an express from Utrecht, but I know not yet what it contains;
only I know the Ministers expect the peace will be signed in
a week, which is a week before the session.   Nite, MD.

27. Parnell's poem is mightily esteemed; but poetry sells
ill.   I am plagued with that . . .[1] poor Harrison's mother;
you would laugh to see how cautious I am of paying her the
£100 I received for her son from the Treasury.   I have asked
every creature I know whether I may do it safely, yet durst
not venture, till my Lord Keeper assured me there was no
danger.   I have not paid her, but will in a day or two: though
I have a great mind to stay till Ppt sends me her opinion,
because Ppt is a great lawyer.   I dined to-day with a mixture of people at a Scotchman's, who made the invitation to
Mr. Lewis and me, and has some design upon us, which we
know very well.   I went afterwards to see a famous moving
picture,[2] and I never saw anything so pretty.   You see a sea
ten miles wide, a town on t'other end, and ships sailing in the
sea, and discharging their cannon.   You see a great sky, with
moon and stars, etc.   I'm a fool.   Nite, dee MD.

28. I had a mighty levee to-day.   I deny myself to everybody, except about half a dozen, and they were all here, and
Mr. Addison was one, and I had chocolate twice, which I
don't like.   Our rainy weather continues.   Coach-hire goes
deep.   I dined with Eltee and his Saturday company, as
usual, and could not get away till nine.   Lord Peterborow
was making long harangues, and Eltee kept me in spite.

[1] Forster reads, "devil's brood"; probably the second word is "bawd."
Cf. p. 510.
[2] Several "moving pictures," mostly brought from Germany, were on view
in London at about this time. See *Tatler*, No. 129, and Gay's *Fables*,
No. 6.

Then I went to see the Bishop of Ossory, who had engaged me in the morning; he is going to Ireland. The Bishop of Killaloe [1] and Tom Leigh was with us. The latter had wholly changed his style, by seeing how the bishops behaved themselves, and he seemed to think me one of more importance than I really am. I put the ill conduct of the bishops about the First-Fruits, with relation to Eltee and me, strongly upon Killaloe, and showed how it had hindered me from getting a better thing for them, called the Crown rents, which the Queen had promised. He had nothing to say, but was humble, and desired my interest in that and some other things. This letter is half done in a week : I believe oo will have it next. Nite MD.

29. I have been employed in endeavouring to save one of your junior Fellows,[2] who came over here for a dispensation from taking orders, and, in soliciting it, has run out his time, and now his fellowship is void, if the College pleases, unless the Queen suspends the execution, and gives him time to take orders. I spoke to all the Ministers yesterday about it ; but they say the Queen is angry, and thought it was a trick to deceive her ; and she is positive, and so the man must be ruined, for I cannot help him. I never saw him in my life ; but the case was so hard, I could not forbear interposing. Your Government recommended him to the Duke of Ormond, and he thought they would grant it ; and by the time it was refused, the fellowship by rigour is forfeited. I dined with Dr. Arbuthnot (one of my brothers) at his lodgings in Chelsea, and was there at chapel ; and the altar put me in mind of Tisdall's outlandish would [3] at your hospital for the soldiers. I was not at Court to-day, and I hear the Queen was not at church. Perhaps the gout has seized her again. Terrible rain all day. Have oo such weather? Nite MD.

30. Morning. I was naming some time ago, to a certain

---

[1] See p. 43.

[2] " Mr. Charles Grattan, afterwards master of a free school at Enniskillen " (Scott).

[3] So given in the MS. Forster suggests that it is a mistake for " wood."

person, another certain person, that was very deserving, and poor and sickly; and t'other, that first certain person, gave me a hundred pounds to give the other, which I have not yet done. The person who is to have it never saw the giver, nor expects one farthing, nor has the least knowledge or imagination of it; so I believe it will be a very agreeable surprise; for I think it is a handsome present enough. At night I dined in the City, at Pontack's,[1] with Lord Dupplin, and some others. We were treated by one Colonel Cleland,[2] who has a mind to be Governor of Barbados, and is laying these long traps for me and others, to engage our interests for him. He is a true Scotchman. I paid the hundred pounds this evening, and it was an agreeable surprise to the receiver. We reckon the peace is now signed, and that we shall have it in three days. I believe it is pretty sure. Nite MD.

31. I thought to-day on Ppt when she told me she suppose[d] I was acquainted with the steward, when I was giving myself airs of being at some lord's house. Sir Andrew Fountaine invited the Bishop of Clogher and me, and some others, to dine where he did; and he carried us to the Duke of Kent's,[3] who was gone out of town; but the steward treated us nobly, and showed us the fine pictures, etc. I have not yet seen Miss Ashe. I wait till she has been abroad,

---

[1] See p. 271.

[2] It is probable that this is Pope's friend, William Cleland, who died in 1741, aged sixty-seven. William Cleland served in Spain under Lord Rivers, but was not a Colonel, though he seems to have been a Major. Afterwards he was a Commissioner of Customs in Scotland and a Commissioner of the Land Tax in England. Colonel Cleland cannot, as Scott suggested (Swift's *Works*, iii. 142, xviii. 137–39, xix. 8), have been the son of the Colonel William Cleland, Covenanter and poet, who died in 1689, at the age of twenty-eight. William Cleland allowed his name to be appended to a letter of Pope's prefixed to the *Dunciad*, and Pope afterwards described him as "a person of universal learning, and an enlarged conversation; no man had a warmer heart for his friends, or a sincerer attachment to the constitution of his country." Swift, referring to this letter, wrote to Pope, "Pray tell me whether your Colonel (*sic*) Cleland be a tall Scots gentleman, walking perpetually in the Mall, and fastening upon everybody he meets, as he has often done upon me?" (Pope's *Works*, iv. 48, vii. 214).

[3] Henry Grey, Lord Lucas (died 1741), who became twelfth Earl of Kent in 1702, was made Duke of Kent in 1710. He held various offices under George I. and George II.

and taken the air. This evening Lady Masham, Dr. Arbuthnot, and I, were contriving a lie for to-morrow, that Mr.
Noble,[1] who was hanged last Saturday, was recovered by his
friends, and then seized again by the sheriff, and is now in a
messenger's hands at the Black Swan in Holborn. We are
all to send to our friends, to know whether they have heard
anything of it, and so we hope it will spread. However, we
shall do our endeavours; nothing shall be wanting on our
parts, and leave the rest to fortune. Nite MD.

April 1. We had no success in our story, though I sent
my man to several houses, to inquire among the footmen,
without letting him into the secret; but I doubt my col-
leagues did not contribute as they ought. Parnell and I
dined with Darteneuf[2] to-day. You have heard of Darteneuf:
I have told you of Darteneuf. After dinner we all went to
Lord Bolingbroke's, who had desired me to dine with him;
but I would not, because I heard it was to look over a dull
poem of one parson Trapp[3] upon the peace. The Swedish
Envoy told me to-day at Court that he was in great apprehen-
sions about his master;[4] and indeed we are afraid that prince
has[5] died among those Turkish dogs. I prevailed on Lord
Bolingbroke to invite Mr. Addison to dine with him on Good
Friday. I suppose we shall be mighty mannerly. Addison
is to have a play of his acted on Friday in Easter Week: 'tis
a tragedy, called Cato; I saw it unfinished some years ago.[6]
Did I tell you that Steele has begun a new daily paper,
called the Guardian?[7] they say good for nothing. I have
not seen it. Nite dee MD.

2. I was this morning with Lord Bolingbroke, and he tells

[1] Forster found, among the MSS. at Narford, the "lie" thus prepared for All
Fools' Day. Richard Noble, an attorney, ran away with a lady who was the
wife of John Sayer and daughter of Admiral Nevill; and he killed Sayer on
the discovery of the intrigue. The incident was made use of by Hogarth in the
fifth scene of "Marriage à la Mode."
[2] See p. 23.   [3] See p. 120.   [4] Charles XII.   [5] "Is" (MS.).
[6] Cibber says that he saw four acts of Cato in 1703; the fifth act, according
to Steele, was written in less than a week. The famous first performance was
on April 14, 1713.
[7] The first number of the Guardian appeared on March 12, and the
paper was published daily until Oct. 1, 1713. Pope, Addison, and Berkeley
were among the contributors.

me a Spanish courier is just come, with the news that the King of Spain has agreed to everything that the Queen desires; and the Duke d'Ossuna has left Paris in order to his journey to Utrecht. I was prevailed on to come home with Trapp, and read his poem and correct it; but it was good for nothing. While I was thus employed, Sir Thomas Hanmer came up to my chamber, and balked me of a journey he and I intended this week to Lord Orkney's at Cliffden;[1] but he is not well, and his physician will not let him undertake such a journey. I intended to dine with Lord Treasurer; but going to see Colonel Disney, who lives with General Withers,[2] I liked the General's little dinner so well, that I stayed and took share of it, and did not go to Lord Treasurer till six, where I found Dr. Sacheverell, who told us that the bookseller had given him £100 for his sermon,[3] preached last Sunday, and intended to print 30,000: I believe he will be confoundedly bit, and will hardly sell above half. I have fires still, though April has begun, against my old maxim; but the weather is wet and cold. I never saw such a long run of ill weather in my life. Nite dee logues MD.

3. I was at the Queen's chapel to-day, but she was not there. Mr. St. John, Lord Bolingbroke's brother, came this day at noon with an express from Utrecht, that the peace is signed by all the Ministers there, but those of the Emperor, who will likewise sign in a few days; so that now the great work is in effect done, and I believe it will appear a most excellent peace for Europe, particularly for England. Addison and I, and some others, dined with Lord Bolingbroke, and sat with him till twelve. We were very civil, but yet when we grew warm, we talked in a friendly manner of party. Addison raised his objections, and Lord Bolingbroke answered them with great complaisance. Addison began Lord Somers's

---

[1] See p. 456.   [2] See p. 389.
[3] The first preached after the period of his suspension by the House of Lords. It was delivered at St. Saviour's, Southwark, before his installation at St. Andrew's, and was published with the title, *The Christian's Triumph, or the Duty of praying for our Enemies.*

health, which went about; but I bid him not name Lord Wharton's, for I would not pledge it; and I told Lord Bolingbroke frankly that Addison loved Lord Wharton as little as I did : so we laughed, etc. Well, but you are glad of the peace, you Ppt the Trimmer, are not you? As for DD I don't doubt her. Why, now, if I did not think Ppt had been a violent Tory, and DD the greater Whig of the two! 'Tis late. Nite MD.

4. This Passion Week, people are so demure, especially this last day, that I told Dilly, who called here, that I would dine with him, and so I did, faith; and had a small shoulder of mutton of my own bespeaking. It rained all day. I came home at seven, and have never stirred out, but have been reading Sacheverell's long dull sermon, which he sent me. It is the first sermon since his suspension is expired ; but not a word in it upon the occasion, except two or three remote hints. The Bishop of Clogher has been sadly bit by Tom Ashe, who sent him a pun, which the Bishop had made, and designed to send to him, but delayed it; and Lord Pembroke and I made Sir Andrew Fountaine write it to Tom. I believe I told you of it in my last; it succeeded right, and the Bishop was wondering to Lord Pembroke how he and his brother could hit on the same thing. I'll go to bed soon, for I must be at church by eight to-morrow, Easter Day. Nite dee MD.

5. Warburton [1] wrote to me two letters about a living of one Foulkes, who is lately dead in the county of Meath. My answer is, that before I received the first letter, General Gorges [2] had recommended a friend of his to the Duke of Ormond, which was the first time I heard of its vacancy, and it was the Provost told me of it. I believe verily that Foulkes was not dead when Gorges recommended the other :

---

[1] Swift's curate at Laracor.

[2] Richard Gorges (died 1728) was eldest son and heir of Dr. Robert Gorges, of Kilbrue, County Meath, by Jane, daughter of Sir Arthur Loftus, and sister of Adam, Viscount Lisburne. He was appointed Adjutant-General of the Forces in Ireland 1697, Colonel of a new Regiment of Foot 1703, Major-General of the Forces 1707, and Lieutenant-General 1710 (Dalton's *Army Lists*, iii. 75).

for Warburton's last letter said that Foulkes was dead the day before the date.—This has prevented me from serving Warburton, as I would have done, if I had received early notice enough. Pray say or write this to Warburton, to justify me to him. I was at church at eight this morning, and dressed and shaved after I came back, but was too late at Court; and Lord Abingdon [1] was like to have snapped me for dinner, and I believe will fall out with me for refusing him; but I hate dining with them, and I dined with a private friend, and took two or three good walks; for it was a very fine day, the first we have had a great while. Remember, was Easter Day a fine day with you? I have sat with Lady Worsley till now. Nite dee MD.

6. I was this morning at ten at the rehearsal of Mr. Addison's play, called *Cato,* which is to be acted on Friday. There were not above half a score of us to see it. We stood on the stage, and it was foolish enough to see the actors prompted every moment, and the poet directing them; and the drab that acts Cato's daughter,[2] out in the midst of a passionate part, and then calling out, "What's next?" The Bishop of Clogher was there too; but he stood privately in a gallery. I went to dine with Lord Treasurer, but he was gone to Wimbledon, his daughter Caermarthen's [3] country seat, seven miles off. So I went back, and dined privately with Mr. Addison, whom I had left to go to Lord Treasurer. I keep fires yet; I am very extravagant. I sat this evening with Sir A. Fountaine, and we amused ourselves with making *ifs* for Dilly. It is rainy weather again; nevle saw ze rike.[4] This letter shall go to-morrow; remember, ung oomens, it is seven weeks since oor last, and I allow oo but five weeks; but oo have been galloping into the country to Swanton's.[5] O pray tell Swanton I had his letter, but cannot contrive how to serve him. If a Governor were to go over, I would recommend him as far as lay in my power, but I can do no more: and you know all employments in Ireland, at

---

[1] See p. 510.   [2] Mrs. Oldfield.   [3] See p. 473.
[4] Never saw the like,   [5] See p. 460.

least almost all, are engaged in reversions. If I were on the spot, and had credit with a Lord Lieutenant, I would very heartily recommend him; but employments here are no more in my power than the monarchy itself. Nite, dee MD.

7. Morning. I have had a visitor here, that has taken up my time. I have not been abroad, oo may be sure; so I can say nothing to-day, but that I rove MD bettle zan ever, if possibbere. I will put this in the post-office; so I say no more. I write by this post to the Dean, but it is not above two lines; and one enclosed to you, but that enclosed to you is not above three lines; and then one enclosed to the Dean, which he must not have but upon condition of burning it immediately after reading, and that before your eyes; for there are some things in it I would not have liable to accident. You shall only know in general that it is an account of what I have done to serve him in his pretensions on these vacancies, etc. But he must not know that you know so much.[1] Does this perplex you? Hat care I? But rove Pdfr, saucy Pdfr. Farewell, deelest MD MD MD FW FW FW, . . . ME, MD Lele.

LETTER LXIII[2]

LONDON, April 7, 1713.

I FANCY I marked my last, which I sent this day, wrong; only 61, and it ought to be 62. I dined with Lord Treasurer, and though the business I had with him is something against Thursday, when the Parliament is to meet, and this is Tuesday, yet he put it off till to-morrow. I dare not tell you what it is, lest this letter should miscarry or be opened; but I never saw his fellow for delays. The Parliament will now certainly sit, and everybody's expectations are ready to burst. At a Council to-night the Lord Chief-Justice Parker, a Whig, spoke against the peace; so did Lord

---

[1] The remainder has been partially obliterated.
[2] Addressed to "Mrs. Dingley," etc. Endorsed "May 4."

Chomley,[1] another Whig, who is Treasurer of the Household. My Lord Keeper [2] was this night made Lord Chancellor. We hope there will soon be some removes. Nite, dee sollahs; Late. Rove Pdfr.[3]

8. Lord Chomley (the right name is Cholmondeley) is this day removed from his employment, for his last night's speech; and Sir Richard Temple,[4] Lieutenant-General, the greatest Whig in the army, is turned out; and Lieutenant-General Palmes [5] will be obliged to sell his regiment. This is the first-fruits of a friendship I have established between two great men. I dined with Lord Treasurer, and did the business I had for him to his satisfaction. I won't tell MD what it was. . . .[6] for zat. The Parliament sits to-morrow for certain. Here is a letter printed in Maccartney's name, vindicating himself from the murder of the Duke of Hamilton. I must give some hints to have it answered; 'tis full of lies, and will give an opportunity of exposing that party. To-morrow will be a very important day. All the world will be at Westminster. Lord Treasurer is as easy as a lamb. They are mustering up the proxies of the absent lords; but they are not in any fear of wanting a majority, which death and accidents have increased this year. Nite MD.

9. I was this morning with Lord Treasurer, to present to him a young son [7] of the late Earl of Jersey, at the desire of the widow. There I saw the mace and great coach ready for Lord Treasurer, who was going to Parliament. Our Society met to-day; but I expected the Houses would sit longer than I cared to fast; so I dined with a friend, and never inquired how matters went till eight this evening, when I went to Lord Orkney's, where I found Sir Thomas Hanmer. The Queen delivered her speech very well, but a little weaker

---

[1] Lord Cholmondeley (see p. 357).   [2] Harcourt.
[3] Forster's reading; the last two words are doubtful.
[4] See p. 52.
[5] Francis Palmes, who was wounded at Blenheim, was made a Lieutenant-General in 1709. In 1707 he was elected M.P. for West Loo; in 1708 he was sent as Envoy Extraordinary to the Duke of Savoy, and in 1710 to Vienna.
[6] Apparently " so heed."
[7] Henry Villiers (died 1743), second son of the first Earl of Jersey and of Barbara, daughter of William Chiffinch (see p. 281).

in her voice. The crowd was vast. The order for the Address[1] was moved, and opposed by Lord Nottingham, Halifax, and Cowper. Lord Treasurer spoke with great spirit and resolution ; Lord Peterborow flirted[2] against the Duke of Marlborough (who is in Germany, you know), but it was in answer to one of Halifax's impertinences. The order for an Address passed by a majority of thirty-three, and the Houses rose before six. This is the account I heard at Lord Orkney's. The Bishop of Chester,[3] a high Tory, was against the Court. The Duchess of Marlborough sent for him some months ago, to justify herself to him in relation to the Queen, and showed him letters, and told him stories, which the weak man believed, and was perverted. Nite MD.

10. I dined with a cousin in the City, and poor Pat Rolt was there. I have got her rogue of a husband leave to come to England from Port-Mahon. The Whigs are much down ; but I reckon they have some scheme in agitation. This Parliament-time hinders our Court meetings on Wednesdays, Thursdays, and Saturdays. I had a great deal of business to-night, which gave me a temptation to be idle, and I lost a dozen shillings at ombre, with Dr. Pratt and another. I have been to see t'other day the Bishop of Clogher and lady, but did not see Miss. It rains every day, and yet we are all over dust. Lady Masham's eldest boy is very ill: I doubt he will not live, and she stays at Kensington to nurse him, which vexes us all. She is so excessively fond, it makes me mad. She should never leave the Queen, but leave everything, to stick to what is so much the interest of the public, as well as her own. This I tell her ; but talk to the winds. Nite MD.

11. I dined at Lord Treasurer's, with his Saturday company. We had ten at table, all lords but myself and the Chancellor of the Exchequer. Argyle went off at six, and was in very

---

[1] See p. 520. The Speech and Address are in the Commons' Journals, xvii. 278, 280. For the draft Address, in Swift's handwriting, see the Portland Papers (1899), v. 276.
[2] Scoffed, jeered.   [3] Dr. Gastrell (see p. 238).

indifferent humour as usual. Duke of Ormond and Lord Bolingbroke were absent. I stayed till near ten. Lord Treasurer showed us a small picture, enamelled work, and set in gold, worth about twenty pounds; a picture, I mean, of the Queen, which she gave to the Duchess of Marlborough, set in diamonds. When the Duchess was leaving England, she took off all the diamonds, and gave the picture to one Mrs. Higgins (an old intriguing woman, whom everybody knows), bidding her make the best of it she could. Lord Treasurer sent to Mrs..Higgins for this picture, and gave her a hundred pounds for it. Was ever such an ungrateful beast as that Duchess? or did you ever hear such a story? I suppose. the Whigs will not believe it. Pray, try them. Takes off the diamonds, and gives away the picture to an insignificant woman, as a thing of no consequence: and gives it to her to sell, like a piece of old-fashioned plate. Is she not a detestable slut? Nite deelest MD.

12. I went to Court to-day, on purpose to present Mr. Berkeley,[1] one of your Fellows of Dublin College, to Lord Berkeley of Stratton. That Mr. Berkeley is a very ingenious man, and great philosopher, and I have mentioned him to all the Ministers, and given them some of his writings; and I will favour him as much as I can. This I think I am bound to, in honour and conscience, to use all my little credit toward helping forward men of worth in the world. The Queen was at chapel to-day, and looks well. I dined at Lord Orkney's with the Duke of Ormond, Lord Arran, and Sir Thomas Hanmer. Mr. St. John, Secretary at Utrecht, expects every moment to return there with the ratification

---

[1] George Berkeley, afterwards Bishop of Cloyne, but then a young man of twenty-eight, came to London in January 1713. He was already known by his *New Theory of Vision* and *Treatise on the Principles of Human Knowledge*, and he brought with him his *Three Dialogues between Hylas and Philonous*. Steele was among the first to welcome him, and he soon made the acquaintance of Addison, Pope, and Swift. On March 27, Berkeley wrote to Sir John Perceval of the breach between Swift and the Whigs: "Dr. Swift's wit is admired by both of them [Addison and Steele], and indeed by his greatest enemies, and . . . I think him one of the best-natured and agreeable men in the world." In November 1713 Swift procured for Berkeley the chaplaincy and secretaryship to Lord Peterborough, the new Envoy to Sicily.

of the peace. Did I tell you in my last of Addison's play called *Cato*, and that I was at the rehearsal of it? Nite MD.

13. This morning my friend, Mr. Lewis, came to me, and showed me an order for a warrant for the three vacant deaneries; but none of them to me. This was what I always foresaw, and received the notice of it better, I believe, than he expected. I bid Mr. Lewis tell Lord Treasurer that I took nothing ill of him but his not giving me timely notice, as he promised to do, if he found the Queen would do nothing for me. At noon, Lord Treasurer hearing I was in Mr. Lewis's office, came to me, and said many things too long to repeat. I told him I had nothing to do but go to Ireland immediately; for I could not, with any reputation, stay longer here, unless I had something honourable immediately given to me. We dined together at the Duke of Ormond's. He there told me he had stopped the warrants for the deans, that what was done for me might be at the same time, and he hoped to compass it to-night; but I believe him not. I told the Duke of Ormond my intentions. He is content Sterne should be a bishop, and I have St. Patrick's; but I believe nothing will come of it, for stay I will not; and so I believe for all oo . . .[1] oo may see me in Dublin before April ends. I am less out of humour than you would imagine: and if it were not that impertinent people will condole with me, as they used to give me joy, I would value it less. But I will avoid company, and muster up my baggage, and send them next Monday by the carrier to Chester, and come and see my willows, against the expectation of all the world. — Hat care I? Nite deelest logues, MD.

14. I dined in the City to-day, and ordered a lodging to be got ready for me against I came to pack up my things; for I will leave this end of the town as soon as ever the warrants for the deaneries are out, which are yet stopped.

[1] Forster reads, "all oo sawcy Ppt can say oo may see me"; but the words are illegible.

Lord Treasurer told Mr. Lewis that it should be determined to-night: and so he will for[1] a hundred nights. So he said yesterday, but I value it not. My daily journals shall be but short till I get into the City, and then I will send away this, and follow it myself; and design to walk it all the way to Chester, my man and I, by ten miles a day. It will do my health a great deal of good. I shall do it in fourteen days. Nite dee MD.

15. Lord Bolingbroke made me dine with him to-day; he[2] was as good company as ever; and told me the Queen would determine something for me to-night. The dispute is, Windsor or St. Patrick's. I told him I would not stay for their disputes, and he thought I was in the right. Lord Masham told me that Lady Masham is angry I have not been to see her since this business, and desires I will come to-morrow. Nite deelest MD.

16. I was this noon at Lady Masham's, who was just come from Kensington, where her eldest son is sick. She said much to me of what she had talked to the Queen and Lord Treasurer. The poor lady fell a shedding tears openly. She could not bear to think of my having St. Patrick's, etc. I was never more moved than to see so much friendship. I would not stay with her, but went and dined with Dr. Arbuthnot, with Mr. Berkeley, one of your Fellows, whom I have recommended to the Doctor, and to Lord Berkeley of Stratton. Mr. Lewis tells me that the Duke of Ormond has been to-day with the Queen; and she was content that Dr. Sterne should be Bishop of Dromore, and I Dean of St. Patrick's; but then out came Lord Treasurer, and said he would not be satisfied but that I must be Prebend[ary] of Windsor. Thus he perplexes things. I expect neither; but I confess, as much as I love England, I am so angry at this treatment that, if I had my choice, I would rather have St. Patrick's. Lady Masham says she will speak to purpose to the Queen to-morrow. Nite, . . . dee MD.

17. I went to dine at Lady Masham's to-day, and she was

---

1 Possibly "see," written in mistake for "say."　　　　2 " J " (MS.).

taken ill of a sore throat, and aguish. She spoke to the
Queen last night, but had not much time. The Queen says
she will determine to-morrow with Lord Treasurer. The
warrants for the deaneries are still stopped, for fear I should
be gone. Do you think anything will be done? I don't
care whether it is or no. In the meantime, I prepare for
my journey, and see no great people, nor will see Lord
Treasurer any more, if I go. Lord Treasurer told Mr. Lewis
it should be done to-night; so he said five nights ago.
Nite MD.

18. This morning Mr. Lewis sent me word that Lord
Treasurer told him the Queen would determine at noon.
At three Lord Treasurer sent to me to come to his lodgings
at St. James's, and told me the Queen was at last resolved
that Dr. Sterne should be Bishop of Dromore, and I Dean
of St. Patrick's; and that Sterne's warrant should be drawn
immediately. You know the deanery is in the Duke of
Ormond's gift; but this is concerted between the Queen,
Lord Treasurer, and the Duke of Ormond, to make room
for me. I do not know whether it will yet be done; some
unlucky accident may yet come. Neither can I feel joy at
passing my days in Ireland; and I confess I thought the
Ministry would not let me go; but perhaps they can't help it.
Nite MD.

19. I forgot to tell you that Lord Treasurer forced me
to dine with him yesterday as usual, with his Saturday
company; which I did after frequent refusals. To-day I
dined with a private friend, and was not at Court. After
dinner Mr. Lewis sent me a note, that the Queen stayed till
she knew whether the Duke of Ormond approved of Sterne
for Bishop. I went this evening, and found the Duke of
Ormond at the Cock-pit, and told him, and desired he would
go to the Queen, and approve of Sterne. He made objections,
desired I would name any other deanery, for he did not like
Sterne; that Sterne never went to see him; that he was
influenced by the Archbishop of Dublin, etc.; so all now is
broken again. I sent out for Lord Treasurer, and told him

this.   He says all will do well; but I value not what he says.
This suspense vexes me worse than anything else.   Nite
MD.

20.   I went to-day, by appointment, to the Cock-pit, to
talk with the Duke of Ormond.   He repeated the same
proposals of any other deanery, etc.   I desired he would put
me out of the case, and do as he pleased.   Then, with great
kindness, he said he would consent; but would do it for no
man alive but me, etc.   And he will speak to the Queen to-
day or to-morrow; so, perhaps, something will come of it.
I can't tell.   Nite dee dee logues, MD.

21.   The Duke of Ormond has told the Queen he is
satisfied that Sterne should be Bishop, and she consents I
shall be Dean; and I suppose the warrants will be drawn in
a day or two.   I dined at an ale-house with Parnell and
Berkeley; for I am not in humour to go among the Ministers,
though Lord Dartmouth invited me to dine with him to-day,
and Lord Treasurer was to be there.   I said I would, if I
were out of suspense.   Nite deelest MD.

22.   The Queen says warrants shall be drawn, but she will
dispose of all in England and Ireland at once, to be teased
no more.   This will delay it some time; and, while it is
delayed, I am not sure of the Queen, my enemies being
busy.   I hate this suspense.   Nite deelest MD.[1]

23.   I dined yesterday with General Hamilton.[2]   I forgot
to tell oo.   I write short journals now.   I have eggs on the
spit.   This night the Queen has signed all the warrants,
among which Sterne is Bishop of Dromore, and the Duke
of Ormond is to send over an order for making me Dean
of St. Patrick's.   I have no doubt of him at all.   I think
'tis now passed.   And I suppose MD is malicious enough

---

[1] Obliterated.   Forster imagined that he read, "Nite dee logues. Poo
Pdfr."
[2] There were two General Hamiltons at this time; probably Swift's
acquaintance was Gustavus Hamilton (1639-1723), who was created Viscount
Boyne in 1717.   Hamilton distinguished himself at the battle of the Boyne
and the capture of Athlone, and was made Brigadier-General in 1696, and Major-
General in 1703.   He took part in the siege of Vigo, and was made a member
of the Privy Council in 1710.

to be glad, and rather have it than Wells.[1] But you see what a condition I am in. I thought I was to pay but six hundred pounds for the house; but the Bishop of Clogher says eight hundred pounds; first-fruits one hundred and fifty pounds, and so, with patent, a thousand pounds in all; so that I shall not be the better for the deanery these three years. I hope in some time they will be persuaded here to give me some money to pay off these debts. I must finish the book I am writing,[2] before I can go over; and they expect I shall pass next winter here, and then I will dun them to give me a sum of money. However, I hope to pass four or five months with MD, and whatever comes on it. MD's allowance must be increased, and shall be too, fais . . .[3] I received oor rettle No. 39 to-night; just ten weeks since I had your last. I shall write next post to Bishop Sterne. Never man had so many enemies of Ireland[4] as he. I carried it with the strongest hand possible. If he does not use me well and gently in what dealings I shall have with him, he will be the most ungrateful of mankind. The Archbishop of York,[5] my mortal enemy, has sent, by a third hand, that he would be glad to see me. Shall I see him, or not? I hope to be over in a month, and that MD, with their raillery, will be mistaken, that I shall make it three years. I will answer oo rettle soon; but no more journals. I shall be very busy. Short letters from henceforward. I shall not part with Laracor. That is all I have to live on, except the deanery be worth more than four hundred pounds a year. Is it? If it be, the overplus shall be divided between MD and FW beside usual allowance of MD. . . .[6] Pray write to me a good-humoured letter immediately, let it be ever so short. This affair was carried with great difficulty, which vexes me. But they say here

---

[1] See p. 427.   [2] *The History of the Peace of Utrecht.*
[3] This is Forster's reading, and appears to be correct. The last word, which he gives as "iss truly," is illegible.
[4] Belonging to Ireland.   [5] See p. 391.
[6] Another excellent reading of Forster's. I cannot decipher the last word, which he gives as "dee rogues."

'tis much to my reputation that I have made a bishop, in spite of all the world, to get the best deanery in Ireland. Nite dee sollahs.

24. I forgot to tell you I had Sterne's letter yesterday, in answer to mine. Oo performed oor commission well, dood dallars both.[1] I made mistakes the three last days, and am forced to alter the number.[2] I dined in the City to-day with my printer, and came home early, and am going to [be] busy with my work. I will send this to-morrow, and I suppose the warrants will go then. I wrote to Dr. Coghill, to take care of passing my patent; and to Parvisol, to attend him with money, if he has any, or to borrow some where he can. Nite MD.

25. Morning. I know not whether my warrant be yét ready from the Duke of Ormond. I suppose it will by to-night. I am going abroad, and will keep this unsealed, till I know whether all be finished. Mollow,[3] sollahs.

I had this letter all day in my pocket, waiting till I heard the warrants were gone over. Mr. Lewis sent to Southwell's clerk at ten; and he said the Bishop of Killaloe[4] had desired they should be stopped till next post. He sent again, that the Bishop of Killaloe's business had nothing to do with ours. Then I went myself, but it was past eleven, and asked the reason. Killaloe is removed to Raphoe, and he has a mind to have an order for the rents of Raphoe, that have fallen due since the vacancy, and he would have all stop till he has gotten that. A pretty request! But the clerk, at Mr. Lewis's message, sent the warrants for Sterne and me; but then it was too late to send this, which frets me heartily, that MD should not have intelligence first from Pdfr. I think to take a hundred pounds a year out of the deanery, and divide it between MD and Pr,[5] and so be one year longer

---

[1] Sentence obliterated.
[2] The number at the beginning of each entry in the *Journal*.
[3] Mr. Ryland's reading.   Forster has "morning, dee."
[4] Dr. Thomas Lindsay (see p. 43).
[5] I think the "MD" is right, though Forster gives "M." The "Pr" is probably an abbreviation of "Pdfr."

in paying the debt; but we'll talk of zis hen I come over. So nite dear sollahs. Lele.[1]

26. I was at Court to-day, and a thousand people gave me joy; so I ran out. I dined with Lady Orkney. Yesterday I dined with Lord Treasurer and his Saturday people as usual; and was so bedeaned! The Archbishop of York says he will never more speak against me. Pray see that Parvisol stirs about getting my patent. I have given Tooke DD's note to prove she is alive. I'll answer oo rettle. . . . Nite.

27. Nothing new to-day. I dined with Tom Harley, etc. I'll seal up this to-night. Pray write soon. . . . MD MD MD FW FW FW ME ME ME Lele, lele.

LETTER LXIV [2]

LONDON, *May* 16 [1713].

I HAD yours, No. 40, yesterday. Your new Bishop acts very ungratefully. I cannot say so bad of it as he deserved. I begged at the same post his warrant and mine went over, that he would leave those livings to my disposal. I shall write this post to him to let him know how ill I take it. I have letters to tell me that I ought to think of employing somebody to set the tithes of the deanery. I know not what to do at this distance. I cannot be in Ireland under a month. I will write two orders; one to Parvisol, and t'other to Parvisol, and a blank for whatever fellow it is whom the last Dean employed; and I would desire you to advise with friends which to make use of: and if the latter, let the fellow's name be inserted, and both act by commission. If the former, then speak to Parvisol, and know whether he can undertake it. I doubt it is hardly to be done by a perfect stranger alone, as Parvisol is. He may perhaps venture at all, to keep up his interest with me; but that is needless, for I am willing to do him any good, that will do me no harm.

---

[1] The last three lines have been obliterated.
[2] Addressed to "Mrs. Dingley," etc. Endorsed "May 22."

Pray advise with Walls and Raymond, and a little with Bishop Sterne for form. Tell Raymond I cannot succeed for him to get that living of Moimed. It is represented here as a great sinecure. Several chaplains have solicited for it; and it has vexed me so, that, if I live, I will make it my business to serve him better in something else. I am heartily sorry for his illness, and that of the other two. If it be not necessary to let the tithes till a month hence, you may keep the two papers, and advise well in the meantime; and whenever it is absolutely necessary, then give that paper which you are most advised to. I thank Mr. Walls for his letter. Tell him that must serve for an answer, with my service to him and her. I shall buy Bishop Sterne's hair as soon as his household goods. I shall be ruined, or at least sadly cramped, unless the Queen will give me a thousand pounds. I am sure she owes me a great deal more. Lord Treasurer rallies me upon it, and I believe intends it; but, *quando?* I am advised to hasten over as soon as possible, and so I will, and hope to set out the beginning of June. Take no lodging for me. What? at your old tricks again? I can lie somewhere after I land, and I care not where, nor how. I will buy your eggs and bacon, DD . . .[1] your caps and Bible; and pray think immediately, and give me some commissions, and I will perform them as far as oo poo Pdfr can.[2] The letter I sent before this was to have gone a post before; but an accident hindered it; and, I assure oo, I wam vely akkree[3] MD did not write to Dean Pdfr, and I think oo might have had a Dean under your girdle for the superscription. I have just finished my Treatise,[4] and must be ten days correcting it. Farewell, deelest MD, MD, MD, FW, FW, FW, ME, ME, ME, Lele.

You'll seal the two papers after my name.

---

[1] Illegible. Forster reads, "and dee deelest Ppt."
[2] The last few words have been partially obliterated.
[3] Am very angry. The last word is scribbled over.
[4] *The History of the Peace of Utrecht.*

" LONDON, *May* 16, 1713.

" I appoint Mr. Isaiah Parvisol and Mr.   to set and let the tithes of the Deanery of St. Patrick's for this present year. In witness whereof, I hereunto set my hand and seal, the day and year above written.   [JONAT. SWIFT." [1]]

" LONDON, *May* 16, 1713.

" I do hereby appoint Mr. Isaiah Parvisol my proctor, to set and let the tithes of the Deanery of St. Patrick's.   In witness whereof, I have hereunto set my hand and seal, the day and year above written.   JONAT. SWIFT."

LETTER LXV[2]

CHESTER, *June* 6, 1713.

I AM come here after six days. I set out on Monday last, and got here to-day about eleven in the morning. A noble rider, fais! and all the ships and people went off yesterday with a rare wind. This was told me, to my comfort, upon my arrival. Having not used riding these three years, made me terrible weary; yet I resolve on Monday to set out for Holyhead, as weary as I am. 'Tis good for my health, mam. When I came here, I found MD's letter of the 26th of May sent down to me. Had you writ a post sooner I might have brought some pins : but you were lazy, and would not write your orders immediately, as I desired you. I will come when God pleases ; perhaps I may be with you in a week. I will be three days going to Holyhead ; I cannot ride faster, say hat oo will. I am upon Stay-behind's mare. I have the whole inn to myself. I would fain 'scape this Holyhead journey ; but I have no prospect of ships, and it will be almost necessary I should be in Dublin before the 25th instant, to take the oaths ; [3] otherwise I must wait to a

---

[1] The signature has been cut off.
[2] Addressed to "Mrs. Dingley," etc.   Endorsed "Chester Letter."
[3] " Others " (MS.).

quarter sessions. I will lodge as I can ; therefore take no lodgings for me, to pay in my absence. The poor Dean can't afford it. I spoke again to the Duke of Ormond about Moimed for Raymond, and hope he may yet have it, for I laid it strongly to the Duke, and gave him the Bishop of Meath's memorial. I am sorry for Raymond's fistula ; tell him so. I will speak to Lord Treasurer about Mrs. South[1] to-morrow. Odso ! I forgot ; I thought I had been in London. Mrs. Tisdall[2] is very big, ready to lie down. Her husband is a puppy. Do his feet stink still ? The letters to Ireland go at so uncertain an hour, that I am forced to conclude. Farewell, MD, MD MD FW FW FW ME ME ME ME.

> Lele lele
> lele logues and
> Ladies bose fair
> and slender.

[*On flyleaf.*]

I mightily approve Ppt's project of hanging the blind parson. When I read that passage upon Chester walls, as I was coming into town, and just received your letter, I said aloud—Agreeable B——tch.

[1] See pp. 86, 301.   [2] See p. 46.

INDEX

in Hill's Expedition, 311 and n., 314.

Barton, Lieut. - Colonel, drowned, 311 and n., 314.

Basto. See *Ombre.*

Bateman, Christopher, the book-seller, 120, 139, 251, 491, 492.

Bath, 185, 186, 188, 190, 194, 207, 213, 247, 278, 409, 410, 425, 429, 432, 445, 526.

Bathurst, Allen, M.P., afterwards Baron and Earl Bathurst, 348 and n.; a member of "the Society," 348, 368, 369; made a peer, 370 note, 371.

Battersea, 253.

"Baudrier, Sieur du," feigned name for Prior, 284 and n., 312. See "*Prior's Journey.*"

Beaufort, Henry Somerset, second Duke of, 385 and n., 529; proposed as a member of "the Society," 390, 391, 397, 403; admitted, 407, 416, 522; proposes his brother-in-law Lord Danby, 416, 417 and n.; shows Swift a poem, 431.

Beaumont, Joseph, a linen merchant of Trim, and an inventor, 1 and n., 19, 21, 22, 27, 155, 250, 427, 441, 444, 475; Swift helps him in his claim on the Government, 6 and n., 8, 13, 16, 26, 211, 232, 250, 333, 349, 368; pleads for the liberties of Trim, 80 and n., 235; asks Swift to get him a collector's place, 213; wants to get a patent, 419; sends Swift some stockings, 475.

Beaumont, Mrs., 139.

Beaumont, Mr., father of Joseph, wishes to be portreeve of Trim, 235 and n., 250.

Beaumont, Sir George, Bart., M.P. for Leicester, 192 and n., 210.

Bedlam, 91 and n.

Beef-Steak Club, the, 52 n.

Beer, October, 152.

Belasyse, Lady, elder daughter of Sir Wm. Armine, Bart., her death, 523 and n.

Belasyse, Sir Henry, sent to Spain on a Commission, 247 and n., 248.

Bell, a grocer, 211.

Bellamont, Lady, wife of Nanfan Coote, Earl of Bellamont, 199 and n.

Bell and Dragon, 312.

Bellasis, Lady. See *Belasyse.*

Bellman, letters sent by the, 6 and n., 33, 54, 65 note, 66, 279, 385, 390, 441, 497.

Benson, Robert, Lord of the Treasury, 41 and n.; Swift presented to, 41 and n.; Chancellor of the Exchequer, 324 and n., 380, 407, 409, 522, 539; received into "the Society," 437, 496; Swift dines with, 480.

Berested's Bridge, 234.

Berkeley, George, afterwards Bishop of Cloyne, 540 and n.; Swift befriends him, 540 and n., 542; Swift dines with, 544.

Berkeley, Countess of, Elizabeth, daughter of Viscount Campden, wife of the second Earl, 218, 297; writes to Swift, 14 and n., 17, 39.

Berkeley, Countess of, Lady Louisa Lennox, daughter of the Duke of Richmond, wife of the third Earl, 134 and n., 230; plays Swift a trick, 230, 231.

Berkeley, Charles, second Earl of, his illness and death, 14 and n., 25, 39 and n.; his former steward, 100; Swift writes an inscription for his tomb, 151.

Berkeley, James, third Earl of, his marriage to Lady Louisa Lennox, 134 and n., 151, 230.

Berkeley Castle, Swift invited to, 14, 17, 25, 39.

Berkeley of Stratton, William Berkeley, fourth Baron, Chancellor of the Duchy of Lancaster, 48 and n., 60, 506 note, 523, 540, 542.

Berkhampstead, 249.

Bernage, an officer serving under Colonel Fielding, 106 and n., 167, 185, 193, 349, 379; seeks Swift's help to obtain a commission, 130, 136; Swift recommends him to the Duke of Argyle, 146, 147, 149, 153, 154, 157, 158, 163; made captain - lieutenant, 158, 172, 173; offers money to

INDEX

of Ireland, 69 and n.; his death, 80.

Freind (?), Colonel, 11 and n.

Freind, John, M.D., 66 and n., 74, 85, 162, 178, 197, 212, 216, 251, 380, 394; Swift dines with, 247, 320, 355, 383; Swift recommends him to be Physician-General, 418, 422, 423, 426.

Freind, Dr. Robert, elder brother of John Freind, Headmaster of Westminster School, 206 and n., 394.

French, Mr., 158.

French Church, the, 495.

French envoys at Windsor, 304.

French priest. See *Gaultier*.

Frenchwoman. See *De Caudres*.

Frowde, Philip, the elder, in difficulties, 336 and n., 337, 338, 351; his son, Addison's friend, see *Proud* (Frowde), 58 and n.

Fruit, Swift seldom eats, 54, 231, 232, 242, 255, 269, 275, 281, 282, 285, 291, 454.

Furmity, 416.

GACCO, 514.

Gallas, Count, the Emperor's Envoy, disgraced, 325 and n.

Galway, the Earl of, lost the battle of Almanza, 36 and n.; a defence of his management of the war, 333 and n.

Garraway's Coffee-house, in Change Alley, 120 and n.

Garter, the, 227, 491.

Garth, Dr. Samuel, author of *The Dispensary*, 32 and n., 64, 274, 341; Swift dines with, 35, 52.

Gasconnade, a, 92.

Gastrell, Dr. Francis, Canon of Christ Church, afterwards Bishop of Chester, 238 and n., 386, 539; Swift dines with him, 253, 309.

Gaultier or Gautier, the Abbé, French emissary, 279 note, 304 and n., 305, 475, 476, 499, 515.

Gay, John, the poet, supposed author of *The State of Wit*, 216 and n.

Gazette, the, 256 and n., 260 and n., 263, 279, 286, 372, 421,

and see *Steele* and *King* and *Ford*.

Gazetteer, 2 note, 8 and n.; Steele loses the place of, for writing a *Tatler* against Harley, 39, 47 and n.; Dr. King made, 374; Ford made, 446, 449.

George, Prince, the husband of Queen Anne, 131 note; his birthday, 413.

Gerard, Digby, Lord, 262 note, 344 note.

Germaine, Lady Betty, daughter of second Earl of Berkeley, and married to Sir John Germaine, 17 and n., 151, 170, 314, 315; Swift dines with, 143, 230, 343; visits Mrs. Vanhomrigh, 158.

Germaine, Sir John, Bart., 17 note, 151.

German, a, of the Queen's music, 398.

Gernon, Stephen, former gauger to Henry Tenison, M.P., 226 and n., 252.

Gery, Betty (Mrs. Elwick), 439 note, 479.

Gery, Mr., Rector of Letcombe, Berks; his marriage, 439 and n., 479.

Gery, Moll (Mrs. Wigmore), 439 note, 502.

Giffard, Lady, sister of Sir William Temple, x, xi, xii, 4 and n., 300, 446, 461; differences between her and Swift, 4 and n., 11, 16, 67, 68, 72; Stella's mother lives with her, 4 and n., 11, 16, 196; holds money of Stella's, 51, 62, 69, 72, 112, 352; holds money of Mrs. Fenton's, 103, 114; Mrs. Fenton with her, 291, 299, 457; invites Swift to Sheen, 299; her footman and Miss Bradley, 446; her picture, 516.

Ginger, preserved, 457.

Glasses. See *Spectacles*.

"Globe" in the Strand, the, 115.

Gloucester, Edward Fowler, D.D., Bishop of, 398 and n.

Gloucester, Duke of, son of Queen Anne, 466 note.

Godfrey, Colonel, Clerk Comptroller

37

88

PRINTED BY MORRISON AND GIBB LIMITED, EDINBURGH

A CATALOGUE OF BOOKS AND ANNOUNCEMENTS OF METHUEN AND COMPANY PUBLISHERS : LONDON 36 ESSEX STREET W.C.

CONTENTS

APRIL 1901

MESSRS. METHUEN'S
ANNOUNCEMENTS

Travel, Adventure and Topography

THE INDIAN BORDERLAND: Being a Personal Record of Twenty Years. By Sir T. H. HOLDICH, K.C.I.E. Illustrated. *Demy 8vo.* 15s. *net.*

This book is a personal record of the author's connection with those military and political expeditions which, during the last twenty years, have led to the consolidation of our present position in the North-West frontier of India. It is a personal history of trans-frontier surveys and boundary demarcations, commencing with Penjdeh and ending with the Pamirs, Chitral, and Tirah.

MODERN ABYSSYNIA. By A. B. WYLDE. With a Map and a Portrait. *Demy 8vo.* 15s. *net.*

An important and comprehensive account of Abyssinia by a traveller who knows the country intimately, and has had the privilege of the friendship of King Menelik.

MANCHURIA. By ALEXANDER HOSIE. With Illustrations and a Map. *Demy 8vo.* 10s. 6d. *net.*

A complete account of this important province by the highest living authority on the subject.

THE RELIEF OF KUMASI. By Captain H. C. J. BISS. With Maps and Illustrations. *Crown 8vo.* 6s.

A narrative both of the siege and of the march of the relieving force, by an officer who took part in the advance.

THE REAL CHINESE QUESTION. By CHESTER HOLCOMBE. *Crown 8vo.* 6s.

A BOOK OF BRITTANY. By S. BARING GOULD. With numerous Illustrations. *Crown 8vo.* 6s.

Uniform in scope and size with Mr. Baring Gould's well-known books on Devon, Cornwall, and Dartmoor.

NAPLES: PAST AND PRESENT. By A. H. NORWAY, Author of 'Highways and Byways in Devon and Cornwall.' With 40 Illustrations by A. G. FERARD. *Crown 8vo.* 6s.

In this book Mr. Norway gives not only a highly interesting description of modern Naples, but a historical account of its antiquities and traditions.

History and Biography

THE PASSING OF THE GREAT QUEEN: A Tribute to the Noble Life of Victoria Regina. By MARIE CORELLI. *Small 4to.* 1s.

In this book Miss Marie Corelli endeavours to interpret the high lessons of the Queen's life and the secret of her extraordinary success. It is a book which deals not only with the personal factor, but also with the commencement of the new era which the death of the Queen has brought about.

PRINTED BY MORRISON AND GIBB LIMITED, EDINBURGH

A HISTORY OF EGYPT, FROM THE EARLIEST TIMES TO
THE PRESENT DAY. Edited by W. M. FLINDERS PETRIE, D.C.L.,
LL.D., Professor of Egyptology at University College. Fully Illus-
trated. In Six Volumes. *Crown 8vo. 6s. each.*
Vol. VI. EGYPT IN THE MIDDLE AGES. By STANLEY LANE-
POOLE, M.A., Litt.D.

A HISTORY OF THE CHURCH OF CYPRUS. By
JOHN HACKETT, M.A. With Maps and Illustrations. *Demy 8vo.*
15s. net.
A work which brings together all that is known on the subject from the introduction
of Christianity to the commencement of the British occupation. A separate
division deals with the local Latin Church during the period of the Western
Supremacy.

A HISTORY OF THE JESUITS IN ENGLAND. By the
Rev. E. L. TAUNTON. *Demy 8vo. 21s. net.*
This book is founded on original research, and contains much curious information
from the state papers and from private sources. The history closes in the year 1773.

THE LIFE OF MRS. LYNN LINTON. By G. S. LAYARD.
With Portraits. *Demy 8vo. 12s. 6d.*

THE LIFE OF SIR HARRY PARKES. By STANLEY LANE-
POOLE. *Crown 8vo. 6s.*

THE LAST OF THE GREAT SCOUTS ('Buffalo Bill.') By
his sister HELEN CODY WETMORE. With Illustrations. *Demy 8vo. 6s.*

A HISTORY OF THE MIDLAND RAILWAY. By CLEMENT
STRETTON. With numerous Illustrations. *Demy 8vo. 12s. 6d.*

BROTHER MUSICIANS: Reminiscences of Edward and
Walter Bache. By CONSTANCE BACHE. *Crown 8vo. 6s. net.*

Theology

THE WAY OF HOLINESS: A Devotional Commentary on
the 119th Psalm. By R. M. BENSON, M.A., of the Cowley Mission,
Oxford. *Crown 8vo. 5s.*

THE SUPERSENSUAL LIFE. By JACOB BEHMEN. Edited
by BERNARD HOLLAND. *Fcap 8vo. 3s. 6d.*

THE IMITATION OF CHRIST. *Crown 8vo. 3s. 6d.*
A new edition in large type of Dr. Bigg's well-known translation.

THE SOUL'S PILGRIMAGE: Devotional Readings from the
published and unpublished writings of GEORGE BODY, D.D.
Selected and Arranged by J. H. BURN, B.D. *Pott 8vo. Gilt top. 2s. 6d.*

Handbooks of Theology

General Editor, A. ROBERTSON, D.D., Principal of King's College, London.

THE PHILOSOPHY OF RELIGION IN ENGLAND AND AMERICA. By ALFRED CALDECOTT, D.D. *Demy 8vo.* 10s. 6d.

A complete history and description of the various philosophies of religion which have been formulated during the last few centuries in England and America.

The Library of Devotion

Pott 8vo.   Cloth 2s.; leather 2s. 6d. net.

THE PSALMS OF DAVID. With an Introduction and Notes by B. W. RANDOLPH, M.A., Principal of the Theological College, Ely.

A devotional and practical edition of the Prayer Book version of the Psalms.

LYRA APOSTOLICA. With an Introduction by Canon SCOTT HOLLAND, and Notes by H. C. BEECHING, M.A.

THE INNER WAY. Selections from the Sermons of F. Tauler. Edited by A. W. HUTTON, M.A.

The Churchman's Bible

General Editor, J. H. BURN, B.D.

Messrs. METHUEN are issuing a series of expositions upon most of the books of the Bible. The volumes will be practical and devotional, and the text of the authorised version is explained in sections, which will correspond as far as possible with the Church Lectionary.

ISAIAH. Edited by W. E. BARNES, D.D. 2 vols. *Fcap 8vo.* 2s. each net.

THE EPISTLE OF ST. JAMES. Edited by H. W. FULFORD. *Fcap 8vo.* 1s. 6d. net.

Belles Lettres

Methuen's Standard Library

THE NATURAL HISTORY OF SELBORNE. By GILBERT WHITE. Edited by L. C. MIALL, F.R.S., assisted by W. WARD FOWLER, M.A. *Crown 8vo.* 6s.

THE JOURNAL TO STELLA. By JONATHAN SWIFT. Edited by G. A. AITKEN, M.A. *Crown 8vo.* 6s.

Little Biographies

Fcap. 8vo.   Each Volume, cloth 3s. 6d. ; leather 4s. net.

THE LIFE OF SAVONAROLA.   By E. L. S. HORSBURGH,
M.A.   With Portraits and Illustrations.

The Little Guides

Pott 8vo.   Cloth, 3s. ; leather, 3s. 6d. net.

THE MALVERN COUNTRY.   By B. C. A. WINDLE, D.Sc.,
F.R.S.   Illustrated by E. H. NEW.

This book, besides dealing with Malvern and its hills, will treat of such places of
interest as can easily be visited from that centre.   The cathedral cities of Worcester
and Hereford, with their history, will be described.   The great abbeys of
Tewkesbury and Pershore and smaller places of beauty and historic note, such as
Deerhurst, Birtsmorton, and Ledbury, will also receive attention.

The Works of Shakespeare

New volume uniform with Professor Dowden's *Hamlet.*

KING LEAR.   Edited by W. J. CRAIG.   *Demy 8vo.   3s. 6d.*

The Novels of Charles Dickens

With Introductions by GEORGE GISSING, Notes by F. G. KITTON,
and Illustrations.

Crown 8vo.   Each Volume, cloth 3s. net, leather 4s. 6d. net.

OLD CURIOSITY SHOP.   With Illustrations by G. M.
BRIMELOW.   *Two volumes.*

BARNABY RUDGE.   With Illustrations by BEATRICE
ALCOCK.   *Two volumes.*

The Little Library

With Introductions, Notes, and Photogravure Frontispieces.

Pott 8vo.   Each Volume, cloth 1s. 6d. net. ; leather 2s. 6d. net.

SELECTIONS FROM WORDSWORTH.   Edited by NOWELL
C. SMITH, Fellow of New College, Oxford.

SELECTIONS FROM WILLIAM BLAKE.   Edited by
M. PERUGINI.

THE PURGATORIO OF DANTE.   Translated by H. F.
CARY.   Edited by PAGET TOYNBEE, M.A.

PRIDE AND PREJUDICE. By JANE AUSTEN. Edited by
E. V. LUCAS. *Two Volumes.*

PENDENNIS. By W. M. THACKERAY. Edited by S. GWYNN.
Three volumes.

LAVENGRO. By GEORGE BORROW. Edited by F. HINDES
GROOME. *Two volumes.*

General Literature

A GARDEN DIARY. By the Hon. EMILY LAWLESS. *Demy 8vo.*
7s. 6d. net.

In this book, Miss Lawless, who is a distinguished amateur, gives her experiences
of the delights and sorrows of a garden.

ON THE OTHER SIDE OF THE LATCH. By SARA
JEANNETTE DUNCAN (Mrs. Cotes), Author of 'A Voyage of Consolation.' *Crown 8vo. 6s.*

In this delightful book Mrs. Cotes recounts her experiences and impressions of an
Indian garden. It is a book similar in character to 'Elizabeth and her German
Garden.'

THE BRITISH GARDENER AND AMATEUR. By W.
WILLIAMSON. Illustrated. *Demy 8vo. 10s. 6d.*

A complete handbook of horticulture by a well-known expert.

EFFICIENCY AND EMPIRE. By ARNOLD WHITE. *Crown
8vo. 6s.*

This book deals with National and Departmental inefficiency, and the root causes of
the muddle that seems inherent in our public affairs. In the preparation of this
book Mr. Arnold White has had the advantage of consulting many of the most
successful business organisers of the day, and consequently the remedial and
constructive side of the problem is principally dealt with.

A KEY TO NOTANDA QUÆDAM. *Fcap 8vo. 2s. net.*

PRACTICAL LICENSING REFORM. By the Hon. SIDNEY
PEEL, late Fellow of Trinity College, Oxford, and Secretary to the
Royal Commission on the Licensing Laws. *Crown 8vo 1s. 6d.*

This book gives in a handy form the results of the present licensing system and the
proposed reforms which are now being urged as a result of the report of the
Commission.

Sporting Books

THE ENGLISH TURF. By CHARLES RICHARDSON. With
over fifty Illustrations and Plans. *Demy 8vo. 15s.*

This book describes the evolution of racing and the racehorse of to-day. It deals
minutely with the lines of blood, the principal racecourses, trainers, jockeys,
steeple-chasing, and, in fact, with every detail of racing under modern conditions.

THE LIGHTER SIDE OF CRICKET. By Captain PHILIP
TREVOR. Illustrated. *Crown 8vo. 6s.*

A book dealing with the humours and comedies of the national pastime.

Scientific

DISEASES OF THE HEART. By E. H. COLBECK, M.D.
With numerous Illustrations. *Demy 8vo.* 12s.

DRAGONS OF THE AIR. By H. G. SEELEY, F.R.S. With
many Illustrations. *Crown 8vo.* 6s.
A popular history of the most remarkable flying animals which ever lived. Their
relations to mammals, birds, and reptiles, living and extinct, are shown by an
original series of illustrations. The scattered remains preserved in Europe and
the United States have been put together accurately to show the varied forms of
the animals. The book is a natural history of these extinct animals, which flew
by means of a single finger.

Fiction

THE SACRED FOUNT. By HENRY JAMES, Author of
'What Maisie Knew.' *Crown 8vo.* 6s.

A GREAT LADY. By ADELINE SERGEANT, Author of 'The
Story of a Penitent Soul.' *Crown 8vo.* 6s.

THE FROBISHERS. By S. BARING-GOULD. *Crown 8vo.* 6s.

A STATE SECRET. By B. M. CROKER, Author of 'Peggy
of the Bartons,' etc. *Crown 8vo.* 3s. 6d.
A volume of stories.

THE SUPREME CRIME. By DOROTHEA GERARD. *Crown
8vo.* 6s.

A SECRETARY OF LEGATION. By HOPE DAWLISH.
Crown 8vo. 6s.

PRINCE RUPERT THE BUCCANEER. By C. J. CUTCLIFFE
HYNE, Author of 'Captain Kettle.' Illustrated. *Crown 8vo.* 6s.
A narrative of the romantic adventures of the famous Prince Rupert, and of his
exploits in the Spanish Indies after the Cromwellian wars.

A NARROW WAY. By MARY FINDLATER, Author of 'Over
the Hills.' *Crown 8vo.* 6s.

TALES THAT ARE TOLD. By J. HELEN FINDLATER,
Author of 'The Green Graves of Balgowrie,' and MARY FINDLATER.
Crown 8vo. 6s.

THE THIRD FLOOR. By Mrs. DUDENEY, Author of 'Folly
Corner.' *Crown 8vo.* 6s.
A vivacious and romantic story of modern life, introducing many scenes of modern
journalism.

THE SALVATION SEEKERS. By NOEL AINSLIE. *Crown
8vo.* 6s.

STRANGE HAPPENINGS. By W. CLARK RUSSELL and
other Authors. *Crown 8vo.* 6s.

THE REDEMPTION OF DAVID CORSON. By C. F.
GOSS. *Crown 8vo.* 6s.

THE BLACK WOLF'S BREED.   By HARRIS DICKSON.
Illustrated.   *Crown 8vo.   6s.*

BELINDA FITZWARREN.   By the EARL OF IDDESLEIGH.
Crown 8vo.   6s.

THE LOST REGIMENT.   By ERNEST GLANVILLE, Author of
'The Kloof Bride.'   *Crown 8vo.   3s. 6d.*

BUNTER'S CRUISE.   By CHARLES GLEIG.   Illustrated.
Crown 8vo.   3s. 6d.

THE ADVENTURE OF PRINCESS SYLVIA.   By Mrs
C. N. WILLIAMSON.   *Crown 8vo.   3s. 6d.*

The Novelist

A monthly series of novels by popular authors at Sixpence. Each
Number is as long as the average Six Shilling Novel. Numbers I. to
XIX. are now ready :—

XVIII. IN THE MIDST OF ALARMS.	ROBERT BARR.
XIX. HIS GRACE.	W. E. NORRIS.
XX. DODO.	E. F. BENSON.
XXI. CHEAP JACK ZITA.	S. BARING GOULD.
	[May.
XXII. WHEN VALMOND CAME TO PONTIAC.	GILBERT PARKER.
	[June.
XXIII. THE HUMAN BOY.	EDEN PHILLPOTTS.
	[July.
XXIV. THE CHRONICLES OF COUNT ANTONIO.	ANTHONY HOPE.
XXV. BY STROKE OF SWORD.	ANDREW BALFOUR.
XXVI. KITTY ALONE.	S. BARING GOULD.

Methuen's Sixpenny Library

NEW VOLUMES

THE GREEN GRAVES OF BALGOWRIE.	JANE H. FINDLATER.
	[April.
THE STOLEN BACILLUS. H. G. WELLS.	*[May.*
MATTHEW AUSTIN. W. E. NORRIS.	*[June.*
THE CONQUEST OF LONDON. DOROTHEA GERARD.	*[July.*
THE MUTABLE MANY. ROBERT BARR.	*[August.*
THE WAR WITH THE BOERS. With Maps and Plans. By H. SIDEBOTHAM. (Double Number, 1s.)	*[September.*

A CATALOGUE OF

MESSRS. METHUEN'S
PUBLICATIONS

◆

Poetry

Rudyard Kipling. BARRACK-ROOM BALLADS. By RUDYARD KIPLING. 68th Thousand. *Crown 8vo. 6s. Leather, 6s. net.*

'Mr. Kipling's verse is strong, vivid, full of character. . . . Unmistakeable genius rings in every line.'—*Times.*

'The ballads teem with imagination, they palpitate with emotion. We read them with laughter and tears; the metres throb in our pulses, the cunningly ordered words tingle with life; and if this be not poetry, what is?'—*Pall Mall Gazette.*

Rudyard Kipling. THE SEVEN SEAS. By RUDYARD KIPLING. 57th Thousand. *Cr. 8vo. Buckram, gilt top. 6s. Leather, 6s. net.*

'The Empire has found a singer; it is no depreciation of the songs to say that statesmen may have, one way or other, to take account of them.'—*Manchester Guardian.*

'Animated through and through with indubitable genius.'—*Daily Telegraph.*

"Q." POEMS AND BALLADS. By "Q." *Crown 8vo. 3s. 6d.*

"Q." GREEN BAYS: Verses and Parodies. By "Q." *Second Edition. Crown 8vo. 3s. 6d.*

E. Mackay. A SONG OF THE SEA. By ERIC MACKAY. *Second Edition. Fcap. 8vo. 5s.*

H. Ibsen. BRAND. A Drama by HENRIK IBSEN. Translated by WILLIAM WILSON. *Third Edition. Crown 8vo. 3s. 6d.*

A. D. Godley. LYRA FRIVOLA. By A. D. GODLEY, M.A., Fellow of Magdalen College, Oxford. *Third Edition. Pott 8vo. 2s. 6d.*

'Combines a pretty wit with remarkably neat versification. . . . Every one will wish there was more of it.'—*Times.*

A. D. Godley. VERSES TO ORDER. By A. D. GODLEY. *Crown 8vo. 2s. 6d. net.*

'A capital specimen of light academic poetry.'—*St. James's Gazette.*

J. G. Cordery. THE ODYSSEY OF HOMER. A Translation by J. G. CORDERY. *Crown 8vo. 7s. 6d.*

Herbert Trench. DEIRDRE WED: and Other Poems. By HERBERT TRENCH. *Crown 8vo. 5s.*

'A notable poem. "Deirdre Wed" will secure for Mr. Trench an acknowledged place—and a high place—among contemporary poets.'—*St. James's Gazette.*

Edgar Wallace. WRIT IN BARRACKS. By EDGAR WALLACE. *Crown 8vo. 3s. 6d.*

'As good as soldier songs can be.'—*Daily Chronicle.*

'Soldier rhymes with much humour and pathos.'—*Outlook.*

A 2

Belles Lettres, Anthologies, etc.

R. L. Stevenson. VAILIMA LET-
TERS. By ROBERT LOUIS STEVEN-
SON. With an Etched Portrait by
WILLIAM STRANG. *Third Edition.*
Crown 8vo. Buckram. 6s.
'A fascinating book.'—*Standard.*
'Unique in Literature.'—*Daily Chronicle.*

G. Wyndham. THE POEMS OF WIL-
LIAM SHAKESPEARE. Edited
with an Introduction and Notes by
GEORGE WYNDHAM, M.P. *Demy
8vo. Buckram, gilt top.* 10s. 6d.
This edition contains the ' Venus,' 'Lucrece,'
and Sonnets, and is prefaced with an
elaborate introduction of over 140 pp.
'We have no hesitation in describing Mr.
George Wyndham's introduction as a
masterly piece of criticism, and all who
love our Elizabethan literature will find a
very garden of delight in it.'—*Spectator.*

Edward FitzGerald. THE RUBAI-
YAT OF OMAR KHAYYAM.
Translated by EDWARD FITZGERALD.
With a Commentary by H. M.
BATSON, and a Biography of Omar by
E. D. ROSS. 6s. Also an Edition
on large paper limited to 50 copies.
' Both introduction and commentary are ex-
cellent.'—*Review of Week.*
'One of the most desirable of the many re-
prints of Omar.'—*Glasgow Herald.*

W. E. Henley. ENGLISH LYRICS.
Selected and Edited by W. E.
HENLEY. *Crown 8vo. Gilt top.*
3s. 6d.
' It is a body of choice and lovely poetry.'—
Birmingham Gazette.

Henley and Whibley. A BOOK OF
ENGLISH PROSE. Collected by
W. E. HENLEY and CHARLES
WHIBLEY. *Crown 8vo. Buckram,
gilt top.* 6s.

H. C. Beeching. LYRA SACRA: An
Anthology of Sacred Verse. Edited
by H. C. BEECHING, M.A. *Crown
8vo. Buckram.* 6s.
'A charming selection, which maintains a
lofty standard of excellence.'—*Times.*

"Q." THE GOLDEN POMP. A Procession of English Lyrics. Arranged
by A. T. QUILLER COUCH. *Crown
8vo. Buckram.* 6s.

W. B. Yeats. AN ANTHOLOGY OF
IRISH VERSE. Edited by W. B.
YEATS. *Revised and Enlarged
Edition. Crown 8vo.* 3s. 6d.
' An attractive and catholic selection.'—
Times.

G. W. Steevens. MONOLOGUES OF
THE DEAD. By G. W. STEEVENS.
Foolscap 8vo. 3s. 6d.

W. M. Dixon. A PRIMER OF
TENNYSON. By W. M. DIXON,
M.A. *Cr. 8vo.* 2s. 6d.
' Much sound and well-expressed criticism.
The bibliography is a boon.'—*Speaker.*

W. A. Craigie. A PRIMER OF
BURNS. By W. A. CRAIGIE.
Crown 8vo. 2s. 6d.
' A valuable addition to the literature of the
poet.'—*Times.*

L. Magnus. A PRIMER OF WORDS-
WORTH. By LAURIE MAGNUS.
Crown 8vo. 2s. 6d.
' A valuable contribution to Wordsworthian
literature.'—*Literature.*

Sterne. THE LIFE AND OPINIONS
OF TRISTRAM SHANDY. By
LAWRENCE STERNE. With an Introduction by CHARLES WHIBLEY,
and a Portrait. 2 *vols.* 7s.

Congreve. THE COMEDIES OF
WILLIAM CONGREVE. With an
Introduction by G. S. STREET, and
a Portrait. 2 *vols.* 7s.

Morier. THE ADVENTURES OF
HAJJI BABA OF ISPAHAN. By
JAMES MORIER. With an Introduc-
tion by E. G. BROWNE, M.A. and a
Portrait. 2 *vols.* 7s.

Walton. THE LIVES OF DONNE,
WOTTON, HOOKER, HERBERT
AND SANDERSON. By IZAAK
WALTON. With an Introduction by
VERNON BLACKBURN, and a Por-
trait. 3s. 6d.

Johnson. THE LIVES OF THE ENGLISH POETS. By SAMUEL JOHNSON, LL.D. With an Introduction by J. H. MILLAR, and a Portrait. 3 *vols.* 10s. 6d.

Burns. THE POEMS OF ROBERT BURNS. Edited by ANDREW LANG and W. A. CRAIGIE. With Portrait. *Second Edition. Demy 8vo, gilt top.* 6s.

'Among editions in one volume, this will take the place of authority.'—*Times.*

F. Langbridge. BALLADS OF THE BRAVE; Poems of Chivalry, Enterprise, Courage, and Constancy. Edited by Rev. F. LANGBRIDGE. *Second Edition. Cr. 8vo.* 3s. 6d. *School Edition.* 2s. 6d.
'The book is full of splendid things.'—*World.*

Methuen's Standard Library

Gibbon. MEMOIRS OF MY LIFE AND WRITINGS. By EDWARD GIBBON. Edited, with an Introduction and Notes, by G. BIRKBECK HILL, LL.D. *Crown 8vo.* 6s.
'An admirable edition of one of the most interesting personal records of a literary life. Its notes and its numerous appendices are a repertory of almost all that can be known about Gibbon.'—*Manchester Guardian.*

Gibbon. THE DECLINE AND FALL OF THE ROMAN EMPIRE. By EDWARD GIBBON. A New Edition, Edited with Notes, Appendices, and Maps, by J. B. BURY, LL.D., Fellow of Trinity College, Dublin. *In Seven Volumes. Demy 8vo. Gilt top.* 8s. 6d. *each. Also Cr. 8vo.* 6s. *each.*
'At last there is an adequate modern edition of Gibbon. . . . The best edition the nineteenth century could produce.— *Manchester Guardian.*
'A great piece of editing.'—*Academy.*
'The greatest of English, perhaps of all, historians has never been presented to the public in a more convenient and attractive form. No higher praise can be bestowed upon Professor Bury than

to say, as may be said with truth, that he is worthy of being ranked with Guizot and Milman.'—*Daily News.*

Dante. LA COMMEDIA DI DANTE ALIGHIERI. The Italian Text edited by PAGET TOYNBEE, M.A. *Crown 8vo.* 6s.
'A carefully-revised text, printed with beautiful clearness.'—*Glasgow Herald.*

C. G. Crump. THE HISTORY OF THE LIFE OF THOMAS ELLWOOD. Edited by C. G. CRUMP, M.A. *Crown 8vo.* 6s.
This edition is the only one which contains the complete book as originally published. It contains a long Introduction and many Footnotes.

Tennyson. THE EARLY POEMS OF ALFRED, LORD TENNYSON, Edited, with Notes and an Introduction by J. CHURTON COLLINS, M.A. *Crown 8vo.* 6s.
An elaborate edition of the celebrated volume which was published in its final and definitive form in 1853. This edition contains a long Introduction and copious Notes, textual and explanatory. It also contains in an Appendix all the Poems which Tennyson afterwards omitted.

The Works of Shakespeare

General Editor, EDWARD DOWDEN, Litt. D.

Messrs. METHUEN have in preparation an Edition of Shakespeare in single Plays. Each play will be edited with a full Introduction, Textual Notes, and a Commentary at the foot of the page.

The first volume is :

HAMLET. Edited by EDWARD DOWDEN. *Demy 8vo.* 3s. 6d.

'An admirable edition. . . . A comely

volume, admirably printed and produced, and containing all that a student of "Hamlet" need require.'—*Speaker.*
'Fully up to the level of recent scholarship, both English and German.'—*Academy.*

ROMEO AND JULIET. Edited by
EDWARD DOWDEN, Litt.D. *Demy*
8vo. 3*s.* 6*d.*
'The edition promises to be one of the best
extant.'—*Glasgow Herald.*

'No edition of Shakespeare is likely to prove
more attractive and satisfactory than this
one. It is beautifully printed and paged
and handsomely and simply bound.'—
St. James's Gazette.

The Novels of Charles Dickens

Crown 8vo. Each Volume, cloth 3s. net ; leather 4s. 6d. net.

Messrs. METHUEN have in preparation an edition of those novels of Charles
Dickens which have now passed out of copyright. Mr. George Gissing,
whose critical study of Dickens is both sympathetic and acute, has written an
Introduction to each of the books, and a very attractive feature of this edition
will be the illustrations of the old houses, inns, and buildings, which Dickens
described, and which have now in many instances disappeared under the
touch of modern civilisation. Another valuable feature will be a series of
topographical and general notes to each book by Mr. F. G. Kitton. The books
will be produced with the greatest care as to printing, paper and binding.

The first volumes are :

THE PICKWICK PAPERS. With
Illustrations by E. H. NEW. *Two
Volumes.*

'As pleasant a copy as any one could desire.
The notes add much to the value of the
edition, and Mr. New's illustrations are
also historical. The volumes promise well
for the success of the edition.'—*Scotsman.*

NICHOLAS NICKLEBY. With
Illustrations by R. J. WILLIAMS.
Two Volumes.

BLEAK HOUSE. With Illustrations
by BEATRICE ALCOCK. *Two volumes.*

OLIVER TWIST. With Illustrations
by G. H. NEW.

Little Biographies

Fcap. 8vo. Each volume, cloth, 3s. 6d.

Messrs. METHUEN are publishing a new series bearing the above title.
Each book will contain the biography of a character famous in war, art,
literature or science, and will be written by an acknowledged expert. The
books will be charmingly produced and will be well illustrated. They
will make delightful gift books.

THE LIFE OF DANTE ALIGHIERI. By PAGET TOYNBEE. With 12
Illustrations.
'This excellent little volume is a clear, compact, and convenient summary of the whole
subject.'—*Academy.*

The Little Library

With Introductions, Notes, and Photogravure Frontispieces.

Pott 8vo. Each Volume, cloth 1s. 6d. net, leather 2s. 6d. net.

'Altogether good to look upon, and to handle.'—*Outlook.*
'In printing, binding, lightness, etc., this is a perfect series.'—*Pilot.*
'It is difficult to conceive more attractive volumes.'—*St. James's Gazette.*
'Very delicious little books.'—*Literature.*
'Delightful editions.'—*Record.*
'Exceedingly tastefully produced.'—*Morning Leader.*

VANITY FAIR. By W. M. THACKERAY. With an Introduction by S. GWYNN.
Three Volumes.

THE PRINCESS. By ALFRED, LORD TENNYSON. Edited by ELIZABETH WORDSWORTH.

IN MEMORIAM. By ALFRED, LORD TENNYSON. Edited, with an Introduction and Notes, by H. C. BEECHING, M.A.

THE EARLY POEMS OF ALFRED, LORD TENNYSON. Edited by J. C. COLLINS, M.A.

MAUD. By ALFRED, LORD TENNYSON. Edited by ELIZABETH WORDSWORTH.

A LITTLE BOOK OF ENGLISH LYRICS. With Notes.

EOTHEN. By A. W. KINGLAKE. With an Introduction and Notes.

CRANFORD. By Mrs. GASKELL. Edited by E. V. LUCAS.

THE INFERNO OF DANTE. Translated by H. F. CARY. Edited by PAGET TOYNBEE.

JOHN HALIFAX, GENTLEMAN. By Mrs. CRAIK. Edited by ANNIE MATHESON. Two volumes.

A LITTLE BOOK OF SCOTTISH VERSE. Arranged and edited by T. F. HENDERSON.

A LITTLE BOOK OF ENGLISH PROSE. Arranged and edited by Mrs. P. A. BARNETT.

The Little Guides

Pott 8vo, cloth 3s. ; leather, 3s. 6d. net.

OXFORD AND ITS COLLEGES. By J. WELLS, M.A., Fellow and Tutor of Wadham College. Illustrated by E. H. NEW. *Fourth Edition.*
'An admirable and accurate little treatise, attractively illustrated.'—*World.*

CAMBRIDGE AND ITS COLLEGES. By A. HAMILTON THOMPSON. Illustrated by E. H. NEW.
'It is brightly written and learned, and is just such a book as a cultured visitor needs.'—*Scotsman.*

SHAKESPEARE'S COUNTRY. By B. C. WINDLE, F.R.S., M.A. Illustrated by E. H. NEW. *Second Edition.*
'One of the most charming guide books. Both for the library and as a travelling companion the book is equally choice and serviceable.'—*Academy.*

SUSSEX. By F. G. BRABANT, M.A. Illustrated by E. H. NEW.
'A charming little book; as full of sound information as it is practical in conception.'—*Athenæum.*
'Accurate, complete, and agreeably written.'—*Literature.*

WESTMINSTER ABBEY. By G. E. TROUTBECK. Illustrated by F. D. BEDFORD.
'A delightful miniature hand-book.'—*Glasgow Herald.*
'In comeliness, and perhaps in completeness, this work must take the first place.'—*Academy.*
'A really first-rate guide-book.'—*Literature.*

Illustrated and Gift Books

Edwin Glasgow. SKETCHES OF WADHAM COLLEGE, OXFORD. By EDWIN GLASGOW. 2s. 6d. net.

Tennyson. THE EARLY POEMS OF ALFRED, LORD TENNYSON. Edited, with Notes and an Introduction by J. CHURTON COLLINS, M.A. With 10 Illustrations in Photogravure by W. E. F. BRITTEN. Demy 8vo. 10s. 6d.
'The illustrations have refinement and reserve and are finely composed.'—Literature.

Gelett Burgess. GOOPS AND HOW TO BE THEM. By GELETT BURGESS. With numerous Illustrations. Small 4to. 6s.
'An amusing volume.'—Glasgow Herald.
'The illustrations are particularly good.'—Spectator.

Gelett Burgess. THE LIVELY CITY OF LIGG. By GELETT BURGESS. With 53 Illustrations, 8 of which are coloured. Small 4to. 6s.
'Lively indeed . . . Modern in the extreme, and ingenious, this picture-story-book should win warm approval.'—Pall Mall Gazette.

Phil May. THE PHIL MAY ALBUM. 4to. 6s.
'There is a laugh in each drawing.'—Standard.

A. H. Milne. ULYSSES; OR, DE ROUGEMONT OF TROY. Described and depicted by A. H. MILNE. Small quarto. 3s. 6d.
'Clever, droll, smart.'—Guardian.

Edmund Selous. TOMMY SMITH'S ANIMALS. By EDMUND SELOUS. Illustrated by G. W. ORD. Fcap. 8vo. 2s. 6d.
A little book designed to teach children respect and reverence for animals.
'A quaint, fascinating little book: a nursery classic.'—Athenæum.

S. Baring Gould. THE CROCK OF GOLD. Fairy Stories told by S. BARING GOULD. Crown 8vo. 6s.
'Twelve delightful fairy tales.'—Punch.

M. L. Gwynn. A BIRTHDAY BOOK. Arranged and Edited by M. L. GWYNN. Demy 8vo. 12s. 6d.
This is a birthday-book of exceptional dignity, and the extracts have been chosen with particular care.

John Bunyan. THE PILGRIM'S PROGRESS. By JOHN BUNYAN. Edited, with an Introduction, by C. H. FIRTH, M.A. With 39 Illustrations by R. ANNING BELL. Crown 8vo. 6s.
'The best "Pilgrim's Progress."'—Educational Times.

F. D. Bedford. NURSERY RHYMES. With many Coloured Pictures by F. D. BEDFORD. Super Royal 8vo. 2s. 6d.

S. Baring Gould. A BOOK OF FAIRY TALES retold by S. BARING GOULD. With numerous Illustrations and Initial Letters by ARTHUR J. GASKIN. Second Edition. Cr. 8vo. Buckram. 6s.

S. Baring Gould. OLD ENGLISH FAIRY TALES. Collected and edited by S. BARING GOULD. With Numerous Illustrations by F. D. BEDFORD. Second Edition. Cr. 8vo. Buckram. 6s.
'A charming volume.'—Guardian.

S. Baring Gould. A BOOK OF NURSERY SONGS AND RHYMES. Edited by S. BARING GOULD, and Illustrated by the Birmingham Art School. Buckram, gilt top. Crown 8vo. 6s.

H. C. Beeching. A BOOK OF CHRISTMAS VERSE. Edited by H. C. BEECHING, M.A., and Illustrated by WALTER CRANE. Cr. 8vo, gilt top. 3s. 6d.

History

Flinders Petrie. A HISTORY OF EGYPT, FROM THE EARLIEST TIMES TO THE PRESENT DAY. Edited by W. M. FLINDERS PETRIE, D.C.L., LL.D., Professor of Egyptology at University College. *Fully Illustrated. In Six Volumes. Cr. 8vo. 6s. each.*

VOL. I. PREHISTORIC TIMES TO XVITH DYNASTY. W. M. F. Petrie. *Fourth Edition.*

VOL. II. THE XVIITH AND XVIIITH DYNASTIES. W. M. F. Petrie. *Third Edition.*

VOL. IV. THE EGYPT OF THE PTOLEMIES. J. P. Mahaffy.

VOL. V. ROMAN EGYPT. J. G. Milne.

'A history written in the spirit of scientific precision so worthily represented by Dr. Petrie and his school cannot but promote sound and accurate study, and supply a vacant place in the English literature of Egyptology.'—*Times.*

Flinders Petrie. RELIGION AND CONSCIENCE IN ANCIENT EGYPT. By W. M. FLINDERS PETRIE, D.C.L., LL.D. Fully Illustrated. *Crown 8vo. 2s. 6d.*

'The lectures will afford a fund of valuable information for students of ancient ethics.'—*Manchester Guardian.*

Flinders Petrie. SYRIA AND EGYPT, FROM THE TELL EL AMARNA TABLETS. By W. M. FLINDERS PETRIE, D.C.L., LL.D. *Crown 8vo. 2s. 6d.*

'A marvellous record. The addition made to our knowledge is nothing short of amazing.'—*Times.*

Flinders Petrie. EGYPTIAN TALES. Edited by W. M. FLINDERS PETRIE. Illustrated by TRISTRAM ELLIS. *In Two Volumes. Cr. 8vo. 3s. 6d. each.*

'Invaluable as a picture of life in Palestine and Egypt.'—*Daily News.*

Flinders Petrie. EGYPTIAN DECORATIVE ART. By W. M. FLINDERS PETRIE. With 120 Illustrations. *Cr. 8vo. 3s. 6d.*

'In these lectures he displays rare skill in elucidating the development of decorative art in Egypt.'—*Times.*

C. W. Oman. A HISTORY OF THE ART OF WAR. Vol. II. : The Middle Ages, from the Fourth to the Fourteenth Century. By C. W. OMAN, M.A., Fellow of All Souls', Oxford. Illustrated. *Demy 8vo. 21s.*

'The whole art of war in its historic evolution has never been treated on such an ample and comprehensive scale, and we question if any recent contribution to the exact history of the world has possessed more enduring value.'—*Daily Chronicle.*

S. Baring Gould. THE TRAGEDY OF THE CÆSARS. With numerous Illustrations from Busts, Gems, Cameos, etc. By S. BARING GOULD. *Fifth Edition. Royal 8vo. 15s.*

'A most splendid and fascinating book on a subject of undying interest. The great feature of the book is the use the author has made of the existing portraits of the Caesars and the admirable critical subtlety he has exhibited in dealing with this line of research. It is brilliantly written, and the illustrations are supplied on a scale of profuse magnificence.' —*Daily Chronicle.*

F. W. Maitland. CANON LAW IN ENGLAND. By F. W. MAITLAND, LL.D., Downing Professor of the Laws of England in the University of Cambridge. *Royal 8vo. 7s. 6d.*

'Professor Maitland has put students of English law under a fresh debt. These essays are landmarks in the study of the history of Canon Law.'—*Times.*

16   MESSRS. METHUEN'S CATALOGUE

H. de B. Gibbins. INDUSTRY IN ENGLAND : HISTORICAL OUTLINES. By H. DE B. GIBBINS, Litt.D., M.A. With 5 Maps. *Second Edition. Demy 8vo.* 10s. 6d.

H. E. Egerton. A HISTORY OF BRITISH COLONIAL POLICY. By H. E. EGERTON, M.A. *Demy 8vo.* 12s. 6d.

'It is a good book, distinguished by accuracy in detail, clear arrangement of facts, and a broad grasp of principles.'— *Manchester Guardian.*

Albert Sorel. THE EASTERN QUESTION IN THE EIGHTEENTH CENTURY. By ALBERT SOREL. Translated by F. C. BRAMWELL, M.A. *Cr. 8vo.* 3s. 6d.

C. H. Grinling. A HISTORY OF THE GREAT NORTHERN RAILWAY, 1845-95. By C. H. GRINLING. With Illustrations. *Demy 8vo.* 10s. 6d.

Mr. Grinling has done for a Railway what Macaulay did for English History.'— *The Engineer.*

W. Sterry. ANNALS OF ETON COLLEGE. By W. STERRY, M.A. With numerous Illustrations. *Demy 8vo.* 7s. 6d.

'A treasury of quaint and interesting reading. Mr. Sterry has by his skill and vivacity given these records new life.'— *Academy.*

G. W. Fisher. ANNALS OF SHREWSBURY SCHOOL. By G. W. FISHER, M.A. With numerous Illustrations. *Demy 8vo.* 10s. 6d.

'This careful, erudite book.'—*Daily Chronicle.*
'A book of which Old Salopians are sure to be proud.'—*Globe.*

J. Sargeaunt. ANNALS OF WESTMINSTER SCHOOL. By J. SARGEAUNT, M.A. With numerous Illustrations. *Demy 8vo.* 7s. 6d.

A. Clark. THE COLLEGES OF OXFORD : Their History and their Traditions. Edited by A. CLARK, M.A., Fellow of Lincoln College. *8vo.* 12s. 6d.

'A work which will be appealed to for many years as the standard book.'— *Athenæum.*

T. M. Taylor. A CONSTITUTIONAL AND POLITICAL HISTORY OF ROME. By T. M. TAYLOR, M.A., Fellow of Gonville and Caius College, Cambridge. *Crown 8vo.* 7s. 6d.

'We fully recognise the value of this carefully written work, and admire especially the fairness and sobriety of his judgment and the human interest with which he has inspired a subject which in some hands becomes a mere series of cold abstractions. It is a work that will be stimulating to the student of Roman history.'—*Athenæum.*

J. Wells. A SHORT HISTORY OF ROME. By J. WELLS, M.A., Fellow and Tutor of Wadham Coll., Oxford. *Third Edition.* With 3 Maps. *Crown 8vo.* 3s. 6d.

This book is intended for the Middle and Upper Forms of Public Schools and for Pass Students at the Universities. It contains copious Tables, etc.
'An original work written on an original plan, and with uncommon freshness and vigour.'—*Speaker.*

O. Browning. A SHORT HISTORY OF MEDIÆVAL ITALY, A.D. 1250-1530. By OSCAR BROWNING, Fellow and Tutor of King's College, Cambridge. *In Two Volumes. Cr. 8vo.* 5s. each.

VOL. I. 1250-1409.—Guelphs and Ghibellines.

VOL. II. 1409-1530.—The Age of the Condottieri.

O'Grady. THE STORY OF IRELAND. By STANDISH O'GRADY, Author of 'Finn and his Companions.' *Crown 8vo.* 2s. 6d.

𝔅𝔶𝔷𝔞𝔫𝔱𝔦𝔫𝔢 𝔗𝔢𝔵𝔱𝔰

Edited by J. B. BURY, M.A.

ZACHARIAH OF MITYLENE. Translated into English by F. J. HAMILTON, D.D., and E. W. BROOKS. *Demy 8vo.* 12s. 6d. net.

EVAGRIUS. Edited by Professor

LÉON PARMENTIER and M. BIDEZ. *Demy 8vo.* 10s. 6d. net.

THE HISTORY OF PSELLUS By C. SATHAS. *Demy 8vo.* 15s. net.

Biography

R. L. Stevenson. THE LETTERS OF ROBERT LOUIS STEVENSON TO HIS FAMILY AND FRIENDS. Selected and Edited, with Notes and Introductions, by SIDNEY COLVIN. *Fourth and Cheaper Edition. Crown 8vo.* 12s.

'Irresistible in their raciness, their variety, their animation . . . of extraordinary fascination. A delightful inheritance, the truest record of a "richly compounded spirit" that the literature of our time has preserved.'—*Times.*

J. G. Millais. THE LIFE AND LETTERS OF SIR JOHN EVERETT MILLAIS, President of the Royal Academy. By his Son, J. G. MILLAIS. With 319 Illustrations, of which 9 are in Photogravure. *Second Edition.* 2 vols. *Royal 8vo.* 32s. net.

'The illustrations make the book delightful to handle or to read. The eye lingers lovingly upon the beautiful pictures.'—*Standard.*
'This splendid work.'—*World.*
'Of such absorbing interest is it, of such completeness in scope and beauty. Special tribute must be paid to the extraordinary completeness of the illustrations.'—*Graphic.*

S. Baring Gould. THE LIFE OF NAPOLEON BONAPARTE. By S. BARING GOULD. With over 450 Illustrations in the Text and 12 Photogravure Plates. *Large quarto. Gilt top.* 36s.

'The main feature of this gorgeous volume is its great wealth of beautiful photo-

gravures and finely-executed wood engravings, constituting a complete pictorial chronicle of Napoleon I.'s personal history from the days of his early childhood at Ajaccio to the date of his second interment.'—*Daily Telegraph.*

W. A. Bettesworth. THE WALKERS OF SOUTHGATE : Being the Chronicles of a Cricketing Family. By W. A. BETTESWORTH. Illustrated. *Demy 8vo.* 15s.

'A volume which every lover of the game of games should add to his library.'—*Outlook.*
'A most engaging contribution to cricket literature . . . a lasting joy.'—*Vanity Fair.*

P. H. Colomb. MEMOIRS OF ADMIRAL SIR A. COOPER KEY. By Admiral P. H. COLOMB. With a Portrait. *Demy 8vo.* 16s.

C. Cooper King. THE STORY OF THE BRITISH ARMY. By Colonel COOPER KING. Illustrated. *Demy 8vo.* 7s. 6d.

'An authoritative and accurate story of England's military progress.'—*Daily Mail.*

R. Southey. ENGLISH SEAMEN (Howard, Clifford, Hawkins, Drake, Cavendish). By ROBERT SOUTHEY. Edited, with an Introduction, by DAVID HANNAY. *Second Edition. Crown 8vo.* 6s.

'A brave, inspiriting book.'—*Black and White.*

A 3

W. Clark Russell. THE LIFE OF ADMIRAL LORD COLLINGWOOD. By W. CLARK RUSSELL. With Illustrations by F. BRANGWYN. *Fourth Edition. Crown 8vo. 6s.*
'A book which we should like to see in the hands of every boy in the country.'— *St. James's Gazette.*

Morris Fuller. THE LIFE AND WRITINGS OF JOHN DAVENANT, D.D. (1571-1641), Bishop of Salisbury. By MORRIS FULLER, B.D. *Demy 8vo. 10s. 6d.*

J. M. Rigg. ST. ANSELM OF CANTERBURY: A CHAPTER IN THE HISTORY OF RELIGION. By J. M. RIGG. *Demy 8vo. 7s. 6d.*

F. W. Joyce. THE LIFE OF SIR FREDERICK GORE OUSELEY. By F. W. JOYCE, M.A. *7s. 6d.*

W. G. Collingwood. THE LIFE OF JOHN RUSKIN. By W. G. COLLINGWOOD, M.A. With Portraits, and 13 Drawings by Mr. Ruskin. *Second Edition. 2 vols. 8vo. 32s. Cheap Edition. Crown 8vo. 6s.*

C. Waldstein. JOHN RUSKIN. By CHARLES WALDSTEIN, M.A. With a Photogravure Portrait, *Post 8vo. 5s.*

A. M. F. Darmesteter, THE LIFE OF ERNEST RENAN. By MADAME DARMESTETER. With Portrait. *Second Edition. Cr. 8vo. 6s.*

W. H. Hutton. THE LIFE OF SIR THOMAS MORE. By W. H. HUTTON, M.A. With Portraits. *Second Edition. Cr. 8vo. 5s.*
'The book lays good claim to high rank among our biographies. It is excellently, even lovingly, written.'—*Scotsman.*

S. Baring Gould. THE VICAR OF MORWENSTOW: A Biography. By S. BARING GOULD, M.A. A new and Revised Edition. With Portrait. *Crown 8vo. 3s. 6d.*
A completely new edition of the well known biography of R. S. Hawker.

Travel, Adventure and Topography

Sven Hedin. THROUGH ASIA. By SVEN HEDIN, Gold Medallist of the Royal Geographical Society. With 300 Illustrations from Sketches and Photographs by the Author, and Maps. *2 vols. Royal 8vo. 20s. net.*
'One of the greatest books of the kind issued during the century. It is impossible to give an adequate idea of the richness of the contents of this book, nor of its abounding attractions as a story of travel unsurpassed in geographical and human interest. Much of it is a revelation. Altogether the work is one which in solidity, novelty, and interest must take a first rank among publications of its class.'—*Times.*

F. H. Skrine and E. D. Ross. THE HEART OF ASIA. By F. H. SKRINE and E. D. ROSS. With Maps and many Illustrations by VERESTCHAGIN. *Large Crown 8vo. 10s. 6d. net.*
This volume will form a landmark in our knowledge of Central Asia. . . . Illuminating and convincing.'—*Times.*

R. E. Peary. NORTHWARD OVER THE GREAT ICE. By R. E. PEARY, Gold Medallist of the Royal Geographical Society. With over 800 Illustrations. *2 vols. Royal 8vo. 32s. net.*
'His book will take its place among the permanent literature of Arctic exploration.'—*Times.*

E. A. FitzGerald. THE HIGHEST ANDES. By E. A. FITZGERALD. With 2 Maps, 51 Illustrations, 13 of which are in Photogravure, and a Panorama. *Royal 8vo,* 30s. *net.* Also a Small Edition on Hand-made Paper, limited to 50 Copies, 4to, £5, 5s.

'The record of the first ascent of the highest mountain yet conquered by mortal man. A volume which will continue to be the classic book of travel on this region of the Andes.'—*Daily Chronicle.*

F. W. Christian. THE CAROLINE ISLANDS. By F. W. CHRISTIAN. With many Illustrations and Maps. *Demy 8vo.* 12s. 6d. *net.*

'A real contribution to our knowledge of the peoples and islands of Micronesia, as well as fascinating as a narrative of travels and adventure.'—*Scotsman.*

H. H. Johnston. BRITISH CENTRAL AFRICA. By Sir H. H. JOHNSTON, K.C.B. With nearly Two Hundred Illustrations, and Six Maps. *Second Edition. Crown 4to.* 18s. *net.*

'A fascinating book, written with equal skill and charm—the work at once of a literary artist and of a man of action who is singularly wise, brave, and experienced. It abounds in admirable sketches.'—*Westminster Gazette.*

L. Decle. THREE YEARS IN SAVAGE AFRICA. By LIONEL DECLE. With 100 Illustrations and 5 Maps. *Second Edition. Demy 8vo.* 10s. 6d. *net.*

A. Hulme Beaman. TWENTY YEARS IN THE NEAR EAST. By A. HULME BEAMAN. *Demy 8vo.* With Portrait. 10s. 6d.

Henri of Orleans. FROM TONKIN TO INDIA. By PRINCE HENRI OF ORLEANS. Translated by HAMLEY BENT, M.A. With 100 Illustrations and a Map. *Cr. 4to, gilt top.* 25s.

J. W. Robertson-Scott. THE PEOPLE OF CHINA. By J. W. ROBERTSON-SCOTT. With a Map. *Crown 8vo.* 3s. 6d.

'A vivid impression . . . This excellent, brightly written epitome.'—*Daily News.* 'Excellently well done. . . . Enthralling.' —*Weekly Dispatch.*

S. L. Hinde. THE FALL OF THE CONGO ARABS. By S. L. HINDE. With Plans, etc. *Demy 8vo.* 12s. 6d.

A. St. H. Gibbons. EXPLORATION AND HUNTING IN CENTRAL AFRICA. By Major A. ST. H. GIBBONS. With full-page Illustrations by C. WHYMPER, and Maps. *Demy 8vo.* 15s.

S. Baring Gould. DARTMOOR: A Descriptive and Historical Sketch. By S. BARING GOULD. With Plans and Numerous Illustrations. *Crown 8vo.* 6s.

'A most delightful guide, companion, and instructor.'—*Scotsman.* 'Informed with close personal knowledge. —*Saturday Review.*

S. Baring Gould. THE BOOK OF THE WEST. By S. BARING GOULD. With numerous Illustrations. *Two volumes.* Vol. I. Devon. *Second Edition.* Vol. II. Cornwall. *Crown 8vo.* 6s. *each.*

'They are very attractive little volumes, they have numerous very pretty and interesting pictures, the story is fresh and bracing as the air of Dartmoor, and the legend weird as twilight over Dozmare Pool, and they give us a very good idea of this enchanting and beautiful district.'—*Guardian.*

S. Baring Gould. THE DESERTS OF SOUTHERN FRANCE. By S. BARING GOULD. 2 vols. *Demy 8vo.* 32s.

J. F. Fraser. ROUND THE WORLD ON A WHEEL. By JOHN FOSTER FRASER. With 100 Illustrations. *Crown 8vo.* 6s.

'A classic of cycling, graphic and witty.'— *Yorkshire Post.*

R. L. Jefferson. A NEW RIDE TO KHIVA. By R. L. JEFFERSON. Illustrated. *Crown 8vo.* 6s.

J. K. Trotter. THE NIGER SOURCES. By Colonel J. K. TROTTER, R.A. With a Map and Illustrations. *Crown 8vo.* 5s.

W. Crooke. THE NORTH-WESTERN PROVINCES OF INDIA: THEIR ETHNOLOGY AND ADMINISTRATION. By W. CROOKE. With Maps and Illustrations. *Demy 8vo.* 10s. 6d.

A. Boisragon. THE BENIN MAS-SACRE. By CAPTAIN BOISRAGON. *Second Edition.* Cr. 8vo. 3s. 6d.
'If the story had been written four hundred years ago it would be read to-day as an English classic.'—*Scotsman.*

H. S. Cowper. THE HILL OF THE GRACES: OR, THE GREAT STONE TEMPLES OF TRIPOLI. By H. S. COWPER, F.S.A. With Maps, Plans, and 75 Illustrations. *Demy 8vo.* 10s. 6d.

W. B. Worsfold. SOUTH AFRICA. By W. B. WORSFOLD, M.A. *With a Map. Second Edition.* Cr. 8vo. 6s.
'A monumental work compressed into a very moderate compass.'—*World.*

Katherine and Gilbert Macquoid. IN PARIS. By KATHERINE and GIL-BERT MACQUOID. Illustrated by THOMAS R. MACQUOID, R.I. With 2 maps. *Crown 8vo.* 1s.
'A useful little guide, judiciously supplied with information.'—*Athenæum.*

A. H. Keane. THE BOER STATES: A History and Description of the Transvaal and the Orange Free State. By A. H. KEANE, M.A. With Map. *Crown 8vo.* 6s.

Naval and Military

F. H. E. Cunliffe. THE HISTORY OF THE BOER WAR. By F. H. E. CUNLIFFE, Fellow of All Souls' College, Oxford. With many Illustrations, Plans, and Portraits. *In 2 vols. Vol. I.*, 15s.
This book contains the narrative of the war from its beginning to the relief of Lady-smith, and is magnificently illustrated. It has been recognised on all hands as the most serious and reasoned contribution to the history of the war, and will remain for many years the standard authority.
'The excellence of the work is double; for the narrative is vivid and temperate, and the illustrations form a picture gallery of the war which is not likely to be rivalled. . . . An ideal gift book.'—*Academy.*

G. S. Robertson. CHITRAL: The Story of a Minor Siege. By Sir G. S. ROBERTSON, K.C.S.I. With numerous Illustrations, Map and Plans. *Second Edition.* Demy 8vo. 10s. 6d.
'A book which the Elizabethans would have thought wonderful. More thrilling, more piquant, and more human than any novel.'—*Newcastle Chronicle.*
'As fascinating as Sir Walter Scott's best fiction.'—*Daily Telegraph.*

R. S. S. Baden-Powell. THE DOWN-FALL OF PREMPEH. A Diary of Life in Ashanti, 1895. By Maj.-Gen. BADEN-POWELL. With 21 Illustrations and a Map. *Third Edition. Large Crown 8vo.* 6s.

R. S. S. Baden-Powell. THE MATA-BELE CAMPAIGN, 1896. By Maj.-Gen. BADEN-POWELL. With nearly 100 Illustrations. *Cheaper Edition. Large Crown 8vo.* 6s.

J. B. Atkins. THE RELIEF OF LADYSMITH. By JOHN BLACK ATKINS. With 16 Plans and Illustrations. *Third Edition. Crown 8vo.* 6s.
'Mr. Atkins has a genius for the painting of war which entitles him already to be ranked with Forbes and Steevens, and encourages us to hope that he may one day rise to the level of Napier and Kinglake.'—*Pall Mall Gazette.*

H. W. Nevinson. LADYSMITH: The Diary of a Siege. By H. W. NEVIN-SON. With 16 Illustrations and a Plan. *Second Edition. Crown 8vo.* 6s.
'There is no exaggeration here, no strain-ing after effect. But there is the truest

realism, the impression of things as they are seen, set forth in well-chosen words and well-balanced phrases, with a measured self-restraint that marks the true artist. Mr. Nevinson is to be congratulated on the excellent work that he has done.'—*Daily Chronicle.*

Barclay Lloyd. A THOUSAND MILES WITH THE C.I.V. By Captain BARCLAY LLOYD. With an Introduction by Colonel MACKINNON, and a Portrait and Map. *Crown 8vo.* 6s.

A personal narrative of the campaign of the C.I.V., lively and realistic. Colonel Mackinnon commends the book.

Filson Young. THE RELIEF OF MAFEKING. By FILSON YOUNG. With Maps and Illustrations. *Crown 8vo.* 6s.
'A very remarkable picture.'—*World.*
'Those who like happy writing should get this book.'—*Daily Chronicle.*
'Vivid.'—*Birmingham Post.*
'Has the courage . o tell the whole of what he saw.'—*Manchester Guardian.*
'Vivid impression.'—*Glasgow Herald.*

J. Angus Hamilton. THE SIEGE OF MAFEKING. By J. ANGUS HAMILTON. With many Illustrations. *Crown 8vo.* 6s.
'A vivid picture.'—*World.*
'A thrilling story.'—*Observer.*

H. F. Prevost Battersby. IN THE WEB OF A WAR. By H. F. PREVOST BATTERSBY. With Plans, and Portrait of the Author. *Crown 8vo.* 6s.
'One of the finest eye-witness books likely to be written about the war.'—*Pall Mall Gazette.*
'The pathos, the comedy, the majesty of war are all in these pages.'—*Daily Mail.*

Howard C. Hillegas. WITH THE BOER FORCES. By HOWARD C. HILLEGAS. With 24 Illustrations. *Second Edition. Crown 8vo.* 6s.
'A most interesting book. It has many and great merits.'—*Athenæum.*
'Has extreme interest and scarcely less value.'—*Pall Mall Gazette.*

E. H. Alderson. WITH THE MOUNTED INFANTRY AND THE MASHONALAND FIELD FORCE, 1896. By Lieut.-Colonel ALDERSON. With numerous Illustrations and Plans. *Demy 8vo.* 10s. 6d.

Seymour Vandeleur. CAMPAIGNING ON THE UPPER NILE AND NIGER. By Lieut. SEYMOUR VANDELEUR. With an Introduction by Sir G. GOLDIE, K.C.M.G. With 4 Maps, Illustrations, and Plans. *Large Crown 8vo.* 10s. 6d.

Lord Fincastle. A FRONTIER CAMPAIGN. By Viscount FINCASTLE, V.C., and Lieut. P. C. ELLIOTT-LOCKHART. With a Map and 16 Illustrations. *Second Edition. Crown 8vo.* 6s.

E. N. Bennett. THE DOWNFALL OF THE DERVISHES: A Sketch of the Sudan Campaign of 1898. By E. N. BENNETT, Fellow of Hertford College. With a Photogravure Portrait of Lord Kitchener. *Third Edition. Crown 8vo.* 3s. 6d.

W. Kinnaird Rose. WITH THE GREEKS IN THESSALY. By W. KINNAIRD ROSE. With Illustrations. *Crown 8vo.* 6s.

G. W. Steevens. NAVAL POLICY: By G. W. STEEVENS. *Demy 8vo.* 6s.

D. Hannay. A SHORT HISTORY OF THE ROYAL NAVY, FROM EARLY TIMES TO THE PRESENT DAY. By DAVID HANNAY. Illustrated. 2 Vols. *Demy 8vo.* 7s. 6d. each. Vol. I., 1200-1688.
'We read it from cover to cover at a sitting, and those who go to it for a lively and brisk picture of the past, with all its faults and its grandeur, will not be disappointed. The historian is endowed with literary skill and style.'—*Standard.*

E. L. S. Horsburgh. WATERLOO: A Narrative and Criticism. By E. L. S. HORSBURGH, M. A. With Plans. *Second Edition. Crown 8vo. 5s.*
'A brilliant essay—simple, sound, and thorough.'—*Daily Chronicle.*

H. B. George. BATTLES OF ENGLISH HISTORY. By H. B. GEORGE, M.A., Fellow of New College, Oxford. With numerous Plans. *Third Edition. Cr. 8vo. 6s.*
'Mr. George has undertaken a very useful task—that of making military affairs intelligible and instructive to non-military readers—and has executed it with a large measure of success.'—*Times.*

General Literature

S. Baring Gould. OLD COUNTRY LIFE. By S. BARING GOULD. With Sixty-seven Illustrations. *Large Cr. 8vo. Fifth Edition. 6s.*
' " Old Country Life," as healthy wholesome reading, full of breezy life and movement, full of quaint stories vigorously told, will not be excelled by any book to be published throughout the year. Sound, hearty, and English to the core.'—*World.*

S. Baring Gould. AN OLD ENGLISH HOME. By S. BARING GOULD. With numerous Plans and Illustrations. *Crown 8vo. 6s.*
'The chapters are delightfully fresh, very informing, and lightened by many a good story. A delightful fireside companion.'—*St. James's Gazette.*

S. Baring Gould. HISTORIC ODDITIES AND STRANGE EVENTS. By S. BARING GOULD. *Fifth Edition. Crown 8vo. 6s.*

S. Baring Gould. FREAKS OF FANATICISM. By S. BARING GOULD. *Third Edition. Cr. 8vo. 6s.*

S. Baring Gould. A GARLAND OF COUNTRY SONG: English Folk Songs with their Traditional Melodies. Collected and arranged by S. BARING GOULD and H. F. SHEPPARD. *Demy 4to. 6s.*

S. Baring Gould. SONGS OF THE WEST: Traditional Ballads and Songs of the West of England, with their Melodies. Collected by S. BARING GOULD, M.A., and H. F. SHEPPARD, M.A. In 4 Parts. *Parts I., II., III., 3s. each. Part IV., 5s. In one Vol., French morocco, 15s.*
'A rich collection of humour, pathos, grace, and poetic fancy.'—*Saturday Review.*

S. Baring Gould. YORKSHIRE ODDITIES AND STRANGE EVENTS. By S. BARING GOULD. *Fifth Edition. Crown 8vo. 6s.*

S. Baring Gould. STRANGE SURVIVALS AND SUPERSTITIONS. By S. BARING GOULD. *Cr. 8vo. Second Edition. 6s.*

Cotton Minchin. OLD HARROW DAYS. By J. G. COTTON MINCHIN. *Cr. 8vo. Second Edition. 5s.*

W. E. Gladstone. THE SPEECHES OF THE RT. HON. W. E. GLADSTONE, M.P. Edited by A. W. HUTTON, M.A., and H. J. COHEN, M.A. With Portraits. *Demy 8vo. Vols. IX. and X., 12s. 6d. each.*

M. N. Oxford. A HANDBOOK OF NURSING. By M. N. OXFORD, of Guy's Hospital. *Crown 8vo. 3s. 6d.*
'The most useful work of the kind that we have seen. A most valuable and practical manual.'—*Manchester Guardian.*

E. V. Zenker. ANARCHISM. By E. V. ZENKER. *Demy 8vo. 7s. 6d.*

A. Silva White. THE EXPANSION OF EGYPT: A Political and Historical Survey. By A. SILVA WHITE. With four Special Maps. *Demy 8vo.* 15s. net.

This is emphatically the best account of Egypt as it is under English control that has been published for many years.'—*Spectator.*

Peter Beckford. THOUGHTS ON HUNTING. By PETER BECKFORD. Edited by J. OTHO PAGET, and Illustrated by G. H. JALLAND. *Demy 8vo.* 10s. 6d.

'Beckford's "Thoughts on Hunting" has long been a classic with sportsmen, and the present edition will go far to make it a favourite with lovers of literature.'—*Speaker.*

E. B. Michell. THE ART AND PRACTICE OF HAWKING. By E. B. MICHELL. With 3 Photogravures by G. E. LODGE, and other Illustrations. *Demy 8vo.* 10s. 6d.

'A book that will help and delight the expert.'—*Scotsman.*
'Just after the hearts of all enthusiasts.'—*Daily Telegraph.*
'No book is more full and authoritative than this handsome treatise.'
—*Morning Leader.*

H. G. Hutchinson. THE GOLFING PILGRIM. By HORACE G. HUTCHINSON. *Crown 8vo.* 6s.

'Without this book the golfer's library will be incomplete.'—*Pall Mall Gazette.*

J. Wells. OXFORD AND OXFORD LIFE. By Members of the University. Edited by J. WELLS, M.A., Fellow and Tutor of Wadham College. *Third Edition. Cr. 8vo.* 3s. 6d.

C. G. Robertson. VOCES ACADEMICÆ. By C. GRANT ROBERTSON, M.A., Fellow of All Souls', Oxford. *With a Frontispiece. Pott 8vo.* 3s. 6d.

Decidedly clever and amusing.'—*Athenæum.*

Rosemary Cotes. DANTE'S GARDEN. By ROSEMARY COTES. With a Frontispiece. *Second Edition. Fcp. 8vo.* 2s. 6d. *Leather,* 3s. 6d. net.

'A charming collection of legends of the flowers mentioned by Dante.'—*Academy.*

Clifford Harrison. READING AND READERS. By CLIFFORD HARRISON. *Fcp. 8vo.* 2s. 6d.

'An extremely sensible little book.'—*Manchester Guardian.*

L. Whibley. GREEK OLIGARCHIES: THEIR ORGANISATION AND CHARACTER. By L. WHIBLEY, M.A., Fellow of Pembroke College, Cambridge. *Crown 8vo.* 6s.

L. L. Price. ECONOMIC SCIENCE AND PRACTICE. By L. L. PRICE, M.A., Fellow of Oriel College, Oxford. *Crown 8vo.* 6s.

J. S. Shedlock. THE PIANOFORTE SONATA: Its Origin and Development. By J. S. SHEDLOCK. *Crown 8vo.* 5s.

'This work should be in the possession of every musician and amateur. A concise and lucid history and a very valuable work for reference.'—*Athenæum.*

A. Hulme Beaman. PONS ASINORUM; OR, A GUIDE TO BRIDGE. By A. HULME BEAMAN. *Fcap 8vo.* 2s.

A practical guide, with many specimen games, to the new game of Bridge.

E. M. Bowden. THE EXAMPLE OF BUDDHA: Being Quotations from Buddhist Literature for each Day in the Year. Compiled by E. M. BOWDEN. *Third Edition. 16mo.* 2s. 6d.

F. Ware. EDUCATIONAL REFORM. By FABIAN WARE, M.A. *Crown 8vo.* 2s. 6d.

Methuen's Sixpenny Library

A New Series of Copyright Books

I. THE MATABELE CAMPAIGN. By Major-General BADEN-POWELL.
II. THE DOWNFALL OF PREM-PEH. By Major-General BADEN-POWELL.
III. MY DANISH SWEETHEART. By W. CLARK RUSSELL.
IV. IN THE ROAR OF THE SEA. By S. BARING-GOULD.
V. PEGGY OF THE BARTONS. By B. M. CROKER.
VI. IN THE MIDST OF ALARMS. By ROBERT BARR.
VII. BADEN-POWELL OF MAFE-KING: A Biography. By J. S. FLETCHER.
VIII. ROBERTS OF PRETORIA. By J. S. FLETCHER.

Philosophy

L. T. Hobhouse. THE THEORY OF KNOWLEDGE. By L. T. HOBHOUSE, Fellow of C.C.C., Oxford. *Demy 8vo.* 21s.
'The most important contribution to English philosophy since the publication of Mr. Bradley's "Appearance and Reality."'—*Glasgow Herald.*

W. H. Fairbrother. THE PHILOSOPHY OF T. H. GREEN. By W. H. FAIRBROTHER, M.A. *Second Edition. Cr. 8vo.* 3s. 6d.

'In every way an admirable book.'— *Glasgow Herald.*

F. W. Bussell. THE SCHOOL OF PLATO. By F. W. BUSSELL, D.D., Fellow of Brasenose College, Oxford. *Demy 8vo.* 10s. 6d.

F. S. Granger. THE WORSHIP OF THE ROMANS. By F. S. GRANGER, M.A., Litt.D. *Crown 8vo.* 6s.

Science

W. C. C. Pakes. THE SCIENCE OF HYGIENE. By W. C. C. PAKES. With numerous Illustrations. *Demy 8vo.* 15s.
'A thoroughgoing working text-book of its subject, practical and well-stocked.' —*Scotsman.*

A. T. Hare. THE CONSTRUCTION OF LARGE INDUCTION COILS. By A. T. HARE, M.A. With numerous Diagrams. *Demy 8vo.* 6s.

J. E. Marr. THE SCIENTIFIC STUDY OF SCENERY. By J. E. MARR, F.R.S., Fellow of St. John's College, Cambridge. Illustrated. *Crown 8vo.* 6s.

'Mr. Marr is distinctly to be congratulated on the general result of his work. He has produced a volume, moderate in size and readable in style, which will be acceptable alike to the student of geology and geography, and to the tourist.' —*Athenæum.*

J. Ritzema Bos. AGRICULTURAL ZOOLOGY. By Dr. J. RITZEMA BOS. Translated by J. R. AINSWORTH DAVIS, M.A. With an Introduction by ELEANOR A. ORMEROD, F.E.S. With 155 Illustrations. *Crown 8vo.* 3s. 6d.

'The illustrations are exceedingly good, whilst the information conveyed is invaluable.'—*Country Gentleman.*

Ed. von Freudenreich. DAIRY BACTERIOLOGY. A Short Manual for the Use of Students. By Dr. ED. VON FREUDENREICH, Translated by J. R. AINSWORTH DAVIS, M.A. *Second Edition, Revised. Crown 8vo.* 2s. 6d.

Chalmers Mitchell. OUTLINES OF BIOLOGY. By P. CHALMERS MITCHELL, M.A. *Illustrated. Cr. 8vo.* 6s.

A text-book designed to cover the new Schedule issued by the Royal College of Physicians and Surgeons.

George Massee. A MONOGRAPH OF THE MYXOGASTRES. By GEORGE MASSEE. With 12 Coloured Plates. *Royal 8vo.* 18s. *net.*

'A work much in advance of any book in the language treating of this group of organisms. Indispensable to every student of the Myxogastres.'—*Nature.*

C. Stephenson and F. Suddards. ORNAMENTAL DESIGN FOR WOVEN FABRICS. By C. STEPHENSON, of The Technical College, Bradford, and F. SUDDARDS, of The Yorkshire College, Leeds. With 65 full-page plates. *Demy 8vo. Second Edition.* 7s. 6d.

'The book is very ably done, displaying an intimate knowledge of principles, good taste, and the faculty of clear exposition.'—*Yorkshire Post.*

C. C. Channer and M. E. Roberts. LACE-MAKING IN THE MIDLANDS, PAST AND PRESENT. By C. C. CHANNER and M. E. ROBERTS. With 16 full-page Illustrations. *Crown 8vo.* 2s. 6d.

'An interesting book, illustrated by fascinating photographs.'—*Speaker.*

Theology

W. R. Inge. CHRISTIAN MYSTICISM. The Bampton Lectures for 1899. By W. R. INGE, M.A., Fellow and Tutor of Hertford College, Oxford. *Demy 8vo.* 12s. 6d. *net.*
'It is fully worthy of the best traditions connected with the Bampton Lectureship.'—*Record.*

S. R. Driver. SERMONS ON SUBJECTS CONNECTED WITH THE OLD TESTAMENT. By S. R. DRIVER, D.D., Canon of Christ Church, Regius Professor of Hebrew in the University of Oxford. *Cr. 8vo.* 6s.
'A welcome companion to the author's famous "Introduction."'—*Guardian.*

T. K. Cheyne. FOUNDERS OF OLD TESTAMENT CRITICISM. By T. K. CHEYNE, D.D., Oriel Professor at Oxford. *Large Crown 8vo.* 7s. 6d.

A historical sketch of O. T. Criticism.

Walter Lock. ST. PAUL, THE MASTER-BUILDER. By WALTER LOCK, D.D., Warden of Keble College. *Crown 8vo.* 3s. 6d.

'The essence of the Pauline teaching is condensed into little more than a hundred pages, yet no point of importance is overlooked. We gladly recommend the lectures to all who wish to read with understanding.'—*Guardian.*

F. S. Granger. THE SOUL OF A CHRISTIAN. By F. S. GRANGER, M.A., Litt.D. *Crown 8vo. 6s.*
A book dealing with the evolution of the religious life and experiences.
'A remarkable book.'—*Glasgow Herald.*
'Both a scholarly and thoughtful book.'—*Scotsman.*

H. Rashdall. DOCTRINE AND DEVELOPMENT. By HASTINGS RASHDALL, M.A., Fellow and Tutor of New College, Oxford. *Cr. 8vo. 6s.*

H. H. Henson. APOSTOLIC CHRISTIANITY: As Illustrated by the Epistles of St. Paul to the Corinthians. By H. H. HENSON, M.A., Fellow of All Souls', Oxford, Canon of Westminster. *Cr. 8vo. 6s.*

H. H. Henson. DISCIPLINE AND LAW. By H. HENSLEY HENSON, B.D., Fellow of All Souls', Oxford. *Fcap. 8vo. 2s. 6d.*

H. H. Henson. LIGHT AND LEAVEN : HISTORICAL AND SOCIAL SERMONS. By H. H. HENSON, M.A. *Crown 8vo. 6s.*

J. Houghton Kennedy. ST. PAUL'S SECOND AND THIRD EPISTLES TO THE CORINTHIANS. With Introduction, Dissertations, and Notes, by JAMES HOUGHTON KENNEDY, D.D., Assistant Lecturer in Divinity in the University of Dublin. *Crown 8vo. 6s.*

Bennett and Adeney. A BIBLICAL INTRODUCTION. By W. H. BENNETT, M.A., and W. F. ADENEY, M.A. *Crown 8vo. 7s. 6d.*
'It makes available to the ordinary reader the best scholarship of the day in the field of Biblical introduction. We know of no book which comes into competition with it.'—*Manchester Guardian.*

W. H. Bennett. A PRIMER OF THE BIBLE. By W. H. BENNETT. *Second Edition. Cr. 8vo. 2s. 6d.*
'The work of an honest, fearless, and sound critic, and an excellent guide in a small compass to the books of the Bible.'—*Manchester Guardian.*

C. F. G. Masterman. TENNYSON AS A RELIGIOUS TEACHER. By C. F. G. MASTERMAN. *Crown 8vo. 6s.*
'A thoughtful and penetrating appreciation, full of interest and suggestion '—*World.*

William Harrison. CLOVELLY SERMONS. By WILLIAM HARRISON, M.A., late Rector of Clovelly. With a Preface by 'LUCAS MALET.' *Cr. 8vo. 3s. 6d.*

Cecilia Robinson. THE MINISTRY OF DEACONESSES. By Deaconness CECILIA ROBINSON. With an Introduction by the Lord Bishop of Winchester. *Cr. 8vo. 3s. 6d.*
'A learned and interesting book.'—*Scotsman.*

E. B. Layard. RELIGION IN BOYHOOD. Notes on the Religious Training of Boys. By E. B. LAYARD, M.A. *18mo. 1s.*

T. Herbert Bindley. THE OECUMENICAL DOCUMENTS OF THE FAITH. Edited with Introductions and Notes by T. HERBERT BINDLEY, B.D., Merton College, Oxford. *Crown 8vo. 6s.*
A historical account of the Creeds.
'Mr. Bindley has done his work in a fashion which calls for our warmest gratitude. The introductions, though brief, are always direct and to the point ; the notes are learned and full, an i serve admirably to elucidate the man; difficulties of the text.'—*Guardian.*

H. M. Barron. TEXTS FOR SERMONS ON VARIOUS OCCASIONS AND SUBJECTS. Compiled and Arranged by H. M. BARRON, B.A., of Wadham College, Oxford, with a Preface by Canon SCOTT HOLLAND. *Crown 8vo. 3s. 6d.*

W. Yorke Fausset. THE *DE CATECHIZANDIS RUDIBUS* OF ST. AUGUSTINE. Edited, with Introduction, Notes, etc., by W. YORKE FAUSSET, M.A. *Cr. 8vo. 3s. 6d.*

F. Weston. THE HOLY SACRIFICE. By F. WESTON, M.A., Curate of St. Matthew's, Westminster. *Pott 8vo. 6d. net.*

À Kempis. THE IMITATION OF CHRIST. By THOMAS À KEMPIS. With an Introduction by DEAN FARRAR. Illustrated by C. M. GERE. *Second Edition. Fcap. 8vo. 3s. 6d. Padded morocco, 5s.*
'Amongst all the innumerable English

editions of the "Imitation," there can have been few which were prettier than this one, printed in strong and handsome type, with all the glory of red initials.'—*Glasgow Herald.*

J. Keble. THE CHRISTIAN YEAR. By JOHN KEBLE. With an Intro-

duction and Notes by W. LOCK, D.D., Warden of Keble College. Illustrated by R. ANNING BELL. *Second Edition. Fcap. 8vo. 3s. 6d. Padded morocco.* 5s.

'The present edition is annotated with all the care and insight to be expected from Mr. Lock.'—*Guardian.*

©xforö Commentaries

General Editor, WALTER LOCK, D.D., Warden of Keble College, Dean Ireland's Professor of Exegesis in the University of Oxford.

THE BOOK OF JOB. Edited, with Introduction and Notes, by E. C. S. GIBSON, D.D., Vicar of Leeds. *Demy 8vo. 6s.*

'The publishers are to be congratulated on the start the series has made.'—*Times.*
'It is in his patient, lucid, interest-sustaining explanations that Dr. Gibson is at his best.'—*Literature.*
'We can hardly imagine a more useful book to place in the hands of an intelligent layman, or cleric, who desires to eluci-

date some of the difficulties presented in the Book of Job.'—*Church Times.*
'The work is marked by clearness, lightness of touch, strong common sense, and thorough critical fairness.
'Dr. Gibson's work is worthy of a high degree of appreciation. To the busy worker and the intelligent student the commentary will be a real boon ; and it will, if we are not mistaken, be much in demand. The Introduction is almost a model of concise, straightforward, prefatory remarks on the subject treated.'—*Athenæum.*

Ibanöbooks of ßbeologg

General Editor, A. ROBERTSON, D.D., Principal of King's College, London.

THE XXXIX. ARTICLES OF THE CHURCH OF ENGLAND. Edited with an Introduction by E. C. S. GIBSON, D.D., Vicar of Leeds, late Principal of Wells Theological College. *Second and Cheaper Edition in One Volume. Demy 8vo. 12s. 6d.*

'We welcome with the utmost satisfaction a new, cheaper, and more convenient edition of Dr. Gibson's book. It was greatly wanted. Dr. Gibson has given theological students just what they want, and we should like to think that it was in the hands of every candidate for orders.'—*Guardian.*

AN INTRODUCTION TO THE HISTORY OF RELIGION. By F. B. JEVONS, M.A., Litt.D., Principal of Bishop Hatfield's Hall. *Demy 8vo. 10s. 6d.*

'The merit of this book lies in the penetration, the singular acuteness and force of the author's judgment. He is at once

critical and luminous, at once just and suggestive. A comprehensive and thorough book.'—*Birmingham Post.*

THE DOCTRINE OF THE INCARNATION. By R. L. OTTLEY, M.A., late fellow of Magdalen College, Oxon., and Principal of Pusey House. *In Two Volumes. Demy 8vo. 15s.*

'A clear and remarkably full account of the main currents of speculation. Scholarly precision . . . genuine tolerance . . . intense interest in his subject—are Mr. Ottley's merits.'—*Guardian.*

AN INTRODUCTION TO THE HISTORY OF THE CREEDS. By A. E. BURN, B.D., Examining Chaplain to the Bishop of Lichfield. *Demy 8vo. 10s. 6d.*

'This book may be expected to hold its place as an authority on its subject.'—*Spectator.*

The Churchman's Library

General Editor, J. H. BURN, B.D., Examining Chaplain to the
Bishop of Aberdeen.

THE BEGINNINGS OF ENGLISH CHRISTIANITY. By W. E. COLLINS, M.A. With Map. *Cr. 8vo.* 3s. 6d.

'An excellent example of thorough and fresh historical work.'—*Guardian.*

SOME NEW TESTAMENT PROBLEMS. By ARTHUR WRIGHT, M.A., Fellow of Queen's College, Cambridge. *Crown 8vo.* 6s.

'Real students will revel in these reverent, acute, and pregnant essays in Biblical scholarship.'—*Great Thoughts.*

THE KINGDOM OF HEAVEN HERE AND HEREAFTER. By CANON WINTERBOTHAM, M.A., B.Sc., LL.B. *Cr. 8vo.* 3s. 6d.

'A most able book, at once exceedingly thoughtful and richly suggestive.'—*Glasgow Herald.*

THE WORKMANSHIP OF THE PRAYER BOOK: Its Literary and Liturgical Aspects. By J. DOWDEN, D.D., Lord Bishop of Edinburgh. *Crown 8vo.* 3s. 6d.

'Scholarly and interesting.'—*Manchester Guardian.*

EVOLUTION. By F. B. JEVONS, Litt.D., Principal of Hatfield Hall, Durham. *Crown 8vo.* 3s. 6d.

'A well-written book, full of sound thinking happily expressed.'—*Manchester Guardian.*

The Churchman's Bible

General Editor, J. H. BURN, D.D.

Messrs. METHUEN are issuing a series of expositions upon most of the books of the Bible. The volumes will be practical and devotional, and the text of the authorised version is explained in sections, which will correspond as far as possible with the Church Lectionary.

THE EPISTLE OF ST. PAUL TO THE GALATIANS. Explained by A. W. ROBINSON, Vicar of All Hallows, Barking. *Fcap. 8vo.* 1s. 6d. net.

'The most attractive, sensible, and instructive manual for people at large, which we have ever seen.'—*Church Gazette.*

ECCLESIASTES. Explained by A. W. STREANE, D.D. *Fcap. 8vo.* 1s. 6d. net.

'Scholarly, suggestive, and particularly interesting.'—*Bookman.*

THE EPISTLE OF PAUL THE APOSTLE TO THE PHILIPPIANS. Explained by C. R. D. BIGGS, B.D. *Fcap. 8vo.* 1s. 6d. net.

'Mr. Biggs' work is very thorough, and he has managed to compress a good deal of information into a limited space.' —*Guardian.*

The Library of Devotion

Pott 8vo, cloth, 2s.; leather, 2s. 6d. net.

'This series is excellent.'—THE BISHOP OF LONDON.
'Very delightful.'—THE BISHOP OF BATH AND WELLS.
'Well worth the attention of the Clergy.'—THE BISHOP OF LICHFIELD.
'The new " Library of Devotion " is excellent.'—THE BISHOP OF PETERBOROUGH.
'Charming.'—*Record.*   'Delightful.'—*Church Bells.*

THE CONFESSIONS OF ST. AUGUSTINE. Newly Translated, with an Introduction and Notes, by C. BIGG, D.D., late Student of Christ Church. *Third Edition.*

'The translation is an excellent piece of English, and the introduction is a masterly exposition. We augur well of a series which begins so satisfactorily.'—*Times.*

THE CHRISTIAN YEAR. By JOHN KEBLE. With Introduction and Notes by WALTER LOCK, D.D., Warden of Keble College, Ireland Professor at Oxford.

'The volume is very prettily bound and printed, and may fairly claim to be an advance on any previous editions.'— *Guardian.*

THE IMITATION OF CHRIST. A Revised Translation, with an Introduction, by C. BIGG, D.D., late Student of Christ Church. *Second Edition.*

A practically new translation of this book, which the reader has, almost for the first time, exactly in the shape in which it left the hands of the author.

'A nearer approach to the original than has yet existed in English.'—*Academy.*

A BOOK OF DEVOTIONS. By J. W. STANBRIDGE, B.D., Rector of Bainton, Canon of York, and sometime Fellow of St. John's College, Oxford.

'It is probably the best book of its kind. It deserves high commendation.'—*Church Gazette.*

LYRA INNOCENTIUM. By JOHN KEBLE. Edited, with Introduction and Notes, by WALTER LOCK, D.D., Warden of Keble College, Oxford.

'This sweet and fragrant book has never been published more attractively.'— *Academy.*

A SERIOUS CALL TO A DEVOUT AND HOLY LIFE. By WILLIAM LAW. Edited, with an Introduction, by C. BIGG, D.D., late Student of Christ Church.

This is a reprint, word for word and line for line, of the *Editio Princeps.*

THE TEMPLE. By GEORGE HERBERT. Edited, with an Introduction and Notes, by E. C. S. GIBSON, D.D., Vicar of Leeds.

This edition contains Walton's Life of Herbert, and the text is that of the first edition.

A GUIDE TO ETERNITY. By Cardinal BONA. Edited, with an Introduction and Notes, by J. W. STANBRIDGE, B.D., late Fellow of St. John's College, Oxford.

Leaders of Religion

Edited by H. C. BEECHING, M.A. *With Portraits, Crown 8vo. 3s. 6d.*

A series of short biographies of the most prominent leaders of religious life and thought of all ages and countries.

The following are ready—

CARDINAL NEWMAN. By R. H. HUTTON.

JOHN WESLEY. By J. H. OVERTON, M.A.

BISHOP WILBERFORCE. By G. W. DANIELL, M.A.

CARDINAL MANNING. By A. W. HUTTON, M.A.

CHARLES SIMEON. By H. C. G. MOULE, D.D.

JOHN KEBLE. By WALTER LOCK, D.D.

THOMAS CHALMERS. By Mrs. OLIPHANT.

LANCELOT ANDREWES. By R. L. OTTLEY, M.A.

AUGUSTINE OF CANTERBURY. By E. L. CUTTS, D.D.

WILLIAM LAUD. By W. H. HUTTON, B.D.

JOHN KNOX. By F. MacCUNN.

JOHN HOWE. By R. F. HORTON, D.D.

BISHOP KEN. By F. A. CLARKE, M.A.

GEORGE FOX, THE QUAKER. By T. HODGKIN, D.C.L.

JOHN DONNE. By AUGUSTUS JESSOPP, D.D.

THOMAS CRANMER. By. A. J. MASON.

BISHOP LATIMER. By R. M. CARLYLE and A. J. CARLYLE, M.A.

Other volumes will be announced in due course.

•

Fiction

Marie Corelli's Novels

Crown 8vo. 6s. each.

A ROMANCE OF TWO WORLDS.
Twenty-first Edition.

VENDETTA. *Sixteenth Edition.*

THELMA. *Twenty-Fourth Edition.*

ARDATH: THE STORY OF A
DEAD SELF. *Twelfth Edition.*

THE SOUL OF LILITH. *Tenth
Edition.*

WORMWOOD. *Tenth Edition.*

BARABBAS: A DREAM OF THE
WORLD'S TRAGEDY. *Thirty-
sixth Edition.*
'The tender reverence of the treatment
and the imaginative beauty of the writing have reconciled us to the daring of
the conception, and the conviction is
forced on us that even so exalted a subject cannot be made too familiar to us,
provided it be presented in the true spirit
of Christian faith. The amplifications
of the Scripture narrative are often conceived with high poetic insight, and this
"Dream of the World's Tragedy" is
a lofty and not inadequate paraphrase
of the supreme climax of the inspired
narrative.'—*Dublin Review.*

THE SORROWS OF SATAN.
Forty-third Edition.
'A very powerful piece of work. . . . The

conception is magnificent, and is likely
to win an abiding place within the
memory of man. . . . The author has
immense command of language, and a
limitless audacity. . . . This interesting
and remarkable romance will live long
after much of the ephemeral literature
of the day is forgotten. . . . A literary
phenomenon . . . novel, and even sub-
lime.'—W. T. STEAD in the *Review
of Reviews.*

THE MASTER CHRISTIAN.
[*150th Thousand.*
'It cannot be denied that "The Master
Christian" is a powerful book ; that it is
one likely to raise uncomfortable questions in all but the most self-satisfied
readers, and that it strikes at the root
of the failure of the Churches—the decay
of faith—in a manner which shows the
inevitable disaster heaping up . . . The
good Cardinal Bonpré is a beautiful
figure, fit to stand beside the good
Bishop in "Les Misérables" . . . The
chapter in which the Cardinal appears
with Manuel before Leo XIII. is char-
acterised by extraordinary realism and
dramatic intensity . . . It is a book with
a serious purpose expressed with absolute unconventionality and passion . . .
And this is to say it is a book worth
reading.'—*Examiner.*

Anthony Hope's Novels

Crown 8vo. 6s. each.

THE GOD IN THE CAR. *Ninth
Edition.*
'A very remarkable book, deserving of
critical analysis impossible within our
limit ; brilliant, but not superficial ;
well considered, but not elaborated ;
constructed with the proverbial art that
conceals, but yet allows itself to be
enjoyed by readers to whom fine literary
method is a keen pleasure.'— *The World.*

A CHANGE OF AIR. *Sixth Edition.*
'A graceful, vivacious comedy, true to
human nature. The characters are
traced with a masterly hand.'—*Times.*

A MAN OF MARK. *Fifth Edition.*
'Of all Mr. Hope's books, "A Man of
Mark" is the one which best compares
with "The Prisoner of Zenda."'—
National Observer.

THE CHRONICLES OF COUNT
ANTONIO. *Fourth Edition.*
'It is a perfectly enchanting story of love
and chivalry, and pure romance. The
Count is the most constant, desperate,
and modest and tender of lovers, a peer-
less gentleman, an intrepid fighter, a
faithful friend, and a magnanimous foe.'
—*Guardian.*

PHROSO. Illustrated by H. R. MILLAR. *Fifth Edition.*
'The tale is thoroughly fresh, quick with vitality, stirring the blood.'—*St. James's Gazette.*
'From cover to cover "Phroso" not only engages the attention, but carries the reader in little whirls of delight from adventure to adventure.'—*Academy.*

SIMON DALE. Illustrated. *Fifth Edition.*
'There is searching analysis of human nature, with a most ingeniously constructed plot. Mr. Hope has drawn the contrasts of his women with marvellous subtlety and delicacy.'—*Times.*

THE KING'S MIRROR. *Third Edition.*
'In elegance, delicacy, and tact it ranks with the best of his novels, while in the wide range of its portraiture and the subtilty of its analysis it surpasses all his earlier ventures.'—*Spectator.*
'"The King's Mirror" is a strong book, charged with close analysis and exquisite irony; a book full of pathos and moral fibre—in short, a book to be read.'—*Daily Chronicle.*

QUISANTE. *Third Edition.*
'The book is notable for a very high literary quality, and an impress of power and mastery on every page.'—*Daily Chronicle.*

Gilbert Parker's Novels

Crown 8vo. 6s. each.

PIERRE AND HIS PEOPLE. *Fifth Edition.*
'Stories happily conceived and finely executed. There is strength and genius in Mr. Parker's style.'—*Daily Telegraph.*

MRS. FALCHION. *Fourth Edition.*
'A splendid study of character.'— *Athenæum.*

THE TRANSLATION OF A SAVAGE.
'The plot is original and one difficult to work out; but Mr. Parker has done it with great skill and delicacy.' —*Daily Chronicle.*

THE TRAIL OF THE SWORD. Illustrated. *Seventh Edition.*
'A rousing and dramatic tale. A book like this, in which swords flash, great surprises are undertaken, and daring deeds done, in which men and women live and love in the old passionate way, is a joy inexpressible.'—*Daily Chronicle.*

WHEN VALMOND CAME TO PONTIAC: The Story of a Lost Napoleon. *Fifth Edition.*
'Here we find romance—real, breathing, living romance. The character of Valmond is drawn unerringly.'—*Pall Mall Gazette.*

AN ADVENTURER OF THE NORTH: The Last Adventures of 'Pretty Pierre.' *Second Edition.*
'The present book is full of fine and moving stories of the great North, and it will add to Mr. Parker's already high reputation.'—*Glasgow Herald.*

THE SEATS OF THE MIGHTY. Illustrated. *Eleventh Edition.*
Mr. Parker has produced a really fine historical novel.'—*Athenæum.*
'A great book.'—*Black and White.*

THE POMP OF THE LAVILET-TES. *Second Edition.* 3s. 6d.
'Living, breathing romance, unforced pathos, and a deeper knowledge of human nature than Mr. Parker has ever displayed before.'—*Pall Mall Gazette.*

THE BATTLE OF THE STRONG: a Romance of Two Kingdoms. Illustrated. *Fourth Edition.*
'Nothing more vigorous or more human has come from Mr. Gilbert Parker than this novel. It has all the graphic power of his last book, with truer feeling for the romance, both of human life and wild nature.'—*Literature.*

S. Baring Gould's Novels

Crown 8vo.   6s. each.

'To say that a book is by the author of "Mehalah" is to imply that it contains a story cast on strong lines, containing dramatic possibilities, vivid and sympathetic descriptions of Nature, and a wealth of ingenious imagery.'—*Speaker.*

'That whatever Mr. Baring Gould writes is well worth reading, is a conclusion that may be very generally accepted. His views of life are fresh and vigorous, his language pointed and characteristic, the incidents of which he makes use are striking and original, his characters are life-like, and though somewhat exceptional people, are drawn and coloured with artistic force. Add to this that his descriptions of scenes and scenery are painted with the loving eyes and skilled hands of a master of his art, that he is always fresh and never dull, and it is no wonder that readers have gained confidence in his power of amusing and satisfying them, and that year by year his popularity widens.'— *Court Circular.*

ARMINELL.   *Fifth Edition.*

URITH.   *Fifth Edition.*

IN THE ROAR OF THE SEA. *Seventh Edition.*

MRS. CURGENVEN OF CURGEN- VEN.   *Fourth Edition.*

CHEAP JACK ZITA. *Fourth Edition.*

THE QUEEN OF LOVE.   *Fifth Edition.*

MARGERY OF QUETHER. *Third Edition.*

JACQUETTA.   *Third Edition.*

KITTY ALONE.   *Fifth Edition.*

NOÉMI. Illustrated. *Fourth Edition.*

THE BROOM-SQUIRE.   Illustrated. *Fourth Edition.*

THE PENNYCOMEQUICKS. *Third Edition.*

DARTMOOR IDYLLS.

GUAVAS THE TINNER.   Illus- trated. *Second Edition.*

BLADYS. Illustrated. *Second Edition.*

DOMITIA. Illustrated. *Second Edition.*

PABO THE PRIEST.

WINEFRED.   Illustrated.   *Second Edition.*

' A telling picture and a capital story.'— *Times.*

' Fine realism.'—*Birmingham Post.*

Conan Doyle. ROUND THE RED LAMP. By A. CONAN DOYLE. *Seventh Edition. Crown 8vo. 6s.*

'The book is far and away the best view that has been vouchsafed us behind the scenes of the consulting-room.'—*Illustrated London News.*

Stanley Weyman. UNDER THE RED ROBE. By STANLEY WEY- MAN, Author of 'A Gentleman of France.' With Illustrations by R. C. WOODVILLE.   *Fifteenth Edition. Crown 8vo. 6s.*

'Every one who reads books at all must read this thrilling romance, from the first page of which to the last the breath- less reader is haled along. An inspira- tion of manliness and courage.'—*Daily Chronicle.*

Lucas Malet. THE WAGES OF SIN. By LUCAS MALET. *Thir- teenth Edition. Crown 8vo. 6s.*

Lucas Malet. THE CARISSIMA. By LUCAS MALET, Author of ' The Wages of Sin,' etc. *Third Edition. Crown 8vo. 6s.*

Lucas Malet.   THE GATELESS BARRIER.   By LUCAS MALET, Author of 'The Wages of Sin.' *Third Edition. Crown 8vo. 6s.*

' The story is told with a sense of style and a dramatic vigour that makes it a pleasure to read. The workmanship arouses en- thusiasm.'—*Times.*

' The story expresses admirably some true aspects of the spiritual life as we know it on this side of the barrier with singular grace of charm.'—*Pilot.*

W. W. Jacobs. A MASTER OF CRAFT. By W. W. JACOBS, Author of 'Many Cargoes.' Illustrated. *Second Edition. Crown 8vo. 6s.*
'Can be unreservedly recommended to all who have not lost their appetite for wholesome laughter.'—*Spectator.*
'The best humorous book published for many a day.'—*Black and White.*

George Gissing. THE TOWN TRAVELLER. By GEORGE GISSING, Author of 'Demos,' 'In the Year of Jubilee,' etc. *Second Edition. Cr. 8vo. 6s.*
'It is a bright and witty book above all things. Polly Sparkes is a splendid bit of work.'—*Pall Mall Gazette.*
"The spirit of Dickens is in it.'—*Bookman.*

George Gissing. THE CROWN OF LIFE. By GEORGE GISSING, Author of 'Demos,' 'The Town Traveller,' etc. *Crown 8vo. 6s.*
'Mr. Gissing is at his best.'—*Academy.*
'A fine novel.'—*Outlook.*

Henry James. THE SOFT SIDE. By HENRY JAMES, Author of 'What Maisie Knew.' *Second Edition. Crown 8vo. 6s.*
'The amazing cleverness marks the great worker.'—*Speaker.*
'The workmanship is simply wonderful. There is amusement, delight, surprise, and admiration.'—*Illustrated London News.*

S. R. Crockett. LOCHINVAR. By S. R. CROCKETT, Author of 'The Raiders,' etc. Illustrated. *Second Edition. Crown 8vo. 6s.*
'Full of gallantry and pathos, of the clash of arms, and brightened by episodes of humour and love. . . .'—*Westminster Gazette.*

S. R. Crockett. THE STANDARD BEARER. By S. R. CROCKETT. *Crown 8vo. 6s.*
'A delightful tale.'—*Speaker.*
'Mr. Crockett at his best.'—*Literature.*

Arthur Morrison. TALES OF MEAN STREETS. By ARTHUR MORRISON. *Fifth Edition. Cr. 8vo. 6s.*
'Told with consummate art and extraordinary detail. In the true humanity of the book lies its justification, the permanence of its interest, and its indubitable triumph.'—*Athenæum.*

'A great book. The author's method is amazingly effective, and produces a thrilling sense of reality. The writer lays upon us a master hand. The book is simply appalling and irresistible in its interest. It is humorous also; without humour it would not make the mark it is certain to make.'—*World.*

Arthur Morrison. A CHILD OF THE JAGO. By ARTHUR MORRISON. *Third Edition. Cr. 8vo. 6s.*
'The book is a masterpiece.'—*Pall Mall Gazette.*
'Told with great vigour and powerful simplicity.'—*Athenæum.*

Arthur Morrison. TO LONDON TOWN. By ARTHUR MORRISON, Author of 'Tales of Mean Streets,' etc. *Second Edition. Crown 8vo. 6s.*
'We have idyllic pictures, woodland scenes full of tenderness and grace. . . . This is the new Mr. Arthur Morrison gracious and tender, sympathetic and human.'—*Daily Telegraph.*

Arthur Morrison. CUNNING MURRELL. By ARTHUR MORRISON, Author of 'A Child of the Jago,' etc. *Crown 8vo. 6s.*
'The plot hangs admirably. The dialogue is perfect.'—*Daily Mail.*
'Admirable. . . . Delightful humorous relief . . . a most artistic and satisfactory achievement.'—*Spectator.*

Max Pemberton. THE FOOTSTEPS OF A THRONE. By MAX PEMBERTON. Illustrated. *Second Edition. Crown 8vo. 6s.*
'Full of original incident.'—*Scotsman.*
'A story of pure adventure, with a sensation on every page.'—*Daily Mail.*

M. Sutherland. ONE HOUR AND THE NEXT. By THE DUCHESS OF SUTHERLAND. *Third Edition. Crown 8vo. 6s.*
'Passionate, vivid, dramatic.'—*Literature.*
'It possesses marked qualities, descriptive, and imaginative.'—*Morning Post.*

Mrs. Clifford. A FLASH OF SUMMER. By Mrs. W. K. CLIFFORD, Author of 'Aunt Anne,' etc. *Second Edition. Crown 8vo. 6s.*
'The story is a very beautiful one, exquisitely told.'—*Speaker.*

Emily Lawless. HURRISH. By the Honble. EMILY LAWLESS, Author of 'Maelcho,' etc. *Fifth Edition. Cr. 8vo. 6s.*

Emily Lawless. MAELCHO : a Sixteenth Century Romance. By the Honble. EMILY LAWLESS. *Second Edition. Crown 8vo. 6s.*
'A really great book.'—*Spectator.*
'One of the most remarkable literary achievements of this generation.'—*Manchester Guardian.*

Emily Lawless. TRAITS AND CONFIDENCES. By the Honble. EMILY LAWLESS. *Crown 8vo. 6s.*

Eden Phillpotts. LYING PROPHETS. By EDEN PHILLPOTTS. *Crown vo. 6s.*

Eden Phillpotts. CHILDREN OF THE MIST. By EDEN PHILLPOTTS. *Crown 8vo. 6s.*

Eden Phillpotts. THE HUMAN BOY. By EDEN PHILLPOTTS, Author of 'Children of the Mist.' With a Frontispiece. *Fourth Edition. Crown 8vo. 6s.*
'Mr. Phillpotts knows exactly what schoolboys do, and can lay bare their inmost thoughts; likewise he shows an all-pervading sense of humour.'—*Academy.*

Eden Phillpotts. SONS OF THE MORNING. By EDEN PHILLPOTTS, Author of 'The Children of the Mist.' *Second Edition. Crown 8vo. 6s.*
'A book of strange power and fascination.' —*Morning Post.*
'Full of charm.'—*Manchester Guardian.*
'A vivid style and a powerful grasp.'— *Athenæum.*
'Inimitable humour.'—*Daily Graphic.*

Jane Barlow. A CREEL OF IRISH STORIES. By JANE BARLOW, Author of 'Irish Idylls.' *Second Edition. Crown 8vo. 6s.*
'Vivid and singularly real.'—*Scotsman.*

Jane Barlow. FROM THE EAST UNTO THE WEST. By JANE BARLOW. *Crown 8vo. 6s.*

Mrs. Caffyn. ANNE MAULEVERER. By Mrs. CAFFYN (Iota), Author of 'The Yellow Aster.' *Second Edition. Crown 8vo. 6s.*

Benjamin Swift. SIREN CITY. By BENJAMIN SWIFT, Author of 'Nancy Noon.' *Crown 8vo. 6s.*

J. H. Findlater. THE GREEN GRAVES OF BALGOWRIE. By

JANE H. FINDLATER. *Fourth Edition. Crown 8vo. 6s.*
'A powerful and vivid story.'—*Standard.*
'A beautiful story, sad and strange as truth itself.'—*Vanity Fair.*
'A very charming and pathetic tale.'—*Pall Mall Gazette.*
'A singularly original, clever, and beautiful story.'—*Guardian.*
'Reveals to us a new writer of undoubted faculty and reserve force.'—*Spectator.*
'An exquisite idyll, delicate, affecting, and beautiful.'—*Black and White.*

J. H. Findlater. A DAUGHTER OF STRIFE. By JANE HELEN FINDLATER. *Crown 8vo. 6s.*

J. H. Findlater. RACHEL. By JANE H. FINDLATER. *Second Edition. Crown 8vo. 6s.*
'A not unworthy successor to "The Green Graves of Balgowrie."'—*Critic.*

Mary Findlater. OVER THE HILLS. By MARY FINDLATER. *Second Edition. Cr. 8vo. 6s.*
'A strong and wise book of deep insight and unflinching truth.'—*Birmingham Post.*

Mary Findlater. BETTY MUSGRAVE. By MARY FINDLATER. *Second Edition. Crown 8vo. 6s.*
'Handled with dignity and delicacy. . . . A most touching story.'—*Spectator.*

Alfred Ollivant. OWD BOB, THE GREY DOG OF KENMUIR. By ALFRED OLLIVANT. *Fourth Edition. Cr. 8vo. 6s.*
'Weird, thrilling, strikingly graphic.'— *Punch.*
'We admire this book. . . . It is one to read with admiration and to praise with enthusiasm.'—*Bookman.*
'It is a fine, open-air, blood-stirring book, to be enjoyed by every man and woman to whom a dog is dear.'—*Literature.*

B. M. Croker. PEGGY OF THE BARTONS. By B. M. CROKER, Author of 'Diana Barrington.' *Fourth Edition. Crown 8vo. 6s.*
'Mrs. Croker excels in the admirably simple, easy, and direct flow of her narrative, the briskness of her dialogue, and the geniality of her portraiture.'—*Spectator.*

Mary L. Pendered. AN ENGLISHMAN. By MARY L. PENDERED. *Crown 8vo. 6s.*

Morley Roberts. THE PLUN-DERERS. By MORLEY ROBERTS, Author of 'The Colossus,' etc. *Crown 8vo. 6s.*

Violet Hunt. THE HUMAN IN-TEREST. By VIOLET HUNT, Author of 'A Hard Woman,' etc. *Crown 8vo. 6s.*
'Clever observation and unfailing wit.'—*Academy.*
'The insight is keen, the irony is delicate.'—*World.*

H. G. Wells. THE STOLEN BA-CILLUS, and other Stories. By H. G. WELLS. *Second Edition. Crown 8vo. 6s.*
'The impressions of a very striking imagination.'—*Saturday Review.*

H. G. Wells. THE PLATTNER STORY AND OTHERS. By H. G. WELLS. *Second Edition. Cr. 8vo. 6s.*
'Weird and mysterious, they seem to hold the reader as by a magic spell.'—*Scotsman.*

Sara Jeannette Duncan. A VOYAGE OF CONSOLATION. By SARA JEANNETTE DUNCAN, Author of 'An American Girl in London.' Illustrated. *Third Edition. Cr. 8vo. 6s.*
'A most delightfully bright book.'—*Daily Telegraph.*
'The dialogue is full of wit.'—*Globe.*

Sara Jeannette Duncan. THE PATH OF A STAR. By SARA JEANNETTE DUNCAN, Author of 'A Voyage of Consolation.' Illustrated. *Second Edition. Crown 8vo. 6s.*

C. F. Keary. THE JOURNALIST. By C. F. KEARY. *Cr. 8vo. 6s.*

W. E. Norris. MATTHEW AUSTIN. By W. E. NORRIS, Author of 'Mademoiselle de Mersac,' etc. *Fourth Edition. Crown 8vo. 6s.*
'An intellectually satisfactory and morally bracing novel.'—*Daily Telegraph.*

W. E. Norris. HIS GRACE. By W. E. NORRIS. *Third Edition. Cr. 8vo. 6s.*

W. E. Norris. THE DESPOTIC LADY AND OTHERS. By W. E. NORRIS. *Crown 8vo. 6s.*

W. E. Norris. CLARISSA FURIOSA. By W. E. NORRIS. *Cr. 8vo. 6s.*
'As a story it is admirable, as a *jeu d'esprit* it is capital, as a lay sermon studded with gems of wit and wisdom it is a model.'—*The World.*

W. E. Norris. GILES INGILBY. By W. E. NORRIS. Illustrated. *Second Edition. Crown 8vo. 6s.*
'Interesting, wholesome, and charmingly written.'—*Glasgow Herald.*

W. E. Norris. AN OCTAVE. By W. E. NORRIS. *Second Edition. Crown 8vo. 6s.*
'A very perfect exposition of the self-restraint, the perfect knowledge of society and its ways, the delicate sense of humour, which are the main characteristics of this very accomplished author.'—*Country Life.*

W. Clark Russell. MY DANISH SWEETHEART. By W. CLARK RUSSELL. Illustrated. *Fourth Edition. Crown 8vo. 6s.*

Robert Barr. IN THE MIDST OF ALARMS. By ROBERT BARR. *Third Edition. Cr. 8vo. 6s.*
'A book which has abundantly satisfied us by its capital humour.'—*Daily Chronicle.*
'Mr. Barr has achieved a triumph.'—*Pall Mall Gazette.*

Robert Barr. THE MUTABLE MANY. By ROBERT BARR. *Second Edition. Crown 8vo. 6s.*
'Very much the best novel that Mr. Barr has yet given us. There is much insight in it, and much excellent humour.'—*Daily Chronicle.*

Robert Barr. THE COUNTESS TEKLA. By ROBERT BARR. *Third Edition. Crown 8vo. 6s.*
'Of these mediæval romances, which are now gaining ground, "The Countess Tekla" is the very best we have seen. The story is written in clear English, and a picturesque, moving style.'—*Pall Mall Gazette.*

Robert Barr. THE STRONG ARM. By ROBERT BARR, Author of 'The Countess Tekla.' Illustrated. *Second Edition. 8vo. 6s.*
'A collection of tales about German chivalry, knightly deeds, and villainous devices of the Middle Ages, by one of the deftest of story-tellers.'—*Illustrated London News.*

Andrew Balfour. BY STROKE OF SWORD. By A. BALFOUR. Illustrated. *Fourth Edition. Cr. 8vo. 6s.*
'A recital of thrilling interest, told with unflagging vigour.'—*Globe.*

Andrew Balfour. TO ARMS! By ANDREW BALFOUR. Illustrated. *Second Edition. Crown 8vo. 6s.*
'The marvellous perils through which Allan passes are told in powerful and lively fashion.'—*Pall Mall Gazette.*

Andrew Balfour. VENGEANCE IS MINE. By ANDREW BALFOUR, Author of 'By Stroke of Sword.' Illustrated. *Crown 8vo. 6s.*
'A vigorous piece of work, well written, and abounding in stirring incidents.'—*Glasgow Herald.*

J. Maclaren Cobban. THE KING OF ANDAMAN: A Saviour of Society. By J. MACLAREN COBBAN. *Crown 8vo. 6s.*
'An unquestionably interesting book. It contains one character, at least, who has in him the root of immortality.'—*Pall Mall Gazette.*

J. Maclaren Cobban. THE ANGEL OF THE COVENANT. By J. MACLAREN COBBAN. *Cr. 8vo. 6s.*

R. Hichens. BYEWAYS. By ROBERT HICHENS. Author of 'Flames, etc.' *Second Edition. Cr. 8vo. 6s.*
'The work is undeniably that of a man of striking imagination.'—*Daily News.*

R. Hichens. TONGUES OF CONSCIENCE. By ROBERT HICHENS, Author of 'Flames.' *Second Edition. Crown 8vo. 6s.*
'Of a strange haunting quality.'—*Glasgow Herald.*
'Powerfully written.'—*Morning Leader.*
'Highly imaginative.'—*Pall Mall Gazette.*

Stephen Crane. WOUNDS IN THE RAIN. WAR STORIES. By STEPHEN CRANE, Author of 'The Red Badge of Courage.' *Second Edition. Crown 8vo. 6s.*
'A fascinating volume.'—*Spectator.*
'Mr. Crane seldom did better work.'—*Daily Mail.*

J. B. Burton. IN THE DAY OF ADVERSITY. By J. BLOUNDELLE-BURTON. *Second Edition. Cr. 8vo. 6s.*

J. B. Burton. DENOUNCED. By J. BLOUNDELLE-BURTON. *Second Edition. Crown 8vo. 6s.*

J. B. Burton. THE CLASH OF ARMS. By J. BLOUNDELLE-BURTON. *Second Edition. Cr. 8vo. 6s.*

J. B. Burton. ACROSS THE SALT SEAS. By J. BLOUNDELLE-BURTON. *Second Edition. Crown 8vo. 6s.*

J. B. Burton. SERVANTS OF SIN. By J. BLOUNDELLE-BURTON, Author of 'The Clash of Arms.' *Second Edition. Crown 8vo. 6s.*
'Admirably told . . . of quite exceptional merit.'—*Scotsman.*

Dorothea Gerard. THE CONQUEST OF LONDON. By DOROTHEA GERARD, Author of 'Lady Baby.' *Second Edition. Crown 8vo. 6s.*
'Bright and entertaining.'—*Spectator.*
'Highly entertaining and enjoyable.'—*Scotsman.*

Ada Cambridge. PATH AND GOAL. By ADA CAMBRIDGE. *Second Edition Crown 8vo. 6s.*
'Admirably told with a fine sympathy.'—*Scotsman.*

Richard Marsh. THE SEEN AND THE UNSEEN. By RICHARD MARSH, Author of 'The Beetle,' 'Marvels and Mysteries,' etc. *Second Edition. Crown 8vo. 6s.*
'Very clever and highly entertaining.'—*Scotsman.*
'Vivid and exciting stories.'—*Country Life.*

E. H. Strain. ELMSLIE'S DRAGNET. By E. H. STRAIN. *Crown 8vo. 6s.*
'Excellent character-studies.'—*Outlook.*

Mrs. Penny. A FOREST OFFICER. By Mrs. PENNY. *Crown 8vo. 6s.*
A story of jungle life in India.
'Most fresh and original—delightful reading.'—*Graphic.*
'A vivid and exciting tale of adventure.'—*Review of the Week.*

W. C. Scully. THE WHITE HECATOMB. By W. C. SCULLY, Author of 'Kafir Stories.' *Cr. 8vo. 6s.*
'Reveals a marvellously intimate understanding of the Kaffir mind.'—*African Critic.*

W. C. Scully. BETWEEN SUN AND SAND. By W. C. SCULLY, Author of 'The White Hecatomb.' *Cr. 8vo. 6s.*

SIR ROBERT'S FORTUNE. By Mrs. OLIPHANT.

THE TWO MARYS. By Mrs. OLIPHANT.

THE LADY'S WALK. By Mrs. OLIPHANT.

MIRRY-ANN. By NORMA LORIMER, Author of 'Josiah's Wife.'

JOSIAH'S WIFE. By NORMA LORIMER.

THE STRONG GOD CIRCUM-STANCE. By HELEN SHIPTON.

MARVELS AND MYSTERIES. By RICHARD MARSH, Author of 'The Beetle.'

CHRISTALLA. By ESMÉ STUART.

THE DESPATCH RIDER. By ERNEST GLANVILLE, Author of 'The Kloof Bride.'

AN ENEMY TO THE KING. By R. N. STEPHENS.

A GENTLEMAN PLAYER. By R. N. STEPHENS, Author of 'An Enemy to the King.'

THE PATHS OF THE PRUDENT. By J. S. FLETCHER.

DANIEL WHYTE. By A. J. DAW-SON.

THE CAPSINA. By E. F. BENSON.

DODO: A DETAIL OF THE DAY. By E. F. BENSON.

THE VINTAGE. By E. F. BENSON. Illustrated by G. P. JACOMB-HOOD.

ROSE À CHARLITTE. By MAR-SHALL SAUNDERS.

WILLOWBRAKE. By R. MURRAY GILCHRIST.

THINGS THAT HAVE HAP-PENED. By DOROTHEA GERARD.

LONE PINE: A ROMANCE OF MEXICAN LIFE. By R. B. TOWNSHEND.

WILT THOU HAVE THIS WOMAN? By J. MACLAREN COBBAN.

A PASSIONATE PILGRIM. By PERCY WHITE.

SECRETARY TO BAYNE, M.P. By W. PETT RIDGE.

ADRIAN ROME. By E. DAWSON and A. MOORE.

THE BUILDERS. By J. S. FLETCHER.

GALLIA. By MÉNIE MURIEL DOWIE.

THE CROOK OF THE BOUGH. By MÉNIE MURIEL DOWIE.

A BUSINESS IN GREAT WATERS. By JULIAN CORBETT.

MISS ERIN. By M. E. FRANCIS.

ANANIAS. By the Hon. Mrs. ALAN BRODRICK.

CORRAGEEN IN '98. By Mrs. ORPEN.

THE PLUNDER PIT. By J. KEIGH-LEY SNOWDEN.

CROSS TRAILS. By VICTOR WAITE.

SUCCESSORS TO THE TITLE. By Mrs. WALFORD.

KIRKHAM'S FIND. By MARY GAUNT.

DEADMAN'S. By MARY GAUNT.

CAPTAIN JACOBUS: A ROMANCE OF THE ROAD. By L. COPE CORN-FORD.

SONS OF ADVERSITY. By L. COPE CORNFORD.

THE KING OF ALBERIA. By LAURA DAINTREY.

THE DAUGHTER OF ALOUETTE. By MARY A. OWEN.

CHILDREN OF THIS WORLD. By ELLEN F. PINSENT.

AN ELECTRIC SPARK. By G. MANVILLE FENN.

UNDER SHADOW OF THE MISSION. By L. S. McCHESNEY.

THE SPECULATORS. By J. F. BREWER.

THE SPIRIT OF STORM. By RONALD ROSS.

THE QUEENSBERRY CUP. By CLIVE P. WOLLEY.

A HOME IN INVERESK. By T. L. PATON.

MISS ARMSTRONG'S AND OTHER CIRCUMSTANCES. By JOHN DAVIDSON.

DR. CONGALTON'S LEGACY. By HENRY JOHNSTON.

TIME AND THE WOMAN. By RICHARD PRYCE.

THIS MAN'S DOMINION. By the Author of 'A High Little World.'

DIOGENES OF LONDON. By H. B. MARRIOTT WATSON.

THE STONE DRAGON. By R. MURRAY GILCHRIST.

A VICAR'S WIFE. By EVELYN DICKINSON.

ELSA. By E. M'QUEEN GRAY.

THE SINGER OF MARLY. By I. HOOPER.

THE FALL OF THE SPARROW. By M. C. BALFOUR.

A SERIOUS COMEDY. By HERBERT MORRAH.

THE FAITHFUL CITY. By HERBERT MORRAH.

IN THE GREAT DEEP. By J. A. BARRY.

BIJLI, THE DANCER. By JAMES BLYTHE PATTON.

THE PHILANTHROPIST. By LUCY MAYNARD.

VAUSSORE. By FRANCIS BRUNE.

THREE-AND-SIXPENNY NOVELS

Crown 8vo.

MANY CARGOES. By W. W. JACOBS.

SEA URCHINS. By W. W. JACOBS.

THE MESS DECK. By W. F. SHANNON.

DERRICK VAUGHAN, NOVEL-IST. 42nd thousand. By EDNA LYALL.

A SON OF THE STATE. By W. PETT RIDGE.

CEASE FIRE! By J. MACLAREN COBBAN. Crown 8vo. 3s. 6d.

THE KLOOF BRIDE. By ERNEST GLANVILLE.

A VENDETTA OF THE DESERT. By W. C. SCULLY.

SUBJECT TO VANITY. By MARGARET BENSON.

FITZJAMES. By LILIAN STREET.

THE SIGN OF THE SPIDER. Fifth Edition. By BERTRAM MITFORD.

THE MOVING FINGER. By MARY GAUNT.

JACO TRELOAR. By J. H. PEARCE.

THE DANCE OF THE HOURS. By 'VERA.'

A WOMAN OF FORTY. By ESMÉ STUART.

A CUMBERER OF THE GROUND. By CONSTANCE SMITH.

THE SIN OF ANGELS. By EVELYN DICKINSON.

AUT DIABOLUS AUT NIHIL. By X. L.

THE COMING OF CUCULAIN. By STANDISH O'GRADY.

THE GODS GIVE MY DONKEY WINGS. By ANGUS EVAN ABBOTT.

THE STAR GAZERS. By G. MANVILLE FENN.

THE POISON OF ASPS. By R. ORTON PROWSE.

THE QUIET MRS. FLEMING. By R. PRYCE.

DISENCHANTMENT. By F. MABEL ROBINSON.

THE SQUIRE OF WANDALES. By A. SHIELD.

A REVEREND GENTLEMAN. By J. M. COBBAN.

A DEPLORABLE AFFAIR. By W. E. NORRIS.

A CAVALIER'S LADYE. By Mrs. DICKER.

THE PRODIGALS. By Mrs. OLIPHANT.

THE SUPPLANTER. By P. NEU-MANN.

A MAN WITH BLACK EYE-LASHES. By H. A. KENNEDY.

A HANDFUL OF EXOTICS. By S. GORDON.

AN ODD EXPERIMENT. By HANNAH LYNCH.

TALES OF NORTHUMBRIA. By HOWARD PEASE.

HALF-CROWN NOVELS
Crown 8vo.

HOVENDEN, V.C. By F. MABEL ROBINSON.

THE PLAN OF CAMPAIGN. By F. MABEL ROBINSON.

MR. BUTLER'S WARD. By F. MABEL ROBINSON.

ELI'S CHILDREN. By G. MAN-VILLE FENN.

A DOUBLE KNOT. By G. MAN-VILLE FENN.

DISARMED. By M. BETHAM EDWARDS.

IN TENT AND BUNGALOW. By the Author of 'Indian Idylls.'

MY STEWARDSHIP. By E. M'QUEEN GRAY.

JACK'S FATHER. By W. E. NORRIS.

A LOST ILLUSION. By LESLIE KEITH.

THE TRUE HISTORY OF JOSHUA DAVIDSON, Christian and Com-munist. By E. LYNN LYNTON. *Eleventh Edition. Post 8vo. 1s.*

The Novelist

MESSRS. METHUEN are making an interesting experiment which constitutes a fresh departure in publishing. They are issuing under the above general title a Monthly Series of Novels by popular authors at the price of Sixpence. Many of these Novels have never been published before. Each Number is as long as the average Six Shilling Novel. The first numbers of 'THE NOVELIST' are as follows :—

I. DEAD MEN TELL NO TALES. E. W. HORNUNG.

II. JENNIE BAXTER, JOURNA-LIST. ROBERT BARR.

III. THE INCA'S TREASURE. ERNEST GLANVILLE.

IV. *Out of print.*

V. FURZE BLOOM. S. BARING GOULD.

VI. BUNTER'S CRUISE. C. GLEIG.

VII. THE GAY DECEIVERS. ARTHUR MOORE.

VIII. PRISONERS OF WAR. A. BOYSON WEEKES.

IX. THE ADVENTURE OF PRIN-CESS SYLVIA. Mrs. C. F. WILLIAMSON.

X. VELDT AND LAAGER: Tales of the Transvaal. E. S. VALEN-TINE.

XI. THE NIGGER KNIGHTS. F. NORREYS CONNELL.

XII. A MARRIAGE AT SEA. W. CLARK RUSSELL.

XIII. THE POMP OF THE LAVI-LETTES. GILBERT PARKER.

XIV. A MAN OF MARK. ANTHONY HOPE.

XV. THE CARISSIMA. LUCAS MALET.

XVI. THE LADY'S WALK. Mrs. OLIPHANT.

XVII. DERRICK VAUGHAN. EDNA LYALL.

Books for Boys and Girls

A Series of Books by well-known Authors, well illustrated.

THREE-AND-SIXPENCE EACH

THE ICELANDER'S SWORD. By S. BARING GOULD.

TWO LITTLE CHILDREN AND CHING. By EDITH E. CUTHELL.

TODDLEBEN'S HERO. By M. M. BLAKE.

ONLY A GUARD-ROOM DOG. By EDITH E. CUTHELL.

THE DOCTOR OF THE JULIET. BY HARRY COLLINGWOOD.

MASTER ROCKAFELLAR'S VOYAGE. By W. CLARK RUSSELL.

SYD BELTON : Or, The Boy who would not go to Sea. By G. MANVILLE FENN.

THE WALLYPUG IN LONDON. By G. E. FARROW.

ADVENTURES IN WALLYPUG LAND. By G. E. FARROW. 5s.

The Peacock Library

A Series of Books for Girls by well-known Authors, handsomely bound, and well illustrated.

THREE-AND-SIXPENCE EACH

THE RED GRANGE. By Mrs. MOLESWORTH.

THE SECRET OF MADAME DE MONLUC. By the Author of ' Mdle. Mori.'

OUT OF THE FASHION. By L. T. MEADE.

DUMPS. By Mrs. PARR.

A GIRL OF THE PEOPLE. By L. T. MEADE.

HEPSY GIPSY. By L. T. MEADE. 2s. 6d.

THE HONOURABLE MISS. By L. T. MEADE.

University Extension Series

A series of books on historical, literary, and scientific subjects, suitable for extension students and home-reading circles. Each volume is complete in itself, and the subjects are treated by competent writers in a broad and philosophic spirit.

Edited by J. E. SYMES, M.A.,

Principal of University College, Nottingham.

Crown 8vo. Price (with some exceptions) 2s. 6d.

The following volumes are ready :—

THE INDUSTRIAL HISTORY OF ENGLAND. By H. DE B. GIBBINS, Litt.D., M.A., late Scholar of Wadham College, Oxon., Cobden Prizeman. *Seventh Edition, Revised. With Maps and Plans.* 3s.

A HISTORY OF ENGLISH POLITICAL ECONOMY. By L. L. PRICE,

M.A., Fellow of Oriel College, Oxon. *Third Edition.*

PROBLEMS OF POVERTY : An Inquiry into the Industrial Conditions of the Poor. By J. A. HOBSON, M.A. *Fourth Edition.*

VICTORIAN POETS. By A. SHARP.

THE FRENCH REVOLUTION. By J. E. SYMES, M.A.

PSYCHOLOGY. By F. S. GRANGER, M.A. *Second Edition.*

THE EVOLUTION OF PLANT LIFE : Lower Forms. By G. MASSEE. *With Illustrations.*

AIR AND WATER. By V. B. LEWES, M.A. *Illustrated.*

THE CHEMISTRY OF LIFE AND HEALTH. By C. W. KIMMINS, M.A. *Illustrated.*

THE MECHANICS OF DAILY LIFE. By V. P. SELLS, M.A. *Illustrated.*

ENGLISH SOCIAL REFORMERS. By H. DE B. GIBBINS, Litt. D., M.A.

ENGLISH TRADE AND FINANCE IN THE SEVENTEENTH CENTURY. By W. A. S. HEWINS, B.A.

THE CHEMISTRY OF FIRE. The Elementary Principles of Chemistry. By M. M. PATTISON MUIR, M.A. *Illustrated.*

A TEXT-BOOK OF AGRICULTURAL BOTANY. By M. C. POTTER, M.A., F.L.S. *Illustrated.* 3s. 6d.

THE VAULT OF HEAVEN. A Popular Introduction to Astronomy. By R. A. GREGORY. *With numerous Illustrations.*

METEOROLOGY. The Elements of Weather and Climate. By H. N. DICKSON, F.R.S.E., F.R. Met. Soc. *Illustrated.*

A MANUAL OF ELECTRICAL SCIENCE. By GEORGE J. BURCH, M.A., F.R.S. *With numerous Illustrations.* 3s.

THE EARTH. An Introduction to Physiography. By EVAN SMALL, M.A. *Illustrated.*

INSECT LIFE. By F. W. THEOBALD, M.A. *Illustrated.*

ENGLISH POETRY FROM BLAKE TO BROWNING. By W. M. DIXON, M.A.

ENGLISH LOCAL GOVERNMENT. By E. JENKS, M.A., Professor of Law at University College, Liverpool.

THE GREEK VIEW OF LIFE. By G. L. DICKINSON, Fellow of King's College, Cambridge. *Second Edition.*

Social Questions of To-day

Edited by H. DE B. GIBBINS, Litt. D., M.A.

Crown 8vo.   2s. 6d.

A series of volumes upon those topics of social, economic, and industrial interest that are at the present moment foremost in the public mind. Each volume of the series is written by an author who is an acknowledged authority upon the subject with which he deals.

The following Volumes of the Series are ready :—

TRADE UNIONISM—NEW AND OLD. By G. HOWELL. *Third Edition.*

THE CO-OPERATIVE MOVEMENT TO-DAY. By G. J. HOLYOAKE. *Second Edition.*

MUTUAL THRIFT. By Rev. J. FROME WILKINSON, M.A.

PROBLEMS OF POVERTY. By J. A. HOBSON, M.A. *Fourth Edition.*

THE COMMERCE OF NATIONS. By C. F. BASTABLE, M.A., Professor of Economics at Trinity College, Dublin. *Second Edition.*

THE ALIEN INVASION. By W. H. WILKINS, B.A.

THE RURAL EXODUS. By P. ANDERSON GRAHAM.

LAND NATIONALIZATION. By HAROLD COX, B.A.

A SHORTER WORKING DAY. By H. DE B. GIBBINS, D.Litt., M.A., and R. A. HADFIELD, of the Hecla Works, Sheffield.

BACK TO THE LAND: An Inquiry into the Cure for Rural Depopulation. By H. E. MOORE.

TRUSTS, POOLS AND CORNERS. By J. STEPHEN JEANS.

THE FACTORY SYSTEM. By R. W. COOKE-TAYLOR.

THE STATE AND ITS CHIL-DREN. By GERTRUDE TUCKWELL.

WOMEN'S WORK. By LADY DILKE, Miss BULLEY, and Miss WHITLEY.

SOCIALISM AND MODERN THOUGHT. By M. KAUFMANN.

THE HOUSING OF THE WORK-ING CLASSES. By E. BOWMAKER.

MODERN CIVILIZATION IN SOME OF ITS ECONOMIC ASPECTS. By W. CUNNINGHAM, D.D., Fellow of Trinity College, Cambridge.

THE PROBLEM OF THE UN-EMPLOYED. By J. A. HOBSON, B.A.

LIFE IN WEST LONDON. By ARTHUR SHERWELL, M.A. *Third Edition.*

RAILWAY NATIONALIZATION. By CLEMENT EDWARDS.

WORKHOUSES AND PAUPER-ISM. By LOUISA TWINING.

UNIVERSITY AND SOCIAL SETTLEMENTS. By W. REASON, M.A.

Classical Translations

Edited by H. F. FOX, M.A., Fellow and Tutor of Brasenose College, Oxford.

ÆSCHYLUS — Agamemnon, Chöe-phoroe, Eumenides. Translated by LEWIS CAMPBELL, LL.D., late Pro-fessor of Greek at St. Andrews. 5*s.*

CICERO—De Oratore I. Translated by E. N. P. MOOR, M.A. 3*s.* 6*d.*

CICERO—Select Orations (Pro Milone, Pro Murena, Philippic II., In Catili-nam). Translated by H. E. D. BLAKISTON, M.A., Fellow and Tutor of Trinity College, Oxford. 5*s.*

CICERO—De Natura Deorum. Trans-lated by F. BROOKS, M.A., late Scholar of Balliol College, Oxford. 3*s.* 6*d.*

CICERO DE OFFICIIS. Translated by G. B. GARDINER, M.A. *Crown 8vo.* 2*s.* 6*d.*

HORACE: THE ODES AND EPODES. Translated by A. GODLEY, M.A., Fellow of Magdalen College, Oxford. 2*s.*

LUCIAN—Six Dialogues (Nigrinus, Icaro - Menippus, The Cock, The Ship, The Parasite, The Lover of Falsehood). Translated by S. T. IRWIN, M.A., Assistant Master at Clifton; late Scholar of Exeter College, Oxford. 3*s.* 6*d.*

SOPHOCLES — Electra and Ajax. Translated by E. D. A. MORSHEAD, M.A., Assistant Master at Win-chester. 2*s.* 6*d.*

TACITUS—Agricola and Germania. Translated by R. B. TOWNSHEND, late Scholar of Trinity College, Cam-bridge. 2*s.* 6*d.*

Educational Books

CLASSICAL

THE NICOMACHEAN ETHICS OF ARISTOTLE. Edited with an Introduction and Notes by JOHN BURNET, M.A., Professor of Greek at St. Andrews. *Demy 8vo. 15s. net.*

This edition contains parallel passages from the Eudemian Ethics, printed under the text, and there is a full commentary, the main object of which is to interpret difficulties in the light of Aristotle's own rules.

'We must content ourselves with saying, in conclusion, that we have seldom, if ever, seen an edition of any classical author in which what is held in common with other commentators is so clearly and shortly put, and what is original is (with equal brevity) of such value and interest.' —*Pilot.*

THE CAPTIVI OF PLAUTUS. Edited, with an Introduction, Textual Notes, and a Commentary, by W. M. LINDSAY, Fellow of Jesus College, Oxford. *Demy 8vo. 10s. 6d. net.*

For this edition all the important MSS. have been re-collated. An appendix deals with the accentual element in early Latin verse. The Commentary is very full.

'This edition bears evidence of profound and accurate grammatical learning on every page.'—*Saturday Review.*
'A work of great erudition and fine scholarship.'—*Scotsman.*

PLAUTI BACCHIDES. Edited with Introduction, Commentary, and Critical Notes by J. M'COSH, M.A. *Fcap. 4to. 12s. 6d.*

A GREEK ANTHOLOGY. Selected by E. C. MARCHANT, M.A., Fellow of Peterhouse, Cambridge, and Assistant Master at St. Paul's School. *Crown 8vo. 3s. 6d.*

PASSAGES FOR UNSEEN TRANSLATION. By E. C. MARCHANT, M.A., Fellow of Peterhouse, Cambridge; and A. M. COOK, M.A., late Scholar of Wadham College, Oxford; Assistant Masters at St. Paul's School. *Crown 8vo. 3s. 6d.*

'We know no book of this class better fitted for use in the higher forms of schools.'— *Guardian.*

TACITI AGRICOLA. With Introduction, Notes, Map, etc. By R. F. DAVIS, M.A., Assistant Master at Weymouth College. *Crown 8vo. 2s.*

TACITI GERMANIA. By the same Editor. *Crown 8vo. 2s.*

HERODOTUS: EASY SELECTIONS. With Vocabulary. By A. C. LIDDELL, M.A. *Fcap. 8vo. 1s. 6d.*

SELECTIONS FROM THE ODYSSEY. By E. D. STONE, M.A., late Assistant Master at Eton. *Fcap. 8vo. 1s. 6d.*

PLAUTUS: THE CAPTIVI. Adapted for Lower Forms by J. H. FREESE, M.A., late Fellow of St. John's, Cambridge. *1s. 6d.*

DEMOSTHENES AGAINST CONON AND CALLICLES. Edited with Notes and Vocabulary, by F. DARWIN SWIFT, M.A. *Fcap. 8vo. 2s.*

EXERCISES IN LATIN ACCIDENCE. By S. E. WINBOLT, Assistant Master in Christ's Hospital. *Crown 8vo. 1s. 6d.*

An elementary book adapted for Lower Forms to accompany the shorter Latin primer.

NOTES ON GREEK AND LATIN SYNTAX. By G. BUCKLAND GREEN, M.A., Assistant Master at Edinburgh Academy, late Fellow of St. John's College, Oxon. *Crown 8vo.* 3*s.* 6*d.*

Notes and explanations on the chief difficulties of Greek and Latin Syntax, with numerous passages for exercise.

NEW TESTAMENT GREEK. A Course for Beginners. By G. RODWELL, B.A. With a Preface by WALTER LOCK, D.D., Warden of Keble College. *Fcap. 8vo.* 3*s.* 6*d.*

THE FROGS OF ARISTOPHANES. Translated by E. W. HUNTINGFORD, M.A., Professor of Classics in Trinity College, Toronto. *Cr. 8vo.* 2*s.* 6*d.*

GERMAN

A COMPANION GERMAN GRAMMAR. By H. DE B. GIBBINS, D. Litt., M.A., Headmaster at Kidderminster Grammar School. *Crown 8vo.* 1*s.* 6*d.*

GERMAN PASSAGES FOR UNSEEN TRANSLATION. By E. M'QUEEN GRAY. *Crown 8vo.* 2*s.* 6*d.*

SCIENCE

GENERAL ELEMENTARY SCIENCE. By J. T. DUNN, D.Sc., and V. A. MUNDELLA. With many Illustrations. *Crown 8vo.* 3*s.* 6*d.* [*Methuen's Science Primers.*

THE WORLD OF SCIENCE. Including Chemistry, Heat, Light, Sound, Magnetism, Electricity, Botany, Zoology, Physiology, Astronomy, and Geology. By R. ELLIOTT STEEL, M.A., F.C.S. 147 Illustrations. *Second Edition.* *Cr. 8vo.* 2*s.* 6*d.*

VOLUMETRIC ANALYSIS. By J. B. RUSSELL, B.Sc., Science Master at Burnley Grammar School. *Cr. 8vo.* 1*s.*
' A collection of useful, well-arranged notes.' —*School Guardian.*

Textbooks of Technology
Edited by PROFESSORS GARNETT and WERTHEIMER.

HOW TO MAKE A DRESS. By J. A. E. WOOD. *Illustrated.* *Second Edition.* *Cr. 8vo.* 1*s.* 6*d.*
' Though primarily intended for students, Miss Wood's dainty little manual may be consulted with advantage by any girls who want to make their own frocks. The directions are simple and clear, and the diagrams very helpful.'—*Literature.*

CARPENTRY AND JOINERY. By F. C. WEBBER. With many Illustrations. *Second Edition. Cr. 8vo.* 3*s.* 6*d.*
' An admirable elementary text-book on the subject.'—*Builder.*

PRACTICAL MECHANICS. By SIDNEY H. WELLS. With 75 Illustrations and Diagrams. *Cr. 8vo.* 3*s.* 6*d.*

PRACTICAL PHYSICS. By H. STROUD, D.Sc., M.A., Professor of Physics in the Durham College of Science, Newcastle-on-Tyne. Fully illustrated. *Crown 8vo.* 3*s.* 6*d.*

MILLINERY, THEORETICAL, AND PRACTICAL. By Miss HILL, Registered Teacher to the City and Guilds of London Institute. With numerous Diagrams. *Crown 8vo.* 2*s.*

PRACTICAL CHEMISTRY. By W. FRENCH, M.A. Part I. With numerous diagrams. *Crown 8vo.* 1*s.* 6*d.*
' An excellent and eminently practical little book.'—*Schoolmaster.*

ENGLISH

ENGLISH RECORDS. A Companion to the History of England. By H. E. MALDEN, M.A. *Crown 8vo.* 3s. 6d.

THE ENGLISH CITIZEN : HIS RIGHTS AND DUTIES. By H. E. MALDEN, M.A. 1s. 6d.

A DIGEST OF DEDUCTIVE LOGIC. By JOHNSON BARKER, B.A. *Crown 8vo.* 2s. 6d.

A CLASS-BOOK OF DICTATION PASSAGES. By W. WILLIAMSON, M.A. *Fourth Edition, Cr. 8vo.* 1s. 6d.

A SHORT STORY OF ENGLISH LITERATURE. By EMMA S. MELLOWS. *Crown 8vo.* 3s. 6d.
'A lucid and well-arranged account of the growth of English literature.' — *Pall Mall Gazette.*

TEST CARDS IN EUCLID AND ALGEBRA. By D. S. CALDER-WOOD, Headmaster of the Normal School, Edinburgh. In three packets of 40, with Answers. 1s. Or in three Books, price 2d., 2d., and 3d.

THE METRIC SYSTEM. By LEON DELBOS. *Crown 8vo.* 2s.
A theoretical and practical guide, for use in elementary schools and by the general reader.

METHUEN'S COMMERCIAL SERIES

Edited by H. DE B. GIBBINS, Litt.D., M.A.

BRITISH COMMERCE AND COLONIES FROM ELIZABETH TO VICTORIA. By H. DE B. GIBBINS, Litt.D., M.A. *Third Edition.* 2s.

COMMERCIAL EXAMINATION PAPERS. By H. DE B. GIBBINS, Litt.D., M.A. 1s. 6d.

THE ECONOMICS OF COMMERCE. By H. DE B. GIBBINS, Litt.D., M.A. 1s. 6d.

FRENCH COMMERCIAL CORRESPONDENCE. By S. E. BALLY, Master at the Manchester Grammar School. *Second Edition.* 2s.

GERMAN COMMERCIAL CORRESPONDENCE. By S. E. BALLY. 2s. 6d.

A FRENCH COMMERCIAL READER. By S. E. BALLY. *Second Edition.* 2s.

A GERMAN COMMERCIAL READER. By S. E. BALLY, M.A. *Crown 8vo.* 2s.

COMMERCIAL GEOGRAPHY, with special reference to the British Empire. By L. W. LYDE, M.A. *Third Edition.* 2s.

A PRIMER OF BUSINESS. By S. JACKSON, M.A. *Third Ed.* 1s. 6d.

COMMERCIAL ARITHMETIC. By F. G. TAYLOR, M.A. *Third Edition.* 1s. 6d.

PRÉCIS WRITING AND OFFICE CORRESPONDENCE. By E. E. WHITFIELD, M.A. 2s.

A GUIDE TO PROFESSIONS AND BUSINESS. By H. JONES. 1s. 6d.

THE PRINCIPLES OF BOOK-KEEPING BY DOUBLE ENTRY. By J. E. B. M'ALLEN, M.A. *Cr. 8vo.* 2s.

COMMERCIAL LAW. By W. DOUGLAS EDWARDS. 2s.

WORKS BY A. M. M. STEDMAN, M.A.

INITIA LATINA: Easy Lessons on Elementary Accidence. *Fourth Edition. Fcap. 8vo.* 1s.

FIRST LATIN LESSONS. *Sixth Edition. Crown 8vo.* 2s.

FIRST LATIN READER. With Notes adapted to the Shorter Latin Primer and Vocabulary. *Fifth Edition revised.* 18mo. 1s. 6d.

EASY SELECTIONS FROM CÆSAR. Part I. T Helvetian War. *Second Edition.* 18mo. 1s.

EASY SELECTIONS FROM LIVY. Part I. The Kings of Rome. 18mo. *Second Edition.* 1s. 6d.

EASY LATIN PASSAGES FOR UNSEEN TRANSLATION. *Seventh Edition. Fcap. 8vo.* 1s. 6d.

EXEMPLA LATINA. First Lessons in Latin Accidence. With Vocabulary. *Crown 8vo.* 1s.

EASY LATIN EXERCISES ON THE SYNTAX OF THE SHORTER AND REVISED LATIN PRIMER. With Vocabulary. *Eighth and cheaper Edition, re-written. Crown 8vo.* 1s. 6d. Issued with the consent of Dr. Kennedy. KEY 3s. *net.*

THE LATIN COMPOUND SENTENCE: Rules and Exercises. *Second Edition. Cr. 8vo.* 1s. 6d. With Vocabulary. 2s.

NOTANDA QUAEDAM: Miscellaneous Latin Exercises on Common Rules and Idioms. *Fourth Edition. Fcap. 8vo.* 1s. 6d. With Vocabulary. 2s.

LATIN VOCABULARIES FOR REPETITION: Arranged according to Subjects. *Ninth Edition. Fcap. 8vo.* 1s. 6d.

A VOCABULARY OF LATIN IDIOMS. 18mo. *Second Edition.* 1s.

STEPS TO GREEK. *Second Edition, Revised.* 18mo. 1s.

A SHORTER GREEK PRIMER. *Crown 8vo.* 1s. 6d.

EASY GREEK PASSAGES FOR UNSEEN TRANSLATION. *Third Edition Revised. Fcap. 8vo.* 1s. 6d.

GREEK VOCABULARIES FOR REPETITION. Arranged according to Subjects. *Second Edition. Fcap. 8vo.* 1s. 6d.

GREEK TESTAMENT SELECTIONS. For the use of Schools. *Third Edition.* With Introduction, Notes, and Vocabulary. *Fcap. 8vo.* 2s. 6d.

STEPS TO FRENCH. *Fifth Edition.* 18mo. 8d.

FIRST FRENCH LESSONS. *Fifth Edition Revised. Crown 8vo.* 1s.

EASY FRENCH PASSAGES FOR UNSEEN TRANSLATION. *Fourth Edition revised. Fcap. 8vo.* 1s. 6d.

EASY FRENCH EXERCISES ON ELEMENTARY SYNTAX. With Vocabulary. *Second Edition. Crown 8vo.* 2s. 6d. KEY 3s. *net.*

FRENCH VOCABULARIES FOR REPETITION: Arranged according to Subjects. *Ninth Edition. Fcap. 8vo.* 1s.

SCHOOL EXAMINATION SERIES

EDITED BY A. M. M. STEDMAN, M.A. *Crown 8vo.* 2s. 6d.

FRENCH EXAMINATION PAPERS IN MISCELLANEOUS GRAMMAR AND IDIOMS. By A. M. M. STEDMAN, M.A. *Eleventh Edition.*

A KEY, issued to Tutors and Private Students only, to be had on application to the Publishers. *Fourth Edition. Crown 8vo.* 6s. *net.*

LATIN EXAMINATION PAPERS IN MISCELLANEOUS GRAMMAR AND IDIOMS. By A. M. M. STEDMAN, M.A. *Tenth Edition.*
KEY (*Fourth Edition*) issued as above. 6s. net.

GREEK EXAMINATION PAPERS IN MISCELLANEOUS GRAMMAR AND IDIOMS. By A. M. M. STEDMAN, M.A. *Sixth Edition.*
KEY (*Second Edition*) issued as above. 6s. net.

GERMAN EXAMINATION. PAPERS IN MISCELLANEOUS GRAMMAR AND IDIOMS. By R. J. MORICH, Clifton College. *Fifth Edition.*
KEY (*Second Edition*) issued as above. 6s. net.

HISTORY AND GEOGRAPHY EXAMINATION PAPERS. By C. H. SPENCE, M.A., Clifton College. *Second Edition.*

SCIENCE EXAMINATION PAPERS. By R. E. STEEL, M.A., F.C.S. *In two vols.*
Part I. Chemistry ; Part II. Physics.

GENERAL KNOWLEDGE EXAMINATION PAPERS. By A. M. M. STEDMAN, M.A. *Third Edition.*
KEY (*Second Edition*) issued as above. 7s. net.

EXAMINATION PAPERS IN ENGLISH HISTORY. By J. TAIT WARDLAW, B.A., King's College, Cambridge. *Crown 8vo.* 2s. 6d.

0 01394 3 105Y

CPSIA information can be obtained
at www.ICGtesting.com
Printed in the USA
LVHW010941181021
700725LV00004B/98